Neoclassical Microeconomics
Volume I

Schools of Thought in Economics

Series Editor: Mark Blaug
Emeritus Professor of the Economics of Education, University of London and Consultant Professor of Economics, University of Buckingham

1. The Keynesian Heritage (Volumes I and II)
   G.K. Shaw

2. Post-Keynesian Economics
   Malcolm C. Sawyer

3. Neoclassical Microeconomics (Volumes I and II)
   Martin Ricketts

4. Sraffian Economics (Volumes I and II)
   Ian Steedman

5. Institutional Economics (Volumes I, II and III)
   Warren J. Samuels

6. Behavioural Economics (Volumes I and II)
   Peter E. Earl

7. Experimental Economics
   Vernon L. Smith

8. Radical Political Economy (Volumes I and II)
   Samuel Bowles and Richard Edwards

9. Marxian Economics (Volumes I, II and III)
   J.E. King

10. Austrian Economics (Volumes I, II and III)
    Stephen Littlechild

11. Monetarism
    K. Alec Chrystal

For greater convenience, a cumulative index to all titles in this series will be published in a separate volume number 12.

Neoclassical Microeconomics Volume I

Edited by

Martin Ricketts

Professor of Economic Organization
University of Buckingham

EDWARD ELGAR

Published by
Edward Elgar Publishing Limited
Gower House
Croft Road
Aldershot
Hants GU11 3HR
England

Gower Publishing Company
Old Post Road
Brookfield
Vermont 05036
USA

British Library Cataloguing in Publication Data

Neoclassical microeconomics. — (Schools of thought in economics; 3)
1. Microeconomics
I. Ricketts, Martin II. Series
338.5

Library of Congress Cataloging-in-Publication Data

Neoclassical microeconomics/edited by Martin J. Ricketts.
p. cm. — (Schools of thought in economics; 3).
Includes index.
1. Neoclassical school of economics. 2. Microeconomics.
I. Ricketts, Martin J. II. Series.
HB98.2.N44 1988 88–16345
338.5 CIP

ISBN 1 85278 054 1 (vol. I)
1 85278 115 7 (2 volume set)

Printed and bound in Great Britain at
The Camelot Press Ltd, Southampton

Contents

Acknowledgements

The editor and publishers wish to thank the following who have kindly given permission for the use of copyright material.

Academic Press Inc. for article: W.D. Shulze (1974), 'The Optimal Use of Non-Renewable Resources: The theory of extraction', *Journal of Environmental Economics and Management*, 1, Part 1, pp. 53–73

American Economic Association for articles: A. Alchian and H. Demsetz (1972), 'Production, Information Costs and Economic Organization', *American Economic Review*, 62 (5), pp. 777–95; W. Niskanen (1968), 'Nonmarket Decision Making: The peculiar economics of bureaucracy', *American Economic Review*, 58 (2) Papers and Proceedings, pp. 293–305; M. Harris and A. Raviv (1978), 'Some Results on Incentive Contracts with Applications to Education and Employment, Health Insurance and Law Enforcement', *American Economic Review*, 68 (1), pp. 20–30; L. Johansen (1978), 'A Calculus Approach to the Theory of the Core of an Exchange Economy', *American Economic Review*, 68 (5), pp. 813–20; D.K. Osborne (1976), 'Cartel Problems', *American Economic Review*, 66 (5), pp. 835–44; M. Spence (1983), 'Contestable Markets and the Theory of Industry Structure: A Review Article', *Journal of Economic Literature*, 21 (3), September, pp. 981–90.

Basil Blackwell Ltd for articles: J. Meade (1972), 'The Theory of Labour-Managed Firms and of Profit Sharing', *Economic Journal*, 82, Special Issue, pp. 402–28; H. Hotelling (1929), 'Stability in Competition', *Economic Journal*, 39 (1), pp. 41–57; G.S. Becker (1965), 'A Theory of the Allocation of Time', *Economic Journal*, 75 (3), pp. 493–517.

The Econometric Society for article: J. Muth (1961), 'Rational Expectations and the Theory of Price Movements', *Econometrica*, 29 (3), July, pp. 315–35.

A. Giuffrè Editore S.p.A. for article: A. Alchian (1965), 'Some Economics of Property Rights', *Il Politico*, 30 (4), pp. 816–29. Reproduced from *Economic Forces at Work*, Liberty Press, 1978.

North Holland Publishing Co. for article: M.G. Allingham and A. Sandmo (1972), 'Income Tax Evasion: A theoretical analysis', *Journal of Public Economics*, 1 (3), pp. 323–38.

Society for Economic Analysis Ltd for articles: A.P. Lerner (1934), 'The Concept of Monopoly and the Measurement of Monopoly Power', *Review of Economic Studies*, 1 (3), pp. 157–75; R.G.D. Allen (1936), 'Professor Slutsky's Theory of Consumers' Choice', *Review of Economic Studies*, 3 (2), pp. 120–9.

Tieto Ltd for article: J.H. Williamson (1966), 'Profit, Growth and Sales Maximization', *Economica*, 33 (1), No. 129, pp. 1–16.

The University of Chicago Press for articles: A. Meltzer and S.F. Richard (1981), 'A Rational Theory of the Size of Government', *Journal of Political Economy*, 89 (5), pp. 914–27; A.C. Harberger (1962), 'The Incidence of the Corporation Income Tax', *Journal of Political Economy*, 70 (3), pp. 215–40; K.J. Lancaster (1966), 'A New Approach to Consumer Theory', *Journal of Political Economy*, 74 (2), pp. 132–57; G.J. Stigler (1961), 'The Economics of Information', *Journal of Political Economy*, 69, pp. 213–25.

John Wiley & Sons Inc. for articles: G.A. Akerlof (1970), 'The Market for "Lemons": Quality uncertainty and the market mechanism', *Quarterly Journal of Economics*, 84 (3), pp. 488–500; J. Hirshleifer (1966), 'Investment Decisions Under Uncertainty: Applications of the State-preference Approach', *Quarterly Journal of Economics*, 80 (2), pp. 252–77.

Every effort has been made to trace all the copyright holders but if any have been inadvertently overlooked the publishers will be pleased to make the necessary arrangement at the first opportunity.

In addition the publishers wish to thank the Library of the London School of Economics and Political Science and the British Library Document Supply Centre for their assistance in obtaining these articles.

Introduction

If an attempt were made to characterize the 'school of thought' that has dominated economics since the end of the nineteenth century, the principal tenets of that school might be summarized under the heading 'neoclassical microeconomics'. During this long period many other 'schools' have flowered in response to the preoccupations of the times, or as a reaction against the dominant paradigm. Behaviouralists, Austrians, Institutionalists, Marxists, and, most spectacularly of all in the post-war era, Keynesians, have challenged the 'orthodoxy' of the neoclassical system. None, however, has succeeded in supplanting neoclassical microeconomic theory as the foundation stone of economics. The professional journals are full of papers in the tradition of neoclassical microeconomic analysis, while macroeconomic analysts turned increasingly during the late 1960s and thereafter to the microfoundations of their subject.

The enormous volume of work published over the years in neoclassical microeconomics presents an obvious editorial problem. In these volumes I have attempted merely to put together a set of papers which exemplify a particular 'view of the world'. They represent the development and use of an 'engine of analysis' which has proved to be of great influence. They are not, and could not be, absolutely comprehensive in the sense of representing the work of every major theorist, covering every sphere of application, charting the historical development of the school, and investigating every theoretical issue or dispute. Although I have included a few classic papers from the pre-war era, I have for the most part preferred to concentrate on the way the school has developed in the last thirty years. The selection inevitably reflects the editor's personal interests and it is not impossible that a different editor would have constructed a substantially different list. In the following paragraphs however the motivation behind the final selection is described, and it is hoped that most readers will feel that, as a group, these papers give an accurate impression of the scope and method of modern neoclassical microeconomics.

As the foundation stone of neoclassical microeconomics there lies the simple proposition that economic agents act as constrained maximizers. Consumers, producers, managers, shareholders, regulators, bureaucrats, politicians, voters, husbands and wives, teachers and students, thieves, archbishops, and any other class of people, know what they want. They cannot have all that they want because they face constraints, and these constraints force economic agents to choose among alternative possible courses of action. Parents cannot spend all their time at work *and* play with their children, consumers cannot buy *all* the goods they could potentially enjoy, philanthropists cannot contribute significant resources to *every* worthy cause, and if, according to President Lincoln, politicians cannot fool all the people all of the time, neither, according to neoclassical microeconomics, is it possible so to *please* them.

Although the objectives of economic agents cannot be observed, and the willingness to sacrifice a little of one goal for more of some alternative goal is a matter of the subjective preference of the individual, the maximizing assumption makes it possible to predict the responses of economic agents to changes in the constraints that they face. These constraints are assumed to be objectively observable – a given budget and given market prices, a given amount of time available, a given endowment of resources or human skills, a given technological environment and so forth. Changes in these constraints can affect the prices or opportunity costs attached to the various goals, and a qualitative response in behaviour may then be predictable. A tax on a good will increase its price in terms of the alternatives sacrificed when a unit is consumed, an increase in the wage rate will increase the 'opportunity cost of leisure', an invention which increases the productivity of resources in a particular area will lower the opportunity cost of production there. All these changes will induce people to modify their behaviour until once more the maximizing condition is satisfied. The use of an extra unit of the constraining resource should yield the same subjective 'payoff' irrespective of the desired goal to which it is devoted.

The consistent and repeated application of these principles is both the strength and distinguishing characteristic of neoclassical microeconomics. Its confidence in the purely computational facility of economic agents is questioned by behaviouralists, its implication of the objectivity of economic constraints is questioned by the subjectivism of the 'Austrians', its thoroughgoing individualist premises are distrusted by many social scientists. Yet however important the objections from a philosophical point of view, the vitality of neoclassical microeconomics and the ability of skilled practitioners to extend its use to areas of inquiry once deemed outside the reach of economic analysis, confirm its continued influence, if not its unquestioned supremacy.

Because microeconomics has at its core the study of constrained maximisation, it is possible to treat the subject in a highly mathematical and formal way. Some mathematical papers are included in this collection and I have not deliberately set out to avoid them. My main concern, however, has been to illustrate the conceptual apparatus, the ingenuity with which it can be used, and the insights to which it has given rise, rather than formal brilliance. An issue related to the place of mathematics in microeconomics is that of the status of general equilibrium theory. General equilibrium theory is very often treated in microeconomics textbooks and it is possible to regard it as one of the greatest intellectual achievements in the tradition of microeconomics. Clearly, whether sets of individual decisions are compatible with constraints which characterize the entire system is a matter of great importance, and the analysis which established the conditions required for the existence and stability of a general equilibrium could be seen as a necessary buttress to the intellectual coherence of microeconomics. No attempt has been made to chart the development of general equilibrium theory however, although a few examples of the general equilibrium approach in the fields of tax incidence and resource depletion are included.

Most of the papers in these volumes are included for their theoretical interest rather than their empirical content. Again I have included a number of papers with a substantial empirical interest but only where this serves to illustrate some important microeconomic concept such as the static efficiency losses associated with housing subsidies or monopoly power. It is debatable how far the advance of quantitative economics can be related to the development of neoclassical microeconomics. Certainly, exponents of the methodology of falsificationism such as Milton Friedman have played a significant role in the development of neoclassical theory, but it is not clear to the editor that there is any *necessary* relationship between the quantitative testing of economic relationships and neoclassical microeconomics as a school of thought. It was the rise of Keynesian macroeconomics which provided the incentive and the testing ground for many quantitative techniques in the post-war era rather than the refinement of microeconomics. I have not therefore felt obliged to maintain a balance of theoretical and empirical papers.

Volume I is devoted to expositions of positive analysis. The first four contributions apply the logic of constrained maximization to consumer and producer behaviour. Allen (1936) presents the now conventional static theory; Lancaster (1966) adds greater sophistication to the discussion of how we should view the 'objects of choice', a contribution which has greatly influenced the theory of imperfect competition and the theory of international trade; Becker (1965) develops a theory of the use of time from which there has grown a large literature on the economics of the family and other social institutions; and Hirshleifer (1966) presents the elements of the neoclassical approach to decision making under uncertainty. The neoclassical approach to intertemporal choice is not represented, but readers can find a discussion of the 'Fisherian' apparatus of capital theory in Volume II (Feldstein 1964) albeit as part of a critique of the normative status of the market rate of interest.

The following six papers on markets introduce some of the main preoccupations of neoclassical theory. Edgeworth (1891) and Johansen (1978) consider the nature of a competitive equilibrium. Lerner (1934) presents a classic analysis of monopoly power. For an economic theory rooted in individual constrained maximization, however, the intermediate cases between monopoly and competition have presented an enormous challenge. Each economic agent will be constrained by, among other things, the induced reactions of rivals. One person's behaviour will therefore depend upon predictions about other people's behaviour. Hotelling (1929) and Osborne (1976) are representative of the response of neoclassical economists to this class of problem. Spence (1983) reviews the concept of a contestable market, a development which illustrates the preference of neoclassical microeconomists for tight and well defined constraints in a resource allocation problem.

During the 1960s and 1970s the information problem increasingly commanded the attention of economists. If the nature of the constraints faced by economic agents was not costlessly and fully known, how could neoclassical theory model the decision making process? Stigler (1961) provides a quintessentially neoclassical answer. People will invest in information acquisition until the marginal benefits and marginal costs of information are equated. People may not face a price in the market which is absolutely *certain* but if they know the probability distribution of offers they can calculate an optimal amount of search.

Search is not the only behavioural consequence of imperfect information however. Most economic decisions (some philosophers would say all decisions) involve forming expectations about the future. Behaviour will therefore be heavily influenced by how these expectations are formed. It is well known that explosive cycles can be generated by producers who decide how much output to supply *next* period on the basis of the price prevailing *this* period. Such behaviour, involving static expectations, would appear irrational however. We might argue that transactors will use all their available information to predict future prices on the basis of the application of neoclassical microeconomic theory. It is this line of reasoning which led Muth (1961) to propose the 'rational expectations' hypothesis, the influence of which on macroeconomics in the 1970s can hardly be overemphasized.

Information is not only imperfect and limited, it will often be distributed unevenly over the transactors in a market. The contributions of Akerlof (1970) and Harris and Raviv (1978) relate to this problem. Akerlof discusses a model of the second hand car market which is very subject to adverse selection as well-informed sellers face less well-informed buyers. Harris and Raviv consider the problem of providing incentives when the monitoring of one of the parties by the other is very costly and agreements are subject to moral hazard.

After the section on information there follows a set of five papers on the theory of the firm. Williamson (1966) compares profit maximizing with 'managerial' theories of the firm. Niskanen (1968) presents a model in which budget maximizing bureaucrats manage to appropriate the maximum that taxpayers are prepared to pay for the services they provide. Meade (1972) looks at the consequences of a labour managed system in which it is assumed that firms will attempt to maximize the average return to each worker in the enterprise. Each of these papers represent models in the tradition of constrained maximization. They differ merely because they postulate differing objectives for the principal decision makers, or place them in differing situations.

Neoclassical economists have an aversion to ad hoc theorizing however. A truly general theory of the firm it might be argued should assume that people have much the same ultimate objectives irrespective of the environment in which they are placed. Differences in behaviour will occur simply because the benefits and costs to individuals of certain actions will vary as constraints vary. This has led to the development of the 'property rights' approach to the firm. As Alchian (1965) puts it 'if we concentrate attention on constraints and classes of permissible action we find ourselves studying the property aspects of behaviour' (p. 128). Not only will differing assignments of rights lead to differing behaviour, but recognition of this relationship may help to explain the development of different types of institution with property rights so structured to induce behaviour which is socially productive. Alchian and Demsetz (1972) discuss the rationale of the classical capitalist firm as well as of alternative institutional forms from this property rights perspective.

The final section of Volume I consists of three papers illustrating other applications of the neoclassical approach. Harberger (1962) is an example of the use of a general equilibrium model to discuss the incidence of the corporation tax. Viewed as a tax on capital in the corporate sector Harberger argues that the tax ultimately falls on capital in general as capital migrates to the non-corporate sector and lowers the after tax rate of return. Allingham and Sandmo (1972) present a model of tax-evasion which bears all the hall marks of neoclassical theory. Self interested individuals with no concept of 'social duty' view tax evasion as a form of gambling. They maximize their expected utility subject to the relevant aspects of their environment, such as the probability of being detected by the tax authorities and the penalty which will be inflicted. Finally Meltzer and Richard (1981) discuss the size of government as the outcome of 'rational choice'. A single 'decisive voter', the person with the median income, views the State as a device to redistribute income. Income redistribution can be effected only by constitutional means and by the use of a linear income tax. The decisive voter picks that rate of tax which maximizes his utility in the full knowledge of the effects which the tax rate will have on work incentives and hence the size of national income. Changes in the voting franchise or changes in the distribution of income will then have predictable effects on the tax rate chosen by the decisive voter.

Part I
Constrained Choice

[1]

Professor Slutsky's Theory of Consumers' Choice

In an article published in 1934,[1] Dr. J. R. Hicks and I attempted to develop a theory of consumers' choice on Paretian lines which would be, at the same time, more consistent and more complete than the theory as left by Pareto himself. Our main object was to show that the theory could be constructed without reference to any determinate or measurable concept of utility. The arbitrary element in the representation of utility was clearly pointed out by Pareto, but his theory of value was never modified to allow for it in any systematic way. In particular, we maintained that the complementary and competitive relations of goods in consumption were most inadequately described by Pareto and we advanced definitions which we considered were theoretically more satisfactory and also more serviceable from the point of view of application. In the article, much use was made of the ideas of the mathematical work of Johnson,[2] but we thought that some of the results attained, as apart from the method of approach, were entirely original. More recently, however, our attention has been drawn to an important article by Professor Slutsky, of Charkov University, entitled *Sulla teoria del biancio del consumatore* and published in the *Giornale degli Economisti* as long ago as 1915. It is now clear that many of our results were first given explicitly by Slutsky in this article and that, though the results were not interpreted in terms of the complementary and competitive relations between goods, yet his own use of them was essentially very similar to ours. The purpose of the present article is to promote wider recognition of the value of Slutsky's work by giving a resumé of the argument of his article, omitting a great deal of the highly involved mathematical development, and by comparing his theory with that developed independently by Hicks and myself.[3]

I

After a number of remarks on Pareto's theory of value and concept of utility, Slutsky states the basis of his own general theory by giving a definition of utility and by setting out three assumptions concerning the utility function so defined. The definition of utility is:

The utility of a combination of goods is a quantity possessing the

[1] A Reconsideration of the Theory of Value, *Economica*, 1934.

[2] The Pure Theory of Utility Curves, *Economic Journal*, 1913.

[3] It is interesting to note the existence of a long time-lag between the publication of a highly mathematical theory, such as those of Johnson and Slutsky, and the general recognition of the main results achieved in the theory. When it is remembered, in addition, that Slutsky's article appeared in a journal of a country actively preparing for war, it cannot be considered as surprising that the work has remained completely unknown to English-speaking economists. Since the present article went to press, Professor Henry Schultz has published a long article on "Interrelations of Demand, Price and Income (*Journal of Political Economy*, August, 1935) in which he gives the essentials of Slutsky's work. It appears that Schultz discovered Slutsky's *Giornale* article rather earlier than, but quite independently of, Hicks and myself.

property of assuming greater or less values according to the degree of preference for the combination expressed by the individual considered.

If u is the utility obtained from the combination consisting of amounts $x_1, x_2, \ldots x_n$ of the various goods bought by the individual in a given period of time, then we write the utility function :

$$u = \psi\,(x_1, x_2, \ldots x_n)$$

Three assumptions are now made :

(1) The assumption of the continuity of the utility function and of its derivatives of the first two orders.
(2) The assumption that the utility function remains unaltered in form during the period of time considered.
(3) The assumption that the increment of utility from one combination of goods to another is not dependent on the mode of variation from the one combination to the other.

The marginal utility of the rth good is represented by the partial derivative of the utility function

$$u_r = \frac{\partial \psi}{\partial x_r}$$

and this is taken as positive since the theory of choice is here limited to consumers who find themselves in positions where they prefer more of any good to less. The second order partial derivatives of the utility function

$$u_{rr} = \frac{\partial^2 \psi}{\partial x_r^2} \quad ; \quad u_{rs} = \frac{\partial^2 \psi}{\partial x_r\, \partial x_s} = \frac{\partial^2 \psi}{\partial x_s\, \partial x_r}$$

then indicate the dependence of the marginal utilities on the amounts of the goods bought. There are two kinds of goods to consider, i.e. those goods for which the marginal utility decreases as more is bought ($u_{rr} < 0$) and those for which the marginal utility increases as more is bought ($u_{rr} > 0$). Goods of the first kind are called " satiable " goods and those of the second kind " non-satiable " goods.

If i is the income of the individual in a given period, if $p_1, p_2, \ldots p_n$ are the prices of the n goods and if $x_1, x_2, \ldots x_n$ are the amounts bought, then

$$p_1x_1 + p_2n_2 + \ldots\ldots + p_nx_n = i \qquad \ldots\ldots (1)$$

For a stable choice, with fixed income and prices, the utility function must have a maximum value consistent with (1). The conditions for this are

$$\frac{u_1}{p_1} = \frac{u_2}{p_2} = \ldots\ldots = \frac{u_n}{p_n} = u' \qquad \ldots\ldots (2)$$

where u' is the marginal utility of money, and

$$d^2u = u_{11}dx_1^2 + u_{22}dx_2^2 + \ldots\ldots + 2u_{12}dx_1dx_2 + \ldots\ldots < 0 \ldots (3)$$

The analysis which follows makes use of a simple determinant notation. Let

$$M = \begin{vmatrix} 0 & p_1 & p_2 & \dots & p_n \\ p_1 & u_{11} & u_{12} & \dots & u_{1n} \\ p_2 & u_{12} & u_{22} & \dots & u_{2n} \\ \dots & \dots & \dots & \dots & \dots \\ p_n & u_{1n} & u_{2n} & \dots & u_{nn} \end{vmatrix}$$

and let M_{or} denote the minor of p_r and M_{rs} the minor of u_{rs} in the determinant M (r and $s = 1, 2, \dots n$). Finally, let R denote the minor of the element of the first row and column of M, i.e.

$$R = \begin{vmatrix} u_{11} & u_{12} & \dots & u_{1n} \\ u_{12} & u_{22} & \dots & u_{2n} \\ \dots & \dots & \dots & \dots \\ u_{1n} & u_{2n} & \dots & u_{nn} \end{vmatrix}$$

These determinants take values dependent on the particular combination of amounts of the goods bought and involve the second order derivatives of the utility function. The determinants other than R also depend on the prices of the goods.

The conditions for stability of choice are given by the inequality (3) provided that the equations (2) are satisfied. A linear transformation connecting the differentials $dx_1, dx_2, \dots dx_n$ with new differentials $d\xi_1, d\xi_2, \dots d\xi_n$ is chosen, so that d^2u takes the form :

$$d^2u = A_1 d\xi_1^2 + A_2 d\xi_2^2 + \dots + A_n d\xi_n^2$$

where the co-efficients $A_1, A_2, \dots A_n$ depend on the values of the second order partial derivatives of u at the equilibrium combination. It is shown[1] that these co-efficients are expressed as the ratios of successive principal minors of the determinant R :

$$A_1 = u_{11}\,; \quad A_2 = \frac{\begin{vmatrix} u_{11} & u_{12} \\ u_{12} & u_{22} \end{vmatrix}}{u_{11}}\,; \quad A_3 = \frac{\begin{vmatrix} u_{11} & u_{12} & u_{13} \\ u_{12} & u_{22} & u_{23} \\ u_{13} & u_{23} & u_{33} \end{vmatrix}}{\begin{vmatrix} u_{11} & u_{12} \\ u_{12} & u_{22} \end{vmatrix}}\,; \text{ etc.}$$

The stability conditions are that d^2u is negative for all values of $d\xi_1, d\xi_2, \dots d\xi_n$ subject to the equations (2). These conditions are shown[2] to depend on the values of the co-efficients $A_1, A_2, \dots A_n$ and on an expression Ω defined so that

$$\Omega = -\frac{M}{R}$$

The conditions can be expressed :

(1) If all the co-efficients $A_1, A_2, \dots A_n$ are negative, the choice is called " normal " and it is always stable.

(2) If one of the co-efficients $A_1, A_2, \dots A_n$ is positive and the others negative, the choice is called " a-normal " and it is stable only in the case where Ω is positive.

[1] Slutsky, *op. cit.*, pp. 7-8. [2] Slutsky, *op. cit.*, pp. 4-11.

(3) If two or more of the co-efficients $A_1, A_2, \ldots A_n$ are positive, the choice is never stable.

The equilibrium conditions (1) and (2), subject to these stability conditions, determine the demands of the individual for the various goods as functions of the income i and of the prices $p_1, p_2, \ldots p_n$. The main problem is to investigate the variation of these demand functions as the income or the prices vary. For the variation of individual demands as functions of the income, we proceed :

The equations (2) can be written

$$u_1 = p_1 u' \,;\ u_2 = p_2 u' \,;\ \ldots\ldots\,;\ u_n = p_n u' \quad \ldots\ldots\ldots\ldots\ldots\ldots \quad (4)$$

Differentiating with respect to i, we obtain

$$\left.\begin{array}{l} u_{11} \dfrac{\partial x_1}{\partial i} + u_{12} \dfrac{\partial x_2}{\partial i} + \ldots + u_{1n} \dfrac{\partial x_n}{\partial i} = p_1 \dfrac{\partial u'}{\partial i} \\ u_{12} \dfrac{\partial x_1}{\partial i} + u_{22} \dfrac{\partial x_2}{\partial i} + \ldots + u_{2n} \dfrac{\partial x_n}{\partial i} = p_2 \dfrac{\partial u'}{\partial i} \\ \ldots\ldots\ldots\ldots\ldots\ldots\ldots\ldots\ldots \\ u_{1n} \dfrac{\partial x_1}{\partial i} + u_{2n} \dfrac{\partial x_2}{\partial i} + \ldots + u_{nn} \dfrac{\partial x_n}{\partial i} = p_n \dfrac{\partial u'}{\partial i} \end{array}\right\} \quad \ldots\ldots\ldots\ldots \quad (5)$$

Differentiating the equation (1) with respect to i, we obtain

$$p_1 \frac{\partial x_1}{\partial i} + p_2 \frac{\partial x_2}{\partial i} + \ldots\ldots + p_n \frac{\partial x_n}{\partial i} = 1 \quad \ldots\ldots\ldots\ldots \quad (6)$$

Solving the set of linear equations (5) and (6),

$$\frac{\partial x_r}{\partial i} = \frac{M_{or}}{M} \qquad (r = 1, 2, \ldots n) \quad \ldots\ldots\ldots\ldots\ldots\ldots \quad (7)$$

No universal results can be deduced concerning the sign of the expression $\frac{\partial x_r}{\partial i}$. It is only known that the expression can be positive in some cases and negative in others. A classification of the goods at any equilibrium position is thus possible ; those goods of which increasing amounts are bought as income increases are called " relatively indispensable " goods and those goods of which decreasing amounts are bought as income increases are called " relatively dispensable " goods. For example, a small increase in the income of a poor family may result in a higher consumption of meat, sugar, and tea, but in a lower consumption of bread and potatoes. Meat, sugar, and tea are thus relatively indispensable, and bread and potatoes relatively dispensable in the case of such a family.

The variation of individual demands as functions of the prices is obtained in a similar way. Differentiating the equations (4) with respect to the price p_r, we obtain

$$\left.\begin{aligned}
u_{11}\frac{\partial x_1}{\partial p_r} + u_{12}\frac{\partial x_2}{\partial p_r} + \ldots\ldots + u_{1n}\frac{\partial x_n}{\partial p_r} &= p_1\frac{\partial u'}{\partial p_r}\\
u_{12}\frac{\partial x_1}{\partial p_r} + u_{22}\frac{\partial x_2}{\partial p_r} + \ldots\ldots + u_{2n}\frac{\partial x_n}{\partial p_r} &= p_2\frac{\partial u'}{\partial p_r}\\
\ldots\ldots\ldots\ldots\ldots\ldots\ldots\ldots\ldots\ldots\\
u_{1r}\frac{\partial x_1}{\partial p_r} + u_{2r}\frac{\partial x_2}{\partial p_r} + \ldots\ldots + u_{rn}\frac{\partial x_n}{\partial p_r} &= p_r\frac{\partial u'}{\partial p_r} + u'\\
\ldots\ldots\ldots\ldots\ldots\ldots\ldots\ldots\ldots\ldots\\
u_{1n}\frac{\partial x_1}{\partial p_r} + u_{2n}\frac{\partial x_2}{\partial p_r} + \ldots\ldots + u_{nn}\frac{\partial x_n}{\partial p_r} &= p_n\frac{\partial u'}{\partial p_r}
\end{aligned}\right\}\ldots\ldots\ldots \quad (8)$$

and, differentiating (1) similarly, we obtain

$$p_1\frac{\partial x_1}{\partial p_r} + p_2\frac{\partial x_2}{\partial p_r} + \ldots\ldots + p_n\frac{\partial x_n}{\partial p_r} = -x_r \qquad \ldots\ldots\ldots \quad (9)$$

Solving the set of linear equations (8) and (9) and reducing the expression of the solution, we have finally

$$\left.\begin{aligned}
\frac{\partial x_r}{\partial p_r} &= u'\frac{M_{rr}}{M} - x_r\frac{M_{or}}{M}\\
\frac{\partial x_s}{\partial p_r} &= u'\frac{M_{rs}}{M} - x_r\frac{M_{os}}{M}
\end{aligned}\right\} (r \text{ and } s = 1, 2, \ldots n) \qquad (10)$$

Write $\qquad k_{rr} = u'\frac{M_{rr}}{M}$ and $k_{rs} = u'\frac{M_{rs}}{M}$

and, using the result (7), the results (10) can be written in the form

$$\left.\begin{aligned}
\frac{\partial x_r}{\partial p_r} &= k_{rr} - x_r\frac{\partial x_r}{\partial i}\\
\frac{\partial x_s}{\partial p_r} &= k_{rs} - x_r\frac{\partial x_s}{\partial i}
\end{aligned}\right\} (r \text{ and } s = 1, 2, \ldots n) \ldots\ldots \quad (11)$$

These last results have very definite economic significance. If the price of the rth good is increased by a small amount dp_r, there is an *apparent deficiency* in the individual's income equal in amount to $x_r dp_r$ since he can only purchase the same amounts of the goods as before the price change if his income is increased by this amount $x_r dp_r$. We shall call a variation dp_r in the price of the rth good accompanied by a variation in the income equal to the apparent deficiency $(x_r dp_r)$ a *compensated variation* in the price of the rth good. For such a compensated price variation, allowing for both the price change and the income change, there is a *residual variation* in the demand for the rth good equal in amount to

$$dx_r = \frac{\partial x_r}{\partial p_r}dp_r + \frac{\partial x_r}{\partial i}di = \left(\frac{\partial x_r}{\partial p_r} + x_r\frac{\partial x_r}{\partial i}\right)dp_r$$

i.e. $$dx_r = k_{rr} dp_r$$

The residual variation in the demand for another good (the sth) is

$$dx_s = \frac{\partial x_s}{\partial p_r} dp_r + \frac{\partial x_s}{\partial i} di = \left(\frac{\partial x_s}{\partial p_r} + x_r \frac{\partial x_s}{\partial i}\right) dp_r$$

i.e. $$dx_s = k_{rs} dp_r$$

Hence, k_{rr} and k_{rs} can be regarded as residual variations in the demands for the rth and sth goods respectively per unit compensated increase in the price of the rth good. They are called, therefore, the ***residual variabilities*** of x_r and x_s respectively for compensated changes in the price of the rth good.

It can now be shown[1] that, in all cases of stable choice (whether normal or a-normal), the ratio of M_{rr} to M is negative, i.e.

$$k_{rr} < 0 \quad (r = 1, 2, \ldots n) \quad \ldots\ldots\ldots\ldots \quad (12)$$

Further, since $M_{rs} = M_{sr}$ by the symmetry of the determinant M which follows from the third assumption concerning the utility function, we have

$$k_{rs} = k_{sr} \quad (r \text{ and } s = 1, 2, \ldots n) \quad \ldots\ldots\ldots\ldots \quad (13)$$

This is the " law of reversibility " of the residual variabilities.

From the results (11), together with (12) and (13), we deduce the following *laws of demand* :

I. If $\frac{\partial x_r}{\partial i} > 0$, then $\frac{\partial x_r}{\partial p_r} < 0$ necessarily,

i.e the demand for a relatively indispensable good must decrease as the price of the good increases and must increase as the price of the good decreases.

II. If $\frac{\partial x_r}{\partial i} < 0$, then it is possible that $\frac{\partial x_r}{\partial p_r} > 0$,

i.e. the demand for a relatively dispensable good may increase as the price of the good increases and decrease as the price of the good decreases.

III. The residual variability of any good for a compensated variation in its price is necessarily negative,

i.e. the demand for any good must decrease when the price of the good increases and when, at the same time, a compensating increase equal to the apparent deficiency occurs in the income.

IV. The residual variability of one good for a compensated variation in the price of a second good is equal to the residual variability of the second good for a compensated variation in the price of the first good.

The formulae (11) belong to a category of relations not previously the object of enquiry in the social sciences. They relate quantities capable of empirical measurement and can be verified by observations of actual consumers' choices. In particular, the empirical confirmation of the law of reversibility, as expressed in the fourth of the above laws of demand, is much needed to demonstrate the truth, or at least the plausibility, of the assumption that increments of utility

[1] Slutsky, *op. cit.*, p. 13.

are not dependent on the mode of variation. It is clear, in fact, that $\frac{\partial^2 \psi}{\partial x_r \, \partial x_s}$ need not equal $\frac{\partial^2 \psi}{\partial x_s \, \partial x_r}$ if this assumption does not correspond to the real phenomena of choice, i.e. M_{rs} need not be equal to M_{sr} and the law of reversibility need not hold.

One particular case of the general theory is of special interest since it has formed the basis of most theories of marginal utility. This is the case where the marginal utility of any one good is a function of the amount of this good only, and not of the amounts of other goods. In this case, $u_{rs} = 0$ (where $r \neq s$) and the stability conditions reduce to

$$d^2u = u_{11}dx_1^2 + u_{22}dx_2^2 + \ldots . + u_{nn}dx_n^2 < 0$$

provided that the equations (2) are satisfied. It follows that

(1) If all the partial derivatives $u_{11}, u_{22}, \ldots u_{nn}$ are negative, the choice is normal and stable in all cases.

(2) If one of the partial derivatives is positive and the others negative, the choice is a-normal and only stable if $\Omega > 0$.

(3) If two or more of the partial derivatives are positive, the choice is never stable.

The variations of the demands of the individual, as income or one of the prices varies, can now be written :

$$\frac{\partial x_r}{\partial i} = \frac{p_r}{u_{rr}\,\Omega}$$

$$\frac{\partial x_r}{\partial p_r} = \frac{u'\left(\Omega - \frac{p_r^2}{u_{rr}}\right) - p_r x_r}{u_{rr}\,\Omega} = u'\,\frac{\Omega - \frac{p_r^2}{u_{rr}}}{u_{rr}\,\Omega} - x_r\,\frac{\partial x_r}{\partial i}$$

and

$$\frac{\partial x_s}{\partial p_r} = -\,\frac{p_s\,(p_r u' + x_r\,u_{rr})}{u_{rr}\,u_{ss}\,\Omega} = -\,u'\,\frac{p_r p_s}{u_{rr}\,u_{ss}\,\Omega} - x_r\,\frac{\partial x_s}{\partial i}$$

where

$$\Omega = \frac{p_1^2}{u_{11}} + \frac{p_2^2}{u_{22}} + \ldots\ldots + \frac{p_n^2}{u_{nn}}$$

The following conclusions can then be drawn. If the choice is normal so that all $u_{11}, u_{22}, \ldots u_{nn}$ are negative, the demand for any good increases when income increases or when the price of the good decreases. If the choice is a-normal, then one of $u_{11}, u_{22}, \ldots u_{nn}$ is positive and the others negative, i.e. one of the goods is non-satiable and the others satiable. If the choice is also stable ($\Omega > 0$) in this case, it follows that, as income increases, the demand for the non-satiable good increases but the demands for all other goods decrease. The demand for the non-satiable good also increases as the price of the good decreases, but similar results need not hold for the other and satiable goods.

II

A comparison of Slutsky's results, as set out above, with those of Hicks and myself is now possible, but some rather general observations on the method of approach to the problem of consumers' choice can be made first.

It is to be noticed that Slutsky's statement of the basis of his theory is not entirely satisfactory. His fundamental definition should refer, not to utility, but to increments of utility if it is to be free from objection. His third assumption should then follow at once to establish the existence of a utility function, "integrating" the increments of utility into a single index of the level of utility. In any case, Slutsky's starting point is different from that of Hicks and myself. Our theory was constructed so as to be independent of the existence of an index of utility and it was only in a special case, the so-called "integrability case," that such an index was taken. This integrability case may be the most interesting and useful of all, but it remains a special case of a more general theory. Slutsky, on the other hand, assumes the special integrability case from the outset and his results are, therefore, unnecessarily limited. This is, of course, perfectly realised by Slutsky himself. His remarks on his law of reversibility, for example, provide sufficient evidence of this. The law does not hold if his third assumption does not apply and so if his utility function does not exist. His plea for statistical evidence on this point is one that we can support most strongly.

But, even when the third assumption is accepted, there still remain innumerable forms possible for the utility function. Slutsky expresses his theory in terms of one selected utility function and its partial derivatives. The arbitrariness of the utility function, however, also appears in the partial derivatives. The values of the determinant M and its various minors, which are used throughout Slutsky's analysis, are thus of no absolute significance themselves. The values vary according to the particular utility function selected from the many possible forms. It can be shown, however, that the particular determinant ratios, involved in the main formulae (7) and (10) deduced by Slutsky, are quite independent of the arbitrary element in the utility function. The results of Slutsky's analysis are thus unobjectionable in this respect ; it is only the method of attaining the results that is open to objection.

It must be admitted, however, that the method of approach to a problem is of some importance. Slutsky's method, in the hands of a less sure mathematician, can lead only too easily to results which are not free from objection. It was for this reason that the theory of choice as given by Hicks and myself was developed from a position where the indeterminateness of any utility function was clearly recognised. We deliberately avoided using a particular utility function and its partial derivatives, and we replaced the concept of marginal utility by the more definite concept of a ratio of marginal utilities, i.e. by what we termed a marginal rate of substitution. From the purely methodological point of view, this seems a development preferable to that of Slutsky.

The advantage of our method of approach does not, however, lie only in the sphere of methodology. The very fact that we rejected the marginal utility concept in favour of the marginal rate of substitution concept lead to the introduction of the ideas of the elasticities of substitution and complementarity. These elasticities are defined as characteristics of the preference scale of an individual and they are of great service in the description of market phenomena. As is pointed out below, the elasticities of substitution and complementarity are proportional, at the level of market phenomena under equilibrium conditions, to Slutsky's residual variabilities. But it must be emphasised that the former are fundamental characteristics of the individual's preferences whereas the latter are not. This means that a more illuminating interpretation of results which are formally identical can be obtained in terms of substitution and complementarity than in terms of Slutsky's residual variabilities. The approach to the formulae (7) and (10) by way of marginal rates of substitution and elasticities of substitution and complementarity has, therefore, much to recommend it as compared with Slutsky's rigidly Paretian approach by way of a utility function and marginal utilities.

Passing to a more detailed comparison, we can notice first that the stability conditions are as essential to Slutsky's theory as they are to the theory of Hicks and myself. The stability conditions as stated by Slutsky in the particular case where a utility function exists are included within the last of the assumptions that Hicks and I make concerning the individual's preference scale.[1] In the more general way in which we express the stability conditions, we see that they imply the principle of increasing marginal rate of substitution.

In the problem of the variation of individual demand, Slutsky's main results, expressed by the formulae (7) and (11) above, are exactly paralleled by the results that Hicks and I obtain and express in terms of the elasticities of demand.[2] Translating the latter into Slutsky's notation, they appear:

$$\frac{\partial x_r}{\partial p_r} = -\frac{x_r}{p_r}\left(1 - \frac{x_r p_r}{i}\right)\sigma_r - x_r\frac{\partial x_r}{\partial i}$$

$$\frac{\partial x_s}{\partial p_r} = -\frac{x_r x_s}{i}\sigma_{sr} - x_r\frac{\partial x_s}{\partial i}$$

where σ_r is the elasticity of substitution between the rth good and all others, and where σ_{sr} is the elasticity of complementarity of the sth good with the rth good against all others.

Each price variation of demand is compounded of two distinct and additive parts. One of the parts is written in the same way in Slutsky's formulae (11) as in our own formulae set out above. This part is due to the variation of real income consequent upon the price change considered. An increase in the price of one good causes a decrease in *real* income, i.e. an apparent deficiency in the fixed *nominal* income. The individual's demands are modified to meet this contraction of real income.

The remaining part of the price variation of demand is expressed in Slutsky's formulae (11) in a way different from that adopted by Hicks and myself. A comparison between the two expressions is interesting. Slutsky

[1] Hicks and Allen, *op. cit.*, p. 203. This reference is to the three goods case which is effectively the general case.

[2] Hicks and Allen, *op. cit.*, p. 67, p. 71, and the formulae (13) and (16) on pp. 208-9.

uses the notion of a change in demand due to a compensated price change, i.e. a price change accompanied by a change in income to make up the apparent deficiency, and the term under consideration appears naturally as a residual variation of demand. Since the residual variation is obtained by eliminating the effect of real income changes, it must be a substitution effect, i.e. it arises because the individual substitutes some goods for others in consumption when the relative price structure alters. This is seen by comparing our version of the direct variation $\partial x_r/\partial p_r$ with Slutsky's. Our elasticity of substitution σ_r is proportional to Slutsky's residual variability k_{rr} with its sign changed. In substitution terms, therefore, Slutsky's third law of demand simply states that the elasticity of substitution σ_r is positive and the residual demand for the rth good falls when the price rises for the reason that other goods are substituted for the good subject to the price increase.

In the same way, the elasticity of complementarity of the sth good with the rth good is proportional to Slutsky's residual variability k_{rs} with the sign changed. If this is positive, we say that the goods are complementary and the residual demand for the sth good falls when the price of the rth good rises. It it is negative, we say that the goods are competitive and the residual demand for the sth good rises with the price of the rth good. These interpretations are clear enough once the definition of complementary and competitive goods is made to depend on a substitution effect and put in a precise and quantitative form. In Slutsky's work, the complementary and competitive interpretation of the formulae remains implicit. It is at this stage, of course, that the difference between the special " integrability " case assumed by Slutsky and our more general case shows itself. It is only in the special case that the complementary or competitive relation of the sth good with the rth good is the same as that of the rth good with the sth good.[1] Slutsky's law of reversibility holds only this special case and asserts the symmetry of the complementary or competitive relation between two goods.

Finally, in the particular case of " independent " goods, Slutsky's results are in agreement with those of Hicks and myself.[2] A set of independent goods can be related in a perfectly " normal " way in the sense that the goods are mutually competitive and that the demand for any one good increases as income increases or as the price of the good decreases. But independent goods can also be related in a very " abnormal " way in the sense that there are strong complementary relations between them and that the demands for all goods except one decrease as income increases. Except for the explicit statement of the complementary and competitive relations, Slutsky has analysed these two possibilities with precision and elegance. In any case, there can be no difficulty about integrability or the law of reversibility when the goods are independent. But the inclusion of the " abnormal " possibility prevents the case being of much use even as a first approximation.

London. R. G. D. Allen.

[1] Hicks and Allen, *op. cit.*, p. 72 and p. 202.
[2] Hicks and Allen, *op. cit.*, pp. 74-6 and pp. 214-7.

[2]

A NEW APPROACH TO CONSUMER THEORY*

KELVIN J. LANCASTER
Johns Hopkins University

I. THE CURRENT STATUS OF CONSUMER THEORY

The theory of consumer behavior in deterministic situations as set out by, say, Debreu (1959, 1960) or Uzawa (1960) is a thing of great aesthetic beauty, a jewel set in a glass case. The product of a long process of refinement from the nineteenth-century utility theorists through Slutsky and Hicks-Allen to the economists of the last twenty-five years,[1] it has been shorn of all irrelevant postulates so that it now stands as an example of how to extract the minimum of results from the minimum of assumptions.

To the process of slicing away with Occam's razor, the author made a small contribution (1957). This brought forth a reply by Johnson (1958) which suggested, somewhat tongue-in-cheek, that the determinateness of the sign of the substitution effect (the only substantive result of the theory of consumer behavior) could be derived from the proposition that goods are goods.

Johnson's comment, on reflection, would seem to be almost the best summary that can be given of the current state of the theory of consumer behavior. All *intrinsic* properties of particular goods, those properties that make a diamond quite obviously something different from a loaf of bread, have been omitted from the theory, so that a consumer who consumes diamonds alone is as rational as a consumer who consumes bread alone, but one who sometimes consumes bread, sometimes diamonds (*ceteris paribus*, of course), is irrational. Thus, the only property which the theory can build on is the property shared by all goods, which is simply that they are goods.

Indeed, we can continue the argument further, since goods are simply what consumers would like more of; and we must be neutral with respect to differences in consumer tastes (some consumers might like more of something that other consumers do not want), that the ultimate proposition is that *goods are what are thought of as goods.*

In spite of the denial of the relevance of intrinsic properties to the pure theory, there has always been a subversive undercurrent suggesting that economists continue to take account of these properties. Elementary textbooks bristle with substitution examples about butter and margarine, rather than about shoes and ships, as though the authors believed that there was something intrinsic to butter and margarine that made them good substitutes and about automobiles and gasoline that made them somehow intrinsically complementary. Market re-

* The author wishes to acknowledge helpful comments from various sources, including Gary Becker, Harry Johnson, and colleagues and students at Johns Hopkins University, especially Carl Christ, F. T. Sparrow, William Poole, C. Blackorby, T. Amemiya, and T. Tsushima.

[1] The American Economic Association *Index of Economic Journals* lists 151 entries under category 2.111 (utility, demand, theory of the household) over the period 1940–63.

searchers, advertisers, and manufacturers also act as though they believe that knowledge of (or belief in) the intrinsic properties of goods is relevant to the way consumers will react toward them.

The clearest case of conflict between a belief that goods do have intrinsic properties relevant to consumer theory but that they are not taken into account has been the long search for a definition of "intrinsic complementarity." The search was successful only where Morishima (1959) turned from traditional theory to an approach somewhat similar to that of the present paper.

Perhaps the most important aspects of consumer behavior relevant to an economy as complex as that of the United States are those of consumer reactions to new commodities and to quality variations. Traditional theory has nothing to say on these. In the case of new commodities, the theory is particularly helpless. We have to expand from a commodity space of dimension n to one of dimension $n + 1$, replacing the old utility function by a completely new one, and even a complete map of the consumer's preferences among the n goods provides absolutely no information about the new preference map. A theory which can make no use of so much information is a remarkably empty one. Even the technique of supposing the existence of a utility function for all possible goods, including those not yet invented, and regarding the prices of nonexistent goods as infinite—an incredible stretching of the consumers' powers of imagination—has no predictive value.

Finally we can note the unsuitability of traditional theory for dealing with many of the manifestly important aspects of actual relationships between goods and consumers in I. F. Pearce's (1964) recent heroic but rather unsuccessful attempts to deal with complementarity, substitution, independence, and neutral want associations within the conventional framework.

II. A NEW APPROACH

Like many new approaches, the one set out in this paper draws upon several elements that have been utilized elsewhere. The chief technical novelty lies in breaking away from the traditional approach that goods are the direct objects of utility and, instead, supposing that it is the properties or characteristics of the goods from which utility is derived.

We assume that consumption is an activity in which goods, singly or in combination, are inputs and in which the output is a collection of characteristics. Utility or preference orderings are assumed to rank collections of characteristics and only to rank collections of goods indirectly through the characteristics that they possess. A meal (treated as a single good) possesses nutritional characteristics but it also possesses aesthetic characteristics, and different meals will possess these characteristics in different relative proportions. Furthermore, a dinner party, a combination of two goods, a meal and a social setting, may possess nutritional, aesthetic, and perhaps intellectual characteristics different from the combination obtainable from a meal and a social gathering consumed separately.

In general—and the richness of the approach springs more from this than from anything else—even a single good will possess more than one characteristic, so that the simplest consumption activity will be characterized by joint outputs. Furthermore, the same characteristic (for example, aesthetic properties) may be included among the joint outputs of many consumption activities so that goods which are apparently unrelated in certain of their characteristics may be related in others.

We shall assume that the structure we have interposed between the goods themselves and the consumer's preferences is, in principle, at least, of an objective kind. That is, the characteristics possessed by a good or a combination of goods are the same for all consumers and, given units of measurement, are in the same quantities,[2] so that the personal element in consumer choice arises in the choice between collections of characteristics only, not in the allocation of characteristics to the goods. The objective nature of the goods-characteristics relationship plays a crucial role in the analysis and enables us to distinguish between objective and private reactions to such things as changes in relative prices.

The essence of the new approach can be summarized as follows, each assumption representing a break with tradition:

1. The good, per se, does not give utility to the consumer; it possesses characteristics, and these characteristics give rise to utility.

2. In general, a good will possess more than one characteristic, and many characteristics will be shared by more than one good.

3. Goods in combination may possess characteristics different from those pertaining to the goods separately.

A move in the direction of the first assumption has already been made by various workers including Strotz (1957, 1959) and Gorman (1959), with the "utility tree" and other ideas associating a particular good with a particular type of utility. The theory set out here goes much further than these ideas. Multiple characteristics, structurally similar to those of the present paper but confined to a particular problem and a point utility function, are implicit in the classical "diet problem" of Stigler (1945), and multidimensioned utilities have been used by workers in other fields, for example, Thrall (1954). The third assumption, of activities involving complementary collections of goods, has been made by Morishima (1959) but in the context of single-dimensioned utility.

A variety of other approaches with similarities to that of the present paper occur scattered through the literature, for example, in Quandt (1956), or in Becker (1965), or in various discussions of investment-portfolio problems. These are typically set out as *ad hoc* approaches to particular problems. Perhaps the most important aspect of this paper is that the model is set out as a general replacement of the traditional analysis (which remains as a special case), rather than as a special solution to a special problem.

It is clear that only by moving to multiple characteristics can we incorporate many of the intrinsic qualities of individual goods. Consider the choice between a gray Chevrolet and a red Chevrolet. On ordinary theory these are either the same commodity (ignoring what may be a relevant aspect of the choice situation) or different commodities (in which case there is no a priori presumption that they are close substitutes). Here we regard them as goods associated with satisfaction vectors which differ in only one component, and we can proceed to look at the situation in much the same way as the consumer—or even the economist, in private life—would look at it.

Traditional theory is forever being forced to interpret quite common real-life

[2] Since the units in which the characteristics are measured are arbitrary, the objectivity criterion relating goods and characteristics reduces to the requirement that the *relative* quantities of a particular characteristic between unit quantities of any pair of goods should be the same for all consumers.

happenings, such as the effects of advertising in terms of "change of taste," an entirely non-operational concept since there is no way of predicting the relationship between preference before and after the change. The theory outlined here, although extremely rich in useful ways of thinking about consumer behavior, may also be thought to run the danger of adding to the economist's extensive collection of non-operational concepts. If this were true, it need not, of course, inhibit the heuristic application of the theory. Even better, however, the theory implies predictions that differ from those of traditional theory, and the predictions of the new approach seem to fit better the realities of consumer behavior.

III. A MODEL OF CONSUMER BEHAVIOR

To obtain a working model from the ideas outlined above, we shall make some assumptions which are, on balance, neither more nor less heroic than those made elsewhere in our present economic theorizing and which are intended to be no more and no less permanent parts of the theory.

1. We shall regard an individual good or a collection of goods as a consumption activity and associate a scalar (the level of the activity) with it. We shall assume that the relationship between the level of activity k, y_k, and the goods consumed in that activity to be both linear and objective, so that, if x_j is the jth commodity we have

$$x_j = \sum_k a_{jk} y_k , \qquad (1)$$

and the vector of total goods required for a given activity vector is given by

$$x = Ay . \qquad (2)$$

Since the relationships are assumed objective, the equations are assumed to hold for all individuals, the coefficients a_{jk} being determined by the intrinsic properties of the goods themselves and possibly the context of technological knowledge in the society.

2. More heroically, we shall assume that each consumption activity produces a fixed vector of characteristics[3] and that the relationship is again linear, so that, if z_i is the amount of the ith characteristic

$$z_i = \sum_k b_{ik} y_k , \qquad (3)$$

or

$$z = By . \qquad (4)$$

Again, we shall assume that the coefficients b_{ik} are objectively determined—in principle, at least—for some arbitrary choice of the units of z_i.

3. We shall assume that the individual possesses an ordinal utility function on characteristics $U(z)$ and that he will choose a situation which maximizes $U(z)$. $U(z)$ is provisionally assumed to possess the ordinary convexity properties of a standard utility function.

The chief purpose of making the assumption of linearity is to simplify the problem. A viable model could certainly be produced under the more general set of relationships

$$F_k(z, x) = 0 , \quad k = 1 \ldots m . \qquad (5)$$

The model could be analyzed in a similar way to that used by Samuelson (1953*b*) and others in analyzing production, although the existence of much jointness among outputs in the present model presents difficulties.

[3] The assumption that the consumption technology A, B is fixed is a convenience for discussing those aspects of the model (primarily static) that are the chief concern of this paper. The consequences of relaxing this particular assumption is only one of many possible extensions and expansions of the ideas presented and are discussed by the author elsewhere (Lancaster, 1966).

In this model, the relationship between the collections of characteristics available to the consumer—the vectors z—which are the direct ingredients of his preferences and his welfare, and the collections of goods available to him—the vectors x—which represent his relationship with the rest of the economy, is not direct and one-to-one, as in the traditional model, but indirect, through the activity vector y.

Consider the relationships which link z and x. These are the equation systems: $x = Ay$ (2) and $z = By$ (4). Suppose that there are r characteristics, m activities, and n goods. Only if $r = m = n$ will there be a one-to-one relationship between z and x. In this case both the B and A matrixes are square (the number of variables equals the number of equations in both sets of equations) and we can solve for y in terms of x, $y = A^{-1}x$, giving $z = BA^{-1}x$. $U(z)$ can be written directly and unambiguously as a function $u(x)$. Otherwise the relations are between vectors in spaces of different dimensions. Consider some x^* in the case in which $m > n$: equation (2) places only n restrictions on the m-vector y, so that y can still be chosen with $m - n$ degrees of freedom. If $r < m$, then there are $m - r$ degrees of freedom in choosing y, given some z, but whether the ultimate relationship gives several choices of z for a given x, or several x for a given z, and whether all vectors z are attainable, depends on the relationships between r, m, and n and the structures of the matrixes A, B. In general, we will expect that the consumer may face a choice among many paths linking goods collections with characteristics collections. The simple question asked (in principle) in the traditional analysis—does a particular consumer prefer collection x_1 or collection x_2—no longer has a direct answer, although the question, does he prefer characteristics collection z_1 or z_2, does have such an answer.

If we take the standard choice situation facing the consumer in a free market, with a linear budget constraint, this situation, in our model, becomes:

$$\begin{aligned}&\text{Maximize } U(z)\\ &\text{subject to } px \leqq k\\ &\text{with} \quad z = By\\ &\qquad\quad x = Ay\\ &\qquad\quad x, y, z \geqq 0\,.\end{aligned}$$

This is a non-linear program of an intractable kind. The problem of solution need not worry us here, since we are interested only in the properties of the solution.

IV. THE SIMPLIFIED MODEL

We shall simplify the model in the initial stages by supposing that there is a one-to-one correspondence between goods and activities so that we can write the consumer-choice program in the simpler form

$$\begin{aligned}&\text{Maximize } U(z)\\ &\text{subject to } px \leqq k\\ &\text{with} \quad z = Bx\\ &\qquad\quad z, x \geqq 0\,.\end{aligned}$$

This is still, of course, a non-linear program, but we now have a single step between goods and characteristics.

The model consists of four parts. There is a maximand $U(z)$ operating on characteristics, that is, U is defined on characteristics-space (C-space). The budget constraint $px \leqq k$ is defined on goods-space (G-space). The equation system $z = Bx$ represents a transformation between G-space and C-space. Finally, there are non-negativity constraints z,

$x \geqq 0$ which we shall assume to hold initially, although in some applications and with some sign conventions they may not always form part of the model.

In traditional consumer analysis, both the budget constraint and the utility function are defined on G-space, and we can immediately relate the two as in the ordinary textbook indifference-curve diagram. Here we can only relate the utility function to the budget constraint after both have been defined on the same space. We have two choices: (1) We can transform the utility function into G-space and relate it directly to the budget constraint; (2) we can transform the budget constraint into C-space and relate it directly to the utility function $U(z)$.

Each of these techniques is useful in different circumstances. In the case of the first, we can immediately write $U(z) = U\ (Bx) = u(x)$, so we have a new utility function directly in terms of goods, but the properties of the function $u(x)$ depend crucially on the structure of the matrix B and this, together with the constraints $x \geqq 0$ and $z = Bx \geqq 0$ give a situation much more complex than that of conventional utility maximization. The second technique again depends crucially on the structure of B and again will generally lead to a constraint of a more complex kind than in conventional analysis.

The central role in the model is, of course, played by the transformation equation $z = Bx$ and the structure and qualitative[4] properties of the matrix B. Most of the remainder of the paper will be concerned with the relationship between the properties of B, which we can call the *consumption technology*[5] of the economy, and the behavior of consumers.

Certain properties of the transformations between G- and C-space follow immediately from the fact that B is a matrix of constants, and the transformation $z = Bx$ is linear. These can be stated as follows, proof being obvious.

a) A convex set in G-space will transform into a convex set in C-space, so that the budget constraint $px \leqq k$, $x \geqq 0$ will become a convex constraint on the z's.

b) An inverse transformation will not necessarily exist, so that an arbitrary vector z in C-space may have no vector x in G-space corresponding to it.

c) Where an inverse transformation does exist from C-space into G-space, it will transform convex sets into convex sets so that, for any set of z's which do have images in G-space, the convexity of the U function on the z's will be preserved in relation to the x's.

The properties are sufficient to imply that utility maximization subject to constraint will lead to determinate solutions for consumer behavior.

V. THE STRUCTURE OF CONSUMPTION TECHNOLOGY

The consumption technology, which is as important a determinant of consumer behavior as the particular shape of the utility function, is described fully only by the A and B matrixes together, but certain types of behavior can be related to more generalized descriptions of the technology. We shall distinguish broadly between structural properties of the technology, such as the relationship between the number of rows and columns of B and/or A and whether A, B are decomposable, and qualitative properties, such as the signs of the elements of A and B.

The leading structural property of the

[4] "Qualitative" is used here in a somewhat more general sense than in the author's work on the properties of qualitatively defined systems for which see Lancaster (1962, 1965).

[5] If the relationship between goods and activities is not one-to-one, the consumption technology consists of the two matrixes B, A, as in the technology of the Von Neumann growth model.

consumption technology is the relationship between the number of characteristics (r) and the number of activities (m), that is, between the number of rows and columns of B. It will be assumed that B contains no linear dependence, so that its rank is the number of rows or columns, whichever is less. We shall assume, unless otherwise stated, a one-to-one relationship between goods and activities.

1. The number of characteristics is equal to the number of goods. In this case, there is a one-to-one relationship between activities vectors and characteristics vectors. We have $z = Bx$, $x = B^{-1}z$. If B is a permutation of a diagonal matrix then there is a one-to-one relationship between each component of z and each component of y, and the model becomes, by suitable choice of units, exactly the same as the traditional model. If B is not a diagonal permutation, the objects of utility are composite goods rather than individual goods, and the model has some important differences from the conventional analysis. Note how specialized is the traditional case in relation to our general model.

If B is a diagonal permutation but there is not a one-to-one relationship between activities and goods so that A is not a diagonal permutation, we have a model similar to that of Morishima (1959).

2. The number of characteristics is greater than the number of goods. In this case, the relationships $Bx = z$ contain more equations than variables x_i so that we cannot, in general, find a goods vector x which gives rise to an arbitrarily specified characteristics vector z. We can take a basis of any arbitrarily chosen n characteristics and consider the reduced $n \times n$ system $\bar{B} = \bar{z}$, which gives a one-to-one relationship between n characteristics and the n goods, with the remaining $r-n$ characteristics being determined from the remaining $r-n$ equations and the goods vector x corresponding to $\bar{z}$. In this case, it is generally most useful to analyze consumer behavior by transforming the utility function into G-space, rather than the budget constraint into C-space. What does the transformed utility function look like?

As shown in the Appendix, the utility function transformed into G-space retains its essential convexity. An intuitive way of looking at the situation is to note that all characteristics collections which are actually available are contained in an n-dimensional slice through the r-dimensional utility function, and that all slices through a convex function are themselves convex. The transformation of this n-dimensional slice into G-space preserves this convexity.

For investigation of most aspects of consumer behavior, the case in which the number of characteristics exceeds the number of goods—a case we may often wish to associate with simple societies—can be treated along with the very special case (of which conventional analysis is a special subcase) in which the number of characteristics and goods is equal. In other words, given the consumption technology, we concern ourselves only with the particular n-dimensional slice of the r-dimensional utility function implied by that technology[6] and, since the slice of the utility function has the same general properties as any n-dimensional utility function, we can proceed as if the utility function was defined on only n characteristics.

[6] Assuming no decomposability or singularities in the consumption technology matrix B, then, if z_n is the vector of any n components of z and B_n, the corresponding square submatrix of B, the subspace of C-space to which the consumer is confined, is that defined by $z_{r-n} = B_{r-n}B_n^{-1} z_n$, where z_{r-n}, B_{r-n} are the vector and corresponding submatrix of B consisting of the components not included in z_n, B_n.

3. In the third case, in which the number of goods exceeds the number of characteristics, a situation probably descriptive of a complex economy such as that of the United States, there are properties of the situation that are different from those of the two previous cases and from the conventional analysis.

Here, the consumption technology, $z = Bx$, has fewer equations than variables so that, for every characteristics vector there is more than one goods vector. For every point in his characteristics-space, the consumer has a choice between different goods vectors. Given a price vector, this choice is a pure efficiency choice, so that for every characteristics vector the consumer will choose the most efficient combination of goods to achieve that collection of characteristics, and the efficiency criterion will be minimum cost.

The efficiency choice for a characteristics vector z^* will be the solution of the canonical linear program

$$\begin{aligned} &\text{Minimize} \quad px \\ &\text{subject to } Bx = z^* \\ &\qquad x \geqq 0 . \end{aligned}$$

Since this is a linear program, once we have the solution x^* for some z^*, with value k^*, we can apply a scalar multiple to fit the solution to any budget value k and characteristics vector $(k/k^*)z^*$. By varying z^*, the consumer, given a budget constraint $px = k$, can determine a characteristics frontier consisting of all z such that the value of the above program is just equal to k. There will be a determinate goods vector associated with each point of the characteristics frontier.

As in the previous case, it is easy to show that the set of characteristics vectors in C-space that are preferred or indifferent to z transforms into a convex set in G-space if it is a convex set in C-space; it is also easy to show that the set of z's that can be obtained from the set of x's satisfying the convex constraint $px \leqq k$ is also a convex set. The characteristics frontier is, therefore, concave to the origin, like a transformation curve. For a consumption technology with four goods and two characteristics, the frontier could have any of the three shapes shown in Figure 1. Note that, in general, if B is a positive matrix, the positive orthant in G-space transforms into a cone which lies in the interior of the positive orthant in C-space, a point illustrated in the diagrams.

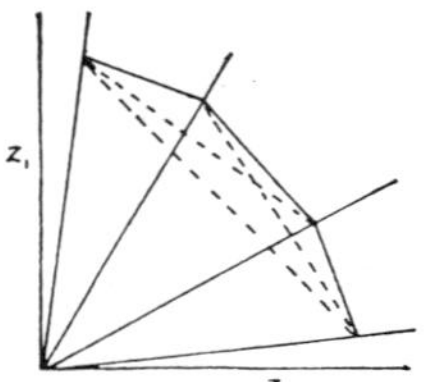

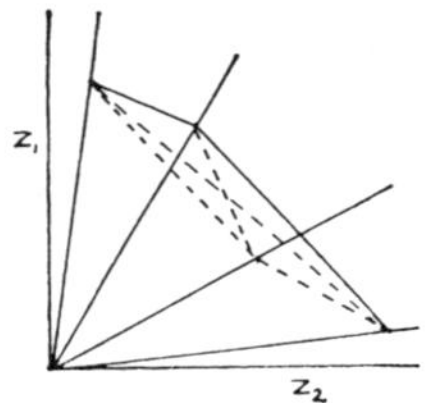

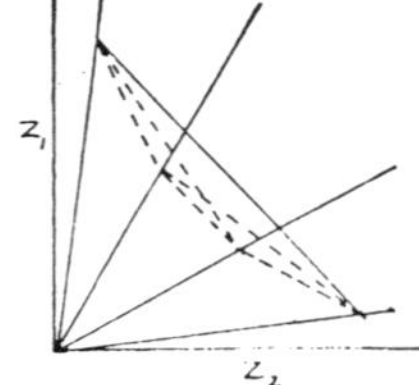

FIG. 1

A consumer's complete choice subject to a budget constraint $px \leqq k$ can be considered as consisting of two parts:

a) An efficiency choice, determining the characteristics frontier and the associated efficient goods collections.

b) A private choice, determining which point on the characteristics frontier is preferred by him.

The efficiency choice is an objective not a subjective choice. On the assumption that the consumption technology is objective, the characteristics frontier is also objective, and it is the same for all consumers facing the same budget constraint. Furthermore the characteristics frontier is expanded or contracted linearly and proportionally to an increase or decrease in income, so that the frontier has the same *shape* for all consumers facing the same prices, income differences simply being reflected in homogeneous expansion or contraction.

We should note that, if the consumption technology matrix has certain special structural properties, we may obtain a mixture of the above cases. For example, a matrix with the structure

$$B \equiv \begin{bmatrix} B_1 0 \\ 0 B_2 \end{bmatrix},$$

where B_1 is an $(s \times k)$ matrix and B_2 is an $(r-s) \times (n-k)$ matrix, partitions the technology into two disconnected parts, one relating s of the characteristics to k of the goods, the other separately relating $r-s$ of the characteristics to $n-k$ of the goods. We can have $s \geqq k$ and $r-s < n-k$ giving a mixed case.

Dropping the assumption of a one-to-one relationship between goods and activities does not add greatly to the difficulties of the analysis. We have, as part of the technology, $x = Ay$, so that the budget constraint $px \leqq k$ can be written immediately as $pAy \leqq k$. The goods prices transform directly into implicit activity prices $q = pA$. Interesting cases arise, of course. If the number of goods is less than the number of activities, then not all q's are attainable from the set of p's; and if the number of goods exceeds the number of activities, different p vectors will correspond to the same q vector. This implies that certain changes in relative goods prices may leave activity prices, and the consumer's choice situation, unchanged.

In most of the succeeding analysis, we will be concerned with the B matrix and the relationship between activities and characteristics, since this represents the most distinctive part of the theory.

VI. THE EFFICIENCY SUBSTITUTION EFFECT AND REVEALED PREFERENCE

At this stage, it is desirable to examine the nature of the efficiency choice so that we can appreciate the role it plays in the consumer behavior implied by our model. Consider a case in which there are two characteristics, a case that can be illustrated diagrammatically, and, say, four activities.

The activities-characteristics portion of the consumption technology is defined by the two equations

$$\begin{aligned} z_1 &= b_{11}y_1 + b_{12}y_2 + b_{13}y_3 + b_{14}y_4 \,; \\ z_2 &= b_{21}y_1 + b_{22}y_2 + b_{23}y_3 + b_{24}y_4 \,. \end{aligned} \qquad (6.1)$$

With activity 1 only, the characteristics will be obtained in proportion, b_{11}/b_{21} (the ray labeled 1 in Fig. 2). Similarly with activities 2, 3, 4, one at a time, characteristics will be obtained in proportions b_{12}/b_{22}, b_{13}/b_{23}, b_{14}/b_{24}, respectively, corresponding to the rays 2, 3, 4 in the diagram.

We are given a budget constraint in goods space of the form $\Sigma_i p_i x_i \leqq k$. If there is a one-to-one correspondence between goods and activities, the prices of the activities are given by p_i. If there is not a one-to-one relationship, but a goods-activities portion of the consumption technology

$$x_i = a_{i1}y_1 + a_{i2}y_2 + a_{i3}y_3 + a_{i4}y_4 \qquad i = 1 \ldots n \,, \qquad (6.2)$$

then the budget constraint can be transformed immediately into characteristics space

$$\Big(\sum_i p_i a_{i1}\Big) y_1 + \Big(\sum_i p_i a_{i2}\Big) y_2 + \Big(\sum_i p_i a_{i3}\Big) y_3 + \Big(\sum_i p_i a_{i4}\Big) y_4 \leqq k \qquad (6.3)$$

where the composite prices $q_j = \Sigma_i p_i a_{ij}$, $j = 1\,..\,4$ represent the prices of each activity. The number of goods in relation to the number of activities is irrelevant at this stage, since each activity has a unique and completely determined price q_j, given the prices of the goods.

Given q_1, q_2, q_3, q_4, and k, the maximum attainable level of each activity in isolation can be written down (corresponding to the points E_1, E_2, E_3, E_4 in Fig. 2,) and the lines joining these points represent combinations attainable subject to the budget constraint. In the diagram it has been assumed that prices are such that combinations of 1 and 2, 2 and 3, 3 and 4 are efficient, giving the characteristics frontier, while combinations 1 and 3, 2 and 4, or 1 and 4 are inefficient.

Suppose that the consumer chooses characteristics in the combination represented by the ray z^*, giving a point E^* on the frontier. Now suppose that relative prices change: in particular, that the price of activity 2 rises so that, with income still at k, the point E_2 moves inward on ray 2. If the movement is small enough, the characteristics frontier continues to have a corner at E_2, and the consumer will continue to obtain characteristics in proportion z^* by a combination of activities 1 and 2. If income is adjusted so that the new frontier goes through E^*, the consumer will use the same activities in the same proportions as before.

If the price of activity 2 rises sufficiently, however, the point E_2 will move inward past the line joining E_1 and E_3 to E_2'. Combinations of 1 and 2 and of 2 and 3 are now inefficient combinations

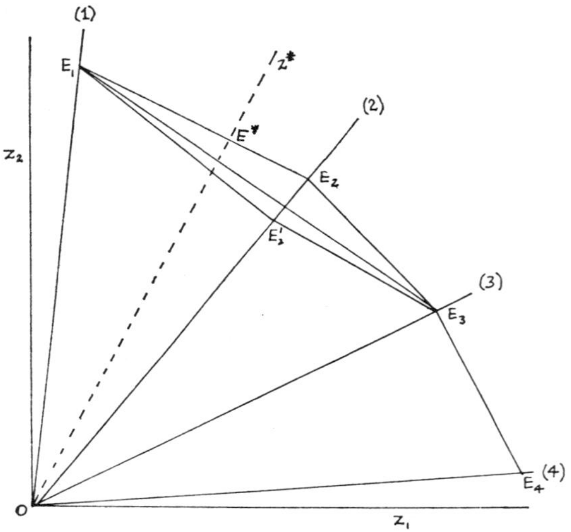

Fig. 2

of activities, their place on the efficiency frontier being taken by a combination of 1 and 3. The consumer will switch from a combination of activities 1 and 2 to a combination of 1 and 3.

Thus there is an efficiency substitution effect which is essentially a switching effect. If price changes are too small to cause a switch, there is no efficiency substitution effect: If they are large enough, the effect comes from a complete switch from one activity to another.

The manifestation of the efficiency substitution effect in goods space depends on the structure of the A (goods-activities) matrix. There are two polar cases:

a) If there is a one-to-one relationship between goods and activities, the efficiency substitution effect will result in a complete switch from consumption of one good to consumption of another. This might be regarded as typical of situations involving similar but differentiated products, where a sufficiently large price change in one of the products will result in widespread switching to, or away from, the product.

b) If there is not a one-to-one relationship between goods and activities and, in particular, if all goods are used in all activities, the efficiency substitution effect will simply result in less consumption of a good whose price rises, not a complete disappearance of that good from consumption. If all cakes require eggs but in different proportions, a rise in the price of eggs will cause a switch from egg-intensive cakes to others, with a decline in the consumption of eggs, but not to zero.

The existence of an efficiency substitution effect depends, of course, on the number of activities exceeding the number of characteristics (otherwise switching of activities will not, in general, occur[7]) but does not require that the number of goods exceed the number of characteristics. In fact, with two goods, two characteristics, and three activities, the effect may occur. With two goods, two characteristics and one hundred activities (well spread over the spectrum), an almost smooth efficiency substitution effect would occur.

Since the efficiency substitution effect implies that consumers may change goods collections as a result of compensated relative price changes, simply in order to obtain the same characteristics collection in the most efficient manner, it is obvious that the existence of substitution does not of itself either require or imply convexity of the preference function on characteristics. In other words, the axiom of revealed preference may be satisfied even if the consumer always consumes characteristics in fixed proportions (and possibly even if the consumers had *concave* preferences), so that the "revelation" may be simply of efficient choice rather than convexity. A formal proof is given in the Appendix.

VII. OBJECTIVE AND SUBJECTIVE CHOICE AND DEMAND THEORY

In an economy or subeconomy with a complex consumption technology (many goods relative to characteristics), we have seen that there are two types of substitution effect:

1. Changes in relative prices may result in goods bundle I becoming an *in-*

[7] This is a somewhat imprecise statement in that, if the B matrix is partitionable into disconnected subtechnologies, for some of which the number of activities exceeds the number of characteristics and for others the reverse, an efficiency-substitution effect may exist over certain groups of activities, although the number of activities is less than the number of characteristics over-all.

efficient method of attaining a given bundle of characteristics and being replaced by goods bundle II even when the characteristics bundle is unchanged.

2. Changes in relative prices, with or without causing efficiency substitutions as in type 1, may alter the slope of the characteristics frontier in a segment relevant to a consumer's characteristics choice. The change in the slope of the frontier is analogous to the change in the budget line slope in the traditional case and, with a convex preference function, will result in a substitution of one characteristics bundle for another and, hence, of one goods bundle for another. Note that, even with smoothly convex preferences, this effect may not occur, since the consumer may be on a corner of the polyhedral characteristics frontier, and thus his characteristics choice could be insensitive to a certain range of slope changes on the facets.

The first effect, the efficiency substitution effect, is universal and objective. Subject to consumer ignorance or inefficiency,[8] this substitution effect is independent of the shapes of individual consumers' preference functions and hence of the effects of income distribution.

The second effect, the private substitution effect, has the same properties, in general, as the substitution effect in traditional theory. In particular, an aggregately compensated relative price change combined with a redistribution of income may result in no substitution effect in the aggregate, or a perverse one.

These two substitution effects are independent—either may occur without the other in certain circumstances—but in general we will expect them both to take place and hence that their effects will be reinforcing, if we are concerned with a complex economy. Thus, the consumer model presented here, in the context of an advanced economy, has, in a sense, more substitution than the traditional model. Furthermore, since part of the total substitution effect arises from objective, predictable, and income-distribution-free efficiency considerations, our confidence in the downward slope of demand curves is increased even when income redistribution takes place.

Since it is well known that satisfaction of the revealed preference axioms *in the aggregate* (never guaranteed by traditional theory) leads to global stability in multimarket models (see, for example, Karlin, 1959), the efficiency substitution effect increases confidence in this stability.

In a simple economy, with few goods or activities relative to characteristics, the efficiency substitution effect will be generally absent. Without this reinforcement of the private substitution effect, we would have some presumption that perverse consumer effects ("Giffen goods," backward-bending supply curves) and lower elasticities of demand would characterize simple economies as compared with complex economies. This seems to be in accord with at least the mythology of the subject, but it is certainly empirically verifiable. On this model, consumption technology as well as income levels differentiate consumers in different societies, and we would not necessarily expect a poor urban American to behave in his consumption like a person at the same real-income level in a simple economy.

[8] One of the properties of this model is that it gives scope for the consumer to be more or less efficient in achieving his desired characteristics bundle, although we will usually assume he is completely efficient. This adds a realistic dimension to consumer behavior (traditional theory never permits him to be out of equilibrium) and gives a rationale for the Consumers' Union and similar institutions.

VIII. COMMODITY GROUPS, SUBSTITUTES, COMPLEMENTS

In a complex economy, with a large number of activities and goods as well as characteristics, and with a two-matrix (A, B) consumption technology, it is obvious that taxonomy could be carried out almost without limit, an expression of the richness of the present approach. Although an elaborate taxonomy is not very useful, discussion of a few selected types of relationships between goods can be of use. One of the important features of this model is that we can discuss relationships between goods, as revealed in the structure of the technology. In the conventional approach, there are, of course, no relationships between goods as such, only properties of individual's preferences.

The simplest taxonomy is that based on the zero entries in the technology matrixes. It may be that both matrixes A, B are almost "solid," in which case there is little to be gained from a taxonomic approach. If, however, the B matrix contains sufficient zeros to be decomposable as follows,

$$B \equiv \begin{bmatrix} B_1 0 \\ 0 B_2 \end{bmatrix}, \qquad (7.1)$$

so that there is some set of characteristics and some set of activities such that these characteristics are derived only from these activities and these activities give rise to no other characteristics, then we can separate that set of characteristics and activities from the remainder of the technology. If, further, the activities in question require a particular set of goods which are used in no other activities (implying a decomposition of the A matrix), then we can regard the goods as forming an *intrinsic commodity group*. Goods within the group have the property that efficiency substitution effects will occur only for relative price changes within the group and will be unaffected by changes in the prices of other goods. If the utility function on characteristics has the conventional properties, there may, of course, be *private* substitution effects for goods within the group when the prices of other goods changes. For an intrinsic commodity group, the whole of the objective analysis can be carried out without reference to goods outside the group.

Goods from different intrinsic commodity groups can be regarded as *intrinsically unrelated*, goods from the same group as *intrinsically related*.

If, within a group, there are two activities, each in a one-to-one relationship with a different good, and if the bundles of characteristics derived from the two goods differ only in a scalar (that is, have identical proportions), we can regard the two goods in question as *intrinsic perfect substitutes*. If the associated characteristics bundles are similar, the goods are *close substitutes*. We can give formal respectability to that traditional butter-margarine example of our texts by considering them as two goods giving very similar combinations of characteristics.

On the other hand, if a certain activity requires more than one good and if these goods are used in no other activity we can consider them as *intrinsic total complements* and they will always be consumed in fixed proportions, if at all.

Many goods within a commodity group will have relationships to each other which are partly complementary and partly substitution. This will be true if two goods, for example, are used in different combinations in each of several activities, each activity giving rise to a similar combination of characteristics. The goods are complements within each activity, but the activities are substitutes.

IX. LABOR, LEISURE, AND OCCUPATIONAL CHOICE

Within the structure of the present theory, we can regard labor as a reversed activity, using characteristics as inputs and producing commodities or a commodity as output. This is similar to the standard approach of generalized conventional theory, as in Debreu (1959).

We can add to this approach in an important way within the context of the present model by noting that a work activity may produce characteristics, as well as the commodity labor, as outputs. This is structurally equivalent to permitting some of the columns of the B matrix to have both negative and positive elements, corresponding to activities that "use up" some characteristics (or produce them in negative quantities) and produce others. In a work activity, the corresponding column of the A matrix will contain a single negative coefficient for the commodity labor, or, more differentiated, for one or more types of labor. If a work activity corresponds to a column of mixed signs in the B matrix, it is a recognition of the obvious truth that some work activities give rise to valued characteristics directly from the work itself.

Consider a very simple model of two characteristics with two commodities, labor and consumption goods. Both labor and consumption goods correspond to separate activities giving rise to the two characteristics in different proportions—perhaps negative in the case of labor. With no income other than labor, and only one good available to exchange for labor, we can collapse work and consumption into a single work-consumption activity. Given the wage rate in terms of the consumption good, the characteristics resulting from the work-consumption activity are given by a linear combination of the characteristics from work and consumption separately, the weights in the combination being given by the wage rate.

Add another activity, leisure, which gives rise to the two characteristics, and the constraint that the weighted sum of the levels of activity labor and activity leisure is a constant.

The model is illustrated in Figure 3. W represents a work-consumption activity giving positive levels of both characteristics, l represents a leisure activity, also giving positive levels of both characteristics. The constraint on total time (so that a linear combination of w and l is a constant) is represented by some line joining w, l.

If the constraint line has, like AB in the diagram, a negative slope, then individual consumers' utility functions will be tangent to the constraint at different points (like m, m') and we will have a neoclassical type of labor-leisure choice in which the proportions depend on individual preferences. Some consumers' preferences may be such that they will choose A (maximum work) or B (maximum leisure), but it is a private choice.

In this model, however, for a certain level of the wage, given the coefficients of the technology, the constraint may have a positive slope as in $A'B$, or AB'. If the constraint is $A'B$ (corresponding, *ceteris paribus*, to a sufficiently low real wage), *all* individuals will choose B, the only efficient point on the constraint set $OA'B$. At a sufficiently high wage, giving constraint set OAB', A, the maximum labor choice, is the only efficient choice and will be chosen by *all* individuals.

The above effect, in which for some wage range there is a private labor-leisure choice between efficient points while outside the range all individuals will take maximum work or maximum leisure, can only occur if both the work-consumption and leisure activities give both characteristics in positive amounts. If the using up of characteristic 2 in labor exceeded the amount of that characteristic gained by consumption, then the work-consumption activity might lie outside the positive quadrant, like w'. In this case, a constraint like $A'B$ can exist, but not one like AB'. Furthermore, if the consumer will choose only positive characteristics vectors, no consumer will choose maximum work.

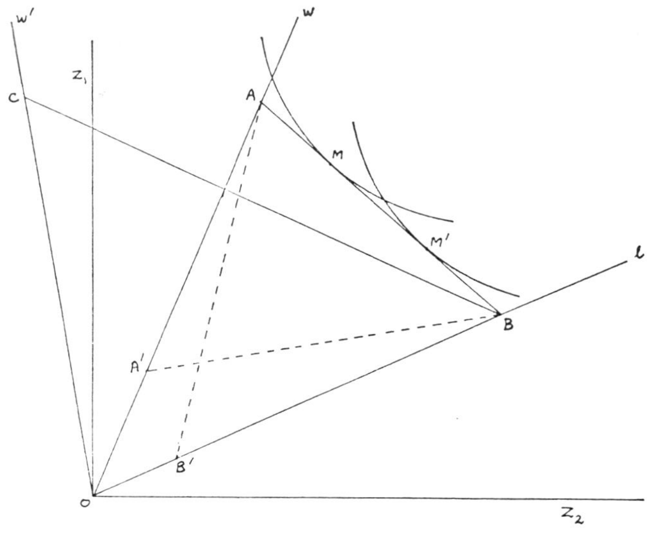

FIG. 3

This model of the labor-leisure choice, which provides for objective and universal efficiency choices as well as private choices, may be the basis for a useful working model for an underdeveloped area. If the "leisure" be defined as "working one's own field," the work-consumption activity as entering the market economy, we see that there will be wages below which no peasant will offer himself as paid labor and that this is an *efficiency* choice and not a private choice.

We can use the same type of model also to analyze occupational choice. Suppose that we have two types of work (occupations) but otherwise the conditions are as above. If and only if the characteristics arising from the work itself are different in the two occupations, the two work-consumption activities will give rise to activities in different combinations. If the work characteristics are in the same proportion, the characteristics of the work-consumption activity will be in the same proportions and one or the other occupation will be the only efficient way to achieve this characteristics bundle.

Figure 4 illustrates one possible set of relationships for such a model. In the diagram, w_1, w_2 represent the characteristics combinations from work-consumption activities in occupations 1 and 2, l the characteristics combinations from leisure. The frontier consists of the lines AC (combinations of w_1 and leisure) and AB (combinations of w_2 and leisure). We shall impose the realistic restriction that an individual can have only a single occupation so that AB is not a possible combination of activities.

The choice of occupation, given the relationships in the figure, depends on personal preferences, being M_1 (combination of w_2 and leisure) for an individual with preferences skewed towards z_2 and M_2 for an individual with preferences skewed towards z_1. But note a special effect. For some individuals whose indifference curves cannot touch BC but can touch AC, the efficient choice will be the corner solution M_3 (= B). There is, in fact, a segment of AC to the left of w_2 (the part of AC to the right of w_2 is dominated by BC), lying below the horizontal through B which is inefficient relative to B and will never be chosen.

In a configuration like the above we have the very interesting effect, where those who choose occupation 1 will work very hard at it; leisure-lovers will choose private combinations of occupation 2 and leisure—surely a good description of effects actually observed.

The loss to certain individuals from confinement to a single occupation is obvious. Could he choose a combination of occupations 1 and 2, the individual at M_2 would do so and be better off than with a combination of occupation 1 and leisure. In a two-characteristic, three-activity model, of course, two activities will be chosen at most, so that leisure plus both occupations will not appear.

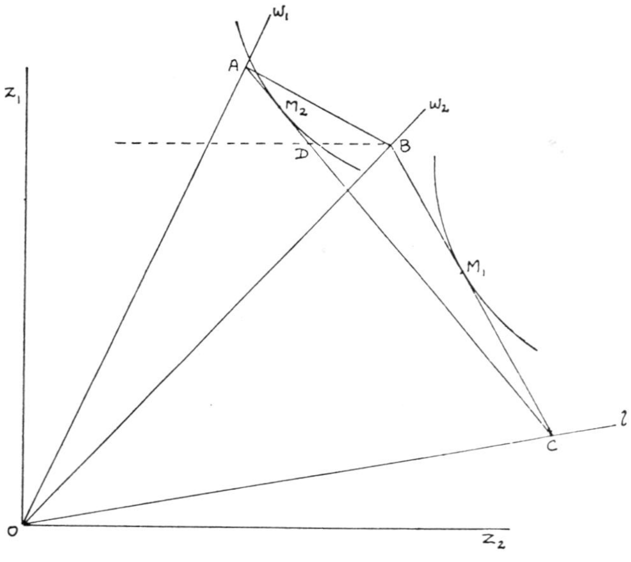

FIG. 4

The configuration in the diagram (Fig. 4) represents the situation for some set of technical coefficients and specific wages in the two occupations. A large number of other configurations is possible. In particular, if the wage rate in occupation 2 fell sufficiently, BC would lie inside AC and occupation 2 would cease to be chosen by any individual. All individuals, in this case, would choose their various personal combinations of occupation 1 and leisure.

Confinement to a single occupation need not result in a welfare loss, even when neither occupation dominates the other in an efficiency sense. If the technical coefficients were different, so that the characteristics vectors representing occupation 2 and leisure changed places, then the work-leisure combinations would be given by *AB* and *BC*, both efficient relative to any combination of occupations 1 and 2. In this case, all individuals would optimize by some combination of leisure and any one of the occupations.

Approaches similar to those outlined above seem to provide a better basis for analysis of occupational choice than the traditional, non-operational, catch-all "non-monetary advantages."

X. CONSUMER DURABLES, ASSETS, AND MONEY

Within the framework of the model, we have a scheme for dealing with durable goods and assets. A durable good can be regarded simply as giving rise to an activity in which the output consists of dated characteristics, the characteristics of different dates being regarded as different characteristics.

Given characteristics as joint outputs and two types of dimension in characteristics space—cross-section and time—any asset or durable good can be regarded as producing a combination of several characteristics at any one time, and that combination need not be regarded as continuing unchanged through time. In the decision to buy a new automobile, for example, the characteristic related to "fashion" or "style" may be present in relative strength in the first season, relatively less in later seasons, although the characteristics related to "transportation" may remain with constant coefficients over several seasons.

Elementary textbooks stress the multidimensional characteristics of money and other assets. The present model enables this multidimensionality to be appropriately incorporated. "Safety," "liquidity," and so forth become workable concepts that can be related to characteristics. We can use analysis similar to that of the preceding sections to show why efficiency effects will cause the universal disappearance of some assets (as in Gresham's Law) while other assets will be held in combinations determined by personal preferences. It would seem that development along these lines, coupled with development of some of the recent approaches to consumer preferences over time as in Koopmans (1960), Lancaster (1963), or Koopmans, Diamond, and Williamson (1964) might eventually lead to a full-blooded theory of consumer behavior with respect to assets—saving and money—which we do not have at present.

In situations involving risk, we can use multiple characteristics better to analyze individual behavior. For example, we might consider a gamble to be an activity giving rise to three characteristics—a mathematical expectation, a maximum gain, and a maximum loss. One consumer's utility function may be such that he gives more weight to the maximum gain than to the maximum loss or the expected value, another's utility function may be biased in the opposite direction. All kinds of models can be developed along these lines, and they are surely more realistic than the models (Von Neumann and Morgenstern, 1944; Friedman and Savage, 1952) in which the expected value, alone, appears in the utility-maximizing decisions.

XI. NEW COMMODITIES, DIFFERENTIATED GOODS, AND ADVERTISING

Perhaps the most difficult thing to do with traditional consumer theory is to introduce a new commodity—an event that occurs thousands of times in the U.S. economy, even over a generation, without any real consumers being unduly disturbed. In the theory of production, where activity-analysis methods have become widely used, a new process or product can be fitted in well enough; but in consumer theory we have traditionally had to throw away our n-dimensional preference functions and replace them by totally new $(n + 1)$ dimensional functions, with no predictable consequences.

In this model, the whole process is extraordinarily simple. A new product simply means addition of one or more activities to the consumption technology. Given the technology (or the relevant portion of it) and given the intrinsic characteristic of the activity associated with the new good, we simply insert it in the appropriate place in the technology, *and we can predict the consequences.*

If a new good possesses characteristics in the same proportions as some existing good, it will simply fail to sell to anyone if its price is too high, or will completely replace the old good if its price is sufficiently low.

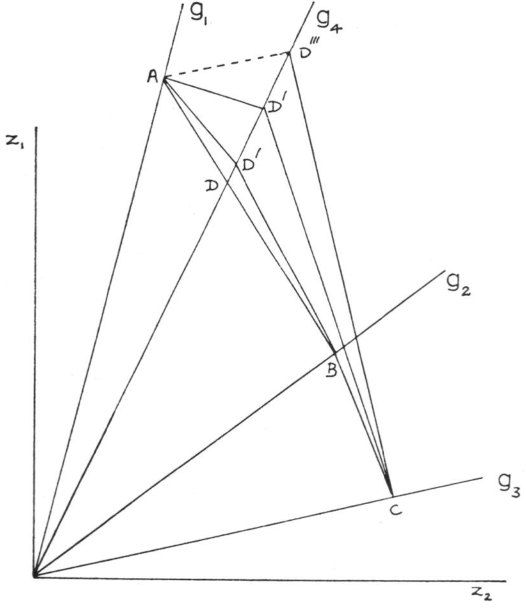

FIG. 5

More usually, we can expect a new good to possess characteristics in somewhat different proportions to an existing good. If its price is too high, it may be dominated by some *combination* of existing goods and will fail to sell. If its price is sufficiently low, it will result in adding a new point to the efficiency frontier. In Figure 5, ABC represents the old efficiency frontier, on which some individuals will consume combinations of goods g_1 and g_2 in various proportions, some combinations of g_2 and g_3. If the price of the new good, g_4, is such that it represents a point, D, on the old efficiency frontier, some persons (those using combinations of g_1 and g_2) will be indifferent between their old combinations and combinations of either g_1 and g_4 or g_2 and g_4. If the price of g_4 is a little lower, it will push the efficiency frontier out to D'. Individuals will now replace combinations of g_1 and g_2 with combinations of g_1 and g_4 or g_2 and g_4, depending on their preferences. The new good will have taken away some of the sales from both g_1 and g_2, but completely replaced neither.

If the price of g_4 were lower, giving point D'', then combinations of g_4 and g_3 would dominate g_2, and g_2 would be replaced. At an even lower price, like D''', combinations of g_4 and g_3 would dominate g_2, and the corner solution g_4 only would dominate all combinations of g_1 and g_4 (since AD''' has a positive slope), so that g_4 would now replace both g_1 and g_2.

Differentiation of goods has presented almost as much of a problem to traditional theory as new commodities. In the present analysis, the difference is really one of degree only. We can regard a differentiated good typically as a new good within an existing intrinsic commodity group, and within that group analyze it as a new commodity. Sometimes there appear new commodities of a more fundamental kind whose characteristics cut across those of existing groups.

We may note that differentiation of goods, if successful (that is, if the differentiated goods are actually sold) represents a welfare improvement since it pushes the efficiency frontier outward an enables the consumer more efficiently to reach his preferred combination of characteristics.

Many economists take a puritanical view of commodity differentiation since their theory has induced them to believe that it is some single characteristic of a commodity that is relevant to consumer decisions (that is, automobiles are only for transportation), so that commodity variants are regarded as wicked tricks to trap the uninitiated into buying unwanted trimmings. This is not, of course, a correct deduction even from the conventional analysis, properly used, but is manifestly incorrect when account is taken of multiple characteristics.

A rather similar puritanism has also been apparent in the economist's approach to advertising. In the neoclassical analysis, advertising, if it does not represent simple information (and little information is called for in an analysis in which a good is simply a good), is an attempt to "change tastes" in the consumer. Since "tastes" are the ultimate datum in welfare judgments, the idea of changing them makes economists uncomfortable.

On the analysis presented here, there is much wider scope for informational advertising, especially as new goods appear constantly. Since the consumption technology of a modern economy is clearly very complex, consumers require a great deal of information concerning that technology. When a new version of a dishwashing detergent is produced which contains hand lotion, we have a product with characteristics different from those of the old. The consumption technology is changed, and consumers are willing to pay to be told of the change. Whether the new product pushes out the efficiency frontier (compared, say, with a combination of dishwasher and hand lotion consumed separately) is, of course, another matter.

In any case, advertising, product design, and marketing specialists, who have a heavy commitment to understanding how consumers actually do behave, themselves act as though consumers regard a commodity as having multiple characteristics and as though consumers weigh the various combinations of characteristics contained in different commodities in reaching their decisions. At this preliminary stage of presenting the model set out here, this is strong evidence in its favor.

XII. GENERAL EQUILIBRIUM, WELFARE, AND OTHER MATTERS

Since the demand for goods depends on objective and universal efficiency effects as well as on private choices, we can draw some inferences relative to equilibrium in the economy.

A commodity, especially a commodity within an intrinsic commodity group, must have a price low enough relative to the prices of other commodities to be represented on the efficiency frontier, otherwise it will be purchased by no one and will not appear in the economy. This implies that if there are n viable commodities in a group, each in a one-to-one relation to an activity, the equilibrium prices will be such that the efficiency frontier has $n-1$ facets in the two-characteristic case. In Figure 6, for example, where the price of commodity 3 brings it to point A on the efficiency frontier, that price could not be allowed to rise to a level bringing it inside point B, or it would disappear from the market; and if its price fell below a level corresponding to C, commodities 2 and 4 would disappear from the market. Thus the limits on prices necessary for the existence of all commodities within a group can be established (in principle) from objective data. Only the demand within that price range depends on consumer preferences.

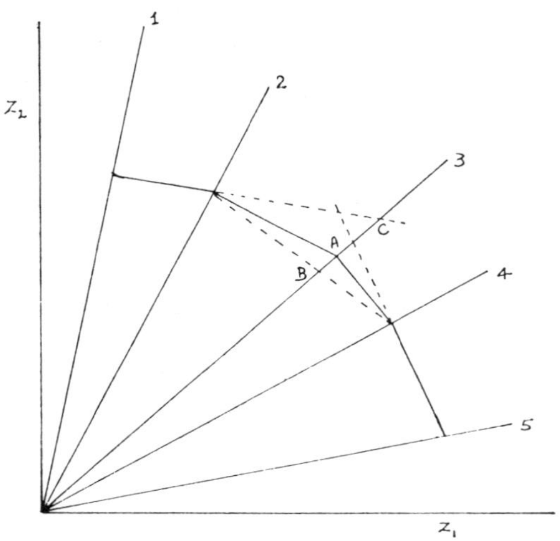

FIG. 6

With a large number of activities relative to characteristics, equilibrium prices would give a many-faceted efficiency frontier that would be approximated by a smooth curve having the general shape of a production possibility curve. For many purposes it may be mathematically simple to analyze the situation in terms of a smooth efficiency frontier. We can then draw on some of the analysis that exists, relating factor inputs to outputs of goods, as in Samuelson (1953*b*). Goods in our model correspond to factors in the production model, and characteristics in our model to commodities in the production model.

The welfare implications of the model set out here are quite complex and deserve a separate treatment. We might note several important aspects of the welfare problem, however, which arise directly from a many-faceted, many-cornered efficiency frontier:

1. Consumers whose choices represent a corner on the efficiency frontier are not, in general, *equating* marginal rates of substitution between characteristics to the ratio of any parameters of the situation or to marginal rates of substitution of other consumers.

2. Consumers whose choices represent points on different facets of the efficiency frontier are equating their marginal rates of substitution between characteristics to different implicit price ratios between characteristics. If there is a one-to-one relationship between goods and activities, the consumers are reacting to relative prices between different sets of goods. The traditional marginal conditions for Paretian exchange optimum do not hold because the price ratio relevant to one consumer's decisions differs from the price ratio relevant to another's. In common-sense terms, the price ratio between a Cadillac and a Continental is irrelevant to my decisions, but the price ratio between two compact cars is relevant, while there are other individuals for whom the Cadillac/Continental ratio is the relevant datum. If the A matrix is strongly connected, however, the implicit price ratios between different activities can correspond to price ratios between the same sets of goods, and the Paretian conditions may be relevant.

Finally, we may note that the shape of the equilibrium efficiency frontier and the existence of the efficiency substitution effect can result in demand conditions with the traditionally assumed properties, even if the traditional, smooth, convex utility function does not exist. In particular, a simple utility function in which characteristics are consumed in constant proportions—the proportions perhaps changing with income—can be substituted for the conventional utility function.

XIII. OPERATIONAL AND PREDICTIVE CHARACTERISTICS OF THE MODEL

In principle, the model set out here can be made operational (that is, empirical coefficients can be assigned to the technology). In practice, the task will be more difficult than the equivalent task of determining the actual production technology of an economy.

To emphasize that the model is not simply heuristic, we can examine a simple scheme for sketching out the efficiency frontier for some commodity group. We shall assume that there is a one-to-one relationship between activities and goods, that at least one characteristic shared by the commodities is capable of independent determination, and that a great quantity of suitable market data is available.

In practice, we will attempt to operate with the minimum number of characteristics that give sufficient explanatory power. These may be combinations of fundamental characteristics (a factor-analysis situation) or fundamental characteristics themselves.

Consider some commodity group such as household detergents. We have a primary objective characteristic, cleaning power, measured in some chosen way. We wish to test whether one or more other characteristics are necessary to describe the consumer-choice situation.

We take a two-dimensional diagram with characteristic "cleaning power" along one axis. Along the axis we mark the cleaning power per dollar outlay of all detergents observed to be sold at the same time. If this is the same for all detergents, this single characteristic describes the situation, and we do not seek further. However, we shall assume this is not so. From our observed market data, we obtain cross-price elasticities between all detergents, taken two at a time. From the model, we know that cross-price elasticities will be highest between detergents with adjacent characteristics vectors, so that the order of the characteristics vectors as we rotate from one axis to the other in the positive quadrant can be established.

The ordering of "cleaning power per dollar" along one axis can be compared with the ordering of the characteristics vectors. If the orderings are the same, an equilibrium efficiency frontier can be built up with two characteristics as in Figure 7a. The slopes of the facets can be determined within limits by the limiting prices at which the various detergents go off the market. If the ordering in terms of cleaning power does not agree with the ordering in terms of cross-elasticity, as in Figure 7b, two characteristics do not describe the market appropriately, since detergent with cleaning power 3 in the figure cannot be on the efficiency frontier. But with a third characteristic, detergent 3 could be adjacent to detergents 2 and 1 in an extra dimension, and we could build up an efficiency frontier in three characteristics.

Other evidence could, of course, be used to determine the efficiency frontier for a given market situation. Among this evidence is that arising from ordinary activity-analysis theory, that, with r characteristics we would expect to find some consumers who used r commodities at the same time, unless all consumers were on corners or edges of the efficiency frontier.

Last, but possibly not least, simply asking consumers about the characteristics associated with various commodities may be much more productive than attempts to extract information concerning preferences within the context of conventional theory.

In general, if consumer preferences are well dispersed (so that all facets of the efficiency frontier are represented in some consumer's choice pattern), a combination of information concerning interpersonal variances in the collections of goods chosen and of the effects of price changes on both aggregate and individual choices can, in principle, be used to ferret out the nature of the consumption technology. Some of the problems that arise are similar to those met by psychologists in measuring intelligence, personality, and other multidimensional traits, so that techniques similar to those used in psychology, such as factor analysis, might prove useful.

Even without specification of the consumption technology, the present theory makes many predictions of a structural kind which may be contrasted with the predictions of conventional theory. Some of these are set out in Chart 1.

XIV. CONCLUSION

In this model we have extended into consumption theory activity analysis, which has proved so penetrating in its application to production theory. The crucial assumption in making this application has been the assumption that goods possess, or give rise to, multiple characteristics in fixed proportions and that it is these characteristics, not goods themselves, on which the consumer's preferences are exercised.

The result, as this brief survey of the possibilities has shown, is a model very many times richer in heuristic explanatory and predictive power than the con-

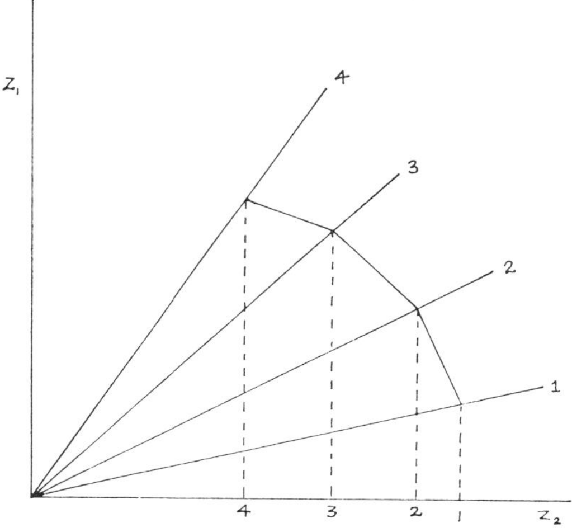

Fig. 7*a*

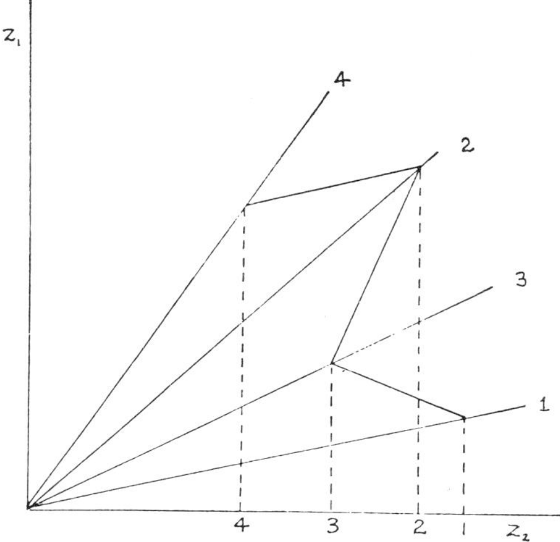

Fig. 7*b*

ventional model of consumer behavior and one that deals easily with those many common-sense characteristics of actual behavior that have found no place in traditional exposition.

This paper is nothing more than a condensed presentation of some of the great number of possible ways in which the model can be used. It is hoped that a door has been opened to a new, rich treasure house of ideas for the future development of the most refined and least powerful branch of economic theory, the theory of the consumer himself.

CHART 1

This Theory	Conventional Theory
Wood will not be a close substitute for bread, since characteristics are dissimilar	No reason except "tastes" why they should not be close substitutes
A red Buick will be a close substitute for a gray Buick	No reason why they should be any closer substitutes than wood and bread
Substitution (for example, butter and margarine) is frequently intrinsic and objective, will be observed in many societies under many market conditions	No reason why close substitutes in one context should be close substitutes in another
A good may be displaced from the market by new goods or by price changes	No presumption that goods will be completely displaced
The labor-leisure choice may have a marked occupational pattern	Labor-leisure choice determined solely by individual preferences; no pattern, other than between individuals, would be predicted
(Gresham's Law) A monetary asset may cease to be on the efficiency frontier, and will disappear from the economy	No ex ante presumption that any good or asset will disappear from the economy
An individual is completely unaffected by price changes that leave unchanged the portion of the efficiency frontier on which his choice rests	An individual is affected by changes in all prices
Some commodity groups may be intrinsic, and universally so	No presumption that commodities forming a group (defined by a break in spectrum of cross-elasticities) in one context will form a group in another context

APPENDIX

I. TRANSFORMATION OF THE UTILITY FUNCTION INTO G-SPACE

Consider some characteristics vector z^* which does have an image x^* in G-space, and consider the set P of all vectors z preferred or indifferent to z^*. If U has the traditional properties, the set P is convex with an inner boundary which is the indifference surface through z^*. Now $z \geqq z^*$ implies z is in P so that every x such that $Bx \geqq z^*$, a set S, is preferred or indifferent to x^*. If we take some other z' in P, every x in S' such that $Bx \geqq z'$ is also preferred or indifferent to x'^*. Similarly for z'' in P and S'' such that that $Bx \geqq z''$, and so on. From the theory of inequalities, the sets S, S', S'' . . . are all convex, and since P is convex, a linear combination of z', z'' is in P, so that a linear combination of x's in S', S'' is also preferred or indifferent to x^*. Hence the set $\bar{P}$ of all x preferred or indifferent to x^* is the linear combination of all the sets $S, S', S'', \ldots$ and so is convex.

Thus the utility function transformed into G-space retains its essential convexity. A more intuitive way of looking at the situation is to note that all characteristics collections which are actually available are contained in an n-dimensional slice through the r-dimensional utility function and that all slices through a convex function are themselves convex. The transformation of this n-dimensional slice into G-space preserves this convexity.

II. "REVEALED PREFERENCE" IN A COMPLEX ECONOMY

We shall use the structural properties of the consumption technology A, B (dropping the assumption of a one-to-one relationship between goods and activities) to show that in a complex economy with more activities than characteristics the efficiency choice always satisfies the weak axiom of revealed preference and will satisfy the strong axiom for sufficiently large price changes, so that satisfaction of even the strong axiom does not "reveal" convexity of the preference function itself.

Consider an economy with a consumption technology defined by

$$z = By\,,$$

$$x = Ay\,,$$

and a consumer subject to a budget constraint of the form $p^*x \leqq k$ who has chosen goods x^* for activities y^*, giving characteristics z^*.

We know that if the consumer has made an efficient choice, y^* is the solution of the program (the value of which is k).

$$\begin{aligned}&\text{Minimize } p^*Ay\ (= p^*x):\\ &\qquad By = z^*\,,\ y \geqq 0\,,\end{aligned} \qquad (8.1a)$$

which has a dual (solution v^*).

$$\text{Maximize } vz^*: vB \leqq p^*A\,. \qquad (8.1b)$$

The dual variables v can be interpreted as the implicit prices of the characteristics themselves. From the Kuh-Tucker Theorem, we can associate the vector v with the slope of the separating hyperplane between the set of attainable z's and the set of z's preferred or indifferent to z^*.

For the same satisfactions vector Z^* and a new price vector p^{**} the efficiency choice will be the solution y^{**} (giving x^{**}), v^{**}, of

$$\begin{aligned}&\text{Min } p^{**}Ay: By = z^*\,,\ y \geqq 0\,,\\ &\text{Max } vz^*: vb \leqq p^{**}A\,.\end{aligned} \qquad (8.2)$$

Since z^* is the same in (8.1) and (8.2), y^{**} is a feasible solution of (8.1) and y^* of (8.2). From the fundamental theorem of linear programing we have

$$p^{**}Ay^* \geqq v^{**}z^* = p^{**}Ay^{**}\,, \qquad (8.3)$$

$$p^*Ay^{**} \geqq v^*z^* = p^*Ay^*\,. \qquad (8.4)$$

A program identical with (8.2) except that z^* is replaced by hz^* will have a solution hy^{**}, v^{**}. Choose h so that $hp^{**}Ay^{**} = p^{**}Ay^*$. From (8.3) $h \geqq 1$. From (8.4),

$$hp^*Ay^{**} \geqq p^*Ay^{**} \geqq p^*Ay^*\,. \qquad (8.5)$$

If we now write p for p^*, p' for p^{**}; $x = Ay^*$, $x' = hAy^{**}$, we have

$$p'x' = p'x \text{ implies } px' \geqq px\,, \qquad (8.6)$$

satisfying the *weak axiom of revealed preference*.

The equality will occur on the right in (8.6) only if equalities hold in *both* (8.3) and (8.4), and these will hold only if y^{**} is optimal as well as feasible in (8.1), and y^* is optimal as well as feasible in (8.2). In general, if the number of activities exceeds the number of characteristics, we can always find two prices p^*, p^{**} so related that neither of the solutions y^{**}, y^* is optimal in the other's program.

Hence, if the number of activities exceeds the number of characteristics (representing the number of primary constraints in the program), we can find prices so related that the strong axiom of revealed preference is satisfied, even though the consumer has obtained characteristics in unchanged proportions (z^*, hz^*) and has revealed nothing of his preference map.

The above effect represents an *efficiency substitution effect* which would occur even if characteristics were consumed in absolutely fixed proportions. If the consumer substitutes between different satisfactions bundles when his budget constraint changes, this private substitution effect is additional to the efficiency substitution effect.

Just as the conceptual experiment implicit in revealed preference implies "overcompensation" in the conventional analysis (see Samuelson 1948, 1953*a*), so the efficiency effect leads to "external overcompensation" additional to private overcompensation.

REFERENCES

Becker, Gary S. "A Theory of the Allocation of Time," *Econ. J.*, September, 1965.

Debreu, Gerald. *Theory of Value*. Cowles Foundation Monograph 17, 1959.

———. "Topological Methods in Cardinal Utility Theory," in K. J. Arrow, S. Karlin, and P. Suppes (eds.). *Mathematical Methods in the Social Sciences, 1959*. Stanford, Calif.: Stanford Univ. Press, 1960.

Friedman, Milton, and Savage, L. J. "The Expected-Utility Hypothesis and the Measurability of Utility," *J.P.E.*, Vol. LX (December, 1952).

Gorman, W. M. "Separable Utility and Aggregation," *Econometrica*, Vol. XXVII (July, 1959).

Johnson, Harry G. "Demand Theory Further Revised or Goods Are Goods," *Economica*, N.S. 25 (May, 1958).

Karlin, S. *Mathematical Methods and Theory in Games, Programming and Economics*. New York: Pergamon Press, 1959.

Koopmans, T. C. "Stationary Ordinal Utility and Impatience," *Econometrica*, Vol. XXIII (April, 1960).

Koopmans, T. C., Diamond, P. A., and Williamson, R. E. "Stationary Utility and Time Perspective," *ibid.*, Vol. XXXII (January–April, 1964).

Lancaster, Kelvin J. "Revising Demand Theory," *Economica*, N.S. 24 (November, 1957).

———. "The Scope of Qualitative Economics," *Rev. Econ. Studies*, Vol. XXIX (1962).

———. "An Axiomatic Theory of Consumer Time Preference," *Internat. Econ. Rev.*, Vol. IV (May, 1963).

———. "The Theory of Qualitative Linear Systems," *Econometrica*, Vol. XXXIII (April, 1965).

———. "Change and Innovation in the Technology of Consumption," *A.E.R.*, Papers and Proceedings, May, 1966 (to be published).

Morishima, M. "The Problem of Intrinsic Complementarity and Separability of Goods," *Metroeconomica*, Vol. XI (December, 1959).

Pearce, I. F. *A Contribution to Demand Analysis*. New York: Oxford Univ. Press, 1964.

Quandt, R. E. "A Probabilistic Theory of Consumer Behaviour," *Q.J.E.*, Vol. LXX (November, 1956).

Samuelson, P. A. "Consumption Theory in Terms of Revealed Preference," *Economica*, N.S. 15 (November, 1948).

———. "Consumption Theorems in Terms of Over-Compensation Rather than Indifference Comparisons," *ibid.*, N.S. 20 (February, 1953). (*a*)

———. "Prices of Factors and Goods in General Equilibrium," *Rev. Econ. Studies*, Vol. XXI (1953). (*b*)

Stigler, G. J. "The Cost of Subsistence," *J. Farm Econ.*, Vol. XXVII (1945).

Strotz, Robert, "The Empirical Implications of a Utility Tree," *Econometrica*, Vol. XXV (April, 1957).

———. "The Utility Tree: A Correction and Further Appraisal," *ibid.*, Vol. XXVII (July, 1959).

Thrall, Robert M., Coombs, C., and Davis, R. L. *Decision Processes*. New York: Wiley & Sons, 1954.

Uzawa, H. "Preference and Rational Choice in the Theory of Consumption," in K. J. Arrow, S. Karlin, and P. Suppes (eds.). *Mathematical Methods in the Social Sciences, 1959*. Stanford, Calif.: Stanford Univ. Press, 1960.

Von Neumann, J., and Morgenstern, O. *Theory of Games and Economic Behaviour*. Princeton, N.J.: Princeton Univ. Press, 1944.

[3]

THE ECONOMIC JOURNAL

SEPTEMBER 1965

A THEORY OF THE ALLOCATION OF TIME

I. Introduction

Throughout history the amount of time spent at work has never consistently been much greater than that spent at other activities. Even a work week of fourteen hours a day for six days still leaves half the total time for sleeping, eating and other activities. Economic development has led to a large secular decline in the work week, so that whatever may have been true of the past, to-day it is below fifty hours in most countries, less than a third of the total time available. Consequently the allocation and efficiency of non-working time may now be more important to economic welfare than that of working time; yet the attention paid by economists to the latter dwarfs any paid to the former.

Fortunately, there is a movement under way to redress the balance. The time spent at work declined secularly, partly because young persons increasingly delayed entering the labour market by lengthening their period of schooling. In recent years many economists have stressed that the time of students is one of the inputs into the educational process, that this time could be used to participate more fully in the labour market and therefore that one of the costs of education is the forgone earnings of students. Indeed, various estimates clearly indicate that forgone earnings is the dominant private and an important social cost of both high-school and college education in the United States.[1] The increased awareness of the importance of forgone earnings has resulted in several attempts to economise on students' time, as manifested, say, by the spread of the quarterly and tri-mester systems.[2]

Most economists have now fully grasped the importance of forgone earnings in the educational process and, more generally, in all investments in human capital, and criticise educationalists and others for neglecting them. In the light of this it is perhaps surprising that economists have not been

[1] See T. W. Schultz, "The Formation of Human Capital by Education," *Journal of Political Economy* (December 1960), and my *Human Capital* (Columbia University Press for the N.B.E.R., 1964), Chapter IV. I argue there that the importance of forgone earnings can be directly seen, *e.g.*, from the failure of free tuition to eliminate impediments to college attendance or the increased enrolments that sometimes occur in depressed areas or time periods.

[2] On the cause of the secular trend towards an increased school year see my comments, *ibid.*, p. 103.

equally sophisticated about other non-working uses of time. For example, the cost of a service like the theatre or a good like meat is generally simply said to equal their market prices, yet everyone would agree that the theatre and even dining take time, just as schooling does, time that often could have been used productively. If so, the full costs of these activities would equal the sum of market prices and the forgone value of the time used up. In other words, indirect costs should be treated on the same footing when discussing all non-work uses of time, as they are now in discussions of schooling.

In the last few years a group of us at Columbia University have been occupied, perhaps initially independently but then increasingly less so, with introducing the cost of time systematically into decisions about non-work activities. J. Mincer has shown with several empirical examples how estimates of the income elasticity of demand for different commodities are biased when the cost of time is ignored;[1] J. Owen has analysed how the demand for leisure can be affected;[2] E. Dean has considered the allocation of time between subsistence work and market participation in some African economies;[3] while, as already mentioned, I have been concerned with the use of time in education, training and other kinds of human capital. Here I attempt to develop a general treatment of the allocation of time in all other non-work activities. Although under my name alone, much of any credit it merits belongs to the stimulus received from Mincer, Owen, Dean and other past and present participants in the Labor Workshop at Columbia.[4]

The plan of the discussion is as follows. The first section sets out a basic theoretical analysis of choice that includes the cost of time on the same footing as the cost of market goods, while the remaining sections treat various empirical implications of the theory. These include a new approach to changes in hours of work and " leisure," the full integration of so-called " productive " consumption into economic analysis, a new analysis of the effect of income on the quantity and " quality " of commodities consumed, some suggestions on the measurement of productivity, an economic analysis of queues and a few others as well. Although I refer to relevant empirical

[1] See his " Market Prices, Opportunity Costs, and Income Effects," in *Measurement in Economics: Studies in Mathematical Economics and Econometrics in Memory of Yehuda Grunfeld* (Stanford University Press, 1963). In his well-known earlier study Mincer considered the allocation of married women between " housework " and labour force participation. (See his " Labor Force Participation of Married Women," in *Aspects of Labor Economics* (Princeton University Press, 1962).)

[2] See his *The Supply of Labor and the Demand for Recreation* (unpublished Ph.D. dissertation, Columbia University, 1964).

[3] See his *Economic Analysis and African Response to Price* (unpublished Ph.D. dissertation, Columbia University, 1963).

[4] Let me emphasise, however, that I alone am responsible for any errors.

I would also like to express my appreciation for the comments received when presenting these ideas to seminars at the Universities of California (Los Angeles), Chicago, Pittsburgh, Rochester and Yale, and to a session at the 1963 Meetings of the Econometric Society. Extremely helpful comments on an earlier draft were provided by Milton Friedman and by Gregory C. Chow; the latter also assisted in the mathematical formulation. Linda Kee provided useful research assistance. My research was partially supported by the IBM Corporation.

work that has come to my attention, little systematic testing of the theory has been attempted.

II. A Revised Theory of Choice

According to traditional theory, households maximise utility functions of the form

$$U = U(y_1, y_2, \ldots, y_n) \qquad (1)$$

subject to the resource constraint

$$\sum p_i' y_i = I = W + V \qquad (2)$$

where y_i are goods purchased on the market, p'_i are their prices, I is money income, W is earnings and V is other income. As the introduction suggests, the point of departure here is the systematic incorporation of non-working time. Households will be assumed to combine time and market goods to produce more basic commodities that directly enter their utility functions. One such commodity is the seeing of a play, which depends on the input of actors, script, theatre and the playgoer's time; another is sleeping, which depends on the input of a bed, house (pills?) and time. These commodities will be called Z_i and written as

$$Z_i = f_i(x_i, T_i) \qquad (3)$$

where x_i is a vector of market goods and T_i a vector of time inputs used in producing the ith commodity.[1] Note that, when capital goods such as refrigerators or automobiles are used, x refers to the services yielded by the goods. Also note that T_i is a vector because, *e.g.*, the hours used during the day or on weekdays may be distinguished from those used at night or on week-ends. Each dimension of T_i refers to a different aspect of time. Generally, the partial derivatives of Z_i with respect to both x_i and T_i are non-negative.[2]

In this formulation households are both producing units and utility maximisers. They combine time and market goods via the "production functions" f_i to produce the basic commodities Z_i, and they choose the best combination of these commodities in the conventional way by maximising a utility function

$$U = U(Z_i, \ldots Z_m) \equiv U(f_1, \ldots f_m) \equiv U(x_1, \ldots x_m;\ T_1, \ldots T_m) \qquad (4)$$

[1] There are several empirical as well as conceptual advantages in assuming that households combine goods and time to produce commodities instead of simply assuming that the amount of time used at an activity is a direct function of the amount of goods consumed. For example, a change in the cost of goods relative to time could cause a significant substitution away from the one rising in relative cost. This, as well as other applications, are treated in the following sections.

[2] If a good or time period was used in producing several commodities I assume that these "joint costs" could be fully and uniquely allocated among the commodities. The problems here are no different from those usually arising in the analysis of multi-product firms.

subject to a budget constraint

$$g(Z_i, \ldots Z_m) = Z \quad . \quad . \quad . \quad . \quad . \quad (5)$$

where g is an expenditure function of Z_i and Z is the bound on resources. The integration of production and consumption is at odds with the tendency for economists to separate them sharply, production occurring in firms and consumption in households. It should be pointed out, however, that in recent years economists increasingly recognise that a household is truly a " small factory ":[1] it combines capital goods, raw materials and labour to clean, feed, procreate and otherwise produce useful commodities. Undoubtedly the fundamental reason for the traditional separation is that firms are usually given control over working time in exchange for market goods, while " discretionary " control over market goods and consumption time is retained by households as they create their own utility. If (presumably different) firms were also given control over market goods and consumption time in exchange for providing utility the separation would quickly fade away in analysis as well as in fact.

The basic goal of the analysis is to find measures of g and Z which facilitate the development of empirical implications. The most direct approach is to assume that the utility function in equation (4) is maximised subject to separate constraints on the expenditure of market goods and time, and to the production functions in equation (3). The goods constraint can be written as

$$\sum_1^m p_i x_i = I = V + T_w \bar{w} \quad . \quad . \quad . \quad . \quad . \quad (6)$$

where p_i is a vector giving the unit prices of x_i, T_w is a vector giving the hours spent at work and $\bar{w}$ is a vector giving the earnings per unit of T_w. The time constraints can be written as

$$\sum_1^m T_i = T_c = T - T_w \quad . \quad . \quad . \quad . \quad . \quad (7)$$

where T_c is a vector giving the total time spent at consumption and T is a vector giving the total time available. The production functions (3) can be written in the equivalent form

$$\left.\begin{aligned} T_i &\equiv t_i Z_i \\ x_i &\equiv b_i Z_i \end{aligned}\right\} \quad . \quad . \quad . \quad . \quad . \quad . \quad . \quad (8)$$

where t_i is a vector giving the input of time per unit of Z_i and b_i is a similar vector for market goods.

The problem would appear to be to maximise the utility function (4) subject to the multiple constraints (6) and (7) and to the production relations (8). There is, however, really only one basic constraint: (6) is not independent of (7) because time can be converted into goods by using less time

[1] See, *e.g.*, A. K. Cairncross, " Economic Schizophrenia," *Scottish Journal of Political Economy* (February 1958).

at consumption and more at work. Thus, substituting for T_w in (6) its equivalent in (7) gives the single constraint [1]

$$\sum p_i x_i + \sum T_i \bar{w} = V + T\bar{w} \quad . \quad . \quad . \quad . \quad . \quad (9)$$

By using (8), (9) can be written as

$$\sum (p_i b_i + t_i \bar{w}) Z_i = V + T\bar{w} \quad . \quad . \quad . \quad . \quad (10)$$

with

$$\left.\begin{aligned} \pi_i &= p_i b_i + t_i \bar{w} \\ S' &= V + T\bar{w} \end{aligned}\right\} \quad . \quad . \quad . \quad . \quad . \quad . \quad . \quad (11)$$

The full price of a unit of Z_i (π_i) is the sum of the prices of the goods and of the time used per unit of Z_i. That is, the full price of consumption is the sum of direct and indirect prices in the same way that the full cost of investing in human capital is the sum of direct and indirect costs.[2] These direct and indirect prices are symmetrical determinants of total price, and there is no analytical reason to stress one rather than the other.

The resource constraint on the right side of equation (10), S', is easy to interpret if $\bar{w}$ were a constant, independent of the Z_i. For then S' gives the money income achieved if all the time available were devoted to work. This achievable income is "spent" on the commodities Z_i either directly through expenditures on goods, $\sum p_i b_i Z_i$, or indirectly through the forgoing of income, $\sum t_i \bar{w} Z_i$, *i.e.*, by using time at consumption rather than at work. As long as $\bar{w}$ were constant, and if there were constant returns in producing Z_i so that b_i and t_i were fixed for given p_i and $\bar{w}$ the equilibrium condition resulting from maximising (4) subject to (10) takes a very simple form:

$$U_i = \frac{\partial U}{\partial Z_i} = \lambda \pi_i \qquad i = 1, \ldots m \quad . \quad . \quad . \quad (12)$$

where λ is the marginal utility of money income. If $\bar{w}$ were not constant the resource constraint in equation (10) would not have any particularly useful interpretation: $S' = V + T\bar{w}$ would overstate the money income achievable as long as marginal wage-rates were below average ones. Moreover, the equilibrium conditions would become more complicated than (12) because marginal would have to replace average prices.

The total resource constraint could be given the sensible interpretation of the maximum money income achievable only in the special and unlikely case when average earnings were constant. This suggests dropping the approach based on explicitly considering separate goods and time constraints and substituting one in which the total resource constraint necessarily equalled the maximum money income achievable, which will be simply called "full income." [3] This income could in general be obtained by devoting all the

[1] The dependency among constraints distinguishes this problem from many other multiple-constraint situations in economic analysis, such as those arising in the usual theory of rationing (see J. Tobin, "A Survey of the Theory of Rationing," *Econometrica* (October, 1952)). Rationing would reduce to a formally identical single-constraint situation if rations were saleable and fully convertible into money income.

[2] See my *Human Capital*, *op. cit.*

[3] This term emerged from a conversation with Milton Friedman.

time and other resources of a household to earning income, with no regard for consumption. Of course, all the time would not usually be spent " at " a job: sleep, food, even leisure are required for efficiency, and some time (and other resources) would have to be spent on these activities in order to maximise money income. The amount spent would, however, be determined solely by the effect on income and not by any effect on utility. Slaves, for example, might be permitted time " off " from work only in so far as that maximised their output, or free persons in poor environments might have to maximise money income simply to survive.[1]

Households in richer countries do, however, forfeit money income in order to obtain additional utility, *i.e.*, they exchange money income for a greater amount of psychic income. For example, they might increase their leisure time, take a pleasant job in preference to a better-paying unpleasant one, employ unproductive nephews or eat more than is warranted by considerations of productivity. In these and other situations the amount of money income forfeited measures the cost of obtaining additional utility.

Thus the full income approach provides a meaningful resource constraint and one firmly based on the fact that goods and time can be combined into a single overall constraint because time can be converted into goods through money income. It also incorporates a unified treatment of all substitutions of non-pecuniary for pecuniary income, regardless of their nature or whether they occur on the job or in the household. The advantages of this will become clear as the analysis proceeds.

If full income is denoted by S, and if the total earnings forgone or " lost " by the interest in utility is denoted by L, the identity relating L to S and I is simply

$$L(Z_1, \ldots, Z_m) \equiv S - I(Z_1, \ldots, Z_m) \quad . \quad . \quad . \quad (13)$$

I and L are functions of the Z_i because how much is earned or forgone depends on the consumption set chosen; for example, up to a point, the less leisure chosen the larger the money income and the smaller the amount forgone.[2] Using equations (6) and (8), equation (13) can be written as

$$\sum p_i b_i Z_i + L(Z_1, \ldots, Z_m) \equiv S \quad . \quad . \quad . \quad . \quad (14)$$

[1] Any utility received would only be an incidental by-product of the pursuit of money income. Perhaps this explains why utility analysis was not clearly formulated and accepted until economic development had raised incomes well above the subsistence level.

[2] Full income is achieved by maximising the earnings function

$$W = W(Z_1, \ldots Z_m) \quad . \quad . \quad . \quad . \quad . \quad . \quad . \quad . \quad . \quad (1')$$

subject to the expenditure constraint in equation (6), to the inequality

$$\sum_1^m T_i \leq T \quad . \quad . \quad . \quad . \quad . \quad . \quad . \quad . \quad . \quad . \quad . \quad (2')$$

and to the restrictions in (8). I assume for simplicity that the amount of each dimension of time used in producing commodities is less than the total available, so that (2′) can be ignored; it is not

This basic resource constraint states that full income is spent either directly on market goods or indirectly through the forgoing of money income. Unfortunately, there is no simple expression for the average price of Z_i as there is in equation (10). However, marginal, not average, prices are relevant for behaviour, and these would be identical for the constraint in (10) only when average earnings, $\bar{w}$, was constant. But, if so, the expression for the loss function simplifies to

$$L = \bar{w}T_c = \bar{w}\sum t_i Z_i \quad . \quad . \quad . \quad . \quad . \quad . \quad . \quad (15)$$

and (14) reduces to (10). Moreover, even in the general case the total marginal prices resulting from (14) can always be divided into direct and indirect components: the equilibrium conditions resulting from maximising the utility function subject to (14) [1] are

$$U_i = T(p_i b_i + L_i), \qquad i = 1, \ldots, m \quad . \quad . \quad . \quad (16)$$

where $p_i b_i$ is the direct and L_i the indirect component of the total marginal price $p_i b_i + L_i$.[2]

Behind the division into direct and indirect costs is the allocation of time and goods between work-orientated and consumption-orientated activities. This suggests an alternative division of costs; namely, into those resulting from the allocation of goods and those resulting from the allocation of time. Write $L_i = \partial L / \partial Z_i$ as

$$L_i = \frac{\partial L}{\partial T_i}\frac{\partial T_i}{\partial Z_i} + \frac{\partial L}{\partial x_i}\frac{\partial x_i}{\partial Z_i} \quad . \quad . \quad . \quad . \quad . \quad . \quad (17)$$

$$= l_i t_i + c_i b_i \quad . \quad . \quad . \quad . \quad . \quad . \quad . \quad . \quad . \quad (18)$$

where $l_i = \dfrac{\partial L}{\partial T_i}$ and $c_i = \dfrac{\partial L}{\partial x_i}$ are the marginal forgone earnings of using more time and goods respectively on Z_i. Equation (16) can then be written as

$$U_i = T[b_i(p_i + c_i) + t_i l_i] \quad . \quad . \quad . \quad . \quad (19)$$

The total marginal cost of Z_i is the sum of $b_i(p_i + c_i)$, the marginal cost of using goods in producing Z_i, and $t_i l_i$, the marginal cost of using time. This division would be equivalent to that between direct and indirect costs only if $c_i = 0$ or if there were no indirect costs of using goods.

difficult to incorporate this constraint. Maximising (1′) subject to (6) and (8) yields the following conditions

$$\frac{\partial W}{\partial Z_i} = \frac{p_i b_i \sigma}{1 + \sigma} \quad . \quad . \quad . \quad . \quad . \quad . \quad . \quad . \quad . \quad . \quad (3')$$

where σ is the marginal productivity of money income. Since the loss function $L = (S - V) - W$, the equilibrium conditions to minimise the loss is the same as (3′) except for a change in sign.

[1] Households maximise their utility subject only to the single total resource constraint given by (14), for once the full income constraint is satisfied, there is no other restriction on the set of Z_i that can be chosen. By introducing the concept of full income the problem of maximising utility subject to the time and goods constraints is solved in two stages: first, full income is determined from the goods and time constraints, and then utility is maximised subject only to the constraint imposed by full income.

[2] It can easily be shown that the equilibrium conditions of (16) are in fact precisely the same as those following in general from equation (10).

The accompanying figure shows the equilibrium given by equation (16) for a two-commodity world. In equilibrium the slope of the full income

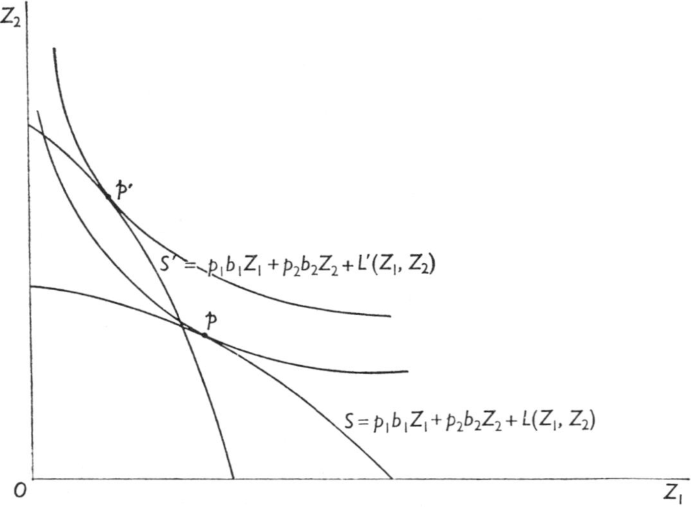

opportunity curve, which equals the ratio of marginal prices, would equal the slope of an indifference curve, which equals the ratio of marginal utilities. Equilibrium occurs at p and p' for the opportunity curves S and S' respectively.

The rest of the paper is concerned with developing numerous empirical implications of this theory, starting with determinants of hours worked and concluding with an economic interpretation of various queueing systems. To simplify the presentation, it is assumed that the distinction between direct and indirect costs is equivalent to that between goods and time costs; in other words, the marginal forgone cost of the use of goods, c_i, is set equal to zero. The discussion would not be much changed, but would be more cumbersome were this not assumed.[1] Finally, until Section IV goods and time are assumed to be used in fixed proportions in producing commodities; that is, the coefficients b_i and t_i in equation (8) are treated as constants.

III. Applications

(a) *Hours of Work*

If the effects of various changes on the time used on consumption, T_c, could be determined their effects on hours worked, T_w, could be found residually from equation (7). This section considers, among other things, the effects of changes in income, earnings and market prices on T_c, and thus on T_w,

[1] Elsewhere I have discussed some effects of the allocation of goods on productivity (see my "Investment in Human Capital: A Theoretical Analysis," *Journal of Political Economy*, special supplement (October 1962), Section 2); essentially the same discussion can be found in *Human Capital, op. cit.*, Chapter II.

using as the major tool of analysis differences among commodities in the importance of forgone earnings.

The relative marginal importance of forgone earnings is defined as

$$\alpha_i = \frac{l_i t_i}{p_i b_i + l_i t_i} \quad . \quad . \quad . \quad . \quad . \quad . \quad . \quad (20)$$

The importance of forgone earnings would be greater the larger l_i and t_i, the forgone earnings per hour of time and the number of hours used per unit of Z_i respectively, while it would be smaller the larger p_i and b_i, the market price of goods and the number of goods used per unit of Z_i respectively. Similarly, the relative marginal importance of time is defined as

$$\gamma_i = \frac{t_i}{p_i b_i + l_i t_i} \quad . \quad . \quad . \quad . \quad . \quad . \quad . \quad (21)$$

If full income increased solely because of an increase in V (other money income) there would simply be a parallel shift of the opportunity curve to the right with no change in relative commodity prices. The consumption of most commodities would have to increase; if all did, hours worked would decrease, for the total time spent on consumption must increase if the output of all commodities did, and by equation (7) the time spent at work is inversely related to that spent on consumption. Hours worked could increase only if relatively time intensive commodities, those with large γ, were sufficiently inferior.[1]

A uniform percentage increase in earnings for all allocations of time would increase the cost per hour used in consumption by the same percentage for all commodities.[2] The relative prices of different commodities would, however, change as long as forgone earnings were not equally important for all; in particular, the prices of commodities having relatively important forgone earnings would rise more. Now the fundamental theorem of

[1] The problem is: under what conditions would

$$\frac{-\partial T_w}{\partial V} = \frac{\partial T_c}{\partial V} = \Sigma t_i \frac{\partial Z_i}{\partial V} < 0 \quad . \quad . \quad . \quad . \quad . \quad . \quad . \quad . \quad (1')$$

when

$$\Sigma(p_i b_i + l_i t_i) \frac{\partial Z_i}{\partial V} = 1 \quad . \quad . \quad . \quad . \quad . \quad . \quad . \quad . \quad . \quad . \quad (2')$$

If the analysis were limited to a two-commodity world where Z_1 was more time intensive, then it can easily be shown that (1′) would hold if, and only if,

$$\frac{\partial Z_1}{\partial V} < \frac{-\gamma_2}{(\gamma_1 - \gamma_2)(p_1 b_1 + l_1 t_1)} < 0 \quad . \quad . \quad . \quad . \quad . \quad . \quad . \quad (3')$$

[2] By a uniform change of β is meant

$$W_1 = (1 + \beta) W_0(Z_1, \ldots Z_n)$$

where W_0 represents the earnings function before the change and W_1 represents it afterwards. Since the loss function is defined as

$$\begin{aligned} L &= S - W - V \\ &= W(\hat{Z}) - W(Z), \end{aligned}$$

then

$$\begin{aligned} L_1 &= W_1(\hat{Z}) - W_1(Z) \\ &= (1 + \beta)\,[W_0(\hat{Z}) - W_0(Z)] = (1 + \beta) L_0 \end{aligned}$$

Consequently, all opportunities costs also change by β.

demand theory states that a compensated change in relative prices would induce households to consume less of commodities rising in price. The figure shows the effect of a rise in earnings fully compensated by a decline in other income: the opportunity curve would be rotated clockwise through the initial position p if Z_1 were the more earnings-intensive commodity. In the figure the new equilibrium p' must be to the left and above p, or less Z_1 and more Z_2 would be consumed.

Therefore a compensated uniform rise in earnings would lead to a shift away from earnings-intensive commodities and towards goods-intensive ones. Since earnings and time intensiveness tend to be positively correlated,[1] consumption would be shifted from time-intensive commodities. A shift away from such commodities would, however, result in a reduction in the total time spent in consumption, and thus an increase in the time spent at work.[2]

The effect of an uncompensated increase in earnings on hours worked would depend on the relative strength of the substitution and income effects. The former would increase hours, the latter reduce them; which dominates cannot be determined *a priori.*

The conclusion that a pure rise in earnings increases and a pure rise in income reduces hours of work must sound very familiar, for they are traditional results of the well-known labour–leisure analysis. What, then, is the relation between our analysis, which treats all commodities symmetrically and stresses only their differences in relative time and earning intensities, and the usual analysis, which distinguishes a commodity having special properties called " leisure " from other more commonplace commodities? It is easily shown that the usual labour–leisure analysis can be looked upon as a special case of ours in which the cost of the commodity called leisure consists entirely of forgone earnings and the cost of other commodities entirely of goods.[3]

[1] According to the definitions of earning and time intensity in equations (20) and (21), they would be positively correlated unless l_i and t_i were sufficiently negatively correlated. See the further discussion later on.

[2] Let it be stressed that this conclusion usually holds, even when households are irrational; sophisticated calculations about the value of time at work or in consumption, or substantial knowledge about the amount of time used by different commodities is not required. Changes in the hours of work, even of non-maximising, impulsive, habitual, etc., households would tend to be positively related to compensated changes in earnings because demand curves tend to be negatively inclined even for such households (see G. S. Becker, " Irrational Behavior and Economic Theory," *Journal of Political Economy* (February 1962)).

[3] Suppose there were two commodities Z_1 and Z_2, where the cost of Z_1 depended only on the cost of market goods, while the cost of Z_2 depended only on the cost of time. The goods-budget constraint would then simply be

$$p_1 b_1 Z_1 = I = V + T_w \bar{w}$$

and the constraint on time would be

$$t_2 Z_2 = T - T_w$$

This is essentially the algebra of the analysis presented by Henderson and Quandt, and their treatment is representative. They call Z_2 " leisure," and Z_1 an average of different commodities. Their

As a description of reality such an approach, of course, is not tenable, since virtually all activities use both time and goods. Perhaps it would be defended either as an analytically necessary or extremely insightful approximation to reality. Yet the usual substitution and income effects of a change in resources on hours worked have easily been derived from a more general analysis which stresses only that the relative importance of time varies among commodities. The rest of the paper tries to go further and demonstrate that the traditional approach, with its stress on the demand for " leisure," apparently has seriously impeded the development of insights about the economy, since the more direct and general approach presented here naturally leads to a variety of implications never yet obtained.

The two determinants of the importance of forgone earnings are the amount of time used per dollar of goods and the cost per unit of time. Reading a book, taking a haircut or commuting use more time per dollar of goods than eating dinner, frequenting a night-club or sending children to private summer camps. Other things the same, forgone earnings would be more important for the former set of commodities than the latter.

The importance of forgone earnings would be determined solely by time intensity only if the cost of time was the same for all commodities. Presumably, however, it varies considerably among commodities and at different periods. For example, the cost of time is often less on week-ends and in the evenings because many firms are closed then,[1] which explains why a famous liner intentionally includes a week-end in each voyage between the United States and Europe.[2] The cost of time would also tend to be less for commodities that contribute to productive effort, traditionally called " productive consumption." A considerable amount of sleep, food and even " play " fall under this heading. The opportunity cost of the time is less because these commodities indirectly contribute to earnings. Productive consumption has had a long but bandit-like existence in economic thought; our analysis does systematically incorporate it into household decision-making.

Although the formal specification of leisure in economic models has ignored expenditures on goods, cannot one argue that a more correct specification would simply associate leisure with relatively important forgone earnings? Most conceptions of leisure do imply that it is time intensive and does not indirectly contribute to earnings,[3] two of the important

equilibrium condition that the rate of substitution between goods and leisure equals the real wage-rate is just a special case of our equation (19) (see *Microeconomic Theory* (McGraw-Hill, 1958), p. 23).

[1] For workers receiving premium pay on the week-ends and in the evenings, however, the cost of time may be considerably greater then.

[2] See the advertisement by United States Lines in various issues of the *New Yorker* magazine: " The S.S. *United States* regularly includes a week-end in its 5 days to Europe, saving [economic] time for businessmen " (my insertion).

[3] For example, *Webster's Collegiate Dictionary* defines leisurely as " characterized by leisure, taking *abundant time* " (my italics); or S. de Grazia, in his recent *Of Time, Work and Leisure*, says, " Leisure is a state of being in which activity is performed for its own sake or as its own end " (New York: The Twentieth Century Fund, 1962, p. 15).

characteristics of earnings-intensive commodities. On the other hand, not all of what are usually considered leisure activities do have relatively important forgone earnings: night-clubbing is generally considered leisure, and yet, at least in its more expensive forms, has a large expenditure component. Conversely, some activities have relatively large forgone earnings and are not considered leisure: haircuts or child care are examples. Consequently, the distinction between earnings-intensive and other commodities corresponds only partly to the usual distinction between leisure and other commodities. Since it has been shown that the relative importance of forgone earnings rather than any concept of leisure is more relevant for economic analysis, less attention should be paid to the latter. Indeed, although the social philosopher might have to define precisely the concept of leisure,[1] the economist can reach all his traditional results as well as many more without introducing it at all!

Not only is it difficult to distinguish leisure from other non-work [2] but also even work from non-work. Is commuting work, non-work or both? How about a business lunch, a good diet or relaxation? Indeed, the notion of productive consumption was introduced precisely to cover those commodities that contribute to work as well as to consumption. Cannot pure work then be considered simply as a limiting commodity of such joint commodities in which the contribution to consumption was nil? Similarly, pure consumption would be a limiting commodity in the opposite direction in which the contribution to work was nil, and intermediate commodities would contribute to both consumption and work. The more important the contribution to work relative to consumption, the smaller would tend to be the relative importance of forgone earnings. Consequently, the effects of changes in earnings, other income, etc., on hours worked then become assimiliated to and essentially a special case of their effects on the consumption of less earnings-intensive commodities. For example, a pure rise in earnings would reduce the relative price, and thus increase the time spent on these commodities, *including the time spent at work*; similarly, for changes in income and other variables. The generalisation wrought by our approach is even greater than may have appeared at first.

Before concluding this section a few other relevant implications of our

[1] S. de Grazia has recently entertainingly shown the many difficulties in even reaching a reliable definition, and *a fortiori*, in quantitatively estimating the amount of leisure. See *ibid.*, Chapters III and IV; also see W. Moore, *Man, Time and Society* (New York: Wiley, 1963), Chapter II; J. N. Morgan, M. H. David, W. J. Cohen and H. E. Brazer, *Income and Welfare in the United States* (New York: McGraw-Hill, 1962), p. 322, and Owen, *op. cit.*, Chapter II.

[2] Sometimes true leisure is defined as the amount of discretionary time available (see Moore, *op. cit.*, p. 18). It is always difficult to attach a rigorous meaning to the word " discretionary " when referring to economic resources. One might say that in the short run consumption time is and working time is not discretionary, because the latter is partially subject to the authoritarian control of employers. (Even this distinction would vanish if households gave certain firms authoritarian control over their consumption time; see the discussion in Section II.) In the long run this definition of discretionary time is suspect too because the availability of alternative sources of employment would make working time also discretionary.

theory might be briefly mentioned. Just as a (compensated) rise in earnings would increase the prices of commodities with relatively large forgone earnings, induce a substitution away from them and increase the hours worked, so a (compensated) fall in market prices would also induce a substitution away from them and increase the hours worked: the effects of changes in direct and indirect costs are symmetrical. Indeed, Owen presents some evidence indicating that hours of work in the United States fell somewhat more in the first thirty years of this century than in the second thirty years, not because wages rose more during the first period, but because the market prices of recreation commodities fell more then.[1]

A well-known result of the traditional labour–leisure approach is that a rise in the income tax induces at least a substitution effect away from work and towards " leisure." Our approach reaches the same result only via a substitution towards time-intensive consumption rather than leisure. A simple additional implication of our approach, however, is that if a rise in the income tax were combined with an appropriate excise on the goods used in time-intensive commodities or subsidy to the goods used in other commodities there need be no change in full relative prices, and thus no substitution away from work. The traditional approach has recently reached the same conclusion, although in a much more involved way.[2]

There is no exception in the traditional approach to the rule that a pure rise in earnings would not induce a decrease in hours worked. An exception does occur in ours, for if the time and earnings intensities (*i.e.*, $l_i t_i$ and t_i) were negatively correlated a pure rise in earnings would induce a substitution towards time-intensive commodities, and thus away from work.[3] Although this exception does illustrate the greater power of our approach, there is no reason to believe that it is any more important empirically than the exception to the rule on income effects.

(b) *The Productivity of Time*

Most of the large secular increase in earnings, which stimulated the development of the labour–leisure analysis, resulted from an increase in the productivity of working time due to the growth in human and physical capital, technological progress and other factors. Since a rise in earnings resulting from an increase in productivity has both income and substitution

[1] See *op. cit.*, Chapter VIII. Recreation commodities presumably have relatively large forgone earnings.

[2] See W. J. Corbett and D. C. Hague, " Complementarity and the Excess Burden of Taxation," *Review of Economic Studies*, Vol. XXI (1953–54); also A. C. Harberger, " Taxation, Resource Allocation and Welfare," in the *Role of Direct and Indirect Taxes in the Federal Revenue System* (Princeton University Press, 1964).

[3] The effect on earnings is more difficult to determine because, by assumption, time intensive commodities have smaller costs per unit time than other commodities. A shift towards the former would, therefore, raise hourly earnings, which would partially and perhaps more than entirely offset the reduction in hours worked. Incidentally, this illustrates how the productivity of hours worked is influenced by the consumption set chosen.

effects, the secular decline in hours worked appeared to be evidence that the income effect was sufficiently strong to swamp the substitution effect.

The secular growth in capital and technology also improved the productivity of consumption time: supermarkets, automobiles, sleeping pills, safety and electric razors, and telephones are a few familiar and important examples of such developments. An improvement in the productivity of consumption time would change relative commodity prices and increase full income, which in turn would produce substitution and income effects. The interesting point is that a very different interpretation of the observed decline in hours of work is suggested because these effects are precisely the opposite of those produced by improvements in the productivity of working time.

Assume a uniform increase only in the productivity of consumption time, which is taken to mean a decline in all t_i, time required to produce a unit of Z_i, by a common percentage. The relative prices of commodities with large forgone earnings would fall, and substitution would be induced towards these and away from other commodities, causing hours of work also to fall. Since the increase in productivity would also produce an income effect,[1] the demand for commodities would increase, which, in turn, would induce an increased demand for goods. But since the productivity of working time is assumed not to change, more goods could be obtained only by an increase in work. That is, the higher real income resulting from an advance in the productivity of consumption time would cause hours of work to *increase*.

Consequently, an emphasis on the secular increase in the productivity of consumption time would lead to a very different interpretation of the secular decline in hours worked. Instead of claiming that a powerful income effect swamped a weaker substitution effect, the claim would have to be that a powerful substitution effect swamped a weaker income effect.

Of course, the productivity of both working and consumption time increased secularly, and the true interpretation is somewhere between these extremes. If both increased at the same rate there would be no change in relative prices, and thus no substitution effect, because the rise in l_i induced by one would exactly offset the decline in t_i induced by the other, marginal forgone earnings ($l_i t_i$) remaining unchanged. Although the income effects would tend to offset each other too, they would do so completely only if the income elasticity of demand for time-intensive commodities was equal to unity. Hours worked would decline if it was above and increase if it was below unity.[2] Since these commodities have probably on

[1] Full money income would be unaffected if it were achieved by using all time at pure work activities. If other uses of time were also required it would tend to increase. Even if full money income were unaffected, however, full real income would increase because prices of the Z_i would fall.

[2] So the " Knight " view that an increase in income would increase " leisure " is not necessarily true, even if leisure were a superior good and even aside from Robbins' emphasis on the substitution effect (see L. Robbins, " On the Elasticity of Demand for Income in Terms of Effort," *Economica* (June 1930)).

the whole been luxuries, such an increase in income would tend to reduce hours worked.

The productivity of working time has probably advanced more than that of consumption time, if only because of familiar reasons associated with the division of labour and economies of scale.[1] Consequently, there probably has been the traditional substitution effect towards and income effect away from work, as well as an income effect away from work because time-intensive commodities were luxuries. The secular decline in hours worked would only imply therefore that the combined income effects swamped the substitution effect, not that the income effect of an advance in the productivity of working time alone swamped its substitution effect.

Cross-sectionally, the hours worked of males have generally declined less as incomes increased than they have over time. Some of the difference between these relations is explained by the distinction between relevant and reported incomes, or by interdependencies among the hours worked by different employees;[2] some is probably also explained by the distinction between working and consumption productivity. There is a presumption that persons distinguished cross-sectionally by money incomes or earnings differ more in working than consumption productivity because they are essentially distinguished by the former. This argument does not apply to time series because persons are distinguished there by calendar time, which in principle is neutral between these productivities. Consequently, the traditional substitution effect towards work is apt to be greater cross-sectionally, which would help to explain why the relation between the income and hours worked of men is less negatively sloped there, and be additional evidence that the substitution effect for men is not weak.[3]

Productivity in the service sector in the United States appears to have advanced more slowly, at least since 1929, than productivity in the goods sector.[4] Service industries like retailing, transportation, education and health, use a good deal of the time of households that never enter into input, output and price series, or therefore into measures of productivity. Incorporation of such time into the series and consideration of changes in its productivity would contribute, I believe, to an understanding of the apparent differences in productivity advance between these sectors.

An excellent example can be found in a recent study of productivity

[1] Wesley Mitchell's justly famous essay " The Backward Art of Spending Money " spells out some of these reasons (see the first essay in the collection, *The Backward Art of Spending Money and Other Essays* (New York: McGraw-Hill, 1932)).

[2] A. Finnegan does find steeper cross-sectional relations when the average incomes and hours of different occupations are used (*see* his " A Cross-Sectional Analysis of Hours of Work," *Journal of Political Economy* (October, 1962)).

[3] Note that Mincer has found a very strong substitution effect for women (see his " Labor Force Participation of Married Women," *op. cit.*).

[4] See the essay by Victor Fuchs, " Productivity Trends in the Goods and Service Sectors, 1929–61: A Preliminary Survey," N.B.E.R. Occasional Paper, October 1964.

trends in the barbering industry in the United States.[1] Conventional productivity measures show relatively little advance in barbers' shops since 1929, yet a revolution has occurred in the activities performed by these shops. In the 1920s shaves still accounted for an important part of their sales, but declined to a negligible part by the 1950s because of the spread of home safety and electric razors. Instead of travelling to a shop, waiting in line, receiving a shave and continuing to another destination, men now shave themselves at home, saving travelling, waiting and even some shaving time. This considerable advance in the productivity of shaving nowhere enters measures for barbers' shops. If, however, a productivity measure for general barbering activities, including shaving, was constructed, I suspect that it would show an advance since 1929 comparable to most goods.[2]

(c) *Income Elasticities*

Income elasticities of demand are often estimated cross-sectionally from the behaviour of families or other units with different incomes. When these units buy in the same market-place it is natural to assume that they face the same prices of goods. If, however, incomes differ because earnings do, and cross-sectional income differences are usually dominated by earnings differences, commodities prices would differ systematically. All commodities prices would be higher to higher-income units because their forgone earnings would be higher (which means, incidentally, that differences in real income would be less than those in money income), and the prices of earnings-intensive commodities would be unusually so.

Cross-sectional relations between consumption and income would not therefore measure the effect of income alone, because they would be affected by differences in relative prices as well as in incomes.[3] The effect of income would be underestimated for earnings-intensive and overestimated for other commodities, because the higher relative prices of the former would cause a substitution away from them and towards the latter. Accordingly, the income elasticities of demand for "leisure," unproductive and time-intensive commodities would be under-stated, and for "work," productive and other goods-intensive commodities over-stated by cross-sectional estimates. Low apparent income elasticities of earnings-intensive commodities and high apparent elasticities of other commodities may simply be illusions resulting from substitution effects.[4]

[1] See J. Wilburn, "Productivity Trends in Barber and Beauty Shops," mimeographed report, N.B.E.R., September 1964.

[2] The movement of shaving from barbers' shops to households illustrates how and why even in urban areas households have become "small factories." Under the impetus of a general growth in the value of time they have been encouraged to find ways of saving on travelling and waiting time by performing more activities themselves.

[3] More appropriate income elasticities for several commodities are estimated in Mincer, "Market Prices . . .," *op. cit.*

[4] In this connection note that cross-sectional data are often preferred to time-series data in estimating income elasticities precisely because they are supposed to be largely free of co-linearity

Moreover, according to our theory demand depends also on the importance of earnings as a source of income. For if total income were held constant an increase in earnings would create only substitution effects: away from earnings-intensive and towards goods-intensive commodities. So one unusual implication of the analysis that can and should be tested with available budget data is that the source of income may have a significant effect on consumption patterns. An important special case is found in comparisons of the consumption of employed and unemployed workers. Unemployed workers not only have lower incomes but also lower forgone costs, and thus lower relative prices of time and other earnings-intensive commodities. The propensity of unemployed workers to go fishing, watch television, attend school and so on are simply vivid illustrations of the incentives they have to substitute such commodities for others.

One interesting application of the analysis is to the relation between family size and income.[1] The traditional view, based usually on simple correlations, has been that an increase in income leads to a reduction in the number of children per family. If, however, birth-control knowledge and other variables were held constant economic theory suggests a positive relation between family size and income, and therefore that the traditional negative correlation resulted from positive correlations between income, knowledge and some other variables. The data I put together supported this interpretation, as did those found in several subsequent studies.[2]

Although positive, the elasticity of family size with respect to income is apparently quite low, even when birth-control knowledge is held constant. Some persons have interpreted this (and other evidence) to indicate that family-size formation cannot usefully be fitted into traditional economic analysis.[3] It was pointed out, however, that the small elasticity found for children is not so inconsistent with what is found for goods as soon as quantity and quality income elasticities are distinguished.[4] Increased expenditures on many goods largely take the form of increased quality–expenditure per pound, per car, etc.—and the increase in quantity is modest. Similarly, increased expenditures on children largely take the form of increased expenditures per child, while the increase in number of children is very modest.

between prices and incomes (see, *e.g.*, J. Tobin, " A Statistical Demand Function for Food in the U.S.A.," *Journal of the Royal Statistical Society*, Series A (1950)).

[1] Biases in cross-sectional estimates of the demand for work and leisure were considered in the last section.

[2] See G. S. Becker, " An Economic Analysis of Fertility," *Demographic and Economic Change in Developed Countries* (N.B.E.R. Conference Volume, 1960); R. A. Easterlin, " The American Baby Boom in Historical Perspective," *American Economic Review* (December 1961); I. Adelman, " An Econometric Analysis of Population Growth," *American Economic Review* (June 1963); R. Weintraub, " The Birth Rate and Economic Development: An Empirical Study," *Econometrica* (October 1962); Morris Silver, *Birth Rates, Marriages, and Business Cycles* (unpublished Ph.D. dissertation, Columbia University, 1964); and several other studies; for an apparent exception, see the note by D. Freedman, " The Relation of Economic Status to Fertility," *American Economic Review* (June 1963).

[3] See, for example, Duesenberry's comment on Becker, *op. cit.*

[4] See Becker, *op. cit.*

Nevertheless, the elasticity of demand for number of children does seem somewhat smaller than the quantity elasticities found for many goods. Perhaps the explanation is simply the shape of indifference curves; one other factor that may be more important, however, is the increase in forgone costs with income.[1] Child care would seem to be a time-intensive activity that is not " productive " (in terms of earnings) and uses many hours that could be used at work. Consequently, it would be an earnings-intensive activity, and our analysis predicts that its relative price would be higher to higher-income families.[2] There is already some evidence suggesting that the positive relation between forgone costs and income explains why the apparent quantity income elasticity of demand for children is relatively small. Mincer found that cross-sectional differences in the forgone price of children have an important effect on the number of children.[3]

(d) *Transportation*

Transportation is one of the few activities where the cost of time has been explicitly incorporated into economic discussions. In most benefit-cost evaluations of new transportation networks the value of the savings in transportation time has tended to overshadow other benefits.[4] The importance of the value placed on time has encouraged experiment with different methods of determination: from the simple view that the value of an hour equals average hourly earnings to sophisticated considerations of the distinction between standard and overtime hours, the internal and external margins, etc.

The transport field offers considerable opportunity to estimate the marginal productivity or value of time from actual behaviour. One could, for example, relate the ratio of the number of persons travelling by aeroplane to those travelling by slower mediums to the distance travelled (and, of course, also to market prices and incomes). Since relatively more people use faster mediums for longer distances, presumably largely because of the greater importance of the saving in time, one should be able to estimate a marginal value of time from the relation between medium and distance travelled.[5]

[1] In *Ibid.*, p. 214 fn. 8, the relation between forgone costs and income was mentioned but not elaborated.

[2] Other arguments suggesting that higher-income families face a higher price of children have generally confused price with quality (see *ibid.*, pp. 214–15).

[3] See Mincer, " Market Prices . . .," *op. cit.* He measures the price of children by the wife's potential wage-rate, and fits regressions to various cross-sectional data, where number of children is the dependent variable, and family income and the wife's potential wage-rate are among the independent variables.

[4] See, for example, H. Mohring, " Land Values and the Measurement of Highway Benefits," *Journal of Political Economy* (June 1961).

[5] The only quantitative estimate of the marginal value of time that I am familiar with uses the relation between the value of land and its commuting distance from employment (see *ibid.*). With many assumptions I have estimated the marginal value of time of those commuting at about 40% of their average hourly earnings. It is not clear whether this value is so low because of errors in these assumptions or because of severe kinks in the supply and demand functions for hours of work.

Another transportation problem extensively studied is the length and mode of commuting to work.[1] It is usually assumed that direct commuting costs, such as train fare, vary positively and that living costs, such as space, vary negatively with the distance commuted. These assumptions alone would imply that a rise in incomes would result in longer commutes as long as space (" housing ") were a superior good.[2]

A rise in income resulting at least in part from a rise in earnings would, however, increase the cost of commuting a given distance because the forgone value of the time involved would increase. This increase in commuting costs would discourage commuting in the same way that the increased demand for space would encourage it. The outcome depends on the relative strengths of these conflicting forces: one can show with a few assumptions that the distance commuted would increase as income increased if, and only if, space had an income elasticity greater than unity.

For let Z_1 refer to the commuting commodity, Z_2 to other commodities, and let

$$Z_1 = f_1(x, t) \quad . \quad . \quad . \quad . \quad . \quad . \quad . \quad (22)$$

where t is the time spent commuting and x is the quantity of space used. Commuting costs are assumed to have the simple form $a + l_1t$, where a is a constant and l_1 is the marginal forgone cost per hour spent commuting. In other words, the cost of time is the only variable commuting cost. The cost per unit of space is $p(t)$, where by assumption $p' < 0$. The problem is to maximise the utility function

$$U = U(x, t, Z_2) \quad . \quad . \quad . \quad . \quad . \quad . \quad . \quad (23)$$

subject to the resource constraint

$$a + l_1t + px + h(Z_2) = S \quad . \quad . \quad . \quad . \quad . \quad . \quad (24)$$

If it were assumed that $U_t = 0$—commuting was neither enjoyable nor irksome—the main equilibrium condition would reduce to

$$l_1 + p'x = 0 \,^{3} \quad . \quad . \quad . \quad . \quad . \quad . \quad . \quad (25)$$

which would be the equilibrium condition if households simply attempt to minimise the sum of transportation and space costs.[4] If $l_1 = kS$, where k

[1] See L. N. Moses and H. F. Williamson, " Value of Time, Choice of Mode, and the Subsidy Issue in Urban Transportation," *Journal of Political Economy* (June 1963), R. Muth, "Economic Change and Rural–Urban Conversion," *Econometrica* (January 1961), and J. F. Kain, *Commuting and the Residential Decisions of Chicago and Detroit Central Business District Workers* (April 1963).

[2] See Muth, *op. cit.*

[3] If $U_t \neq 0$, the main equilibrium condition would be

$$\frac{U_t}{U_x} = \frac{l_1 + p'x}{p}$$

Probably the most plausible assumption is that $U_t < 0$, which would imply that $l_1 + p'x < 0$.

[4] See Kain, *op. cit.*, pp. 6–12.

is a constant, the effect of a change in full income on the time spent commuting can be found by differentiating equation (25) to be

$$\frac{\partial t}{\partial S} = \frac{k(\epsilon_x - 1)}{p''x} \quad . \quad . \quad . \quad . \quad . \quad . \quad (26)$$

where ϵ_x is the income elasticity of demand for space. Since stability requires that $p'' > 0$, an increase in income increases the time spent commuting if, and only if, $\epsilon_x > 1$.

In metropolitan areas of the United States higher-income families tend to live further from the central city,[1] which contradicts our analysis if one accepts the traditional view that the income elasticity of demand for housing is less than unity. In a definitive study of the demand for housing in the United States, however, Margaret Reid found income elasticities greater than unity.[2] Moreover, the analysis of distance commuted incorporates only a few dimensions of the demand for housing; principally the demand for outdoor space. The evidence on distances commuted would then only imply that outdoor space is a " luxury," which is rather plausible [3] and not even inconsistent with the traditional view about the total elasticity of demand for housing.

(e) *The Division of Labour Within Families*

Space is too limited to do more than summarise the main implications of the theory concerning the division of labour among members of the same household. Instead of simply allocating time efficiently among commodities, multi-person households also allocate the time of different members. Members who are relatively more efficient at market activities would use less of their time at consumption activities than would other members. Moreover, an increase in the relative market efficiency of any member would effect a reallocation of the time of all other members towards consumption activities in order to permit the former to spend more time at market activities. In short, the allocation of the time of any member is greatly influenced by the opportunities open to other members.

IV. Substitution Between Time and Goods

Although time and goods have been assumed to be used in fixed proportions in producing commodities, substitution could take place because different commodities used them in different proportions. The assumption of fixed proportions is now dropped in order to include many additional implications of the theory.

It is well known from the theory of variable proportions that households

[1] For a discussion, including many qualifications, of this proposition see L. F. Schnore, " The Socio-Economic Status of Cities and Suburbs," *American Sociological Review* (February 1963).

[2] See her *Housing and Income* (University of Chicago Press, 1962), p. 6 and *passim*.

[3] According to Reid, the elasticity of demand for indoor space is less than unity (*ibid.*, Chapter 12). If her total elasticity is accepted this suggests that outdoor space has an elasticity exceeding unity.

would minimise costs by setting the ratio of the marginal product of goods to that of time equal to the ratio of their marginal costs.[1] A rise in the cost of time relative to goods would induce a reduction in the amount of time and an increase in the amount of goods used per unit of each commodity. Thus, not only would a rise in earnings induce a substitution away from earnings-intensive commodities but also a substitution away from time and towards goods in the production of each commodity. Only the first is (implicitly) recognised in the labour–leisure analysis, although the second may well be of considerable importance. It increases one's confidence that the substitution effect of a rise in earnings is more important than is commonly believed.

The change in the input coefficients of time and goods resulting from a change in their relative costs is defined by the elasticity of substitution between them, which presumably varies from commodity to commodity. The only empirical study of this elasticity assumes that recreation goods and " leisure " time are used to produce a recreation commodity.[2] Definite evidence of substitution is found, since the ratio of leisure time to recreation goods is negatively related to the ratio of their prices. The elasticity of substitution appears to be less than unity, however, since the share of leisure in total factor costs is apparently positively related to its relative price.

The incentive to economise on time as its relative cost increases goes a long way towards explaining certain broad aspects of behaviour that have puzzled and often disturbed observers of contemporary life. Since hours worked have declined secularly in most advanced countries, and so-called " leisure " has presumably increased, a natural expectation has been that " free " time would become more abundant, and be used more " leisurely " and " luxuriously." Yet, if anything, time is used more carefully to-day than a century ago.[3] If there was a secular increase in the productivity of working time relative to consumption time (see Section III (*b*)) there would be an increasing incentive to economise on the latter because of its greater expense (our theory emphatically cautions against calling such time " free "). Not surprisingly, therefore, it is now kept track of and used more carefully than in the past.

Americans are supposed to be much more wasteful of food and other

[1] The cost of producing a given amount of commodity Z_i would be minimised if

$$\frac{\partial f_i/\partial x_i}{\partial f_i/\partial T_i} = \frac{P_i}{\partial L/\partial T_i}$$

If utility were considered an indirect function of goods and time rather than simply a direct function of commodities the following conditions, among others, would be required to maximise utility:

$$\frac{\partial U/\partial x_i}{\partial U/\partial T_i} \equiv \frac{\partial Z_i/\partial x_i}{\partial Z_i/\partial T_i} = \frac{p_i}{\partial L/\partial T}$$

which are exactly the same conditions as above. The ratio of the marginal utility of x_i to that of T_i depends only on f_i, x_i and T_i, and is thus independent of other production functions, goods and time. In other words, the indirect utility function is what has been called " weakly separable " (see R. Muth, " Household Production and Consumer Demand Functions," unpublished manuscript).

[2] See Owen, *op. cit.*, Chapter X.

[3] See, for example, de Grazia, *op. cit.*, Chapter IV.

goods than persons in poorer countries, and much more conscious of time: they keep track of it continuously, make (and keep) appointments for specific minutes, rush about more, cook steaks and chops rather than time-consuming stews and so forth.[1] They are simultaneously supposed to be wasteful—of material goods—and overly economical—of immaterial time. Yet both allegations may be correct and not simply indicative of a strange American temperament because the market value of time is higher relative to the price of goods there than elsewhere. That is, the tendency to be economical about time and lavish about goods may be no paradox, but in part simply a reaction to a difference in relative costs.

The substitution towards goods induced by an increase in the relative cost of time would often include a substitution towards more expensive goods. For example, an increase in the value of a mother's time may induce her to enter the labour force and spend less time cooking by using pre-cooked foods and less time on child-care by using nurseries, camps or baby-sitters. Or barbers' shops in wealthier sections of town charge more and provide quicker service than those in poorer sections, because waiting by barbers is substituted for waiting by customers. These examples illustrate that a change in the quality of goods [2] resulting from a change in the relative cost of goods may simply reflect a change in the methods used to produce given commodities, and not any corresponding change in *their* quality.

Consequently, a rise in income due to a rise in earnings would increase the quality of goods purchased not only because of the effect of income on quality but also because of a substitution of goods for time; a rise in income due to a rise in property income would not cause any substitution, and should have less effect on the quality of goods. Put more dramatically, with total income held constant, a rise in earnings should increase while a rise in property income should decrease the quality chosen. Once again, the composition of income is important and provides testable implications of the theory.

One analytically interesting application of these conclusions is to the recent study by Margaret Reid of the substitution between store-bought and home-delivered milk.[3] According to our approach, the cost of inputs into the commodity " milk consumption at home " is either the sum of the price of milk in the store and the forgone value of the time used to carry it home or simply the price of delivered milk. A reduction in the price of store relative to delivered milk, the value of time remaining constant, would reduce the cost of the first method relatively to the second, and shift production towards the first. For the same reason a reduction in the value of time, market prices

[1] For a comparison of the American concept of time with others see Edward T. Hall, *The Silent Language* (New York: Doubleday, 1959), Chapter 9.

[2] Quality is usually defined empirically by the amount spent per physical unit, such as pound of food, car or child. See especially S. J. Prais and H. Houthakker, *The Analysis of Family Budgets* (Cambridge, 1955); also my " An Economic Analysis of Fertility," *op. cit.*

[3] See her " Consumer Response to the Relative Price of Store versus Delivered Milk," *Journal of Political Economy* (April 1963).

of milk remaining constant, would also shift production towards the first method.

Reid's finding of a very large negative relation between the ratio of store to delivered milk and the ratio of their prices, income and some other variables held constant, would be evidence both that milk costs are a large part of total production costs and that there is easy substitution between these alternative methods of production. The large, but not quite as large, negative relation with income simply confirms the easy substitution between methods, and indicates that the cost of time is less important than the cost of milk. In other words, instead of conveying separate information, her price and income elasticities both measure substitution between the two methods of producing the same commoditity, and are consistent and plausible.

The importance of forgone earnings and the substitution between time and goods may be quite relevant in interpreting observed price elasticities. A given percentage increase in the price of goods would be less of an increase in commodity prices the more important forgone earnings are. Consequently, even if all commodities had the same true price elasticity, those having relatively important forgone earnings would show lower apparent elasticities in the typical analysis that relates quantities and prices of goods alone.

The importance of forgone earnings differs not only among commodities but also among households for a given commodity because of differences in income. Its importance would change in the same or opposite direction as income, depending on whether the elasticity of substitution between time and goods was less or greater than unity. Thus, even when the true price elasticity of a commodity did not vary with income, the observed price elasticity of goods would be negatively or positively related to income as the elasticity of substitution was less or greater than unity.

The importance of substitution between time and goods can be illustrated in a still different way. Suppose, for simplicity, that only good x and no time was initially required to produce commodity Z. A price ceiling is placed on x, it nominally becomes a free good, and the production of x is subsidised sufficiently to maintain the same output. The increased quantity of x and Z demanded due to the decline in the price of x has to be rationed because the output of x has not increased. Suppose that the system of rationing made the quantity obtained a positive function of the time and effort expended. For example, the quantity of price-controlled bread or medical attention obtained might depend on the time spent in a queue outside a bakery or in a physician's office. Or if an appointment system were used a literal queue would be replaced by a figurative one, in which the waiting was done at "home," as in the Broadway theatre, admissions to hospitals or air travel during peak seasons. Again, even in depressed times the likelihood of obtaining a job is positively related to the time put into job hunting.

Although x became nominally a free good, Z would not be free, because the time now required as an input into Z is not free. The demand for Z

would be greater than the supply (fixed by assumption) if the cost of this time was less than the equilibrium price of Z before the price control. The scrambling by households for the limited supply would increase the time required to get a unit of Z, and thus its cost. Both would continue to increase until the average cost of time tended to the equilibrium price before price control. At that point equilibrium would be achieved because the supply and demand for Z would be equal.

Equilibrium would take different forms depending on the method of rationing. With a literal " first come first served " system the size of the queue (say outside the bakery or in the doctor's office) would grow until the expected cost of standing in line discouraged any excess demand;[1] with the figurative queues of appointment systems, the " waiting " time (say to see a play) would grow until demand was sufficiently curtailed. If the system of rationing was less formal, as in the labour market during recessions, the expected time required to ferret out a scarce job would grow until the demand for jobs was curtailed to the limited supply.

Therefore, price control of x combined with a subsidy that kept its amount constant would not change the average private equilibrium price of Z,[2] but would substitute indirect time costs for direct goods costs.[3] Since, however, indirect costs are positively related to income, the price of Z would be raised to higher-income persons and reduced to lower-income ones, thereby redistributing consumption from the former to the latter. That is, women, the poor, children, the unemployed, etc., would be more willing to spend their time in a queue or otherwise ferreting out rationed goods than would high-earning males.

V. Summary and Conclusions

This paper has presented a theory of the allocation of time between different activities. At the heart of the theory is an assumption that households are producers as well as consumers; they produce commodities by combining inputs of goods and time according to the cost-minimisation rules of the traditional theory of the firm. Commodities are produced in quantities determined by maximising a utility function of the commodity set subject to prices and a constraint on resources. Resources are measured by what is called full income, which is the sum of money income and that forgone or " lost " by the use of time and goods to obtain utility, while commodity prices are measured by the sum of the costs of their goods and time inputs.

[1] In queueing language the cost of waiting in line is a " discouragement " factor that stabilises the queueing scheme (see, for example, D. R. Cox and W. L. Smith, *Queues* (New York: Wiley 1961)).

[2] The social price, on the other hand, would double, for it is the sum of private indirect costs and subsidised direct costs.

[3] Time costs can be criticised from a Pareto optimality point of view because they often result in external diseconomies: *e.g.*, a person joining a queue would impose costs on subsequent joiners. The diseconomies are real, not simply pecuniary, because time is a cost to demanders, but is not revenue to suppliers.

The effect of changes in earnings, other income, goods prices and the productivity of working and consumption time on the allocation of time and the commodity set produced has been analysed. For example, a rise in earnings, compensated by a decline in other income so that full income would be unchanged, would induce a decline in the amount of time used at consumption activities, because time would become more expensive. Partly goods would be substituted for the more expensive time in the production of each commodity, and partly goods-intensive commodities would be substituted for the more expensive time-intensive ones. Both substitutions require less time to be used at consumption, and permit more to be used at work. Since the reallocation of time involves simultaneously a reallocation of goods and commodities, all three decisions become intimately related.

The theory has many interesting and even novel interpretations of, and implications about, empirical phenomena. A few will be summarised here.

A traditional " economic " interpretation of the secular decline in hours worked has stressed the growth in productivity of working time and the resulting income and substitution effects, with the former supposedly dominating. Ours stresses that the substitution effects of the growth in productivity of working and consumption time tended to offset each other, and that hours worked declined secularly primarily because time-intensive commodities have been luxuries. A contributing influence has been the secular decline in the relative prices of goods used in time-intensive commodities.

Since an increase in income partly due to an increase in earnings would raise the relative cost of time and of time-intensive commodities, traditional cross-sectional estimates of income elasticities do not hold either factor or commodity prices constant. Consequently, they would, among other things, be biased downward for time-intensive commodities, and give a misleading impression of the effect of income on the quality of commodities consumed. The composition of income also affects demand, for an increase in earnings, total income held constant, would shift demand away from time-intensive commodities and input combinations.

Rough estimates suggest that forgone earnings are quantitatively important and therefore that full income is substantially above money income. Since forgone earnings are primarily determined by the use of time, considerably more attention should be paid to its efficiency and allocation. In particular, agencies that collect information on the expenditure of money income might simultaneously collect information on the " expenditure " of time. The resulting time budgets, which have not been seriously investigated in most countries, including the United States and Great Britain, should be integrated with the money budgets in order to give a more accurate picture of the size and allocation of full income.

Gary S. Becker

Columbia University.

[4]

INVESTMENT DECISION UNDER UNCERTAINTY: APPLICATIONS OF THE STATE-PREFERENCE APPROACH

J. Hirshleifer

An earlier article[1] examined alternative approaches to the problem of investment decision under uncertainty. It was shown there that the various formulations differ essentially in specifying the *objects of choice* (commodities). Two such specifications were reviewed in detail: (1) The *mean, variability* approach — this reduces the assets or securities traded in the market to underlying objects of choice in the form of mean-return and variability-of-return measures which, it is alleged, enter into investors' preference functions.[2] (2) The *state-preference* (or, more fully, *time-state-preference*) approach — which resolves the assets or securities into distributions of dated contingent claims to income defined over the set of all possible "states of the world."[3]

The predecessor article showed that the more familiar mean, variability formulation has never been completed so as to constitute an acceptable choice-theoretic structure. If mean-return and variability-of-return are to be regarded as commodities, the analysis must go beyond the individual level of decision to show how the relative "prices" for mean-return and variability-of-return are determined in the market. There seem to be rather considerable difficulties facing theorists who attempt to fulfill this program.[4] In contrast, the state-preference approach was demonstrated to be the

1. Investment Decision Under Uncertainty: Choice-Theoretic Approaches," this *Journal*, LXXIX (Nov. 1965).

2. The most complete development is in H.M. Markowitz, *Portfolio Selection* (New York: Wiley, 1959); see also D.E. Farrar, *The Investment Decision Under Uncertainty* (Englewood Cliffs, N.J.: Prentice-Hall, 1962).

3. See K. J. Arrow, "The Role of Securities in the Optimal Allocation of Risk-Bearing," *Review of Economic Studies*, XXI (April 1964); G. Debreu, *Theory of Value* (New York: Wiley, 1959), Chap. 7; J. Hirshleifer, "Efficient Allocation of Capital in an Uncertain World," *American Economic Review*, LIV (May 1964), 77–85.

4. The furthest development to date seems to be that of W. F. Sharpe, "Capital Asset Prices: A Theory of Market Equilibrium Under Conditions of Risk," *Journal of Finance*, XIX (Sept. 1964). This may be regarded as a theory of prices for mean and variability in the "very short run," with fixed supplies of productive and financial assets.

natural generalization of Fisher's theory of intertemporal choice,[5] into the domain of uncertainty. Where Fisher's objects of choice are titles to consumption as of differing dates, the generalization takes the fundamental commodities, underlying all market assets, to be contingent time-state claims — titles to consumption for specified dates and states of the world. While various assets may package these underlying claims into more or less complex bundles, the "market-clearing" or "conservation" equations determine prices for the elementary time-state claims to which asset prices must conform. The idealizing assumptions, necessary for this formal theoretical structure to hold, are in some respects akin to those of standard theory in requiring a kind of precision of knowledge or belief as to preferences and opportunities that is only very approximately true of the real world. Thus, the theory that results contains uncertainty, imperfect knowledge as to the state of the world that will actually obtain in the future, but does not contain the "vagueness" we usually find psychologically associated with uncertainty.

The present article is devoted to an examination of some implications and applications of the time-state-preference approach, that reveal its power by casting light upon a number of unresolved controversies. These include: (1) the nature and extent of risk aversion; (2) whether there is an optimal "debt-equity mix" in financing corporate undertakings (the Modigliani-Miller problem); and (3) the "appropriate" rate of discount to employ in cost-benefit calculations for government investments not subject to the market test.

In the very simplest illustration of time-state-preference, there is one commodity ("corn"), only one possible current state (i.e., the *present* is certain), and just two possible and mutually exclusive future states. The objects of choice then can be symbolized: c_0, c_{1a}, c_{1b} — present titles to consumption of, respectively, current or time-0 corn, corn at time-1 provided that state a obtains, and corn at time-1 provided that state b obtains. Each individual has an endowment of such claims, has preference relations ordering the combinations he could possibly hold,[6] and has certain opportunities for transforming his endowed bundle into alternative combinations. The possible transformations can take the form of market trading ("financial opportunities") or else of physical conversions ("productive oppor-

5. Irving Fisher, *The Theory of Interest* (New York: Macmillan, 1930; reprinted, Augustus M. Kelley, 1955).

6. Note that he can *hold* present claims or titles to both c_{1a} and c_{1b}, although he cannot ultimately *consume* both since only one of the two states will actually obtain.

tunities") — transactions in the one case with other individuals, in the other case with Nature.

I. State Preference, Risk Aversion, and the Utility-of-Income Function

In this section we restrict ourselves to synchronous choice among claims to consumption in alternative future states; i.e., we are isolating the problem of risky choice from the problem of time choice. Under these circumstances the individual's situation may be portrayed as in Figure I, which shows an indifference map and financial

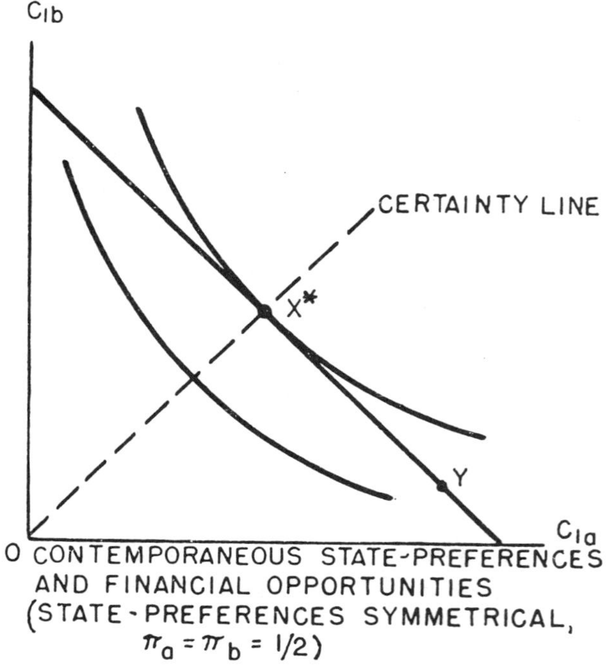

CONTEMPORANEOUS STATE-PREFERENCES AND FINANCIAL OPPORTUNITIES (STATE-PREFERENCES SYMMETRICAL, $\pi_a = \pi_b = 1/2$)

Figure I

or market opportunities for converting endowment Y into alternative combinations of c_{1a} and c_{1b}. The assumption here is that the state probabilities $\pi_a = \pi_b = \frac{1}{2}$. The wealth constraint upon the market opportunities can be written $W = P_0c_0 + P_{1a}c_{1a} + P_{1b}c_{1b}$, where P_0, P_{1a}, and P_{1b} are the prices of the respective time-state claims, with c_0 here taken to be a constant holding of current corn. The wealth is in turn fixed by the value of the endowment: $W = P_0y_0$

$+ P_{1a}y_{1a} + P_{1b}y_{1b}$ — where the y's represent elements of the endowment vector. The 45° "certainty line" connects combinations for which $c_{1a} = c_{1b}$.

The convexity of the indifference curves between the commodities c_{1a} and c_{1b}, which corresponds to one concept of *risk aversion*, may be justified by appeal to the general principle of diminishing marginal rate of substitution that holds for ordinary commodities. A more convincing defense, perhaps, is the observation of "nonspecialization" — that individuals almost universally prefer to hedge against many contingencies rather than place all their bets on one. It is of interest to relate this formulation to the Neumann-Morgenstern utility-of-income function $v(c_1)$ that permits use of the expected-utility theorem in rationalizing risky choice.[7] It was shown in the predecessor article that a concave $v(c_1)$ function, as plotted in Figure II ("diminishing marginal utility of consumption income") is equivalent to a convex indifference map as in Figure I. In addition, the rather strong theorem was obtained that under these con-

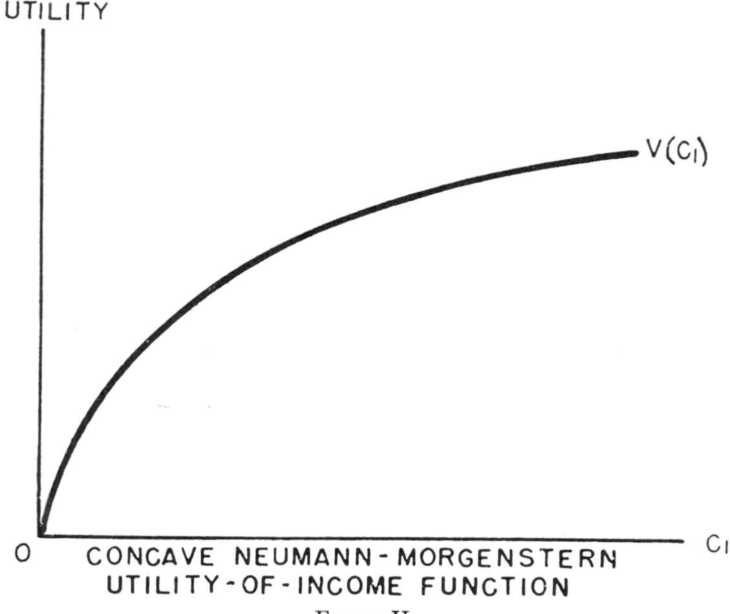

FIGURE II

7. As discussed, for example, in M. Friedman and L. J. Savage, "The Utility Analysis of Choices Involving Risk," *Journal of Political Economy*, LVI (Aug. 1948). Reprinted in American Economic Association, *Readings in Price Theory* (Homewood, Ill.: Irwin, 1952). Page references are to the latter volume.

ditions, if the probability ratio for the two states π_b/π_a is equal to the price ratio P_{1b}/P_{1a}, the individual's optimum must be on the certainty line. This is completely consistent with the Friedman-Savage formulation in terms of the Neumann-Morgenstern function, which under the same conditions leads to the conclusions that a fair gamble would not be accepted and that the individual would be willing to insure at fair odds.[8]

However, one observes in the world instances of risk-preferring behavior. Some gambles are accepted at fair, or even adverse odds. We will be considering in this section alternative explanations for this phenomenon. First, however, it is necessary to clarify one point on which error is often committed. Whether a particular contract is a *gamble* — i.e., an arrangement moving the individual farther from the 45° certainty line — or a particular asset a risky one depends not upon the terms of the contract or the nature of the asset in isolation but upon the individual's total portfolio and endowed position. While common stocks are often regarded as riskier than bonds, their purchase may stabilize an overall portfolio with respect to the hazard of inflation; i.e., may move an investor *closer* to the 45° line. Similarly, for some individuals a futures contract may be very risky, but for a hedger the same contract is "insurance" rather than a gamble. The hedger, of course, is someone who starts with a risky endowment — i.e., he has an unbalanced endowed state-distribution of income — and a contract with an *offsettingly* uneven state-distribution of return serves to bring him nearer the certainty line.

The predecessor article also showed that it was possible, by relaxing the assumption of *uniqueness* of the Neumann-Morgenstern $v(c_1)$ function, to combine convex indifference curves with solutions at fair odds that are off the 45° line (see Figure III). The assumption of a single $v(c_1)$ function implies a symmetry as to state preferences such that — adjusting for probabilities — marginal incomes, at any given level of income, are valued equivalently in all states. But since the definition of a state of the world incorporates a description of an entire world-environment, there may well be "nonpecuniary" aspects of the respective situations that would warrant biasing the pecuniary-wealth position at fair odds. There would then be a different $v(c_1)$ function for each state, as portrayed for the two-state situation in Figure IV, where the functions $v_a(c_{1a})$ and $v_b(c_{1b})$ are defined so as to continue permitting the use of the expected-utility theorem to rationalize uncertain choice. This relaxation leads to the conclusion that basically conservative behavior is still consis-

8. *Ibid.*, pp. 73–77.

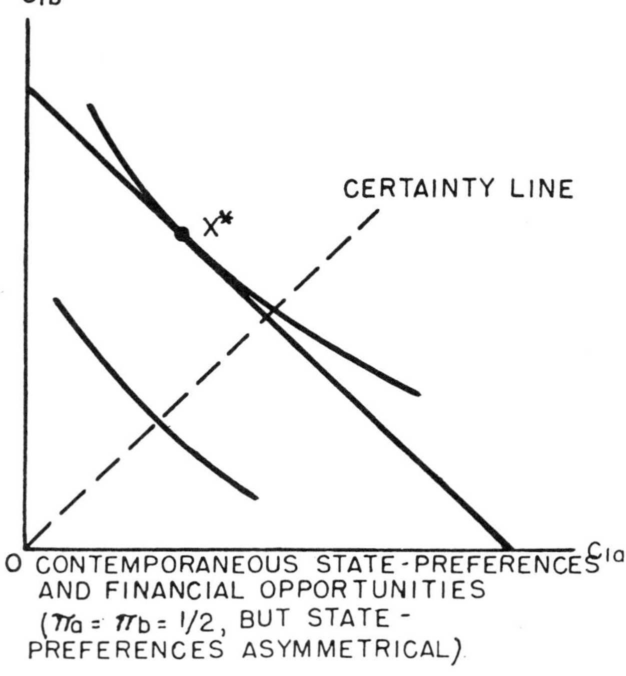

CONTEMPORANEOUS STATE-PREFERENCES AND FINANCIAL OPPORTUNITIES ($\pi_a = \pi_b = 1/2$, BUT STATE-PREFERENCES ASYMMETRICAL)

FIGURE III

tent with a certain amount of seeming risk preference — the risk preference being a kind of illusion due to looking only at the *pecuniary* income distribution. Still, this explanation hardly accounts for what we observe at Las Vegas, though it may tell us why bachelors commonly do not buy life insurance.[9]

A different explanation for the observed mixture of risk-avoiding and risk-preferring behavior has been offered by Friedman and Savage. They argue that in economic activities such as choices of occupation, business undertakings, and purchases of securities and real property, people generally prefer both low-risk and high-risk activities to moderate-risk activities. This is, assertedly, evidenced by relatively low realized average return (after allowance for unsuccessful as well as successful outcomes) on the former categories

9. While a responsible family man in his current decisions will attach considerable significance to income for his beneficiaries contingent upon his own death, a bachelor with only remote heirs has very asymmetrical state-preferences with respect to income accruing to him under the contingencies "Alive" or "Dead."

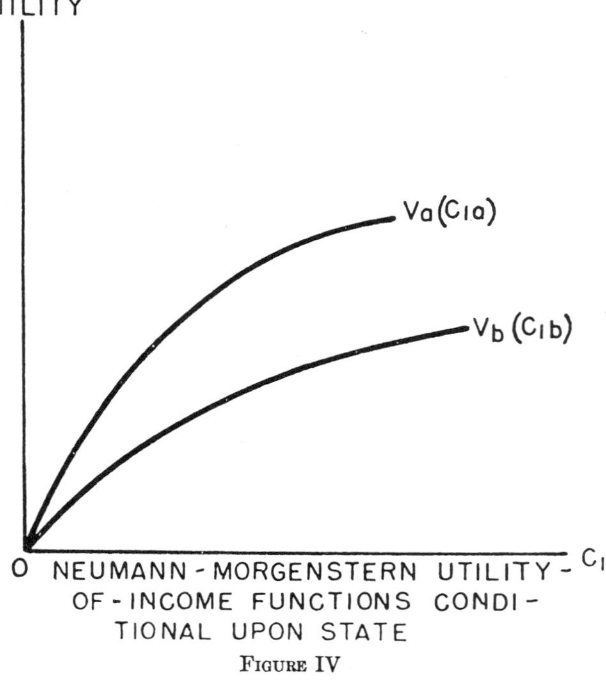

NEUMANN-MORGENSTERN UTILITY-OF-INCOME FUNCTIONS CONDITIONAL UPON STATE

FIGURE IV

as compared with the latter.[1] To explain this, and certain other observed behavior patterns — of which the most significant is the simultaneous purchase of insurance and lottery tickets by low-income individuals — Friedman and Savage construct a Neumann-Morgenstern utility-of-income function of the special shape[2] illustrated in Figure V.

This doubly-inflected curve has a concave segment at the low-income end, a convex segment for middle incomes, and finally another concave segment at the high-income end. For a lottery with only two outcomes, the relative desirability of taking or refusing the lottery is found by comparing the height along the straight line connecting the utilities of the outcomes (i.e., the expected utility of the lottery) with the height of the corresponding point along the doubly-inflected curve — the utility of the certain income alternative. If the lottery is fair, the corresponding points are vertically aligned.[3]

1. Friedman and Savage, *op. cit.*, pp. 63–66.
2. *Ibid.*, p. 85.
3. Justifications of these assertions are omitted because of their familiarity and availability in the cited source. The key to the proofs is the use of the expected-utility principle for risky outcomes.

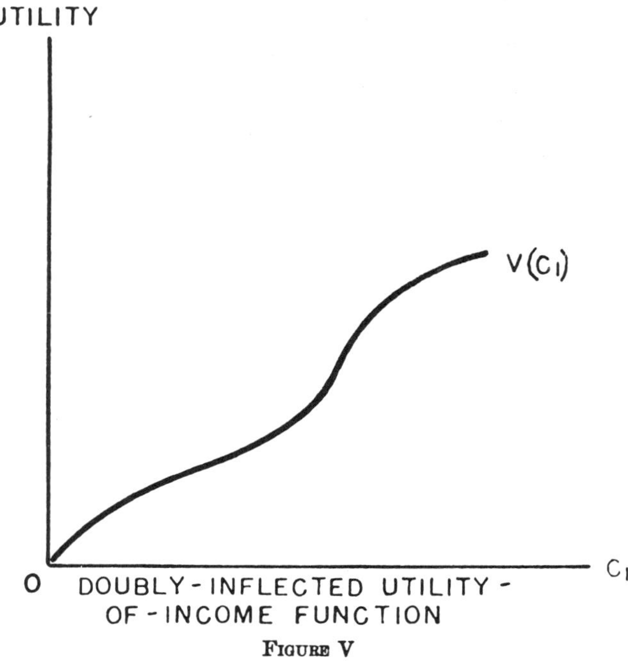

DOUBLY-INFLECTED UTILITY-OF-INCOME FUNCTION

FIGURE V

The following may then be inferred: (1) For individuals in the middle convex segment, small-scale fair lotteries at roughly even odds (e.g., bets on heads in tosses of a coin) are preferred to certainties, become increasingly desirable as the scale of the lottery increases up to a point, after which as scale increases further the lotteries become decreasingly desirable. (2) Low-income individuals, especially if they are toward the upper end of the initial concave segment, would be inclined to buy fair "long-shot" lotteries, giving them at low cost a small chance at a relatively big prize. On the other hand, if they find themselves subject to a hazard threatening (though with low probability) a relatively large loss, they will be inclined to escape it by purchasing insurance at fair odds. (3) High-income individuals, especially if toward the lower end of their concave segment, will be inclined to bet heavily at fair odds on "short shots" (strong favorites, offering a large chance of a small gain and a small chance of a great loss) and, what amounts to the same thing, they will be inclined to avoid purchasing insurance.

Following the lead of Friedman and Savage, testable inferences can be derived if we interpret the three segments as corresponding at least roughly to three income classes. The behavior implied for the low-income class (most particularly, as we have noted, for the upper end of the low-income segment) is to some extent verified by common observation: many poor people place long-shot bets, and many purchase insurance to protect their modest sources of wealth. Actually, the data cited by Friedman-Savage[4] indicate that poorer people buy proportionately *less* insurance than other income groups; furthermore, the fraction of families purchasing insurance seems to rise smoothly with income. There is thus no indication of a risk-preferring middle segment. This evidence does not, therefore, support their position as against the alternative hypothesis of general risk aversion. The smaller purchases by poorer people may, perhaps, be explained away as due to relatively heavier transactions costs on smaller policies (leading to adverse "loading" of rates) or to possession of fewer insurable assets in proportion to income.

The behavior implied by the Friedman-Savage hypothesis for the upper-income group seems somewhat strange. Do we really see rich people failing to insure their *major* sources of wealth[5] — or, correspondingly, do we commonly observe them hazarding major sums on short-odds bets?[6] A possible defense here would be to bring in the asymmetrical income-tax treatment of gambling and casualty gains and losses, and the favorable treatment of insurance reserves — all of which combine to induce rich people to insure more and to gamble less than they otherwise would. On the other hand, it seems doubtful whether conservative behavior in these respects was really uncharacteristic of rich people even before the income tax.

But the crucial failure of the Friedman-Savage model lies in its implied behavior for the middle classes. This group, if they behaved as pictured, would be plungers of an extreme sort. They would stand ready, at any moment, to accept at fair odds a gamble of such a scale as to thrust them out of the convex segment and into (depending on the outcome) the poor-man or rich-man class. In addition, as we have remarked, it is the individual at the upper end

4. *Ibid.*, pp. 66 f.

5. Rich people would, on any risk-preference assumption, tend to self-insure (to save the transactions cost) against hazards threatening losses involving only minor fractions of their wealth. Thus we would expect to see them often foregoing the purchase of automobile collision insurance. But the Friedman-Savage assertion implies that they would omit insuring against potentially great losses such as those associated with accident liability claims, and physical disability or death of the main income-earner. Again their own evidence does not support Friedman and Savage here.

6. Occasional racetrack betting on favorites, so long as the scale is minor, means little here. The main point of the Friedman-Savage assumption is that the rich man is willing, at fair odds, to accept a hazard that (if it eventuated) would thrust him entirely out of the concave segment — out of the rich-man class! This requires betting on a scale considered pathological in our culture (see Dostoyevsky, *The Gambler*).

of the low-income segment who is most inclined to take long-shot bets, and the individual at the lower end of the high-income segment who is most inclined to take short-odds bets. Thus, the model would have us believe, the solid risk-avoiders of our society are only the poorer poor, and the richer rich. Aside from the notorious lack of direct confirmation of these assertions, it is of interest to note how they conflict with observed stability patterns of the various income classes. With behavior as postulated, the middle ranks of incomes would be rapidly depopulated, the end result being a U-shaped distribution piled up at the extremes. Needless to say, this is not observed.

There is one important observation that should be considered part of the behavior that needs explaining in constructing a risk-preference model (utility-of-income function): Gambling on a scale at all likely to *impoverish* is rarely observed in middle- and upper-income groups. One way to reconcile this observation with the Friedman-Savage model would be to shrink the middle convex segment to a narrow range.[7] To do this is, however, to lose the main point of the Friedman-Savage argument, since then risk aversion would be the predominant behavior pattern after all.[8] And the problem remains of combining the risk aversion necessary for observed diversification of assets and purchase of insurance with the existence of at least a modest amount of gambling at all income levels.[9]

An easy way out of the difficulty lies in recognizing that many people take pleasure in gambling per se (i.e., as a consumption good). A modest amount of *pleasure-oriented* gambling would then not be inconsistent with risk aversion (a concave utility-of-income function) for serious *wealth-oriented* activities.[1] To make this distinction workable, however, it must be possible to distinguish observationally between pleasure-oriented and wealth-oriented gambling, the latter being defined as a deliberate attempt to change wealth

7. At one point (*op. cit.*, p. 92) Friedman and Savage do suggest that relatively few individuals are in the middle segment.

8. Substantial numbers of individuals in the middle segment are necessary to explain the alleged observation of preference for low-risk or high-risk as against moderate-risk economic activities.

9. One possible way out would be to assert that the middle segment is small and, in addition, slides up and down as the individual's income level changes — see H. Markowitz "The Utility of Wealth," *Journal of Political Economy*, LX (April 1952) — so that he is always willing to undertake a small amount of gambling from his present income level. As in the case of Ptolemy's geocentric system, when it becomes necessary to incorporate such *ad hoc* "epicycles" to save the phenomena, it is time for a new conception.

1. The following may perhaps be an illuminating analogy. Men like to live in houses on solid foundations, with square corners, and level floors. And yet they may pay money to spend a few minutes at an amusement park in a "crazy-house" with quite the reverse characteristics.

status. Fortunately, the two motives for gambling are observably distinct, because they imply radically different wagering procedures. If gambling is wealth-oriented, it will take the form of hazarding great sums (proportionate to one's endowment and hopes) on a single turn of a wheel or flip of a coin. Repetitive gambling at relatively small stakes would be absurd: the law of large numbers shrinks the variance of the overall outcome, whereas wealth-oriented gamblers are trying to achieve large changes. While repetitive small-stake gambling does not quite guarantee a final result near the mean, the likelihood of such outcomes is greatly increased; in any case, the average time required to win the desired sum (or lose the fortune hazarded) will be enormously extended. What we observe at Las Vegas is, of course, very much the repetitive, small-stake pattern. The combination of adverse odds and limited stakes assures a high probability that the final outcome for the gambler will be a modest loss — the price paid for the pleasure of gambling. All this is not to say that we never observe wealth-oriented gambling, but rather that it is not a sufficiently important phenomenon to dictate the main lines of our theory of risk.[2]

On our hypothesis, therefore, we expect to see risk aversion predominating in wealth-oriented activities at all income levels — thus explaining purchase of insurance all along the wealth scale. We also expect to see a moderate amount of pleasure-oriented gambling, again all along the wealth scale. Wealth-oriented gambling will not be a very important phenomenon, but such as exists would be concentrated among the poor.[3] This is in sharp contrast with the view of Friedman and Savage, whose theory indicates that wealth-oriented gambling will be very significant, and concentrated among

2. Some wealth-oriented gambling is based on "hunches" or "inside information" that, if true, would make the bet a lottery at *favorable* odds rather than the adverse gamble it appears — to others! Of course, given the belief in favorable odds, even a risk-avoider might gamble. There is also strictly rational wealth-oriented gambling, as in the classic case of the embezzler who plunges his remaining cash in the hope of being able to straighten out his accounts prior to an audit. Here the dollar in hand that the gambler risks is almost costless, as he cannot hope to salvage much of his illegal taking by conservative behavior. A somewhat similar argument may partially explain lower-class gambling: the floor on consumption provided by public-assistance payments — where such payments are liable to be withheld or reduced if the would-be gambler conserved his assets — permits the individual to gamble with dollars that do not fully represent sacrifices of consumption to him. Finally, there is the gambling behavior that would generally be regarded as pathological; this would be associated with subnormal or aberrant mental conditions.

3. See footnote above concerning the effect of relief payments (consumption floor) upon the propensity to gamble. Also, ill-informed believers in hunches, and subnormal or aberrant mental types, will tend to have low income status.

the middle classes. We, on the contrary, would expect to find the middle classes to be the most insurance-minded. Insurance purchases by the poor would be deterred by the substantially higher transactions cost on the one hand, and the relief floor on the other. As for the rich, they are likely to possess a sufficient diversity of assets as to make self-insurance feasible (this consideration being counterbalanced somewhat by tax advantages where life insurance is concerned).

Leaving the sphere of gambling versus insurance, the most significant class of economic activity, in terms of implications for attitudes toward risk, is choice of occupation. Except in the very highest income brackets, this decision determines the nature of the major source of wealth. In addition, it is difficult to insure or diversify against certain hazards associated with occupational choice, such as cyclical unemployment and technological obsolescence. Insurance is available against physical hazards — but there will typically be penalty rates to pay for life or disability insurance in dangerous occupations. Consequently, on our hypothesis we would expect to observe relatively low returns in occupations that are highly secure in almost all respects, like teaching and civil service. In hazardous occupations such as mining, and insecure activities such as business entrepreneurship, we would expect higher average returns — even after allowing for injuries and failures. Unfortunately, the evidence available is difficult to interpret because of differences in personal qualities of individuals, nonpecuniary returns and differences of tastes with respect to them, tax and relief effects, and numerous difficulties with the data.[4]

The evidence on return to property in relation to risk is fortunately somewhat clearer. We must be careful to recollect here, however, that the "riskiness" (imbalance in the state-distribution of income) relevant for decisions is not that of particular assets in isolation. It is the variability of the state-distribution of consumption possibilities yielded by overall *portfolios* that is relevant. For some classes of assets (securities, in particular) it is relatively easy to obtain considerable diversification while holding individually

4. Friedman and Savage allege (*op. cit.*, pp. 63–66) that higher returns are received on (reflecting aversion to) moderate risks — and that the average returns to high-risk activities like auto-racing, piloting aircraft, business undertakings in untried fields, and the professions of law and medicine (?) are so low as to evidence an inclination in favor of bearing extreme risks. The evidence presented for these assertions is weak, to say the least. The following will illustrate one of the many problems of interpreting such data as exist: for high-risk occupations there is likely to be a selection bias (since those who overestimate the chance of success are more likely to enter) so that adverse average results are not necessarily evidence of risk preference.

risky assets. The main problem is posed by the overall swings of the business cycle, which limit the variance-minimizing effect of diversification by imposing high correlation among security returns — and, probably even more important, high correlation between overall property income and overall wage or other personal income. Consequently, and especially because of the intrinsically risky situation involved in occupational choice, the risk-aversion hypothesis would predict relatively high average return on procyclical securities and relatively low on stable or anticyclical securities. This is borne out by the historically realized yields on equities (highly procyclical in real terms).[5] Comparison of the cyclically unstable "industrial" equities with the more stable "utility" equities provides another confirmation.[6]

Thus, a combination of a risk-aversion hypothesis for wealth-oriented activities with recognition that, for many individuals, repetitive small-stake gambling (i.e., gambling guaranteed not to drastically transform the wealth level) is a pleasurable activity, serves to explain the available evidence. In contrast, the attempt to explain both insurance and gambling as reflecting a single utility-of-income function of peculiar shape leads to contradictions — in which the supposed risk-preferring group is first large and then small, first a stable and then a disappearing element, etc. — and is in conflict with more direct knowledge about the risk-seeking propensities of the various income groups.

II. Optimal Capital Structure

The analysis of risky investment decision in terms of state preferences may be applied in the area of corporate finance to the controversial "Proposition I" of Modigliani and Miller: "The market value of any firm is independent of its capital structure and is given by capitalizing its expected return at the rate ρ_k appropriate to its class."[7] Our main concern here will be with the first part of the proposition, the assertion that market value is independent of capital structure. Symbolically, the contention is that $D_0 + E_0 = V_0 = \overline{X}/\rho_k$, a constant — where D_0 is present (or mar-

5. H. A. Latané, "Portfolio Balance — The Demand for Money, Bonds, and Stock," *Southern Economic Journal*, XXIX (Oct. 1962).

6. Most of the difference is realized in the form of capital gains. See *Historical Statistics of the United States, Colonial Times to 1957* (Washington, 1960), p. 657.

7. F. Modigliani and M. H. Miller, "The Cost of Capital, Corporation Finance and the Theory of Investment," *American Economic Review*, XLVIII (June 1958), 268.

ket) value of the debt, E_0 the value of the equity, V_0 is the assertedly constant value of the firm, and $\overline{X}$ is the firm's given operating income. The language in the second part of the proposition, and elsewhere in their paper, indicate that Modigliani and Miller were employing a mean, variability approach to risk-bearing.[8]

In the predecessor to this article, Fisher's analysis of individuals' investment decisions under certainty was generalized to include investment decisions of *firms*. The result was obtained, in equation (6‴), that the market value (wealth) of the firm under certainty equals the present value of debt repayments plus (if the firm has productive opportunities that lead to an increase of wealth) the present value of any equity increment. This looks very much like the Modigliani-Miller theorem. In fact, it is easy to extend this result, via a state-preference analysis, to decisions under uncertainty so as to validate the Modigliani-Miller theorem. The extension is based on the premise that individuals and firms form a closed system, so that all assets or claims must be held by, and only by, individuals or firms. Furthermore, looking at the situation *ex post* of the production decisions (i.e., after commitment of funds to investment), the social totals of each time-state class of assets must then be constant. What this rules out are "external drains" of which the most crucial are personal and corporate taxes. Bankruptcy penalties, transactions and underwriting costs, etc., must also be excluded.

Continuing to employ our simplifying assumption of only two time-periods (times 0 and 1), with only one present state but two future states (a and b), we first develop equations for the firm's capital input and the distribution of returns.

(1) $\quad -q_0 = d_0 + e_0 \qquad$ Capital input balance

Here q_0 is the total of corporate funds committed to investment at time 0; d_0 is the portion coming from borrowings, and e_0 the portion from equity funds.[9] (In the predecessor article we assumed $e_0 = 0$, all-debt financing being possible under certainty.)

8. In their paper the assumption is made throughout that the expected yield on equities exceeds the yield on riskless bonds; they associate the premium with "financial risk" due at least in part to variance of outcome (p. 271). Modigliani and Miller claim that their propositions do not depend upon any assumption about individual risk preferences (p. 279); this statement is correct on the level of the individual (who can maximize asset value regardless of personal risk preferences), but on the market level the existence of a premium reflects the need on balance for compensation to induce bearing of variability risk.

9. It is assumed that the firm does not consume and has null endowment. Hence all funds for investment must be obtained from outside, and also the firm has no use for funds except to invest them. While actual firms do

$$(2)\qquad \begin{cases} q_{1a} = d_{1a} + e_{1a} \\ q_{1b} = d_{1b} + e_{1b} \end{cases} \qquad \text{Firm's financial distributions}$$

Equations (2) say that all gross asset earnings, in either state, are fully distributed and that the only recipients are the debt and equity owners. Here d_{1a} is the gross return to debtholders if state a obtains; the other claims are defined correspondingly. If the debt is riskless, $d_{1a} = d_{1b} = d_0\ (1 + r^*)$, where r^* is the promised interest rate on the bond. If the debt is risky so that in state b, let us say, $d_{1b} < d_0\ (1 + r^*)$ then $e_{1b} = 0$ — since the debt is a senior claim that must be paid first before equity receives any return.

We have here three types of future time-state claims: (physical) asset claims (q_{1a} and q_{1b}), debt claims (d_{1a} and d_{1b}) and equity claims (e_{1a} and e_{1b}). Under the single-price law of markets, unit claims to the same commodity must sell at the same price. Hence, unless there are differentiations due to such features as tax status (excluded by our assumption above), the single price P_{1a} must apply to q_{1a}, d_{1a}, and e_{1a} — and correspondingly P_{1b} is the price of q_{1b}, d_{1b}, and e_{1b}. Taking c_0 as numeraire so that $P_0 = 1$, the prices for the future claims can be written in the form $P_{1a} = 1/(1 + r_{1a})$ and $P_{1b} = 1/(1 + r_{1b})$, where r_{1a} and r_{1b} are the "time-and-risk" discount rates for contingent future incomes. There is a possible source of confusion here: it might be thought that the equity claim e_{1b} is "riskier" than the debt claim d_{1b}, for example, and so should sell at a lower price. But risk has already been taken account of in the *quantification* of d_{1b} and e_{1b} — in the example given just above, if state b obtains so that d_{1b} is less than $d_0(1 + r^*)$, then the junior claim $e_{1b} = 0$. Conditionally upon the occurrence of the specified state, the various claims all become certainties.[1]

If we define present values of the firm, of the debt, and of the equity return in the natural way for this problem (*ex post* of the investment decision),[2] we obtain:

$$(3)\qquad \begin{cases} V_0 = P_{1a}q_{1a} + P_{1b}q_{1b} \\ D_0 = P_{1a}d_{1a} + P_{1b}d_{1b} \\ E_0 = P_{1a}e_{1a} + P_{1b}e_{1b} \end{cases}$$

Here again there is a possible source of confusion, in that it might

make use of "internal" funds, we regard such funds as distributed to stockholders and returned to the firm for reinvestment.

1. Modigliani and Miller describe an "arbitrage" process which has the effect of enforcing this single-price law (pp. 69–71). While their argument has been the subject of controversy, it seems unexceptionable under the provisos of the model here discussed — in particular, under the assumption that the several types of claim do not diverge in tax status.

2. That is, *after* the commitment of current funds (which being "sunk," do not enter into present worth) but *before* the payout of returns to investors.

seem plausible that the relative constancy of the *d*'s as compared with the *e*'s would be reflected by a kind of premium in the value D_0 as compared with E_0, given predominant risk aversion. But since each form of security is only a package of elementary claims to contingent incomes, market equilibrium requires that the value of the package equal the sum of the values of the components.[3]

The Modigliani-Miller Theorem follows immediately from (2) and (3):

(4) $$V_0 = D_0 + E_0.$$

Our formulation makes it possible to observe that the proposition in question is a special case of a Fisherian theorem. Financing operations (i.e., market conversions among claims to income) take place *within* a wealth constraint — they do not change wealth. In the familiar Fisherian analysis of choices involving time, the market value of the productive solution determines wealth; borrowing and lending can then take place to achieve a different distribution of timed income claims, but all such transformations leave wealth unchanged. In the model considered here, the productive solution determines wealth by the condition $V_0 = \overline{X}/\rho_k$; financing via alternative debt-equity ratios then represent different possible ways of distributing this wealth over time-state claims. But all the attainable distributions have the same wealth-value.

We may now examine further the significance of the "closed system" or "no external drains" proviso stated earlier. Let us suppose that there is no corporate tax, but that equity claims are given preferential treatment with respect to the external drain of the *personal* income tax on the system composed of the individuals and firms.[4] This factor, other things equal, would raise the price (lower the discounting rate) of an equity claim relative to a debt claim — and also relative to asset claims assuming these latter have to be financed by mixes of debt and equity. Then the single-price law, for claims conditioned on a given state, could not be applied, and

3. Consider the following analogy. Bread and butter are complements for most people, and possibly substitutes for some careful calorie-watchers — but, regardless, a package of bread and butter in competitive equilibrium must sell for the sum of the bread price and the butter price. Any divergence could only be due to a possible saving of transactions cost, but such costs are a form of "external drain" assumed away in our model. (The assumption of competitive conditions also rules out "tie-in sales" as a device for capitalizing on monopoly power.)

4. The capital gains feature applies to both debt and equity securities, though in practice equity benefits more. The unique advantage to equity is the opportunity to reinvest via "retained earnings," escaping personal tax in the process. (In our analysis, the "retention" is a mere fiction — which is not the whole story, of course.)

equations (3) and (4) would not hold. Alternatively, if we ignored the personal income tax but assumed the existence of an external drain on the corporation in the form of a *corporate* income tax, equations (2) would be modified so as to become (t_{1a} and t_{1b} indicating conditional tax liabilities):

$$(2') \qquad \begin{cases} q_{1a} = d_{1a} + e_{1a} + t_{1a} \\ q_{1b} = d_{1b} + e_{1b} + t_{1b}. \end{cases}$$

Equations (2′) indicate that there is an opportunity to increase wealth by tax-minimizing devices. Under the corporate income tax, debt and equity earnings are differentially treated; tax liability can be reduced by a high debt/equity fraction. The sum $d_{1a} + e_{1a}$ then, for example, would not be a constant independent of the ratio of the two — so that even though the prices (or discounting rates) for asset, debt, and (after-tax) equity earnings are identical, equation (4) would not follow.

We may conclude this section by noting that we have gone only a small step toward solving the problem of optimal capital structure in terms of a state-preference analysis. Doing so would require an integration of the personal-tax and corporate-tax effects, and consideration of other factors (such as the magnitude of bankruptcy penalties) to yield the optimal balance of debt and equity financing.[5] The limited purpose here was only to illustrate the use of a state-preference analysis in order to suggest the range of applicability and the crucial limitations of the much debated Modigliani-Miller "Proposition I."

III. Uncertainty and the Discount Rate for Public Investment

The final application to be presented here of the model of time-state-preference concerns the much controverted question: What is the "appropriate" discount rate, for use under uncertainty, in present-worth calculations evaluating government investments not subject to the market test? Many conflicting recommendations have been expressed on this question, but only two of these will be examined here for consistency with Pareto efficiency in an uncertain world.[6] Of these, the first prescribes that the government employ as

5. For a more complete analysis see J. Lintner, "Dividends, Earnings, Leverage, Stock Prices and the Supply of Capital to Corporations," *Review of Economics and Statistics*, XLIV (Aug. 1962). The result here differs from Lintner's in showing that uncertainty *alone* is not sufficient to negate the Modigliani-Miller theorem.

6. Among the points of view not considered here are those which reject the market evidence on time preference or time productivity in favor of a "social discount rate" excogitated from value judgments or planners' time

discount rate for a public project the same rate as would be applied, in principle, by a company evaluating a "comparable" project in the private sphere. The opposing position would have the government take advantage of its power to finance exceptionally cheaply by undertaking projects that are profitable when the returns are evaluated at the government's low borrowing rate. We may think of these two as prescriptions to employ, in the first case, a *risky*, and in the second case a *riskless*, rate — to discount the mathematical expectations of the uncertain returns.

The argument for use of the risky rate runs somewhat as follows.[7] The market rate of interest is generated by an equilibrium between marginal time preferences of consumers and the marginal time productivity of resources. If neither private nor public projects involved risk, it would obviously be inefficient to depart from this equilibrium rate in evaluating intertemporal transfers of income (i.e., investments) in the public sphere. It is true that in a risky world there are many "impure" time-plus-risk interest rates rather than one pure time-rate, but the way to take this into account is to use in the public sphere the rate employed for "comparable" investments in the private sphere. Thus, if a power project would in the private sector be financed half from debt sources paying 4 per cent (this being a riskless rate, let us say) and half from equity sources requiring an expected return of 6 per cent, the government discount rate for a comparable project should be the same 5 per cent the private company must employ. Then the marginally desirable project would, in either sector, yield 5 per cent in terms of probabilistic expectation. (If corporate income tax is taken into account, the marginally desirable project in the private sphere must have an expected yield around 8.5 per cent, and so the discount rate for government investment should be correspondingly higher.) [8]

preferences. This point of view can be defended as a way of compensating for market bias due to private "myopia" or intertemporal "selfishness," but it raises issues beyond the scope of the Pareto-efficiency criterion. For discussions of this position see O. Eckstein, "A Survey of the Theory of Public Expenditure Criteria," my "Comment," and Eckstein's "Reply" in the National Bureau of Economic Research volume, *Public Finances: Needs, Sources, and Utilization* (Princeton University Press, 1961), and S. Marglin, "The Social Rate of Discount and the Optimal Rate of Investment," this *Journal*, LXXVII (Feb. 1963).

7. The argument is based on that offered in J. Hirshleifer, J. C. DeHaven, and J. W. Milliman, *Water Supply: Economics, Technology, and Policy* (University of Chicago Press, 1960), pp. 139–50.

8. It might be argued that the corporate income tax is an equalizing adjustment designed to compensate the community for certain costs imposed on it by the corporate form of business — in contrast with partnerships, proprietorships, cooperatives, government enterprises, etc. This argument raises issues which are best avoided here; the principle in contention remains the

Failure to abide by this rule leads to obviously inefficient results. If the government, merely because it can finance entirely by riskless borrowing at, say 4 per cent, employed the latter rate in its calculations, the marginally adopted project in the public sector would yield on the average but 4 per cent while private projects with higher expected yields were failing of adoption.

The opposing recommendation is based upon the contention that the higher rates required to secure funds for private investments (e.g., the 6 per cent equity yield in the illustration above) are a reflection of risk aversion — and that risk aversion is a private, not a social cost. The possibility of *pooling* independent risks is essential to this argument. A.T.&T. can pool more risks than can a small local telephone company; it will therefore, be able to finance more cheaply and so to undertake projects with a lower expected yield than the small company can. The federal government can pool risks far more effectively than A.T.&T., and so is as a practical matter quite justified in treating the expected project yield as if it were riskless. Consequently, the 4 per cent riskless discount rate is the relevant one for its calculations.[9] (It should be noted, however, that the conclusion of this argument only follows in a "second-best" sense. For, granted the premises, it would clearly be most efficient for the government to borrow in order to subsidize the higher-expected-yield private investments — a larger subsidy to the small telephone company, a smaller one to A.T.&T. — rather than for the purpose of undertaking lower-yield public investments. Only if this possibility is ruled out does it follow that lower-yielding government investments should be undertaken.)

A simple numerical illustration will indicate the incorrectness of the "pooling" argument *within the time-state model developed here*. Suppose the society consists of J identically placed individuals with identical tastes, and let the social endowment consist of $100J$ units of income (say, "corn") in time 0, $150J$ units in the time-state $1a$, and $50J$ units in time-state $1b$. Let the numeraire $P_0 = 1$. Suppose, for arithmetical convenience, that the state-probabilities $\pi_a = \pi_b = 1/2$, and that with this distribution of consumption opportunities there is on the margin zero time preference with respect to

same, though in one case the divergence is only between 4 per cent and 5 per cent and in the other case between 4 and 8.5 per cent.

9. Many prominent theorists have repeated this argument. Among recent examples are the discussions by P. A. Samuelson and W. Vickrey at the *Principles of Efficiency* session, Papers and Proceedings of the 76th Annual Meeting, *American Economic Review*, LIV (May 1964). See also, Robert M. Solow, *Capital Theory and the Rate of Return* (Chicago: Rand-McNally, 1964), pp. 70–71.

certainties: thus, the price of a unit of future certain income $P_1 = 1$ (and the riskless discount rate $r_1 = 0$ per cent) [1] where, of course, $P_1 = P_{1a} + P_{1b}$. Since by hypothesis there is risk aversion, it must be the case that the overall value of the time-1 endowment for each person — 150 (P_{1a}) + 50 (P_{1b}) — must be less than the value of the average holding as a certainty, i.e., less than $100(P_{1a})+100(P_{1b}) = 100$. (If the prices P_{1a} and P_{1b} were such that the average holding certain *could* be purchased within the endowment wealth constraint, it *would* be, given risk aversion.) This requires that P_{1a} be less than ½. For concreteness, let $P_{1a} = .4$, and hence $P_{1b} = .6$, thus determining the "impure" time-and-state discount rates $r_{1a} = 150$ per cent, and $r_{1b} = 66⅔$ per cent.[2]

Now consider various investment opportunities, all of infinitesimal scale so that we can hold the price relationships unchanged (the opportunities are infinitesimal on the social scale, but not necessarily on the individual scale). It is immediately clear that, in terms of efficiency, either a private or public project whose returns fall *exclusively* in state 1*a* should have these returns discounted at the rate of 150 per cent. To attempt to make a distinction between public and private here would be equivalent to charging different prices for the same commodity — c_{1a}. If the returns all fell in state 1*b*, the discount rate should be 66⅔ per cent. For an investment yielding returns equally in either state (i.e., an investment whose returns are certain), the 0 per cent rate would be appropriate. For a project yielding in the ratio of 3 in state 1*a* to 1 in state 1*b* (that is, in the same proportions as the private and social endowments) the appropriate discount (for application to the mathematical expectation of returns) is approximately 11.1 per cent.[3] The appropriate discount rate would be much lower if, with the same mathematical expectation of returns, the state-distribution were reversed so as to pay off more heavily in the less well-endowed state 1*b* (the rate to use would be *minus* 9.1 per cent, on our assumptions). In every case, of course, the "appropriate" discount rate is that which correctly distinguishes

1. Since $P_1 = 1/(1 + r_1)$.
2. Since $P_{1a} = 1/(1 + r_{1a})$, and $P_{1b} = 1/(1 + r_{1b})$.
3. This figure is derived as follows. Let x be the scale of return per dollar invested. We seek the averaged discount rate r_1^* such that the present-worth calculations in terms of r_1^* and the averaged returns lead to the same result as the explicit calculation in terms of the state-distributed returns and the corresponding r_{1a} and r_{1b}. We determine r_1^* in the equation: $-1 + 3x/(1 + r_{1a}) + x/(1 + r_{1b}) = -1 + 2x/(1 + x_1^*)$. With $r_{1a} = 150$ per cent and $r_{1b} = 66⅔$ per cent the numerical result in the text is obtained.

efficient from inefficient projects by showing positive or negative values in a present-worth calculation.

The foregoing indicates that there is a single definite discount rate to be used, *whether a project is private or public*, in making efficiency calculations for any given state-pattern of returns. This result supports, therefore, the "risky discount rate" position on the normative issue in question. The crucial proviso is that when the recommendation is made to employ for government investments the private market discount rate for "comparable" projects, it must be understood that *"comparable" projects are those having the same proportionate time-state distribution of returns*. In particular, note that the "risky" rate might be *lower* than the riskless rate.

It is correspondingly clear that within this model the position recommending the use of the riskless discount rate with the mathematical expectation of returns must be incorrect. We have just seen that it would fail to distinguish between, on the one hand, a project paying off more heavily in the better-endowed state and, on the other hand, a project with a quantitatively identical but reversed state-pattern paying off more heavily in the more urgently desired income of the poorer-endowed state. Or, to take another example, a project yielding only a dollar in state $1a$ would have that dollar reduced to $.50 in taking the expectation, and then be discounted at the riskless rate (0 per cent here). This is equivalent to letting $r_{1a} = 100$ per cent, too lax a criterion since the correct $r_{1a} = 150$ per cent. On the other hand, if the dollar were returned in state $1b$ the recommendation would indicate too stringent a criterion, employing 100 per cent instead of the correct $66\frac{2}{3}$ per cent. The basic reason, of course, is that the process of taking mathematical expectations considers dollars equivalent when they appertain to equally probable states — but as between two such states, the dollars in one may be much more highly-valued on the margin than in the other. In other words, dollars in distinct time-states are different commodities within the model considered here, and it is as incorrect to average them as it would be to average shoes and apples.

We may now turn to the "pooling" argument. Suppose it were possible to pool two projects, one yielding a dollar in state $1a$ and the other a dollar in state $1b$. Since the pooled return is thus riskless, it may seem plausible to employ the riskless rate 0 per cent for the two, viewed in combination. But this is definitely incorrect. If the two projects were *necessarily* tied together, then the recommended procedure would be appropriate. But if they are really separable, they should be evaluated separately (for simplicity, we set aside complications such as possible interactions between the two). It could easily happen that the combination, if forced upon us as a combination, might be desirable — but that it might be more efficient to adopt one component and not the other, if we could separate the two. In short, the device of pooling provides no justification in efficiency terms for adopting what is incrementally a bad project, if in fact we can adopt the good one separately from the bad.[4]

Even if the "pooling" argument is rejected, it could still be maintained that the discount rate on public projects ought "usually" to be lower than those of private projects. All that is required to support this view is that government projects be "usually" (in contrast with private projects) such that they pay off in less well-endowed states. For example, a federal irrigation project pays off disproportionately when there would otherwise be a drought. Of course, some special argument is required to explain why private initiative does not exploit such opportunities. But if such opportunities are not privately exploited, then in fact the "usual" private investments would not be the *comparable* ones in the sense required by the "risky-discount-rate" position.

It may seem surprising, however, that so little can be made of "pooling" in view of the plausible arguments adduced in its favor. One can, in fact, construct a model in which the pooling argument makes more sense, and it will be instructive to compare that model with ours above. The key is to distinguish between private "states" and social "states." The idea here is related to a maxim often (rather too sweepingly) expressed in connection with life insurance calculations: "We don't know who will die next year, but we do know how many!" Similarly, the social total of endowments might be constant (thus, there is really only one social state, ignoring distribution) and yet for each individual the endowment might be uncertain.[5] For concreteness, imagine the following situation. If state a obtains, every odd-numbered individual has an endowment of 50 and every even-numbered individual an endowment of 150; if state b obtains the positions are reversed. Let us suppose, in order to make the case as strong as possible, that the investments available to even and odd classes of individuals will have returns propor-

4. Precisely this error is committed in the so-called "basin account" doctrine. This theory, put forward by proponents of certain large river basin plans, maintains that benefit-cost evaluations of component projects should be ignored so long as the overall plan shows a surplus of benefits over costs. Federal legislation has adopted this doctrine for the gigantic Missouri Basin Project. See Report of the President's Water Resources Policy Commission, Vol. 2, *Ten Rivers in America's Future* (Washington, 1950), p. 250.

5. This may have been the assumption made in Arrow's original formulation of the state-preference model. See Arrow, *op. cit.*, equation (5).

tionate to their respective endowment distributions. Then the "even" individuals will, on the basis of risk aversion, have a bias against the investments available to them, and the "odd" individuals similarly against their investments — whereas, if pooled, the investments would tend to become certainties justifying no risk discount.

Consider investments of the form requiring a time-0 input of $1, and yielding a time-1 return of $1.50 in an individual's better-endowed and $.50 in his worse-endowed state, the states again assumed equally probable. If the subjective marginal value of a dollar in an individual's better-endowed state is .4 and in his poorer-endowed state is .6 (as before), then each individual would assign a present worth of – $.10 to the investment opportunity. But if an "odd" and an "even" investment opportunity were pooled, the return would be certain; at the riskless 0 per cent rate the combination would have a zero present worth, and so be on the margin of desirability. Here pooling does not sneak in a bad project under the mantle of a good one. Rather, two projects separately bad (in terms of private calculations) may become a good project in terms of social calculations!

A model of this kind is what lies behind the usual "pooling" argument justifying the use of the riskless rate for evaluating government investments. The model diverges in two essential ways from that presented earlier justifying the employment of the risky rate. First is the assumption, already mentioned, that risk is private rather than social — i.e., that there is only one state with respect to social totals [6] but more than one state in terms of possible individual distributions within that total. Second, and this is the really critical point, is the assumption that markets are so imperfect that it is impossible for the individuals better-endowed in state a to trade claims to income in that state against the claims to income in state b that other individuals would like to sell. In short, *the single-price law of markets must be violated.*

Continuing our numerical example, the commodity c_{1a} had a subjective value equal to .4 for even-numbered individuals and .6 for odd-numbered individuals. If trade were permitted between the two classes, the two values would have to come into equality.

6. In an unpublished paper, Kenneth Arrow has employed the somewhat more general assumption of multiple social states, but where the social incomes (endowments) for the several states are *uncorrelated* with the returns from incremental investments in the private states. This also leads to the result that private risks are (on the average) socially irrelevant, and so that market rates of return reflecting private risk aversion should not influence the government's discount rate.

Holding to the assumption that a riskless future claim has unit present value ($P_{1a} + P_{1b} = 1$), P_{1a} and P_{1b} would then each have to equal .5. Then strictly private calculations, without any pooling, would show that the private investment opportunities of the example were on the margin of desirability. The discount rate for the "comparable" private investments would be 0 per cent, so that proponents of the so-called "risky discount rate" for evaluation of public investment would be led by their analysis to the correct 0 per cent rate in this case. In contrast, as we have seen, proponents of the so-called "riskless rate" — while also correct in favoring 0 per cent as the discount rate *in this case* — would be led into definite error under conditions where private risks *are* reflective of social risks.

We may conclude, therefore, that the pooling argument rests ultimately for support upon market imperfections that prevent equivalent time-state claims from selling at a uniform price, thus hindering the possibility of private movements away from risky (unbalanced with respect to state) endowments by trading. Such imperfections may, of course, be very prevalent. One important example concerns assets whose productiveness has a personal element. Such an asset may be worth much in the hands of some Mr. X, but little if traded to anyone else. It will, therefore, be difficult to reduce the riskiness associated with holding such assets.[7] Here is a case where, granted the other conditions in our illustration above, the pooling argument would have real force. But it is clear that the argument is incorrect on the level of generality at which it is usually propounded. If time-state claims can be regarded as commodities traded in perfect markets, the prescription for the use of the so-called "risky rate" — the discount rate implicit in the valuation of private projects with the *same proportionate time-state distribution of returns* — has been shown to be generally correct.

IV. Concluding Remarks

To rationalize the process of investment decision under uncertainty, and to explain the price relationships among risky assets,

7. The most important such asset is labor power. Riskiness might deter both a Mr. X and a Mr. Y. from investing to improve their personal labor capacities. Yet, the state-distributions of the returns from the two investments might in combination represent a certainty. This would suggest that Mr. X and Mr. Y form a partnership, so that each has 50 per cent of the certain combination (i.e., each sells the other half his claims). But, it is possible that one or both will work less productively when he only receives 50 per cent of the benefit of his personal efforts. This possibility would, therefore, inhibit such trading.

two main conceptions of the choice process have been put forward by economic theorists. Both conceptions *reduce* the observed assets traded in the marketplace into more fundamental entities — choice-objects assertedly desired by investors. Under the first and more familiar approach, the more fundamental entities are represented by mean and variability measures, μ and σ, of overall return provided by any given portfolio of assets; under the second approach, the assets are regarded as packages of more fundamental contingent claims to income at specified dates and states of the world.

In the predecessor to this article, it was shown that the state-preference formulation was the logical extension, to the world of uncertain choice, of Fisher's model of certain intertemporal choice. The various topics covered in this article were intended to serve as illustrations of the power and relevance of the state-preference approach, to show that some interesting and novel results in a number of areas can be obtained thereby. (1) As to risk aversion, under the mean vs. variability approach the investor's attitude toward risk (whether σ is for him a good or a "bad") is a personal characteristic. It remains unclear how the risk-loving or risk-avoiding propensities of individuals are composed into an overall market premium or discount for risk. In contrast, under the state-preference approach the very elementary principle of nonspecialization of choice among time-state claims, leads to the inference that in their wealth-oriented decisions, and if asset prices represent fair odds, investors seek portfolios with balanced state-distributions of income. In general, however, they will not actually achieve perfect balance (zero σ), because the endowments and productive opportunities available to society are not symmetrically distributed over all the possible states. (2) As to the unresolved question about the existence of an optimal debt-equity ratio for financing corporate investment, the state-preference formulation leads directly to a set of idealizing assumptions ("no external drains") under which all possible ratios are equivalent in market value. Where the idealized conditions do not hold, there *will* in general be an optimal ratio. (3) With regard to the appropriate discount rate for evaluating government investments, rather vaguely stated ideas concerning risk aversion as a social or a private cost can be precisely formulated in terms of time-state preferences. It was shown that the efficient discount rate, assuming perfect markets, is the market rate implicit in the valuation of private assets whose returns are "comparable" to the public investment in question — where "comparable" means having the same proportionate time-state distribution of returns. The argument often encountered, to the effect that "risk aversion is a private cost and not a social cost," was shown to be mistaken unless two restrictive conditions both hold: (a) Private risks exist, but these do not represent social risks (as when the aggregate social endowment is constant, but its distribution over the individuals varies with state). (b) Markets are imperfect, so that the single-price law of markets does not hold for contingent time-state-claims as commodities.

Going beyond the ground covered by this article, there seem to be considerable difficulties of an operational nature in more direct empirical tests employing a state-preference formulation. The mean and the variability of return embodied in a given set of assets are already only implicitly observable; when the assets are interpreted instead as packages of claims to incomes in underlying hypothetical states of the world, the fundamental choice-objects have an even higher degree of invisibility. Assets ordinarily encountered in capital markets, such as corporate bonds or equities, represent complex aggregates of claims to income in an embarrassing multiplicity of possible states of the world. Nevertheless, in some cases the interpretation may be reasonably clear. Thus, the course of stock and bond prices since 1929 has certainly reflected investors' changing views of the probabilities of more and less prosperous states of the world occurring. Here, as elsewhere, progress will depend upon the discovery of strategic simplifications that reduce seemingly intractable problems into at least partially manageable ones.[8]

University of California
Los Angeles

8. One possible line of simplification is exemplified by the "good year/bad year" dichotomy in H. A. Latané, "Investment Criteria: A Three Asset Portfolio Balance Model," *Review of Economics and Statistics,* XLVI (Feb. 1964).

Part II
Markets

[5]

(β)

ON THE DETERMINATENESS OF ECONOMIC EQUILIBRIUM

[This is a translation of an article which appeared under a slightly different title in the *Giornale degli Economisti*, 1891. The inquiry takes its start from a passage in the then recently published second edition of Marshall's *Principles*, where he adduces from the present writer's essay on *Mathematical Psychics* a construction there largely employed in the investigation of economic equilibrium, the *contract-curve*. Apart from this connection the discourse is not closely related to the text. For Marshall in the passage cited has in view a market in a special sense distinguished from normal, whereas the process which I analyse has much in common with the determination of normal equilibrium. Besides, as argued by Mr. Berry in the same volume (XL.) of the *Giornale*, the term "determinate" is used by Marshall in a somewhat different sense from that which I have adopted.

Apropos, it may be remarked that there is a certain indeterminateness about the use of the term "determinate" by economists. Thus Pareto has demurred to the description (above, **E**) of the transactions between two monopolists as indeterminate. There being more equations than unknowns, the problem, he thinks, cannot properly be described as "mathematically indeterminate."

I dispute no man's definition of terms; concerned, rather, with the truth of propositions. The proposition which I seek to establish here relates to a typical market consisting of two groups of individuals, say A's and B's: the A's offering the commodity a in exchange for β supplied by B's. Each A makes agreements with B's independently of and not in concert with other A's; and the B's likewise act independently. The term "market" applied to this transaction is not to be understood in a sense opposed to "normal" or "natural." Rather there is conceived to be a certain normality about the proceedings. They need not be supposed to take up a long period; rather the contrary, since the disposition and circumstances of the parties are assumed to remain throughout constant. But it is supposed that agreements are renewed or varied many times. A " final settlement " is not reached until the market has hit upon a set of agreements which cannot be varied with advantage to all the re-contracting parties. The re-contract most favourable to the disturbance of a temporary equilibrium is one in which an A deals with a great many B's. If that power is not used, *e.g.*, if each A confines himself to dealing with one B, it is quite possible (as will appear below) that re-contract thus hampered would not disturb the equilibrium. Thus the condition that perfect finality should be reached may be stated as follows, in the case, say, of equal numbers on both sides of the market, m A's and m B's; it must be impossible for any number of A's, say $m-n$, dealing (each for himself) with any number of B's to enter into a new set of agreements with advantage to all the re-contracting parties. Since in general the less restriction there is on the number of B's who re-contract the greater is the possibility of a new equilibrium, the condition is adequately expressed by the proviso that it should not be possible for $(m-n)$ A's to re-contract with *all* the B's. This " all " has proved a stumbling-block to a critic who writes in the same *Giornale* for June, 1891. But I think it might have been difficult to recall the explanation above given by any other concise phrase. I trust that I shall not suffer like the plaintiff in the old state of the English Law who lost his case because in describing an article which had been stolen from him he spoke of a " ham " where he should have used the words " part of a ham." At any rate before condemnation is passed, reference should be made to the writer's essay on *Mathematical Psychics*; on which the article in the *Giornale* is largely based. In the reproduction of the article here presented I have omitted several long passages which purported to be restatements of theories more accurately enunciated in that essay.

I illustrate the theory of determinate equilibrium by two examples in which first appearances are deceptive. There is first the case in which the marginal utility of both articles for at least one of the parties varies with the terms of an agreement. This circumstance may seem at first sight unfavourable to determinateness. It may be to some kinds of determinateness, but not to that which has been above defined. Rather, it is the general rule that both articles should vary in respect of final utility for both parties. If we have to do not with the general problem, but with the particular case in which the marginal utility of one commodity remains constant—as in the instance cited below from Auspitz and Lieben—the equilibrium does not on that account, I think, become more determinate than in the general case, theoretically at least, and apart from "friction."

If this view is correct, indeterminateness is not to be attributed to the labour market, because the marginal utility of money varies with the price of labour that may be set up. But a certain indeterminateness is to be attributed to that market for a quite different reason, namely, the circumstance that a man cannot, or at least does not, simultaneously serve two masters. This point is disputed by the aforesaid critic in the *Giornale* (June, 1891). But, as appears from the passages cited below from the *Giornale*, he seems not to have taken account of an essential condition in our problem, viz., that the competing work-people should not act in concert.]

The theory of Exchange is founded on the principle of Barter, which has been discussed by Marshall with remarkable originality and accuracy. He has avoided the common error of attributing to two persons who are bargaining with each other a fixed rate of exchange governing the whole transaction. A uniform rate of exchange, he remarks, is applicable only to the case of a perfect market. By way of example he puts the case of A having a basket of apples and B a basket of nuts; A desiring nuts and B apples. Referring to this example, I would express the process of barter mathematically in the following manner.

Let the abscissa x denote the number of apples given by A and received by B; the ordinate y, the number of nuts given by B and received by A. Thus every point in the plane (x, y) represents a barter of so many apples for so many nuts. Let u be the utility, or satisfaction, of A so far as it depends on the one hand on the number of nuts that he gains, and on the other hand the number of apples that he retains, that is the number initially in the basket less by the number that he has parted with. Let v be the similarly defined advantage of B.[1] Bartering will continue as long as it is possible for both parties to gain thereby. Let Δx be the *quid* given by A and Δy the *pro quo* received by him at any stage of the transaction. The process of exchange

[1] It may assist the formation of correct conceptions to put $u \equiv \phi_1(a - x) + \psi_1(y)$, where a is the original stock of apples; with a corresponding expression for v. But we are not limited to this simple form. We are at liberty to use for it an expression of the form $\chi(a-x, y)$.

can only continue as long as the gain (of satisfaction) by A and likewise B's gain is positive; in symbols,

$$\frac{du}{dx}\Delta x + \frac{du}{dy}\Delta y > 0. \quad \frac{dv}{dx}\Delta x + \frac{dv}{dy}\Delta y > 0.$$

Now this condition will cease to be fulfilled when the total quantities exchanged, x and y, are such as to satisfy the equation

$$\frac{du}{dx}\frac{dv}{dy} = \frac{dv}{dx}\frac{du}{dy}.$$

The locus thus represented I have called the *contract-curve.*

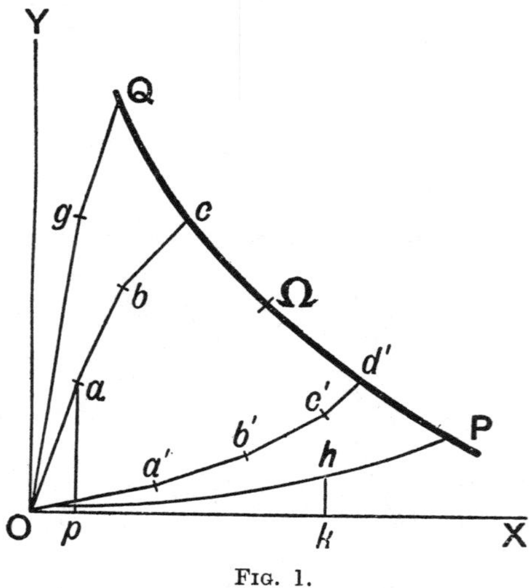

Fig. 1.

In Fig. 1 any point, for instance a, denotes the exchange of, or contract for the exchange of, the number of nuts represented by the ordinate ap against the number of apples expressed by the abscissa Op. The series of short lines Oa, ab, bc, corresponds to successive barters (at different rates of exchange) of a few nuts for a few apples. The broken line $Oa'b'c'd'$ indicates a possible set of exchanges more favourable to B.

Alike at c and at d' the bartering comes to a stop, those points being situated on the contract-curve PQ. Of this curve the only part with which we are concerned is that which is intercepted by the *curves of constant satisfaction*, or *curves of indifference*, for A and B respectively which pass through O; viz., OhP and OgQ. The *curve of indifference* which passes through a given point is the locus of all the contracts that procure to the contractor the same satisfaction as the contract designated by the given point. For instance, the contract designated by the point *h*, that is *Ok* apples given for *hk* nuts, or, again, the contract designated by *P*, procures for the contractor A the same satisfaction as the contract (or absence thereof) designated by *O*. It is indifferent to A whether he makes either of the first two deals, or none at all. Similarly, it is indifferent to B whether the dealing is represented by the point *O*, or *g*, or *Q*.

At what point on the tract of contract-curve between *P* and *Q* the process of bartering will come to a stop cannot be predicted. The position of equilibrium may be described as indeterminate. The essential condition of this indeterminateness is the absence of competition.

The essential condition is not to be sought in an incident of the case before us, namely, that the marginal utility of both the commodities varies in the course of the dealing. The phenomenon of indeterminateness may very well exist without that incident. Whether or not the marginal utility of one commodity, say *y*, is regarded as varying with the additions or subtractions incidental to exchange, there will always remain—in the case of barter between two individuals—an indeterminate tract on the contract-curve, every point of which is a position of equilibrium. True, the curve will sometimes degenerate into a right line parallel to one of the axes.[1] An example is furnished by Messrs. Auspitz and Lieben in that part of their important book in which they discuss the contract between a monopolist entrepreneur and a union of operatives. Assuming that the marginal utility of money may be treated as constant, they justly observe that "the determination of price seems to be between wide limits arbitrary."

Thus the imperfections of the labour market do not depend on the circumstance that the marginal utility of money varies for the work-people according to their bargain with the employers, according as their wages afford only bare necessities or superabundant luxuries. The imperfections of that market are rather

[1] In symbols if the final utility of y is constant for both dealers, we may put for u the satisfaction of the contractor A the expression $\phi_1(a-x) + \alpha y$, and for v (pertaining to B) $\phi_2(x) + \beta y$; where α and β are constants. Accordingly we obtain for the contract-curve $\frac{\phi_1'(a-x)}{\alpha} = \frac{\phi_2'(x)}{\beta}$; or $x =$ constant; representing a line parallel to the axis of y. This line fulfils the characteristic condition of the contract-curve that at any point of the locus the inclination of the tangent to a curve of indifference passing through that point should be the same for both parties.

to be sought in certain peculiarities which Marshall has pointed out, as noticed at the conclusion of this paper.

Apropos of impediments to the play of competition in the labour market there may be observed from the point of view here adopted two incidents which are more curious than important.

Suppose that every A can contract with only one B, and likewise every B with only one A. Then it is no longer possible that $(m-n)$ A's—each acting independently—should form a set of new contracts with all—or any number of—the B's (and likewise impossible for $(m-n)$ B's to re-contract); which variation of contracts—when it can be effected with advantage to all the re-contracting parties—is here regarded as the essential attribute of competition. Accordingly, the equilibrium would be in the case supposed as indeterminate for a set of couples, as we have seen that it is in the case of a single couple. There may possibly exist types of domestic service which fulfil the supposed condition. But practical importance is not claimed for this *curiosum*.

There is another unobserved peculiarity of the labour-market which is the more curious in that it constitutes a positive advantage to the work-people in their dealings with entrepreneurs. Suppose that the system of contracts is initially at any point on the contract-curve (Fig. 1) d' on the right of the position hereinafter defined Ω; that is to the advantage of the B's who supply the article y. It may be shown that the advantage which the B's thus possess is lost through the action of $(m-n)$ of their number who carry off, so to speak, the whole (or a large part) of the A group.* Suppose now that the A's are work-people, the B's entrepreneurs. The terms first proposed may be very much to the advantage of the entrepreneurs. But they will lose that advantage through competition against each other. Assuming that an entrepreneur can employ several men, it will be to his advantage to offer to some of his rivals' workmen better terms than they were receiving, and so carry them off. And this process will theoretically continue until the system of agreements reaches the position of stable equilibrium symbolised by the point Ω, the point at which the demand curves (not shown in the figure) intersect on the contract-curve. Analogously it might be supposed that if the terms are at first too favourable for the work-people, if, for instance, the point c (left of Ω) represented an initial system of contracts, the work-people would lose that advantage, by mutual competition. But such competition would imply, according to our analysis, that a workman

* See note at end of article.

takes on several entrepreneurs; that a man *can* serve two masters simultaneously. In the case of painters, no doubt, and many home-workers plurality of employers is common. Still, the general rule is that no man can serve two masters, and so far as this is true the work-people have an advantage over the entrepreneurs in that they cannot equally beat down the price of their services by mutual competition.

I do not, however, regard these nice points as more than *curiosa*, of little practical importance in comparison with the conditions of the labour-market on which Marshall has dwelt; in particular, the tendency of any accidental disadvantage under which the work-people may be suffering to become perpetuated through the lowering of their vitality and efficiency, and the fact that employers are few in comparison with the number of work-people. In this field Marshall has thoroughly reaped the harvest, leaving nothing to those who come after him but to glean some logical niceties.

(Note referring to p. 318.)

[The argument that if a rate of exchange unduly favourable to the work-people is set up they will not beat the price down by their mutual competition is disputed by an able critic in the June number (1891) of the *Giornale*, on grounds of which the following quotation (*loc. cit.* p. 553) contains the gist. "Though it is true that 'no man can serve two masters,' yet it is quite possible for a number of work-people to increase the number of entrepreneurs whom they serve. If, on average, 100 work-people serve one employer, 500 may at pleasure renew their contract with six or with four. The first proceeding tends, according to Professor Edgeworth's reasoning, to favour the entrepreneurs, the second the work-people."

To which I reply in the October number of the *Giornale* (1891) suggesting that the critic has not taken account of the condition that the work-people should not act in concert.

"Say five entrepreneurs employ each on average 100 men. Four of these entrepreneurs are disposed to employ a larger number of workmen, and they offer higher wages, each finding that he can thus make a bargain more advantageous for himself and for his employees. What can be simpler? But now consider the opposite case. How can 400 work-people originally employed by four entrepreneurs find occupation with five entrepreneurs by way of an initiative on the part of the work-people, each acting independently, and not in concert with others. This case is not analogous to the first; because it is not in the power of any operative to purchase, so to speak, a fraction of an entrepreneur, other than, or in addition to, that which he already enjoys in virtue of his present engagement."]

[6]

A Calculus Approach to the Theory of the Core of an Exchange Economy

By LEIF JOHANSEN*

The theory of the shrinking of the core of an exchange economy to the competitive equilibrium (or set of equilibria) when the number of participants increases is one of the most important and interesting contributions to general equilibrium theory in recent decades, and ought to become part of standard courses in economic theory. It is important to have an exposition of this idea which appears as a simple and natural extension of the tools of analysis familiar to most students of economics. The purpose of the present paper is to make an attempt at such an exposition along traditional calculus lines. The paper does not contain results which are new to specialists in the field. In the literature there are, of course, some expositions which point in the direction taken here, but I have not seen the approach spelled out in the way it is done in the sequel. (Some relevant references are given at the end of the paper.)

I. Background and Perspectives

Let me first state very briefly why I consider the result mentioned to be interesting and important. It is then necessary to emphasize the difference between the meaning of the concepts of competitive equilibrium and core allocations.

A competitive equilibrium presupposes the existence of a price system. Under this system individual agents act in isolation in the sense that each of them decides how much to supply and how much to demand of the various commodities on the basis of his own preferences, without making conscious and explicit arrangements with other agents. Each agent considers prices as given in an impersonal way, not subject to bargaining or manipulation through his own supply and demand. We have equilibrium if prices are such that supply and demand for all agents taken together are equal for each commodity. Provided that we have somehow established equilibrium prices in this sense, they solve a complicated multiagent problem by transforming it into a set of rather simple individual decision problems. (It is not necessary for our purpose to go into the problem of how the prices are established and the associated dynamic stability problems.)

A core allocation is defined by an entirely different approach. In this case we consider only a set of agents with initial holdings of commodities who may improve their positions by reallocation, but we do not presuppose the existence of a price system. We start at a more basic level, assuming only that there are possibilities for the agents to communicate and make agreements to reallocate commodities between them—by unilateral gifts, by bilateral exchange, or by some more complicated multilateral exchange arrangement. The individuals are free to form "coalitions" for the purpose of improving the situation for members of the coalition. In our context a coalition is simply a group of agents who agree on a certain reallocation of the initial quantities of goods held by its members. It should be observed that the initial quantities are individually owned, and ownership respected in the sense that nothing can be taken away from an agent without his consent, as part of a voluntary exchange or reallocation. We may now ask whether it is possible to predict the outcome of the exchange or reallocation process in such a system. The "core" gives an answer to this question. It is based on the following observation: Consider an outcome which is feasible in the

*Professor of economics, University of Oslo. I am grateful to a referee for useful remarks and suggestions.

sense that the total amounts of commodities held after the exchange or reallocation are equal to the total initial amounts. This outcome implies a specific bundle of commodities for each agent. If there is at least one group of agents such that these agents could improve their situations by redistributing their own initial holdings instead of agreeing to the proposed outcome, then this outcome will not be realized. It will be "blocked" by the group or coalition mentioned, that is, they will refuse to accept it, because there is another arrangement which they can realize without requiring the cooperation of other agents, and which is better for each of them. It is then natural to ask: Is there a feasible outcome, or a set of outcomes, which will not be blocked by any coalition that can be formed by some agents of the economy (including degenerate coalitions consisting of single agents, and the grand coalition comprising all agents). If such an outcome, or set of outcomes exists, then this is the core.

An outcome belonging to the core is stable in a very important sense, different from the usual dynamic stability concept. It is stable against attempts by individuals and coalitions to find something better, because no possible coalition can do better by refusing to accept the outcome, and instead manage on the basis of the initial holdings of the members of the coalition.

We can now compare the allocation defined by the competitive equilibrium with core allocations. It is a simple matter to show, for exchange economies which we shall consider here, that the competitive equilibrium allocation belongs to the core. The result referred to above as the theory of the "shrinking of the core of an exchange economy to the competitive equilibrium (or set of equilibria) when the number of participants increases" is more striking and also more complicated to prove, and it is to this theme the present paper will be devoted. This connection between competitive equilibria and the core may, in my opinion, give rise to rather far-reaching speculations about economic systems and institutions.

The establishing of a core allocation by means of tentative formations of coalitions of all sizes and compositions, and comparisons of feasible outcomes for the various coalitions, will for an economy with more than a handful of agents represent a large effort in terms of communication and negotiations. In comparison the mechanism of competitive equilibrium is strikingly simple, requiring only individual decisions (when correct prices are given). If an economy has, so to speak, invented the price mechanism, and competitive equilibrium prices have been established, then an enormous organizational problem is solved in an easy manner, and the solution is stable in the sense described above, that is, any group which might contemplate breaking out of the market system will in the end find that it cannot improve its situation by doing so. Furthermore, if the economy consists of a number of agents "approaching infinity," then outcomes corresponding to the set of competitive equilibria are the *only* outcomes which satisfy this kind of stability requirement. I think these considerations go a long way towards explaining why competitive market mechanisms have appeared in almost all corners of the world and, under almost all conceivable circumstances, why they have proved to be so robust, why other arrangements tend to be less permanent, and why attempts to abolish the market mechanism have often failed in the sense that markets reappear unofficially parallel with the official nonmarket system. (These are, of course, sweeping statements which should not be taken too literally. They are meant only as suggestions of the perspectives opened up by a seemingly rather formal and esoteric theory.)

II. Strategy of Reasoning

As already suggested, this paper will treat only exchange economies, although extensions to production economies are possible. The main idea is to get as far as we can by means of simple calculus tools of analysis. We must then assume more of "smoothness" than necessary in more advanced expositions and proofs. In fact, we shall assume strictly convex preferences, representable by differentiable utility functions. The advantage gained by this is that we can exploit the possibility of approximating a utility function by its tangent in certain neighborhoods.

The strategy of the reasoning is first to limit considerations to Pareto optimal points since both competitive equilibria and core allocations belong to the set of Pareto optima. (The last part of this statement is true because the coalition of all agents would block, in the sense indicated above, any allocation which is not Pareto optimal. This, by the way, points to a limitation of the core theory in the form considered here. Whenever we consider, as we often do in welfare theory, situations which are not Pareto optimal, then we must implicitly assume some sorts of difficulties which prevent the formation of coalitions. It is, however, beyond the scope of this paper to pursue this idea.) Then we consider the various Pareto optimal allocations to see whether there are coalitions which would block them, and we shall find that, for any such allocation which does not belong to the set of competitive equilibria, we can construct such a coalition, that is, prove that the allocation does not belong to the core, provided that the number of agents is sufficiently large. (A certain regularity may be required concerning the way in which the number of agents is made large.)

III. Description of the Economy and Notation

I now introduce the notation necessary to describe the exchange economy to be considered. Let there be M perfectly divisible commodities indexed $i = 1, \ldots, M$ and G "types" of individuals, indexed $j = 1, \ldots, G$. All individuals of the same type have the same initial quantities of the various commodities and the same utility functions. The following notation is also introduced:

N_j = the number of individuals of type $j\,(j = 1, \ldots, G)$.

$\bar{x}_{ij}$ = *initial quantity* of commodity i held by a person of type j $(i = 1, \ldots, M; j = 1, \ldots, G)$.

x_{ij} = quantity of commodity i held by a person of type j after the exchange $(i = 1, \ldots, M; j = 1, \ldots, G)$. I call these *final quantities*.

U_j = $U_j(x_{1j}, \ldots, x_{Mj})$ = utility function of an individual of type $j\,(j = 1, \ldots, G)$. Assumptions about the utility functions have already been mentioned in Section II above.

u_{ij} = $\partial U_j / \partial x_{ij}$ = marginal utility of commodity i for an individual of type $j\,(i = 1, \ldots, M; j = 1, \ldots, G)$. I assume $u_{ij} > 0$ for all i, j.

The collection of all $\bar{x}_{ij}$ will be called the *initial allocation* or *initial point* and symbolized by $\bar{x}$. The collection of all x_{ij}, symbolized by x, will be called the *final allocation* or *final point*. I shall, furthermore, use x^*_{ij} and x^* to symbolize a Pareto optimal allocation.

An allocation which is feasible for the economy as a whole must satisfy

$$(1) \quad N_1 x_{i1} + \ldots + N_G x_{iG} = N_1 \bar{x}_{i1} + \ldots + N_G \bar{x}_{iG} \qquad (i = 1, \ldots, M)$$

IV. Pareto Optimal Allocations and Competitive Equilibria

As already pointed out it follows from the definition of the core that a point which is not Pareto optimal cannot belong to the core. Hence, we need only consider Pareto optimal points as candidates for belonging to the core. Furthermore we shall consider as candidates only Pareto optimal points where individuals of the same type receive the same amounts of the various goods. This implies some loss in generality, but hardly serious for our purpose. Indeed, if $N_1, N_2, \ldots, N_G$ have a greatest common divisor which is greater than one, then a very simple argument given by Jerry R. Green, which need not be repeated here, shows that core allocations have this "equal treatment property." (Convexity of preferences, as assumed above, is used in establishing this result.)

For our calculus approach it is assumed

that the optimizations defining Pareto optimal points yield interior solutions. Pareto optimal points with equal treatment as just described can then be characterized by the following conditions:

$$(2)\quad \frac{u_{1j}}{\lambda_1} = \ldots = \frac{u_{Mj}}{\lambda_M} = \mu_j \quad (j = 1, \ldots, G)$$

Pareto optimal allocations are allocations which satisfy these conditions in addition to the balances (1).

The symbols μ_j in (2), one for each type $1, \ldots, G$, are introduced for convenience as the common value of the proportions to the left. The factors of proportionality $\lambda_1, \ldots, \lambda_M$ in formula (2) can, of course, be interpreted as prices, but they are used here only as coefficients to characterize a Pareto optimal allocation, not to describe any particular institutional arrangement. Let x^*_{ij} denote the quantities corresponding to some Pareto optimal allocation, that is, an allocation satisfying (1) and (2).

I now introduce *imputed wealth*. For an individual of type j the imputed wealth in an arbitrary allocation x is defined by

$$(3)\quad y_j = \lambda_1 x_{1j} + \ldots + \lambda_M x_{Mj} \qquad (j = 1, \ldots, G)$$

where the factors of proportionality are used from (2). For the initial allocation and for the Pareto optimal allocation we have, in particular, imputed wealth $\bar{y}_j$ and y^*_j respectively, defined by

$$(4)\quad \bar{y}_j = \lambda_1 \bar{x}_{1j} + \ldots + \lambda_M \bar{x}_{Mj} \qquad (j = 1, \ldots, G)$$

$$(5)\quad y^*_j = \lambda_1 x^*_{1j} + \ldots + \lambda_M x^*_{Mj} \qquad (j = 1, \ldots, G)$$

For the Pareto optimal allocation considered we do not necessarily have $y^*_j = \bar{y}_j$. If $y^*_j = \bar{y}_j$, then x^* represents a competitive equilibrium with prices $\lambda_1, \ldots, \lambda_M$ since the relations (2) then signify the adaptation of the various individuals to these prices and $y^*_j = \bar{y}_j$ represents the budget balance of an individual of type j. If $y^*_j \neq \bar{y}_j$ for some j, then we have a Pareto optimal point which is not a competitive equilibrium. It is well known that we may have more than one competitive equilibrium, that is, a set of equilibria. This does not matter for the following arguments.

V. The Blocking of Pareto Optimal Allocations which are not Competitive Equilibria

I now raise the question as to whether a Pareto optimal point which is not necessarily a competitive equilibrium can be blocked by any coalition. Let a possible coalition consist of $n_1, n_2, \ldots, n_G$ individuals of the various types. This coalition can, on the basis of its own initial quantities, reach any final point x which satisfies the balance relations

$$(6)\quad n_1 x_{i1} + \ldots + n_G x_{iG} = n_1 \bar{x}_{i1} + \ldots + n_G \bar{x}_{iG} \qquad (i = 1, \ldots, M)$$

The imputed wealth for individuals of type j in such a point is then given by (3).

The question now is whether there exists any feasible final point x for the coalition which is considered by all members to be better than the given Pareto optimal point x^*. It follows from what has been explained that, in order to show that x^* does not belong to the core, it is sufficient to construct *one* such coalition for which *one* such point exists. We then look for a simple way to do this, not for the most general characterization of the possibilities of blocking. If we tentatively limit attention to points x which are in the neighborhood of x^*, then imputed wealth can be used as a criterion to compare x and x^*. Since we have, approximately,

$$(7)\quad U_j(x_{1j}, \ldots, x_{Mj}) - U_j(x^*_{1j}, \ldots, x^*_{Mj}) \approx u_{1j} \cdot (x_{1j} - x^*_{1j}) + \ldots + u_{Mj} \cdot (x_{Mj} - x^*_{Mj}) = [\lambda_1(x_{1j} - x^*_{1j}) + \ldots + \lambda_M(x_{Mj} - x^*_{Mj})]\mu_j = (y_j - y^*_j)\mu_j$$

and since $\mu_j > 0$, we have for x in the neighborhood of x^*:

(8) $y_j > y^*_j \Longrightarrow$ an individual of type j is better off in x than in x^* $(j = 1, \ldots, G)$

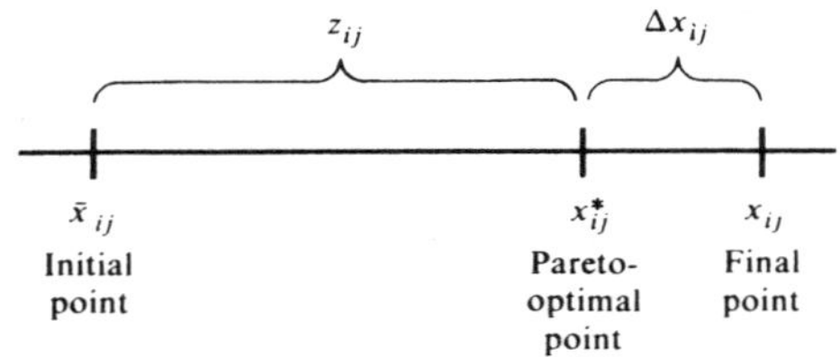

FIGURE 1

The question can now be posed as follows: Can we make $y_j > y_j^*$ hold for all j when the final point x is constrained by (6)? Introduce the following terms

$$\Delta x_{ij} = x_{ij} - x_{ij}^* \tag{9}$$

$$z_{ij} = x_{ij}^* - \bar{x}_{ij} \tag{10}$$

that is, Δx_{ij} is the deviation between the final point and the Pareto optimal point we are testing for possible blocking, and z_{ij} is the deviation between the Pareto optimal point and the initial point, as suggested in Figure 1.

We will now see if a change from x^* to x which, for each type, changes the quantities proportionately with z_{ij} will do for the purpose of blocking x^*, that is, for producing a final point which all members of the coalition find superior to x^*. We may think of this in the commodity space as drawing a straight line between the initial point $\bar{x}$ and the Pareto optimal point x^*, and then moving the final point for each group away from x^* along this ray, either towards $\bar{x}$ or further away from $\bar{x}$. Introduce the ratio

$$s_j = \Delta x_{ij}/z_{ij} \qquad (i = 1, \ldots, M; \; j = 1, \ldots, G) \tag{11}$$

If $s_j > 0$, then individuals of type j are moved further away than x^* from the initial point; if $s_j < 0$, then they are moved some distance back towards $\bar{x}$. (We may have $z_{ij} > 0$ or $z_{ij} < 0$. If, by coincidence, $z_{ij} = 0$ for some i, then also $\Delta x_{ij} = 0$, and s_j takes the value suitable for the changes in the quantities of the other commodities. If, for some j, we should happen to have $z_{ij} = 0$ for all i, then s_j is arbitrary. In the explanations which follow I shall, for brevity, neglect this special case.)

If such moves are feasible for the coalition considered, that is, satisfy (6), then we must have

$$n_1(x_{i1} - \bar{x}_{i1}) + \ldots + n_G(x_{iG} - \bar{x}_{iG}) = 0 \qquad (i = 1, \ldots, M)$$

which by use of (9)–(11) can be written as

$$n_1(1 + s_1)z_{i1} + \ldots + n_G(1 + s_G)z_{iG} = 0 \qquad (i = 1, \ldots, M) \tag{12}$$

According to (8) individuals of type j are better off at x than at x^* if we have

$$y_j - y_j^* = \lambda_1(x_{1j} - x_{1j}^*) + \ldots + \lambda_M(x_{Mj} - x_{Mj}^*) > 0$$

or, in view of (9) and (11),

$$y_j - y_j^* = (\lambda_1 z_{1j} + \ldots + \lambda_M z_{Mj})s_j > 0 \tag{13}$$

Using (4), (5), and (10), this can also be written as

$$y_j - y_j^* = (y_j^* - \bar{y}_j)s_j > 0 \tag{14}$$

This requirement determines the sign of s_j for each type j. For members of the coalition belonging to each type j we must have

$$s_j \gtrless 0 \quad \text{according as} \quad y_j^* \gtrless \bar{y}_j \tag{15}$$

This condition means that members of the coalition who have a larger imputed wealth at the Pareto optimal point considered than at the initial point should be moved further away from $\bar{x}$ through x^*, whereas members with higher imputed wealth in the initial situation than in the Pareto optimal point considered should be moved somewhat back from x^* towards $\bar{x}$.

I have not yet said anything about possible members for whom $y_j^* = \bar{y}_j$. This is a special case which will be disposed of later. For the moment it is assumed

$$\bar{y}_j \neq y_j^* \text{ for } j = 1, \ldots, G \tag{16}$$

We have now considered feasibility and a criterion for positive gain by members of the coalition of the various types. The feasibility condition is dependent upon the number of members of the coalition belonging to each type, i.e., on $n_1, \ldots, n_G$. The crucial question now is whether it is possible to compose the coalition, that is, determine the numbers $n_1, \ldots, n_G$, in such a way that the feasibility condition (12) is fulfilled, while at the same time the condition (15) for a gain by all members in comparison with x^* is fulfilled.

For studying this it is convenient to introduce the proportions ν_j which members of each type form in the total coalition, i.e.,

$$(17) \quad \nu_j = \frac{n_j}{n_1 + \ldots + n_G} = \frac{n_j}{n} \qquad (j = 1, \ldots, G)$$

In terms of these proportions the feasibility requirement (12) can be written as

$$(18) \quad \nu_1(1 - s_1)z_{i1} + \ldots + \nu_G(1 + s_G)z_{iG} = 0 \qquad (i = 1, \ldots, M)$$

Observe that this condition is fulfilled for

$$(19) \quad \nu_1 = N_1/N, \ldots, \nu_G = N_G/N$$
$$s_1 = \ldots = s_G = 0$$

where $N_1, \ldots, N_G$ are the total number of individuals of each type, and N is the total number of individuals, i.e., $N = N_1 + \ldots + N_G$. This follows from the fact that the Pareto optimal point x^* must be feasible for the exchange economy as a whole, that is, we must have

$$(20) \quad N_1 x^*_{i1} + \ldots + N_G x^*_{iG} = N_1 \bar{x}_{i1} + \ldots + N_G \bar{x}_{iG} \qquad (i = 1, \ldots, M)$$

which is the feasibility condition (1) applied to the Pareto optimal point considered.

The statement just made simply means that a coalition with a composition proportional to the composition in the complete set of individuals can reach the Pareto optimal point under consideration on the basis of its own initial amounts. In order to construct a coalition which blocks the Pareto optimal point considered we shall try to find an allocation in the neighborhood of x^* which all members of the coalition prefer to x^*. We must then alter the composition of the coalition somewhat, but shall keep it *approximately* similar to the composition given by the first line of (19).

Now, in order that all members of the coalition gain by a move away from x^*, we must make $s_1, \ldots, s_G$ different from zero according to the sign pattern determined by (15). In order not to do violence to the local nature of the criterion that we use, we let $s_1, \ldots, s_G$ deviate only a little from zero. Let us for the moment treat $\nu_1, \ldots, \nu_G$ as free variables in the neighborhood of the values given by (19), restricted only by $\Sigma \nu_j = 1$. (This is a crucial point to which I shall return.) Then, for any given set of values for $s_1, \ldots, s_G$, some positive and some negative according to (15), we can clearly satisfy all equations in (18) by simply setting

$$(21) \quad \nu_1 = \frac{\alpha}{1 + s_1}\frac{N_1}{N}, \ldots, \nu_G = \frac{\alpha}{1 + s_G}\frac{N_G}{N}$$

since (18) by this insertion reduces to (20), which is known to be fulfilled. Here α is a parameter which is adjusted to that $\Sigma \nu_j = 1$.

By the procedure outlined above we have succeeded in constructing a coalition together with a feasible final point for the coalition which is superior to the Pareto optimal point x^* for all members of the coalition. By the definition of the core, we can accordingly conclude that x^* does not belong to the core. The argument is, however, not yet quite complete because of a couple of points which were temporarily put off in the development of the idea given above. Let us now return to these points.

VI. Some Special Points Needed to Complete the Argument

Let us first consider the assumption made by (16). If the Pareto optimal point considered should be such that for some type, $\bar{y}_j = y^*_j$, then individuals of this type cannot gain anything by being moved away from x^* in any direction according to the construction used above. However, it may be necessary to include a suitable number of individuals of this type in the coalition in order to give it the desired composition. For these members we set $s_j = 0$. We will then have $\nu_j = \alpha N_j/N$ according to (21). We now need these as members of the coalition, but they do not gain anything by it as compared with the Pareto optimal point x^*. However, since other members of the coalition, for whom $\bar{y}_j \neq y_j^*$, make a strictly positive gain, then a slight transfer so as to make these special members gain also could always be carried out if this is necessary for involving them in the coalition.

As already mentioned before the case in which $\bar{y}_j = y_j^*$ for *all* $j = 1, \ldots, G$ is the case in which x^* is the special Pareto optimal point representing the competitive equilibrium, or one of these if the competitive equilibrium is not unique. In this case the procedure outlined above will not succeed in constructing another feasible final point for a coalition which is superior to x^* for all members of the coalition. This is as it should be. It is well known that the competitive equilibrium belongs to the core so that no coalition can be constructed which can block such a point. (The fact that the competitive equilibrium belongs to the core is proved by elementary methods in many expositions and will not be taken up for further consideration here.)

In connection with the comparison between y_j and y_j^*, the following point may be observed. Consider equation (14). The difference $y_j^* - \bar{y}_j$ here decides the sign of s_j. If we multiply these differences by the number of individuals of each type and add over types we get

$$(22)\quad \sum_{j=1}^{G} N_j(y_j^* - \bar{y}_j) = \sum_{i=1}^{M} \lambda_i\Big(\sum_{j=1}^{G} N_j x_{ij}^* - \sum_{j=1}^{G} N_j \bar{x}_{ij}\Big) = 0$$

The last equality here follows from (1) which must hold for x^*. Since all $N_j > 0$ it follows from this that when some $y_j^* > \bar{y}_j$, then there must be at least one j for which the opposite inequality holds, and vice versa. Thus, if not all $y_j^* = \bar{y}_j$, then there will be at least one j for which $s_j > 0$, and at least one j for which $s_j < 0$.

The second point which must be taken up refers to the assumption temporarily made that we could consider $\nu_1, \ldots, \nu_G$, i.e., the proportions of the representation of each type in the coalition considered, as free variables (restricted only by nonnegativity and $\Sigma\nu_j = 1$). When N is a finite integer and also $N_1, \ldots, N_G$ are integers, then we are in fact not entirely free in determining $\nu_1, \ldots, \nu_G$. These variables are defined by (17), and $n_1, \ldots, n_G$ must also be integers and restricted by $0 \leqq n_j \leqq N_j$. Suppose that we have tentatively determined $s_1, \ldots, s_G$ with correct signs and sufficiently small so as not to invalidate the application of our local criterion for gains. Then there may be no integers satisfying $0 \leqq n_j \leqq N_j$ which used in (17) produce the required $\nu_1, \ldots, \nu_G$ according to (21). The natural idea then is to make some small adjustments in $s_1, \ldots, s_G$ (without altering their signs) so as to make (21) hold good with values of $\nu_1, \ldots, \nu_G$ which can be produced by (17) with permissible integers for $n_1, \ldots, n_G$.

Now, this may be impossible if $N_1, \ldots, N_G$ are small integers. However, if $N_1, \ldots, N_G$ are large, then we are much more free in choosing $n_1, \ldots, n_G$, and it is easier to produce proportions $\nu_1, \ldots, \nu_G$ which satisfy the requirements needed for some sufficiently small $s_1, \ldots, s_G$ with correct signs. (According to what was said above in connection with (22), some of the types will be "overrepresented" in the coalition in the sense that $\nu_j > N_j/N$, and some types will be "underrepresented" in the sense that $\nu_j < N_j/N$. The factor α used to secure $\Sigma\nu_j = 1$ will be near to unity when $s_1, \ldots, s_G$ are small.)

If we increase $N_1, \ldots, N_G$ beyond all limits, then we approach a situation in which the restriction that $n_1, \ldots, n_G$ have to be integers is no longer an effective restriction on the possibilities for choosing $\nu_1, \ldots, \nu_G$. Then the construction of the coalitions as given above can be carried out for any Pareto optimal point x^* which is not a competitive equilibrium, that is, for any x^* for which at least one type (and then necessarily at least two) have $y_j^* \neq \bar{y}_j$. This shows that when the number of individuals of all types increases beyond all limits, then only competitive equilibrium solutions remain in the core. (In order to make the comparison between smaller and larger economies meaningful, it is easiest to think of the larger economy as one in which the number of individuals of each type has been blown up proportionately. Then we may speak about "the same point" x^* in the smaller and the larger economy, the only difference being in the absolute numbers of individuals enjoying the various commodity bundles.)

VII. A Final Remark

The construction presented above can also be used to say something more intuitive about the size of the core when the number of individuals is finite, and in general other (Pareto optimal) points besides the competitive equilibrium belong to the core. For instance, if the indifference surfaces corresponding to the utility functions of individuals of the various types are very strongly curved, then there will be less freedom in the choice of $s_1, \ldots, s_G$, while smaller curvature makes for wider ranges of permissible choices of $s_1, \ldots, s_G$. The less free we are in choosing $s_1, \ldots, s_G$, the more difficult will it be to find permissible $\nu_1, \ldots, \nu_G$ when we have a limited number of individuals of each type to select $n_1, \ldots, n_G$ from. Thus, for an economy with a given number of individuals, the blocking procedure used here seems to be more powerful in excluding points from the core when there is a moderate curvature than when there is strong curvature in the indifference surfaces in the neighborhood of the point tested. By similar reasoning one may also get the impression that it will normally be easier to exclude points which are far away from the competitive equilibrium than points in its neighborhood. However, these suggestions are only hints about directions in which the arguments can be developed. A complete analysis of the question as to which points belong to the core and which ones do not, for a given number of individuals of each type, is a much more difficult task than the one tackled above. In order to show that a point does *not* belong to the core, it is sufficient to construct *one* particular coalition which is able to block the point in *one* particular way as we have done above. In order to show that a point belongs to the core, one must show that all possible coalitions with all their feasible reallocations fail to produce a point which is superior to the point considered for all members. Except for competitive equilibrium points, this is usually a complicated matter.

REFERENCES

G. Debreu and H. Scarf, "A Limit Theorem on the Core of an Economy," *Int. Econ. Rev.*, Sept. 1963, *4*, 235–46.

______ and ______, "The Limit of the Core of an Economy," in C. B. McGuire and Roy Radner, eds., *Decision and Organization: A Volume in Honor of Jacob Marschak*, Amsterdam 1972.

J. R. Green, "On the Inequitable Nature of Core Allocations," *J. Econ. Theory*, Apr. 1972, *4*, 132–43.

Edmond Malinvaud, *Lectures on Microeconomic Theory*, Amsterdam 1972.

Peter Newman, *The Theory of Exchange*, Englewood Cliffs 1965.

L. S. Shapley and M. Shubik, "Concepts and Theories of Pure Competition," in Martin Shubik, ed., *Essays in Mathematical Economics in Honor of O. Morgenstern*, Princeton 1967.

M. Shubik, "Edgeworth Market Games," in A. W. Tucker and Robert D. Luce, eds., *Contributions to the Theory of Games, Annals of Mathematical Studies*, Vol. IV, Princeton 1959.

[7]

STABILITY IN COMPETITION [1]

AFTER the work of the late Professor F. Y. Edgeworth one may doubt that anything further can be said on the theory of competition among a small number of entrepreneurs. However, one important feature of actual business seems until recently to have escaped scrutiny. This is the fact that of all the purchasers of a commodity, some buy from one seller, some from another, in spite of moderate differences of price. If the purveyor of an article gradually increases his price while his rivals keep theirs fixed, the diminution in volume of his sales will in general take place continuously rather than in the abrupt way which has tacitly been assumed.

A profound difference in the nature of the stability of a competitive situation results from this fact. We shall examine it with the help of some simple mathematics. The form of the solution will serve also to bring out a number of aspects of a competitive situation whose importance warrants more attention than they have received. Among these features, all illustrated by the same simple case, we find (1) the existence of incomes not properly belonging to any of the categories usually discussed, but resulting from the discontinuity in the increase in the number of sellers with the demand; (2) a socially uneconomical system of prices, leading to needless shipment of goods and kindred deviations from optimum activities; (3) an undue tendency for competitors to imitate each other in quality of goods, in location, and in other essential ways.

Piero Sraffa has discussed [2] the neglected fact that a market is commonly subdivided into regions within each of which one seller is in a quasi-monopolistic position. The consequences of this phenomenon are here considered further. In passing we remark that the asymmetry between supply and demand, between buyer and seller, which Professor Sraffa emphasises is due to the condition that the seller sets the price and the buyers the quanti-

[1] Presented before the American Mathematical Society at New York, April 6, 1928, and subsequently revised.

[2] " The Laws of Returns Under Competitive Conditions," ECONOMIC JOURNAL, Vol. XXXVI. pp. 535–550, especially pp. 544 ff. (December 1926).

ties they will buy. This condition in turn results from the large number of the buyers of a particular commodity as compared with the sellers. Where, as in new oil-fields and in agricultural villages, a few buyers set prices at which they will take all that is offered and exert themselves to induce producers to sell, the situation is reversed. If in the following pages the words " buy " and " sell " be everywhere interchanged, the argument remains equally valid, though applicable to a different class of businesses.

Extensive and difficult applications of the Calculus of Variations in economics have recently been made, sometimes to problems of competition among a small number of entrepreneurs.[1] For this and other reasons a re-examination of stability and related questions, using only elementary mathematics, seems timely.

Duopoly, the condition in which there are two competing merchants, was treated by A. Cournot in 1838.[2] His book went apparently without comment or review for forty-five years until Walras produced his *Théorie Mathématique de la Richesse Sociale*, and Bertrand published a caustic review of both works.[3] Bertrand's criticisms were modified and extended by Edgeworth in his treatment of duopoly in the *Giornale degli Economisti* for 1897,[4] in his criticism of Amoroso,[5] and elsewhere. Indeed all writers since Cournot, except Sraffa and Amoroso,[6] seem to hold that even apart from the likelihood of combination there is an essential instability in duopoly. Now it is true that such competition lacks complete stability; but we shall see that in a very general class of cases the independent actions of two competitors not in collusion lead to a type of equilibrium much less fragile than in the examples of Cournot, Edgeworth and Amoroso. The solution which we shall obtain can break down only in case of an express or tacit understanding which converts the supposed

[1] For references to the work of C. F. Roos and G. C. Evans on this subject see the paper by Dr. Roos, " A Dynamical Theory of Economics," in the *Journal of Political Economy*, Vol. XXXV. (1927), or that in the *Transactions of the American Mathematical Society*, Vol. XXX. (1928), p. 360. There is also an application of the Calculus of Variations to depreciation by Dr. Roos in the *Bulletin of the American Mathematical Society*, Vol. XXXIV. (1928), p. 218.

[2] *Recherches sur les Principes Mathématiques de la Théorie des Richesses.* Paris (Hachette). Chapter VII. English translation by N. T. Bacon, with introduction and bibliography by Irving Fisher (New York, Macmillan, 1897 and 1927).

[3] *Journal des Savants* (1883), pp. 499–508.

[4] Republished in English in Edgeworth's *Papers Relating to Political Economy* (London, Macmillan, 1925), Vol. I. pp. 116–26.

[5] ECONOMIC JOURNAL, Vol. XXXII. (1922), pp. 400–7.

[6] *Lezioni di Economia Mathematica* (Bologna, Zanichelli, 1921).

competitors into something like a monopoly, or in case of a price war aimed at eliminating one of them altogether.

Cournot's example was of two proprietors of mineral springs equally available to the market and producing, without cost, mineral water of identical quality. The demand is elastic, and the price is determined by the total amount put on the market. If the respective quantities produced are q_1 and q_2 the price p will be given by a function

$$p = f(q_1 + q_2).$$

The profits of the proprietors are respectively

$$\pi_1 = q_1f(q_1 + q_2)$$

and

$$\pi_2 = q_2f(q_1 + q_2).$$

The first proprietor adjusts q_1 so that, when q_2 has its current value, his own profit will be as great as possible. This value of q_1 may be obtained by differentiating π_1, putting

$$f(q_1 + q_2) + q_1f(q_1 + q_2) = 0.$$

In like manner the second proprietor adjusts q_2 so that

$$f(q_1 + q_2) + q_2f(q_1 + q_2) = 0.$$

There can be no equilibrium unless these equations are satisfied simultaneously. Together they determine a definite (and equal) pair of values of q_1 and q_2. Cournot showed graphically how, if a different pair of q's should obtain, each competitor in turn would readjust his production so as to approach as a limit the value given by the solution of the simultaneous equations. He concluded that the actual state of affairs will be given by the common solution, and proceeded to generalise to the case of n competitors.

Against this conclusion Bertrand brought an "objection péremptoire." The solution does not represent equilibrium, for either proprietor can by a slight reduction in price take away all his opponent's business and nearly double his own profits. The other will respond with a still lower price. Only by the use of the quantities as independent variables instead of the prices is the fallacy concealed.

Bertrand's objection was amplified by Edgeworth, who maintained that in the more general case of two monopolists controlling commodities having correlated demand, even though not identical, there is no determinate solution. Edgeworth gave a variety of examples, but nowhere took account of the stabilising effect of masses of consumers placed so as to have a natural preference for one seller or the other. In all his illustrations of competition one merchant can take away his rival's entire business by undercutting his price ever so slightly. Thus discontinuities appear, though a discontinuity, like a vacuum, is abhorred by nature. More typical of real situations is the case in which the quantity sold by each merchant is a continuous function of two variables, his own price and his competitor's. Quite commonly a tiny increase in price by one seller will send only a few customers to the other.

I

The feature of actual business to which, like Professor Sraffa, we draw attention, and which does not seem to have been generally taken account of in economic theory, is the existence with reference to each seller of groups of buyers who will deal with him instead of with his competitors in spite of a difference in price. If a seller increases his price too far he will gradually lose business to his rivals, but he does not lose all his trade instantly when he raises his price only a trifle. Many customers will still prefer to trade with him because they live nearer to his store than to the others, or because they have less freight to pay from his warehouse to their own, or because his mode of doing business is more to their liking, or because he sells other articles which they desire, or because he is a relative or a fellow Elk or Baptist, or on account of some difference in service or quality, or for a combination of reasons. Such circles of customers may be said to make every entrepreneur a monopolist within a limited class and region—and there is no monopoly which is not confined to a limited class and region. The difference between the Standard Oil Company in its prime and the little corner grocery is quantitative rather than qualitative. Between the perfect competition and monopoly of theory lie the actual cases.

It is the gradualness in the shifting of customers from one merchant to another as their prices vary independently which is ignored in the examples worked out by Cournot, Amoroso and Edgeworth. The assumption, implicit in their work, that all buyers deal with the cheapest seller leads to a type of instability which disappears when the quantity sold by each is considered as a continuous function of the differences in price. The use of such a continuous function does, to be sure, seem to violate the doctrine that in one market there can at one time be only one price. But this doctrine is only valid when the commodity in question is absolutely standardised in all respects and when the

" market " is a point, without length, breadth or thickness. It is, in fact, analogous to the physical principle that at one point in a body there can at one time be only one temperature. This principle does not prevent different temperatures from existing in different parts of a body at the same time. If it were supposed that any temperature difference, however slight, necessitates a sudden transfer of all the heat in the warmer portion of the body to the colder portion—a transfer which by the same principle would immediately be reversed—then we should have a thermal instability somewhat resembling the instability of the cases of duopoly which have been discussed. To take another physical analogy, the earth is often in astronomical calculations considered as a point, and with substantially accurate results. But the precession of the equinoxes becomes explicable only when account is taken of the ellipsoidal bulge of the earth. So in the theory of value a market is usually considered as a point in which only one price can obtain; but for some purposes it is better to consider a market as an extended region.

Consider the following illustration. The buyers of a commodity will be supposed uniformly distributed along a line of

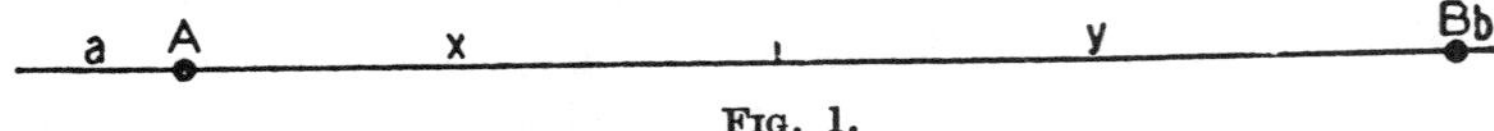

FIG. 1.

Market of length $l = 35$. In this example $a = 4$, $b = 1$, $x = 14$, $y = 16$.

length l, which may be Main Street in a town or a transcontinental railroad. At distances a and b respectively from the two ends of this line are the places of business of A and B (Fig. 1). Each buyer transports his purchases home at a cost c per unit distance. Without effect upon the generality of our conclusions we shall suppose that the cost of production to A and B is zero, and that unit quantity of the commodity is consumed in each unit of time in each unit of length of line. The demand is thus at the extreme of inelasticity. No customer has any preference for either seller except on the ground of price plus transportation cost. In general there will be many causes leading particular classes of buyers to prefer one seller to another, but the ensemble of such consideration is here symbolised by transportation cost. Denote A's price by p_1, B's by p_2, and let q_1 and q_2 be the respective quantities sold.

Now B's price may be higher than A's, but if B is to sell anything at all he must not let his price exceed A's by more than the cost of transportation from A's place of business to his own. In fact he will keep his price p_2 somewhat below the figure p_1 —

$c(l - a - b)$ at which A's goods can be brought to him. Thus he will obtain all the business in the segment of length b at the right of Fig. 1, and in addition will sell to all the customers in a segment of length y depending on the difference of prices and lying between himself and A. Likewise A will, if he sells anything, sell to all the buyers in the strips of length a at the left and of length x to the right of A, where x diminishes as $p_1 - p_2$ increases.

The point of division between the regions served by the two entrepreneurs is determined by the condition that at this place it is a matter of indifference whether one buys from A or from B. Equating the delivered prices we have

$$p_1 + cx = p_2 + cy.$$

Another equation between x and y is

$$a + x + y + b = l.$$

Solving we find

$$x = \tfrac{1}{2}\left(l - a - b + \frac{p_2 - p_1}{c}\right),$$

$$y = \tfrac{1}{2}\left(l - a - b + \frac{p_1 - p_2}{c}\right),$$

so that the profits are

$$\pi_1 = p_1q_1 = p_1(a + x) = \tfrac{1}{2}(l + a - b)p_1 - \frac{p_1^2}{2c} + \frac{p_1p_2}{2c},$$

and $$\pi_2 = p_2q_2 = p_2(b + y) = \tfrac{1}{2}(l - a + b)p_2 - \frac{p_2^2}{2c} + \frac{p_1p_2}{2c}.$$

If p_1 and p_2 be taken as rectangular co-ordinates, each of the last equations represents a family of hyperbolas having identical asymptotes, one hyperbola for each value of π_1 or π_2. Some of these curves are shown in Fig. 2, where (as also in Fig. 1) we have taken $l = 35$, $a = 4$, $b = 1$, $c = 1$.

Each competitor adjusts his price so that, with the existing value of the other price, his own profit will be a maximum. This gives the equations

$$\frac{\partial \pi_1}{\partial p_1} = \tfrac{1}{2}(l + a - b) - \frac{p_1}{c} + \frac{p_2}{2c} = 0,$$

$$\frac{\partial \pi_2}{\partial p_2} = \tfrac{1}{2}(l - a + b) + \frac{p_1}{2c} - \frac{p_2}{c} = 0,$$

from which we obtain

$$p_1 = c\left(l + \frac{a - b}{3}\right),$$

$$p_2 = c\left(l - \frac{a - b}{3}\right);$$

and
$$q_1 = a + x = \tfrac{1}{2}\left(l + \frac{a-b}{3}\right),$$
$$q_2 = b + y = \tfrac{1}{2}\left(l - \frac{a-b}{3}\right).$$

The conditions $\partial^2\pi_1/\partial p_1^2 < 0$ and $\partial^2\pi_2/\partial p_2^2 < 0$, sufficient for a maximum of each of the functions π_1 and π_2, are obviously satisfied.

If the two prices are originally the co-ordinates of the point Q in Fig. 2, and if A is the more alert business man of the two, he

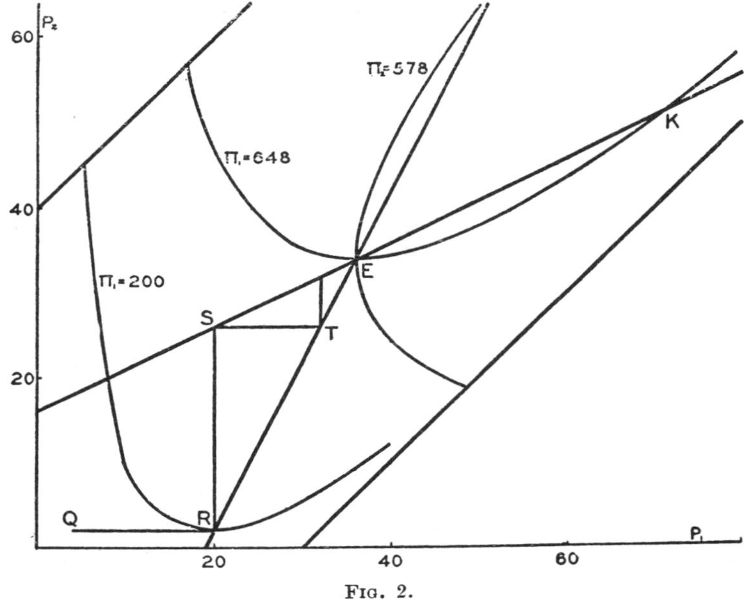

Fig. 2.

Conditions of competition for the market of Fig. 1. The co-ordinates represent the prices at A's and B's shops for the same article. The straight lines through E are the two lines of maximum profit. On one of the curves through E, A's profit is everywhere 648; on the other, B's is 578. The lower curve is the locus on which A's profit is 200.

will change his price so as to make his profit a maximum. This is represented graphically by a horizontal motion to the point R on the line $\partial\pi_1/\partial p_1 = 0$. This line has the property that every point on it represents a greater profit for A than any other point having the same ordinate. But presently B discovers that his profits can be increased by a vertical motion to the point S on his own line of maximum profit. A now moves horizontally to T. Thus there is a gradual approach to the point E at the intersection of the two lines; its co-ordinates are given by the values of p_1 and

p_2 found above. At E there is equilibrium, since neither merchant can now increase his profit by changing his price. The same result is reached if instead of Q the starting point is any on the figure.[1]

Now it is true that prices other than the co-ordinates of the equilibrium point may obtain for a considerable time. Even at this point one merchant may sacrifice his immediate income to raise his price, driving away customers, in the hope that his rival will do likewise and thus increase both profits. Indeed if A moves to the right from E in Fig. 2 he may reasonably expect that B will go up to his line of maximum profit. This will make A's profit larger than at E, provided the representing point has not gone so far to the right as K. Without this proviso, A's position will be improved (and so will B's as compared with E) if only B will sufficiently increase p_2. In fact, since the demand is inelastic, we may imagine the two alleged competitors to be amicably exploiting the consumers without limit by raising their prices. The increases need not be agreed upon in advance but may proceed by alternate steps, each seller in turn making his price higher than the other's, but not high enough to drive away all business. Thus without a formal agreement the rivals may succeed in making themselves virtually a monopoly. Something of a tacit understanding will exist that prices are to be maintained above the level immediately profitable in order to keep profits high in the long run.

But understandings between competitors are notoriously fragile. Let one of these business men, say B, find himself suddenly in need of cash. Immediately at hand he will have a resource: Let him lower his price a little, increasing his sales. His profits will be larger until A decides to stop sacrificing business

[1] The solution given above is subject to the limitation that the difference between the prices must not exceed the cost of transportation from A to B. This means that E must lie between the lines $p_1 - p_2 = \pm c(l - a - b)$ on which the hyperbolic arcs shown in Fig. 2 terminate. It is easy to find values of the constants for which this condition is not satisfied (for example, $l = 20$, $a = 11$, $b = 8$, $c = 1$). In such a case the equilibrium point will not be E and the expressions for the p's, q's and π's will be different; but there is no essential difference either in the stability of the system or in the essential validity of the subsequent remarks. A's locus of maximum profit no longer coincides with the line $\partial\pi_1/\partial p_1 = 0$, but consists of the portion of this line above its intersection with $p_1 - p_2 = c(l - a - b)$, and of the latter line below this point. Likewise B's locus of maximum profit consists of the part of the line $\partial\pi_2/\partial p_2 = 0$ to the right of its intersection with $p_2 - p_1 = c(l - a - b)$, together with the part of the last line to the left of this point. These two loci intersect at the point whose co-ordinates are, for $a > b$,

$$p_1 = c(3l - 3a - b), \quad p_2 = 2c(l - a),$$

and the type of stability is the same as before.

and lowers his price to the point of maximum profit. B will now be likely to go further in an attempt to recoup, and so the system will descend to the equilibrium position E. Here neither competitor will have any incentive to lower his price further, since the increased business obtainable would fail to compensate him.

Indeed the difficulties of maintaining a price-fixing agreement have often been remarked. Not only may the short-sighted cupidity of one party send the whole system crashing through price-cutting; the very fear of a price cut will bring on a cut. Moreover, a price agreement cannot be made once for all; where conditions of cost or of demand are changing the price needs constant revision. The result is a constant jarring, an always obvious conflict of interests. As a child's pile of blocks falls to its equilibrium position when the table on which it stands is moved, so a movement of economic conditions tends to upset quasi-monopolistic schemes for staying above the point E. For two independent merchants to come to an agreement of any sort is notoriously difficult, but when the agreement must be made all over again at frequent intervals, when each has an incentive for breaking it, and when it is frowned upon by public opinion and must be secret and perhaps illegal, then the pact is not likely to be very durable. The difficulties are, of course, more marked if the competitors are more numerous, but they decidedly are present when there are only two.

The details of the interaction of the prices and sales will, of course, vary widely in different cases. Much will depend upon such market conditions as the degree of secrecy which can be maintained, the degree of possible discrimination among customers, the force of habit and character as affecting the reliance which each competitor feels he can put in the promises of the other, the frequency with which it is feasible to change a price or a rate of production, the relative value to the entrepreneur of immediate and remote profits, and so on. But always there is an insecurity at any point other than the point E which represents equilibrium. Without some agreement, express or tacit, the value of p_1 will be less than or equal to the abscissa of K in Fig. 2; and in the absence of a willingness on the part of one of the competitors to forgo immediate profits in order to maintain prices, the prices will become the co-ordinates of E.

One important item should be noticed. The prices may be maintained in a somewhat insecure way *above* their equilibrium values but will never remain *below* them. For if either A or B has a price which is less than that satisfying the simultaneous equations it will pay him *at once* to raise it. This is evident from the figure. Strikingly in contrast with the situation pictured by Bertrand, where prices were for ever being cut below their calculated values, the stabilising effect of the intermediate customers who shift their purchases gradually with changing prices makes itself felt in the existence of a pair of minimum prices. For a prudent investor the difference is all-important.

It is, of course, possible that A, feeling stronger than his opponent and desiring to get rid of him once for all, may reduce his price so far that B will give up the struggle and retire from the business. But during the continuance of this sort of price war A's income will be curtailed more than B's. In any case its possibility does not affect the argument that there is stability, since stability is by definition merely the tendency to return after *small* displacements. A box standing on end is in stable equilibrium, even though it can be tipped over.

II

Having found a solution and acquired some confidence in it, we push the analysis further and draw a number of inferences regarding a competitive situation.

When the values of the p's and q's obtained on p. 46 are substituted in the previously found expressions for the profits we have

$$\pi_1 = \frac{c}{2}\left(l + \frac{a-b}{3}\right)^2, \quad \pi_2 = \frac{c}{2}\left(l - \frac{a-b}{3}\right)^2.$$

The profits as well as the prices depend directly upon c, the unit cost of transportation. These particular merchants would do well, instead of organising improvement clubs and booster associations to better the roads, to make transportation as difficult as possible. Still better would be their situation if they could obtain a protective tariff to hinder the transportation of their commodity between them. Of course they will not want to impede the transportation of the supplies which come to them; the object of each is merely to attain something approaching a monopoly.

Another observation on the situation is that incomes exist which do not fall strictly within any of the commonly recognised categories. The quantities π_1 and π_2 just determined may be classified as monopoly profits, but only if we are ready to extend the term " monopoly " to include such cases as have been considered, involving the most outright competition for the marginal customer but without discrimination in his favour, and with no sort of open or tacit agreement between the sellers. These profits certainly do not consist of wages, interest or rent, since we have assumed no cost of production. This condition of no cost is not essential to the existence of such profits. If a constant cost of production per unit had been introduced into the calculations above, it would simply have been added to the prices without affecting the profits. Fixed overhead charges are to be subtracted from π_1 and π_2, but may leave a substantial residuum. These gains are not compensation for risk, since they represent a minimum return. They do not belong to the generalised type of "rent," which consists of the advantage of a producer over the marginal producer, since each makes a profit, and since, moreover, we may suppose a and b equal so as to make the situation symmetrical. Indeed π_1 and π_2 represent a special though common sort of profit which results from the fact that the number of sellers is finite. If there are three or more sellers, income of this kind will still exist, but as the number increases it will decline, to be replaced by generalised "rent" for the better-placed producers and poverty for the less fortunate. The number of sellers may be thought of as increasing as a result of a gradual increase in the number of buyers. Profits of the type we have described will exist at all stages of growth excepting those at which a new seller is just entering the field.

As a further problem, suppose that A's location has been fixed but that B is free to choose his place of business. Where will he set up shop? Evidently he will choose b so as to make

$$\pi_2 = \frac{c}{2}\left(l + \frac{b - a}{3}\right)^2$$

as large as possible. This value of b cannot be found by differentiation, as the value thus determined exceeds l and, besides, yields a minimum for π_2 instead of a maximum. But for all smaller values of b, and so for all values of b within the conditions of the problem, π_2 increases with b. Consequently B will seek to make b as large as possible. This means that he will come just as close to A as other conditions permit. Naturally, if A is not exactly in the centre of the line, B will choose the side of A towards the more extensive section of the market, making b greater than a.[1]

[1] The conclusion that B will tend to gravitate *infinitesimally* close to A requires a slight modification in the particular case before us, but not in general. In the footnote on p. 48 it was seen that when A and B are sufficiently close together, the analytic expressions for the prices, and consequently the profits,

This gravitation of B towards A increases B's profit at the expense of A. Indeed, as appears from the expressions on p. 46, if b increases so that B approaches A, both q_2 and p_2 increase while q_1 and p_1 diminish. From B's standpoint the sharper competition with A due to proximity is offset by the greater body of buyers with whom he has an advantage. But the danger that the system will be overturned by the elimination of one competitor is increased. The intermediate segment of the market acts as a cushion as well as a bone of contention ; when it disappears we have Cournot's case, and Bertrand's objection applies. Or, returning to the analogy of the box in stable equilibrium though standing on end, the approach of B to A corresponds to a diminution in size of the end of the box.

It has become common for real-estate subdividers in the United States to impose restrictions which tend more or less to fix the character of future businesses in particular locations. Now we find from the calculations above that the total profits of A and B amount to

$$\pi_1 + \pi_2 = c\left[l^2 + \left(\frac{a-b}{3}\right)^2\right].$$

Thus a landlord or realtor who can determine the location of future stores, expecting to absorb their profits in the sales value of the land, has a motive for making the situation as unsymmetrical as possible; for, the more the lack of symmetry, the greater is $(a - b)^2$, which appears in the expression above for $\pi_1 + \pi_2$.

Our example has also an application to the question of capitalism *v.* socialism, and contributes an argument to the socialist side. Let us consider the efficiency of our pair of merchants in serving the public by calculating the total of transportation charges paid by consumers. These charges for the strip of length a amount to $c\int_0^a tdt$, or $\frac{1}{2}ca^2$. Altogether the sum is

$$\tfrac{1}{2}c(a^2 + b^2 + x^2 + y^2).$$

are different. By a simple algebraic calculation which will not here be reproduced it is found that B's profits π_2 will increase as B moves from the centre towards A, only if the distance between them is more than four-fifths of the distance from A to the centre. If B approaches more closely his profit is given by $\pi_2 = bc(3l - a - 3b)$, and diminishes with increasing b. This optimum distance from A is, however, an adventitious feature of our problem resulting from a discontinuity which is necessary for simplicity. In general we should consider q_1 and q_2 as continuous functions of p_1 and p_2, instead of supposing, as here, that as $p_2 - p_1$ falls below a certain limit, a great mass of buyers shift suddenly from B to A.

Now if the places of business are both fixed, the quantities a, b and $x + y$ are all determined. The minimum total cost for transportation will be achieved if, for the given value of $x + y$, the expression $x^2 + y^2$ is a minimum. This will be the case if x and y are equal.

But x and y will not be equal unless the prices p_1 and p_2 are equal, and under competition this is not likely to be the case. If we bar the improbable case of A and B having taken up symmetrical positions on the line, the prices which will result from each seeking his own gain have been seen to be different. If the segment a in which A has a clear advantage is greater than b, then A's price will be greater than B's. Consequently some buyers will ship their purchases from B's store, though they are closer to A's, and socially it would be more economical for them to buy from A. If the stores were conducted for public service rather than for profit their prices would be identical in spite of the asymmetry of demand.

If the stores be thought of as movable, the wastefulness of private profit-seeking management becomes even more striking. There are now four variables, a, b, x and y, instead of two. Their sum is the fixed length l, and to minimise the social cost of transportation found above we must make the sum of their squares as small as possible. As before, the variables must be equal. This requires A and B to occupy symmetrical positions at the quartiles of the market. But instead of doing so they crowd together as closely as possible. Even if A, the first in the field, should settle at one of these points, we have seen that B upon his arrival will not go to the other, but will fix upon a location between A and the centre and as near A as possible.[1] Thus some customers will have to transport their goods a distance of more than $\frac{1}{2}l$, whereas with two stores run in the public interest no shipment should be for a greater distance than $\frac{1}{4}l$.

If a third seller C appears, his desire for as large a market as possible will prompt him likewise to take up a position close to A or B, but not between them. By an argument similar to that just used, it may be shown that regard only for the public interest would require A, B and C each to occupy one of the points at distances one-sixth, one-half and five-sixths of the way from one end of the line to the other. As more and more sellers of the same commodity arise, the tendency is not to become distributed in the socially optimum manner but to cluster unduly.

The importance and variety of such agglomerative tendencies

[1] With the unimportant qualification mentioned in the footnote on p. 48.

become apparent when it is remembered that distance, as we have used it for illustration, is only a figurative term for a great congeries of qualities. Instead of sellers of an identical commodity separated geographically we might have considered two competing cider merchants side by side, one selling a sweeter liquid than the other. If the consumers of cider be thought of as varying by infinitesimal degrees in the sourness they desire, we have much the same situation as before. The measure of sourness now replaces distance, while instead of transportation costs there are the degrees of disutility resulting from a consumer getting cider more or less different from what he wants. The foregoing considerations apply, particularly the conclusion that competing sellers tend to become too much alike.

The mathematical analysis thus leads to an observation of wide generality. Buyers are confronted everywhere with an excessive sameness. When a new merchant or manufacturer sets up shop he must not produce something exactly like what is already on the market or he will risk a price war of the type discussed by Bertrand in connection with Cournot's mineral springs. But there is an incentive to make the new product very much like the old, applying some slight change which will seem an improvement to as many buyers as possible without ever going far in this direction. The tremendous standardisation of our furniture, our houses, our clothing, our automobiles and our education are due in part to the economies of large-scale production, in part to fashion and imitation. But over and above these forces is the effect we have been discussing, the tendency to make only slight deviations in order to have for the new commodity as many buyers of the old as possible, to get, so to speak, *between* one's competitors and a mass of customers.

So general is this tendency that it appears in the most diverse fields of competitive activity, even quite apart from what is called economic life. In politics it is strikingly exemplified. The competition for votes between the Republican and Democratic parties does not lead to a clear drawing of issues, an adoption of two strongly contrasted positions between which the voter may choose. Instead, each party strives to make its platform as much like the other's as possible. Any radical departure would lose many votes, even though it might lead to stronger commendation of the party by some who would vote for it anyhow. Each candidate "pussyfoots," replies ambiguously to questions, refuses to take a definite stand in any controversy for fear of losing votes. Real differences, if they ever exist, fade gradually with time though the issues may be as important as ever. The Democratic party, once opposed to protective tariffs, moves gradually to a position almost, but not quite, identical with that of the Republicans. It need have no fear of fanatical free-traders, since they will still prefer it to the Republican party, and its advocacy of a continued high tariff will bring it the money and votes of some intermediate groups.

The reasoning, of course, requires modification when applied to the varied conditions of actual life. Our example might have been more complicated. Instead of a uniform distribution of customers along a line we might have assumed a varying density, but with no essential change in conclusions. Instead of a linear market we might suppose the buyers spread out on a plane. Then the customers from one region will patronise A, those from another B. The boundary between the two regions is the locus of points for which the difference of transportation costs from the two shops equals the difference of prices, *i.e.* for which the delivered price is the same whether the goods are bought from A or from B. If transportation is in straight lines (perhaps by aeroplane) at a cost proportional to the distance, the boundary will be a hyperbola, since a hyperbola is the locus of points such that the difference of distances from the foci is constant. If there are three or more sellers, their regions will be separated from each other by arcs of hyperbolas. If the transportation is not in straight lines, or if its cost is given by such a complicated function as a railroad freight schedule, the boundaries will be of another kind; but we might generalise the term hyperbola (as is done in the differential geometry of curved surfaces) to include these curves also.

The number of dimensions of our picture is increased to three or more when we represent geometrically such characters as sweetness of cider, and instead of transportation costs consider more generally the decrement of utility resulting from the actual commodity being in a different place and condition than the buyer would prefer. Each homogeneous commodity or service or entrepreneur in a competing system can be thought of as a point serving a region separated from other such regions by portions of generalised hyperboloids. The density of demand in this space is in general not uniform, and is restricted to a finite region. It is not necessary that each point representing a service or commodity shall be under the control of a different entrepreneur from every other. On the other hand, everyone who sells an article in different places or who sells different articles in the same place may be said to control the prices at several points of the symbolic space. The mutual gravitation will now take the form of a tendency of the outermost entrepreneurs to approach the cluster.

Two further modifications are important. One arises when it is possible to discriminate among customers, or to sell goods at a delivered price instead of a fixed price at store or factory plus transportation. In such cases, even without an agreement between sellers, a monopoly profit can be collected from some consumers while fierce competition is favouring others. This seems to have been the condition in the cement industry about which a controversy raged a few years ago, and was certainly involved in the railroad rebate scandals.

The other important modification has to do with the elasticity of demand. The problem of the two merchants on a linear market might be varied by supposing that each consumer buys an amount of the commodity in question which depends on the delivered price. If one tries a particular demand function the mathematical complications will now be considerable, but for the most general problems elasticity must be assumed. The difficulty as to whether prices or quantities should be used as independent variables can now be cleared up. This question has troubled many readers of Cournot. The answer is that either set of variables may be used; that the q's may be expressed in terms of the p's, and the p's in terms of the q's. This was not possible in Cournot's example of duopoly, nor heretofore in ours. The sum of our q's was constrained to have the fixed value l, so that they could not be independent, but when the demand is made elastic the constraint vanishes.

With elastic demand the observations we have made on the solution will still for the most part be qualitatively true; but the tendency for B to establish his business excessively close to A will be less marked. The increment in B's sales to his more remote customers when he moves nearer them may be more than compensation to him for abandoning some of his nearer business to A. In this case B will definitely and apart from extraneous circumstances choose a location at some distance from A. But he will not go as far from A as the public welfare would require. The tempting intermediate market will still have an influence.

In the more general problem in which the commodities purveyed differ in many dimensions the situation is the same. The elasticity of demand of particular groups does mitigate the tendency to excessive similarity of competing commodities, but not enough. It leads some factories to make cheap shoes for the poor and others to make expensive shoes for the rich, but all the shoes are too much alike. Our cities become uneconomically large and the business districts within them are too concentrated. Methodist and Presbyterian churches are too much alike; cider is too homogeneous.

HAROLD HOTELLING

Stanford University,
California.

[8]

The Concept of Monopoly and the Measurement of Monopoly Power[1]

I

MONOPOLY, says the dictionary, is the exclusive right of a person, corporation or state to sell a particular commodity. Economic science, investigating the economic aspects of this legal right, found that they all resolved themselves into the implications of the power of the monopolist—as distinguished from a seller in a competitive market—arbitrarily to decide the price of the commodity, leaving it to the buyers to decide how much they will buy at that price, or, alternatively, to decide the quantity he will sell, by so fixing the price as to induce buyers to purchase just this quantity. Technically this is expressed by saying that the monopolist is confronted with a falling demand curve for his product or that the elasticity of demand for his product is less than infinity, while the seller in a purely[2] competitive market has a horizontal demand curve or the elasticity of demand for his product is equal to infinity.

The monopolist is normally assumed to tend to fix the price at the level at which he makes the greatest profit or " monopoly revenue." This monopoly revenue constitutes a levy upon the consumers that the monopolist is able to appropriate for himself purely in virtue of his restrictive powers *qua* monopolist, and it is the consumers' objection to paying this levy that lies at the base of popular feeling against the monopolist.

In addition to this it is claimed that monopoly is harmful in a more objective sense. A levy which involves a mere transference from buyer to monopolist cannot be said to be harmful from a social point of view unless it can be shown that the monopolist is less deserving of the levy than the people who have to pay it ; either because he is in general a less deserving kind of person, or because the transference will increase the evils of inequality of incomes. But the levy is not a mere transference. The method of raising it, namely, by increasing the price of the monopolised commodity, causes buyers to divert their expenditure to other, less satisfactory, purchases. This constitutes a loss to the consumer which is not balanced by any gain reaped by the monopolist, so that there is a net social loss.

The nature of the loss here loosely expressed seems to have defied attempts at more exact exposition, the difficulties encountered on these attempts having

[1] The great advances made in the subject of this article since the major part of it was written —particularly in the work of Mr. Chamberlin and Mrs. Robinson—have rendered many parts of it out of date. In preparing it for publication, while cutting out some of these parts, I have been so much under the influence of this recent work that I cannot say how much of what is here published is really my own.—A. P. LERNER.

[2] " Pure " competition is different from " perfect " competition. The former implies perfection of competition only in respect of the complete absence of monopoly and abstracts from other aspects of perfection in competition. This useful distinction is suggested by Chamberlin. See his *Theory of Monopolistic Competition*, p. 6.

even induced some to declare that this commonsense view of a social loss is an illusion, while more careful sceptics prefer to say that nothing " scientific " can be said about it. The account given above clearly will not do as a general and accurate description of the nature of the social loss. Where a consumer spends as much as before on the monopolised commodity when the price is raised, he cannot be said to divert expenditure to other and less satisfactory channels, and where he spends more[1] upon the commodity than at the lower competitive price it might even be argued that there is a net social gain in so far as the consumer is induced to spend more on the commodity which is more urgently needed and less on other commodities! There seems little to choose between this argument and the counter-argument, that as long as the elasticity is greater than zero some consumer (or unit of consumption) is induced to change the direction of his expenditure so that he suffers the uncompensated inconvenience which constitutes the net social loss. Does this mean that if a man's demand is completely inelastic (so that the increased price brings no diminution in the amount of the monopolised commodity consumed and the whole of the levy is sacrificed ultimately in the form of other commodities) the expenditure of the income, as diminished by the amount of the levy, is not interfered with by the existence of the monopoly ?—i.e. that if he had paid the levy in cash and prices were not affected he would have reduced his consumption of other commodities in the same way ? Or is it more reasonable to suppose that a rise in a particular price will always tend to diminish purchases of the dearer commodity, where a cash levy (prices remaining unchanged) would diminish all expenditures in the same proportion so that if the same amount of the monopolised commodity is bought at the higher price, a cash diminution in income of the size of the levy would

[1] Where as much or more is spent on a commodity when the price is raised the elasticity of demand is equal to or less than unity. This may appear incompatible with the condition of monopolistic equilibrium that elasticity of demand shall be greater than unity (as long as marginal cost is positive). There is, however, no incompatibility, for the two elasticities of demand are different things. The elasticity that has to be greater than unity for monopolistic equilibrium is the elasticity at the *point* on the demand curve corresponding to the position of monopolistic equilibrium. The elasticity that is equal to or less than unity when the amount spent on the commodity remains unchanged or increases as the price is raised, is the elasticity over the *arc* of the demand curve from the point of competitive equilibrium to the point of monopolistic equilibrium. The arc elasticity in this sense will normally be less than the point elasticity, as will appear from the diagram. If tT is the demand curve (here drawn a straight line), P' the point of competitive equilibrium, and P the point of monopolistic equilibrium, then the *point* elasticity at the monopoly equilibrium will be $\frac{PT}{Pt}$ while the *arc* elasticity will be $\frac{P'T}{Pt}$, which is smaller. The arc elasticity must be smaller unless the demand curve is so concave (upwards) that it shows a constant or increasing point elasticity as price is lowered. The point elasticity at the competitive position will, of course, be $\frac{P'T}{P't}$. For the explanation of this definition of " arc elasticity," see my note on " The Diagrammatical Representation of Elasticity of Demand," in No. I of the REVIEW.

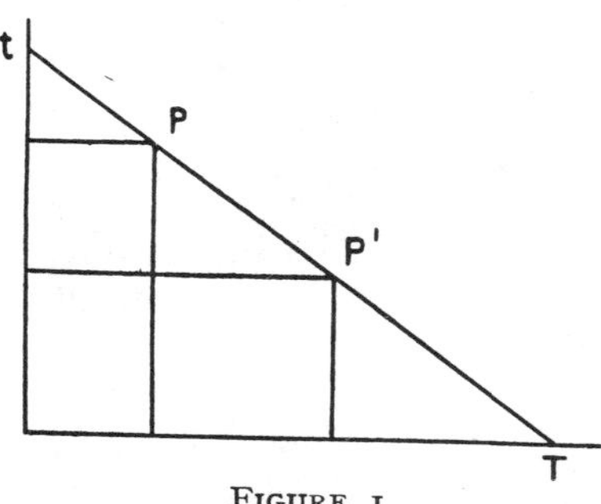

FIGURE I

have *increased* the demand for that commodity? The problems do not seem to be amenable to treatment on these lines.[1]

The commonsense attitude is, however, not easily balked. Another attempt was made to deal with the problem by Marshall, by means of the apparatus of consumers' surplus. If it is assumed that the marginal utility of money is unchanged, or that the change is so small that it may legitimately be neglected, it can be shown that the money value of the consumers' surplus lost is greater than the monopoly revenue gained, so that we have a theoretical measure of the net social loss due to the monopoly. There are, of course, many important weaknesses in this treatment, and some ways of applying it are completely wrong. The marginal utility of money can be considered unchanged only if we are considering a small change in the price of only one commodity. This makes it impossible to add the consumers' surplus obtained by an individual from different goods. Quite wrong is any attempt to speak of the consumers' surplus of a community and to derive it from the communal demand curve. And there are other traps to be avoided in this connection which are quite well known. But the exclusive preoccupation of teachers of economics with putting their pupils on their guard against these insufficiencies and dangers has tended to make them deny the problem with which the concept of consumers' surplus was intended to deal—the net social loss and its nature. It is not intended here to deny or even to belittle the dangers and confusions attendant on the use of the concept of consumers' surplus, but it does seem that some light can be thrown on the problem by its use.

From the consumers' surplus approach there has emerged a clarification of the rent element in monopoly revenue. It is only in the case of constant or decreasing average cost that the amount of monopoly revenue is necessarily less than the loss of consumers' surplus. The monopoly revenue will be greater if the average cost curve rises steeply enough. This gave the impression that the monopolistic restriction brought about a net social gain so that the competitive output was too great and it would be beneficial to tax industries which were "subject to diminishing returns." In correcting this view it was shown that against the monopoly revenue was to be reckoned not only the loss of consumers' surplus, but also the reduction in rents as compared with those receivable under competition. If the reductions of rent is not allowed for, the diminution of costs of the marginal units, as output is restricted, is attributed to all the *infra*-marginal costs where there has been no reduction in social costs, but only a transference of income from the receivers of rent. In the accompanying Fig. 2 AR is the average revenue or demand curve (which, to avoid the quarrels over consumers' surplus, we can consider as the sum of a number of identical demand curves of similar individuals), MR is the marginal revenue curve, AC is average costs, and MC is marginal costs. P' will be the competitive point where output is OM' and price is $M'P'$, and P, which is perpendicularly above

[1] In the last few months Dr. J. R. Hicks and Mr. R. G. D. Allen have been making investigations on these lines and have demonstrated by means of the indifference curve apparatus that, with continuous indifference curves, an absolutely inelastic demand curve must be accompanied by a negatively sloping expenditure curve. This means that a change in income (prices remain unchanged) would bring about a change *in inverse direction* of the amount of the commodity bought. They have not been interested, however, in the problems dealt with in this article.

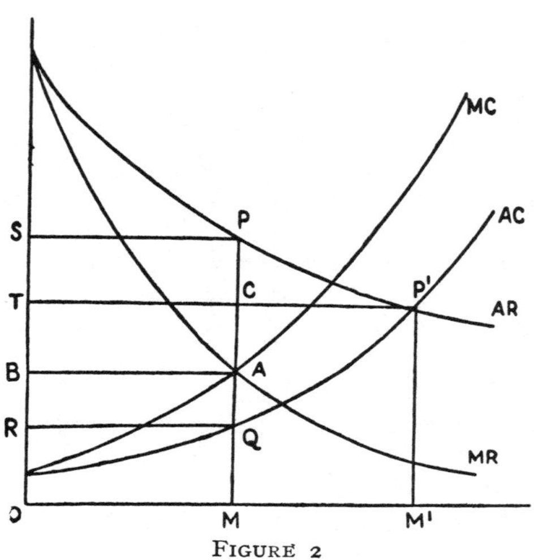

FIGURE 2

A, where MR and MC cut, will be the monopoly point where output is OM and price is MP. Consumers' surplus lost is equal to $SPP'T$, while monopoly revenue is $SPQR$, which may be greater. But against this must be reckoned the loss in rents, $RQP'T$, so that there is a net social loss of PQP'.

One is tempted to divide the monopoly revenue $SPQR$ into two parts, $SPCT$ and $RQCT$, and to say that the former is the monopoly revenue extracted from consumers while the latter is the monopoly revenue extracted from receivers of rent or producers' surplus. It is exactly parallel to the extraction of monopoly revenue from the receivers of consumers' surplus, but is obtained in virtue of the monopolist being confronted with a rising supply curve instead of with a falling demand curve. It is a gain obtained by a " single " buyer instead of a gain obtained by a " single " seller. The appropriate parallel name for it would be *Monopsony Revenue*.[1] This dichotomy of the monopoly revenue is based on a comparison of the monopoly position with the competitive position.[2] PC is the rise in price and QC is the fall in average cost, so that these quantities multiplied by the monopolistic output give the monopoly revenue and the monopsony revenue respectively.

It will, however, not do to compare the monopoly position with the competitive position for the purpose of making the dichotomy, for by this procedure it is made to depend upon the shape of the curves for outputs between the monopolistic output OM and the competitive output OM', which may be a long way from it. It does not seem reasonable that the degree of monopsony or monopoly at output OM should be dependent upon what happens to demand or cost curves in the vicinity of output OM'. And apart from this the taking of the competitive output and price as a base from which everything is to be measured leads to more concrete inconsistencies. Thus we may attempt to find the amount of monopoly revenue, (in the more exact sense, that is, not including monopsony revenue) by considering what it would be if the average cost were constant at the competitive level so that there was no monopsony. AC and MC would then coincide with TP', and the monopoly

[1] Joan Robinson, in *The Economics of Imperfect Competition*, introduces the word Monopsony, but does not speak of Monopsony Revenue.

[2] By monopoly position is meant a position in which the demand curve does not appear horizontal to all the firms in the industry. The simplest case of this is when there is only one firm which coincides with the whole industry, and that is what is shown in Fig. 2 at the monopoly position P. Monopoly is essentially a property of *firms* and by a monopolistic industry is meant nothing more than an industry in which *firms* have downward sloping demand curves. And, of course, only a firm is interested in maximising monopoly revenue. If the demand curve for the whole industry is horizontal, the industry is in a competitive condition, but that is only because in this case every firm in the industry must also have a horizontal demand curve—even if there is only one firm.

revenue would not be *SPCT* but some other larger amount, for the output could not be *OM* but some other amount. If we reverse this process, assuming that the demand curve and the *MR* curve are horizontal, we again find that the monopsony revenue is not *RQCT* but some other larger amount, and the output is not *OM* but, again, some other amount.[1]

The direct comparison of monopolistic with competitive equilibrium further assumes that cost conditions are the same and that demand conditions are the same. Neither of these is likely, and the combination of both is much less likely.

A more reasonable procedure for the allocation of the gains as between monopoly and monopsony revenue is to take as a basis not the price which would obtain if there were neither monopoly nor monopsony, but instead of that the actual conditions of the monopoly-monopsony equilibrium. With the given demand curve pure[2] monopoly output could only be *OM* if the horizontal *AC* curve were coincident with *AB*, in which case the monopoly revenue would be equal to *SPAB*. With the given *AC* curve the pure monopsony output could only be *OM* if the horizontal demand curve is coincident with *AB*, in which case the monopsony revenue would be equal to *RQAB*, and *RQAB* and *SPAB* do add up to the monopoly-monopsony ıevenue *SPQR*.

From this it appears that the monopoly revenue per unit of output, *AP*, is the excess of price over marginal cost, so that the mark of the absence of monopoly is the equality of price or *average* receipts to *marginal* cost, and the mark of the absence of monopsony is the equality of *average* cost to *marginal* receipts.[3]

The test more usually accepted is the equality of average costs to price or average receipts. It is this equation which is regularly given as the definition of

[1] In Fig. 2, where both *AR* and *AC* are concave upwards, the output under monopoly without monopsony would be less than *OM*, and the output under monopsony without monopoly would be greater than *OM*. The outputs are given by the abscissae of the points where *TP'* is cut by *MR* and *MC* respectively. If *AR* and *AC* are convex, the outputs would move in the opposite direction. If they are straight lines, or if the convexity of one is just offset by the concavity of the other, the output will be the same as when the monopoly and monopsony are found in combination. If the elimination of monopsony changes the output in one direction, the elimination of monopoly would change output in the other direction, and *vice versa*.

[2] By *pure monopoly* is meant a case where one is confronted with a falling demand curve for the commodity one sells, but with a horizontal supply curve for the factors one has to buy for the production of the commodity ; so that one sells as a monopolist but buys in a perfect market. Similarly, *pure monopsony* stands for perfect competition in the market where one sells, but monopsony in the market where one buys—being confronted with a horizontal demand curve but a rising supply curve. *Pure monopoly* is monopoly free from all elements of monopsony. *Pure monopsony* is monopsony free from all elements of monopoly. *Pure competition* stands for freedom from all elements of both monopoly and monopsony. The *purity* of monopoly or of monopsony has nothing to do with the *degree* of monopoly or monopsony.

[3] *Marginal* cost and *marginal* receipts are, of course, always equal to each other in any equilibrium, whether monopolistic or monopsonistic, or both or neither. It is, therefore, possible to express the same relationships in terms of the equality of price or average receipts to marginal receipts and the equality of average costs to marginal costs. But this procedure rules out conditions of disequilibrium together with monopoly or monopsony, so that to affirm this would be merely to say in other words that the demand or supply curve is horizontal, so that by definition there is no monopoly or monopsony. The relationships given in the text are not the merely mathematical relationships between an average and its corresponding marginal curve, but between real conditions of costs on the one hand and of receipts on the other. It will be seen below that these relationships will not always coincide with the tautologous alternatives suggested in this footnote.

" competitive " position,[1] and a suggestion like the one here given is likely to meet with a lecture on the impropriety of comparing averages with marginal values. It would seem, however, that the orthodox point of view is not only based upon too great a readiness to consider perfect competition as the ideal type of economic phenomena towards which all things tend, but are deterred more or less only by " frictions " (for in perfect competition all these equations become identical), but is in some measure induced by the habit of using straight lines in diagrams dealing with monopoly, and thus missing the problem. For in this case, AB of Fig. 2 would coincide with $P'T$, and the two dichotomies of the monopoly-cum-monopsony revenue are identical.

The point at issue is not merely a verbal one of definition—a quibble as to what it is better to call the " competitive " position. The importance of the competitive position lies in its implications of being a position which in some way or another is better than other positions. It is the position in which the " Invisible Hand " has exerted its beneficial influences to the utmost. It has become the symbol for the social optimum. Its importance for us here is in giving us a basis against which we can compare the effect of monopoly in order to see the social loss, if any, that the existence of a monopoly brings about. Is the social optimum that position at which prices are equal to average cost, or that at which price equals marginal cost and average cost equals marginal revenue ?

The social optimum relative to any distribution of resources (or income) between different individuals (and we cannot here go into the problems connected with optimum distribution) will be reached only if the resources which are to be devoted to satisfying the wants of each individual are so allocated between the different things he wants, that his total satisfaction would not be increased by any transference of resources from the provision of any one of the things he gets to any other thing he wants. This would show itself in the impossibility of any individual being put in a preferred position without putting another individual in a worse position. We may adopt this as our criterion or test of the achievement of the relative optimum. If in any set of circumstances it is possible to move one individual into a preferred position without moving another individual into a worse position (i.e. such that the original position is preferred to it by the individual affected), we may say that the relative optimum is not reached ; but if such a movement is impossible, we may say that the relative optimum has been attained. The conditions which must be satisfied if the optimum is attained can be formulated quite simply.

Any change in the position of any individual means a change in the quantity of goods (and services) he consumes. For any such a change to take place it is necessary that there shall be either (*a*) a *similar* change in the total quantity of goods produced or (*b*) an *opposite* change in the total quantity of goods consumed by others, or (*c*) some combination of (*a*) and (*b*). In the case of (*a*), consumption by other people need not be interfered with by the change,

[1] Even Mrs. Robinson defines " competitive output " and " competitive price " as that output or price at which $AC=AR$ or price (*op. cit.*, p. 160), although she demonstrates most clearly in other parts of the book how this condition ($AC=AR$) is also reached in monopolistic or imperfectly competitive equilibrium.

the whole change in the consumption by one individual being covered by changes in production. In the case of (*b*), there need be no change in production, any increase in the consumption of particular goods by one individual be provided by decreases in their consumption by others, and any decreases in the consumption of other goods by one individual being covered by increases in their consumption by others. In case (*c*) both kinds of compensating movements take place, but these can be separated and dealt with as cases of (*a*) and (*b*) so that no special treatment is necessary.

If a change in the consumption of various goods by one individual which improves his position is compensated solely by a movement of type (*a*), consumption by all other individuals need not be affected. This means that the effect of the movement from the previous position was to make one individual better off without making any other individual worse off. The previous position could not, therefore, have been an optimum position. One condition, then, of the optimum position is that any change in the quantity of goods consumed by any individual which improves his position cannot be compensated by a movement of type (*a*).

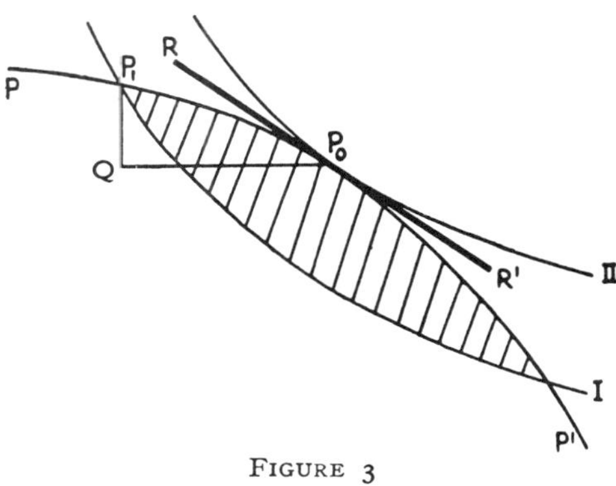

FIGURE 3

This is illustrated in Fig. 3,[1] PP' is a section of the displacement cost curve (or productive indifference curve) of the whole community. I and II are consumption indifference curves of one individual. The indifference curves are superimposed upon the displacement cost curve, so that the point on the indifference map which represents the quantities of the commodities X (measured horizontally) and Y (measured vertically), consumed by the individual in the initial position, coincides with the point on the communal displacement cost curve which represents the total amount of the commodities (X and Y) produced in the whole community in the initial position. If P_1 is this position, a movement from P_1 to any point above I represents a movement favourable to one individual. Compensating movements of type (*a*) from P_1 are, however, limited to points below PP'. The shaded area in the diagram represents positions to which movements from P_1 are favourable to one individual and can be compensated by movements of type (*a*). Thus a movement from P_1 to P_0 represents a diminution in the production of Y by an amount P_1Q and an increase in the production of X by an amount QP_0;[2] accompanied by a similar change in one individual's con-

[1] I am indebted to Mr. V. Edelberg for the suggestion of the application of the indifference curve apparatus to the problem in this manner.

[2] It is not necessary that all or any of the identical units of factors set free from the production of Y should be used in the production of X. They, or a part of them, may go to the production of a third commodity Z, as substitutes for other factors which are released to produce the additional X; and there may be any number of such steps. This, of course, does not mean that every commodity is a *direct* displacement cost for every other commodity at the margin (in the

sumption which moves him on to the higher indifference curve *II* ; while the quantities of goods remaining to be consumed by other people are unaffected.

It is, of course, not necessary that any improvement should go up to the highest possible point—here P_0. A movement from P_1 to any other point in the shaded area indicates an improvement, but leaves room for still further improvement.

Such a movement is possible as long as the indifference curve cuts the displacement cost curve, giving an overlapping (shaded) area. Our first condition for the optimum position can be expressed by saying that these curves must not cut.

If the curves are smooth this will mean that they are tangential as at P_0, but our condition is satisfied without the tangency of the curves, if either (or both) of the curves changes directions suddenly at the point where the curves meet or that it forms an angle. What is necessary is merely that the curves shall meet at P_0 without cutting. This condition must be fulfilled for every individual in the community.

The movement of one individual to a preferred position, may, however, be covered by opposite changes in the consumption of others. This, too, can be examined in the same diagram. Let *I* and *II* represent the same indifference curves as before, but let *PP'* represent now not the displacement cost curve, but the indifference curve of any other individual, turned through 180° around the common point which shows the combinations of goods consumed by the individual. If the indifference curves cut, as they do in our diagram if P_1 is the common point, there is an overlapping area, shaded in the diagram, showing the possibility of improving the position of one without worsening the position of the other. A movement from P_1 to P_0 improves the position of *one* individual and leaves the other at another point on the same indifference curve *PP'*, and, therefore, not worse off. Movements from P_1 to any intermediate point in the shaded area would make both individuals better off. In order to satisfy the condition of the optimum it is therefore again necessary that there should be no gap between the curves, i.e. that they should not cut. If they are smooth, it means that they are tangential, and that the slopes of the indifference curves of both individuals were parallel in the initial position, since the turning of a curve through 180° does not change any slopes.

The diagrammatical treatment restricts one to the consideration of only two commodities. This does not matter for the present purpose, since the relationships described have to obtain for every pair of all the commodities in the economy. This is because the failure of the conditions to be satisfied for *any* pair of commodities shows a possibility for improvement which is incompatible with an optimum position.

If both of these conditions are satisfied, as between each individual's indifference curves and the communal displacement costs curve on the one

sense that factors can move directly from one to the other without economic loss), as would be the case if each factor had the same marginal productivity in all uses—universal substitutability of factors at the margin. It only means that there is some path, however indirect, whereby a diminution in the production of one commodity permits an increase in the production of any other commodity, leaving the quantity of the rest of the commodities unaffected. That is what is meant by drawing a displacement cost curve for any two commodities.

hand, and as between each individual's indifference curves and every other individual's (inverted) indifference curves, on the other hand, it is impossible to improve the position of any individual without worsening the position of some other individual. The optimum position, relative to the distribution of income between individuals, is attained.

Can we make any use of such a complicated set of conditions? If it were necessary to investigate separately the slopes of the indifference curves of all individuals for all pairs of commodities in order to discover whether the conditions are satisfied, it would be most profitable to discontinue this analysis at once. But there is no need for all this. We need merely assume that some of the indifference curves are smooth at the positions representing the amounts consumed by the individuals, and that each individual, in buying goods for his own consumption, considers the price as given. Under these conditions the relative prices of each pair of goods in the market will accurately reflect the slopes of the indifference curves where these are smooth; and for those cases, where an indifference curve forms an angle, the ratio between the prices will give a line (RR' in Fig. 3) of such slope that the indifference curve will lie wholly *above* it, meeting it but not cutting it if it is superimposed on the consumption point P_0. The mere existence of a free market in consumption goods thus satisfies the second of our two conditions.

The first condition is satisfied if the price ratio on the market, represented by the slope of the line RR', is such that the displacement curve lies wholly *below* it, meeting it at the production-consumption point P_0, but not cutting it. If the displacement cost curve is smooth and, therefore, tangential to RR', this will mean that the price ratio is proportional to the marginal displacement costs, which condition is satisfied if *price is equal to marginal cost.*

From this analysis we see that the optimum is reached when the price reflects the alternatives given up at the margin, whether this alternative is considered in physical terms of some other commodity or whether we go direct to the satisfactions that the physical alternatives represent. The loss involved in monopoly can be seen in the divergence between price and this marginal cost. The loss involved in monopsony is of exactly the same nature, and a parallel analysis is rendered unnecessary if we translate the rising supply curve that is seen by the monopsonist into a falling demand curve by considering the purchase of A for B as the sale of B for A. This loss is avoided only if price to the consumer (AR) is equal to marginal cost (MC), and if the wages of labour (AC) are equal to its marginal product ($=MR$). If we prefer we may put the latter statement in the form of demand. The price of leisure demanded by labourers (AR) (which is his wage) must be equal to the marginal cost of his leisure (MC) (which is equal to the marginal product of the labour withdrawn).

II

In considering the degree of monopoly in a particular field one's first inclination seems to be to hark back to the etymological meaning of the word and to see how close the situation is to the conditions which accompany a "single seller." On this line one would say that there is complete monopoly if there is actually only one seller, and that the monopoly element diminishes as the number of sellers increases. One could construct some kind of index of the degree of monopoly, such as the inverse of the number of sellers, which would give values ranging from unity in the case of this kind of "complete" monopoly to zero in the case of an infinite number of sellers.

The most obvious of the many reasons why this will not do is that there may be a very high degree of monopoly (in any sense other than that of the formula for such an index), even where there are many sellers, if one or two sellers control a sufficiently large proportion of the total supply. For this reason one turns instead to discover how great a proportion of the total supply is controlled by one or a few individuals or organisations. The same information may also be sought more indirectly by inquiries into the size of firms.

This procedure, however, is still quite inappropriate for measuring the degree of monopoly if we are interested in its economic and social implications of control over price and social loss as discussed in the first part of this paper. This is seen most clearly when we observe that control by a single firm of 100 per cent. of the supply of a commodity for which the demand is infinitely elastic (which will always be the case if there is some equally satisfactory substitute available at a constant price) is absolutely unimportant and has no economic significance, while a "partial" monopoly of a commodity for which the demand is inelastic may be able to raise price by reducing output and is clearly a much more effective case of monopoly.

The statistical method of measuring monopoly, besides missing the main issue in this way, encounters enormous practical difficulties in which investigators can hardly hope to avoid getting entangled. The problems of allowing for changes in taste and technique, in transport and in business organisation, of dealing with firms making many products and of discovering the degree to which different firms compete with one another or mitigate the competition by Gentlemen's Agreements, trade conventions, business alliances, and so on, are just a few worth mentioning, but there is one that interests us particularly here, and that is the relatively simple one of defining the commodity.

A man may have a considerable degree of monopolistic power although he is in control of only a very small part of the supply of a commodity if he is afforded some protection from the competition of the rest of the supply by the cost of transporting other supplies to his market. Under these conditions the price of the commodity will be different in different places. The best way of dealing with this is to declare that objects having the same physical characteristics are not the same goods if they are at different places. Location is an essential and distinguishing characteristic of economic goods, and the only relationship between the prices of similar goods in different places is that which results from the possibilities of transforming the one good into the other by transporting it from the one place to the other.

And location is not the only variant of this kind, but rather the simplest species of a large genus, and is useful for a simplified exposition of the problems involved. Every specialised gradation of every particular quality of every "commodity" may be treated as "distance," and the cost of changing the quality to a particular grade as the cost of "transport." Some of these problems are dealt with by Hotelling in his article, " Stability in Competition," *Economic Journal*, 1929, p. 41, where he gives examples ranging from the sweetness of cider to the service of churches.

To these variants must be added also all fictitious variations, such as are successfully imposed upon the minds of buyers by skilful advertising, as well as the tendencies of customers to buy from one seller rather than from another by sheer force of habit. Here the " distance " is the fictitious difference in quality or the goodwill of the customer, while the " transport costs " are the costs involved in overcoming the " goodwill " whether by reducing price or by counter-advertisement.

This splitting up of the conception of a commodity of course multiplies the number of commodities indefinitely, and seems to create monopolies in the most unexpected places. Carried to its logical extreme, every firm now becomes a monopoly, since it is impossible for more than one unit of product to be in the same place. But even without going to such extremes it becomes impossible to apply the simple measures of monopoly that we are criticising. Further difficulties are yet to arise.

While the idea of considering the same things at different places as different goods seems to have spread considerably, the full revolutionary implications of this step forward in the picturing of the equilibrial forces do not seem to have been quite realised.

In calling the same thing at different places different commodities, we have rejected the criterion of physical similarity as a basis for the recognition or classification of commodities and have put in its place the principle of substitutability at the margin.

If the same thing at a different place is not the same commodity it is only because the difference in its location prevents it from being substituted for, or used in the same way as, the same thing here. But this principle can be applied in the converse form too. With substitutability as the principle it is no longer necessary for different units of the same commodity to have the same physical characteristics as long as they are substitutable at the margin for the purpose that the buyer wants them. This means that if one pound of coal gives me the same heating power as four pounds of wood, that both of these items cost the same on the market, and I am indifferent as to which I have, then one pound of coal and four pounds of wood represent the same number of units of the same commodity. It means, further, that if I am indifferent as to whether I have one hundredweight of coal every week during the winter, or an overcoat to keep me warm, then a winter's coal and an overcoat are equal quantities of the same commodity. Further still, if I am indifferent as to whether I have a wireless set for £10 or whether I have the satisfaction of saving ten Chinese children from starvation, the wireless set in London is the same quantity of the same commodity as £10 worth of rice in China; while if I get the same satisfaction from a £100 motor-car here and now as I could from a Mediterranean cruise next year, which costs £100 plus the accumulated interest on the money, then the motor-car here and now and the Mediterranean cruise next year are equal quantities of the same commodity. Physical qualities, spacial and temporal position are irrelevant now that we have the ultimate criterion of substitutability at the margin. If any quantity or complex of goods and services can be substituted at the margin for any other quantity of goods and services (and therefore have the same market value), then they are both equal quantities of the same commodity. It would perhaps be best to give terminological recognition to such a break with traditional usage by speaking of " units of accommodation " instead of units of commodities.

If this way of looking at things seems paradoxical, it is only because we have not yet completely freed ourselves from the crudely materialistic conception of goods with which the Physiocrats and Adam Smith were the first to wrestle. The inadequacy of a purely physical criterion of commodities is obvious when we consider the enormous physical difference which we neglect if they do not affect the qualities in which we are interested (that is which affect our satisfactions), of which we are often completely unconscious, but which are of so much importance to Mr. Sherlock Holmes. Physically there are no two similar articles even apart from location. If two objects are considered to be items of the same good, it is only because they are " good for " the same purpose—always, ultimately, the satisfaction of a want. It is futile to say that the motor-car and the Mediterranean cruise satisfy different wants until we are able to define " similar " wants otherwise than as wants that are satisfied by physically similar objects. There is no *qualitative* criterion of wants. Wants can only be considered as similar when the person who feels them displays equal concern for their satisfaction and thus shows them to be equal in *quantity*. To follow any other course is to sacrifice the logic of the science to the irrelevant convenience of the shopkeeper.

It may be objected that this concept of commodity is so abstract and elusive as to be unusable. That is perfectly correct. But therein lies a great part of its advantages. It cannot be used like the more material conception to drown the theory in irrelevant statistics. It puts an end to attempts, here, to find a measure of monopoly in terms of the proportion of the supply of a commodity under single control and clears the way to a better understanding.

Another line of approach that suggests itself is to compare the amount of monopoly revenue with the total receipts, and to take this ratio as a measure of the degree of monopoly power. Allowance is thus made for the size of the industry or the firm. We will obtain values ranging from 0 in the case of perfect competition to 1 where the whole of receipts is monopoly revenue, and at first glance all seems well.

This procedure will, however, not do, for what we want in the measure of monopoly is not the amount of tribute individuals can obtain for themselves from the rest of the community, by being in an advantageous monopolistic position, but the divergence of the system from the social optimum that is reached in perfect competition. From this point of view the monopolist gains are not to be distinguished from rents of scarce property that he owns, or any other source of individual income. The independence of the monopolist gain from the social loss can perhaps most clearly be brought out by a consideration of how far they can vary independently. The limiting case is seen where the demand curve for the product of a monopolist coincides over considerable range with his average cost curve. Here the monopoly revenue is zero wherever the monopolist produces within this range, yet he has control over price, and the social loss will be different according to what output the monopolist decides to produce. It clearly will not do to say that the degree of monopoly power in such a case is zero.

If the average cost curve is horizontal such a divergence cannot occur. The firm can only change output while keeping monopoly revenue zero if the demand curve is also horizontal, and that means perfect competition in either case and no social loss. But in such a case we are comparing not merely monopoly revenue with total receipts, which is the same as the ratio between average receipts minus costs and average receipts (and which is also seen in the ratio between average costs and average receipts), but also *marginal costs* with *average receipts*, and it is in divergence between these, as we have seen above, that the essence of monopoly is to be found.

In such cases (where the cost curve is horizontal) the ratio of monopoly revenue to total receipts coincides exactly with the ratio of the divergence of price from marginal cost to price, and it is this latter formula that I wish to put forward as the measure of monopoly power. If P = price and C = marginal cost, then the index of the degree of monopoly power is $\frac{P-C}{P}$.

It will be observed that this formula looks like the inverse of the formula for the elasticity of demand. It differs from it only in that the item marginal cost replaces the item marginal receipts. In equilibrium as normally conceived marginal costs coincide with marginal receipts so that our formula becomes identical with the inverse of the elasticity of demand. It will be best to consider this as a special case.

In this special case we can find the degree of monopoly power via the elasticity of demand. The determination of this elasticity of demand is not to be confused with that of Pigou and Schultz in finding the elasticity of demand (as part of the demand function) for a materially (physically) defined commodity on a market. What we want here is the elasticity of demand for the product of a particular firm. This is much easier to obtain, for it is only when he knows the shape of the demand curve for his product that any entrepreneur can obtain his maximum profit ; and he is, therefore, always applying himself energetically to obtaining as accurate an estimate as possible of this elasticity. This does not mean that the entrepreneur will be able to fill in the elasticity of demand on a questionnaire form. He will rarely know what the term means. But his unfamiliarity with the technical jargon of economists must not be held to show an ignorance of so primary a principle for intelligent business management as the urgency of knowing the effect of price changes on sales. His behaviour in running the business for maximum profit will enable any student to deduce the (estimated) elasticity of demand from the firm's cost curve and the selling price. From the average cost curve the marginal cost curve can be derived. The marginal cost is equal to the marginal receipt, output being adjusted so as to make them equal if profit is maximised. The elasticity of demand is equal to the price divided by the difference between price and marginal cost—it is the inverse of our formula for the measurement of the degree of monopoly power.

In finding the degree of monopoly in this special case " via the elasticity of demand " we found that the easiest way of finding the elasticity of demand was via the degree of monopoly. We may, therefore, leave out the elasticity of demand altogether and just keep to our formula all the time. In the special case both come to the same thing, but we must use the new formula and not the inverse of the elasticity of demand whenever we consider cases where the maximum monopoly revenue is not obtained in practice.

This may be accidental, as when the monopolist does not know the shape of his demand curve and his estimate of the elasticity of demand at the actual output is erroneous ; or it may be intentional. The price and output may intentionally be fixed in a manner which does not give the maximum monopoly revenue :

(*a*) When the monopolist is not working on purely business principles, but for social, philanthropic or conventional reasons sells *below* this price commodities which it is considered socially desirable to cheapen—as when a public authority supplies cheap transport facilities—or sells *above* this price commodities which are considered socially harmful—as may be done by a State liquor monopoly.

(*b*) When the monopolist is working on purely business principles, but keeps the price and his profits lower than they might be so as to avoid political opposition or the entry of new competitors. The second could, perhaps, better be considered as a case where the demand is more elastic in the long period, taking into account the contingent competition, than in the short period, and where the monopolist takes a long period view.

In all such cases our formula is not equal to the inverse of the elasticity of demand ; but wherever there appears a divergence between the two it is our formula and not the inverse of the elasticity of demand which gives the measure of what we want. In the first case—where the monopolist's estimate of the elasticity of demand is erroneous—the consumers will in every way be in exactly the same position as if the elasticity were what the monopolist thinks it is. If he over-estimates the elasticity of demand he will sell a larger amount at a lower price. If he thinks the elasticity is infinite—i.e. that if he produced less he would not be able to get a better price—he will make price equal to marginal cost, and the effect on consumers will be the same as if there were perfect competition.[1] The unused monopoly power will be there, but being unknown and unused it is, economically, as if it were not there. For practical purposes we must read monopoly power not as *potential* monopoly, but as monopoly *in force.*

If the monopolist underestimates the elasticity of demand he will sell a

[1] Mrs. Robinson has pointed out to me that the delusion that elasticity is infinite would persist only if *MC* happened to equal price already. This is the easiest case for the correction of a mistaken estimate in the process of adjustment to it. The same possibility exists with any estimated elasticity of demand as long as the marginal cost and the estimated marginal receipts do not coincide and so preclude any adjustments.

smaller quantity and at a higher price than at the point of maximum monopoly revenue. The only difference between this and the previous case is that the monopolist's error brings a loss to consumers instead of a gain. The monopolist himself, of course, loses by the error in either case. The consumer here has to pay a higher price or else do without. It is again just as if the elasticity of demand were what the monopolist thinks it is. This may sound as if the monopoly *in force* is here greater than the *potential* monopoly power, but the inverse of the elasticity of demand at the maximum revenue point does not really give the potential monopoly power. It gives just that degree of monopoly power which it is necessary to put into force in order to obtain the maximum revenue and which is in force where the maximum revenue is being obtained. The monopolist always has powei in excess of this ; but as the employment of it can only bring him a loss, he normally does not use it intentionally. If he chooses to use it he can, of course, for the exercise of this power consists of diminishing the amount he produces. Potential monopoly power is only used to its maximum when the monopolist stops all production. What our formula gives is the degree of monopoly power in force.

The same arguments apply to cases where the maximum monopoly revenue is not obtained for social, philanthropic or conventional reasons or for the purpose of avoiding political opposition or contingent competition. In the last case, our procedure saves us all further investigation into the complications involved in considering the length of the period upon which the demand curve is based. The appropriate costs to be reckoned are those of the present, or rather of the immediate future, so as to enable us to measure temporary monopolies. The degree of monopoly over a long period is perhaps best expressed in an average of the short-period monopolies over the period.

The primary unit to which our measure of monopoly applies is the firm in the very shortest period. In order to get a measure of monopoly over a period we had to take an average of such coefficients of monopoly. In order to get a measure of monopoly over an industry we have to follow the same procedure and find an average of monopoly of the separate firms included in the industry. The " industry " is to be considered as a group of firms, chosen for the purpose of the special investigation. It is quite unnecessary, for this purpose, to say anything at all about the " commodity " which the " industry " produces, nor is there any need to be able to draw demand or supply curves for the industry. All the difficulties of definition of " commodity " or " industry " are completely avoided.

More strictly a simple average of the degrees of monopoly in firms may be used to indicate the degree of monopoly in an industry only in the very limited sense of the degree of monopoly *at that stage*. It is not a measure of the degree to which the application of the resources of the community to the production of the products of the " industry " diverges from the social optimum. That depends upon two other sets of conditions in addition to this *local* element of monopoly.

The first of these is the degree of monopoly in the firms (or " industries ") producing the raw materials for all the previous stages in the production of the products. The restriction of productions in any stage has its effects in all the succeeding stages. The final degree of reduction of product will depend upon the degree of monopoly in all the preceding stages. These have to be aggregated so as to give the tendency to divergence from the social optimum in the whole series of the production stages of the product ; this phenomenon may be called the transitiveness of monopoly.

Theoretically, this can be done quite simply. What we want is the divergence between the price of the product and its marginal *social* cost. If in all the previous stages price is equal to marginal cost, the marginal cost to the firm is also the marginal social cost. If in any stage there is a divergence, price being above marginal cost, that divergence is a gap in the social cost. The social cost can then be calculated by multiplying the price by a factor for each stage in production, each factor being the ratio of the marginal cost to the price in the corresponding stage. Thus, if there are five stages and in each stage the degree of monopoly is $\frac{1}{5}$, marginal cost over price in each stage is $\frac{4}{5}$, the social cost is $(\frac{4}{5})^5$ of the price of the final product, and by our formula the " social " degree of monopoly is $1-(\frac{4}{5})^5$.

Practical difficulties that arise in attempts to measure the " social " degree of monopoly, or different products may be attacked by any of the tricks of the trade of mathematical statistics. It may be necessary to assume average degrees of monopoly in separate stages and to calculate " social " degree of monopoly by the number of stages, and so on ; but it is not intended here to discuss anything but the simplest theoretical implications.

The second set of complicating considerations arise when we ask the even more ambitious question : What is the (social) degree of monopoly in the society as a whole ? From this general point of view the conditions for that optimum distribution of resources between different commodities that we designate the absence of monopoly are satisfied if prices are all *proportional* to social marginal cost. If the " social " degree of monopoly is the same for *all* final products (including leisure) there is no monopolistic alteration from the optimum at all. The absolute height of " social " degrees of monopoly becomes completely unimportant.

This is because if the "social " degree of monopoly is the same for all products it *must* be equal to zero in real terms. For from the social point of view, the marginal cost of any product is always some other product. If the " social " degree of monopoly for product A is positive, this means that the price of A is greater than the price of some other product B which is the alternative foregone. The price of B cannot then be greater than the price of A. If both degrees of monopoly are equal they must both be zero.

What is important is the deviations between the degrees of monopoly ; and it is this which must be measured in order to answer our question. A suitable measure for this is the standard deviation of the " social " degrees of monopoly of all final products in the society.

Another complication arises in the growingly important cases where it is found to be profitable to extend or maintain the amount sold, not by reducing price but by expenditure on advertising, salesmanship, gifts, coupons and beautiful wrappings—all of which can be subsumed under the heading of " marketing costs." In such cases what becomes of the elasticity of demand ?

In the recent cost controversy, "marketing costs" were eagerly seized upon in attempts at a conciliation between decreasing costs and competitive equilibrium.[1] Such arguments may be described with some justification as contriving to exhibit decreasing costs at peace with competitive equilibrium by the device of leaving out of account the marketing element in the costs which is increasing so rapidly that *total costs* are not decreasing at all; the contradiction being hidden by a separation of "productive" from "marketing" costs.

This solution of the problem cannot, however, be dismissed as mere word-jugglery. It does show the actual working of the forces involved, and it is only the terminology that is unfortunate. What we have here is not perfect competition but *monopolistic* or *imperfect* competition. Chamberlain and Robinson have developed a more satisfactory line of attack on these problems, but how are we to find the falling demand curve which will entitle us to put these cases into this category and enable us to deal with them in the same way?

In order to obtain this it is essential to separate productive from marketing costs. The marketing costs involved in selling a given quantity of product must be subtracted from the gross receipts, just as if they were all direct or indirect reductions in price, leaving a definite total and average net receipts. For each quantity produced different prices may be charged and different marketing costs incurred. For each output some combination of prices charged and marketing costs incurred will leave a maximum average (and total) residue after subtracting the average (or total) marketing costs, and this maximum is the relevant Average Net Receipts for that output. The locus of such points will be the Average Net Receipts curve for the firm, and this is the "demand curve" which we need. This average net receipts curve and the corresponding marginal net receipts curve have to be used in conjunction with the "productive" cost curves which we may call "net" cost curves.

If the average net receipts curve is negatively inclined, one proceeds just as in the simple analysis of imperfect competition where there are no selling costs. The firm equates its marginal net cost to its marginal net receipts, and the degree of monopoly is equal to average net receipts over average net receipts minus marginal net costs, and the divergence of the position from the social optimum is illustrated by the fact that production is not carried on at the minimum average cost, but the firm produces less than this optimum output, stopping at a point where the average net cost curve is tangential to the average net receipts curve. The social loss, if any, due to the expenditure of resources on advertising is *not* taken into account in the measurement of monopoly. The measure will be the same whether the marketing costs are large or small, and whether they are given to the consumer in forms corresponding to cash, or whether they have important influences on his tastes for good or for bad. The social effects of different kinds of advertising constitute a quite separate problem.

If the average net receipts curve is horizontal where the marginal net costs curve cuts it, there is no monopoly. The existence of marketing costs is quite another matter.

[1] As by R. Harrod in his article on "The Law of Decreasing Costs," *Economic Journal*, Dec. 1931.

But there is no reason why the average net receipts curve should not slope upwards! It may well be that a larger quantity can be sold at a higher price at the same or a smaller *average* cost of marketing, and there is no ground for considering such a combination of circumstances as in any way exceptional. We must apply the same analysis here and not be deterred if the results at first appear a little strange.

If the firm with a rising average net revenue curve has a constant cost curve, or can acquire more of the product from other firms without affecting its marketing possibilities, we have another form of the paradox of the incompatibility of equilibrium with a horizontal demand curve and a falling average cost curve below it. The marginal revenue and the marginal cost curves cannot meet until the conditions are changed. Either the receipts curves must begin to fall or the cost curves must rise.

The interesting case—the one which can remain in equilibrium in these conditions—is the case where the average costs of the firm rise after a time as output increases, and where it cannot obtain more from other firms at the same price, either because the other firms' costs rise or because to do this would interfere with the reputation of the firm and upset its marketing possibilities.

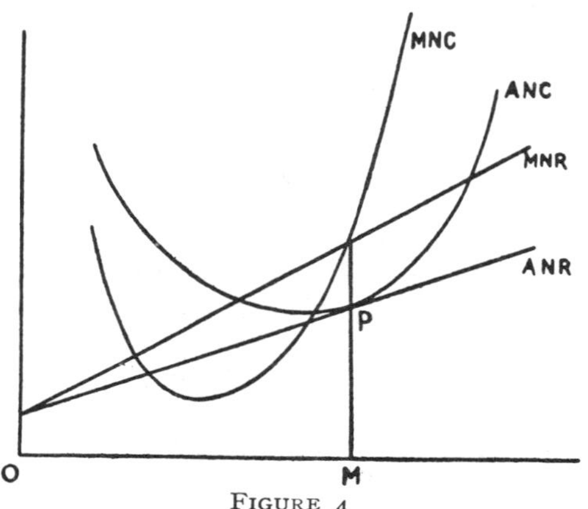

FIGURE 4

This is shown in Fig. 4, where the firm is in equilibrium producing an output *OM*.

Average net receipts (*ANR*) are equal to average net costs (*ANC*), and marginal net receipts (*MNR*) are equal to marginal net costs (*MNC*). The degree of monopoly is here *negative* since marginal cost is greater than average receipts. This may appear surprising, but it merely means that the divergence from the social optimum is in the direction opposite to that usually brought about by monopolies. Instead of the firm producing *less* than it should, it is producing *more*; the same kind of social harm is done, and it is reflected in the same way by the excess of the average cost over the minimum.

In finding an average degree of monopoly in an " industry," positive and negative monopolies may cancel out in whole or in part. Does this harm our apparatus?

I do not think it does this at all. It rather brings out the true nature of our measure as an index of *divergence* from an optimum. In any group of firms taken together to make an " industry," divergences may, and should, be expected to some extent to cancel out. For we are now considering the application of resources to this " industry " as against the rest of the economy. If of two firms within the " industry," one is producing too much and the other too little from the point of view of the economy as a whole; the industry may not be producing either too much or too little. The maladjustment becomes a local affair which we must neglect in this larger consideration.

When our " industry " becomes the whole society, there cannot be too much or too little resources used, and as we have seen above, all the individual positive and negative monopolies must cancel out. This does not mean that society as a whole must always be in an optimum position, nor does it take any meaning away from the concept. It only means that the larger the fraction of the whole society one wishes to examine, the less legitimate is it to use particular analysis. In applying the particular mechanism to the whole economy we get the appropriate *reductio ad absurdum*. What is relevant for general analysis is not the *sum* of individual degrees of monopoly but their *deviations*. The standard deviations as suggested above may perhaps be used one day to give an estimate of the divergence of society from the social optimum of production relative to a given distribution of income.

A. P. LERNER.

London.

[9]

Cartel Problems

By D. K. Osborne*

A cartel faces one external and four internal problems. The external problem, to which we here give only passing attention, is to predict (and if possible, discourage) production by nonmembers. The internal problems are, first, to locate the contract surface; second, to choose a point on that surface (the sharing problem); third, to detect, and fourth, to deter, cheating. Of these we are concerned with the problems of sharing the output and deterring cheating.

Locating the contract surface and detecting cheating are evidently serious problems. Indeed, they are the *only* serious internal problems. Solve them and the cartel will be internally stable. This might seem surprising. Standard theory teaches us that cartels are inherently *unstable*, mainly because of the sharing and deterring problems. Apart from the rare conditions of identical profit functions, the members will disagree about the appropriate point on the contract surface; some members will feel victimized and be tempted to cheat. Even those who don't feel victimized will have powerful incentives to cheat, because of the positive marginal profits (*ceteris paribus*) at the output quota. The reasoning can be explained in terms of the two-member case diagrammed in Figure 1: x_i^q is the output quota of member i ($i=1,2$); q is the point selected by the cartel as best on the contract curve; $I_i^1, \ldots, I_i^4$ are portions of four of member i's isoprofit contours, with profit along I_i^1 being greater than profit along $I_i^2, \ldots$, and

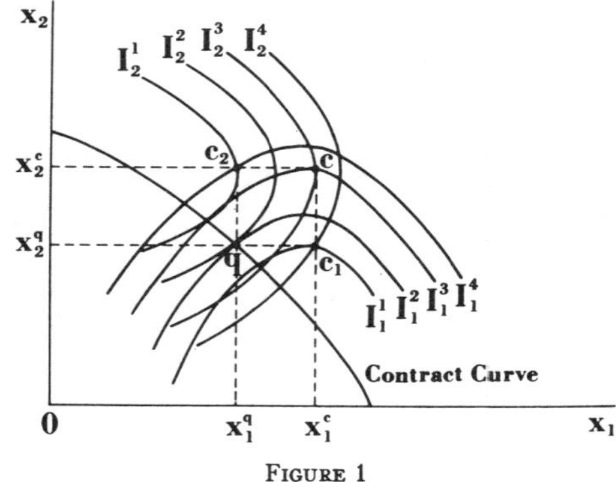

FIGURE 1

profit along I_i^3 being greater than the profit along I_i^4. Member i's profit at the cartel point q is $F_i(x_1^q, x_2^q)$. As is well known, and illustrated by the diagram,

$$\frac{\partial F_i(x_1^q, x_2^q)}{\partial x_i} > 0$$

If member i expects the other to observe the quota x_j^q he can maximize his profit by producing x_i^c; that is,

$$F_1(x_1^c, x_2^q) > F_1(x_1^q, x_2^q) \tag{1}$$

$$F_2(x_1^q, x_2^c) > F_2(x_1^q, x_2^q)$$

If each expects the other to observe the quota, and produces x_i^c, they will end up at the cheating point c, where the profits are $F_i(x_1^c, x_2^c)$. Evidently,

$$F_1(x_1^q, x_2^q) > F_1(x_1^c, x_2^c) \tag{2}$$

$$F_2(x_1^q, x_2^q) > F_2(x_1^c, x_2^c)$$

and so both members will be worse off at c than at q. However, it is also true that

* Federal Reserve Bank of Dallas. The views expressed in this article are solely those of the author and do not necessarily represent those of the Federal Reserve System.

$$(3) \qquad F_1(x_1^c, x_2^c) > F_1(x_1^q, x_2^c)$$

$$F_2(x_1^c, x_2^c) > F_2(x_1^c, x_2^q)$$

If one member cheats the other is better off cheating than observing the quota. Since the other is better off cheating even when the one observes the quota, it appears that cheating dominates observing the quota.

If we think of the cartel members as playing a game of strategy, where each member must choose one of two strategies (observe the quota or cheat), and regard the profits made at the points q, c_1, c_2, and c as payoffs, we can set up the following payoff matrix:

	member 2	
member 1	observe the quota	cheat
observe the quota	$F_1(x_1^q, x_2^q)$, $F_2(x_1^q, x_2^q)$	$F_1(x_1^q, x_2^c)$, $F_2(x_1^q, x_2^c)$
cheat	$F_1(x_1^c, x_2^q)$, $F_2(x_1^c, x_2^q)$	$F_1(x_1^c, x_2^c)$, $F_2(x_1^c, x_2^c)$

Choosing eight convenient numbers satisfying relations (1)–(3) we get

	observe	cheat
observe	4,3	2,4
cheat	5,1	3,2

Whether the outcome is in column 1 or 2, member 1 prefers to cheat; and whether the outcome is in row 1 or 2, member 2 prefers to cheat. Of the four strategy vectors, only (cheat, cheat) is Pareto dominated; the other three belong to the Pareto optimal set for this game. But since each of these Pareto optimal strategy vectors has at least one dominated component, it appears that the cartel faces a prisoners' dilemma.[1]

A prisoners' dilemma can be resolved satisfactorily by an enforceable contract. If such is available, the cartel can pool revenues and share them out according to some negotiated rule. This is the device used by what Joe Bain calls *perfect cartels*, the theory of which was given by Don Patinkin. *Imperfect* cartels (those without revenue pooling) are not able to resolve their dilemma in this manner and, apparently, are thus doomed to collapse.

This reasoning certainly seems plausible; and it tends to comfort. If the cartel is inherently unstable because of the sharing and deterring problems, let us wait a while and it will go away. Indeed, when the Organization of Petroleum Exporting Countries (*OPEC*) formed their cartel in October 1973, many economists (myself included) predicted that it would collapse within a year. It is now thirty-six months later, and the cartel seems pretty healthy.[2] Of course not all of the returns are in yet, and everything must crumble eventually (entropy); but how much time must pass before the theory is proved wrong? While we are waiting perhaps we should reexamine the theory which led us to predict so poorly.

I shall argue that the problems of sharing and deterring are easily solved if the locating and detecting problems are solved—that for all its plausibility, the reasoning along the prisoners' dilemma line is incorrect. From this argument we will see that a cartel is not inherently unstable internally unless the locating and detecting problems are inherently insoluble; and we will see how mistaken are the proposals of civil servants and political leaders in the oil-importing countries to create a central international buying agency to deal with *OPEC*. If carried out these proposals would have the effect of solving the detecting problem for the car-

[1] A prisoners' dilemma is a game in which no Pareto optimal outcome can be reached unless at least one player plays a dominated strategy. See R. D. Luce and H. Raiffa for a discussion.

[2] Crude oil prices began to fall a bit early in 1975. Far from being a sign of imminent collapse of the cartel this is more likely an adjustment to the greater long-run demand elasticity, and might be a sign of successful adjustment to change.

tel, and thus remove its most important internal source of instability; they would almost certainly support the price of crude oil at a large multiple of long-run marginal cost.[3]

I. Definitions and Assumptions

Let us assume that the nonmember, locating, and detecting problems are solved, so that the cartel has located the contract surface and always knows the outputs of all members, who together produce the entire industry output. Let us also assume the following, where f_j is the inverse demand function and F_j is the profit function of member j $(j=1, \ldots, n)$, and $x=(x_1, \ldots, x_n)$ is the vector of outputs:[4]

ASSUMPTION 1: For $j=1, \ldots, n$, $F_j(x)$ is differentiable, strictly concave in x_j, and concave and decreasing in $x_i (i \neq j)$; i.e., $F_j(x)$ is concave in x.

ASSUMPTION 2: $\partial f_j/\partial x_i = \partial f_i/\partial x_j$ for $i,j=1, \ldots, n$; i.e., the effect of member i's output on member j's demand equals the effect of member j's output on member i's demand.

These effects are made up of the cross-substitution and cross-income effects. Since the cross-substitution effects are always equal, Assumption 2 implies that the cross-income effects are either equal or negligible (see John Hicks, p. 310).

From Assumption 2 and the relation

$$\frac{\partial F_j}{\partial x_i} = x_j \frac{\partial f_j}{\partial x_i} \text{ for } i \neq j$$

we get

$$x_i \frac{\partial F_j}{\partial x_i} = x_j \frac{\partial F_i}{\partial x_j} \tag{4}$$

[3] Morris Adelman estimates the long-run marginal cost, inclusive of a 20 percent rate of return on investment, at about 10 cents per barrel in 1968 prices.

[4] The analysis is not limited to profit maximization, but holds for any set of objective functions $F_1, \ldots, F_n$ of which Assumptions 1–3 are true.

Note that (4) does not imply

$$x_2 \frac{\partial F_1}{\partial x_2} = x_3 \frac{\partial F_1}{\partial x_3} = \ldots = x_n \frac{\partial F_1}{\partial x_n}$$

The cross effect between members i and j need not equal the cross effect between members j and k. Assumption 2 permits but does not imply perfect substitutes.

ASSUMPTION 3: $F(x) \equiv F_1(x) + \ldots + F_n(x)$ has an interior maximum (not necessarily unique).

Because of Assumption 1, F is the sum of concave functions and is thus itself concave. Therefore, the first-order conditions for an interior maximum are also sufficient conditions, and Assumption 3 implies:

x^0 maximizes $F(x)$ if and only if

$$\sum_{j=1}^{n} \frac{\partial F_j(x^0)}{\partial x_i} = 0 \text{ for } i = 1, \ldots, n \tag{5}$$

Let M be the set of points maximizing $F(x)$. The concavity of F implies that M is connected, from which it follows that exactly one maximizer x^0 has the property

$$Var\,[F_1(x^0), \ldots, F_n(x^0)] \text{ is minimal in } M \tag{6}$$

We shall use this fact to derive an optimal quota rule for the cartel.

The *contract surface* C is the set of points (output vectors x) that maximize $F_i(x)$ for constant $F_j(x)$, $i,j=1, \ldots, n$, $j \neq i$. At a point on C member i's isoprofit surface is tangent to a hyperplane H_i. The hyperplanes $H_1, \ldots, H_n$ intersect in a line L to which the n isoprofit surfaces are mutually tangent. Thus to each point $x \in C$ there corresponds one line $L(x)$ to which the isoprofit surfaces are tangent at x. See Figure 2 for an illustration in two dimensions.

A point $\bar{x} \in C$ has the *ray property* whenever $L(\bar{x})$ is a ray from the origin (as in Figure 2). All points on the boundary of C have the ray property (for example, the monopoly points $(x_1^m, 0)$ and $(0, x_2^m)$ in Fig-

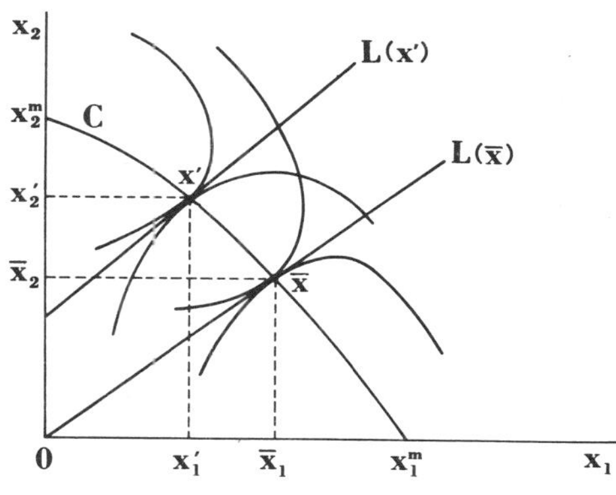

FIGURE 2

ure 2) but it is not obvious that any interior points have this property.

Define *grad* $F_i(x)$ as

$$(\partial F_i(x)/\partial x_1, \ldots, \partial F_i(x)/\partial x_n)$$

the gradient vector of member i's profit function at the point x. This vector is normal to member i's isoprofit surface at x; hence it is orthogonal to the line $L(x)$. If x lacks the ray property $L(x)$ does not pass through the origin; in that case the output vector x does not lie on $L(x)$ and is thus not orthogonal to *grad* $F_i(x)$ for any i. But each output vector $\bar{x}$ with the ray property is orthogonal to *grad* $F_i(\bar{x})$, i.e., $\bar{x} \cdot grad\, F_i(\bar{x}) = 0$ for $i = 1, \ldots, n$ if and only if $\bar{x}$ has the ray property. Hence the following system of equations holds if and only if $\bar{x}$ has the ray property:

$$(7) \qquad \sum_{j=1}^{n} \bar{x}_j \frac{\partial F_i(\bar{x})}{\partial x_j} = 0 \text{ for } i = 1, \ldots, n$$

Now let us return to system (5) and multiply equation i of that system by $\overset{0}{x}_i$.

$$(8) \quad \sum_{j=1}^{n} \overset{0}{x}_i \frac{\partial F_j(x^0)}{\partial x_i} = 0 \text{ for } i = 1, \ldots, n$$

Because of Assumption 3, system (8) holds if and only if system (5) does. Now use (4) to rewrite (8) in the equivalent form:

$$(9) \quad \sum_{j=1}^{n} \overset{0}{x}_j \frac{\partial F_i(x^0)}{\partial x_j} = 0 \text{ for } i = 1, \ldots, n$$

This system holds if and only if x^0 is an interior maximizer of $F(x)$; it evidently has the same solutions as (7), which holds if and only if $\bar{x}$ has the ray property. Hence an interior point maximizes joint profits if and only if it has the ray property. (Thus $\bar{x}$ in Figure 2 maximizes joint profits.)

The *cartel point* is the unique point $x^\circ \in C$ which satisfies (6).

II. A Quota Rule

If the cartel were merely to assign the quota $\overset{0}{x}_i$ to member i, where x^0 is the cartel point, it would maximize joint profits provided no member cheated. But of course each member would gain by cheating, even if found out. The assignment would not resolve the prisoners' dilemma. To resolve that dilemma the cartel must assign each member a quota *rule*, an operating rule incorporating a deterrent to cheating; and the deterrent must take the form of a credible threat of retaliation. The cartel has such a rule, and that rule solves the sharing problem as well.

Let

$$s_i = \frac{\overset{0}{x}_i}{\sum_{j=1}^{n} \overset{0}{x}_j}$$

be member i's market share at the cartel point, and consider the following

(10) *Quota Rule for Member* i: Produce

$$\max\{\overset{0}{x}_i, \overset{0}{x}_i + \frac{s_i}{s_j} \Delta x_j\}$$

where Δx_j is the amount by which member j's output deviates from his quota $\overset{0}{x}_j$.[5]

[5] A more complete rule is, "Produce

$$\max\{\overset{0}{x}_i, \overset{0}{x}_i + s_i \sum_{j \in J} \Delta x_j / \sum_{j \in J} s_j\}$$

where each member j in J deviates from his quota by Δx_j." The ensuing discussion applies, *mutatis mutandis*, to this rule as well.

Upon discovering that member j cheats, member i increases his output so that when all the other loyal members increase their outputs according to rule, all market shares are preserved. This rule operates to keep the output vector x on the ray $L(x^0)$; it gives the smallest increase in output that can be shared *pro rata* between the loyal members and that will punish the cheater; it is a "cheapest deterrent."

Member j will not cheat if he expects the other members to obey their quota rules; he (and the other members) would end up somewhere beyond x^0 on the line $L(x^0)$, thus losing profits. The n quota rules, regarded as strategies, form a Nash equilibrium point in the space of all strategies; i.e., no member can gain by a unilateral departure *of any kind* from his assigned quota rule.

Moreover, member j has every reason to expect the other members to follow their quota rules and retaliate to his cheating, for in so doing they will lose less than by standing pat at x_i^0. This important fact can be understood with the help of Figure 3.

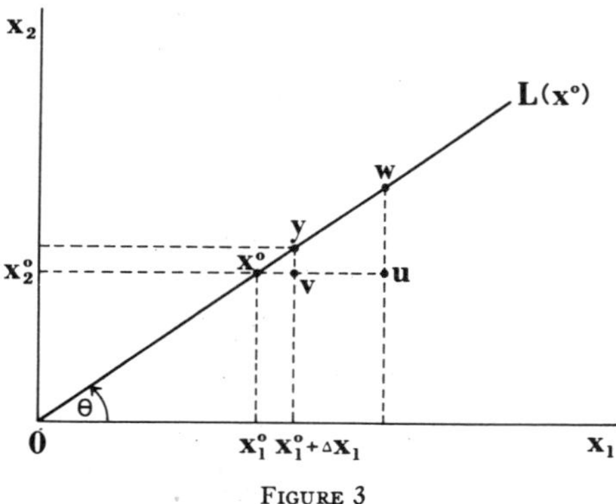

FIGURE 3

If member 1 increases his output by a small amount Δx_1 and member 2 retaliates according to rule, the output vector will move to y. Member 2's profit will change by the amount $\Delta x_1 D_y F_2(x^0)$, where

$$D_y F_2(x^0) = \cos\theta\ \partial F_2(x^0)/\partial x_1 + \sin\theta\ \partial F_2(x^0)/\partial x_2$$

is the directional derivative, in the direction from x^0 to y, of F_2 at x^0. Let

$$d = \sqrt{(x_1^0)^2 + (x_2^0)^2}$$

so that $\cos\theta = \overset{0}{x_1}/d, \quad \sin\theta = \overset{0}{x_2}/d$

then the directional derivative has the form

$$D_y F_2(x^0) = \frac{\overset{0}{x_1}}{d}\frac{\partial F_2(x^0)}{\partial x_1} + \frac{\overset{0}{x_2}}{d}\frac{\partial F_2(x^0)}{\partial x_2}$$

On the other hand, if member 2 stands pat the output vector will move to v and his profit will change by $\Delta x_1 D_v F_2(x^0)$, where

$$D_v F_2(x^0) = \partial F_2(x^0)/\partial x_1$$

is the directional derivative in the direction of v. Member 2 will lose less by retaliating than by standing pat if $D_y F_2(x^0) > D_v F_2(x^0)$, i.e., if

$$\frac{\partial F_2(x^0)}{\partial x_2} > \frac{d - \overset{0}{x_1}}{x_2^0}\frac{\partial F_2(x^0)}{\partial x_1} \tag{11}$$

This inequality certainly holds because the left side is positive and the right side is negative. Hence $F_2(y) > F_2(v)$ and member 2 is better off retaliating than not. The quota rule thus incorporates a credible threat.

It is true that member 2 will not necessarily lose less by retaliating in full to a *large* increase in x_1 (i.e., $F_2(u)$ might be greater than $F_2(w)$, see Figure 3); but he is better off retaliating at least in part, because of (11). And the cheater will lose money by *any* retaliation: since $L(x^0)$ is tangent to his isoprofit surface at x^0 any outward movement along it will reduce his profit. Unlike the prisoners' dilemma, no member is tempted to cheat unless he can escape detection by all members. The quota rule therefore solves the problem of deterring.

The rule also solves the problem of sharing. This is particularly obvious if $F(x)$ has a unique maximizer x^0. Let x' be any proposed solution of the sharing problem. In order to get his cooperation the cartel must allow member i to earn as much per period at x' as he could earn by buying up the other members and becoming a monopolist.[6] As a monopolist member i would obtain $F(x^0)$ per period; to buy out the other members would cost him the capitalized value of their per period profits

$$\sum_{\substack{j=1\\ j\neq i}}^{n} F_j(x')$$

Hence x' must have the property

$$\frac{F_i(x')}{r} \geq \frac{F(x^0)}{r} - \left[\frac{F_1(x')+\ldots+F_{i-1}(x')+F_{i+1}(x')+\ldots F_n(x')}{r}\right]$$

for $i=1,\ldots,n$, where r is the appropriate rate of interest (assuming an infinite time horizon for simplicity). This implies

$$\sum_{i=1}^{n} F_i(x') \geq F(x^0)$$

and since x^0 maximizes $F(x)$ the cooperation can be obtained only at the joint maximum.

A deeper reason why the quota rule solves the sharing problem is found in the ray property of x^0. If a proposed sharing solution x' lacked the ray property then the cartel would have more trouble with the deterring problem. Suppose $L(x')$ is not a ray and let s_i' be member i's market share at x'. If, *first*, the cartel told member i to produce

$$\max\left\{x_i', x_i' + \frac{s_i'}{s_j'}\Delta x_j\right\}$$

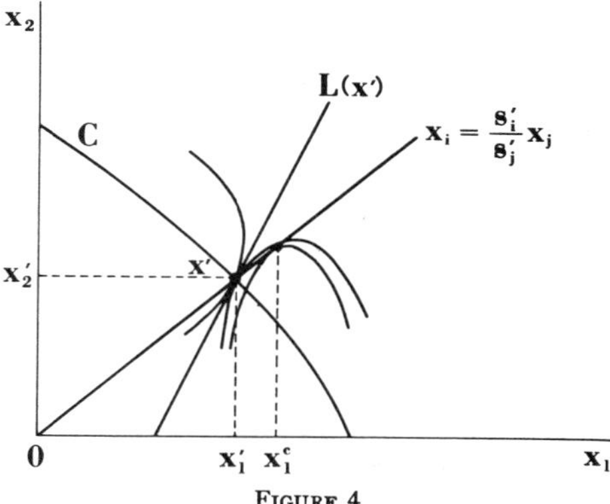

FIGURE 4

then at least one member j would be tempted to cheat even if he were certain to be caught; for in that case x_j' would not maximize $F_j(x)$ against the quota rules of the other members.[7] The ray through x' would intersect a better isoprofit surface of member j than the isoprofit surface through x' (see Figure 4, illustrating how, given member 2's observance of his quota rule, member 1 could get more profit by producing x_1^c than by producing x_1'). Only when a market-sharing quota rule is expressed in terms of a point with the ray property will this temptation disappear. If, *second*, the cartel told member i to produce x_i' if every other member j produces x_j' but to move out along the line $L(x')$ if the others produce more, then some members will lose market share by retaliating. (Only along a ray are the market shares constant.) Those members standing to lose market share would have a less credible threat, and so the deterrent would be weaker.

In case more than one point maximizes joint profits, the unique point that minimizes the variance of profits in M also minimizes jealousy and resentment; it is an obvious "focal point" (see Thomas Schelling).

[6] This possibility may not exist in the case of an international cartel of nationalized firms.

[7] The set of quota rules would not be a Nash equilibrium point.

The quota rule (10) thus neatly solves the sharing and deterring problems in one fell swoop. We cannot expect it to be overlooked by cartels which are able to solve their other problems. Their managers may have been to Harvard Business School.

III. Nonmember and Locating Problems

Part of the problem of locating the contract surface is to predict the behavior of the firms that remain outside the cartel. Variations in the total output of these firms change the members' profit functions and thus shift the contract surface about. As these variations are likely to depend on the cartel's output the contract surface is not exogenously given, but varies with cartel production. In the best case—from the point of view of a cartel which cannot control it—the external production is wholly predictable, a known function of cartel production. To each cartel output there will then correspond one position of the contract surface, and the cartel will be able to choose the output which places the surface in the best position.

The external firms are likely to behave as Cournot followers. The cartel can then act as a Stackelberg leader, maximizing its profit subject to the Cournot reaction functions of the external firms. In this position, though its profit will be lower than it would be if no external firms existed, the cartel is doing the best it can subject to the existence of such firms. Total industry profit will not be maximized, but it will be be positive.[8] We should not underestimate this problem, but neither should we exaggerate it; it does not appear to be a source of inherent instability in itself, but is most serious in connection with the detection problem.

The other, and more important, parts of the location problem are not so much sources of instability to actual cartels as obstacles that many potential cartels never overcome. Bjarke Fog has reported some of the differences of opinion that prevent the formation of cartels. People have differing views about the availability of substitutes, differing expectations about the future course of the market, and differing time preferences. The latter is especially troublesome. If some member j takes a longer view than the majority, more lightly discounting the future, he might well think that the contract surface is higher, i.e., that F is maximized by a larger x than the majority thinks. He will reckon the present value of his earnings to be higher at an output larger than x_j^0; he will "cheat" and be better off (in his own view) even if the other members retaliate according to rule. Obviously, if the members can't agree on the joint profit-maximizing output they will not agree on their shares.[9] Still, these differences are sometimes resolved. Cartels do get formed. In any case public policy can do little to exacerbate the locating problem. Perhaps we could adopt a policy of deliberate misinformation, making demand appear to be more elastic than it is.[10]

IV. Detecting

It is to the problem of detecting cheating that we must turn for a source of instability more amenable to public policy. This problem is not inherently insoluble (suppose there are only two members), but it is difficult. George Stigler has studied

[8] If new entry can occur the cartel might practice limit pricing, along the lines considered by Morton Kamien and Nancy Schwartz, or the author.

[9] Cartels composed of national and private firms are especially prone to this source of disagreement. The nationalized firms, especially in underdeveloped countries, are likely to take the *shorter* view. Owing to frequent changes of government, the civil servants and politicians who make the decisions must discount the future very heavily.

[10] With respect to the demand for crude oil, the opposite effect is achieved by the civil servants and political figures in the consuming countries who soberly extrapolate the yearly growth of consumption of $3 oil to determine the "national needs" for $10 oil.

some aspects of the problem; to his excellent discussion I have only a little to add.

With respect to output a cartel could find itself in one of four positions. First, it could know the output of each member (perhaps after a brief lag). In this position the cartel has solved the detection problem completely, and can adopt the quota rule explained above. Second, the cartel can know the total output of all members taken together, but not the output of individual members. In this second-best position the cartel can modify the quota rule and still preserve some of its deterrent effect.

(12) *Modified Quota Rule for Member i*:

Produce $\max\{x_i^0, x_i^0 + ns_iz\}$

where $1/n$ is the average quota share and z is the amount by which cartel output deviates from

$$\sum_{i=1}^{n} x_i^0$$

Member i is thus told to assume that the unknown cheater has an average quota, and to increase output accordingly.

This modified rule operates to keep the *expected* output vector on $L(x^0)$; it incorporates a credible threat, just as rule (10) does, and thus deters cheating on the average, but it might not deter cheating by any member with an exceptionally small quota. Such a member might still gain profit by cheating because his actual market share increases enough to overmatch the price depressing effect of the greater total cartel output. This problem is more severe the greater the variance of quota shares. One possible solution is to modify rule (10) in a different manner—to tell member i to produce the larger of x_i^0 and $x_i^0+(s_i/s^*)z$, where s^* is the smallest quota share. This will deter, but perhaps at a cost which is unnecessarily high (an unduly large increase in cartel output). Other modifications could be considered, but none can be wholly effective. This second position is therefore a true second best.

Third, the cartel could know the total industry output, but not the total output of the cartel. Evidently, this position can arise only when some producers remain outside the cartel; with respect to the detection problem it is equivalent to the fourth position, in which the cartel is ignorant of total industry output. These are the positions in which public policy must try to place cartels.

Given the fondness of the bureaucracy of all developed nations for publishing output statistics (some of them useful), public policy cannot place *domestic* cartels in the third or fourth positions. But if some important producers remain independent, the situation is different in the case of international cartels. We can illustrate with reference to the *OPEC* cartel.

With only the shortest of lags, world shipments of crude oil are known by all interested parties. The information is collected and reported by trade journals and various national and international agencies, and could in any case be inferred from a number of sources (for example, tanker charterings). All producers know their current market shares to a high degree of accuracy, and can thus learn if someone is cheating; they cannot so easily learn *who* is cheating. The members are sovereign states; they can attempt to keep their sales statistics secret if they wish. And some important producers (for example, Mexico) remain outside the cartel. *OPEC* thus finds itself in the third of the four positions. The likely consequences are a matter for speculation, but the following events are possible.

An increase in world shipments reduces the market shares of the loyal members who, however, cannot detect its source. If they assume the source to be external and remain at x_i^0 they will, in effect, demonstrate the profitability of cheating; those least loyal to the cartel will then secretly increase their output. On the other hand, if the loyal members assume the source to be internal and obey their quota rules (however modified), they will risk a needless increase in cartel output. With either choice the additional cartel output, added to the original increase from the unknown source, reduces prices. Distrust grows. Discipline weakens generally, and can be expected ultimately to disappear. Each member must look out for himself. Plenty of business can be done at a dollar under the cartel price; but it must be done quickly, for the buyers are daily demanding better terms. There is a general scurry for orders, and long-term commitments are made at $1, then $2, then $5 and $6 under the cartel price. The cartel has collapsed.

This outcome is by no means certain; it is possible, and we must nurture the possibility. It will be *impossible* if the consuming nations establish a central purchasing agency through which all orders are funneled. Sellers will be identified. Undetected cheating will be impossible and known by all to be impossible. The agency will have solved the severest problem that the cartel faced, thus placing it in the first of the four positions. In these circumstances who would be rash enough to predict anything but a *stable* oil cartel?

V. Summary

A cartel is inherently unstable only if it faces inherently insoluble problems. Of the five problems that we noticed, the three most serious are those of locating the contract surface, which requires information about demand and costs, predicting and if possible discouraging production by external firms (which affects the demands for members' output and is thus a species of the location problem), and detecting cheating by members. We considered these problems only in enough detail to see that, while difficult, they are not inherently insoluble. The two remaining problems are to determine quotas and deter cheating. We treated them jointly because a good solution of the one also solves the other, and we saw that a quota rule expressed in terms of the ray through the cartel point deters cheating (unless it is undetected) and embodies a credible threat of retaliation. This rule has the further advantages of being the simplest rule with that property and requiring the smallest retaliatory increase in output that can be shared *pro rata* by the loyal members. Thus the sharing and deterring problems are not inherently insoluble either. A cartel is not inherently unstable.

From this it does not follow that a cartel is stable. Though it can solve its problems in principle, it might nevertheless fail to solve them in practice. But to recognize that a cartel might collapse because it cannot control external production or detect cheating is quite different from believing that all are necessarily doomed. So much depends on the particular features of their environments that no general prediction about the durability of cartels is justified.[11]

[11] Note added in proof: Further research into cartel history, undertaken after this article was written, convinces me that there is one justifiable prediction: a cartel will last—possibly succumbing to epidemics of cheating from time to time, but soon thereafter re-forming itself—until new substitutes appear at a price near its marginal cost. I can find no record of a cartel which died of internal problems alone, but plenty which fell to new substitutes. I therefore regret my suggestion that external production is a problem comparable to the internal ones. It is not; it is the one fatal problem. But this does not mean that collective purchasing would only be a trivial mistake. It would still delay and shorten the outbreaks of price competition that normally occur from time to time even in cartels protected from substitutes; but more significantly, it would also delay, and possibly prevent, the development of substitutes. The delegates to the collective purchasing agencies would sooner or later vest their interest in the orderly operation of established arrangements, and would perceive new substitutes as nothing more than a threat to settled practice. This they naturally would resist.

A cartel of raw material producers is well placed with respect to the nonmember problem. Its chief difficulty is the detection of cheating, a problem that public policy should exacerbate if possible and avoid solving in any case. The correct policy here as in so many areas is more easily expressed in negative than in positive terms: Take no action that will lead to the identification of individual transactors—it will only discourage cheating and preserve the cartel.

Though we considered the detection problem with reference to *OPEC* the analysis applies more generally. The success of this cartel has planted seeds in many minds in those countries which export primary materials. We can expect some of them to bear fruit, the more so if an international oil-buying agency keeps *OPEC* in business. We will hear proposals for the establishment of international agencies to present a "united front" to the banana, coffee, copper, tin, . . . , and bauxite cartels, to share the reduced output "on an equitable basis," or, depending on who does the proposing, to guarantee to the cartel an "orderly marketing arrangement" in exchange for a dollar or two off its price. These proposals are gravely mistaken.

REFERENCES

M. A. Adelman, *The World Petroleum Market,* London, Baltimore 1972.

J. S. Bain, "Output Quotas in Imperfect Cartels," *Quart. J. Econ.,* Aug. 1948, *62,* 617–22.

B. Fog, "How Are Cartel Prices Determined?," *J. Ind. Econ.,* Nov. 1956, *5,* 16–23.

J. R. Hicks, *Value and Capital,* 2d ed., Oxford 1946.

M. I. Kamien and N. L. Schwartz, "Limit Pricing and Uncertain Entry," *Econometrica,* May 1971, *39,* 441–54.

R. D. Luce and H. Raiffa, *Games and Decisions,* New York 1957.

D. K. Osborne, "On the Rationality of Limit Pricing," *J. Ind. Econ.,* Sept. 1973, *22,* 71–80.

D. Patinkin, "Multi-Plant Firms, Cartels, and Imperfect Competition," *Quart. J. Econ.,* Feb. 1947, *61,* 173–205.

T. Schelling, *The Strategy of Conflict,* Cambridge 1960.

G. J. Stigler, "A Theory of Oligopoly," *J. Polit. Econ.,* Feb. 1964, *72,* 44–61.

[10]

Journal of Economic Literature
Vol. XXI (September 1983), pp. 981–990

Contestable Markets and the Theory of Industry Structure: A Review Article*

By MICHAEL SPENCE
Harvard University

THE NEW BOOK by William J. Baumol, John C. Panzar and Robert D. Willig is the culmination of several years of research on the related problems of understanding multiproduct cost structures and their implications for competition and market performance. It is a significant book for several reasons. The empirical reality that forms the starting point for the theoretical work is, I think, widely recognized to be important. Cost structures constitute one of the foundations of competitive strategy, and strongly influence industry structure. Notwithstanding this fact, the amount of microeconomic theory directed toward competitively relevant attributes of costs has been, if not minimal, then certainly more limited than the subject deserves. In fact, prior to the work of our authors, economists and business strategists did not have a language or a set of concepts with which to talk precisely about scale economies in a multiproduct setting. We now have at least the beginnings of such a language, and a body of theory that provides a grammar for using it.

The theory of contestable markets was the subject of Baumol's presidential address at the American Economic Association meetings in Washington in December 1981. Both the theory and its presentation have generated controversy, useful controversy I think, because it helps clarify issues that need attention. I shall have remarks to offer later in this review concerning the normative and descriptive relevance of the contestable markets hypothesis.

My plan for this review is as follows. I begin by outlining some of the principal definitions and propositions of the theory. This outline should not be mistaken for a complete summary of the book. But the economist who has not yet read the book needs a reasonably detailed picture of the approach. Few of the propositions require long proofs: in fact once they are stated, the proofs are often simple exercises.

Having outlined some of the principal concepts, I comment upon their usefulness for understanding markets. And finally, I conclude by suggesting some ways in which the general subject may be pursued from this point forward.

What Is the Theory of the Contestable Market?

This theory is best thought of as a generalization of the theory of perfect competition. As students of microeconomic theory know, the conditions under which perfectly competitive outcomes are likely or possible, are rather stringent. The conditions include constant or diminishing returns to scale, or scale economies that are small in relation to the size of the market. For normative purposes, the absence of externalities at the level of costs is also essential. Contestable markets theory says nothing at the moment about externalities.

* *Contestable Markets and the Theory of Industry Structure.* By William J. Baumol, John C. Panzar and Robert D. Willig. New York: Harcourt, Brace Jovanovich, Inc., 1982.

But it does tackle the problem of scale economies head on.

At one level, then, the theory is an attempt to provide a substitute for the theory of perfect competition, one that is applicable in a world characterized by scale economies or by the multiproduct analogues or scale economies. Perfect competition theory serves two functions in economics. It is sometimes a reasonable approximation to reality in the descriptive sense, and perhaps more importantly it is a welfare standard. In the absence of externalities, perfectly competitive equilibria are Pareto optimal. The problem is that such equilibria do not exist in certain market environments. And even when they do, it is sometimes hard to believe that the competitive model accurately describes what is taking place.

The contestable market theory then provides a more robust welfare standard. In particular, it locates or points to properties of efficient vectors of prices. Still more important, it deals with efficient (in the sense of cost minimizing) industry structures. The efficient industry structure issue does not quite disappear in the perfectly competitive world, but it isn't very interesting or visible. With scale economies and multiproduct firms, it is.

The critical assumption in perfect competition is price-taking behavior. The reader is entitled to know what behavioral postulate replaces price-taking in the new theory and serves the same or a similar role. The answer is entry. Entry is free in the sense that there are potential competitors with the same cost functions, who can enter and leave without loss of capital within the time frame required for incumbents to change prices. Lest the reader close the *Journal* at this point, remember that we are talking for the moment about a theory that provides a normative standard against which market outcomes can be judged. There may also be conditions under which the theory is a reasonable descriptive approximation to reality as well. But I want to defer that discussion until later.

As said, the theory replaces price-taking with rapid entry and exit. It then focusses on cost structures, principally multiproduct cost structures in an attempt to identify the properties of those costs that influence industry structure, cost minimizing configurations, and market performance.

What is set aside in the theory are elements of strategic interaction that we have come to associate with entry deterrence; matters such as preempting market positions by making irreversible moves first. These strategic problems are set aside because they arise in contexts in which entry or investment or both are at least partially irreversible: i.e., in contexts in which there are sunk costs. It is quite clear the authors are aware that these strategic or game theoretic problems have been set aside. The debate will center on the empirical importance of some of these deliberately neglected aspects of industry structure. The book and Baumol's presidential address might have been clearer on the range of applicability of the models. Though sunk costs and related aspects of structure are important influences on the dynamic aspects of competition, I think it perfectly appropriate to develop a theory that focusses on some other important structural aspect of many markets. It is neither fair nor reasonable to require microeconomic models to capture all relevant aspects of reality. No model that is tractable and informative does. The only caution is that because models do leave things out, one needs to exercise some discretion and judgment in using them.

Some Critical Definitions, Concepts and Propositions

All firms have the same cost function, $c(.)$. Let y^i be the vector of outputs of firm i, and let m be the number of firms. $Q(p)$ is industry multiproduct demand, and p is the vector of prices. An industry configuration is a vector $(m, y^1, \ldots, y^m, p)$.

DEF: $(m, y^1, \ldots, y^m, p)$ is a feasible configuration if

$$\sum_{i=1}^{m} y^i = Q(p),$$
$$py^i - c(y^i) \geq 0, \; i = 1, \ldots, m, \tag{1}$$
$$\text{and } y^i \geq 0.$$

That is to say, a configuration is feasible if production is sufficient to meet demand, and no firm is losing money.

DEF: $(m, y^1, \ldots, y^m, p)$ is sustainable if it is

(1) feasible and

(2) $p^e y^e \geq c(y^e)$ for all $p^e \geq p$ and $y^e \geq Q(p^e)$. (2)

No outside potential competitor can enter by cutting prices and make money supplying quantities that do not exceed total market demands at those prices.

DEF: A perfectly contestable market is a market in which sustainability is a necessary condition for equilibrium: (3)

i.e., a contestable market is one subject to hit-and-run entry. It is not prefectly clear what else is required for an equilibrium. Were it not for hit-and-run entry, some firm might want to lower its quantity and raise prices. But hit-and-run entry prevents positive profits. I think it is acceptable to think of a sustainable configuration as an equilibrium of a particular kind.

DEF: $(m, y^1, \ldots, y^m, p)$ is a long-run equilibrium if it is feasible and if for all y, $py \geq c(y)$. (4)

This is the conventional definition of equilibrium. No firm is losing money, and at the prevailing prices, no firm (incumbent or potential entrant) can find a vector of outputs that makes money.

PROP: A long-run equilibrium is sustainable. (5)

PROP: A sustainable configuration is not necessarily a long-run equilibrium. (6)

Both of these propositions follow automatically from the definitions. If a configuration is a long run equilibrium, then there is no output vector y that is profitable. Thus there is no output vector $y \geq Q(p)$ that is profitable. Cutting price won't help. Thus there is no $p \geq p$ and $y \geq Q(\bar{p})$ that is profitable. So the configuration is sustainable by definition. On the other hand, a single firm with declining average costs in a single product industry pricing at average cost is sustainable but not a long-run equilibrium. Remember that "long-run equilibrium" is a technical term. A long-run equilibrium involves price-taking behavior. Price-taking is the more stringent concept, because it doesn't require the firm to imagine that it is constrained by the market demand. In the presence of scale economies, that difference is not trivial. One might object that a monopoly will not take prices as given. That is precisely the point. Moreover it won't set marginal revenue equal to marginal cost; it is faced with potential competition. Contestable market theory is a theory of what it will do. The competing theory is conventional entry theory, which has its problems.

What then are the properties of sustainable outcomes? In what follows, superscripts refer to firms and subscripts to products.

PROP: If $(m, y^1, \ldots, y^m, p)$ is sustainable then

(1) $py^i - c(y^i) = 0$: zero profit,

(2) let the set of products be $N = \{1, \ldots, n\}$. Let S be a subset of N. Then $P_S y_S^i \geq c(y^i) - c(y_{N\text{-}S}^i)$. (7)

(3) $P_j \geq \partial\, c(y^i)/\partial y_j^i$.

The notion y_S means a vector with elements equal to those of y for products k in the set S, and zeros elsewhere. The zero profit property is clear cut. Property 2 says that the revenues from a subset of the products exceed the incremental costs of those products. If that weren't true the firm could drop that subset and make money. Note that from (1), each firm is breaking even on the full set. The third part states that prices are at or above marginal costs. Otherwise the firm could reduce y_j, and make money, counter to the sustainability hypothesis.

PROP: If $(m, y^1, \ldots, y^m, p)$ is sustainable and if $y_j^k < \sum_{i-1}^{m} y_j^i$, then $P_j = \partial c(y^k)/\partial y_j^k$. (8)

That is to say if more than one firm is supplying a good, its price is equal to marginal cost for all supplying firms, who must therefore have the same marginal cost for that good.

PROOF: Given the assumptions of the proposition, if $P_j > \partial c(y^k)/\partial y_j^k$, then someone could enter supplying the vector $y^k + \epsilon e_j \geq Q(p)$, and $\epsilon > 0$, and make positive profits counter to sustainability.

PROP: If $(m, y^1, \ldots y^m, p)$ is sustainable and if some other set of output vectors $(\bar{y}^1, \ldots, \bar{y}^n)$ produces the same industry output, $\sum_j \bar{y}^j = \sum_i$, then $\sum_j c(\bar{y}^j) \geq \sum_i c(y^i)$. (9)

This proposition says that sustainable configurations are cost-minimizing configurations for the industry. In outline, the argument is as follows: if the proposition were not true then we could find a lower cost output mix across firms. But that would imply that industry profits with the new output vector are positive because industry revenues are the same and costs are lower. That in turn implies that there is at least one profitable firm. By definition, that is inconsistent with sustainability of the original set of output vectors. In summary, if an industry is not minimizing costs, costless entry will cause the industry configuration to change, so that the starting point cannot be an equilibrium.

These propositions are simultaneously quite simple and quite powerful in characterizing industry outcomes. Of course hit-and-run entry is a powerful constraining force. It is also striking how elegantly certain aspects of the multiproduct case are handled. It is not much more complicated than the single product case.

At this point, it is tempting to digress to discuss the important question of the circumstances under which the theory is a good description of reality. I will resist that temptation (with the promise to return to it later) in order to pursue the logic of the authors' conceptual apparatus.

It is clear from the propositions above that hit-and-run entry eliminates technical inefficiency at the industry level. It also eliminated "excess" profits though that is not the same as achieving constrained allocative efficiency as we know from Ramsey pricing theory. The reader will find a discussion of Ramsey optimal prices in Baumol and David Bradford (1970). Ramsey optimal prices are optimal (meaning surplus maximizing) prices when there is a binding non-negative profit constraint.

The question naturally arises, what do efficient industry structures (i.e., vectors, $y^1, \ldots, y^m$) look like and on what properties of the cost function do they depend? One might ask "Who cares?" if the market gets it right whatever it (meaning cost-minimizing structure) is. But, of course, not all markets actually function this way. And thus if one wants to be able to compare actual market structures with industry cost-minimizing ones, then it is important to be able to map properties of cost functions into efficient market structures. The authors have made significant progress in this difficult area.[1]

Multiproduct Cost Structures

The following is a partial outline of the treatment of multiproduct cost structures as it is developed in the book.

Let $P = \{T_1, \ldots, T_k\}$ be a non-trivial partition of SN (a nontrivial partition is a set of non-empty disjoint subsets of a larger set, whose union is the larger set).

DEF: There are strict economies of scope at y_S with respect to the partition P if (10)

$$\sum_{i=1}^{k} c(y_{T_i}) > c(y_S).$$

The term on the left side is the total cost of producing the bundle of goods y_S in k distinct firms, while the term on the right is the cost of producing y_S with a single firm. If the strict inequality is replaced by equal to or greater than, then the economies of scope are said to be weak. That is, there is no loss from multiproduct operations, and there may be a gain. Economies of scope occur when it is cheaper to produce y_S than the components $y_{T_1}, \ldots, y_{T_k}$ separately.[2]

The authors also need to be able to talk about scale economies in a multiproduct setting. Un-

[1] One might object that if the object is to study technically efficient industry structures, why not take the problem directly. The book convinced me that hit-and-run entry is not a bad analytical device for studying multiproduct, multifirm cost minimization problems.

[2] Economies of scale and scope are referred to as global if they occur at every point, and in the case of economies of scope, with respect to all partitions of N.

like the single product case, there is no single measure of scale economies in the multiproduct setting. But there are properties of the cost function that are closely akin to single-product scale economies, that influence cost minimizing industry configurations.

The authors measure scale economies in several ways. One relevant type of scale economy occurs along a ray pointing out from the origin. Define the function $f(t) = c(ty)/t$, where t is a scalar, and let $\nabla c(y)$ stand for the gradient of the function $c(y)$. It is the vector of first partial derivatives of $c(y)$, i.e. $c(y) = (\partial c/\partial y_1, \ldots, \partial c/\partial y_k)$. Then differentiating log $f(t)$ with respect to log t we have:

$$\frac{d\log f}{d\log t} = \frac{y\nabla c(y)}{c}, \tag{11}$$

at $t = 1$. This ratio tells us the percentage increase in costs per percentage point increase in output, with the proportions of various products in the output vector held constant. The degree of scale economies $s_N(y)$ is defined to be the inverse of this derivative:

$$s_N(y) = c/[y\nabla c(y)]. \tag{12}$$

Thus if $s_N(y) = 1$, costs increase in percentage terms on a one for one basis with percentage changes in output along a ray. If $s_N(y) > 1$, costs increase less than output, i.e., there are economies of scale. And if $s_N(y) < 1$, costs increase more than output, i.e., there are diseconomies of scale.

In addition to scale economies along a ray, there are incremental costs. Let TN be a proper subset of N. The incremental cost of y_T, starting from $y - y_T$, is

$$IC_T(y) = c(y) - c(y_{N-T}). \tag{13}$$

Average incremental cost is

$$AIC_T(y) = IC_T(y)/\left[\sum_{j\epsilon T} y_j\right]. \tag{14}$$

The sum in the denominator seems slightly odd as it involves adding non-comparable units, unless T has one element. I have no explanation for why this particular measure of average incremental costs is the right one to adopt. Incremental costs are costs associated with adding products to the bundle.

There is another concept that proves useful, called trans-ray convexity. It is related to the shapes of iso-cost curves, and it will not be surprising to economists that the properties of these are relevant.

DEF: $c(y)$ is trans-ray convex through y^* if there exist $w_1, \ldots, w_n$, with $w_i > 0$ such that for all y^a and y^b in the plane $\Sigma(w_i y_i - y_i^*) = 0$ and for any $\alpha \epsilon (0, 1)$ (15)

$$c(\alpha y^a + (1-\alpha)y^b) \leq \alpha c(y^a) + (1-\alpha)c(y^b). \tag{16}$$

Trans-ray convexity requires that the production cost of a weighted average of a pair of output bundles, y^a and y^b, is not greater than the weighted average of the costs of producing each of them in isolation. That is to say, complementarities in production outweigh scale effects. A graph of this concept can be found in Baumol, Bailey and Willig (1977).

As far as I can tell, trans-ray convexity is a very strong restriction. Let me illustrate. Suppose there are two goods, and that the cost function is

$$c(y) = F(y_1 + y_2)$$

with F concave, so that there are economies of scale. Think of this case as the same good produced subject to economies of scale, and sold into distinct markets, as in an international trade setting. Here I follow the standard economic convention of identifying goods not only by their production technologies but also by the markets into which they are sold.

There are clearly economies of scope since

$$\begin{aligned} c(y) &= F(y_1 + y_2) < F(y_1) + F(y_2) \\ &= c(y_1, 0) + c(0, y_2). \end{aligned} \tag{17}$$

On the other hand, select any pair of output vectors, y^a and y_b. Then, with $e = (1,1)$, we have,

$$\begin{aligned} c(\alpha y^a &+ (1-\alpha)y^b) \\ &= F(\alpha y^a \cdot e + (1-\alpha)y^b \cdot e) \\ &\leq \alpha F(y^a \cdot e) + (1-\alpha)F(y^b \cdot e) \\ &= \alpha c(y^a) + (1-\alpha)c(y^b). \end{aligned} \tag{18}$$

Further, the inequality holds only if $y^a \cdot e = y^b \cdot e$. Thus this particular multiproduct cost function which exhibits strong economies of scope induced by scale economies, nevertheless is weakly trans-ray convex. That is to say, in terms of the definition, with $w_1 = w_2 = 1$,

$$c(\alpha y^a + (1-\alpha)y^b) = \alpha c(y^a) + (1-\alpha)c(y^b). \quad (19)$$

For all other weights, the inequality is the opposite of that required for trans-ray convexity.

One important source of economies of scope is economies of scale in components of costs that are shared by several products. But at least in the example above, this type of economy of scope does not seem to lead to trans-ray convexity in a strong form. At the moment, I am not able to provide a further exposition of circumstances that will lead to trans-ray convexity. The importance of the concept lies in the fact that it is required to ensure that Ramsey optimal prices are sustainable.

The following propositions characterize outcomes in perfectly contestable markets.

PROP: A multiproduct firm must have weak economies of scope over the set of goods it produces. If the cost function exhibits strict economies of scope at all points, then there must be at least one multiproduct firm. (20)

PROP: Any product with declining average incremental costs throughout is produced by a single firm. (21)

PROP: If all goods have product-specific economies of scale and if there are economies of scope among them all, then there will be only one firm. (22)

PROP: Trans-ray convexity and economies of scale at every point imply that there will be a monopoly.[3] (23)

PROP: If there are two or more firms producing each good, the outcome is first best optimal. (24)

REMARK: I remind the reader that there are no externalities on the cost side (spillovers, shared learning, depletion of resources) and there is no imperfect competition among firms protected by entry barriers of the conventional type. Thus the proposition follows directly from the fact that any good with two or more producers is priced at marginal cost in any sustainable configuration.

Sunk Costs, Fixed Costs, Entry and Economies of Scale

A certain amount of controversy has centered around the notion of hit-and-run entry and its relation to scale economies. Martin Weitzman has argues that with very rapid entry and exit, there can't be scale economies (Martin Weitzman, 1982). Let me begin by noting that for hit-and-run entry one needs essentially two assumptions:

(1) If t is the response time required for incumbents to make price changes and if τ is the period for which a new entrant's costs are sunk, after which the investment is costlessly reversible, then $t > \tau$.

(2) Demand responds instantaneously to price changes or to price differentials. Under these conditions, entry directly constrains market prices in the manner described by the theory. If demand fails to respond instantly, then entrants do not receive the full return on their investment immediately. That will deter entry and alter the ground rules in comparison with contestable market theory.

The Theory as a Descriptive Model

There are two possible objections to this theory as a descriptive model. One is that the assumptions, particularly (1) above, are usually not satisfied. That is an empirical issue. It seems to me that scale economies and sunk costs, that is, costs not consistent with assumption (1), are positively though not perfectly correlated in reality. My personal view is that the range of applicability of the theory as a descriptive tool for analyzing short and medium run industry configurations is limited by the widespread existence of partial irreversibility of investment. And while point (2) is a simplification we often

[3] And under the same conditions, a monopoly charging Ramsey optimal prices is a sustainable configuration. There are certain other technical conditions required for this second deduction. Ramsey optimal prices in a multiproduct context are prices that emerge from maximizing the total surplus subject to a non-negative profit constraint. For a thorough treatment, see Baumol and Bradford (1970).

adopt, it is also at best a crude approximation. And here it is perhaps somewhat more crucial than elsewhere, for it is reasonably well known that sluggishness on the demand side creates market power, and sometimes entry barriers.

I do not mean to suggest that there are no cases in which capital or resources or both are sufficiently reversibly mobile to make the model descriptively useful. In some of the service industries the conditions may be met. If capital can be rented and has multiple uses, one can see the potential applicability of the model. It is useful to remember that the theory does not predict a great deal of actual entry and exit. It is the potential entry that constrains structure and price.

The second kind of objection is related more to the logic of the model than to its empirical relevance. Suppose that the cost function exhibits scale economies, but that rapid costless entry and exit are possible. A firm could produce at efficient scale for short bursts, cease production and sell the product off over an interval which is a multiple of the production interval. The multiple would be set equal to the ratio of minimum efficient scale to quantity demanded at the price equal to average cost at minimum efficient scale. By making the intervals short without changing this ratio, the carrying cost of the inventory can be eliminated, so that average costs approach the theoretical minimum, even when the market is smaller than minimum efficient scale.

For example, suppose that minimum efficient scale is 1000 units per month, but that the market will absorb only 100 units per month. With costless entry and exit, you can produce for a week, a day, an hour etc. and then stop and resume production after 10 weeks, days, hours etc. As the interval is shortened, the average stocks of inventory decline, and hence the inventory carrying cost. In the limit, average costs are at the minimum. The conclusion is that with costless entry and exit, minimizing costs with respect to output over time leads to a cost function that exhibits *constant* returns to scale. That is the essence of the Weitzman argument. This argument assumes that the goods are not perishable.

Economies of scale will not be eliminated by hit-and-run entry of this type if (1) there are sunk costs which impede hit-and-run entry or, (2) the good is perishable in the sense that it must be delivered at the time it is produced (example: flying on an airplane), or (3) production takes time regardless of the scale. The last would prevent the complete elimination of inventory carrying costs. The second eliminates the possibility of inventories, and the first makes the "run" part of hit-and-run entry expensive or impossible.

Sunk costs would include the cost of shutting down and opening up plants (labor, machine set-up, etc.). These are generally not proportional to the time interval. They are more like fixed costs, and they would and do offset inventory carrying cost reductions. This kind of cost restores scale economies, but also gets in the way of hit-and-run entry.

Once again it is an empirical issue whether there is a significant subset of industries or markets for which hit-and-run constraints are a reasonable approximation to reality. There are certainly major industries in which the product is not storable. The service industries present numerous examples. In addition, the services associated with selling most goods are not storable. Thus it seems plausible that for many goods, the package, consisting of the physical good and some associated services that is delivered to consumers, is not perfectly storable. The implication is that there may be returns to scale without sunk costs. On the other hand, I am not yet persuaded that sunk costs are negligible for most goods. But my impressions should not substitute for empirical research. The Weitzman argument is helpful clarifying some of the issues concerning the range of applicability of the theory as a descriptive model.

How We Can Use the Theory

My judgment is that the theory's use is primarily in the analysis of multiproduct costs and efficient industry structures, and in providing a welfare standard that is more relevant and useful than the perfect competition paradigm in industries characterized by returns to scale and scope of a variety of kinds. These applications of the theory do not require us to throw out the concepts of sunk costs, irreversibility and strategy.

Stepping back from contestable market models, observed industry equilibria are the product of a number of elements of structure. Among them are:

1. costs or technology
2. demand
3. irreversibility
4. competitive or strategic interactions

The contestable market theory focuses on costs and technology. Demand plays a minimal role. The only role for demand functions in contestable market theory is to set the size of the various markets. Roughly, the market sizes are the levels of demand when prices are in the neighborhood of average costs. The properties of demand at prices above marginal or average costs are not centrally important in this theory. These properties of demand functions *are* crucial in other models such as those that deal with product differentiation and monopolistic competition. Structure and conduct falling under (3) are assumed away and strategic behavior (4) isn't plausible in the absence of (3).

Thus, to summarize, the applications of the theory seem to me to be

(a) in studying cost structures in all markets
(b) in analyzing normative properties of equilibria in all markets
(c) and in descriptive analysis in industries in which the good is perishable (services) and in which sunk costs are minimal.

I also have a strong feeling, for which I cannot give a rigorous defense, that in the long run, costs and technology ultimately dominate the fine structure of demand, while sunk costs give rise to the vagaries of history and the play of competitive strategy in determining industry structure. This feeling is based partly upon (or is perhaps equivalent to) another intuition or conjecture, and that is that entry barriers lack permanence or durability. If this is correct, it follows that for certain analytical purposes relating to the long-run evolution of industries, the theory's range of descriptive applicability may be greater than many of us whose eyes are trained mainly upon competitive strategy and entry barriers might imagine.

Welfare Analysis

Chapter 11 of the book contains some interesting welfare analysis of sustainable industry configurations. I summarize the section on normative analysis briefly.

The authors discuss three different forms of a Ramsey optimum. Let $w(p)$ be the multiproduct surplus.

(1) A viable industry Ramsey optimum (VIRO) is the solution to the problem:

$$\max W(p) + \sum_{i=1}^{m} (py^i - c(y^i))$$
$$\text{subject to} \qquad (25)$$
$$Q(p) = \sum_i y^i \text{ and } \sum_i py^i - c(y^i) \geq 0.$$

Generally, there may be an unprofitable firm in the solution to the problem above, so that the solution would not be a sustainable configuration. The reason for the unprofitable firm is that the constraint only prevents industry profits from falling below zero. If in the solution, all firms are alike, then each will be profitable. But if the solution requires asymmetries among firms, as it may well, then there is no guarantee that all will be profitable.

The second and more stringent welfare standard is

(2) The Viable Firm Ramsey Optimum (VFRO): It is the solution to

$$\max W(p) + \sum_{i=1}^{m} (py^i - c(y^i))$$
$$\text{subject to} \qquad (26)$$
$$Q(p) = \Sigma y^i \text{ and } py^i - c(y^i) \geq 0, \text{ for all } i.$$

Obviously requiring every firm to be profitable will force the industry to be profitable. Thus the constraints in the VFRO are more stringent than in the VIRO—i.e., the feasible set is smaller. Generally in the solution to this problem, two firms producing the same product will not necessarily have equal marginal costs for that product. The reason is that there will be firm specific multipliers associated with the constraints $py^i \geq c(y^i)$. If the solution requires asymmetries among firms as it may well, then the multipliers will differ among firms. Since prices are uniform, marginal costs will differ across firms as a result. The solution will not, in those cases, be sustainable.

The third welfare standard is referred to as

the Autarkic Ramsey Optimum (ARO). An autarkic Ramsey optimum is a feasible configuration $(p, m, y^1, \ldots, y^m)$ with the property that no firm can find prices $\bar{p}$ and output $\bar{y}$ that increase the value of

$$W(p) + p \cdot \bar{y} - c(y) \qquad (27)$$

taking other firms' prices and quantities as given and subject to the constraint that revenues cover costs. Welfare here would be lower than with the other two cases because the conditions are more restrictive. In fact the constraints in the ARO are those in the viable firm optimum (VFRO), but with the additional constraints that no firms can break away and increase the sum of its profits and the consumer surplus.

The authors' conjecture that an ARO is sustainable. If true, that is quite an important proposition.

Other Thoughts and a Few Criticisms

I have a few relatively minor complaints about the book in its present form. It is very much in need of a road map for the reader, an explanation of which chapters do what and why. At the moment, one does not know as one reads along when one is building a new block of the analysis, continuing an old one, or embellishing something already established. It is hard to separate important definitions and concepts from others of secondary interest. And several of the theorems are hard to follow. The reader has to hunt for a complete statement of the theorem, and the proofs are often difficult to locate and follow. The net effect is that reading the book is harder work than it need be. Subsequent revisions will doubtless profit from readers' criticism.

The book would also benefit from more frequent use of illustrative parameterized cost functions as examples. Nearly all the examples of cost functions appear near the end of the book in Chapter 15 under the heading "Toward Empirical Analysis." I suspect that a considerable amount of illustrative theory could be done with sufficiently flexible parameterized examples. And it would help to have some idea in advance of how to translate the authors' definitions into parameter restrictions.

The book does make frequent and effective use of graphical analysis to illustrate and motivate the more formal arguments.

These criticisms are minor compared to the principal achievement of the book. It makes the analysis of market structure in multiproduct industries accessible, really for the first time.

Future Applications and Development of the Subject

There are a number of important areas of microeconomic research for which the multiproduct structure of costs is of central significance to the problem. So I can best conclude this review by outlining one or two of these areas briefly and by indicating the directions that further research might take.

1. *Segmented Markets and International Competition*

There are many industries in which products are sold by producers in different (noninteracting) markets. If those products are developed and produced subject to economies of scale, the effect is to create a certain specific form of economies of scope which affect strategy, relative cost positions, comparative advantage and policy. This broad class of problems has barely begun to be analyzed. Most of them are specific versions of problems involving economies of scope. For example, R&D is generally a fixed cost that generates scale economies. These scale advantages are not truncated by national boundaries. Thus a firm selling the same or slightly differentiated products in several national markets will have economies of scope advantages relative to its single country competitors. As a matter of semantics one might want to call this scale economies. So let me change the example slightly. The products really are different, but they share components that are produced subject to economies of scale. Again it is a question of semantics. But it is important to understand that the multiproduct cost function will exhibit economies of scope. The cost function for the shared components will exhibit scale economies. The concepts are closely related.

2. *The Vertical Structure of Costs*

It is well known that there are numerous steps in the value-added chain ranging from R&D through manufacturing to marketing and distribution. Each of these components is subject to scale economies, and some of the components are shared by several products. This creates a rich structure that generates economies of scale and scope that in turn affect industry structure including vertical integration.

I believe that future progress in these and related areas will result from the analysis of particular types of cost structures that emerge from studies of particular industries or industry chains. In studying generic types of cost structures, derived from problems of global competition and other sources, we will, I think, be able to refine and expand the analysis of the properties of cost functions and their implications for competition and industry performance. And we shall certainly be much better armed with conceptual weapons as a result of the theory that is developed in this book.

REFERENCES

BAUMOL, WILLIAM J. AND BRADFORD, DAVID. "Optimal Departures from Marginal Cost Pricing," *Amer. Econ. Rev.*, June 1970, *60*(3), pp. 265–83.

———; BAILEY, ELIZABETH E. AND WILLIG, ROBERT D. "Weak Invisible Hand Theorems on the Sustainability of Multiproduct Natural Monopoly," *Amer. Econ. Rev.*, June 1977, *67*(3), pp. 350–65.

WEITZMAN, MARTIN. "Fixed Costs and Sunk Costs," Unpubl., MIT, Mar. 1982.

Part III
Information Problems

THE JOURNAL OF
POLITICAL ECONOMY

Volume LXIX JUNE 1961 *Number 3*

THE ECONOMICS OF INFORMATION[1]

GEORGE J. STIGLER
University of Chicago

One should hardly have to tell academicians that information is a valuable resource: knowledge *is* power. And yet it occupies a slum dwelling in the town of economics. Mostly it is ignored: the best technology is assumed to be known; the relationship of commodities to consumer preferences is a datum. And one of the information-producing industries, advertising, is treated with a hostility that economists normally reserve for tariffs or monopolists.

There are a great many problems in economics for which this neglect of ignorance is no doubt permissible or even desirable. But there are some for which this is not true, and I hope to show that some important aspects of economic organization take on a new meaning when they are considered from the viewpoint of the search for information. In the present paper I shall attempt to analyze systematically one important problem of information—the ascertainment of market price.

[1] I have benefited from comments of Gary Becker, Milton Friedman, Zvi Griliches, Harry Johnson, Robert Solow, and Lester Telser.

I. THE NATURE OF SEARCH

Prices change with varying frequency in all markets, and, unless a market is completely centralized, no one will know all the prices which various sellers (or buyers) quote at any given time. A buyer (or seller) who wishes to ascertain the most favorable price must canvass various sellers (or buyers)—a phenomenon I shall term "search."

The amount of dispersion of asking prices of sellers is a problem to be discussed later, but it is important to emphasize immediately the fact that dispersion is ubiquitous even for homogeneous goods. Two examples of asking prices, of consumer and producer goods respectively, are displayed in Table 1. The automobile prices (for an identical model) were those quoted with an average amount of "higgling": their average was $2,436, their range from $2,350 to $2,515, and their standard deviation $42. The prices for anthracite coal were bids for federal government purchases and had a mean of $16.90 per ton, a range from $15.46 to $18.92, and a standard deviation of $1.15. In both cases the range of prices was significant on almost any criterion.

Price dispersion is a manifestation—and, indeed, it is the measure—of ignorance in the market. Dispersion is a biased measure of ignorance because there is never absolute homogeneity in the commodity if we include the terms of sale within the concept of the commodity. Thus, some automobile dealers might perform more service, or carry a larger range of varieties in stock, and a portion of the observed dispersion is presumably attributable to such differences. But it would be metaphysical, and fruitless, to assert that all dispersion is due to heterogeneity.

TABLE 1

ASKING PRICES FOR TWO COMMODITIES

A. CHEVROLETS, CHICAGO, FEBRUARY, 1959*

Price (Dollars)	No. of Dealers
2,350–2,400	4
2,400–2,450	11
2,450–2,500	8
2,500–2,550	4

B. ANTHRACITE COAL, DELIVERED (WASHINGTON, D.C.), APRIL, 1953†

Price per Ton (Dollars)	No. of Bids
15.00–15.50	2
15.50–16.00	2
16.00–16.50	2
16.50–17.00	3
17.00–18.00	1
18.00–19.00	4

* Allen F. Jung, "Price Variations Among Automobile Dealers in Metropolitan Chicago," *Journal of Business*, XXXIII (January, 1960), 31–42.

† Supplied by John Flueck

At any time, then, there will be a frequency distribution of the prices quoted by sellers. Any buyer seeking the commodity would pay whatever price is asked by the seller whom he happened to canvass, if he were content to buy from the first seller. But, if the dispersion of price quotations of sellers is at all large (relative to the cost of search), it will pay, on average, to canvass several sellers. Consider the following primitive example: let sellers be equally divided between asking prices of \$2 and \$3. Then the distribution of minimum prices, as search is lengthened, is shown in Table 2. The buyer who canvasses two sellers instead of one has an expected saving of 25 cents per unit, etc.

The frequency distributions of asking (and offering) prices have not been studied sufficiently to support any hypothesis as to their nature. Asking prices are probably skewed to the right, as a rule, because the seller of reproducible goods will have some minimum but no maximum limit on the price he can accept. If the distribution of asking prices is normal, the distributions of minimum prices encountered in searches of one, two, and three sellers will be those displayed in Figure 1. If the distribution is rectangular, the corresponding distributions would be those shown in Panel B. The latter assumption does not receive strong support from the evidence, but it will be used for a time because of its algebraic simplicity.

TABLE 2

DISTRIBUTION OF HYPOTHETICAL MINIMUM PRICES BY NUMBERS OF BIDS CANVASSED

No. of Prices Canvassed	Probability of Minimum Price of \$2.00	Probability of Minimum Price of \$3.00	Expected Minimum Price
1	.5	.5	\$2.50
2	.75	.25	2.25
3	.875	.125	2.125
4	.9375	.0625	2.0625
∞	1.0	0	2.00

In fact, if sellers' asking prices (p) are uniformly distributed between zero and one, it can be shown that:[2] (1) The dis-

[2] If $F(p)$ is the cumulative-frequency function of p, the probability that the minimum of n observations will be greater than p is

$$[1-F(p)]^n=\left[\int^1 dx\right]^n.$$

tribution of minimum prices with n searches is

$$n(1-p)^{n-1}, \quad (1)$$

(2) the average minimum price is

$$\frac{1}{n+1},$$

and (3) the variance of the average minimum price is

$$\frac{n}{(n+1)^2(n+2)}.$$

Whatever the precise distribution of prices, it is certain that increased search will yield diminishing returns as measured by the expected reduction in the minimum asking price. This is obviously true of the rectangular distribution, with an expected minimum price of $1/(n+1)$ with n searches, and also of the normal distributions.[3] In fact, if a distribution of asking prices did not display this property, it would be an unstable distribution for reasons that will soon be apparent.[4]

For any buyer the expected savings from an additional unit of search will be approximately the quantity (q) he wishes to purchase times the expected reduction in price as a result of the search,[5] or

$$q\left|\frac{\partial P_{\min}}{\partial_n}\right|. \quad (2)$$

The expected saving from given search will be greater, the greater the dispersion of prices. The saving will also obviously be greater, the greater the expenditure on the commodity. Let us defer for a time the problem of the time period to which the expenditure refers, and hence the amount of expenditure, by considering the purchase of an indivisible, infrequently purchased good—say, a used automobile.

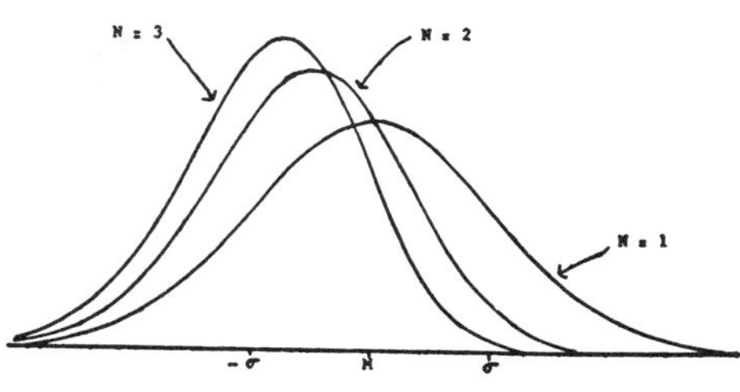

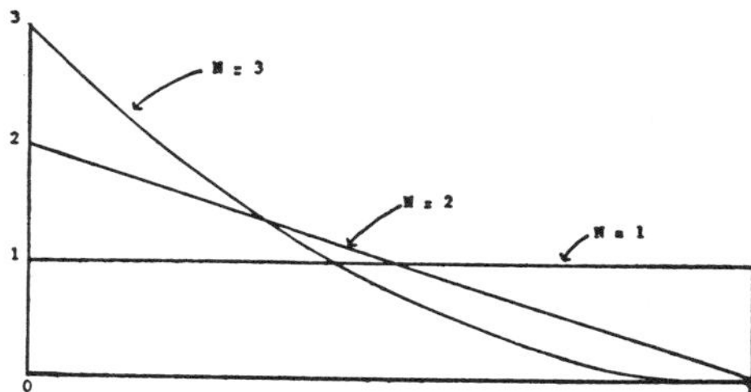

FIG. 1.—Distribution of minimum prices with varying amounts of search.

[3] The expected minimum prices with a normal distribution of mean M and standard deviation σ are

Search	Expected Minimum Price
1	M
2	$M - .564\sigma$
3	$M - .846\sigma$
4	$M - 1.029\sigma$
5	$M - 1.163\sigma$
6	$M - 1.267\sigma$
7	$M - 1.352\sigma$
8	$M - 1.423\sigma$
9	$M - 1.485\sigma$
10	$M - 1.539\sigma$

[4] Robert Solow has pointed out that the expected value of the minimum of a random sample of n observations,

$$E(n) = n\int_0^\infty p(1-F)^{n-1}F'dp,$$

is a decreasing function of n, and

$$[E(n+2) - E(n+1)] - [E(n+1) - E(n)]$$

is positive so the minimum decreases at a decreasing rate. The proofs involve the fact that the density function for the rth observation from the maximum in a sample of n is

$$n\binom{n-1}{r-1}F^{n-r}(1-F)^{r-1}F'dp.$$

[5] The precise savings will be (*a*) the reduction in price times the quantity which would be purchased at the higher price—the expression in the text—*plus* (*b*) the average saving on the additional purchases induced by the lower price. I neglect this quantity, which will generally be of a smaller order of magnitude.

The cost of search, for a consumer, may be taken as approximately proportional to the number of (identified) sellers approached, for the chief cost is time. This cost need not be equal for all consumers, of course: aside from differences in tastes, time will be more valuable to a person with a larger income. If the cost of search is equated to its expected marginal return, the optimum amount of search will be found.[6]

Of course, the sellers can also engage in search and, in the case of unique items, will occasionally do so in the literal fashion that buyers do. In this—empirically unimportant—case, the optimum amount of search will be such that the marginal cost of search equals the expected increase in receipts, strictly parallel to the analysis for buyers.

With unique goods the efficiency of personal search for either buyers or sellers is extremely low, because the identity of potential sellers is not known—the cost of search must be divided by the fraction of potential buyers (or sellers) in the population which is being searched. If I plan to sell a used car and engage in personal search, less than one family in a random selection of one hundred families is a potential buyer of even a popular model within the next month. As a result, the cost of search is increased more than one hundredfold per price quotation.

The costs of search are so great under these conditions that there is powerful inducement to localize transactions as a device for identifying potential buyers and sellers. The medieval markets commonly increased their efficiency in this respect by prohibiting the purchase or sale of the designated commodities within a given radius of the market or on non-market days. The market tolls that were frequently levied on sellers (even in the absence of effective restrictions on non-market transactions) were clear evidence of the value of access to the localized markets.

Advertising is, of course, the obvious modern method of identifying buyers and sellers: the *classified* advertisements in particular form a meeting place for potential buyers and sellers. The identification of buyers and sellers reduces drastically the cost of search. But advertising has its own limitations: advertising itself is an expense, and one essentially independent of the value of the item advertised. The advertising of goods which have few potential buyers relative to the circulation of the advertising medium is especially expensive. We shall temporarily put advertising aside and consider an alternative.

The alternative solution is the development of specialized traders whose chief service, indeed, is implicitly to provide a meeting place for potential buyers and sellers. A used-car dealer, turning over a thousand cars a year, and presumably encountering three or five thousand each of buying and selling bids, provides a substantial centralization of trading activity. Let us consider these dealer markets, which we shall assume to be competitive in the sense of there being many independent dealers.

Each dealer faces a distribution of (for example) buyers' bids and can vary his selling prices with a corresponding effect upon purchases. Even in the markets for divisible (and hence non-unique) goods there will be some scope for higgling (discrimination) in each individual transaction: the buyer has a maximum price given by the lowest price he encounters among the dealers he has searched (or

[6] Buyers often pool their knowledge and thus reduce the effective cost of search; a few remarks are made on this method below.

plans to search), but no minimum price. But let us put this range of indeterminacy aside, perhaps by assuming that the dealer finds discrimination too expensive,[7] and inquire how the demand curve facing a dealer is determined.

Each dealer sets a selling price, p, and makes sales to all buyers for whom this is the minimum price. With a uniform distribution of asking prices by dealers, the number of buyers of a total of N_b possible buyers who will purchase from him is

$$N_i = K N_b n (1-p)^{n-1}, \qquad (3)$$

where K is a constant.[8] The number of buyers from a dealer increases as his price is reduced, and at an increasing rate.[9] Moreover, with the uniform distribution of asking prices, the number of buyers increases with increased search if the price is below the reciprocal of the amount of search.[10] We should generally expect the high-price sellers to be small-volume sellers.

The stability of any distribution of asking prices of dealers will depend upon the costs of dealers. If there are constant returns to scale, the condition of equal rates of return dictates that the difference between a dealer's buying and selling prices be a constant. This condition cannot in general be met: any dealer can buy low, and sell high, provided he is content with a small volume of transactions, and he will then be earning more than costs (including a competitive rate of return). No other dealer can eliminate this non-competitive rate of profit, although by making the same price bids he can share the volume of business, or by asking lower prices he can increase the rewards to search and hence increase the amount of search.

With economies of scale, the competition of dealers will eliminate the profitability of quoting very high selling and very low buying prices and will render impossible some of the extreme price bids. On this score, the greater the decrease in average cost with volume, the smaller will be the dispersion of prices.[11] Many distributions of prices will be inconsistent with any possible cost conditions of dealers,[12] and it is not evident that strict equalities of rates of return for dealers are generally possible.

If economies of scale in dealing lead to

[7] This is the typical state of affairs in retailing xcept for consumer durable goods.

[8] Since $n(1-p)^{n-1}$ is a density function, we must multiply it by a dp which represents the range of prices between adjacent price quotations. In addition, if two or more sellers quote an identical price, they will share the sales, so $K = dp/r$, where r is the number of firms quoting price p.

[9] For

$$\frac{\partial N_i}{\partial p} = -\frac{(n-1)N_i}{(1-p)} < 0,$$

and

$$\frac{\partial^2 N_i}{\partial p^2} = \frac{(n-1)(n-2)N_i}{(1-p)^2} > 0$$

if $n > 2$.

[10] Let

$$\log N_i = \log K + \log N_b + \log n + (n-1)\log(1-p).$$

Then

$$\frac{1}{N_i}\frac{\partial N_i}{\partial n} = \frac{1}{n} + \log(1-p) = \frac{1}{n} - p,$$

approximately.

[11] This argument assumes that dealers will discover unusually profitable bids, given the buyers' search, which is, of course, only partly true: there is also a problem of dealers' search with respect to prices.

[12] With the rectangular distribution of asking prices, if each buyer purchases the same number of units, the elasticity of demand falls continuously with price, so that, if average cost equaled price at every rate of sales (with one seller at each price), marginal costs would have to be negative at large outputs. But, of course, the number of sellers can be less at lower prices.

a smaller dispersion of asking prices than do constant costs of dealing, similarly greater amounts of search will lead to a smaller dispersion of observed selling prices by reducing the number of purchasers who will pay high prices. Let us consider more closely the determinants of search.

DETERMINANTS OF SEARCH

The equation defining optimum search is unambiguous only if a unique purchase is being made—a house, a particular used book, etc. If purchases are repetitive, the volume of purchases based upon the search must be considered.

If the correlation of asking prices of dealers in successive time periods is perfect (and positive!), the initial search is the only one that need be undertaken. In this case the expected savings of search will be the present value of the discounted savings on all future purchases, the future savings extending over the life of the buyer or seller (whichever is shorter).[13] On the other hand, if asking prices are uncorrelated in successive time periods, the savings from search will pertain only to that period,[14] and search in each period is independent of previous experience. If the correlation of successive prices is positive, customer search will be larger in the initial period than in subsequent periods.[15]

The correlation of successive asking prices of sellers is usually positive in the handful of cases I have examined. The rank correlation of anthracite price bids (Table 1) in 1953 with those in 1954 was .68 for eight bidders; that for Chevrolet dealers in Chicago February and August of 1959 was .33 for twenty-nine dealers—but, on the other hand, it was zero for Ford dealers for the same dates. Most observed correlations will, of course, be positive because of stable differences in the products or services, but our analysis is restricted to conditions of homogeneity.

As a rule, positive correlations should exist with homogeneous products. The amount of search will vary among individuals because of differences in their expenditures on a commodity or differences in cost of search. A seller who wishes to obtain the continued patronage of those buyers who value the gains of search more highly or have lower costs of search must see to it that he is quoting relatively low prices. In fact, goodwill may be defined as continued patronage by customers without continued search (that is, no more than occasional verification).

A positive correlation of successive asking prices justifies the widely held view that inexperienced buyers (tourists)

[13] Let the expected minimum price be $p_1 = f(n)_1$ in period 1 (with $f' < 0$) and let the expected minimum price in period 2, with r a measure of the correlation between sellers' successive prices, be

$$p_2 = \left(\frac{p_1}{f(n_2)}\right)^r f(n_2) .$$

If the cost of search is λ per unit, total expenditures for a fixed quantity of purchases (Q) per unit of time are, neglecting interest,

$$E = Q(p_1 + p_2) + \lambda(n_1 + n_2) .$$

Expenditures are a minimum when

$$\frac{\partial E}{\partial n_1} = Qf'(n_1) + Qr[f(n_1)]^{r-1} \times [f(n_2)]^{1-r} f'(n_1) + \lambda = 0$$

and

$$\frac{\partial E}{\partial n_2} = (1-r)Q[f(n_1)]^r \times [f(n_2)]^{-r} f'(n_2) + \lambda = 0 .$$

If $r = 1$, $n_2 = 0$, and n_1 is determined by $Qf'(n_1) = -\lambda/2$, the cost of search is effectively halved.

[14] See n. 13; if $r = 0$, $n_1 = n_2$.

[15] Let $f(n) = e^{-n}$. Then, in the notation of our previous footnotes,

$$n_1 - n_2 = \frac{2r}{1-r},$$

approximately.

pay higher prices in a market than do experienced buyers.[16] The former have no accumulated knowledge of asking prices, and even with an optimum amount of search they will pay higher prices on average. Since the variance of the expected minimum price decreases with additional search, the prices paid by inexperienced buyers will also have a larger variance.

If a buyer enters a wholly new market, he will have no idea of the dispersion of prices and hence no idea of the rational amount of search he should make. In such cases the dispersion will presumably be estimated by some sort of sequential process, and this approach would open up a set of problems I must leave for others to explore. But, in general, one approaches a market with some general knowledge of the amount of dispersion, for dispersion itself is a function of the average amount of search, and this in turn is a function of the nature of the commodity:

1. The larger the fraction of the buyer's expenditures on the commodity, the greater the savings from search and hence the greater the amount of search.
2. The larger the fraction of repetitive (experienced) buyers in the market, the greater the effective amount of search (with positive correlation of successive prices).
3. The larger the fraction of repetitive sellers, the higher the correlation between successive prices, and hence, by condition (2), the larger the amount of accumulated search.[17]
4. The cost of search will be larger, the larger the geographical size of the market.

An increase in the number of buyers has an uncertain effect upon the dispersion of asking prices. The sheer increase in numbers will lead to an increase in the number of dealers and, *ceteris paribus*, to a larger range of asking prices. But, quite aside from advertising, the phenomenon of pooling information will increase. Information is pooled when two buyers compare prices: if each buyer canvasses s sellers, by combining they effectively canvass $2s$ sellers, duplications aside.[18] Consumers compare prices of some commodities (for example, liquor) much more often than of others (for example, chewing gum)—in fact, pooling can be looked upon as a cheaper (and less reliable) form of search.

SOURCES OF DISPERSION

One source of dispersion is simply the cost to dealers of ascertaining rivals' asking prices, but even if this cost were zero the dispersion of prices would not vanish. The more important limitation is provided by buyers' search, and, if the conditions and participants in the market were fixed in perpetuity, prices would immediately approach uniformity. Only those differences could persist which did not remunerate additional search. The condition for optimum search would be (with perfect correlation of successive prices):

$$q\left|\frac{\partial p}{\partial n}\right| = i \times \text{marginal cost of search},$$

where i is the interest rate. If an additional search costs \$1, and the interest rate is 5 per cent, the expected reduction in price with one more search would at equilibrium be equal to \$0.05/q—a quantity which would often be smaller than the smallest unit of currency. But, indivisibilities aside, it would normally be

[16] For that matter, a negative correlation would have the same effects.

[17] If the number of sellers (s) and the asking-price distributions are the same in two periods, but k are new sellers, the average period-1 buyer will have lost proportion k/s of his period-1 search.

[18] Duplications will occur more often than random processes would suggest, because pooling is more likely between buyers of similar location, tastes, etc.

unprofitable for buyers or sellers to eliminate all dispersion.

The maintenance of appreciable dispersion of prices arises chiefly out of the fact that knowledge becomes obsolete. The conditions of supply and demand, and therefore the distribution of asking prices, change over time. There is no method by which buyers or sellers can ascertain the new average price in the market appropriate to the new conditions except by search. Sellers cannot maintain perfect correlation of successive prices, even if they wish to do so, because of the costs of search. Buyers accordingly cannot make the amount of investment in search that perfect correlation of prices would justify. The greater the instability of supply and/or demand conditions, therefore, the greater the dispersion of prices will be.

In addition, there is a component of ignorance due to the changing identity of buyers and sellers. There is a flow of new buyers and sellers in every market, and they are at least initially uninformed on prices and by their presence make the information of experienced buyers and sellers somewhat obsolete.

The amount of dispersion will also vary with one other characteristic which is of special interest: the size (in terms of both dollars and number of traders) of the market. As the market grows in these dimensions, there will appear a set of firms which specialize in collecting and selling information. They may take the form of trade journals or specialized brokers. Since the cost of collection of information is (approximately) independent of its use (although the cost of dissemination is not), there is a strong tendency toward monopoly in the provision of information: in general, there will be a "standard" source for trade information.

II. ADVERTISING

Advertising is, among other things, a method of providing potential buyers with knowledge of the identity of sellers. It is clearly an immensely powerful instrument for the elimination of ignorance—comparable in force to the use of the book instead of the oral discourse to communicate knowledge. A small \$5 advertisement in a metropolitan newspaper reaches (in the sense of being read) perhaps 25,000 readers, or fifty readers per penny, and, even if only a tiny fraction are potential buyers (or sellers), the economy they achieve in search, as compared with uninstructed solicitation, may be overwhelming.

Let us begin with advertisements designed only to identify sellers; the identification of buyers will not be treated explicitly, and the advertising of price will be discussed later. The identification of sellers is necessary because the identity of sellers changes over time, but much more because of the turnover of buyers. In every consumer market there will be a stream of new buyers (resulting from immigration or the attainment of financial maturity) requiring knowledge of sellers, and, in addition, it will be necessary to refresh the knowledge of infrequent buyers.

Suppose, what is no doubt too simple, that a given advertisement of size a will inform c per cent of the potential buyers in a given period, so $c = g(a)$.[19] This contact function will presumably show diminishing returns, at least beyond a certain size of advertisement. A certain fraction, b, of potential customers will be "born" (and "die") in a stable population, where "death" includes not only

[19] The effectiveness of the advertisement is also a function of the skill with which it is done and of the fraction of potential buyers who read the medium, but such elaborations are put aside.

departure from the market but forgetting the seller. The value of b will obviously vary with the nature of the commodity; for example, it will be large for commodities which are seldom purchased (like a house). In a first period of advertising (at a given rate) the number of potential customers reached will be cN, if N is the total number of potential customers. In the second period $cN(1 - b)$ of these potential customers will still be informed, cbN new potential customers will be informed, and

$$c[(1-b)n - cN(1-b)]$$

old potential customers will be reached for the first time, or a total of

$$cN[1 + (1-b)(1-c)] .$$

This generalizes, for k periods, to

$$cN[1 + (1-b)(1-c) + \ldots + (1-b)^{k-1}(1-c)^{k-1}] ,$$

and, if k is large, this approaches

$$\frac{cN}{1-(1-c)(1-b)} = \lambda N . \quad (4)$$

The proportion (λ) of potential buyers informed of the advertiser's identity thus depends upon c and b.

If each of r sellers advertises the same amount, λ is the probability that any one seller will inform any buyer. The distribution of N potential buyers by the number of contacts achieved by r sellers is given by the binomial distribution:

$$N(\lambda + [1-\lambda])^r ,$$

with, for example,

$$\frac{Nr!}{m!(r-m)!}\lambda^m(1-\lambda)^{r-m}$$

buyers being informed of exactly m sellers' identities. The number of sellers known to a buyer ranges from zero to r, with an average of $r\lambda$ sellers and a variance of $r\lambda(1 - \lambda)$.[20]

The amount of relevant information in the market, even in this simple model, is not easy to summarize in a single measure—a difficulty common to frequency distributions. If all buyers wished to search s sellers, all buyers knowing less than s sellers would have inadequate information, and all who knew more than s sellers would have redundant information, although the redundant information would not be worthless.[21] Since the value of information is the amount by which it reduces the expected cost to the buyer of his purchases, if these expected reductions are $\Delta C_1, \Delta C_2, \ldots$, for searches of $1, 2, \ldots$, the value of the information to buyers is approximately

$$\sum_{m=1}^{r}\frac{r!}{m!(r-m)!}\lambda^m(1-\lambda)^{r-m}\Delta C_m .$$

The information possessed by buyers, however, is not simply a matter of chance; those buyers who spend more on the commodity, or who search more for a given expenditure, will also search more for advertisements. The buyers with more information will, on average, make more extensive searches, so the value of information will be greater than this last formula indicates.

We may pause to discuss the fact that advertising in, say, a newspaper is normally "paid" for by the seller. On our analysis, the advertising is valuable to the buyer, and he would be willing to pay

[20] This approach has both similarities and contrasts to that published by S. A. Ozga, "Imperfect Markets through Lack of Knowledge," *Quarterly Journal of Economics*, LXXIV (February, 1960), 29–52.

[21] The larger the number of sellers known, the larger is the range of prices among the sellers and the lower the expected minimum price after s searches. But this effect will normally be small.

more for a paper with advertisements than for one without. The difficulty with having the sellers insert advertisements "free" and having the buyer pay for them directly is that it would be difficult to ration space on this basis: the seller would have an incentive to supply an amount of information (or information of a type) the buyer did not wish, and, since numerous advertisements are supplied jointly, the buyer could not register clearly his preferences regarding advertising. (Catalogues, however, are often sold to buyers.) Charging the seller for the advertisements creates an incentive for him to supply to the buyer only the information which is desired.

It is commonly complained that advertising is jointly supplied with the commodity in the sense that the buyer must pay for both even though he wishes only the latter. The alternative of selling the advertising separately from the commodity, however, would require that the advertising of various sellers (of various commodities) would be supplied jointly: the economies of disseminating information in a general-purpose periodical are so great that some form of jointness is inescapable. But the common complaint is much exaggerated: the buyer who wishes can search out the seller who advertises little (but, of course, enough to be discoverable), and the latter can sell at prices lower by the savings on advertising.

These remarks seem most appropriate to newspaper advertisements of the "classified" variety; what of the spectacular television show or the weekly comedian? We are not equipped to discuss advertising in general because the problem of quality has been (and will continue to be) evaded by the assumption of homogeneous goods. Even within our narrower framework, however, the use of entertainment to attract buyers to information is a comprehensible phenomenon. The assimilation of information is not an easy or pleasant task for most people, and they may well be willing to pay more for the information when supplied in an enjoyable form. In principle, this complementary demand for information and entertainment is exactly analogous to the complementary demand of consumers for commodities and delivery service or air-conditioned stores. One might find a paradox in the simultaneous complaints of some people that advertising is too elaborate and school *houses* too shoddy.

A monopolist will advertise (and price the product) so as to maximize his profits,

$$\pi = Npq\lambda - \phi(N\lambda q) - ap_a ,$$

where $p = f(q)$ is the demand curve of the individual buyer, $\phi(Nq\lambda)$ is production costs other than advertising, and ap_a is advertising expenditures. The maximum profit conditions are

$$\frac{\partial \pi}{\partial q} = N\lambda\left(p + q\frac{\partial p}{\partial q}\right) - \phi' N\lambda = 0 \quad (5)$$

and

$$\frac{\partial \pi}{\partial a} = Npq\frac{\partial \lambda}{\partial a} - \phi' Nq\frac{\partial \lambda}{\partial a} - p_a = 0 \,. \quad (6)$$

Equation (5) states the usual marginal cost–marginal revenue equality, and equation (6) states the equality of (price − marginal cost) with the marginal cost $[p_a/Nq(\partial\lambda/\partial a)]$ of advertising.[22]

[22] The marginal revenue from advertising expenditure,

$$\frac{Npq}{p_a}\frac{\partial \lambda}{\partial a},$$

equals the absolute value of the elasticity of demand by equations (5) and (6); see R. Dorfman and P. O. Steiner, "Optimal Advertising and Optimal Quality," *American Economic Review*, XLIV (1954), 826.

With the Cournot spring (where production costs $\phi = 0$) the monopolist advertises up to the point where price equals the marginal cost of informing a buyer: the monopolist will not (cannot) exploit ignorance as he exploits desire. The monopolist will advertise more, the higher the "death" rate (b), unless it is very high relative to the "contact" rate (c).[23] The monopolistic situation does not invite comparison with competition because an essential feature—the value of search in the face of price dispersion—is absent.

A highly simplified analysis of advertising by the competitive firm is presented in the Appendix. On the assumption that all firms are identical and that all buyers have identical demand curves and search equal amounts, we obtain the maximum-profit equation:

$$\text{Production cost} = p\left(1 + \frac{1}{\eta_{qp} + \eta_{Kp}}\right), \quad (7)$$

where η_{qp} is the elasticity of a buyer's demand curve and η_{K_p} is the elasticity of the fraction of buyers purchasing from the seller with respect to his price. The latter elasticity will be of the order of magnitude of the number of searches made by a buyer. With a uniform distribution of asking prices, increased search will lead to increased advertising by low-price sellers and reduced advertising by high-price sellers. The amount of advertising by a firm decreases as the number of firms increases.

Price advertising has a decisive influence on the dispersion of prices. Search now becomes extremely economical, and the question arises why, in the absence of differences in quality of products, the dispersion does not vanish. And the answer is simply that, if prices are advertised by a large portion of the sellers, the price differences diminish sharply. That they do not wholly vanish (in a given market) is due simply to the fact that no combination of advertising media reaches all potential buyers within the available time.

Assuming, as we do, that all sellers are equally convenient in location, must we say that some buyers are perverse in not reading the advertisements? Obviously not, for the cost of keeping currently informed about all articles which an individual purchases would be prohibitive. A typical household probably buys several hundred different items a month, and, if, on average, their prices change (in some outlets) only once a month, the number of advertisements (by at least several sellers) which must be read is forbiddingly large.

The seller's problem is even greater: he may sell two thousand items (a modest number for a grocery or hardware store), and to advertise each on the occasion of a price change—and frequently enough thereafter to remind buyers of his price—would be impossibly expensive. To keep the buyers in a market informed on the current prices of all items of consumption would involve perhaps a thousandfold increase of newspaper advertising.

From the manufacturer's viewpoint, uncertainty concerning his price is clearly disadvantageous. The cost of search is a cost of purchase, and consumption will therefore be smaller, the greater the dispersion of prices and the greater the optimum amount of search. This is presumably one reason (but, I conjecture, a very minor one) why uniform prices are set by

[23] Differentiating equation (6) with respect to b, we find that $\partial a/\partial b$ is positive or negative according as

$$b \lessgtr \frac{c}{1-c}.$$

If $c \geq \frac{1}{2}$, the derivative must be positive.

sellers of nationally advertised brands: if they have eliminated price variation, they have reduced the cost of the commodity (including search) to the buyer, even if the dealers' margins average somewhat more than they otherwise would.

The effect of advertising prices, then, is equivalent to that of the introduction of a very large amount of search by a large portion of the potential buyers. It follows from our discussion in Section I that the dispersion of asking prices will be much reduced. Since advertising of prices will be devoted to products for which the marginal value of search is high, it will tend to reduce dispersion most in commodities with large aggregate expenditures.

III. CONCLUSIONS

The identification of sellers and the discovery of their prices are only one sample of the vast role of the search for information in economic life. Similar problems exist in the detection of profitable fields for investment and in the worker's choice of industry, location, and job. The search for knowledge on the quality of goods, which has been studiously avoided in this paper, is perhaps no more important but, certainly, analytically more difficult. Quality has not yet been successfully specified by economics, and this elusiveness extends to all problems in which it enters.

Some forms of economic organization may be explicable chiefly as devices for eliminating uncertainties in quality. The department store, as Milton Friedman has suggested to me, may be viewed as an institution which searches for the superior qualities of goods and guarantees that they are good quality. "Reputation" is a word which denotes the persistence of quality, and reputation commands a price (or exacts a penalty) because it economizes on search. When economists deplore the reliance of the consumer on reputation—although they choose the articles they read (and their colleagues) in good part on this basis—they implicitly assume that the consumer has a large laboratory, ready to deliver current information quickly and gratuitously.

Ignorance is like subzero weather: by a sufficient expenditure its effects upon people can be kept within tolerable or even comfortable bounds, but it would be wholly uneconomic entirely to eliminate all its effects. And, just as an analysis of man's shelter and apparel would be somewhat incomplete if cold weather is ignored, so also our understanding of economic life will be incomplete if we do not systematically take account of the cold winds of ignorance.

APPENDIX

Under competition, the amount of advertising by any one seller (i) can be determined as follows. Each buyer will engage in an amount s of search, which is determined by the factors discussed above (Sec. 1). He will on average know

$$(r-1)\lambda+\lambda_i$$

sellers, where λ_i is defined by equation (4) for seller i. Hence,

$$\frac{\lambda_i}{(r-1)\lambda+\lambda_i}$$

per cent of buyers who know seller i will canvass him on one search, and

$$\left(1-\frac{\lambda_i}{(r-1)\lambda+\lambda_i}\right)^s$$

per cent of the buyers who know i will not canvass him in s searches,

$$s\leq(r-1)\lambda+\lambda_i\,.$$

Therefore, of the buyers who know i, the proportion who will canvass him at least once is[24]

$$1-\left(1-\frac{\lambda_i}{(r-1)\lambda+\lambda_i}\right)^s.$$

If we approximate

$$\frac{\lambda_i}{(r-1)\lambda+\lambda_i}$$

by

$$\frac{\lambda_i}{r\lambda}$$

and take only the first two terms of the binomial expansion, this becomes

$$\frac{s\lambda_i}{r\lambda}.$$

The receipts of any seller then become the product of (1) The number of buyers canvassing him,

$$\frac{s\lambda_i}{r\lambda}\lambda_i N = T_i\,,$$

(2) the fraction K of those canvassing him who buy from him, where K depends upon his relative price (and the amount of search and the number of rivals), and (3) sales to each customer, pq. If $\phi(T_i Kq)$ is production costs and ap_a advertising costs, profits are

$$\pi = T_i K p q - \phi\,(T_i K q) - a p_a\,.$$

The conditions for maximum profits are

$$\frac{\partial\pi}{\partial p} = T_i\left(K\frac{\partial pq}{\partial p}+pq\frac{\partial K}{\partial p}\right) - T_i\phi'\left(K\frac{\partial q}{\partial p}+q\frac{\partial K}{\partial p}\right)=0 \qquad (8)$$

and

$$\frac{\partial\pi}{\partial a} = Kpq\frac{\partial T_i}{\partial a} - \phi' Kq\frac{\partial T_i}{\partial a} - p_a = 0\,. \qquad (9)$$

[24] The formula errs slightly in allowing the multiple canvass of one seller by a buyer.

The former equation can be rewritten in elasticities as

$$\phi' = p\left(1+\frac{1}{\eta_{qp}+\eta_{Kp}}\right) \qquad (8a)$$

Price exceeds marginal cost, not simply by $(-p/\eta_{qp})$ as with monopoly, but by the smaller amount

$$\frac{-p}{\eta_{qp}+\eta_{Kp}},$$

where η_{Kp} will generally be of the order of magnitude of the number of searches made by a buyer.[25] Equation (2) states the equality of the marginal revenue of advertising with its marginal cost. By differentiating equation (2) with respect to s and taking ϕ' as constant, it can be shown that increased search by buyers will lead to increased advertising by low-price sellers and reduced advertising by high-price sellers (with a uniform distribution of prices).[26]

By the same method it may be shown that the amount of advertising by the firm will decrease as the number of rivals increases.[27] The aggregate amount of advertising by the industry may either increase or decrease with an increase in the number of firms, s, depending on the relationship between λ and a.

[25] In the case of the uniform distribution, η_{Kp} is

$$\frac{-(s-1)p}{1-p}.$$

[26] The derivative $\partial a/\partial s$ has the sign of $(1+\eta_{Ks})$, and this elasticity equals

$$1 + s\log\,[1-p]$$

with a uniform distribution of prices.

[27] By differentiation of equation (2) with respect to r one gets

$$r\frac{\partial a}{\partial r}\left\{\lambda_i\frac{\partial^2\lambda_i}{\partial a^2}+\left(\frac{\partial\lambda_i}{\partial a}\right)^2\right\} = \lambda_i\frac{\partial\lambda_i}{\partial a}\left(1-\frac{r}{K}\frac{\partial K}{\partial r}\right).$$

The term in brackets on the left side is negative by the stability condition; the right side is positive.

[12]

Econometrica, Vol. 29, No. 3 (July 1961)

RATIONAL EXPECTATIONS AND THE THEORY OF PRICE MOVEMENTS[1]

BY JOHN F. MUTH

In order to explain fairly simply how expectations are formed, we advance the hypothesis that they are essentially the same as the predictions of the relevant economic theory. In particular, the hypothesis asserts that the economy generally does not waste information, and that expectations depend specifically on the structure of the entire system. Methods of analysis, which are appropriate under special conditions, are described in the context of an isolated market with a fixed production lag. The interpretative value of the hypothesis is illustrated by introducing commodity speculation into the system.

1. INTRODUCTION

THAT EXPECTATIONS of economic variables may be subject to error has, for some time, been recognized as an important part of most explanations of changes in the level of business activity. The "ex ante" analysis of the Stockholm School—although it has created its fair share of confusion—is a highly suggestive approach to short-run problems. It has undoubtedly been a major motivation for studies of business expectations and intentions data.

As a systematic theory of fluctuations in markets or in the economy, the approach is limited, however, because it does not include an explanation of the way expectations are formed. To make dynamic economic models complete, various expectations formulas have been used. There is, however, little evidence to suggest that the presumed relations bear a resemblance to the way the economy works.[2]

What kind of information is used and how it is put together to frame an estimate of future conditions is important to understand because the character of dynamic processes is typically very sensitive to the way expectations are influenced by the actual course of events. Furthermore, it is often necessary to make sensible predictions about the way expectations would change when either the amount of available information or the struc-

[1] Research undertaken for the project, *Planning and Control of Industrial Operations*, under contract with the Office of Naval Research. Contract N-onr-760-(01), Project NR 047011. Reproduction of this paper in whole or in part is permitted for any purpose of the United States Government.

An earlier version of this paper was presented at the Winter Meeting of the Econometric Society, Washington, D.C., December 30, 1959.

I am indebted to Z. Griliches, A. G. Hart, M. H. Miller, F. Modigliani, M. Nerlove, and H. White for their comments.

[2] This comment also applies to dynamic theories in which expectations do not explicitly appear. See, for example, Arrow, Block, and Hurwicz [**3, 4**].

ture of the system is changed. (This point is similar to the reason we are curious about demand functions, consumption functions, and the like, instead of only the reduced form "predictors" in a simultaneous equation system.) The area is important from a statistical standpoint as well, because parameter estimates are likely to be seriously biased towards zero if the wrong variable is used as the expectation.

The objective of this paper is to outline a theory of expectations and to show that the implications are—as a first approximation—consistent with the relevant data.

2. THE "RATIONAL EXPECTATIONS" HYPOTHESIS

Two major conclusions from studies of expectations data are the following:

1. Averages of expectations in an industry are more accurate than naive models and as accurate as elaborate equation systems, although there are considerable cross-sectional differences of opinion.

2. Reported expectations generally underestimate the extent of changes that actually take place.

In order to explain these phenomena, I should like to suggest that expectations, since they are informed predictions of future events, are essentially the same as the predictions of the relevant economic theory.[3] At the risk of confusing this purely descriptive hypothesis with a pronouncement as to what firms ought to do, we call such expectations "rational." It is sometimes argued that the assumption of rationality in economics leads to theories inconsistent with, or inadequate to explain, observed phenomena, especially changes over time (e.g., Simon [**29**]). Our hypothesis is based on exactly the opposite point of view: that dynamic economic models do not assume enough rationality.

The hypothesis can be rephrased a little more precisely as follows: that expectations of firms (or, more generally, the subjective probability distribution of outcomes) tend to be distributed, for the same information set, about the prediction of the theory (or the "objective" probability distributions of outcomes).

The hypothesis asserts three things: (1) Information is scarce, and the economic system generally does not waste it. (2) The way expectations are formed depends specifically on the structure of the relevant system describing the economy. (3) A "public prediction," in the sense of Grunberg and Modigliani [**14**], will have no substantial effect on the operation of the economic system (unless it is based on inside information). This is not quite the same thing as stating that the marginal revenue product of economics is zero,

[3] We show in Section 5 that the hypothesis is consistent with these two phenomena.

because expectations of a single firm may still be subject to greater error than the theory.

It *does not* assert that the scratch work of entrepreneurs resembles the system of equations in any way; nor does it state that predictions of entrepreneurs are perfect or that their expectations are all the same.

For purposes of analysis, we shall use a specialized form of the hypothesis. In particular, we assume:

1. The random disturbances are normally distributed.
2. Certainty equivalents exist for the variables to be predicted.
3. The equations of the system, including the expectations formulas, are linear.

These assumptions are not quite so strong as may appear at first because any one of them virtually implies the other two.[4]

3. PRICE FLUCTUATIONS IN AN ISOLATED MARKET

We can best explain what the hypothesis is all about by starting the analysis in a rather simple setting: short-period price variations in an isolated market with a fixed production lag of a commodity which cannot be stored.[5] The market equations take the form

$$
\begin{aligned}
C_t &= -\beta p_t && \text{(Demand)}\,, \\
P_t &= \gamma p_t^e + u_t\,, && \text{(Supply)}\,, \\
P_t &= C_t && \text{(Market equilibrium)}\,,
\end{aligned}
\tag{3.1}
$$

where: P_t represents the number of units produced in a period lasting as long as the production lag,

C_t is the amount consumed,

p_t is the market price in the tth period,

p_t^e is the market price expected to prevail during the tth period on the basis of information available through the $(t-1)$'st period,

u_t is an error term—representing, say, variations in yields due to weather.

All the variables used are deviations from equilibrium values.

[4] As long as the variates have a finite variance, a linear regression function exists if and only if the variates are normally distributed. (See Allen [**2**] and Ferguson [**12**].) The certainty-equivalence property follows from the linearity of the derivative of the appropriate quadratic profit or utility function. (See Simon [**28**] and Theil [**32**].)

[5] It is possible to allow both short- and long-run supply relations on the basis of dynamic costs. (See Holt *et al.* [**17**, esp. Chapters 2-4, 19]). More difficult are the supply effects of changes in the number of firms. The relevance of the cost effects has been emphasized by Buchanan [**7**] and Akerman [**1**]. To include them at this point would, however, take us away from the main objective of the paper.

The quantity variables may be eliminated from (3.1) to give

$$p_t = -\frac{\gamma}{\beta}p_t^e - \frac{1}{\beta}u_t . \tag{3.2}$$

The error term is unknown at the time the production decisions are made, but it is known—and relevant—at the time the commodity is purchased in the market.

The prediction of the model is found by replacing the error term by its expected value, conditional on past events. If the errors have no serial correlation and $Eu_t = 0$, we obtain

$$Ep_t = -\frac{\gamma}{\beta}p_t^e . \tag{3.3}$$

If the prediction of the theory were substantially better than the expectations of the firms, then there would be opportunities for the "insider" to profit from the knowledge—by inventory speculation if possible, by operating a firm, or by selling a price forecasting service to the firms. The profit opportunities would no longer exist if the aggregate expectation of the firms is the same as the prediction of the theory:

$$Ep_t = p_t^e . \tag{3.4}$$

Referring to (3.3) we see that if $\gamma/\beta \neq -1$ the rationality assumption (3.4) implies that $p_t^e = 0$, or that the expected price equals the equilibrium price. As long as the disturbances occur only in the supply function, price and quantity movements from one period to the next would be entirely along the demand curve.

The problem we have been discussing so far is of little empirical interest, because the shocks were assumed to be completely unpredictable. For most markets it is desirable to allow for income effects in demand and alternative costs in supply, with the assumption that part of the shock variable may be predicted on the basis of prior information. By retracing our steps from (3.2), we see that the expected price would be

$$p_t^e = -\frac{1}{\beta + \gamma} Eu_t . \tag{3.5}$$

If the shock is observable, then the conditional expected value or its regression estimate may be found directly. If the shock is not observable, it must be estimated from the past history of variables that can be measured.

Expectations with Serially Correlated Disturbances. We shall write the u's as a linear combination of the past history of normally and independently distributed random variables ε_t with zero mean and variance σ^2:

$$u_t = \sum_{i=0}^{\infty} w_i \varepsilon_{t-i}\,, \qquad E\varepsilon_j = 0\,, \qquad E\varepsilon_i\varepsilon_j = \begin{cases} \sigma^2 \text{ if } i = j\,, \\ 0 \ \text{ if } i \neq j\,. \end{cases} \tag{3.6}$$

Any desired correlogram in the u's may be obtained by an appropriate choice of the weights w_i.

The price will be a linear function of the same independent disturbances; thus

$$p_t = \sum_{i=0}^{\infty} W_i \varepsilon_{t-i}\,. \tag{3.7}$$

The expected price given only information through the $(t-1)$'st period has the same form as that in (3.7), with the exception that ε_t is replaced by its expected value (which is zero). We therefore have

$$p_t^e = W_0 E\varepsilon_t + \sum_{i=1}^{\infty} W_i \varepsilon_{t-i} = \sum_{i=1}^{\infty} W_i \varepsilon_{t-i}\,. \tag{3.8}$$

If, in general, we let $p_{t,L}$ be the price expected in period $t+L$ on the basis of information available through the tth period, the formula becomes

$$p_{t-L,L} = \sum_{i=L}^{\infty} W_i \varepsilon_{t-i}\,. \tag{3.9}$$

Substituting for the price and the expected price into (3.1), which reflect the market equilibrium conditions, we obtain

$$W_0 \varepsilon_t + \left(1 + \frac{\gamma}{\beta}\right) \sum_{i=1}^{\infty} W_i \varepsilon_{t-i} = -\frac{1}{\beta} \sum_{i=0}^{\infty} w_i \varepsilon_{t-i}\,. \tag{3.10}$$

Equation (3.10) is an identity in the ε's; that is, it must hold whatever values of ε_j happen to occur. Therefore, the coefficients of the corresponding ε_j in the equation must be equal.

The weights W_i are therefore the following:

$$W_0 = -\frac{1}{\beta} w_0\,, \tag{3.11a}$$

$$W_i = -\frac{1}{\beta + \gamma} w_i \qquad (i = 1,2,3,\ldots)\,. \tag{3.11b}$$

Equations (3.11) give the parameters of the relation between prices and price expectations functions in terms of the past history of independent shocks. The problem remains of writing the results in terms of the history of observable variables. We wish to find a relation of the form

$$p_t^e = \sum_{j=1}^{\infty} V_j p_{t-j}\,. \tag{3.12}$$

We solve for the weights V_j in terms of the weights W_j in the following manner. Substituting from (3.7) and (3.8), we obtain

$$\sum_{i=1}^{\infty} W_i \varepsilon_{t-i} = \sum_{j=1}^{\infty} V_j \sum_{i=0}^{\infty} W_i \varepsilon_{t-i-j} = \sum_{i=1}^{\infty}\left(\sum_{j=1}^{i} V_j W_{i-j}\right) \varepsilon_{t-i} . \tag{3.13}$$

Since the equality must hold for all shocks, the coefficients must satisfy the equations

$$W_i = \sum_{j=1}^{i} V_j W_{i-j} \qquad (i = 1,2,3,\ldots) . \tag{3.14}$$

This is a system of equations with a triangular structure, so that it may be solved successively for the coefficients V_1, V_2, $V_3, \ldots$.

If the disturbances are independently distributed, as we assumed before, then $w_0 = -1/\beta$ and all the others are zero. Equations (3.14) therefore imply

$$p_t^e = 0 , \tag{3.15a}$$

$$p_t = p_t^e + W_0 \varepsilon_t = -\frac{1}{\beta}\varepsilon_t . \tag{3.15b}$$

These are the results obtained before.

Suppose, at the other extreme, that an exogenous shock affects all future conditions of supply, instead of only the one period. This assumption would be appropriate if it represented how far technological change differed from its trend. Because u_t is the sum of all the past ε_j, $w_i = 1$ $(i = 0,1,2,\ldots)$. From (3.11),

$$W_0 = -1/\beta , \tag{3.16a}$$

$$W_i = -1/(\beta + \gamma) . \tag{3.16b}$$

From (3.14) it can be seen that the expected price is a geometrically weighted moving average of past prices:

$$p_t^e = \frac{\beta}{\gamma} \sum_{j=1}^{\infty} \left(\frac{\gamma}{\beta + \gamma}\right)^j p_{t-j} . \tag{3.17}$$

This prediction formula has been used by Nerlove [**26**] to estimate the supply elasticity of certain agricultural commodities. The only difference is that our analysis states that the "coefficient of adjustment" in the expectations formula should depend on the demand and the supply coefficients. The geometrically weighted moving average forecast is, in fact, optimal under slightly more general conditions (when the disturbance is composed of both permanent and transitory components). In that case the coefficient will depend on the relative variances of the two components as well as the supply and demand coefficients. (See [**24**].)

Deviations from Rationality. Certain imperfections and biases in the expectations may also be analyzed with the methods of this paper. Allowing for cross-sectional differences in expectations is a simple matter, because their aggregate effect is negligible as long as the deviation from the rational forecast for an individual firm is not strongly correlated with those of the others. Modifications are necessary only if the correlation of the errors is large and depends systematically on other explanatory variables. We shall examine the effect of over-discounting current information and of differences in the information possessed by various firms in the industry. Whether such biases in expectations are empirically important remains to be seen. I wish only to emphasize that the methods are flexible enough to handle them.

Let us consider first what happens when expectations consistently over- or under-discount the effect of current events. Equation (3.8), which gives the optimal price expectation, will then be replaced by

$$p_t^e = f_1 W_1 \varepsilon_{t-1} + \sum_{i=2}^{\infty} W_i \varepsilon_{t-i} \,. \tag{3.18}$$

In other words the weight attached to the most recent exogenous disturbance is multiplied by the factor f_1, which would be greater than unity if current information is over-discounted and less than unity if it is under-discounted.

If we use (3.18) for the expected price instead of (3.8) to explain market price movements, then (3.11) is replaced by

$$W_0 = -\frac{1}{\beta} w_0 \,, \tag{3.19a}$$

$$W_1 = -\frac{1}{\beta + f_1 \gamma} w_1 \,, \tag{3.19b}$$

$$W_i = -\frac{1}{\beta + \gamma} w_i \qquad (i = 2,3,4,\ldots) \,. \tag{3.19c}$$

The effect of the biased expectations on price movements depends on the statistical properties of the exogenous disturbances.

If the disturbances are independent (that is, $w_0 = 1$ and $w_i = 0$ for $i \geqslant 1$), the biased expectations have no effect. The reason is that successive observations provide no information about future fluctuations.

On the other hand, if all the disturbances are of a permanent type (that is, $w_0 = w_1 = \ldots = 1$), the properties of the expectations function are significantly affected. To illustrate the magnitude of the differences, the parameters of the function

$$p_t^e = \sum_{j=1}^{\infty} V_j p_{t-j}$$

are compared in Figure 3.1 for $\beta = 2\gamma$ and various values of f_1. If current information is under-discounted ($f_1 = 1/2$), the weight V_1 attached to the latest observed price is very high. With over-discounting ($f_1 = 2$), the weight for the first period is relatively low.

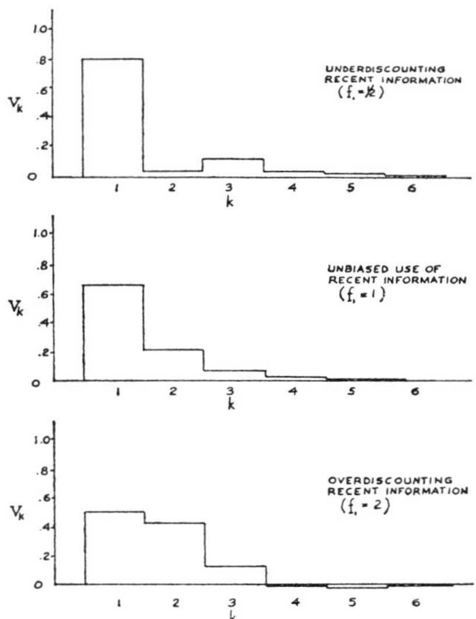

FIGURE 3.1.—Autoregression Coefficients of Expectations for Biased Use of Recent Information. ($w_0 = w_1 = \ldots = 1$).

The model above can be interpreted in another way. Suppose that some of the firms have access to later information than the others. That is, there is a lag of one period for some firms, which therefore form price expectations according to (3.8). The others, with a lag of two periods, can only use the following:

$$p_t^{e'} = \sum_{i=2}^{\infty} W_i \varepsilon_{t-i} . \tag{3.20}$$

Then the aggregate price expectations relation is the same as (3.18), if f_1 represents the fraction of the firms having a lag of only one period in obtaining market information (that is, the fraction of "insiders").

4. EFFECTS OF INVENTORY SPECULATION

Some of the most interesting questions involve the economic effects of inventory storage and speculation. We can examine the effect by adjoining to (3.1) an inventory demand equation depending on the difference between the expected future price and the current price. As we shall show, the price expectation with independent disturbances in the supply function then turns out to have the form

$$p_t^e = \lambda p_{t-1} , \tag{4.1}$$

where the parameter λ would be somewhere between zero and one, its value depending on the demand, supply, and inventory demand parameters.

Speculation with moderately well-informed price expectations reduces the variance of prices by spreading the effect of a market disturbance over several time periods, thereby allowing shocks partially to cancel one another out. Speculation is profitable, although no speculative opportunities remain. These propositions might appear obvious. Nevertheless, contrary views have been expressed in the literature.[6]

Before introducing inventories into the market conditions, we shall briefly examine the nature of speculative demand for a commodity.

Optimal Speculation. We shall assume for the time being that storage, interest, and transactions costs are negligible. An individual has an opportunity to purchase at a known price in the tth period for sale in the succeeding period. The future price is, however, unknown. If we let I_t represent the speculative inventory at the end of the tth period,[7] then the profit to be realized is

$$\pi_t = I_t(p_{t+1} - p_t) . \tag{4.2}$$

Of course, the profit is unknown at the time the commitment is to be made. There is, however, the expectation of gain.

The individual demand for speculative inventories would presumably be based on reasoning of the following sort. The size of the commitment depends on the expectation of the utility of the profit. For a sufficiently small range of variation in profits, we can approximate the utility function by the first few terms of its Taylor's series expansion about the origin:

$$u_t = \phi(\pi_t) = \phi(0) + \phi'(0)\pi_t + \frac{1}{2}\phi''(0)\pi_t^2 + \dots . \tag{4.3}$$

The expected utility depends on the moments of the probability distribution of π:

$$Eu_t = \phi(0) + \phi'(0)E\pi_t + \frac{1}{2}\phi''(0)E\pi_t^2 + \dots . \tag{4.4}$$

[6] See Baumol [**5**]. His conclusions depend on a nonspeculative demand such that prices would be a pure sine function, which may always be forecast perfectly.

[7] Speculative inventories may be either positive or negative.

From (4.2) the first two moments may be found to be

$$E\pi_t = I_t(p^e_{t+1} - p_t)\,, \tag{4.5a}$$

$$E\pi^2_t = I^2_t[\sigma^2_{t,1} + (p^e_{t+1} - p_t)^2]\,, \tag{4.5b}$$

where p^e_{t+1} is the conditional mean of the price in period $t+1$ (given all information through period t) and $\sigma^2_{t,1}$ is the conditional variance. The expected utility may therefore be written in terms of the inventory position as follows:

$$Eu_t = \phi(0) + \phi'(0)I_t(p^e_{t+1} - p_t) + \frac{1}{2}\phi''(0)I^2_t[\sigma^2_{t,1} + (p^e_{t+1} - p_t)^2] + \dots . \tag{4.6}$$

The inventory therefore satisfies the condition

$$\frac{dEu}{dI_t} = \phi'(0)(p^e_{t+1} - p_t) + \phi''(0)I_t[\sigma^2_{t,1} + (p^e_{t+1} - p_t)^2] + \dots = 0\,. \tag{4.7}$$

The inventory position would, to a first approximation, be given by

$$I_t = -\frac{\phi'(0)(p^e_{t+1} - p_t)}{\phi''(0)[\sigma^2_{t,1} + (p^e_{t+1} - p_t)^2]}\,. \tag{4.8}$$

If $\phi'(0) > 0$ and $\phi''(0) < 0$, the above expression is an increasing function of the expected change in prices (as long as it is moderate).

At this point we make two additional assumptions: (1) the conditional variance, $\sigma^2_{t,1}$, is independent of p^e_t, which is true if prices are normally distributed, and (2) the square of the expected price change is small relative to the variance. The latter assumption is reasonable because the original expansion of the utility function is valid only for small changes. Equation (4.8) may then be simplified to[8]

$$I_t = \alpha(p^e_{t+1} - p_t)\,, \tag{4.9}$$

where $\alpha = -\phi'(0)/\phi''(0)\sigma^2_{t,1}$.

Note that the coefficient α depends on the commodity in only one way: the variance of price forecasts. The aggregate demand would, in addition, depend on who holds the stocks as well as the size of the market. For some commodities, inventories are most easily held by the firms.[9] If an organized futures exchange exists for the commodity, a different population would

[8] This form of the demand for speculative inventories resembles that of Telser [**31**] and Kaldor [**20**].

[9] Meat, for example, is stored in the live animals or in any curing or ageing process.

be involved. In a few instances (in particular, durable goods), inventory accumulation on the part of households may be important.

The original assumptions may be relaxed, without affecting the results significantly, by introducing storage or interest costs. Margin requirements may, as well, limit the long or short position of an individual. Although such requirements may primarily limit cross-sectional differences in positions, they may also constrain the aggregate inventory. In this case, we might reasonably expect the aggregate demand function to be nonlinear with an upper "saturation" level for inventories. (A lower level would appear for aggregate inventories approaching zero.)

Because of its simplicity, however, we shall use (4.9) to represent inventory demand.

Market Adjustments. We are now in a position to modify the model of Section 3 to take account of inventory variations. The ingredients are the supply and demand equations used earlier, together with the inventory equation. We repeat the equations below (P_t represents production and C_t consumption during the tth period:

$$C_t = -\beta p_t \qquad \text{(Demand)}, \tag{4.10a}$$

$$P_t = \gamma p_t^e + u_t \qquad \text{(Supply)}, \tag{4.10b}$$

$$I_t = \alpha(p_{t+1}^e - p_t) \qquad \text{(Inventory speculation)}. \tag{4.10c}$$

The market equilibrium conditions are

$$C_t + I_t = P_t + I_{t-1}. \tag{4.11}$$

Substituting (4.10) into (4.11), the equilibrium can be expressed in terms of prices, price expectations, and the disturbance, thus

$$-(\alpha+\beta)p_t + \alpha p_{t+1}^e = (\alpha+\gamma)p_t^e - \alpha p_{t-1} + u_t. \tag{4.12}$$

The conditions above may be used to find the weights of the regression functions for prices and price expectations in the same way as before. Substituting from (3.6), (3.7), and (3.8) into (4.12), we obtain

$$\begin{aligned} &-(\alpha+\beta)\sum_{i=0}^{\infty} W_i \varepsilon_{t-i} + \alpha \sum_{i=1}^{\infty} W_i \varepsilon_{t+1-i} \\ &= (\alpha+\gamma)\sum_{i=1}^{\infty} W_i \varepsilon_{t-i} - \alpha \sum_{i=0}^{\infty} W_i \varepsilon_{t-1-i} + \sum_{i=0}^{\infty} w_i \varepsilon_{t-i}. \end{aligned} \tag{4.13}$$

In order that the above equation hold for all possible ε's, the corresponding coefficients must, as before, be equal. Therefore, the following system of equations must be satisfied:[10]

(4.14a) $$-(\alpha+\beta)W_0+\alpha W_1=w^0\,,$$

(4.14b) $$\alpha W_{i-1}-(2\alpha+\beta+\gamma)W_i+\alpha W_{i+1}=w_i \qquad (i=1,2,3,\ldots)\,.$$

Provided it exists, the solution of the homogeneous system would be of the form

(4.15) $$W_k=c\lambda_1^k\,,$$

where λ_1 is the smaller root of the characteristic equation

(4.16) $$\alpha-(2\alpha+\beta+\gamma)\lambda+\alpha\lambda^2=\alpha(1-\lambda)^2-(\beta+\gamma)\lambda=0\,.$$

λ_1 is plotted against positive values of $\alpha/(\beta+\gamma)$ in Figure 4.1.

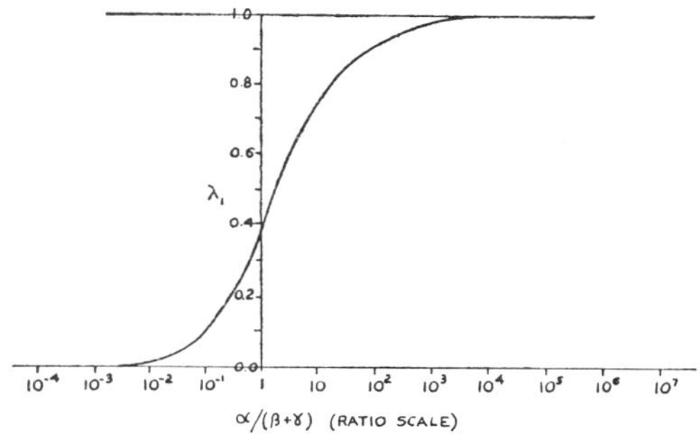

FIGURE 4.1.—Characteristic Root as a Function of $\alpha/(\beta+\gamma)$.

A unique, real, and bounded solution to (4.14) will exist if the roots of the characteristic equation are real. The roots occur in reciprocal pairs, so that if they are real and distinct exactly one will have an absolute value less than unity. For a bounded solution the coefficient of the larger root vanishes; the initial condition is then fitted to the coefficient of the smaller root.

The response of the price and quantity variables will be dynamically stable, therefore, if the roots of the characteristic equation are real. It is easy to see that they will be real if the following inequalities are satisfied:

(4.17a) $$\alpha>0\,,$$

(4.17b) $$\beta+\gamma>0\,.$$

The first condition requires that speculators act in the expectation of gain (rather than loss). The second is the condition for Walrasian stability. Hence an assumption about dynamic stability implies rather little about

[10] The same system appears in various contexts with embarrassing frequency. See Holt *et al.* [**17**] and Muth [**24**].

the demand and supply coefficients. It should be observed that (4.17) are not necessary conditions for stability. The system will also be stable if both inequalities in (4.17) are reversed (!) or if $0 > \alpha/(\beta + \gamma) > -1/4$. If $\alpha = 0$, there is no "linkage" from one period of time to another, so the system is dynamically stable for all values of $\beta + \gamma$.

Suppose, partly by way of illustration, that the exogenous disturbances affecting the market are independently distributed. Then we can let $w_0 = 1$ and $w_i = 0$ $(i \geqslant 1)$. The complementary function will therefore be the complete solution to the resulting difference equation. By substituting (4.15) into (4.14a), we evaluate the constant and find

$$W_k = -\frac{1}{(\alpha + \beta) - \alpha\lambda_1}\lambda_1^k . \tag{4.18}$$

The weights V_k may be found either from (3.14) or by noting that the resulting stochastic process is Markovian. At any rate, the weights are

$$V_k = \begin{cases} \lambda_1, & k = 1 , \\ 0, & k > 1 . \end{cases} \tag{4.19}$$

The expected price is therefore correlated with the previous price, and the rest of the price history conveys no extra information, i.e.,

$$p_t^e = \lambda_1 p_{t-1} , \tag{4.20}$$

where the parameter depends on the coefficients of demand, supply, and inventory speculation according to (4.16) and is between 0 and 1. If inventories are an important factor in short-run price determination, λ_1 will be very nearly unity so that the time series of prices has a high positive serial correlation.[11] If inventories are a negligible factor, λ_1 is close to zero and leads to the results of Section 3.

Effects of Inventory Speculation. Substituting the expected price, from (4.20), into (4.10), we obtain the following system to describe the operation of the market:

$$C_t = -\beta p_t , \tag{4.21a}$$

$$P_t = \gamma\lambda_1 p_{t-1} + \varepsilon_t , \tag{4.21b}$$

$$I_t = -\alpha(1 - \lambda_1) p_t . \tag{4.21c}$$

The market conditions can be expressed in terms of supply and demand by including the inventory carryover with production and inventory carry-

[11] If the production and consumption flows are negligible compared with the speculative inventory level, the process approaches a random walk. This would apply to daily or weekly price movements of a commodity whose production lag is a year. Cf. Kendall [**22**].

TABLE 4.1

EFFECTS OF INVENTORY SPECULATION

Description	Symbol	General Formula	Approximation for Small α
1. Characteristic root	λ_1	[eq. (4.16)]	$\alpha/(\beta+\gamma)$
2. Standard deviation of prices	σ_p	$\lvert W_0\rvert(1-\lambda_1^2)^{-1/2}\sigma$	$\frac{1}{\beta}\left(1-\frac{\alpha}{\beta}\right)\sigma$
3. Standard deviation of expected price	σ_p^e	$\lambda_1\sigma_p$	$\frac{\alpha}{\beta(\beta+\gamma)}\sigma$
4. Standard deviation of output	σ_P	$(\sigma^2+\gamma^2\lambda_1^2\sigma_p^2)^{1/2}$	$\left[1+\frac{\alpha\gamma}{2\beta(\beta+\gamma)}\right]\sigma$
5. Mean producers' revenue	$EP_t p_t$	$\gamma\lambda_1^2\sigma_p^2+W_0\sigma^2$	$-\frac{1}{\beta}\left(1-\frac{\alpha}{\beta}\right)\sigma^2$
6. Mean speculators' revenue	$EI_t(p_{t+1}-p_t)$	$\alpha(1-\lambda_1)^2\sigma_p^2$	$\alpha\sigma^2$
7. Mean consumers' expenditure	EC_tp_t	$-\beta\sigma_p^2$	$-\frac{1}{\beta}\left(1-\frac{2\alpha}{\beta}\right)\sigma^2$

Notes: (1) σ is the standard deviation of the disturbance in the supply function (4.10b) with $w_0 = 1$ and $w_1 = w_2 = \ldots = 0$.
(2) $W_0 = -1/[\beta+\alpha(1-\lambda_1)]$.

forward with consumption; thus,

$$Q_t = C_t + I_t \quad \text{(Demand)},$$
$$Q_t = P_t + I_{t-1} \quad \text{(Supply)}. \tag{4.22}$$

Substituting from (4.21) we obtain the system:

$$Q_t = -[\beta+\alpha(1-\lambda_1)]p_t \quad \text{(Demand)}, \tag{4.23a}$$

$$Q_t = [\gamma\lambda_1-\alpha(1-\lambda_1)]p_{t-1}+\varepsilon_t \quad \text{(Supply)}. \tag{4.23b}$$

The coefficient in the supply equation is reduced while that of the demand equation is increased. The conclusions are not essentially different from those of Hooton [**18**]. The change is always enough to make the dynamic response stable.

If price expectations are in fact rational, we can make some statements about the economic effects of commodity speculation. (The relevant formulas are summarized in Table 4.1.) Speculation reduces the variance of prices by spreading the effect of a disturbance over several time periods. From Figure 4.2, however, we see that the effect is negligible if α is much less than the sum of β and γ. The standard deviation of expected prices first increases with α because speculation makes the time series more predictable and then decreases because of the small variability of actual prices. The variability of factor inputs and production follows roughly the same pattern (cf. Kaldor [**20**]).

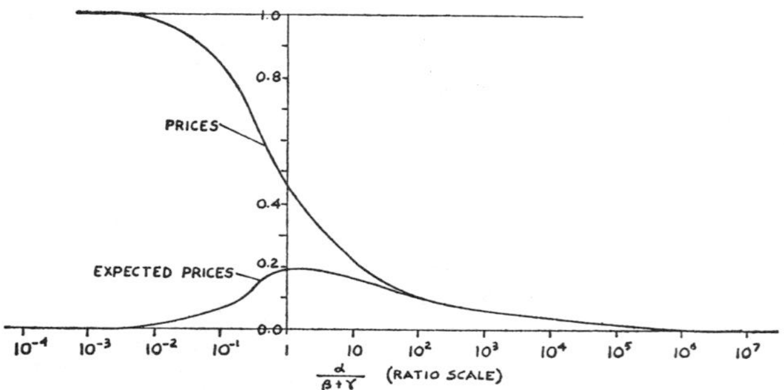

FIGURE 4.2.—Standard Deviation of Prices and Expected Prices as a Function of $\alpha/(\beta+\gamma)$ for $\beta = \gamma$.

In Figure 4.3 we see that mean income to speculators is always positive and has a maximum value slightly to the left of that for expected prices. Producers' revenue and consumers' expenditures both increase with α. Consumers' expenditures increase at first a little faster than the revenue of the producers. The effect of speculation on welfare is therefore not obvious.

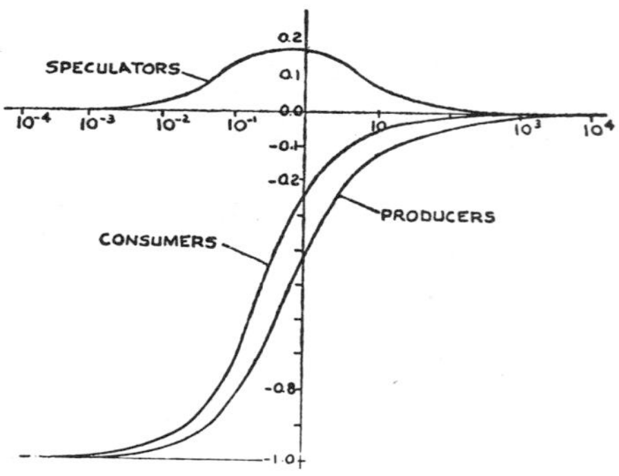

FIGURE 4.3.—Mean Income of Producers and Speculators, and Mean Expenditures of Consumers as a Function of $\alpha/(\beta+\gamma)$ for $\beta = \gamma$.

The variability of prices for various values of γ/β is plotted as a function of α/β in Figure 4.4. The general shape of the curve is not affected by values of γ/β differing by as much as a factor of 100. The larger the supply coefficient, however, the sharper is the cut-off in price variability.

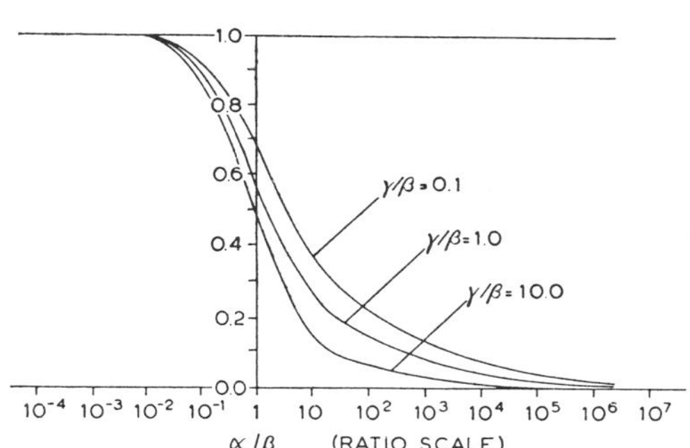

FIGURE 4.4—Standard Deviation of Prices for Various Values of γ/β as a Function of α/β.

5. RATIONALITY AND COBWEB THEOREMS

It is rather surprising that expectations have not previously been regarded as rational dynamic models, since rationality is assumed in all other aspects of entrepreneurial behavior. From a purely theoretical standpoint, there are good reasons for assuming rationality. First, it is a principle applicable to all dynamic problems (if true). Expectations in different markets and systems would not have to be treated in completely different ways. Second, if expectations were not moderately rational there would be opportunities for economists to make profits in commodity speculation, running a firm, or selling the information to present owners. Third, rationality is an assumption that can be modified. Systematic biases, incomplete or incorrect information, poor memory, etc., can be examined with analytical methods based on rationality.

The only real test, however, is whether theories involving rationality explain observed phenomena any better than alternative theories. In this section we shall therefore compare some of the empirical implications of the rational expectations hypothesis with those of the cobweb "theorem." The effects of rational expectations are particularly important because the cobweb theorem has often been regarded as one of the most successful attempts at dynamic economic theories (e.g., Goodwin [**13**]). Few students of agricultural problems or business cycles seem to take the cobweb theorem very seriously, however, but its implications do occasionally appear. For example, a major cause of price fluctuations in cattle and hog markets is sometimes believed to be the expectations of farmers themselves (Jesness [**19**]). Dean and Heady [**10**] have also suggested more extensive governmental forecasting and outlook services in order to offset an increasing tendency toward instability of hog prices due to a secular decrease in the elasticity of demand.

Implications of Cobweb Theorems. If the market equilibrium conditions of (3.1) are subjected to independent shocks in the supply function, the prediction of the theory would be

$$E(p_t \mid p_{t-1}, p_{t-2}, \ldots) = -\frac{\gamma}{\beta} p_t^e . \tag{5.1}$$

As a result, the prediction of the cobweb theory would ordinarily have the sign opposite to that of the firms. This, of course, has been known for a long time. Schultz noted that the hypothesis implies farmers do not learn from experience, but added: "Such a behavior is not to be ruled out as extremely improbable" [**27**, p. 78].

The various theories differ primarily in what is assumed about price expectations. The early contributors (through Ezekiel [**11**]) have assumed that the expected price is equal to the latest known price. That is,

$$p_t^e = p_{t-1} . \tag{5.2}$$

Goodwin [**13**] proposed the extrapolation formula,

$$p_t^e = p_{t-1} - \varrho(p_{t-1} - p_{t-2}) . \tag{5.3}$$

That is, a certain fraction of the latest change is added on to the latest observed price. Depending on the sign of ϱ, which should be between -1 and $+1$, we can get a greater variety of behavior. It is still the case, however, that farmers' expectations and the prediction of the model have the opposite sign.

A third expectations formula is much more recent. The adaptive expectations model, used by Nerlove [**25**], satisfies the following equation:

$$p_t^e = p_{t-1}^e + \eta(p_{t-1} - p_{t-1}^e) . \tag{5.4}$$

The forecast is changed by an amount proportional to the most recently observed forecast error. The solution of the difference equation gives the price expectation as a geometrically weighted moving average:

$$p_t^e = \eta \sum_{j=0}^{\infty} (1-\eta)^j p_{t-j} . \tag{5.5}$$

Certain properties of the cobweb models are compared with the rational model in Table 5.1 for shocks having no serial correlation. Such comparisons are a little treacherous because most real markets have significant income effects in demand, alternative costs in supply, and errors in both behavioral equations. To the extent that these effects introduce positive serial correlation in the residuals, the difference between the cobweb and rational models would be diminished. Subject to these qualifications, we shall compare the two kinds of models according to the properties of firms' expectations and the cyclical characteristics of commodity prices and output.

Expectations of Firms. There is some direct evidence concerning the quality of expectations of firms. Heady and Kaldor [**16**] have shown that, for the period studied, average expectations were considerably more

TABLE 5.1
PROPERTIES OF COBWEB MODELS

	Expectation p_t^e	Prediction $E(p_t \mid p_{t-1}, \ldots)$	Stability Conditions
(A) Classical (Schultz-Tinbergen-Ricci)	p_{t-1}	$-\frac{\gamma}{\beta} p_t^e$	$\gamma < \beta$
(B) Extrapolative (Goodwin)	$(1-\varrho)p_{t-1} + \varrho p_{t-2}$ $(-1 < \varrho < 1)$	$-\frac{\gamma}{\beta} p_t^e$	$\frac{\gamma}{\beta} < \begin{cases} \frac{1}{1-2\varrho}, & \varrho \leqslant \frac{1}{3} \\ \frac{1}{\varrho}, & \varrho \geqslant \frac{1}{3} \end{cases}$
(C) Adaptive (Nerlove)	$\eta \sum_{j=1}^{\infty} (1-\eta)^{j-1} p_{t-j}$ $(0 < \eta < 1)$	$-\frac{\gamma}{\beta} p_t^e$	$\frac{\gamma}{\beta} < \frac{2}{\eta} - 1$
(D) Rational	0	0	$\beta + \gamma \neq 0$
(E) Rational (with speculation)	$\lambda_1 p_{t-1}$ $(0 < \lambda_1 < 1)$	$\lambda_1 p_{t-1}$	$\alpha > 0$ $\beta + \gamma > 0$

Note: The disturbances are normally and independently distributed with a constant variance.

accurate than simple extrapolation, although there were substantial cross-sectional differences in expectations. Similar conclusions concerning the accuracy have been reached, for quite different expectational data, by Modigliani and Weingartner [**23**].

If often appears that reported expectations underestimate the extent of changes that actually take place. Several studies have tried to relate the two according to the equation:

$$p_t^e = b p_t + v_t', \tag{5.6}$$

where v_t' is a random disturbance. Estimated values of b are positive, but less than unity (see, e.g., Theil [**33**]). Such findings are clearly inconsistent with the cobweb theory, which ordinarily requires a negative coefficient. We shall show below that they are generally consistent with the rational expectations hypothesis.

Bossons and Modigliani [**6**] have pointed out that the size of the estimated coefficient, $\hat{b}$, may be explained by a regression effect. Its relevance may be seen quite clearly as follows. The rational expectations hypothesis states that, in the aggregate, the expected price is an unbiased predictor of the actual price. That is,

$$p_t = p_t^e + v_t , \qquad Ep_t^e v_t = 0 , \qquad Ev_t = 0 . \tag{5.7}$$

The probability limit of the least squares estimate of b in (5.6) would then be given by

$$\text{Plim } \hat{b} = (\text{Var } p^e)/(\text{Var } p) < 1 . \tag{5.8}$$

Cycles. The evidence for the cobweb model lies in the quasi-periodic fluctuations in prices of a number of commodities. The hog cycle is perhaps the best known, but cattle and potatoes have sometimes been cited as others which obey the "theorem." The phase plot of quantity with current and lagged price also has the appearance which gives the cobweb cycle its name.

A dynamic system forced by random shocks typically responds, however, with cycles having a fairly stable period. This is true whether or not any characteristic roots are of the oscillatory type. Slutzky [**30**] and Yule [**34**] first showed that moving-average processes can lead to very regular cycles. A comparison of empirical cycle periods with the properties of the solution of a system of differential or difference equations can therefore be misleading whenever random shocks are present (Haavelmo [**15**]).

The length of the cycle under various hypotheses depends on how we measure the empirical cycle period. Two possibilities are: the interval

TABLE 5.2

CYCLICAL PROPERTIES OF COBWEB MODELS

	Serial Correlation Of Prices, r_1	Mean Interval Between Successive Upcrosses, L	Mean Interval Between Successive Peaks or Troughs, L'
(A) Classical	$r_1 = -\dfrac{\gamma}{\beta} < 0$		
(B) Extrapolative	$r_1 = \dfrac{-\gamma(1-\varrho)}{\beta + \gamma\varrho} < 0$	$2 \leqslant L \leqslant 4$	$2 \leqslant L' \leqslant 3$
(C) Adaptive	$-\dfrac{\eta\gamma}{\beta} \leqslant r_1 \leqslant 0$		
(D) Rational	$r_1 = 0$	$L = 4$	$L' = 3$
(E) Rational - with storage	$r_1 = \lambda_1 > 0$	$L > 4$	$3 \leqslant L' \leqslant 4$

Note: The disturbances are assumed to be normally and independently distributed with a constant variance. β and γ are both assumed to be positive.

between successive "upcrosses" of the time series (i.e., crossing the trend line from below), and the average interval between successive peaks or troughs. Both are given in Table 5.2, which summarizes the serial correlation of prices and mean cycle lengths for the various hypotheses.[12]

That the observed hog cycles were too long for the cobweb theorem was first observed in 1935 by Coase and Fowler [**8**, **9**]. The graph of cattle prices presented given by Ezekiel [**11**] as evidence for the cobweb theorem implies an extraordinarily long period of production (five to seven years). The interval between successive peaks for other commodities tends to be longer than three production periods. Comparisons of the cycle lengths should be interpreted cautiously because they do not allow for positive serial correlation of the exogenous disturbances. Nevertheless, they should not be construed as supporting the cobweb theorem.

Carnegie Institute of Technology

REFERENCES

[**1**] Akerman, G.: "The Cobweb Theorem; A Reconsideration," *Quarterly Journal of Economics*, 71: 151–160 (February, 1957).

[**2**] Allen, H. V.: "A Theorem Concerning the Linearity of Regression," *Statistical Research Memoirs*, 2: 60–68 (1938).

[**3**] Arrow, K. J., and L. Hurwicz: "On the Stability of Competitive Equilibrium I," *Econometrica*, 26: 522–552 (October, 1958).

[**4**] Arrow, K. J., H. D. Block, and L. Hurwicz: "On the Stability of Competitive Equilibrium II," *Econometrica*, 27: 82–109 (January, 1959).

[**5**] Baumol, W. J.: "Speculation, Profitability, and Stability," *Review of Economics and Statistics*, 39: 263–271 (August, 1957).

[**6**] Bossons, J. D., and F. Modigliani: "The Regressiveness of Short Run Business Expectations as Reported to Surveys—An Explanation and Its Implications," *Unpublished*, no date.

[**7**] Buchanan, N. S.: "A Reconsideration of the Cobweb Theorem," *Journal of Political Economy*, 47: 67–81 (February, 1939).

[**8**] Coase, R. H., and R. F. Fowler: "The Pig-Cycle in Great Britain: An Explanation," *Economica*, 4 (NS): 55–82 (1937).

[**9**] ———: "Bacon Production and the Pig-Cycle in Great Britain," *Economica*, 2 (NS): 143–167 (1935). Also "Reply" by R. Cohen and J. D. Barker, pp. 408–422, and "Rejoinder" by Coase and Fowler, pp. 423–428 (1935).

[**10**] Dean, G. W., and E. O. Heady: "Changes in Supply Response and Elasticity For Hogs," *Journal of Farm Economics*, 40: 845–860 (November, 1958).

[**11**] Ezekiel, M.: "The Cobweb Theorem," *Quarterly Journal of Economics*, **52**: 255–280 (February, 1938). Reprinted in *Readings in Business Cycle Theory*.

[**12**] Ferguson, T.: "On the Existence of Linear Regression in Linear Structural Relations," *University of California Publications in Statistics*, Vol. 2, No. 7, pp. 143–166 (University of California Press, 1955).

[12] See Kendall [**21**, Chapters 29 and 30, especially pp. 381 ff.] for the relevant formulas.

[13] GOODWIN, R. M.: "Dynamical Coupling With Especial Reference to Markets Having Production Lags," *Econometrica*, 15 : 181–204 (1947).

[14] GRUNBERG, E., AND F. MODIGLIANI: "The Predictability of Social Events," *Journal of Political Economy*, 62: 465–478 (December, 1954).

[15] HAAVELMO, T.: "The Inadequacy of Testing Dynamic Theory by Comparing Theoretical Solutions and Observed Cycles," *Econometrica*, 8: 312–321 (1940).

[16] HEADY, E. O., AND D. R. KALDOR: "Expectations and Errors in Forecasting Agricultural Prices," *Journal of Political Economy*, 62: 34–47 (February, 1954).

[17] HOLT, C. C., F. MODIGLIANI, J. F. MUTH, AND H. A. SIMON: *Planning Production, Inventories, and Work Force* (Prentice-Hall, 1960).

[18] HOOTON, F. G.: "Risk and the Cobweb Theorem," *Economic Journal*, 60: 69–80 (1950).

[19] JESNESS, O. B.: "Changes in the Agricultural Adjustment Program in the Past 25 Years," *Journal of Farm Economics*, 40: 255–264 (May, 1958).

[20] KALDOR, N.: "Speculation and Economic Stability," *Rev. Economic Studies*, 7: 1–27 (1939–1940).

[21] KENDALL, M. G.: *The Advanced Theory of Statistics*, Vol. II (Hafner, 1951).

[22] ———: "The Analysis of Economic Time-Series—Part I: Prices," *Journal of the Royal Statistical Society, Series A*, 116 : 11–34 (1953).

[23] MODIGLIANI, F., AND H. M. WEINGARTNER: "Forecasting Uses of Anticipatory Data on Investment and Sales," *Quarterly Journal of Economics*, 72: 23–54 (February, 1958).

[24] MUTH, J. F.: "Optimal Properties of Exponentially Weighted Forecasts," *Journal of the American Statistical Association* 55: 299–306 (June, 1960).

[25] NERLOVE, M.: "Adaptive Expectations and Cobweb Phenomena," *Quarterly Journal of Economics*, 73: 227–240 (May, 1958).

[26] ———: *The Dynamics of Supply: Estimation of Farmers' Response to Price* (John Hopkins Press, 1958).

[27] SCHULTZ, H.: *The Theory and Measurement of Demand* (University of Chicago Press, 1958).

[28] SIMON, H. A.: "Dynamic Programming Under Uncertainty with a Quadratic Criterion Function," *Econometrica*, 24: 74–81 (1956).

[29] ———: "Theories of Decision-Making in Economics," *American Economic Review*, 49: 223–283 (June, 1959).

[30] SLUTZKY, E.: "The Summation of Random Causes as the Source of Cyclic Processes," *Econometrica*, 5: 105–146 (April, 1937).

[31] TELSER, L. G.: "A Theory of Speculation Relating Profitability and Stability," *Review of Economics and Statistics*, 61 : 295–301 (August, 1959).

[32] THEIL, H.: "A Note on Certainty Equivalence in Dynamic Planning," *Econometrica*, 25: 346–349 (April, 1957).

[33] ———: *Economic Forecasts and Policy* (North-Holland, 1958).

[34] YULE, G. U.: "On a Method of Investigating Periodicity in Disturbed Series," *Transactions of the Royal Society*, London, A, 226: 267–298 (1927).

[13]

THE MARKET FOR "LEMONS": QUALITY UNCERTAINTY AND THE MARKET MECHANISM *

George A. Akerlof

I. Introduction

This paper relates quality and uncertainty. The existence of goods of many grades poses interesting and important problems for the theory of markets. On the one hand, the interaction of quality differences and uncertainty may explain important institutions of the labor market. On the other hand, this paper presents a struggling attempt to give structure to the statement: "Business in underdeveloped countries is difficult"; in particular, a structure is given for determining the economic costs of dishonesty. Additional applications of the theory include comments on the structure of money markets, on the notion of "insurability," on the liquidity of durables, and on brand-name goods.

There are many markets in which buyers use some market statistic to judge the quality of prospective purchases. In this case there is incentive for sellers to market poor quality merchandise, since the returns for good quality accrue mainly to the entire group whose statistic is affected rather than to the individual seller. As a result there tends to be a reduction in the average quality of goods and also in the size of the market. It should also be perceived that in these markets social and private returns differ, and therefore, in some cases, governmental intervention may increase the welfare of all parties. Or private institutions may arise to take advantage of the potential increases in welfare which can accrue to all parties. By nature, however, these institutions are nonatomistic, and therefore concentrations of power — with ill consequences of their own — can develop.

* The author would especially like to thank Thomas Rothenberg for invaluable comments and inspiration. In addition he is indebted to Roy Radner, Albert Fishlow, Bernard Saffran, William D. Nordhaus, Giorgio La Malfa, Charles C. Holt, John Letiche, and the referee for help and suggestions. He would also like to thank the Indian Statistical Institute and the Ford Foundation for financial support.

The automobile market is used as a finger exercise to illustrate and develop these thoughts. It should be emphasized that this market is chosen for its concreteness and ease in understanding rather than for its importance or realism.

II. The Model with Automobiles as an Example

A. *The Automobiles Market*

The example of used cars captures the essence of the problem. From time to time one hears either mention of or surprise at the large price difference between new cars and those which have just left the showroom. The usual lunch table justification for this phenomenon is the pure joy of owning a "new" car. We offer a different explanation. Suppose (for the sake of clarity rather than reality) that there are just four kinds of cars. There are new cars and used cars. There are good cars and bad cars (which in America are known as "lemons"). A new car may be a good car or a lemon, and of course the same is true of used cars.

The individuals in this market buy a new automobile without knowing whether the car they buy will be good or a lemon. But they do know that with probability q it is a good car and with probability $(1-q)$ it is a lemon; by assumption, q is the proportion of good cars produced and $(1-q)$ is the proportion of lemons.

After owning a specific car, however, for a length of time, the car owner can form a good idea of the quality of this machine; i.e., the owner assigns a new probability to the event that his car is a lemon. This estimate is more accurate than the original estimate. An asymmetry in available information has developed: for the sellers now have more knowledge about the quality of a car than the buyers. But good cars and bad cars must still sell at the same price — since it is impossible for a buyer to tell the difference between a good car and a bad car. It is apparent that a used car cannot have the same valuation as a new car — if it did have the same valuation, it would clearly be advantageous to trade a lemon at the price of new car, and buy another new car, at a higher probability q of being good and a lower probability of being bad. Thus the owner of a good machine must be locked in. Not only is it true that he cannot receive the true value of his car, but he cannot even obtain the expected value of a new car.

Gresham's law has made a modified reappearance. For most cars traded will be the "lemons," and good cars may not be traded at all. The "bad" cars tend to drive out the good (in much the same way that bad money drives out the good). But the analogy with Gresham's law is not quite complete: bad cars drive out the good because they sell at the same price as good cars; similarly, bad money drives out good because the exchange rate is even. But the bad cars sell at the same price as good cars since it is impossible for a buyer to tell the difference between a good and a bad car; only the seller knows. In Gresham's law, however, presumably both buyer and seller can tell the difference between good and bad money. So the analogy is instructive, but not complete.

B. Asymmetrical Information

It has been seen that the good cars may be driven out of the market by the lemons. But in a more continuous case with different grades of goods, even worse pathologies can exist. For it is quite possible to have the bad driving out the not-so-bad driving out the medium driving out the not-so-good driving out the good in such a sequence of events that no market exists at all.

One can assume that the demand for used automobiles depends most strongly upon two variables — the price of the automobile p and the average quality of used cars traded, μ, or $Q^d = D(p, \mu)$. Both the supply of used cars and also the average quality μ will depend upon the price, or $\mu = \mu\ (p)$ and $S = S(p)$. And in equilibrium the supply must equal the demand for the given average quality, or $S(p) = D(p, \mu(p))$. As the price falls, normally the quality will also fall. And it is quite possible that no goods will be traded at any price level.

Such an example can be derived from utility theory. Assume that there are just two groups of traders: groups one and two. Give group one a utility function

$$U_1 = M + \sum_{i=1}^{n} x_i$$

where M is the consumption of goods other than automobiles, x_i is the quality of the ith automobile, and n is the number of automobiles.

Similarly, let

$$U_2 = M + \sum_{i=1}^{n} 3/2 x_i$$

where M, x_i, and n are defined as before.

Three comments should be made about these utility functions: (1) without linear utility (say with logarithmic utility) one gets needlessly mired in algebraic complication. (2) The use of linear utility allows a focus on the effects of asymmetry of information; with a concave utility function we would have to deal jointly with the usual risk-variance effects of uncertainty and the special effects we wish to discuss here. (3) U_1 and U_2 have the odd characteristic that the addition of a second car, or indeed a kth car, adds the same amount of utility as the first. Again realism is sacrificed to avoid a diversion from the proper focus.

To continue, it is assumed (1) that both type one traders and type two traders are von Neumann-Morgenstern maximizers of expected utility; (2) that group one has N cars with uniformly distributed quality x, $0 \leqq x \leqq 2$, and group two has no cars; (3) that the price of "other goods" M is unity.

Denote the income (including that derived from the sale of automobiles) of all type one traders as Y_1 and the income of all type two traders as Y_2. The demand for used cars will be the sum of the demands by both groups. When one ignores indivisibilities, the demand for automobiles by type one traders will be

$$D_1 = Y_1/p \qquad \mu/p > 1$$
$$D_1 = 0 \qquad \mu/p < 1.$$

And the supply of cars offered by type one traders is

$$S_2 = pN/2 \qquad p \leqq 2 \tag{1}$$

with average quality

$$\mu = p/2. \tag{2}$$

(To derive (1) and (2), the uniform distribution of automobile quality is used.)

Similarly the demand of type two traders is

$$D_2 = Y_2/p \qquad 3\mu/2 > p$$
$$D_2 = 0 \qquad 3\mu/2 < p$$

and

$$S_2 = 0.$$

Thus total demand $D(p, \mu)$ is

$$D(p, \mu) = (Y_2 + Y_1)/p \qquad \text{if } p < \mu$$
$$D(p, \mu) = Y_2/p \qquad \text{if } \mu < p < 3\mu/2$$
$$D(p, \mu) = 0 \qquad \text{if } p > 3\mu/2.$$

However, with price p, average quality is $p/2$ and therefore at no price will any trade take place at all: in spite of the fact that *at any given price* between 0 and 3 there are traders of type one who are willing to sell their automobiles at a price which traders of type two are willing to pay.

C. Symmetric Information

The foregoing is contrasted with the case of symmetric information. Suppose that the quality of all cars is uniformly distributed, $0 \leqq x \leqq 2$. Then the demand curves and supply curves can be written as follows:

Supply

$S(p) = N$ $\quad p>1$

$S(p) = 0$ $\quad p<1.$

And the demand curves are

$D(p) = (Y_2+Y_1)/p$ $\quad p<1$

$D(p) = (Y_2/p)$ $\quad 1<p<3/2$

$D(p) = 0$ $\quad p>3/2.$

In equilibrium

(3) $p = 1$ $\quad$ if $Y_2<N$

(4) $p = Y_2/N$ $\quad$ if $2Y_2/3<N<Y_2$

(5) $p = 3/2$ $\quad$ if $N<2Y_2/3.$

If $N<Y_2$ there is a gain in utility over the case of asymmetrical information of $N/2$. (If $N>Y_2$, in which case the income of type two traders is insufficient to buy all N automobiles, there is a gain in utility of $Y_2/2$ units.)

Finally, it should be mentioned that in this example, if traders of groups one and two have the same probabilistic estimates about the quality of individual automobiles — though these estimates may vary from automobile to automobile — (3), (4), and (5) will still describe equilibrium with one slight change: p will then represent the expected price of one quality unit.

III. Examples and Applications

A. Insurance

It is a well-known fact that people over 65 have great difficulty in buying medical insurance. The natural question arises: why doesn't the price rise to match the risk?

Our answer is that as the price level rises the people who insure themselves will be those who are increasingly certain that they will need the insurance; for error in medical check-ups, doctors' sympathy with older patients, and so on make it much easier for the applicant to assess the risks involved than the insurance company. The result is that the average medical condition of insurance applicants deteriorates as the price level rises — with the result that no insurance sales may take place at any price.[1] This is strictly analogous to our automobiles case, where the average quality of used cars supplied fell with a corresponding fall in the price level. This agrees with the explanation in insurance textbooks:

> Generally speaking policies are not available at ages materially greater than sixty-five. . . . The term premiums are too high for any but the most pessimistic (which is to say the least healthy) insureds to find attractive. Thus there is a severe problem of adverse selection at these ages.[2]

The statistics do not contradict this conclusion. While demands for health insurance rise with age, a 1956 national sample survey of 2,809 families with 8,898 persons shows that hospital insurance coverage drops from 63 per cent of those aged 45 to 54, to 31 per cent for those over 65. And surprisingly, this survey also finds average medical expenses for males aged 55 to 64 of $88, while males over 65 pay an average of $77.[3] While noninsured expenditure rises from $66 to $80 in these age groups, insured expenditure declines from $105 to $70. The conclusion is tempting that insurance companies are particularly wary of giving medical insurance to older people.

The principle of "adverse selection" is potentially present in all lines of insurance. The following statement appears in an insurance textbook written at the Wharton School:

> There is potential adverse selection in the fact that healthy term insurance policy holders may decide to terminate their coverage when they become older and premiums mount. This action could leave an insurer with an undue proportion of below average risks and claims might be higher than anticipated. Adverse selection "appears (or at least is possible) whenever the individual or group insured has freedom to buy or not to buy, to choose the amount or plan of insurance, and to persist or to discontinue as a policy holder."[4]

Group insurance, which is the most common form of medical insurance in the United States, picks out the healthy, for generally

1. Arrow's fine article, "Uncertainty and Medical Care" (*American Economic Review*, Vol. 53, 1963), does not make this point explicitly. He emphasizes "moral hazard" rather than "adverse selection." In its strict sense, the presence of "moral hazard" is equally disadvantageous for both governmental and private programs; in its broader sense, which includes "adverse selection," "moral hazard" gives a decided advantage to government insurance programs.

2. O. D. Dickerson, *Health Insurance* (Homewood, Ill.: Irwin, 1959), p. 333.

3. O. W. Anderson (with J. J. Feldman), *Family Medical Costs and Insurance* (New York: McGraw-Hill, 1956).

4. H. S. Denenberg, R. D. Eilers, G. W. Hoffman, C. A. Kline, J. J. Melone, and H. W. Snider, *Risk and Insurance* (Englewood Cliffs, N. J.: Prentice Hall, 1964), p. 446.

adequate health is a precondition for employment. At the same time this means that medical insurance is least available to those who need it most, for the insurance companies do their own "adverse selection."

This adds one major argument in favor of medicare.[5] On a cost benefit basis medicare may pay off: for it is quite possible that every individual in the market would be willing to pay the expected cost of his medicare and buy insurance, yet no insurance company can afford to sell him a policy — for at any price it will attract too many "lemons." The welfare economics of medicare, in this view, is *exactly* analogous to the usual classroom argument for public expenditure on roads.

B. The Employment of Minorities

The Lemons Principle also casts light on the employment of minorities. Employers may refuse to hire members of minority groups for certain types of jobs. This decision may not reflect irrationality or prejudice — but profit maximization. For race may serve as a good *statistic* for the applicant's social background, quality of schooling, and general job capabilities.

Good quality schooling could serve as a substitute for this statistic; by grading students the schooling system can give a better indicator of quality than other more superficial characteristics. As T. W. Schultz writes, "The educational establishment *discovers* and cultivates potential talent. The capabilities of children and mature students can never be known until *found* and cultivated."[6] (Italics added.) An untrained worker may have valuable natural talents, but these talents must be certified by "the educational establishment" before a company can afford to use them. The certifying establishment, however, must be credible; the unreliability of slum schools decreases the economic possibilities of their students.

This lack may be particularly disadvantageous to members of

5. The following quote, again taken from an insurance textbook, shows how far the medical insurance market is from perfect competition:

> ". . . insurance companies must screen their applicants. Naturally it is true that many people will voluntarily seek adequate insurance on their own initiative. But in such lines as accident and health insurance, companies are likely to give a second look to persons who voluntarily seek insurance without being approached by an agent." (F. J. Angell, *Insurance, Principles and Practices*, New York: The Ronald Press, 1957, pp. 8–9.)

This shows that insurance is *not* a commodity for sale on the open market.

6. T. W. Schultz, *The Economic Value of Education* (New York: Columbia University Press, 1964), p. 42.

already disadvantaged minority groups. For an employer may make a rational decision not to hire any members of these groups in responsible positions — because it is difficult to distinguish those with good job qualifications from those with bad qualifications. This type of decision is clearly what George Stigler had in mind when he wrote, "in a regime of ignorance Enrico Fermi would have been a gardener, Von Neumann a checkout clerk at a drugstore." [7]

As a result, however, the rewards for work in slum schools tend to accrue to the group as a whole — in raising its average quality — rather than to the individual. Only insofar as information in addition to race is used is there any incentive for training.

An additional worry is that the Office of Economic Opportunity is going to use cost-benefit analysis to evaluate its programs. For many benefits may be external. The benefit from training minority groups may arise as much from raising the average quality of the group as from raising the quality of the individual trainee; and, likewise, the returns may be distributed over the whole group rather than to the individual.

C. The Costs of Dishonesty

The Lemons model can be used to make some comments on the costs of dishonesty. Consider a market in which goods are sold honestly or dishonestly; quality may be represented, or it may be misrepresented. The purchaser's problem, of course, is to identify quality. The presence of people in the market who are willing to offer inferior goods tends to drive the market out of existence — as in the case of our automobile "lemons." It is this possibility that represents the major costs of dishonesty — for dishonest dealings tend to drive honest dealings out of the market. There may be potential buyers of good quality products and there may be potential sellers of such products in the appropriate price range; however, the presence of people who wish to pawn bad wares as good wares tends to drive out the legitimate business. The cost of dishonesty, therefore, lies not only in the amount by which the purchaser is cheated; the cost also must include the loss incurred from driving legitimate business out of existence.

Dishonesty in business is a serious problem in underdeveloped countries. Our model gives a possible structure to this statement and delineates the nature of the "external" economies involved. In particular, in the model economy described, dishonesty, or the

7. G. J. Stigler, "Information and the Labor Market," *Journal of Political Economy*, Vol. 70 (Oct. 1962), Supplement, p. 104.

misrepresentation of the quality of automobiles, costs 1/2 unit of utility per automobile; furthermore, it reduces the size of the used car market from N to 0. We can, consequently, directly evaluate the costs of dishonesty — at least in theory.

There is considerable evidence that quality variation is greater in underdeveloped than in developed areas. For instance, the need for quality control of exports and State Trading Corporations can be taken as one indicator. In India, for example, under the Export Quality Control and Inspection Act of 1963, "about 85 per cent of Indian exports are covered under one or the other type of quality control." [8] Indian housewives must carefully glean the rice of the local bazaar to sort out stones of the same color and shape which have been intentionally added to the rice. Any comparison of the heterogeneity of quality in the street market and the canned qualities of the American supermarket suggests that quality variation is a greater problem in the East than in the West.

In one traditional pattern of development the merchants of the pre-industrial generation turn into the first entrepreneurs of the next. The best-documented case is Japan,[9] but this also may have been the pattern for Britain and America.[1] In *our* picture the important skill of the merchant is identifying the quality of merchandise; those who can identify used cars in our example and can guarantee the quality may profit by as much as the difference between type two traders' buying price and type one traders' selling price. These people are the merchants. In production these skills are equally necessary — both to be able to identify the quality of inputs and to certify the quality of outputs. And this is one (added) reason why the merchants may logically become the first entrepreneurs.

The problem, of course, is that entrepreneurship may be a scarce resource; no development text leaves entrepreneurship unemphasized. Some treat it as central.[2] Given, then, that entrepreneurship is scarce, there are two ways in which product variations impede development. First, the pay-off to trade is great for would-be entrepreneurs, and hence they are diverted from production; second, the amount of entrepreneurial time per unit output is greater, the greater are the quality variations.

8. *The Times of India*, Nov. 10, 1967, p. 1.

9. See M. J. Levy, Jr., "Contrasting Factors in the Modernization of China and Japan," in *Economic Growth: Brazil, India, Japan*, ed. S. Kuznets, *et. al.* (Durham, N. C.: Duke University Press, 1955).

1. C. P. Kindleberger, *Economic Development* (New York: McGraw-Hill, 1958), p. 86.

2. For example, see W. Arthur Lewis, *The Theory of Economic Growth* (Homewood, Ill.: Irwin, 1955), p. 196.

D. Credit Markets in Underdeveloped Countries

(1) Credit markets in underdeveloped countries often strongly reflect the operation of the Lemons Principle. In India a major fraction of industrial enterprise is controlled by managing agencies (according to a recent survey, these "managing agencies" controlled 65.7 per cent of the net worth of public limited companies and 66 per cent of total assets).[3] Here is a historian's account of the function and genesis of the "managing agency system":

> The management of the South Asian commercial scene remained the function of merchant houses, and a type of organization peculiar to South Asia known as the Managing Agency. When a new venture was promoted (such as a manufacturing plant, a plantation, or a trading venture), the promoters would approach an established managing agency. The promoters might be Indian or British, and they might have technical or financial resources or merely a concession. In any case they would turn to the agency because of its reputation, which would encourage confidence in the venture and stimulate investment.[4]

In turn, a second major feature of the Indian industrial scene has been the dominance of these managing agencies by caste (or, more accurately, communal) groups. Thus firms can usually be classified according to communal origin.[5] In this environment, in which outside investors are likely to be bilked of their holdings, either (1) firms establish a reputation for "honest" dealing, which confers upon them a monopoly rent insofar as their services are

3. *Report of the Committee on the Distribution of Income and Levels of Living,* Part I, Government of India, Planning Commission, Feb. 1964, p. 44.

4. H. Tinker, *South Asia: A Short History* (New York: Praeger, 1966), p. 134.

5. The existence of the following table (and also the small per cent of firms under mixed control) indicates the communalization of the control of firms. *Source*: M. M. Mehta, *Structure of Indian Industries* (Bombay: Popular Book Depot, 1955), p. 314.

DISTRIBUTION OF INDUSTRIAL CONTROL BY COMMUNITY

	1911	1931 (number of firms)	1951
British	281	416	382
Parsis	15	25	19
Gujratis	3	11	17
Jews	5	9	3
Muslims	—	10	3
Bengalis	8	5	20
Marwaris	—	6	96
Mixed control	28	28	79
Total	341	510	619

Also, for the cotton industry see H. Fukuzawa, "Cotton Mill Industry," in V. B. Singh, editor, *Economic History of India, 1857–1956* (Bombay: Allied Publishers, 1965).

limited in supply, or (2) the sources of finance are limited to local communal groups which can use communal — and possibly familial — ties to encourage honest dealing *within* the community. It is, in Indian economic history, extraordinarily difficult to discern whether the savings of rich landlords failed to be invested in the industrial sector (1) because of a fear to invest in ventures controlled by other communities, (2) because of inflated propensities to consume, or (3) because of low rates of return.[6] At the very least, however, it is clear that the British-owned managing agencies tended to have an equity holding whose communal origin was more heterogeneous than the Indian-controlled agency houses, and would usually include both Indian and British investors.

(2) A second example of the workings of the Lemons Principle concerns the extortionate rates which the local moneylender charges his clients. In India these high rates of interest have been the leading factor in landlessness; the so-called "Cooperative Movement" was meant to counteract this growing landlessness by setting up banks to compete with the local moneylenders.[7] While the large banks in the central cities have prime interest rates of 6, 8, and 10 per cent, the local moneylender charges 15, 25, and even 50 per cent. The answer to this seeming paradox is that credit is

6. For the mixed record of industrial profits, see D. H. Buchanan, *The Development of Capitalist Enterprise in India* (New York: Kelley, 1966, reprinted).

7. The leading authority on this is Sir Malcolm Darling. See his *Punjabi Peasant in Prosperity and Debt*. The following table may also prove instructive:

	Commonest rates for —		
	Secured loans (per cent)	Unsecured loans (per cent)	Grain loans (per cent)
Punjab	6 to 12	12 to 24 (18 ¾ commonest)	25
United Provinces	9 to 12	24 to 37 ½	25 (50 in Oudh)
Bihar		18 ¾	50
Orissa	12 to 18 ¾	25	25
Bengal	8 to 12	9 to 18 for "respectable clients" 18 ¾ to 37 ½ (the latter common to agriculturalists)	
Central Provinces	6 to 12	15 for proprietors 24 for occupancy tenants 37 ½ for ryots with no right of transfer	25
Bombay	9 to 12	12 to 25 (18 commonest)	
Sind		36	
Madras	12	15 to 18 (in insecure tracts 24 not uncommon)	20 to 50

Source: Punjabi Peasant in Prosperity and Debt, 3rd ed. (Oxford University Press, 1932), p. 190.

granted only where the granter has (1) easy means of enforcing his contract or (2) personal knowledge of the character of the borrower. The middleman who tries to arbitrage between the rates of the moneylender and the central bank is apt to attract all the "lemons" and thereby make a loss.

This interpretation can be seen in Sir Malcolm Darling's interpretation of the village moneylender's power:

> It is only fair to remember that in the Indian village the money-lender is often the one thrifty person amongst a generally thriftless people; and that his methods of business, though demoralizing under modern conditions, suit the happy-go-lucky ways of the peasant. He is always accessible, even at night; dispenses with troublesome formalities, asks no inconvenient questions, advances promptly, and if interest is paid, does not press for repayment of principal. He keeps in close personal touch with his clients, and in many villages shares their occasions of weal or woe. *With his intimate knowledge of those around him he is able, without serious risk, to finance those who would otherwise get no loan at all.* [Italics added.] [8]

Or look at Barbara Ward's account:

> A small shopkeeper in a Hong Kong fishing village told me: "I give credit to anyone who anchors regularly in our bay; but if it is someone I don't know well, then I think twice about it unless I can find out all about him." [9]

Or, a profitable sideline of cotton ginning in Iran is the loaning of money for the next season, since the ginning companies often have a line of credit from Teheran banks at the market rate of interest. But in the first years of operation large losses are expected from unpaid debts — due to poor knowledge of the local scene.[1]

IV. Counteracting Institutions

Numerous institutions arise to counteract the effects of quality uncertainty. One obvious institution is guarantees. Most consumer durables carry guarantees to ensure the buyer of some normal expected quality. One natural result of our model is that the risk is borne by the seller rather than by the buyer.

A second example of an institution which counteracts the effects of quality uncertainty is the brand-name good. Brand names

8. Darling, *op. cit.*, p. 204.

9. B. Ward, "Cash or Credit Crops," *Economic Development and Cultural Change*, Vol. 8 (Jan. 1960), reprinted in *Peasant Society: A Reader*, ed. G. Foster *et al.* (Boston: Little Brown and Company, 1967). Quote on p. 142. In the same volume, see also G. W. Skinner, "Marketing and Social Structure in Rural China," and S. W. Mintz, "Pratik: Haitian Personal Economic Relations."

1. Personal conversation with mill manager, April 1968.

not only indicate quality but also give the consumer a means of retaliation if the quality does not meet expectations. For the consumer will then curtail future purchases. Often too, new products are associated with old brand names. This ensures the prospective consumer of the quality of the product.

Chains — such as hotel chains or restaurant chains — are similar to brand names. One observation consistent with our approach is the chain restaurant. These restaurants, at least in the United States, most often appear on interurban highways. The customers are seldom local. The reason is that these well-known chains offer a better hamburger than the *average* local restaurant; at the same time, the local customer, who knows his area, can usually choose a place he prefers.

Licensing practices also reduce quality uncertainty. For instance, there is the licensing of doctors, lawyers, and barbers. Most skilled labor carries some certification indicating the attainment of certain levels of proficiency. The high school diploma, the baccalaureate degree, the Ph.D., even the Nobel Prize, to some degree, serve this function of certification. And education and labor markets themselves have their own "brand names."

V. Conclusion

We have been discussing economic models in which "trust" is important. Informal unwritten guarantees are preconditions for trade and production. Where these guarantees are indefinite, business will suffer — as indicated by our generalized Gresham's law. This aspect of uncertainty has been explored by game theorists, as in the Prisoner's Dilemma, but usually it has not been incorporated in the more traditional Arrow-Debreu approach to uncertainty.[2] But the difficulty of distinguishing good quality from bad is inherent in the business world; this may indeed explain many economic institutions and may in fact be one of the more important aspects of uncertainty.

University of California, Berkeley
Indian Statistical Institute — Planning Unit, New Delhi

2. R. Radner, "Équilibre de Marchés à Terme et au Comptant en Cas d'Incertitude," in *Cahiers d'Econometrie*, Vol. 12 (Nov. 1967), Centre National de la Recherche Scientifique, Paris.

[14]

Some Results on Incentive Contracts with Applications to Education and Employment, Health Insurance, and Law Enforcement

By MILTON HARRIS AND ARTUR RAVIV*

When decision-making authority is delegated from one agent to another, contractual arrangements are often used to allocate resources and outputs. Such situations may be analyzed using the theory of principal-agent relationships. This theory seeks to characterize optimal contracts and explain observed arrangements. Examples which fit the "agency paradigm" include employer-employee, insurer-insured, and owner-manager relations. In this paper, we report some results which significantly extend the theory of agency to situations characterized by a divergence of incentives between the two parties and asymmetric information with opportunities for acquiring information. In addition, we discuss several applications of this theory.

The theory of optimal contracts under conditions of uncertainty has received considerable attention. Kenneth Arrow and Robert Wilson (1968) were concerned with the optimal sharing of purely exogenous risk. Wilson (1969) and Stephen Ross considered situations in which the risk could be affected by the actions of the agents. They analyze contracts which induce similar attitudes toward risk on the part of the agents, thus allowing the possibility that decentralized decision making will be optimal. Conditions under which such arrangements are indeed Pareto optimal are also investigated. In their models, incentive problems arise purely as a consequence of diverse attitudes toward risk among the agents. A. Michael Spence and Richard Zeckhauser, in the context of insurance contracts, introduced the problem of a divergence in incentives due to the action of an agent together with differential information among agents. More recently, Joseph Stiglitz (1975a) analyzed incentive contracts between employers and employees. With regard to differential information, both Spence-Zeckhauser and Stiglitz assume one of two extreme cases: either the agent's action is known by everyone with certainty (in which case there is no differential information), or no information about the agent's action is available to anyone except the agent himself. A somewhat intermediate case was analyzed by Robert Townsend in which the exact information possessed by one agent can be made available to the other at some cost.

Two important aspects of agency relationships are not fully explored in the literature on the theory of contracts. First, most agency relationships must deal with incentive problems which arise because the agent would prefer to work less, other things equal, while the principal is indifferent to the level of the agent's effort, other things (i.e., his share of the payoff) equal. This type of incentive problem is somewhat different from the one considered by Wilson (1969) and Ross in which a divergence in incentives results only from different attitudes toward risk. Second, in most instances an agent may acquire information about other agents' actions. This possibility was discussed in interesting papers by Armen Alchian and Harold Demsetz and by C. Michael Jensen and William Meckling. The quality of the information obtained through monitoring (or supervising) depends on the resources committed to this activity as well as on the available monitoring technology. Furthermore, as Stiglitz

*Carnegie-Mellon University. We would like to acknowledge helpful discussions with Ed Prescott and Rob Townsend, as well as suggestions of Stephen Ross, Martin Hellwig, an anonymous referee, and the managing editor of this *Review*.

points out, "... the amount (or quality) of supervision will affect both the optimal incentive scheme which will be used and the level of expected utility which the individual will attain" (1975a, p. 572). Consequently, the optimal incentive contract will depend on the available monitoring technology. In this paper, we explore these aspects of the agency problem.

Our analysis is based on a model in which there are two individuals: one, denoted the agent, takes an action which together with the realization of an exogenous random variable results in the payoff to be divided between the agent and the other individual, denoted the principal. Incentive problems arise because the agent has a disutility for the action while the principal does not. We distinguish two versions of this model. In the first, the agent is assumed to take his action without any information regarding the realization of the exogenous random state. In the second version, the agent is assumed to know the value of the random state before taking his action. In both versions, the object of the analysis is to discover the form of the Pareto optimal contract, that is, how the optimal sharing arrangement for the payoff depends on the observed variables. In particular, our analysis deals with the following issues: When would we expect to observe performance-contingent contracts, and what would be the form of such contracts; when performance is not observable, under what conditions would we expect contracts to depend on imperfect estimates of performance, what types of estimators would be used, and how would they be incorporated into the contract.

Our results are discussed in terms of the employer-employee relationship. They are, however, more general, and we discuss their implications for three other agency relationships.

The first application is to the analysis of employment contracts based on training or education and ability. Here we show under what conditions and in what form it is optimal to make employment contracts contingent on training or ability. In particular we show when the type of contract used in the "signaling literature" (see Spence, 1973, 1974, 1976; John Riley; Stiglitz, 1975b) is Pareto optimal.

The second application is to health insurance contracts. We show when indemnity insurance, that is, contracts in which the insurance payment depends only on the degree of illness, is optimal. We also show when the optimal policy provides payment contingent on the level of medical care chosen. The case in which the level of medical care chosen is not directly observable is also considered.

The third application of the analysis is to the problem of procuring the optimal amount of law enforcement, an issue which was addressed by Gary Becker and George Stigler. We exhibit conditions on the information structure under which the standard type of compensation arrangement for the enforcer (i.e., a salary) would lead to an inefficiently large degree of malfeasance or nonfeasance (shirking). We also show under what conditions these inefficiencies could be resolved by the use of contracts which we exhibit. In particular, we provide conditions under which some suggestions of Becker and Stigler would be optimal.

I. The Agency Model

In this section we describe the model with which we address the issues mentioned above (a more detailed and formal treatment may be found in the authors' working paper). In this model there are two individuals, "the principal" and "the agent." For concreteness, in describing the model and results, we refer to these individuals as the employer and worker, respectively.

The worker chooses a level of effort (or action) a, which together with the realization of some exogenous random variable θ determines the value of the worker's product x (the payoff). The random variable θ may be interpreted as the result of any exogenous uncertain event which affects the worker's productivity, for example, the weather, equipment failure, the price of the product, etc. We represent the relationship among the value of the worker's output, the worker's effort, and the realization of the random variable by a production function X, that is,

$$(1) \qquad x = X(a, \theta)$$

We assume that greater effort by the worker results in greater output for any value of θ (i.e., $X_1 > 0$ for all a, θ).

Two important cases may be distinguished regarding the information available to the worker when he decides upon his level of effort. First, in Model 1, we assume that he does *not* know the value of θ when he chooses his effort. For example, a sharecropper may not know what the weather will be when he plants his crop; a lawyer, when he prepares his case, may not know which judge will preside. Second, in Model 2, we assume that the worker *does* observe the value of θ and chooses his effort contingent on this observation. For example, a salesman may observe the state of demand before deciding how many calls to make.

The division of the product will be determined by a function which may depend on any variable which is observable by both parties, that is, whose value is known by both parties when the product is divided. This assumption rules out contracts which are not incentive compatible. The function and its list of arguments denoted $(S; z)$ will be called a *contract*. The value of $S(z)$ is interpreted as the worker's share of the product while the employer's share is $x - S(z)$. The product x is assumed always to be observable by both parties. In addition to x, the list z might include the effort a, provided, of course, that it is observable. If a is not observable, z might include an estimator, denoted α of a. For example, an estimator of the sharecropper's effort might be the amount of time he spends in the field. An estimator of the salesman's effort might be the number of miles he drives. When available, the estimator will be called a *monitor*, that is, a monitor is a random variable whose distribution is conditional on a. The class of available monitors is referred to as the *monitoring technology*.

Associated with the worker is a utility function U, whose first argument is the worker's share of the product and whose second argument is his effort. The worker is assumed to prefer less effort to more effort, other things equal. We therefore assume that

$$(2) \qquad U_1 > 0; \qquad U_2 < 0$$

We will often assume that the worker is risk averse, that is, that U is strictly concave in the first argument.

Given a contract $(S; z)$, in Model 1 the worker determines his effort by solving the following maximization problem:

$$(3) \qquad \max_a E_\theta U[S(z), a]$$

In Model 2, the worker chooses a as a function of θ to solve

$$(3') \qquad \max_a U[S(z), a]$$

In both models, the effort chosen will depend on the functional form of S; in Model 2, it will also depend on the realization of the exogenous random variable.

Associated with the employer is a utility function V, which is a function *only* of his share of the product. We assume V is monotone increasing, concave (i.e., the employer is either risk neutral or risk averse). Given a contract $(S; z)$, and a level of effort a chosen by the worker according to either (3) or (3′), the employer's utility is

$$(4) \qquad E_\theta V[X(a, \theta) - S(z)]$$

This concludes our presentation of the model. We turn in the next section to a description of our results.

II. Results

Our results characterize the Pareto optimal contracts under various assumptions concerning the availability of information. In particular, optimal contracts are investigated under alternative assumptions on the observability of the worker's effort and the random variable and on the existing technology for monitoring the worker's effort. We are interested in Pareto optimal contracts on the supposition that observed contracts will have the property that, given the availability of information, neither agent's expected utility can be increased without decreasing the expected utility of the other agent. Thus we seek to characterize the contracts which we expect to arise under various information structures. Our results are simply discussed here without formal derivations; these may be found in our earlier paper.

To begin, suppose that the realization of the random variable (also referred to as "the state of nature" or simply "the state") is freely observable by both employer and worker when the product is distributed. In this case, our first result implies that making the contract contingent on the worker's effort provides no gains over contracts which depend only on output and the observed value of θ. Therefore, if the state is freely observable, we would *not* expect to observe contracts contingent on worker effort. Thus *ex post* uncertainty as to the relationship between the effort and the product is essential if contracts based on worker performance are to be observed. For future reference we state this result as

PROPOSITION 1: *The expected utilities achieved under any contract which depends on the product, the effort, and the state can also be achieved under a contract which depends on the product and the state, but not on the effort. This result holds for both Models* 1 *and* 2.

The above result does not yield information as to the form of the optimal contract when the state is freely observable. This information is provided by

PROPOSITION 2: *The Pareto optimal contract which depends on the product and the state specifies a "standard" output contingent on the state. The worker receives an amount which depends on the standard output and perhaps on the state, plus the difference between the actual output and the standard. The employer receives an amount which depends only on the state and is therefore unaffected by the worker's level of effort. This result holds for both Models* 1 *and* 2.

To illustrate this result, consider the sharecropper example mentioned above. In this case, Propositions 1 and 2 imply that if the weather is the only exogenous random factor affecting the crop, we would expect to observe an arrangement in which the tenant "pays" the landlord an amount of output contingent only on the weather and keeps the remainder of the crop.

Note that Propositions 1 and 2 hold regardless of attitudes toward risk of the employer (landlord) and worker (tenant). Thus the determination of the variables on which the contract will depend (if all are observable) is independent of attitudes toward risk. For example, if output, effort, and the weather are all observable, the contract will depend only on output and weather. This result does depend, however, on the ability of both parties to agree *ex ante* on which types of weather are possible, what the probability attached to each type is, and how weather affects output. It also depends on the ability of both parties to observe *ex post* which type of weather occurred. Attitudes toward risk do play a role in determining the sharing function. For example, if the landlord is risk neutral, the contract will be such that if the tenant puts in sufficient effort to produce the (weather-contingent) standard output, then the tenant's share will be independent of the weather. If the tenant does not render the effort implicit in the standard output, however, his share may be weather-dependent. The landlord's share (i.e., rent) *will* depend on the weather, in general, if the tenant is risk averse.

Attitudes toward risk also play an important role in determining the variables on which the optimal contract will depend when the state is not observable, *ex post*. The next result states that risk aversion on the part of the worker is a necessary and sufficient condition for contracts which depend explicitly on effort to be superior to contracts which depend only on the output. Intuitively, if the worker is risk neutral, it will be optimal for him to bear all the risk associated with uncertain productivity. In this case, all effects of the worker's performance are internalized, and thus incentive problems are resolved without the use of performance-contingent contracts. When the worker is risk averse, optimality requires some sharing of risk, and therefore the employer bears some of the consequences of the worker's choice of effort. In this case, performance-contingent contracts are superior to contracts based only on output.

PROPOSITION 3: (i) *If the worker is risk neutral, any contract which depends only on output and effort can be dominated (in the Pareto sense) by a contract which depends only on output.*

(ii) *If the worker is risk averse, any contract which depends only on output can be strictly dominated by a contract which depends on both output and effort.*

(iii) *If the worker is risk averse, any contract which depends only on output can be strictly dominated by a contract which depends only on output and the state and is of the form given in Proposition* 2.

These results hold for Models 1 and 2.[1] Next we characterize the form of Pareto optimal contracts which depend on output and effort.

PROPOSITION 4: *Any Pareto optimal contract in the class of contracts depending only on output and effort has the property that the worker's share depends only on the output, provided his effort meets a prespecified criterion. If not, he receives nothing. This result holds for Model* 1.

Thus when the worker's effort is freely observable, and the worker is risk averse, we would expect to observe contracts which stipulate a particular choice of effort by the worker. Since the worker will always choose to meet the requirement, we refer to this contract as a forcing contract.[2]

With respect to the sharecropping paradigm, these results imply that if the tenant is risk averse, and output and effort, *but not the weather,* are observable *ex post,*[3] we would expect the sharing arrangement to include a stipulation of how much effort the tenant is expected to expend. If the tenant puts in the required effort (and he will if his effort is perfectly observable), he will receive a share of the product. This share will depend on the product and the attitudes toward risk of the landlord and tenant. For example if the landlord is risk neutral (and not the tenant), the tenant will get a fixed wage independent of output (or the weather). If, on the other hand, the tenant (and not the landlord) is risk neutral, contracts stipulating the tenant's effort are unnecessary; we expect to observe the landlord receiving a fixed rent with the tenant keeping the residual.

We now turn to some results regarding the use of imperfect estimators of effort as a contingency affecting the distribution of the product. Clearly we would not expect to observe the use of imperfect monitors of effort when there are no gains to using actual effort. We have exhibited above two situations in which there are no gains to acquiring information about the worker's effort (even if such information is available costlessly). Moreover we have shown that in all other cases there are gains to acquiring information, that is, if information of "sufficient quality" can be obtained at a "sufficiently low price," then both individuals can be made better off. The two conditions

[1] For Model 2 the utility function of the worker is assumed to be separable and the production function is one-to-one in the state.

[2] This terminology was suggested to us by Ross.

[3] With respect to the sharecropping example, one might question the assumption that the tenant's effort is observable while the weather is not. We agree that these assumptions are not particularly appropriate to sharecropping. Our model is, however, applicable to a large class of situations, and for many of these, the assumptions are appropriate (see Section III). We use the sharecropping example here only for the purpose of illustrating all our results with a consistent example.

under which there are no gains to monitoring the worker's effort are (a) when the realization of θ, the exogenous random variable affecting output, is observable, and (b) when the worker is risk neutral. From a methodological point of view, these results imply that it is not possible to simplify the analysis of monitoring by assuming away either exogenous uncertainty or risk aversion on the part of the worker.

In general, even when there are gains to perfect information on effort, these gains may be impossible to realize through imperfect monitoring. The introduction of imperfect information on the worker's effort into a contract produces two opposing effects on the welfare of the parties to the contract. First, since the information is imperfect, additional uncertainty is introduced. Since both the employer and worker are risk averse, this additional uncertainty tends to reduce welfare. Second, inclusion of monitoring can motivate the worker to choose a level of effort which, neglecting the first effect, would make both parties better off.

Because the minimum (necessary) conditions for monitoring to be valuable appear to be very difficult to formulate, we explore several sets of sufficient conditions. These results are derived using forcing type contracts. This type of contract specifies that the worker is paid only if the monitoring reveals his effort to be "acceptable," and the size of the payment does not depend on the results of monitoring in any other way. The forcing contract thus requires that a decision be made based on the realization of the monitor. This statistical decision problem is the test of the following hypothesis: the worker's level of effort is one of a set of acceptable levels. The precision of the monitor, in this case, is summarized by the probabilities of type I and type II errors. The conditions on the monitoring technology referred to below are assumptions as to the availability of monitors with various probabilities of type I and type II errors.

Our results regarding the use of contracts based on imperfect monitoring of worker effort can be summarized as follows:

i) First, we establish general sufficient conditions under which the potential gains to monitoring may be realized.

ii) Under additional assumptions on the monitoring technology, we show that any Pareto optimal contract can be approximated to any degree of precision by a forcing type of contract.

iii) Under another set of assumptions on the monitoring technology and the worker's utility function, we show that all the results achievable under perfect information can be obtained even when information is imperfect, using a forcing contract.

The above results are obtained only for Model 1.

III. Applications

In this section, three applications of the results of the previous section are analyzed. These results are used to describe the Pareto optimal contractual arrangements, and therefore the contracts we would expect to observe in some interesting situations. First, we analyze employment contracts based on education, training, or ability. We compare our results to those of the signaling literature (for example, Spence, 1973, 1974). Second, we consider optimal health insurance contracts and explain indemnity insurance. Finally, the problem of optimal compensation of law enforcers is discussed. Here we relate our results to those of Becker and Stigler.

A. *Ability, Training, and Employment Contracts*

There has recently been considerable interest in the relationship between education and other "signals" and the allocation of labor in job markets. For example, Spence (1973, 1974, 1976) stresses the use of education as a signal for native ability in the hiring of employees (see also Riley, Stiglitz, 1975b). In this literature, a particular payment structure for the worker, based on the signal, is assumed. This structure involves paying the worker a fixed wage which depends only on his education level. These papers provide no analysis to justify the use of such a payment schedule, nor do they consider the possibility that the use of the signal in this way may be Pareto inferior to some other contractual arrangement. The present section is devoted to a clarification of this issue. We characterize the Pareto optimal contract in several situations similar to those analyzed in the signaling literature. In particular we exhibit conditions under which an *optimal* contract will depend on the education level of the worker (as well as things like recommendations, transcripts, previous experience, etc.), even when education is not a perfect measure of acquired ability or productivity. Thus our results may be viewed as complementary with the signaling literature.

To apply our model to the present problem, we reinterpret the effort as the ability the worker has acquired to perform the task, and the state as his native ability. We assume that neither the worker nor his prospective employer knows the worker's native ability at the time the contract is agreed on. Finally, each worker is assumed to know his own *acquired* ability.

With this interpretation, our results of Section II are applicable and imply:

i) If native ability is known or observable *ex post*, it follows from Propositions 1 and 2 that the optimal contract specifies that the employer receives an amount which depends only on the worker's native ability. In particular, the employer specifies a standard output to be produced by the worker contingent on his native ability. The employer's payoff is a certain share (which may depend on the worker's native ability) of this "standard output" while the worker receives the remainder of the standard revenue plus any output generated in excess of the standard (or minus any shortfall of actual output from standard output). This arrangement is equivalent to specifying a standard level of acquired ability required from a worker in this particular job and allowing workers with different levels of acquired ability to participate and accept the full consequences if their acquired ability is different from the one required.

ii) If workers are risk neutral, from Proposition 3, the Pareto optimal contract will specify a given payoff to employers independent of output, the worker's acquired ability, or his native ability level. Therefore, the worker receives the entire output minus some constant, that is, the worker purchases the right to use the production function for a given price.

iii) If workers are risk averse, contracts which depend only on the output are inefficient relative to contracts which depend on the native ability and/or acquired ability of the worker as well as the output. Pareto-superior results can be obtained if the acquired ability is observable and is included in the contract. From Proposition 4 it follows that Pareto optimal contracts when only output and acquired ability are observable are of the form "workers with acquired ability level of (at least) a^* will be paid $S(x)$, others need not apply," where $S(x)$ is some function of the output. For example, if years of education is a perfect correlate of acquired ability, this result implies that it is Pareto inferior not to make employment and/or salaries contingent on the education of the worker. Even if acquired ability is not observable (nor is something perfectly correlated with it) there may be imperfect measures which are sufficiently precise to make using them Pareto efficient. Examples of such monitors include years of education, interviews, transcripts, recommendations, etc. In this case we have shown sufficient conditions under which it is Pareto inferior not to include such monitors of acquired ability. The contract used is of the forcing type and specifies a minimum required level of the observable monitor of acquired ability. The above analysis provides an explanation for compensation schedules which are functions of education level. According to our analysis it is optimal for workers to receive *fixed wages* contingent on education level when employers are risk neutral. If employers are risk averse, a worker's compensation will depend on his output if he meets the education requirement.

B. *Health Insurance Contracts*

It has for some time been recognized that when insurance payments depend on a decision of the insured as well as the state of nature, then an optimal allocation of resources and risk will not be achieved by a simple arrangement in which the insured pays a given price (premium) in return for various payments contingent on the state of nature. This problem arises because the insured has an incentive to "overspend" on insured expenses. It has been called "moral hazard" in the insurance literature (see, for example, Arrow, chs. 5, 8, 9; Pauly, 1968). One way to mitigate the inefficiency is to impose some of the cost of medical care on the insured. Zeckhauser illustrates the tradeoff between risk spreading and incentives. He suggests that insurance payments should depend on the degree of illness as well as the cost of the associated health care. Pauly (1971) refers to this type of insurance as "indemnity" insurance. The results of Section II can be applied to the case of health insurance to show under what conditions moral hazard causes inefficiencies and how appropriate contractual arrangements such as indemnity insurance can resolve this problem. Therefore, the results of Zeckhauser and Pauly (1971) can be obtained as special cases of our results.

To apply our results, we view the insurer as the principal and the insured as the agent. The random state θ is interpreted as the degree of illness. There are two possible interpretations of the agent's action, a. First, a may be the level of preventive care purchased by the insured or a general decision made by him *before* the state is realized as to the amount and quality of health care to be purchased when and if he becomes ill. The second interpretation of the agent's action is as a decision made *after* becoming ill on the amount and quality of health care to purchase. These two interpretations correspond to the assumptions of Models 1 and 2, respectively. The payoff x is interpreted as the amount spent on health care.[4]

Applying the results of Section II yields the following:

i) If the insurer can observe the degree of illness of the insured θ, then from Propositions 1 and 2 the optimal insurance contract specifies a given amount to be paid by the insurer for each possible degree of illness, that is, indemnity insurance. The amount paid by the insurer is thus independent of the choice of medical care taken by the insured. The insured under this contract can choose a level of medical care which costs more or less than the amount which the insurer agrees to pay. Moreover, since the insured is obviously risk averse, Propositions 1, 2, and 3 imply that indemnity insurance is *strictly* Pareto superior to insurance based only on the cost of the medical care. All of the above results hold whether the choice of medical care is taken before or after the occurrence of an illness.

ii) If the degree of illness cannot be observed by the insurer, but the insured's choice of medical care can be observed, then from Proposition 3 there are contracts which depend on both the cost of medical care and the insured's choice of medical care which are *strictly* Pareto superior to contracts which depend only on the cost. This result holds whether the choice of medical care is taken before or after the occurrence of illness. Furthermore, when the insured chooses his level of medical care *before* the occurrence of an illness, from Proposition 4, the Pareto optimal contract (when only the total cost and the insured's choice of care are observable) stipulates that the insurer pays some share of the cost *provided that the insured chooses some prespecified level of medical care*. Otherwise, the insurer pays nothing. Even when the insured's choice of medical care is not itself

[4]Note that these interpretations of a and x require opposite assumptions on the signs of the first derivatives of U and V than were made in Section I. It is easy to check that all the results continue to hold.

directly observable, it may be optimal to employ some indirect and imperfect measure of the level of care (for example, frequency of visits to a doctor). When these measures are sufficiently precise estimates of the insured's actual choice of medical care, the optimal policy will be essentially the same as when the choice is directly observable.

C. *Compensation of Law Enforcers*

In a very interesting paper, Becker and Stigler analyze the law enforcement problem and suggest two alternative methods for improving the incentives given enforcers. Here we recast the law enforcement problem in our framework and employ the results of the previous section to obtain the optimal contract between the state and enforcers. Our results provide a firm foundation for the suggestions of Becker and Stigler. In particular, we show explicitly under what conditions each suggestion is Pareto optimal.

Becker and Stigler explore the economic incentives for malfeasance in law enforcement. They conclude that officials responsible for enforcement might lack sufficient incentives to enforce certain laws. Moreover, there may also be incentives for them to engage in malfeasance. Becker and Stigler suggest two methods for improving the incentives given enforcers. The first suggestion discourages malfeasance and lack of proper enforcement by penalizing the enforcer if such behavior is detected. The penalty is set such that it more than offsets the gain from malfeasance. This method is made operational by requiring the enforcers to "post a bond equal to the temptation of malfeasance, receive the income on the bond as long as they are employed, and have the bond returned if they behave themselves until retirement" (Becker and Stigler, p. 9). If the state detects malfeasance on the part of the enforcer, he is fired and loses the bond he posted. The second suggestion is to allow free entry into the enforcement industry. Enforcers would be rewarded based on their performance. Becker and Stigler argue that the amount of enforcement would be optimal if successful enforcers were paid the fines levied against convicted violators. These fines would equal the damages to society caused by the violator divided by the probability of conviction.

The situation described by Becker and Stigler can be stated in terms of Models 1 and 2 of Section I. The state (society) and the enforcer can be viewed as the principal and agent, respectively. The payoff x to the law enforcement activity is the revenue generated via the fine levied on convicted violators net of the costs associated with trying the accused. These latter costs include both costs borne by the accused (for example, time lost) and those borne by the state (for example, court costs). As is the case in the Becker-Stigler paper, we are not concerned with the problem of *crime prevention* or the effects of law enforcement on the level of criminal activity. In fact, we assume here that the level and type of criminal activity is completely exogenous. The schedule of fines is also taken to be exogenous. The state is interested in the degree of law enforcement as measured by the revenue generated from fine collection.

Two important aspects of the incentive problem for law enforcers may be distinguished. These aspects correspond to two distinct interpretations of the agent's action a, and the exogenous random variable θ (recall that a and θ jointly determine the payoff x). In the first, the effort of the enforcer can be interpreted as his level of investment in crime detection and apprehension capabilities and the levels of activities such as patrolling, etc. These decisions must occur *before* θ, *the level of crime activity, is known.* In this case, the problem is to provide, in an efficient contract, the proper incentives for investment in crime detection and apprehension capabilities. This problem may be analyzed using Model 1, since the agent's action (investment and patrolling) is taken before the realization of the exogenous random state (level of criminal activity).

In the second interpretation, the random state θ is the type of crimes committed, the identities of the criminals, and other details associated with the crimes (for example, evidence, etc.). The action of the enforcer a is the effort expended in apprehending the criminals, creating cases, and the extent to which the enforcer refrains from engaging in malfeasance (for example, taking bribes, etc.). We assume for the purpose of this analysis that the enforcer knows all the details of the crimes (including the identities of the criminals) before taking his action. Society, as represented by the state, may or may not know these details. In any case, we assume contracts are agreed upon before crimes are committed. This version of the problem can be analyzed using Model 2.

Our results indicate the following:

i) With regard to the first problem, suppose the level of criminal activity can be observed *ex post*, both by the state and by enforcers. In this case, it follows from Propositions 1 and 2 that the optimal contract specifies that the state receives an amount which depends only on the level of criminal activity. In particular, the state specifies a standard for the revenue generated by enforcement activities contingent on the level of criminal activity. It then receives a certain share of this standard revenue while enforcers receive the remainder of the standard revenue plus any revenues generated in excess of the standard (or minus any shortfall of actual revenue from standard revenue). Essentially, the optimal arrangement is equivalent to one in which the state specifies a given level of investment in enforcement capability and enforcers accept full responsibility for any deviations from this level.

Regarding the second problem, when both the state and enforcers can observe the particulars of the crimes which occur, Propositions 1 and 2 imply essentially the same result but with a slightly different interpretation. Here the state specifies a total amount to be recovered by the enforcer, contingent on the particular circumstances of the crimes which have occurred. The state receives a share of this specified amount, independent of the enforcer's action. The enforcer receives the remainder of the specified amount, plus or minus any deviation of the actual amount recovered from the specified amount. All consequences of malfeasance are borne by the enforcer.

ii) If law enforcers are risk neutral, as assumed by Becker and Stigler, the Pareto optimal contract in both interpretations specifies that enforcers receive the entire payoff minus, perhaps, some constant. This follows directly from Proposition 3 and is similar to Becker and Stigler's second suggestion. In this case, enforcers purchase for a fixed amount the right to enforce laws and collect fines. There is no point in observing either the enforcer's action or the random state when the enforcers are risk neutral.

iii) If law enforcers are risk averse, contracts which depend only on the revenue generated may be inefficient. In the second interpretation, by Proposition 3, Pareto-superior results can be achieved if the particulars of the crimes committed can be observed by both parties. In this case the particular form of the Pareto optimal contract is as described in (i). Also, if there is a one-to-one relationship between the payoff and the crimes committed for any given action by the enforcer, then Pareto-superior results can be obtained if the enforcer's action can be observed.

In the first interpretation, Pareto-superior results can be achieved if either the action or the level of criminal activity can be observed by both parties. Moreover there are potential gains to monitoring (imperfectly) the activities of enforcers including detection of shirking. Under certain conditions on the monitoring technology, forcing contracts will be Pareto optimal. Under this type of contract, the enforcer would receive an amount which depends on the payoff if monitoring reveals that his action is "acceptable" (for example, there was no shirking). If his action is found to be unacceptable, he would receive a smaller amount or pay a penalty. This contract is similar to the first method suggested by Becker and Stigler, in which enforcers are required to post a bond. In order for such an arrangement to be Pareto superior to compensation which depends only on the revenue, the state must possess means of detecting unacceptable performance by enforcers which have low probabilities of error. The restrictions on the quality of the detection mechanism needed to guarantee Pareto superiority of the Becker-Stigler proposal are quite severe.

REFERENCES

A. Alchian and H. Demsetz, "Production, Information Costs, and Economic Organization," *Amer. Econ. Rev.*, Dec. 1972, *62*, 777–95.

Kenneth J. Arrow, *Essays in the Theory of Risk Bearing,* Chicago 1970.

G. S. Becker and G. J. Stigler, "Law Enforcement, Malfeasance, and Compensation of Enforcers," *J. Legal Stud.*, Jan. 1974, *3*, 1–18.

M. Harris and A. Raviv, "Optimal Incentive Contracts with Imperfect Information," Grad. Sch. Ind. Adm., work. paper no. 70-75-76, Carnegie-Mellon Univ., April 1976.

C. M. Jensen and W. H. Meckling, "Theory of the Firm: Managerial Behavior, Agency Costs and Ownership Structure," *J. Finan. Econ.*, Oct. 1976, *3*, 305–60.

M. V. Pauly, "The Economics of Moral Hazard," *Amer. Econ. Rev.*, June 1968, *58*, 531–37.

———, "Idemnity Insurance for Health Care Efficiency," *Econ. Bus. Bull.*, Fall 1971, *24*, 53–59.

J. G. Riley, "Competitive Signalling," *J. Econ. Theory*, Apr. 1975, *10*, 174–86.

S. A. Ross, "The Economic Theory of Agency: The Principal's Problem," *Amer. Econ. Rev. Proc.*, May 1973, *63*, 134–39.

A. Michael Spence, *Market Signaling: Information Transfer in Hiring and Related Processes*, Cambridge, Mass. 1973.

———, "Competitive and Optimal Responses to Signals: An Analysis of Efficiency and Distribution," *J. Econ. Theory,* Mar. 1974, *8*, 1296–332.

———, "Competition in Salaries, Credentials, and Signaling Prerequisites for Jobs," *Quart. J. Econ.*, Feb. 1976, *90*, 51–74.

——— **and R. Zeckhauser,** "Insurance, Information, and Individual Action," *Amer. Econ. Rev. Proc.*, May 1971, *61*, 380–87.

J. E. Stiglitz, (1975a) "Incentives, Risk and Information: Notes Toward a Theory of Hierarchy," *Bell J. Econ.*, Autumn 1975, *6*, 552–79.

———, (1975b) "The Theory of 'Screening', Education, and Distribution of Income," *Amer. Econ. Rev.*, June 1975, *65*, 283–300.

R. M. Townsend, "Efficient Contracts with Costly State Verification," Grad. Sch. Ind. Admin., work. paper no. 14-77-78, Carnegie-Mellon Univ. 1976.

R. B. Wilson, "On the Theory of Syndicates," *Econometrica*, Jan. 1968, *36*, 119–32.

———, "The Structure of Incentives for Decentralization Under Uncertainty," in *La Decision*, Paris 1969.

R. Zeckhauser, "Medical Insurance: A Case Study of the Tradeoff between Risk Spreading and Appropriate Incentives," *J. Econ. Theory*, Mar. 1970, *2*, 10–26.

Part IV
Theory of the Firm

[15]

Profit, Growth and Sales Maximization[1]

By John Williamson

1. Introduction

One of the more discredited concepts in the theory of the firm is that of an "optimum size" of firm. Empirical evidence has provided no substantiation for the thesis of a long-run U-shaped cost curve and, since firms are not restricted to the sale of a single product or even a particular range of products, there is no more reason to expect profitability to decline with size than there is evidence to suggest that it does. This raises the question as to what does limit the size of a firm. The answer that has been given is that there are important costs entailed in *expanding* the size of a firm and that these expansion costs tend to increase with the firm's rate of growth. This view was first advanced by Edith Penrose [7], has been most fully developed by Robin Marris [5], and has received its most elegant formulation in a paper by Professor Baumol [2].[2]

The development of a theory of growth of the firm was a necessary prerequisite to another feature of the last two analyses just cited—the consideration of alternative assumptions about managerial objectives. Only static profit-maximization and Baumol's static sales maximization hypothesis [1] (with its seemingly arbitrary minimum profit constraint) can be analyzed other than in a growth context. Many economists, the author included, would judge that these are less realistic assumptions than that management wishes to maximize growth or a discounted sum of future sales. Whether they in fact are is an empirical question whose resolution demands a technique for elucidating the alternative implications of different objectives. The principal purpose of this paper is to construct a model which will permit one to derive the differences in behaviour that would follow from the objectives of maximizing profits, maximizing growth and maximizing (discounted) sales.

The framework in which this is accomplished is that of a permanent growth model of the firm. The model is based upon that presented by Baumol [2], but has been considerably extended. It is developed in section 2, simplified in section 3 and solved in section 4. The basic assumption of a permanent growth model is that unit costs and revenues are independent of the absolute scale involved, although they

[1] The author is indebted to William Baumol, Keith Hartley, Alan Peacock and Alan Williams for useful comments on an earlier draft. Responsibility for any errors and opinions expressed is that of the author alone.

[2] References in square brackets are listed on p. 16, below.

depend in the traditional ways on the level of the firm's operations relative to its present size. It therefore follows that, if prices and technology are unchanging or altering in appropriately offsetting ways, management is able to make a once-for-all selection of the values of its policy variables. (Where these are not expressed in ratio form, the appropriate value of the variable will increase at a constant proportionate rate over time.) Of course, if at some future date (contrary to the expectations presently held with certainty) there were a change in external circumstances, or a change in management's objectives, or a change in management (perhaps as a result of take-over) with a consequential change in objectives, then the values of these variables would change to new "permanent" levels.

The (economic) policy variables on which any firm has to reach decisions may conveniently be classified into four categories, though the firm actually has only three degrees of freedom in selecting them. First, there are the decisions on input levels required to satisfy the efficiency conditions—the selection of least-cost input combinations, the optimal distribution of given investment funds among alternative projects, and the optimal distribution of sales effort.[1] Second, there is the other decision that is analyzed in traditional price theory, that of the output, price or sales[2] level in the current period; this will be referred to as the output decision. Third, there are the financial decisions embracing the division of profits between dividends and retained earnings, the flotation of new equity and the raising of new capital by bond finance. Fourth, there is the decision as to how much should be spent on expanding the size of the firm—the investment decision.

The present paper is largely confined to a consideration of the output decision, the retention ratio and the flotation of new equity. The reasons for this restriction are as follows. The efficiency conditions are irrelevant to our aims since they will be satisfied by a firm successfully pursuing any of the objectives under investigation (or, for that matter, virtually any other consistent aim apart from an easy life). If the firm sells bonds, it will not be able to increase the ratio of debt to assets (i.e. its "gearing" or "leverage") indefinitely because of the added risk involved ([5], p. 206). The extra investment funds that accrue from this source will therefore bear a constant ratio to the funds obtainable from the other two sources, so that inclusion of this complication would not add any qualitatively different conclusions. Finally, the investment decision need not be considered explicitly as it is implied by the net revenue and the financial decisions of the firm —this is the missing degree of freedom.

Given the framework outlined, and in particular the basic assumption of rather stationary external circumstances that is necessary to construct

[1] This is intended to include the decision as to whether to raise price in order to finance, say, extra advertising, given whatever constraint is imposed by the "output decision".

[2] The existence of a demand curve implies that these are equivalent.

a permanent growth model, only weak additional assumptions are necessary to prove the following results:

A. The growth rate of the firm cannot be increased by resort to additional equity finance.

B. Growth is never limited by lack of finance as such, as postulated by Baumol [2] and Downie [3], but by the fear of takeover, as postulated by Marris [5].

C. A profit or growth maximizer will grow at a positive rate if it is a profitable firm; a sales maximizer need not.

D. It is not possible, as Baumol has claimed [2], to derive the static sales maximization model from the assumption of growth maximization. (It can, however, be derived from a long-run sales maximization assumption.)

E. A profit and growth maximizer would reach the same output decision, but a sales maximizer would, except in a limiting case, produce more.

F. A profit maximizer would, except in a limiting case, distribute more of its profits than a growth maximizer.

2. Development of the Model

We define the following variables, where lower-case letters denote ratios and capitals denote other variables. Where no time subscript appears, that variable is to be interpreted as applying to time zero. (The time subscript for period zero is included in those equations where variables for other periods appear as well.) Since the rate of interest is assumed constant and the permanent growth context implies that retention ratio and rate of new issue are maintained constant, the variables i, r, and f never carry a time subscript.

(*a*) Policy variables:

S=value of sales or total revenue; r=retention ratio; f=(permanent) growth rate of equity.

(*b*) Exogenous variables:

$$k=\frac{\textit{value of firm at which it would be taken over}}{\textit{potential maximum value of firm}};$$

i=rate of interest.

(*c*) Variables which are exogenous at time zero but endogenous thereafter:

K=capital; F=equity.

(*d*) Endogenous variables:

R=net revenue (profits), which consists of total revenue less those costs which the firm would incur to maintain current output if it were not growing; $X\equiv C+I$=expansion costs (i.e., all other costs incurred by the firm); I=(net) investment, i.e. addition to capital; C=non-investment expansion costs; M=market value of firm; g=future (permanent) growth rate of S_t, R_t, K_t, X_t, I_t, C_t; $m \equiv M/F$=value of share.

Most of these definitions are self-explanatory. The exceptions are k, which will be explained in section 4, and g, the future permanent growth rate of the firm. This, it should be noted, is an endogenous variable whose value is determined by the particular decisions made regarding the firm's policy variables. In order to assess the generality of the model, it is necessary to investigate briefly the plausibility of the assumption that the six variables listed will all grow at the same rate.

Consider a perfectly competitive firm with an unchanging linear homogenous production function facing constant prices, and assume that the increasing costs of growth arise because the process of expanding management requires existing managers to spend some of their time training new managers and integrating them into the managerial team. Then increasing output by a certain proportion, g, over its present level would increase total revenue, costs and hence net revenue in this same proportion. Moreover, the output expansion would require an equal proportionate increase in the capital stock, since with unchanging technology the firm would wish to maintain the ratio of capital to output found optimal in the present period. A growth of g in the present period requires a certain level of spending on management training, C; an equal proportionate increase in the next period requires an expenditure of $(1+g)C$, since the unit cost of training managers is maintained constant by the increased stock of existing managers to do the training, but the number needing to be trained increases by the proportion g. In this simple case, therefore, it is easy to show that total revenue, net revenue, the capital stock and the various forms of expansion costs all increase at the same rate g.

Although it cannot be demonstrated in an equally rigorous manner, the implication of recent discussion is that much the same conclusion is likely to apply to a diversified, oligopolistic firm. Suppose that the general level of output prices is constant; then total revenue will expand at the same rate as output provided that the firm is not forced to cut its prices in order to move down existing demand curves. But the virtually unlimited opportunities for diversification remove any such necessity. Net revenue will also expand at this rate, not only if factor prices and technology are constant, but also if they offset one another; this would occur if wages increased at the same rate as productivity rose due to neutral technical progress. It is well known that with neutral technical progress the capital-output ratio is constant, so that the capital stock and therefore investment will also increase at the same rate. No modification of the argument in the previous paragraph is required so far as C is concerned. Consequently, it is not unreasonable to postulate that S, R, K, X, I and C will all increase at the same rate as output if the price level is constant. (If prices were increasing at a constant rate, these variables would all increase at the same rate in real terms but an appropriately magnified rate in money terms.)

The first relationship we shall derive, that between sales and net revenue, comes from the standard theory of the firm. As output expands (in the current period), net and total revenue both increase initially but eventually both reach maxima. Net revenue reaches a maximum first due to positive marginal costs, and the position of maximum total revenue marks the end of the economically interesting output range. The relationship may therefore be summarized as

(1) $R=R(S)$ $\qquad R''<0.$

Second, let us analyze expansion costs. By definition, these consist of the cost of adding to the capital stock to keep it in line with the planned greater sales in the following period plus such other costs as the firm must incur in the process of expansion. Assuming a constant capital-output ratio and constant prices, it is evident that $I=gK$. More interesting are the other expansion costs, which were the principal interest in Mrs. Penrose's enquiry [7] and have been extensively discussed by Marris [5]. They consist largely of the managerial diseconomies involved in growing fast and the costs of research, development and sales promotion entailed in diversification. The literature on this point may conveniently be summarized for our purposes by the assumptions made about $C(g)$ below, although the last one—that the marginal cost of growth is negligible for very small growth rates —is less firmly founded than the others.

(2) $X\equiv I+C=gK+C(g)$ $\qquad C'>0$

$C''>0$

$C(0)\equiv 0$

$C'(0)\approx 0.$

Taking the inverse function of equation (2), one derives

(3) $g=g(X)$ $\qquad g'>0, g''<0.$

The statement that growth depends on the amount spent on expansion, but that there are decreasing returns to such expenditure, is actually weaker than the assumptions from which it was derived. As a matter of fact, the latter are needed only in the proof of result C.

The sources from which expansion funds may be obtained are retained earnings and the proceeds of new equity issues. Retained earnings are defined as the product of the retention ratio and net revenue. (Of course, insofar as the tax laws permit some expansion costs to be counted as current costs, the conceptual retention ratio differs from the published ratio of a firm.) The amount raised by floating new equity is the product of the price for which the shares are sold and the number that are sold. The number sold in period O is the product of the proportionate increase in the number of shares and the number outstanding at the start of the period, or fF. Their price is computed on the assumption that dividends are paid on existing shares prior to selling the new shares, so that the amount that investors will be willing to pay for the new shares is the price of a share in period 1, m_1, discounted to the present period. It follows that

$$(4)\quad X_0 = rR_0 + \frac{m_1}{1+i} fF_0 = rR_0 + \frac{fM_1}{(1+i)(1+f)}.$$

The market value of the firm is given by the discounted future earnings of the shares at present outstanding.[1] In period t, the firm will earn a net revenue of $(1+g)^t R$, but it will only pay out $(1-r)(1+g)^t R$. Moreover, some of this will accrue to those who purchase new securities issued between time zero and t; only $F/(1+f)^t F$ will accrue to those who own shares at the beginning. Discounting these future earnings and summing yields the market value of the firm as

$$(5)\quad M = \sum_{t=0}^{\infty} \left[\frac{1+g}{(1+f)(1+i)}\right]^t (1-r)R$$

$$= \left[\frac{1}{1 - \dfrac{1+g}{(1+f)(1+i)}}\right](1-r)R = \frac{(1-r)(1+f)(1+i)R}{i-g+f+if}$$

provided that $(1+f)(1+i) > 1+g$ so that the geometric series converges. A sufficient condition for this is $i > g$. Although we have listed i as an exogenous variable, there is an overwhelming economic reason for believing that $i > g(R)$; since otherwise a firm which invested slightly less than R would have an infinite valuation by the stock market, the interest rate would be revised upwards by the stock market till this ceased to be true. And it will be shown in section 3 that $i > g(R)$ is a sufficient condition to ensure that $i > g$. It may also be noted that, since $R_1 = (1+g)R_0$ and all other factors in equation (5) are invariant over time, one has

$$(6)\quad M_1 = (1+g)M_0.$$

3. Simplification of the Model

It is interesting to analyze a frequent assumption to the effect that there is an absolute limit to the amount of finance a firm can obtain for expenditure on expansion.[2] The reasoning is that with low pay-out rates any increase in dividends is so effective in raising share prices as to permit a greater augmentation of external finance than the loss of internal finance; and *vice versa* when pay-out rates are high. Consequently there is a trade-off between external and internal finance

[1] This is only one of several possible ways in which the stock-market value of the firm may be computed. It is what Miller and Modigliani [6] term the "stream of dividends approach" to valuation, and is the simplest one to apply in the present model. The other approaches are logically equivalent since we are implicitly assuming absence of transactions costs, taxes and uncertainty. It may be noted that the permanent growth context permits one to dispense with consideration of undistributed profits or capital stocks.

[2] See, for example, Baumol [2] pp. 1085–86, Downie [3] p. 66.

and some optimum financial policy which maximizes access to total funds. At this point expansion funds reach an absolute maximum.

To investigate this proposition, one substitutes equations (5) and (6) into (4) to yield

$$(7) \quad X = rR + \frac{(1-r)(1+g)fR}{i-g+f+if}.$$

To find that combination of the firm's financial policy variables which maximizes the finance available for expansion (and therefore its growth rate), one differentiates (7) with respect to r and f.

$$(8) \quad \frac{\partial X}{\partial r} = R + \frac{fR}{(i-g+f+if)^2}\left[(1-r)(1+i)(1+f)\partial g/\partial r - (1+g)(i-g+f+if)\right].$$

At $r=1$, this simplifies to $\frac{\partial X}{\partial r} = \frac{(1+f)(i-g)R}{i-g+f+if} > 0$, provided that $i > g$.

Since the first term in the square brackets in (8) is positive when $r<1$, it follows that $\partial X/\partial r > 0$ throughout the feasible range of r and irrespective of the value of f.

$$\frac{\partial X}{\partial f} = \frac{(l-r)R}{(i-g+f+if)^2}\left[(1+g)(i-g) + f(1+i)(1+f)\,\partial g/\partial f\right] > 0.$$

Assuming that as $f \rightarrow \infty$ the growth rate approaches a finite limiting value g_0, one has, however,

$$(9) \quad \lim_{f\rightarrow\infty} X = rR + (1-r)(1+g_0)R/(1+i).$$

One concludes that there is no optimum retention ratio and rate of equity creation which maximize the availability of new finance. An increase in the rate of selling shares will always increase the funds available, though these funds will approach a finite limiting value. Similarly, any increase in the retention ratio will increase the availability of funds.

The maximum funds that would be available through retentions are R. This exceeds the maximum available if new equity is issued, since the value of equation (7) is always less than R provided $r<1$; and if $r=1$ then $X=R$ and all funds are raised internally. But when the retention ratio is unity the value of the firm is zero by equation (5). Marris has argued that this is not an economically significant solution ([5], chapter 1), since when a potentially profitable firm is depressed to a low market value it creates the risk of provoking a take-over raid.[1] This indeed seems by far the most powerful reason for believing that firms will be constrained at some determinate point in their desire to grow.

Result A of section 1 was proved in the last paragraph; growth can never be increased by resort to additional equity finance. The significance of this conclusion may be assessed by supposing that the firm has

[1] Analytically, take-over means that new values of the policy variables are selected, presumably with the aim of raising M. The raiders will make a profit provided that the new value of M exceeds that which existed under the policies of the previous management. (We assume a perfect capital market.)

made its investment decision, so that X and therefore g are determined, and its output decision, so that R is specified. Then from equation (7) the rate of equity creation, f, needed to finance X will depend on r by the formula

$$f=\frac{(i-g)\,(X/R-r)}{(i-g)r+(1+g)-X/R(1+i)}.$$

Substituting in (5) and simplifying yields[1]

$M=(1+i)\,(R-X)/(i-g)$. In other words, we are living in a Miller and Modigliani [6] type of world where, because there are no transactions costs, taxes or uncertainty, the purely financial decisions of the firm have no impact on its value or on the rate of return enjoyed by investors. There is therefore no compelling reason for a firm to choose any particular method of raising finance. However, it is a familiar fact that management prefers to raise finance internally and that new equity issues are comparatively unusual occurrences, and this is presumably explicable in terms of the frictions involved in equity flotation that are ignored in our model. The analysis therefore suggests that the essential rôle of new issues is to finance occasional bursts of abnormal expansion where increasing returns are present rather than permanent, steady growth. In view of the above, it is possible to simplify the analysis of section 4 very considerably by assuming that all finance is raised internally with no loss of generality.

Result B was that the restraint on growth always consists of a fear of take-over rather than that there exists some absolute maximum on the amount of funds the firm could obtain; this proposition was also established above. Although not immediately obvious, this conclusion is intuitively plausible. Essentially, a firm could always increase its expansion funds at the cost of its present shareholders, either by reducing its dividends or by promising a higher proportion of future dividends to new shareholders, were it not for the power of present shareholders to sell out to a new management which would engage in fewer expansion activities which are so costly as to earn a return below the current rate of interest.

Finally, it may be noted that we have also established that $i>g(R)$ is sufficient to ensure $i>g$. By definition, X cannot exceed R when $f=0$. And we also established that $r<1$ implies $X<R$. Consequently, expansion funds cannot exceed net revenue,[2] so that the assumption that the stock market behaves in such a way as to give the firm a finite value ensures that no firm can ever (i.e. even with the aid of new issues) achieve a permanent growth rate as large as the interest rate.

[1] It may be noted that this bears a close similarity to Baumol's equation (3) ([2], p. 1081), except that we have provided, by breaking down his $C(g)$ into $\sum\left(\frac{1+g}{1+i}\right)^t X$, a rather convincing reason for expecting his second-order conditions to be fulfilled.

[2] It should be noted that, if we were to take account of bond finance, the maximum funds available to the firm could exceed R. Consequently, the condition $i>g(R)$ would require strengthening.

4. A Comparison of Profit, Growth and Sales Maximization

Profit maximization is, of course, interpreted as the desire to maximize the present value of the firm, M. Neither is there any difficulty in interpreting the meaning of growth maximization in the context of a permanent growth model, since total revenue, net revenue, and assets all expand permanently at the same rate g. Slightly less obvious is the appropriate definition of sales maximization, since the total sales of a firm between now and infinity are obviously infinite. But so, of course, are total profits over this period: they are reduced to a well-defined value by the technique of discounting. It seems quite plausible to suppose that managements which derive utility from the size of the undertaking they control will similarly discount future sales. After all, most managers must anticipate retirement or coronory thrombosis in the less than infinitely far distant future, so that it is reasonable to suppose that they will prefer an increase in sales in the present to an equal increase in the future. We therefore assume that management applies a discount rate s to future sales, and therefore seeks to maximize a function H of the form

$$(10)\quad H=\sum_{t=0}^{\infty}\left(\frac{1+g}{1+s}\right)^{t} S=\frac{1+s}{s-g} S,$$

provided that $s>g$ so that the geometric series converges. It must be admitted that there is no particularly convincing reason for believing that $s>g$ analogous to that for assuming $i>g$; if the condition does not hold, presumably management is in a state of bliss. Or perhaps it just satisfices.

(a) Profit Maximization

It was shown in section 3 that it is possible to assume that all finance is raised internally without loss of generality. One may therefore set $f=0$ in equation (5), so that the problem of the profit-maximizing firm is to select S and r so as to maximize

$$(11)\quad M=(1-r)(1+i)R/(i-g),$$

subject to $g=g(rR)$ $\qquad g'>0,\ g''<0$

$R=R(S)$ $\qquad R''<0$

$$\text{Now } \frac{\partial M}{\partial R}=\frac{(i-g)(1-r)(1+i)+(1-r)(1+i)R\partial g/\partial R}{(i-g)^2}>0$$

so that the profit-maximizing firm will select that output level S^* that maximizes net revenue (R*).

One also has

$$(12)\quad \frac{\partial M}{\partial r}=\frac{-(i-g)(1+i)R+(1-r)(1+i)R\partial g/\partial r}{(i-g)^2}=0, \text{ or } 1-r=\frac{i-g}{\partial g/\partial r} \text{ as}$$

the first-order condition for a profit-maximizing retention ratio.

This result is most easily interpreted diagrammatically. By substituting R^* into $g=g(rR)$, one obtains a unique relationship between the retention ratio and the growth rate that this permits, and from the signs on the derivatives of g this has the shape shown by $g(rR^*)$ in Figure 1. Intuitively, for a given level of net revenue—which happens to be the maximum possible level since the firm desires to maximize profits—the amount of finance available for expansion is a linear function of the retention ratio, but the assumption of increasing costs of expansion leads to a situation in which the permitted rate of growth increases less than in proportion to the retention ratio.

One may also plot on this diagram a series of curves which reflect the extent to which the objective function of the firm is met, i.e. a set of curves which show all those combinations of r and g at which the value of the firm would be equal to some particular level of M. We shall borrow the term "iso-valuation line" from Marris ([5], p. 252) to describe these loci of points at which the value of M is constant. Each one is labelled with the value of M that it represents when R has the value specified after M. The iso-valuation lines show a relationship between g and r and may therefore be derived by rearranging equation (11) to yield

$$g=i-\frac{(1+i)R}{M}+\frac{(1+i)R}{M}r.$$

Hence all of the iso-valuation lines converge on the point A at which $r=1$ and $g=i$, although they do not do anything quite as embarrassing as meet at this point since M is undefined when $g=i$. They are all upward-sloping straight lines: higher growth is needed to compensate for reduced dividends if the value of the firm is to remain unchanged. Finally, the less steep is the line—i.e. the higher it appears—the greater is the value of M that it represents.

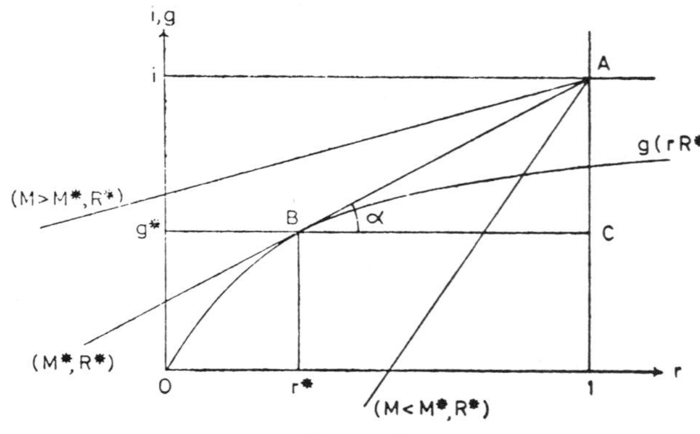

FIGURE 1

The object of the profit-maximizing firm is therefore to reach the highest possible iso-valuation line. This occurs in the diagram at B, the point of tangency to $g(rR^*)$. We shall denote the value of the firm at this point by M^*. At B it is evident that $BC=AC/\tan\alpha$, i.e., $1-r = \dfrac{i-g}{\partial g/\partial r}$ which is the first-order condition (12) for a profit-maximizing retention ratio. It is apparent that the assumption of decreasing returns to expansion expenditure reflected in the shape of $g(rR^*)$ ensures that the second-order condition will be satisfied.

There is nothing in the diagram to show that this tangency condition need occur at a positive g. However, the assumptions made about $C(g)$ in equation (2) imply that in the neighbourhood of $g=0$, we have $gK\approx X=Rr$, so that $\partial g/\partial r\approx R/K$. Now the definition of a profitable firm is one that earns a rate of return on capital employed greater than the rate of interest, so that, if the firm is profitable, $R/K>i$, which implies $\partial g/\partial r>i$ at $g=0$. At this point, therefore, the left-hand side of (12) exceeds the right-hand side, and reducing this inequality requires a higher r and g. Since it is by definition true that a growth-maximizing firm will grow at least as fast as a profit-maximizing one, this establishes that (profitable) profit and growth maximizers will grow at a positive rate, which was the first part of Proposition C.

(b) Growth Maximization

It was shown in section 3 that the constraint on a growth-maximizer arises from the danger of being taken over. A firm is likely to be taken over when its market value sinks to a low level in comparison with what the new owners could expect to make out of it.[1] The measure that Marris adopts as an indicator of the value of the firm to a take-over raider is the value of its net assets which, in our model, are represented by K. However, a more appropriate norm would seem to be M^*, since it is in general reasonable to expect that a new management would not change the total nature of the trading activities in which the firm engages. It will therefore be assumed that management wishes to prevent the stock market value of the firm falling below a specified proportion, k, of its potential maximum value, in order to safeguard its job security. This proportion k will vary inversely with the efficiency of existing management relative to that which would be provided by the potential raiders; it will tend to vary directly with the extent to which these raiders are themselves "profit-motivated". Without some sort of general equilibrium analysis beyond the scope of the present paper, it is necessary to take k as exogenous.

The problem of the growth maximizer is therefore to select S and r

so as to maximize $g=g(rR)$

subject to $M\geq kM^*$ $\quad 0<k\leq 1$

$R=R(S)$.

Since $\partial g/\partial R>0$, the growth maximizer will select the same output

[1] For his development of a theory of take-over, on which the present remarks are largely based, see Marris [5] chapter 1.

level S^* as the profit-maximizer; both will seek the highest possible level of current net revenue.[1] This is the first part of result E; it has the (happy?) consequence that the voluminous literature on pricing policy may be applied without modification to growth-maximizing firms. It also establishes that it is not possible to derive the static sales maximization model from the postulate of growth maximization, as was stated in proposition D.[2]

Since $\partial g/\partial r > 0$ and $\partial M/\partial r < 0$ for values of $r > r^*$, it is obvious that the constraint will be exactly satisfied and r_g, the growth-maximizing retention ratio, will be given by a corner solution. The diagrammatic solution to the problem is shown in Figure 2. If one draws any horizontal from AB to the iso-valuation line (M^*, R^*), and then divides this horizontal in the ratio $1-k:k$, the iso-valuation line passing through the resulting point is (kM^*, R^*). The intersection of this iso-valuation line with $g(rR^*)$ yields the maximum possible growth rate, g_{max} which is clearly greater than the profit-maximizing growth rate g^* unless $k=1$.

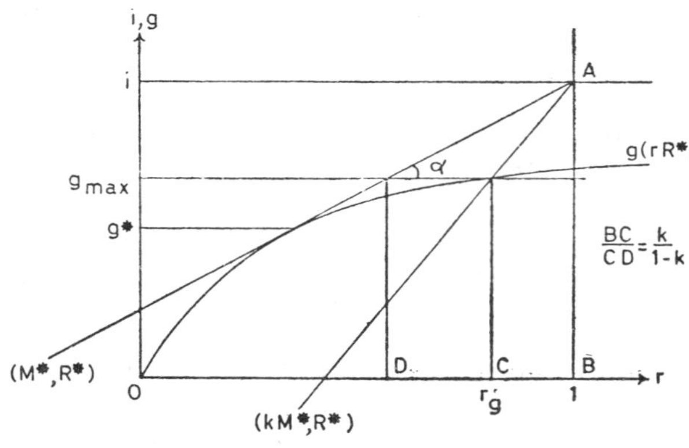

FIGURE 2

[1] Intuitively, one might have expected a growth-maximizer to keep his initial sales down so as to "keep the base small". While this factor would operate in any finite period model (and this constitutes an additional reason for believing that the sales-maximization hypothesis may be fruitful), it is inoperative in a permanent growth context since it would involve keeping subsequent sales down correspondingly as well.

[2] Baumol's error arose from a confusion between the firm's current net revenue, R, and what one may term its profitability (the excess of revenue over *all* costs), $R-X$. Specifically, he argued that since faster growth involves lower profits (meaning profitability), the sales level needed to maximize growth would be determined as a compromise between the desire to earn profits to finance expansion and the reduction in profits (here equated to net revenue) caused by this faster growth. But it is clear that a growth-maximizer will never be prepared to forego current net revenue, unless one introduces some quite different postulate such as that future expansion costs will be less if sales are pushed further in the present. (A rationale for this might be the creation of consumer goodwill.) In other words, the unprofitable activities that a growth-maximizer engages in are those involved in pushing g beyond g^* and not those arising from pushing S beyond S^*. See [2] section III.

Formally, one derives $M=\frac{(1-r)(1+i)R^*}{i-g}=\frac{k(1-r^*)(1+i)R^*}{i-g^*}=kM^*$,

or $\frac{1-r}{k}=\frac{1-r^*}{i-g^*}(i-g)=\frac{(i-g)}{\tan\alpha}$

which is satisfied at g_{max} since $(i-g)/\tan\alpha=BC+CD=BC/k=(1-r)/k$.

It may be noted that the only case in which the growth maximizer and profit maximizer would distribute the same proportion of their profits is that in which they stand in imminent danger of take-over, i.e. when $k=1$. This is the result asserted in proposition F.

(*c*) *Sales Maximization*

At the beginning of section 4 we concluded that the problem of the sales-maximizer is to select r and S so as to maximize

(10) $H=\frac{1+s}{s-g}S$ (provided $s>g$)

subject to $M\geqq kM^*$, $g=g(rR)$, $R=R(S)$.

Now $\partial H/\partial g>0$, $\partial g/\partial r>0$ and $\partial M/\partial r<0$ imply that the sales-maximizer will also exhaust such slack as may be provided by $k<1$ and exactly satisfy the constraint. It follows that $1-r=\frac{kR^*}{R}\frac{1-r^*}{i-g^*}(i-g)$, so that one could construct the relevant iso-valuation line on Figure 2 by making $\frac{BC}{CD}=\frac{kR^*/R_s}{1-kR^*/R_s}$ if one knew R_s, the sales maximizing value of R. There is, however, no way of determining R_s from this diagram. If we assume that R_s is known and is less than R^*, then the optimal iso-valuation line (kM^*, R_s) would lie between (kM^*, R^*) and (M^*, R^*). The equilibrium r would occur at the highest intersection of this line with $g(rR_s)$, which would lie to the right of $g(rR^*)$. However, this diagram does not yield any very interesting information for the sales-maximizing case.

Consider instead the way in which g will vary with S, given that the constraint is exactly satisfied. As sales increase to S^*, g will rise to reach a maximum of g_{max} and then start to decline as the "surplus" is used to finance unprofitable sales rather than unprofitable growth. One therefore obtains a curve with the properties of $g=h(S)$ in Figure 3. An increase in k would reduce the height of this curve throughout its length.

One may also derive a series of iso-H curves by rearranging (10) to read $g=s-\frac{1+s}{H}S$.

The iso-H curves therefore all approach the point ($S=0$, $g=s$), though they do not actually reach it since H is undefined at this point. They are all downward-sloping straight lines. Higher curves represent larger values of H.

It is obvious that the highest attainable value of H is H_2, where the iso-H curve is tangential to $h(S)$. It is easy to confirm that this is the maximum by differentiating (10) with respect to S to get the first-order condition for the sales-maximizing level of sales S_s, and it is apparent

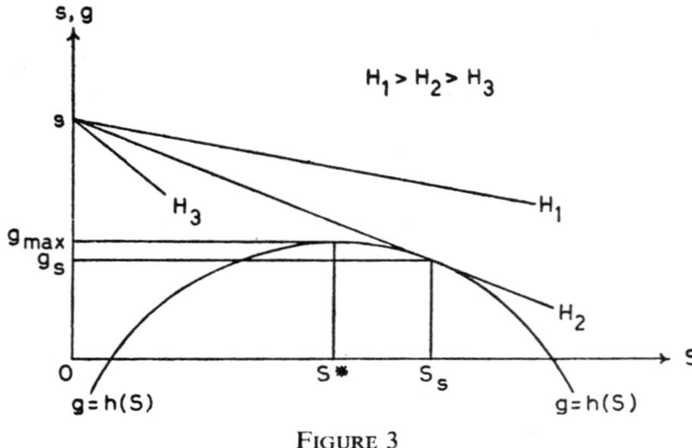

FIGURE 3

from the diagram that the second-order condition will also be satisfied provided the demand curve is monotonic:

$$\frac{\partial H}{\partial S}=\frac{(s-g)\ (1+s)+(1+s)S\partial g/\partial S}{(s-g)^2}=0, \text{ or } s-g+S\frac{\partial g}{\partial S}=0.$$

It is obvious that this condition is satisfied at $S=S_s$, $g=g_s$. If management's time preference is sufficiently high, i.e. if s is large enough (and k is small enough), it is evident that the sales-maximizer, unlike the profit and growth-maximizers, will not in fact grow, as is asserted in the second part of result C. It is also evident that $s>g_{max}$ ensures that $S_s>S^*$ unless $k=1$, when the curve $g=h(S)$ (which is defined to include the stock-market constraint) is compressed to the single point $S=S^*$, $g=g^*$. This was the second part of result E.

Finally, suppose that the sales-maximizer were considering its output decision subject to the constraints that it wished to avoid being taken over and that it wished to grow at g_s. This is logically equivalent to the problem

maximize S, subject to $R\geqq R_s$.

This demonstrates that Baumol's static hypothesis, that firms try to maximize sales subject to a minimum profit constraint, can be derived from the long-run sales maximization hypothesis, as asserted in result D.

5. CONCLUSION

In a paper such as this one cannot delve into the vast body of theory underlying many of the relationships assumed. For example, a large part of the books by Edith Penrose and Robin Marris are devoted to investigating the theory behind the restrictions that we have placed on the shape of $g(X)$. Similarly, we have joined Joan Robinson [8] in sweeping aside all the complications of oligopolistic interdependence by assuming that the output decision is taken on the basis of well-defined demand curves. What a permanent growth model of the type developed in this paper is capable of providing, however, is a means of linking such problems as these together in a simple and systematic way.

We have demonstrated that doing this enables one to establish a number of interesting results, some of which are far from trivial. The most interesting were listed in the Introduction, so that there is no point in repeating them here. The most general conclusion is one that one would hesitate to state explicitly were it not for the suspicion it still seems to engender in certain quarters: that in all cases except where profitability is at best the minimum sum necessary to prevent take-over,[1] the policies the firm pursues will depend on the form of its objectives. Profit, growth and sales-maximizers will act differently.

One could easily extend the above analysis to include more general managerial utility functions such as $U(g, M)$ or $U(g, S)$. The former would yield indifference curves tangential to $g(rR^*)$ above r^* in Figure 1, the latter indifference curves tangential to some point on the downward-sloping part of $h(S)$ in Figure 3. But no very interesting insights seem to emerge from such a generalization.

Of more interest is the observation that any one of the three objectives is capable of yielding a set of comparative-statics theorems. For example, inspection of Figures 1 and 2 makes it clear that an increase in the rate of interest would reduce the growth rate and the retention ratio for both profit and growth-maximizing firms. Changes in the efficiency of the firm or the prices of its factors would have straightforward implications for the position of such curves as $g(rR^*)$ and $h(S)$, which could similarly lead to comparative statics predictions. It does not seem to be possible to predict the effect of a proportional profits tax on the retention ratio without making assumptions additional to those contained in the paper; I suspect that one requires some condition such as $g''' =$constant to get a definite solution.

Finally, it is interesting to draw attention to an empirical finding which has caused a certain amount of discomfort in the past but for which we are able to offer a superior explanation to "systematic irrationality on the part of the investing public" (Miller and Modigliani, [6], p. 432), or discount rates that vary with the futurity of the return (Marris [5], p. 221). This is the finding that "when stock prices are related to current dividends and retained earnings, higher dividend payout is usually associated with higher price-earnings ratios" (Friend and Puckett [4], p. 657). The reason that this has caused dismay is that "investors should be indifferent if the present value of the additional

[1] Baumol's conclusion in [1] that a sales-maximizer who could only just satisfy his minimum profit constraint would act in the same way as a profit-maximizer is, of course, a special case of this result.

future returns resulting from earnings retention equals the amount of dividends foregone" (*idem.*), whereas apparently they are not. But, of course, investors are irrational in preferring dividends only if the present value of the additional future returns actually *does* equal the amount of dividends foregone, and if the firm is a growth (or for that matter a sales) maximizer then it is obvious from Figure 2 that they do not, for the retention ratio is pushed beyond the point at which the value of the firm is maximized. With a great deal of ingenuity Friend and Puckett manage to cast a certain amount of doubt on the conventional findings, but the bulk of the empirical evidence would still seem to indicate that dividends are more highly valued. Since this is consistent with the view that shareholders are rational in seeking to maximize their wealth, and that management rationally seeks objectives other than profit maximization, while any other interpretation assumes that at least one of these parties acts irrationally, one may conclude that there is substantial empirical evidence favouring abandonment of the time-honoured profit-maximization assumption.

University of York.

References

[1] Baumol, W. J., *Business Behavior, Value and Growth* (New York, 1959).

[2] ——, "On the Theory of Expansion of the Firm", *American Economic Review*, December 1962.

[3] Downie, J., *The Competitive Process*, (1958).

[4] Friend, I. and Puckett, M., "Dividends and Stock Prices", *American Economic Review*, September 1964.

[5] Marris, R., *The Economic Theory of 'Managerial' Capitalism* (1964).

[6] Miller, M. H. and Modigliani, F., "Dividend Policy, Growth, and the Valuation of Shares", *Journal of Business*, October 1961.

[7] Penrose, E., *The Theory of the Growth of the Firm* (Oxford, 1959).

[8] Robinson, J. *The Economics of Imperfect Competition* (1933).

[16]

NONMARKET DECISION MAKING
THE PECULIAR ECONOMICS OF BUREAUCRACY

By William A. Niskanen
Institute for Defense Analyses

I. *Introduction*

Economics does not now provide a theory of the maximizing bureaucrat. The currently dominant approach to public administration is to provide the organizational structure, information system, and analysis to bureaucrats who, for whatever reason, want to be efficient. This approach, however, does not develop, or explicitly recognize as relevant, the conditions for which the personal objectives of the bureaucrat are consistent with the efficiency of the bureaucracy.

At present, with a large and increasing proportion of economic activity being conducted in bureaus, economists have made no substantial contribution to answering the following questions: What are the distinguishing characteristics of bureaucracies? What are the critical elements of a theory of bureaucracy? Specifically, what do bureaucrats maximize and under what external conditions? What are the consequences of maximizing behavior under these conditions? For example, what is the equilibrium output and budget of a bureau for given demand and cost conditions? What are the effects of changes in demand and cost conditions? What are the welfare consequences of bureaucratic organization of economic activity? What changes in organization and the structure of rewards would improve the efficiency of a bureaucracy? This paper presents a simple model of the maximizing bureaucrat and, based on this model, a set of tentative qualitative answers to these questions.

II. *The Model*

The model outlined in this section is based on the following two critical characteristics of bureaus: (1) Bureaucrats maximize the total budget of their bureau, given demand and cost conditions, subject to the constraint that the budget must be equal to or greater than the minimum total costs at the equilibrium output. (2) Bureaus exchange a specific output (or combination of outputs) for a specific budget. For this paper, thus, bureaus are defined by these two characteristics.

Among the several variables that may enter the bureaucrat's utility function are the following: salary, perquisites of the office, public reputation, power, patronage, ease of managing the bureau, and ease of making changes. All of these variables, I contend, are a positive monotonic function of the total budget of the bureau.[1] Budget maximization should be an adequate proxy even for those bureaucrats with a relatively low pecuniary motivation and a relatively high motivation for making changes in the public interest. It is an interesting observation that the most distinguished public servants of recent years have substantially increased the budgets of the bureaus for which they are responsible.

The second characteristic—bureaus exchange their output for a total budget rather than at a per unit rate—is generally recognized, but the implications of this characteristic for the behavior of a bureau are not. This characteristic gives the bureau the same type of "market" power as a monopoly that presents the market with an all-or-nothing choice.[2] A bureau, thus, can appropriate all of the consumer surplus. As is shown later, however, this characteristic leads to significantly different output, budget, and welfare conditions for a bureau than for a monopoly.[3]

The equilibrium conditions for a bureau, as defined by these two characteristics, are developed below by considering a bureau faced by linear demand and cost conditions. First, consider a bureau that buys factors in a competitive market and for which

$$V = a - bQ$$

and

$$C = c + 2dQ,$$ [4]

where

$V \equiv$ marginal value to consumers
$C \equiv$ minimum marginal cost to bureau

and

$Q \equiv$ output of bureau.

For these conditions, then,

$$B = aQ - \frac{b}{2}Q^2$$

[1] This paper develops only the static model of a bureau and does not explore the time dimension of budget maximization.

[2] I am indebted to Gordon Tullock for this powerful insight.

[3] This characteristic applies strictly to a "pure" bureau, such as the Department of Defense. Many economic institutions such as the Post Office, most colleges and universities, and most hospitals sell part of their output at a per unit rate and a substantial proportion of their output for a budget.

[4] The marginal cost function for a bureau that is not a discriminating monopsonist includes the factor surplus. The average cost function to this bureau and the corresponding marginal cost functions for a monopoly or bureau which is a discriminating monopsonist would be $C=c+dQ$.

and

$$TC = cQ + dQ^2,$$

where

$B \equiv$ total budget of bureau

and

$TC \equiv$ minimum total cost to bureau.

The equilibrium level of Q, for these conditions, is determined as follows: Maximization of B leads to an upper level of $Q = a/b$. The constraint that B must be equal to or greater than TC, under some conditions, leads to a lower level of $Q = 2(a-c)/b+2d$. These two levels of Q are equal where $a = 2bc/b-2d$. For a bureau that buys factors in a competitive market, the equilibrium level of Q, thus, is where

$$Q \begin{cases} = \dfrac{2(a - c)}{b + 2d} & \text{for } a < \dfrac{2bc}{b - 2d} \cdot \\ = \dfrac{a}{b} & \text{for } a \geq \dfrac{2bc}{b - 2d} \cdot \end{cases}$$

Figure 1 illustrates these equilibrium levels of output for representative demand and cost conditions.

For the lower demand condition represented by V_1, the equilibrium output of a bureau will be in the budget-constrained region where the area of the polygon ea_1hi is equal to the area of the rectangle $efgi$. At the equilibrium level of output, there is no "fat" in this bureau; the total budget just covers the minimum total costs, and no cost-effectiveness analysis will reveal any wasted resources. The output of this bureau, however, is higher than the Pareto-optimal level. The equilibrium level of output is in a region where the minimum achievable marginal costs ig are substantially higher than the marginal value to consumers ih, offsetting all of the consumer surplus that would be generated by efficient operation at lower budget levels. If minimum marginal costs increase with output as a consequence of increasing per-unit factor costs (rather than diminishing productivity), this bureau will generate a substantial factor surplus equal to the triangle cfg—larger than would be generated at the lower, Pareto-optimal output. Legislatures predominantly representing factor interests understandably prefer the provision of public services through bureaus.

For the higher demand conditions represented by V_2, the equilibrium output of a bureau will be in the demand-constrained region where the marginal value of output is zero. In this case the total budget will be

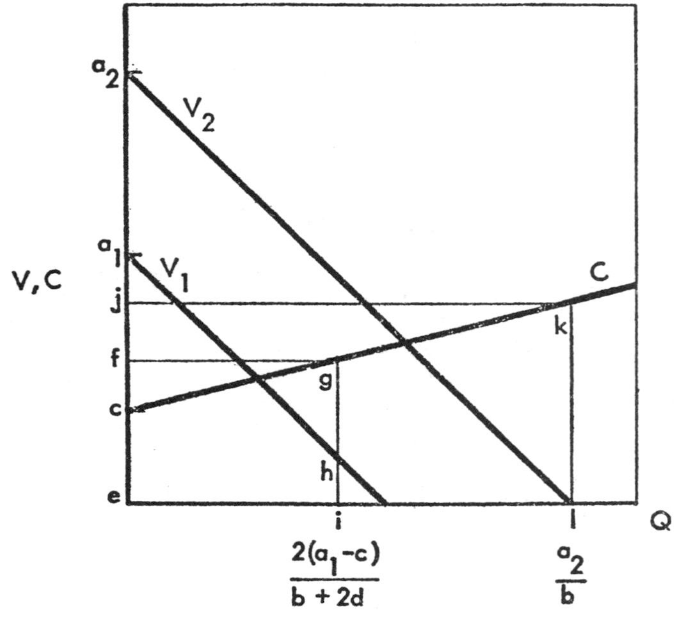

FIGURE 1
EQUILIBRIUM OUTPUT OF BUREAU

equal to the triangle ea_2l and will be larger than the minimum total costs equal to the rectangle *ejkl*. At the equilibrium level of output, there is "fat" in this bureau. A careful analysis would indicate that the same output could be achieved at a lower budget, but the analyst should expect no cooperation from the bureau since it has no incentive to either know or reveal its minimum cost function. In this region, the equilibrium level of output is dependent only on demand conditions. The output of this bureau is also higher than the Pareto-optimal level, operating at an output level where the minimum marginal costs are equal to *lk* and the marginal value to consumers is zero, again offsetting all of the consumer surplus. The factor surplus generated by this bureau, of course, is also substantially larger than would be generated by a lower, Pareto-optimal output level.

III. *Comparison of Organizational Forms*

A better understanding of the consequences of bureaucratic organization of economic activity can be gained by comparison with the consequences of other forms of economic organization facing the same demand and cost conditions. Table 1 presents the equilibrium levels of output and related variables for a private monopoly which buys factors on a competitive market, a private monopoly which discriminates among factor suppliers, a competitive industry, a bureau which buys factors on a competitive market, and a bureau that discriminates among factor suppliers. Each form of organization faces the same following demand and cost conditions:

$$V = 200 - 1.00\,Q$$

$$C = 75 + .25\,Q.^{5}$$

TABLE 1
EQUILIBRIUM CONDITIONS FOR ALTERNATIVE FORMS OF ECONOMIC ORGANIZATION FACING SAME DEMAND AND COST CONDITIONS

Product Market	Monopoly		Competitive	Bureau	
Factor Market	Competitive	Monopsony	Competitive	Competitive	Monopsony
Measures					
Output	50	55.6	100	166.7	200
Revenue:					
Total	7,500	8,024.7	10,000	19,444.4	20,000
Average	150	144.4	100	116.7	100.0
Marginal	100	88.9	100	33.3	0
Costs:					
Total	4,375	4,552.5	10,000	19,444.4	20,000
Average	87.5	81.9	100	116.7	100.0
Marginal	100.0	88.9	100	158.3	125.0
Profits	3,125	3,472.2	0	0	0
Consumer surplus	1,250	1,543.3	5,000	0	0
Factor surplus	312.5	0	1,250	3,472.2	0

The traditional concern about private monopolies is that they produce too little output. Operating in an output region where marginal value is greater than marginal cost, they do not generate as much surplus value as would a competitive industry. For the demand and cost conditions shown in Table 1, a private monopoly would generate a sum of profit plus consumer and factor surplus around 75 percent that of a competitive industry.

For these demand and cost conditions, a bureau that buys factors on a competitive market will have an equilibrium output around two-thirds more than the competitive industry. This bureau will generate no profits or consumer surplus but will generate a factor surplus around 55 percent of the total surplus from a competitive industry. For these conditions,

[5] This is the average cost function to a monopoly or bureau that is not a discriminating monopolist, the marginal cost function to a discriminating monopsonist, and the supply function to a competitive industry.

a bureau that discriminates among factor suppliers will have an equilibrium output twice that of a competitive industry and will generate no profits or surplus value.

A comparison of the supply and cost conditions is also helpful. A monopoly has no supply function; it will set an output such that marginal revenue equals marginal cost, with the output sold at a uniform price. A bureau also has no supply function; it will exchange increments of output at the demand price for each increment to an output level such that the budget equals the minimum achievable costs or the marginal value of the increment is zero. In a sense, a bureau also has no separate marginal cost function. The incremental resource withdrawal for a budget-maximizing bureau will be equal to the demand value, as the difference between this value and the minimum incremental cost will be financed from the consumer surplus appropriated at lower output levels. Only if a bureau is efficient at lower output levels, for whatever reason, would the incremental resource withdrawal be equal to the minimum incremental cost. One implication of this condition is that an analyst may not be able to identify a demand-constrained bureau's minimum cost function from budget and output behavior. All this may yield is the bureau's estimate of its demand function; in the static case, all bureaus will appear to have declining marginal costs and in a sense they do. An estimate of a demand-constrained bureau's minimum marginal cost function must be constructed from detailed estimates of the production function and factor costs—creating an extraordinary demand for analysis.

For different reasons, in summary, both private monopolies and bureaus operate in output regions that are inherently nonoptimal. The substitution of a bureau for a monopoly to provide some product or service, however, solves no problems; this substitution will reduce the aggregate surplus value and serve only the interests of the owners of specific factors.

IV. *Effects of Changes in Demand and Cost Conditions*

The model outlined in Section II may also be used to estimate a bureau's response to changes in demand and cost conditions.

Demand Shifts. Figure 2 illustrates the changes in a bureau's equilibrium output and budget, for given cost conditions, in response to shifts in demand.

In the budget-constrained output region, the output of a bureau will grow by more than the amount of a demand shift, even when faced by increasing marginal costs. A bureau producing an output at constant marginal costs will grow at twice the rate of a competitive industry under the same conditions. In this region, the budget per unit output

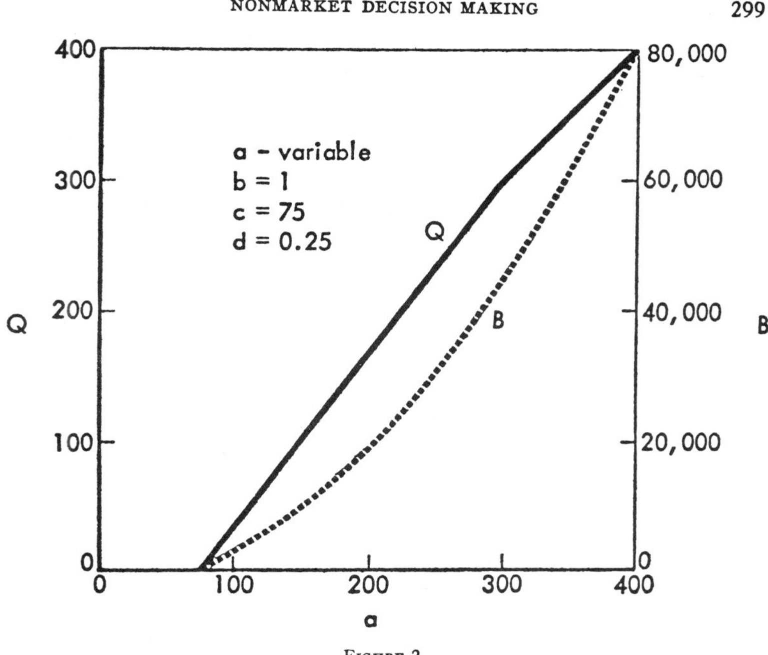

FIGURE 2
EFFECTS OF DEMAND SHIFT

will increase only by the amount of the increase in the minimum unit costs.

In the demand-constrained output region, the output of a bureau will grow by the same amount as the demand shift, regardless of the slope of the minimum marginal cost function. The slower rate of growth of a bureau in this region is still higher than the rate of growth of a competitive industry facing increasing marginal costs. In this region, the budget per unit output increases rapidly, by an amount proportionate to the demand shift, regardless of the slope of the minimum marginal cost function.

A bureau, like a private monopoly, will often find it rewarding to try to shift its demand function. The incremental budget that would result from a demand shift will be particularly high in the demand-constrained output region. One would expect, therefore, that bureaucrats would spend a significant part of their time on various promotional activities, supported by the owners of specific factors.

Changes in the Demand Slope. Figure 3 illustrates the changes in a bureau's equilibrium output and budget, for given cost conditions, in response to changes in the slope of the demand function. The indicated changes in the intercept and slope are such that the output of a competitive industry, given the same cost conditions, would be constant at a level of 100 for each combination.

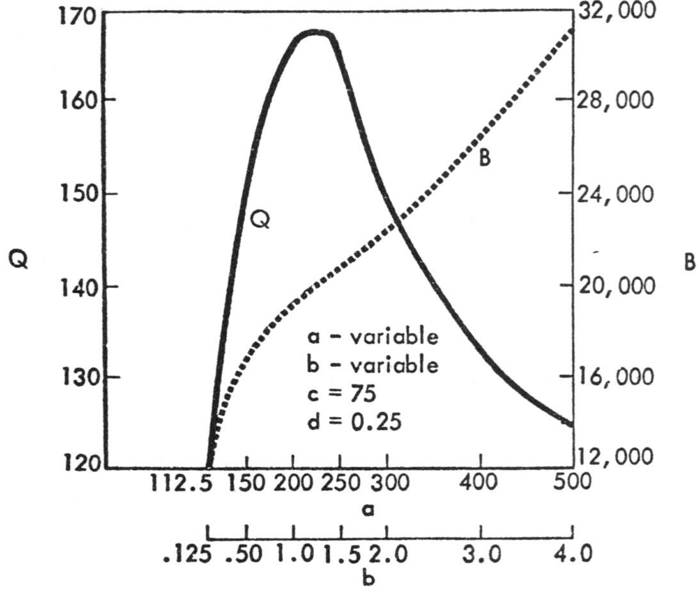

FIGURE 3
EFFECTS OF CHANGES IN THE DEMAND SLOPE

In the budget-constrained output region, the equilibrium output of a bureau will increase with increasing (negative) demand slopes; in the demand-constrained region, output will decline with increasing demand slopes. A bureau faced by a nearly horizontal demand function will produce an output at a budget per unit output only slightly higher than that of a competitive industry, but the total budget and the budget per unit output will increase monotonically with higher demand slopes. This suggests that a bureau may find it rewarding to try to increase the slope of the demand function for its output by promotional activities citing public "need" or military "requirement" to be fulfilled regardless of cost. A more important suggestion is that a bureau operating in a highly competitive output market would be relatively efficient. However, the present environment of bureaucracy—with severe constraints on the creation of new bureaus or new outputs by existing bureaus, and the passion of reformers to consolidate bureaus with similar output—seems diabolically designed to reduce the competition among bureaus and increase the inefficiency (and, not incidentally, the budget) of the bureaucracy.

Cost Shifts. Figure 4 illustrates the changes in a bureau's equilibrium output and budget, for given demand conditions, in response to shifts in the minimum marginal cost function.

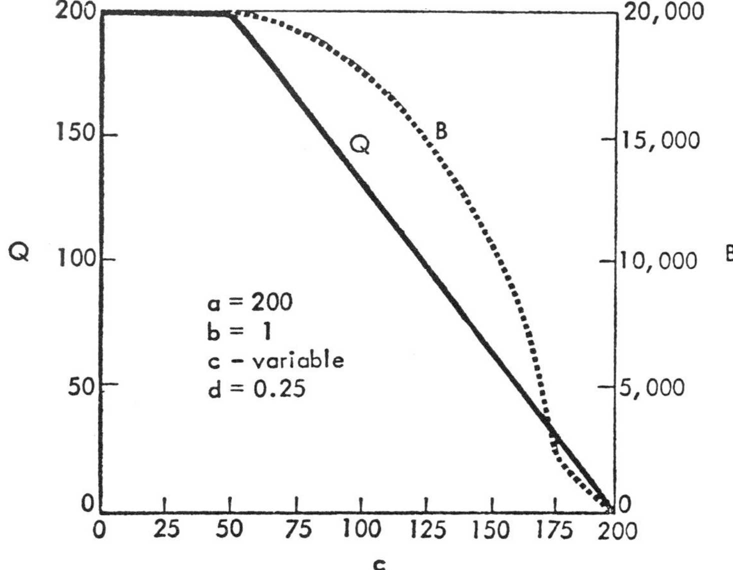

FIGURE 4
EFFECTS OF COST SHIFTS

In the budget-constrained output region, a downward shift of the minimum marginal cost function will increase the equilibrium output of a bureau at a rapid rate. A bureau producing an output at constant minimum marginal cost will grow at twice the rate of a competitive industry for the same downward cost shift. The bureau's budget will grow rapidly with the initial cost reductions and then very slowly as output approaches the demand-constrained output level. In the higher output region, further reductions in cost will not increase either the equilibrium output or budget.

These effects suggest that new bureaus or those facing exogenous increases in costs will be very cost conscious. Such bureaus will have an incentive to determine their minimum marginal cost function and to try to reduce the level of this function. Older bureaus or those facing a rapid increase in demand couldn't care less on either count. Tullock has been intrigued by the observation that bureaus both attempt to reduce costs and manifestly waste huge amounts of resources. This model

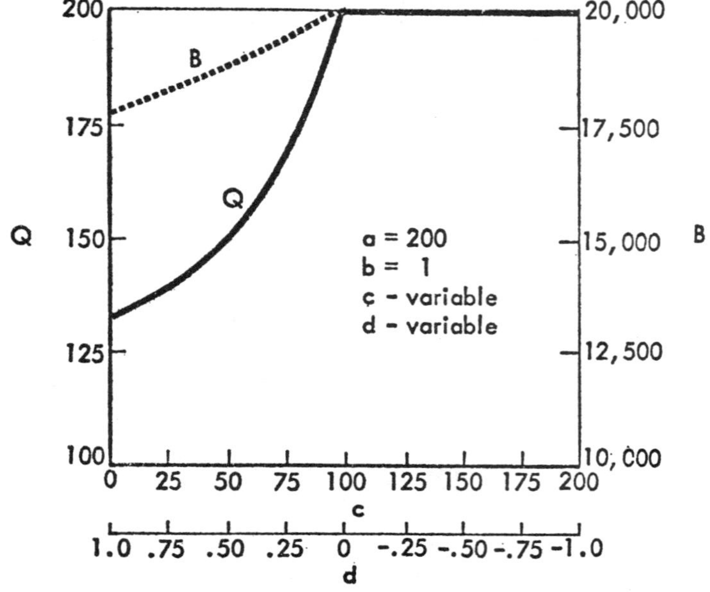

FIGURE 5
EFFECTS OF CHANGES IN THE COST SLOPE

suggests that, in equilibrium, a single-product bureau will be in one or the other of these conditions. A multiproduct bureau, such as Department of Defense, should be expected to attempt to reduce costs on the budget-constrained outputs and to assure that costs are sufficiently high to exhaust the obtainable budget on the demand-constrained outputs.

Changes in the Slope of the Minimum Unit Cost Function. Figure 5 illustrates the changes in a bureau's equilibrium output and budget, for given demand conditions, in response to changes in the slope of the minimum marginal cost function. The indicated changes in the intercept and slope are such that the output of a competitive industry, given the same demand conditions, would be constant at a level of 100 for each combination.

In the budget constrained output region, the equilibrium output of a bureau that buys factors on a competitive market will increase with a reduction of the slope of the minimum unit cost function to a level, with constant unit costs, that is twice the output of a competitive industry. The bureau's budget will also increase with a reduction in the slope of this function, but relatively slowly. Both output and budget are invariant to changes in the slope of the cost function in the demand-constrained output region.

These effects suggest that bureaus may have an incentive to use production processes with a higher cost at low output levels and a lower cost at high output levels. In the static case, however, this incentive is not very strong and may be offset in part by pressure through the legislature from the owners of specific factors.

V. *Critical Tests of This Model*

This model suggests an image of a bureau with a level and rate of growth of output that is up to twice that of a competitive industry facing the same conditions. Demand by consumers may be the basis for establishing a bureau, but the interests of this group in preserving the bureau will diminish or disappear as the bureau creates no consumer surplus, except by negligence. A bureau, however, creates a substantially larger factor surplus than would a competitive industry, and the primary interests in continuing the bureau (or a war) are likely to originate from the bureau itself and the owners of specific factors. In the demand-constrained output region, a bureau's only concern about costs is to assure that they exhaust the obtainable budget. A bureau should be expected to engage in considerable promotion, in cooperation with the owners of specific factors, to augment the demand for its output, and to reduce—through persuasion, restrictions on entry, and consolidation—the elasticity of this demand.

These are serious charges. A set of critical tests of these assertions are difficult to pose. The best tests that I can conceive are to compare the output and costs of a bureau with those of a private firm with the same type of product. A comparison of the Social Security Administration and insurance companies, public and private hospitals, public and private statistics gathering organizations, or public and private police and garbage disposal services may be sufficient. Such tests, however, will be difficult as the existence of potential competition may present the bureau with a highly elastic demand, and some of the private firms producing a similar product have some of the characteristics of bureaus. A test of these assertions about a bureau that is the sole producer of a set of products, such as the Department of Defense, is even more difficult and probably more important. For such bureaus, an internal comparison at different points of time or, possibly, with bureaus producing a similar product in another political jurisdiction could be made.

VI. *Further Implications for Analysis and Policy*

Analytic Developments. The static model of a single-product bureau outlined in Section II should be extended in several dimensions. First, the consequences of the time-dimension of budget maximization should be developed. Louis DeAlessi's preliminary analysis suggests that a bureaucrat's concept of his property rights will lead to a preference for capital-intensive production processes. Second, the behavior of a multiproduct bureau that receives a single budget (or several budgets not specific to product type) should be explored. And third, the behavior of "mixed" bureaus, such as the Post Office, educational institutions, and public hospitals should be explored.

Policy Implications. This model of a bureau, if the suggested tests fail to disconfirm its assertions, has important implications for the organization for the production of the large and increasing proportion of our national output now produced by bureaus. What changes could be made to improve the efficiency of the production of these goods and services?

First, and probably most interesting, bureaucratic provision of these goods and services could be maintained, but each bureau would operate in a competitive environment and face a highly elastic demand function. The creation of new bureaus would be encouraged. Existing bureaus would be permitted and encouraged to produce products now provided by other bureaus. "Antitrust" restrictions would prevent collusive behavior to divide products or output among bureaus and to prevent the dominance of one bureau in a single product. The legislature would be willing to shift some part of the output of one agency to another, based on output and budget performance. The resulting bureaucracy would consist of many single and multiproduct bureaus without any obvious relation (in use) of the products offered by any single bureau. (As such, it would look a little like the corporate sector of our economy.)

Second, the incentives of bureaucrats could be changed to encourage them to minimize the budget for a given output or set of outputs. For example, the salaries of the top 5 percent of the personnel of a bureau could be a negative function of the budget of a bureau for a given set of outputs. This would still permit a political determination of the output level for the combination of bureaus providing the same product. Such a system would require more precise measurement of output than now, but would not require the monetary valuation of this output.

Such a system may also attract better managers to the bureaucracy.

Third, the type of goods and services now provided by bureaus could be financed through government or foundations as is now the case, but the provision of these services would be contracted to private, profit-seeking economic institutions. The bureaucracy, as such, would disappear, except for the review and contracting agencies. This system would also require better measures of output than now, but better measures are necessary for improved efficiency under any organizational form.

[17]

THE THEORY OF LABOUR-MANAGED FIRMS AND OF PROFIT SHARING[1]

ONE important problem in industrial economics which deserves more attention from economic theorists than it has received in the past is the effects of different forms of industrial organisation upon economic efficiency. To take one such question, what would happen if workers hired capital instead of capitalist entrepreneurs hiring workers? Professor J. Vanek has recently made an important contribution to this subject. Building on the work of two other economists,[2] he has produced a full-scale textbook on the theory of labour-managed economies.[3] In this book he investigates the properties of a system in which workers get together and form collectives or partnerships to run firms; they hire capital and purchase other inputs and they sell the products of the firm at the best prices they can obtain in the markets for inputs and outputs; they themselves bear the risk of any unexpected gain or loss and distribute the resulting surplus among themselves, all workers of any one given grade or skill receiving an equal share of the surplus; their basic objective is assumed to be to maximise the return per worker. For shorthand we will in what follows refer to this as the Co-operative system.

Professor Vanek contrasts the micro- and macro-results of such a system with those of the textbook capitalist model in which an entrepreneur hires all the inputs (including labour) and sells all the outputs of a firm at market prices, bears the risks and runs the firm in such a way as to maximise the total surplus of revenues from the sale of outputs over costs of the purchase of inputs. For ease of reference I shall call this the Entrepreneurial system.

Many essential features of the contrast between the two systems are not basically affected by the question whether the capital resources of the community are privately owned or are socialised and owned by the State. In the case of a Co-operative the workers may be hiring their capital resources either in a competitive capital market fed by private savings or else from a central governmental organisation which lends out the State's capital resources at rentals which will clear the market. The contrasting features of the Entrepreneurial system are equally well portrayed by a system in which the managers of socialised plants are told to hire inputs and sell outputs at given prices, the managers operating so as to maximise the total surplus of the plant and the State setting the prices so as to clear the markets.

[1] The author would like to thank Professors A. B. Atkinson, E. H. Phelps Brown and R. C. O. Matthews for many helpful comments in the preparation of this article.

[2] B. Ward, " The Firm in Illyria: Market Syndicalism," *American Economic Review*, September 1953. B. Ward, *The Socialist Economy* (Random House, 1967). E. Domar, " The Soviet Collective Farm as a Producer Co-operative," *American Economic Review*, September 1966.

[3] Jaroslav Vanek, *The General Theory of Labor-Managed Market Economies* (Cornell University Press, Ithaca and London, 1970).

II

Let us start then with an enumeration of what appear to us to be the five main differences which Professor Vanek notes between the two systems.

Difference (1): Incentives

A worker hired at a given hourly wage in an Entrepreneurial firm will have to observe the minimum standard of work and effort in order to keep his job; but he will have no immediate personal financial motive and, particularly in the case of a large concern, may well have little or no social participatory motivation to behave in a way which will promote the profitability of the enterprise. He may, of course, take a pride in his work; and he may well wish to stand well with his employer in order to achieve security and promotion in his job. But any extra profit due to his extra effort will in the first place accrue to the entrepreneur. It is difficult and in many cases impossible to overcome this problem by a system of piece-rate wages; and in any case the problem is not one simply of incentives to work harder and to produce more.

Let us go to the other extreme and consider a one-man Co-operative, *i.e.*, a single self-employed worker who hires his equipment. He can balance money income against leisure and other amenities by pleasing himself over hours of work, holidays, the pace and concentration of work, tea-breaks or the choice of equipment and methods of work which will make his work more pleasant at the cost of profitability. Any innovative ideas which he has, he can apply at once and reap the whole benefit himself. And so on over a whole range of qualities and conditions of his working life.

The trouble is, of course, that there are economies of scale which mean that a one-man firm must normally be ruled out. In an n-man Co-operative the individual worker who shares the profit with his fellows will still get some direct benefit from any additional profit due to his own effort; but it will be only $\frac{1}{n}$th of the result of his own efforts. If to reap the technical advantages of scale n must be large, then the direct advantage in financial incentives of the Co-operative over the Entrepreneurial firm may be small. But even in this case the sense of participation may be greater and thus provide a stronger social motivation to do the best for the firm as a whole, *i.e.*, for the whole partnership of fellow workers.

This last consideration takes one out of the realms of strict economic analysis into those of the industrial and social psychologists and sociologists; and it must be left to them to consider what is perhaps in fact the decisive question, namely whether or not there would be difficulties of disciplined administration in a self-governing Co-operative which would offset in part or whole the improved incentives which it would enjoy. One conclusion, however, may be reached. The most efficient scale for a Co-operative is likely to be smaller than for an Entrepreneurial firm; for in the case of the former but not of the latter a reduction in the number of workers increases the direct economic incentives for efficiency of the individual worker.

So much for *difference (1)*. If we abstract from this difference in incentives and also from any differences due to the effects of risks, it can be shown that both the Co-operative and the Entrepreneurial systems will lead to the same Pareto-optimal equilibrium situations in the long-run, provided that there is perfect mobility of factors, including perfectly free and costless entry and exit of new firms in any industry and that there is perfect competition in the sense that no individual economic agent can by his own decisions affect appreciably any market price. Differences become apparent, however, as soon as we (i) consider the short run, (ii) modify the assumption of free and costless entry of firms, or (iii) allow for monopolistic conditions. We will consider each of these three cases below under *differences (2), (3) and (4)* respectively. But before we do so, we must consider the long-run Pareto-optimal outcome of the two systems.

Let us do this first by considering a firm in an industry in which there are only two inputs—a homogeneous worker (L) who works a given number of hours at a given intensity, and a fixed capital good (K), these two factors producing an output (X) with a production function $X = X(L, K)$ in which there is some substitutability between L and K.[1] Let P_x be the price of a unit of X and W the market wage rate of labour in an Entrepreneurial firm. If the price of a machine (a unit of K) is P_k and if i is the market rate of interest, then iP_k is the rental paid for the hire of a machine. In an Entrepreneurial firm more (or less) labour will be hired if the value of the marginal product of labour $\left(P_x \frac{\partial X}{\partial L}\right)$ is greater (less) than the wage rate of labour (W); and more (or less) machinery will be hired if the value of the marginal product of a machine $\left(P_x \frac{\partial X}{\partial K}\right)$ is greater (less) than the rental payable for a machine (iP_k). These relationships are shown in columns 1 and 2 of the Table.

In a Co-operative machinery is hired in the same way as in an Entre-

[1] The firm's production function may be such as to result, with given prices of the two inputs, in either a U-shaped or an L-shaped long-run cost curve:

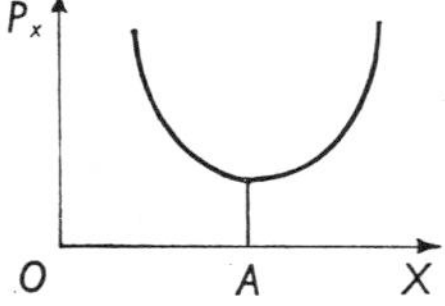

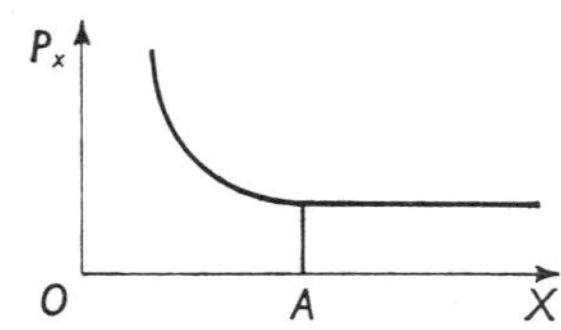

In order to rule out the one-man firm the cost per unit must at first fall because of economies of large-scale production, but in order that perfect competition should be possible the total demand for the industry's output must be many times the amount OA which, for an individual firm, is sufficient to lead to minimum cost per unit.

preneurial firm and the same rule is, therefore, relevant. Machinery will be hired up to the point at which the value of its marginal product is equal to its rental. But the considerations governing the size of the labour force are different. If one more partner is accepted into a Co-operative, he will add

	Entrepreneurial.	Co-operative.	Inegalitarian Co-operative.	Joint-Stock.	Inegalitarian Joint-Stock.	Inegalitarian Joint-Stock-Co-operative.
1.	2.	3.	4.	5.	6.	7.
Increase or Decrease K according as $P_x \frac{\partial X}{\partial K} \gtreqless$	iP_k	iP_k	iP_k	$\frac{P_xX - WL}{K}$	rP_k	rP_k
Increase or Decrease L according as $P_x \frac{\partial X}{\partial L} \gtreqless$	W	$\frac{P_xX - iP_kK}{L}$	E_o	W	W	E_o

to the revenue of the Co-operative an amount equal to the value of his marginal product $\left(P_x \frac{\partial X}{\partial L}\right)$; in a Co-operative he will receive the same share of the total surplus as do all the other partners $\left(\frac{P_xX - iP_kK}{L}\right)$; if, therefore, $P_x \frac{\partial X}{\partial L} > \frac{P_xX - iP_kK}{L}$, he will add to the surplus of the Co-operative something more than the existing surplus per head, so that the surplus per head can be raised for all the partners. Thus the existing partners will wish to build up the partnership until the value of the marginal product of labour is equal to the average earnings per worker. These relationships are shown for the Co-operative in column 3 of the Table.

It is now easy to see why both systems lead to the same (i) long-run, (ii) free-entry-and-exit, and (iii) perfect-competition solution. As far as K is concerned, in both cases it is attracted from points where the value of its marginal product is low to points where it is high by a competitive process in which either the Entrepreneurial manager is attempting to maximise the surplus for the entrepreneur's or state's pocket or else the Co-operative partners are attempting to maximise the surplus for distribution between them. As far as L is concerned, in the Entrepreneurial firm the same competitive process will attract it to the uses in which the value of its marginal product is highest. In the Co-operative the process is different, but the final result the same. First, in each Co-operative L will be attracted until the value of its marginal product is equal to the average earnings of the existing workers in that firm. Second, if as a result of this the average earnings are higher in one industry than another workers will be attracted from Co-operatives in the industry of low earnings to set up new Co-operatives in the industry of high earnings; the output of the high earning product will rise and its price will fall, until earnings, and so the value of marginal products of labour, are equalised in all industries.

Difference (2): Short-Run Adjustment

The short-run process of adjustment is, however, very different. Let us suppose that the capital is fixed in amount in each firm in the short run, but that the number of workers is variable. Suppose that we start in a full equilibrium and that then the demand price for the particular product X rises, while all other demand prices remain unchanged. In the Entrepreneurial system labour will be attracted into the X-industry, since the value of the marginal product of L is now higher in the production of X; and this is a Pareto-optimal process of adjustment, since L can be shifted from its low-valued to its high-valued uses, even though K is *ex hypothesi* not shiftable immediately from its low-valued to its high-valued uses.

But the short-run effect in the Co-operative system will be to reduce, not to increase, the levels of employment and output which will maximise earnings per head in the X-industry firms. A rise in the selling price of X will, of course, in itself raise both the value of the marginal product of labour and the average earnings per head in the X-industry firms; but it will raise the value of the marginal product of labour less than the average earnings [1] and it will thus mean that the average earnings could be still further raised if one worker was dismissed. The value of the reduction in the firm's output would be less than the amount paid by the Co-operative to the dismissed worker; and the remaining partners would gain by his dismissal.

This relationship is shown in Fig. 1.

Measure the number of workers on the horizontal axis and money payments per worker on the vertical axis. Draw a rectangular hyperbola MN such that the rectangle $STUO$ has a constant value of iP_kK, the total rental payable for the hire of K. Then TU measures $\frac{iP_kK}{L}$ or the burden of debt payment per worker when the number of workers is OU. Draw a curve PQ such that its height measures $\frac{P_xX}{L}$ or the total value of receipts per worker, *i.e.*, output per head multiplied by the price of output. Net earn-

[1] Suppose $P_x = £1$, $\frac{\partial X}{\partial L} = 1$, $X = 100$, $iP_kK = £50$, and $L = 50$.

Then $P_x \frac{\partial X}{\partial L} = £1$ and $\frac{P_xX - iP_kK}{L} = \frac{£100 - £50}{50} = £1$.

If P_x rises to £1·1, $P_x \frac{\partial X}{\partial L}$ rises to £1·1; but $\frac{P_xX - iP_kK}{L}$ rises to $\frac{£110 - £50}{50} = £1{\cdot}2$.

ings per head are then the excess of the height of the curve PQ over the height of the curve $MN\left(i.e., \frac{P_xX}{L} - \frac{iP_kK}{L}\right)$. These earnings are maximised at CB, where the slope of the curve PQ is the same as that of the curve MN. The optimum number of worker-partners is thus OA.

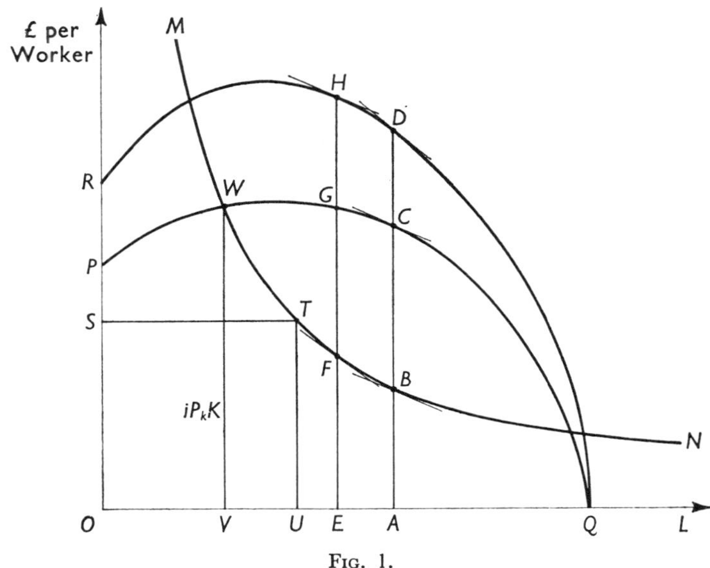

FIG. 1.

Suppose now that P_x rises by 10%, then the curve PQ is replaced by the curve RQ which is 10% higher than the curve PQ at every value of L. Consider now a volume of labour OE which is somewhat less than OA. Since $HG = 10\%$ of GE and $DC = 10\%$ of CA and since $GE > CA$, HG must be $> DC$. In other words the slope of RQ at D is steeper than the slope of PQ at C which is equal to the slope of MN at B. Since the slope of RQ is greater than the slope of MN with employment at OA, it will be possible by reducing the number of workers to OE (where the slope of RQ at H is equal to the slope of MN at F) to raise average earnings. The rise in P_x will itself raise earnings ($DB > CB$); but these can be raised still more if the number of workers is reduced ($HF > DB$).

The commonsense of this result can easily be seen in the following way. (1) With a fixed debt interest it is to the interest of the workers-partners to have a large partnership so that debt per head may be small. (2) With decreasing returns to labour applied to a given amount of capital it is desirable to have a small partnership so that the value of output per head may be high. A rise in the selling price of the product or a fall in the rental of capital will increase the importance of influence (2) relatively to influence (1) and will, therefore, work in the direction of a smaller partnership.[1]

Professor Vanek seems to assume tacitly in most of his analysis that the rules of a Co-operative would somehow permit the dismissal of a worker if it were to the advantage of the remaining workers, even if it were to the detriment of the dismissed worker.[2] In this case the short-run supply curve of X would be backward-sloping; and this would be highly perverse and inefficient. Pareto-optimality requires that in the short run the variable factor L should be attracted to, not pushed away from, its more highly valued uses.

At a later stage (Section V below) we will return to the question whether a rule which allowed the dismissal of a partner against his will is appropriate. But even if such dismissals are not allowed, there would be no

[1] As a *curiosum* it may be noted that if the production function were of a Cobb–Douglas variety with $X = K^{\alpha} L^{1-\alpha}$, then the backward-sloping short-run supply curve of X in terms of its price P_x would take the form of a rectangular hyperbola. In a Co-operative L is always adjusted until the earnings of labour are equal to the value of their marginal product; with constant returns to scale this means that what is left over (namely iP_kK) will be just sufficient to pay to each unit of capital the value of its marginal product; and with a Cobb–Douglas function capital will in such an equilibrium always be paid a constant proportion α of the value of the output; thus the equation $iP_kK = \alpha P_xX$ with iP_kK as well as α constant in the short run provides the short-run supply curve for X, as depicted in Fig. 2.

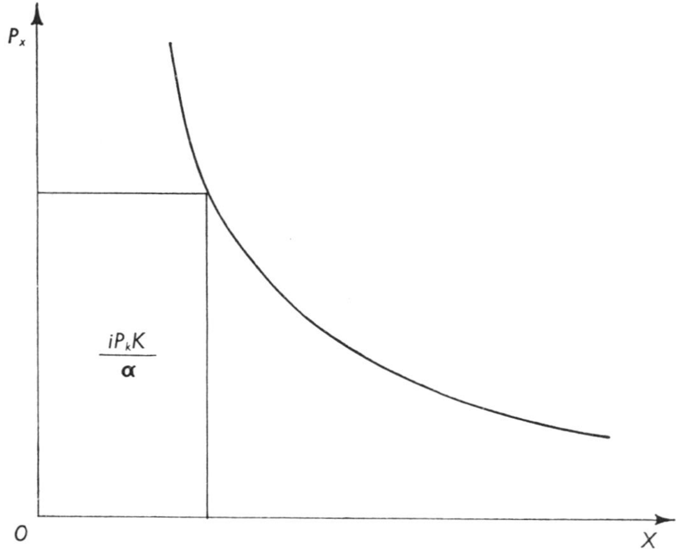

FIG. 2.

[2] Professor B. Ward makes the assumption explicitly when he writes (*The Socialist Economy*, p. 186, footnote 5), " Conflicts might arise in case the criterion by the workers' council would lead to layoffs. But as long as these amounted to less than half the work force (and less than half of the members of the workers' council) a majority decision would still follow the criterion."

Professor Joan Robinson very pertinently queries this assumption (" The Soviet Collective Farm as a Producer Co-operative: Comment," *American Economic Review*, March 1967).

mechanism inducing the existing partners to take the positive step of admitting more partners when the selling price of their product went up and when, in consequence, it would pay each existing partner to reduce rather than to increase the size of the partnership. The short-run supply curve of a Co-operative would at least be highly inelastic—certainly less elastic than the Pareto-optimal Entrepreneurial short-run supply curve.

The rather startling result that a rise in the selling price of a Co-operative's product will in the short run lead to a reduction in the amount produced and a reduction in the volume of employment rests upon the assumption that the firm employs only one variable input, namely L, to produce only one product, namely X. But, as Professor Vanek points out, if we allow for the fact that the firm may well produce more than one product (*e.g.*, products X and Y) and may employ not only labour, L, but also a raw material, M, as a factor which is variable in the short run, these results may need to be modified.

The case of a multi-product firm is easy to understand. If the price of X goes up, the Co-operative may well shift from the production of the now relatively unprofitable Y on to the now relatively profitable X. If X and Y are very easy substitutes in the firm's production programme, a rise in the price of X may thus well lead to an increase in the output of X even though, for the reasons already discussed at length, the Co-operative were to reduce the absolute level of its employment and total production.

The case of a Co-operative which uses inputs of materials as well as of labour needs a little more explanation. When the price of its output X goes up, the Co-operative which buys its material M in the market will, just like an Entrepreneurial firm, find that the cost-price of M is now less than the value of the marginal product of M. For example, when the selling price of cars goes up a firm assembling cars, whether it be a Co-operative or an Entrepreneurial firm, will wish to purchase more components to assemble because the profit margin on each assembled set of components has risen. Suppose now (1) that the marginal product of M does not fall at all rapidly as more X is produced (that is to say, with the existing capital equipment K a greater throughput on the assembly line is fairly readily possible); and suppose further (2) that labour L and materials M are rather highly complementary (that is to say, it is difficult to reduce the labour per car assembled). Then the possibility of extra profit because of the increased margin between the cost of M and the selling price of X may be more important in leading to an increased need for labour than the factors which we have previously examined can be in leading to a contraction in the labour force.

For these reasons with firms with many outputs and with many variable inputs the extreme paradoxical results of an increased selling price leading to reduced employment and output may disappear. But this in no way modifies what is the result of major importance which our previous analysis revealed. If the selling price of something produced by a Co-operative does go up, clearly the workers in that firm can improve their average earnings whether this is accompanied by a rise or by a fall in output or in employment. Moreover, the new level of employment which will maximise earnings per head will always be that which equates the value of the marginal product of labour to its average earnings. This bit of our previous analysis is in no way modified; one can always raise earnings per head by taking on one more worker so long as what he adds net to total revenue is greater than the existing level of earnings per head. Thus in the new equilibrium situation the average earnings and so the value of the marginal product of labour in the firm in question will be higher than before and will thus be higher than it is in the other outside occupations whose situation has not been improved. The Co-operative, unlike the Entrepreneurial firm, will, therefore, fail in the short run to attract the variable factor L from points in which the value of its marginal product is low to points where it is high. This is the essential point.

Difference (3): The Importance of Free Entry

In the Co-operative system this situation is ultimately restored only by the free entry of new firms into any industry which has become exceptionally lucrative as a result of a rise in its selling prices. It is thus clear that the competitive pressures of free entry play a much more important role in a Co-operative than they do in an Entrepreneurial system. This can be illustrated in the following way. Consider a competitive industry with a large number of firms producing at constant returns to scale, *i.e.*, firms with L-shaped cost curves of the kind shown in the footnote on page 404 above, each producing an output appreciably greater than OA. P_x then rises. In an Entrepreneurial system firms take on more labour until the value of the marginal product of labour $\left(P_x \frac{\partial X}{\partial L}\right)$ has fallen again to the ruling wage rate (W) partly as a result of the reduction in the marginal physical product of labour $\left(\frac{\partial X}{\partial L}\right)$ as more L is applied to the fixed amount of K and partly as a result of the reduction in P_x as more X is produced. The value of the marginal product of capital $\left(P_x \frac{\partial X}{\partial K}\right)$ will now be greater than the ruling rental (iP_k) because P_x will still be somewhat greater than before and the physical marginal product of capital $\left(\frac{\partial X}{\partial K}\right)$ will also have been raised because more L is now applied to the given amount of K. The Entrepreneurial firm will, therefore, invest in more K. The process will go on until P_x has fallen to its initial level (since the long-run cost curve is horizontal) and an increased X is produced by the use of more K and more L, both K and L being increased in the same proportion as X. The process does not in this case r... ...ire the entry of any new firms, though new firms may come in.

In the Co-operative the first effect of the rise in P_x is to reduce L and X. This will go on until the marginal product of labour is so raised (as a result of the reduced application of L to the given amount of K) that the value of the marginal product of labour $\left(P_x \frac{\partial X}{\partial L}\right)$ has been raised once more as high as the amount of net average earnings per worker $\left(\frac{P_x X - iP_k K}{L}\right)$.[1] If and when a new equilibrium is reached, the earnings of workers will be equal to the value of their marginal products. With constant returns to scale what is then " left over " as a return to capital (namely, $iP_k K$) will be just sufficient to pay to each unit of capital the value of marginal product $\left(P_x \frac{\partial X}{\partial K} K\right)$. The reduction in the amount of L will have reduced the marginal product of K until $P_x \frac{\partial X}{\partial K}$, which had been raised above iP_k by the rise in P_x, is once more reduced to equality with iP_k as a result of the fall in $\frac{\partial X}{\partial K}$.[2] The situation will then be that the existing Co-operatives are producing less X with the same amount of K and with less L in circumstances in which (i) the value of the marginal product of labour is equal to the average earnings in the firms concerned but is greater than the value of the marginal product and the earnings of labour in other industries, and (ii) the value of the marginal product of capital is equal to the rental of capital, so that the existing firms have no incentive to invest in more capital. This is a Pareto non-optimal situation; restoration of the situation rests wholly upon the possibility of the free entry of new firms; and it should be emphasised that free entry involves workers who are unemployed as a result of the contraction of the firms in the X-industry getting together with workers in other industries who are earning less than the X-industry workers, and setting up new firms in the X-industry. The costs and institutional problems involved in such company promotion are not analysed in Professor Vanek's book.

Difference (4): Monopolistic Behaviour

A closely related difference is that in any given monopolistic conditions the Co-operative will always be more restrictive than the corresponding

[1] We must assume that the demand curve for X is sufficiently price-elastic. If it were very inelastic, P_x might rise so quickly as the output X was reduced that, with a backward-sloping supply curve of X, the excess demand was not eliminated.

[2] $P_x \frac{\partial X}{\partial L} = \frac{P_x X - iP_k K}{L}$ as a result of the adjustment in L. Since with constant returns to scale $P_x X = P_x L \frac{\partial X}{\partial L} + P_x K \frac{\partial X}{\partial K}$, it follows that $P_x \frac{\partial X}{\partial K} = iP_k K$.

Entrepreneurial firm. The reason for this can be seen in the following way. Let us start with an Entrepreneurial firm making a positive monopoly profit of $M = P_xX - iP_kK - WL$. If this firm has maximised its monopoly profit it will be in a position in which a small reduction in L will cause no change in M. It follows that a small reduction in L will cause a rise in $\frac{M}{L}$. But $\frac{M}{L} = \frac{P_xX - iP_kK}{L} - W$. With W constant, it follows that a small reduction in L will cause a rise in $\frac{P_xX - iP_kK}{L}$, *i.e.* in the average earnings of L in a corresponding Co-operative. In other words in any given monopolistic situation the Co-operative will produce less than the corresponding Entrepreneurial firm.

A particular example of this tendency may be of interest. Consider a case of a monopolistic Entrepreneurial concern with an L-shaped cost curve facing a big demand, so that, as illustrated in Fig. 3, it produces on the constant-cost part of its cost curve.

The Entrepreneurial firm produces OB where the marginal cost curve cuts the marginal revenue curve and sells the output at the price BC.

The Co-operative will, however, always produce less than OA (the output which is sufficient to make the average cost curve virtually horizontal), for the following reason. If there are constant returns to scale a 10% reduction in L and K would reduce X by 10%. But if P_x and iP_k were both constant, this 10% reduction in L, K and X would leave $\frac{P_xX - iP_kK}{L}$ unchanged. But if as a result of the monopolistic situation P_x goes up when X is reduced by 10%, then $\frac{P_xX - iP_kK}{L}$ rises when L, K and X are all reduced by 10%. In other words, in order to maximise surplus per unit of L, there will always in monopolistic situations be an incentive for a Co-operative to reduce output so long as there are constant returns to scale. Output will be reduced below OA, until the tendency for real costs per unit to rise as output is reduced offsets the tendency for a rise in the selling price of X to raise income per unit of factor inputs.

Professor Vanek concludes from this analysis that in conditions of monopolistic competition each Co-operative will tend to be smaller than the corresponding Entrepreneurial firm; but, he argues, in the Co-operative economy there will be more competing firms than in the Entrepreneurial economy. This argument rests on the assumption that there will be full employment in the Co-operative economy or, more precisely, that there will not be more unemployment in the Co-operative economy than in the Entrepreneurial economy. If there were the same number of firms but each firm were smaller then there would be more unemployment in the Co-operative economy. If these unemployed got together and set up new firms, then there would be more, but smaller, firms in the Co-operative economy.[1] This in Professor Vanek's view justifies the view that in a very real, and desirable, sense the Co-operative economy will be more competitive than the Entrepreneurial economy. This is a somewhat paradoxical, but to the present reviewer a convincing conclusion.[2]

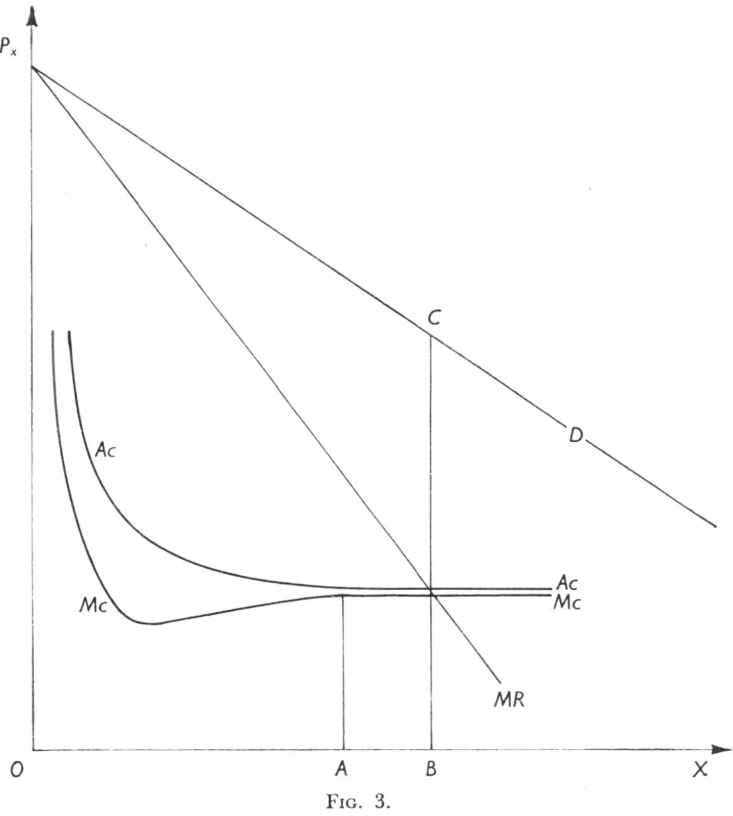

FIG. 3.

Difference (5): Macro-Economic Effects

As a result of the great difference in the short-run behaviour of firms (see *difference (2)* above), the problems of macro-economic control of inflations and deflations of price and employment would be strikingly different.

[1] This conclusion is reinforced by the argument (see pp. 403–4 above) that because of the effect on incentives the most efficient size of the firm is likely to be smaller in the Co-operative than in the Entrepreneurial economy.

[2] Professor Vanek also claims that there will be less expenditure on advertisement in the Co-operative economy. The relevant question here is presumably not whether the individual small Co-operative will spend less absolutely on advertisement than the individual large Entrepreneurial firm, but whether advertisement expenditure per unit of total output will be smaller in the Co-operative than in the Entrepreneurial economy. After covering many sheets of paper with clumsy and inelegant differential calculus the present reviewer can find no plausible reason for giving an emphatic answer " Yes " to the latter question. It seems to him that it might go either way.

A fluctuation in the total money demand for goods as a whole would cause much greater fluctuations in price in the Co-operative than in the Entrepreneurial economy. In an Entrepreneurial economy an increase in total money expenditure engineered through monetary or fiscal policy may lead to some increase in prices, but if there is any considerable initial volume of unemployment it will lead also and importantly to increased employment and output. In a Co-operative economy it will not give any incentive to existing firms to increase output and may indeed, for the reasons discussed in connection with *difference* (2) above, lead to a reduction in employment and output.[1] Prices are thus likely to fluctuate up and down much more in a Co-operative than in an Entrepreneurial economy, as total money expenditures fluctuate.

But Professor Vanek argues that at the same time it may be much easier in a Co-operative system to avoid a continuing upward inflation of money prices, since there can in a Co-operative economy *ex hypothesi* be no simple straightforward wage-cost inflation. Workers take what money earnings are left over after the firm has conducted its operations; they do not set money wage rates on which employers construct their cost prices. But may not this argument be too *simpliste*? In an Entrepreneurial system wage-earners push up money wage rates; employers then push up prices to maintain their profit margins; and the government permits or engineers a rise in total money expenditures sufficient to maintain full employment at the higher money price level. In a Co-operative system may not workers push up their selling prices directly and the government then permit or engineer a rise in total money expenditures sufficient to equate demand to supply at the higher price level? [2]

But however that may be, the implications for employment policy are very far-reaching. To rely in a Co-operative system on Keynesian policies to expand effective demand in times of unemployment would be at best ineffective, and at worst might lead to a reduction in output and employ-

[1] Whether it causes an actual decline in output will depend *inter alia* upon the way in which the hire of K by the Co-operative workers is financed. (*a*) At the one extreme let us suppose that the existing K is financed by a long-term debt whose service is fixed in terms of money. In this case the workers will have a fixed sum (R) to pay in the service of debt. (*b*) At the other extreme let us suppose that the workers pay a rental of iP_k per unit of K, the terms i and P_k being adjusted from day to day to correspond to market changes in the short-term rate of interest (i) and the market price of a machine (P_k). We start with a firm in equilibrium with

$$P_x \frac{\partial X}{\partial L} = \frac{P_x X - R}{L} \text{ in case } (a) \text{ and } \frac{P_x X - iP_k K}{L} \text{ in case } (b).$$

If P_x and P_k are both inflated by 10% while R remains unchanged the equilibrium is not disturbed in case (*b*), but in case (*a*) $P_x \frac{\partial X}{\partial L}$ rises less than $\frac{P_x X - R}{L}$ and there will be an incentive to reduce the size of the firm of the kind examined in connection with *difference* (2) above. Thus in case (*b*) a general inflation of commodity prices will leave output unchanged, while in case (*a*) it may actually cause a reduction in output and employment.

[2] With some possible adverse effect on total employment if the finance of fixed capital is by long-term fixed interest loans as in case (*a*) of the previous footnote.

ment. Indeed, as a short-run policy to induce existing firms to give more employment it would be necessary to *decrease* total demand or to *increase* the fixed overhead cost which firms had to face, for example by *raising* some fixed tax on each firm. But it is pretty clear that such policies would be ill-advised. If the short-run elasticities of supply of existing firms are low, then employment cannot be substantially increased except by setting up new firms, a process which may take considerable time both because of the organisational–promotional problems involved and also because of the gestation period for the production of the necessary new fixed capital equipment.

In a Co-operative economy unemployment may well exist. If it does exist, its cure must be found in a longer-term structural policy aimed at promoting the institution of new firms by the unemployed in order to help them in their desire to enjoy the average earnings of an employed worker rather than the pittance of unemployment benefit. This relative short-run intractability of the unemployment problem may seem to be a serious disadvantage of the Co-operative system. But as Professor Vanek rightly points out one must set on the other side of the balance sheet the fact that if a long-run structure is achieved which gives full employment, then it will be much easier to maintain full employment than is the case in an Entrepreneurial system, since fluctuations in total demand will no longer lead to large fluctuations in output and employment. Prices, not output, will bear the brunt of the change.

So far only the macro-economic effects of effective demand on output and employment, but not those of output and employment on effective demand have been considered. We may perhaps assume that the consumption function (the effect of real income and employment on consumption) would be the same in both systems. As for the incentive to invest in new capital goods by existing firms, perhaps we might also consider it to be the same, namely a function of the relationship between the cost of financing new capital goods and the value of the marginal product of new capital goods, investment by an existing firm being greater, the lower was iP_k and the higher $P_x \frac{\partial X}{\partial K}$.[1] If this is so, it points to a very fundamental difference in the workings of the two systems. Suppose that there is an initial increase in effective demand. As we have seen (page 414 above) in an Entrepreneurial firm this will lead to an increase in output and employment and will also thereby lead to an increase in the value of the marginal product of capital in existing firms who will then (in the absence of any rise in the rate of interest) have an incentive to expand their capital equipment. In the Co-operative, however, there will be no increase in employment and, therefore, no rise in

[1] Professor Vanek (*op. cit.*, pages 168–172) discusses at length possible differences in the case of investment by Co-operative and Entrepreneurial firms. There is no space to discuss his views in this article.

the physical marginal product of capital. Indeed, in the case in which labour can be dismissed from an existing partnership and in which there were constant returns to scale, employment and output would be reduced until the value of the marginal product of capital were equal to its rental (see page 411 above). There would be no incentive to invest by existing firms as a result of an increase in effective demand.

But as we have seen, in a Co-operative we must rely much more on investment to set up new firms as a means for coping with unemployment. Suppose then that there is some automatic or government sponsored mechanism for promoting the setting up of new firms, such promotion being intensified as the volume of unemployment grows. Then if there were a reduction in employment and output, there would be a rise in the scale of investment to set up new firms to cope with the increased volume of unemployment.

But what a perverse universe this is! With the Entrepreneurial system a fall in effective demand reduces employment which reduces the marginal product of capital which reduces investment which reduces effective demand which reduces employment . . ., a vicious circle of positive feedback. With the Co-operative system a rise in effective demand reduces employment which increases unemployment which increases investment to set up new firms which increases effective demand which increases unemployment . . ., another vicious circle of positive feedback. The stability conditions of these two systems might be compared with some interest.[1] But on the face of it the devil seems to win whichever institutional arrangement we may adopt.

III

So much for the main features of Professor Vanek's analysis. It is interesting to consider what are the basic institutional features which give rise to these differences in the workings of the two systems. We may ask whether the differences are due (i) to the fact that in a Co-operative the objective is to maximise a residual surplus per unit of a factor input (*i.e.*, earnings per worker) whereas in an Entrepreneurial firm the objective is to maximise a residual total surplus (*i.e.*, total company profit), or (ii) to the fact that in a Co-operative the factor which is variable in the short-run (L) is the hiring factor whereas in an Entrepreneurial system it is a hired factor.

We can answer this question by considering an institutional set-up in which owners of machines (K) get together, put their machines into a common enterprise, hire labour (L) and sell the output (X) on the best terms which they can obtain on the market, and run the concern so as to maximise the return per machine. This system which for ease of reference

[1] The reader is referred to Professor Vanek's consideration of the stability of his labour-managed economy (*op. cit.*, pp. 204–9).

we will call a Joint-Stock system is exactly analogous to a Co-operative except that it is the factor which is fixed in the short-run (K) which hires the factor which is variable in the short-run (L) instead of the other way round. In conditions of perfect competition the management rules for maximising the return per unit of K for the existing K-partners will be (i) to hire more labour until the value of the marginal product of labour is equal to the market wage rate and (ii), if possible, to expand the size of the partnership by getting more adventurers to put machines into the enterprise so long as the value of the marginal product of machines $P_x \frac{\partial X}{\partial K}$ is greater than the average return per machine in the enterprise as it exists at present $\left(\frac{P_x X - WL}{K}\right)$. These rules are shown in column 5 of the Table on page 405.

As far as labour incentives are concerned (*difference* (*1*) above), Joint-Stock and Entrepreneurial firms are similar, since in both of these labour is hired at a given wage and told what to do. Moreover, in so far as the short period in which K is fixed is concerned, the objective of an Entrepreneurial firm to maximise a total surplus leads to exactly the same result as the objective of a Joint-Stock firm to maximise surplus per unit of the fixed amount of K. For this reason, as far as the short-run competitive behaviour of the systems are concerned (*differences* (*2*), (*3*) *and* (*5*) above), once more Joint-Stock and Entrepreneurial economies are similar and are to be contrasted with a Co-operative economy in which the variable factor (L) does the hiring.[1]

But so far as monopolistic behaviour is concerned (*difference* (*4*)) a Joint-Stock firm is very similar in its effects to a Co-operative. A Joint-Stock firm and a Co-operative are more restrictive than an Entrepreneurial firm because they aim at maximising a surplus per unit of a factor input instead of the total surplus of the firm. The similarity in this connection between a Joint-Stock firm and a Co-operative can be appreciated by simply substituting K for L and L for K in the analysis given above on pages 411–13. For example, a monopolistic Joint-Stock firm like a monopolistic Co-operative will always have an incentive to reduce output so long as it is

[1] At first sight it seems very paradoxical that when P_x rises because of an increased demand for X, there should in the short run be an increase in the production of X if the fixed factor (K) hires the variable factor (L) but a reduction in the production of X if the variable factor (L) hires the fixed factor (K). But when one factor hires another factor, a rise in the selling price of the product by reducing the real cost of the hired factor will induce each unit of the hiring factor to employ a greater amount of the hired factor. Thus when K is the hiring factor a rise in P_x will induce a rise in $\frac{L}{K}$ which, in the short-run with K constant, means a rise in L. But when L is the hiring factor, a rise in P_x will induce a rise in $\frac{K}{L}$ which, in the short-run with K constant, implies a reduction in L. In the long run, of course, in both systems if there are constant returns to scale L, K, and X will all increase in the same proportion until the selling price of the product, P_x, has fallen once more to the old unchanged long-run cost of production.

producing with constant returns to scale. For if a 10% reduction in K and L would lead to a 10% reduction in X, then the return per machine $\frac{P_x X - WL}{K}$ would remain unchanged if the market prices P_x and W remained unchanged. But if P_x rose as X was reduced, $\frac{P_x X - WL}{K}$ would rise. Output would be reduced until the increase in real cost due to the low scale of operations offset the ability to raise earnings per machine by raising the price of the output.

In monopolistic conditions there is thus a real difference between an Entrepreneurial firm and a Joint-Stock firm. In what does this consist? An Entrepreneurial firm may be typified by a capitalist firm in which all the capital has been financed by the issue of fixed interest debentures, the entrepreneur being someone who simply bears the risk that the difference between the revenue of the firm and the total bill for interest and wages may be a high or low positive or negative figure. At first sight it might be thought [1] that a Joint-Stock firm could be typified by a capitalist firm in which all the capital was financed by the issue of ordinary shares and in which, therefore, the existing shareholders would wish to maximise surplus per existing share rather than total surplus and would issue new shares to finance an increase in K if and only if this would raise the return per existing share. For reasons which will become clear later, we will refer to such a firm as an Inegalitarian Joint-Stock firm.

In fact, however, this is not so: there is a world of difference between a Joint-Stock firm in which the objective is the maximisation of return per machine and an Inegalitarian Joint-Stock firm in which the objective is the maximisation of return per share. Let us consider the rules which an Inegalitarian Joint-Stock firm must follow. Since labour is hired at a wage rate W, in perfect competition labour will be hired in the same way as in an Entrepreneurial firm or a Joint-Stock firm up to the point at which the value of its marginal product is equal to the wage rate $\left(P_x \frac{\partial X}{\partial L} = W\right)$.

As far as capital is concerned, we assume that there is a perfectly competitive capital market in which there rules a price (P_s) at which the ordinary shares (S) of the firm can be sold. We are assuming that all capital is financed by the issue of ordinary shares, *i.e.*, that all profits are distributed in dividends and none used for the internal finance of development. The yield on the ordinary shares S is thus $\frac{P_x X - WL}{P_s S}$; let us call this r. The total return per existing ordinary share $\frac{P_x X - WL}{S}$ can be raised by the

[1] The author of this paper presented this thought to a seminar at the Delhi School of Economics, but realised his mistake as he lay in bed that evening. He was thus fortunately able to correct his mistake when the seminar met again on the following day.

issue of new shares to finance new capital equipment if the value of the marginal product of a machine $P_x \frac{\partial X}{\partial K}$ is greater than rP_k. For suppose that £100 worth of new shares are issued. This enables $\frac{£100}{P_k}$ new machines to be purchased and this will add $\frac{£100}{P_k} P_x \frac{\partial X}{\partial K}$ to total revenue at the current marginal productivity of machines. But the dividends which must be paid out to the new shareholders at the current rate of dividend per share will be r £100. If $\frac{£100}{P_k} P_x \frac{\partial X}{\partial K} > r$ £100, *i.e.*, if $P_x \frac{\partial X}{\partial K} > r\ Pk$, there will be some net gain which can be used to raise the dividend for all shareholders. These rules are shown in column 6 of the Table on page 405.

It is clear that the rule for investing more capital in an Inegalitarian Joint-Stock firm is quite different from that for investment in a Joint-Stock firm but is very similar to that in an Entrepreneurial firm with the exception that we are concerned with the earnings yield on ordinary shares (r) instead of the rate of interest on debentures (i).[1]

Why is this so? The answer becomes clear when we substitute the value $r = \frac{P_xX - WL}{P_sS}$ in the expression $P_x \frac{\partial X}{\partial K} \lesseqgtr r\ P_k$ and obtain $P_x \frac{\partial X}{\partial K} \lesseqgtr \frac{P_kK}{P_sS} \frac{P_xX - WL}{K}$.

There are now two influences at work tending to lead to an increase in K:

(i) As in a Joint-Stock firm there is an incentive to increase K if the value of the marginal product of a machine $\left(P_x \frac{\partial X}{\partial K}\right)$ is high relatively to the existing return per machine $\left(\frac{P_xX - WL}{K}\right)$.

(ii) But now there is an additional incentive to expand K if the valuation ratio $\left(\frac{P_sS}{P_kK}\right)$ is high, *i.e.*, if the market value of the share capital is high relatively to the market price of the machinery which it finances.

[1] This similarity applies to monopolistic as well as to competitive conditions. Let $P_x\left(1 - \frac{1}{ed}\right)$ represent the marginal revenue obtained from the sale of an additional unit of X. The Entrepreneurial firm will wish to invest in more K so long as the marginal revenue from the marginal product of K is greater than the rental for a unit of K, *i.e.*, so long as $P_x\left(1 - \frac{1}{ed}\right) > iP_k$. The Inegalitarian Joint-Stock firm will wish to invest in more capital so long as the marginal revenue from the marginal product of K is greater than the additional dividends which must be paid on the value of the shares issued to finance the purchase of K, *i.e.*, so long as $P_x\left(1 - \frac{1}{ed}\right) > r\ P_k$.

Point (ii) means that while shareholders are treated equally, not all shareholders " own," as it were, the same number of machines per £100 subscribed in money capital. Suppose that an Inegalitarian Joint-Stock firm is set up. The original shareholders purchase 100 shares at £1 a share and with the £100 so subscribed purchase 100 machines at £1 a machine. The company does well and the market value of a share rises from £1 to £2. Another 50 shares are issued raising £100 with which 100 additional machines are purchased again at £1 a machine. The company now owns 200 machines and has issued 150 shares. The first shareholders who own $\frac{2}{3}$ of the shares " own " as it were $\frac{2}{3}$ of the 200 machines, *i.e.*, $133\frac{1}{2}$ machines as a result of subscribing £100 which financed the purchase of only 100 machines; the second lot of shareholders own $\frac{1}{3}$ of the shares and thus " own " as it were $\frac{1}{3}$ of the 200 machines, *i.e.*, $66\frac{2}{3}$ machines as a result of subscribing £100 which financed the purchase of no less than 100 machines.

It should now be clear why we have nicknamed this an *Inegalitarian* Joint-Stock firm. Partners do not participate in the partnership according to the amount of real resources which they have put in. Early partners (the original shareholders) can determine the conditions on which new partners (the later shareholders) can come in; and if the early partners, having taken the first risks, find that they are on to a good thing they may admit new partners on less favourable terms than those which they enjoy themselves. It is interesting to see the effects of applying this principle to a Co-operative; and this we shall do in Section VI.

V

Before we outline the structure of what we will call an Inegalitarian Co-operative it will be useful to consider in more detail some of the rules which are appropriate for the running of all forms of labour Co-operatives.

(i) It is clear that in order to give some security to those owners of capital who lend capital to a Co-operative there must be some regulations governing the use of its real capital by a Co-operative. In this respect a Co-operative is in the same position as an Entrepreneurial firm. It must not be possible for a group of workers any more than for an entrepreneur to borrow money, use the proceeds for riotous living, and then go bankrupt. While the commercial decisions as to what is the most profitable form for the use of the borrowed funds must be left to the worker managers, there must clearly be some " company-law " regulations which require the labour managers to make proper use of proper depreciation allowances to maintain the capital of the concern intact in some accepted accounting sense; and if the concern should go bankrupt, then the capital assets would revert to the ownership of those who had lent funds to the concern. The loans to the concern would be secured on the real capital assets of the concern, which the labour managers would be required by law to maintain intact in some accepted accounting sense.[1]

(ii) As for the rules governing the expansion of the number of worker-partners in a Co-operative, it would seem obvious that a new partner should enter the concern only if two conditions are fulfilled, namely (*a*) that the new partner wished to come in and (*b*) that the old partners wish to accept him.

(iii) The rules under (ii) seem obviously fair and acceptable. We will now argue, what is not perhaps quite so obvious, that there must be two analogous conditions for the withdrawal of an existing partner from a Co-operative, namely (*a*) that the partner concerned wishes to leave and (*b*) that he should obtain from the remaining partners permission to withdraw.

Rule (iii) (*a*) is incompatible with the rule of the dismissal of partners by majority decision mentioned in the footnote on page 408. There is presumably no absolute right or wrong about such a rule; but it would appear to the present reviewer that a fully participatory Co-operative must have a rule like (iii) (*a*). In any case the following analysis is an analysis of what will occur if one does have such a rule.[2]

Rule (iii) (*b*) requires somewhat more discussion. Why should any individual worker-partner not be free to leave any Co-operative at any time if he so wishes without any cost to himself? Consider the following case in terms of Fig. 1 on page 407 above. Suppose the Co-operative to be confronted with the curve PQ for its average revenue per head $\left(\frac{P_xX}{L}\right)$. Suppose that it starts with the optimum size of the Co-operative (namely, OA) at which its average earnings $\left(CB = \frac{P_xX - i\,P_kK}{L}\right)$ are at a maximum. But suppose that the average earnings which partners might be able to get if they

[1] This points to an important consideration concerning incentives. We have already argued (page 417 above) that as far as labour incentives are concerned, Entrepreneurial and Joint-Stock firms are similar (in that labour is hired at a given wage and is told what to do), and are to be contrasted with a Co-operative (where labour manages itself). But economic efficiency depends not only on labour incentives, but also upon incentives to maintain the value of the real capital stock. In this respect Entrepreneurial and Co-operative firms are similar (in that those who receive the residual profit on the firm's operations have no direct interest in the wealth of the ultimate owners of the capital) and are to be contrasted with Joint-Stock firms (in which those who enjoy the residual profit themselves own the capital and have, therefore, a much more direct incentive to pay regard to the maintenance or improvement of its value).

[2] Incidentally the existence of such a rule removes a serious problem which would otherwise arise from self-financing of Co-operatives to which Professor Vanek draws attention (*op. cit.*, p. 307). Consider a Co-operative which puts aside undistributed profits and thereby pays off the whole of its outside indebtedness. In terms of Fig. 1 $i\,P_kK$ is reduced to zero and the curve MN collapses to coincide with the two axes. The size of a competitive partnership which will maximise earnings per head is now that which will maximise output per head, which, in the absence of any increasing returns to scale, would with any given amount of real capital involve the reduction of the partnership to one man. With no debt there is no incentive to enlarge the partnership in order to share the debt burden; and the remaining partner will be left endowed with an enormous equipment of real capital financed out of the savings of his previous partners who have been dismissed without compensation.

were free to join new Co-operatives in other industries were greater than the earnings inside the existing partnership, $\left(i.e., E_0 > CB = \frac{P_xX - iP_kK}{L}\right.$ where E_0 measures the average earnings available outside the partnership$\left.\right)$. Some workers might be better able than others to take the opportunity of withdrawal to a more remunerative Co-operative. Suppose the size of the Co-operative is reduced to OE; then the remaining partners can earn only GF so that E_0 is now even greater than before relatively to $GF = \frac{P_xX - i\,P_kK}{L}$. This may go on until what may be called the starvation–bankruptcy size of the Co-operative is reached at a Co-operative size OV where the revenue is just sufficient to cover the debt interest and the remaining workers' earnings are zero.

The point is simply that as partners withdraw the remaining partners are left to hold the debt baby. If the debt obligation has been willingly incurred by all the partners, it is not a true participatory Co-operative if any individual partner can without any obligation just walk out and leave his other partners with the full debt burden. All must sink or swim together.

What then should be the rules for the closure of a Co-operative? What does bankruptcy mean?

One possibility would be that the partners could always in agreement decide to close down the concern leaving the debt holders with the ownership of the capital assets of the concern. Or, in the interests of the debt holders, it might be ruled that the existing partners could not take such action simply because they could do better elsewhere, but only if their earnings, after paying debt interest and maintaining capital intact, fell below some stated level. Indeed different rules, giving different degrees of security to the debt holders, might be freely negotiable between the partners and the debt holders when the partnership was first formed.[1]

VI

Let us then consider a Co-operative with rules (i), (ii) (*a*), (ii) (*b*), (iii) (*a*), and (iii) (*b*); and let us with these rules contrast the operation of a Co-operative (as described on page 402 above) with that of an Inegalitarian Co-operative whose mode of working is as follows. Each individual L-partner on joining the partnership is allotted a share l in the total surplus $(P_xX - iP_kK)$ of the partnership. This share is such that (*a*) it pays the new partner to come in and (*b*) it pays the existing partners to let him in. A partner once in can (apart from death and retirement for reasons of age or ill-

[1] Such rules would make schemes for capital reorganisation possible. If the debt holders were as a result of a " bankruptcy " left holding the real assets of some defunct concern, they might by cutting the debt interest (reducing $i\,P_kK$ and so the curve MN in Fig. 1) bring the concern to life again with a different, or indeed the same, set of worker–partners.

health) withdraw only if (*a*) it pays him to do so and (*b*) he can make it worthwhile for the remaining partners to release him. The shares allotted to the individual partners are not necessarily the same. They may differ because different partners with different skills and trainings may have different values to the partnerships, but they may also differ for partners with the same skills and trainings, because the partners have joined the partnership at different times.

The objective of the Inegalitarian Co-operative as it exists at any moment of time will be to maximise the return per share

$$a = \frac{P_x X - iP_k K}{l_1 + l_2 + \ldots . + l_n}$$

where $l_1 \ldots . . l_n$ are the shares allotted to individuals $l \ldots n$ who make up the existing partnership. Given the distribution of the shares, it is a fully participatory partnership in the sense that every partner has the same motive that the concern should be so managed as to maximise the return per share.

Let us consider the operation of Rules (ii) and (iii) above for the expansion and contraction of such an Inegalitarian Co-operative.

The rules for expansion are straightforward. Suppose that $E_0 < P_x \frac{\partial X}{\partial L}$, *i.e.*, that the average earnings outside are less than the value of the marginal product of labour in the partnership. Then all that is necessary is for the existing partners to agree on a share l_{n+1} for a new partner such that

$$E_0 < al_{n+1} < P_x \frac{\partial X}{\partial L}$$

The new partner will wish to join because $E_0 < al_{n+1}$. The existing partners will wish him to join because $al_{n+1} < P_x \frac{\partial X}{\partial L}$; for since the addition to the revenue of the concern as a result of his joining will be greater than his share of the surplus, the return to all existing workers will be raised.

The rules for withdrawal are a little more complicated. Let us suppose that $E_0 > P_x \frac{\partial X}{\partial L}$. Now there are three cases to be considered.

(i) Suppose that some existing partner j has a share in the partnership (l_j) such that

$$E_0 > al_j > P_x \frac{\partial X}{\partial L}$$

Then the partner will wish to withdraw because $E_0 > al_j$; and the existing partners will willingly let him go because $al_j > P_x \frac{\partial X}{\partial L}$, that is to say, they they will lose less in revenue than they save on his share of the surplus.

(ii) But suppose that for all the existing partners

$$al > E_0 > P_x \frac{\partial X}{\partial L}$$

The existing partners would like to see any individual partner withdraw because $al > P_x \frac{\partial X}{\partial L}$; but no existing partner will wish to go because $al > E_0$. However, there is a net gain to everyone concerned of $E_0 - P_x \frac{\partial X}{\partial L}$ if one partner does withdraw, since that partner will earn E_0 and the existing partnership will lose only $P_x \frac{\partial X}{\partial L}$. In this case the existing partners might bribe one of their number to withdraw, perhaps by allowing him to retain some of his shares in the partnership even if he goes and works elsewhere. In this case L will be reduced so long as $E_0 > P_x \frac{\partial X}{\partial L}$.

(iii) Suppose that for all existing partners

$$E_0 > P_x \frac{\partial X}{\partial L} > al$$

Then an individual partner will want to withdraw because $E_0 > al$, but the other partners will not want to release him since $P_x \frac{\partial X}{\partial L} > al$. But once again there is a net gain of $E_0 - P_x \frac{\partial X}{\partial L}$ and an individual partner should be able to purchase his release from his colleagues.[1] Once again L will be reduced so long as $E_0 > P_x \frac{\partial X}{\partial L}$.

An Inegalitarian Co-operative, in the same way as a Co-operative, will have an incentive to borrow money to expand its capital equipment so long as the value of the marginal product of machinery is greater than its rental $\left(P_x \frac{\partial X}{\partial K} > i\, P_k K\right)$. The resulting rules for an Inegalitarian Co-operative are shown in column 4 of the Table on page 405.

[1] For example, if the withdrawing partner pays to the partnership the present value of earnings of $E = \frac{1}{2}\left(E_0 + P_x \frac{\partial X}{\partial L}\right) - al$, the gain will be shared equally between the withdrawing partner who will gain $E_0 - al - E = \frac{1}{2}\left(E_0 - P_x \frac{\partial X}{\partial L}\right)$ and the remaining partners who will gain $al - P_x \frac{\partial X}{\partial L} + E = \frac{1}{2}\left(E_0 - P_x \frac{\partial X}{\partial L}\right)$.

For simplicity of exposition we have presented the argument without reference to the fact that not only the particular partnership which we have been examining, but also all the other concerns in the community, may be organised as Inegalitarian Co-operatives. Suppose this to be so and that the value of the marginal product of labour in one industry is greater than in another $\left(e.g., P_y \frac{\partial Y}{\partial L} > P_x \frac{\partial X}{\partial L}\right)$. Then there is a net gain for everyone concerned of $P_y \frac{\partial Y}{\partial L} - P_x \frac{\partial X}{\partial L}$ if one unit of L moves from the X- to the Y-industry. There must be some bargain which will involve the choice of the share which the migrant worker will receive in the Y-industry and which may involve him in purchasing his release from his X-colleagues which improves the lot of everyone—the existing Y-partners, the migrant worker and the remaining X-partners. Thus labour will move from X to Y if $P_y \frac{\partial Y}{\partial Y} > P_x \frac{\partial X}{\partial L}$. The short-run adjustment process of the Inegalitarian Co-operative, unlike that of the Co-operative, becomes Pareto-optimal.

But this result is achieved only at the expense of a distributional principle which may involve two workers of equal age, sex, ability, skill, etc., working side by side at the same job at the same work-bench, but receiving different shares in the product. As with the shareholders in the Inegalitarian Joint-Stock firm, the worker–partners in an Inegalitarian Co-operative who come in early bearing the initial risks in a concern which turns out to do well will earn more than those workers who come in later when the success of the enterprise is already established.

VII

There is no reason why one should not go the whole hog in participation and profit-sharing and apply the same principle both to those who supply the capital and to those who supply the labour. Such a set-up would be a combination of an Inegalitarian Joint-Stock firm (as far as the supply of capital was concerned) and an Inegalitarian Co-operative (as far as the supply of labour was concerned). Let us call the resulting structure an Inegalitarian Joint-Stock-Co-operative firm. Let S represent the number of shares issued to those who have subscribed capital. Let there be three skills or types of Labour (L, M, and N) and let $l_1, l_2, \ldots, m_1, m_2 \ldots, n_1, n_2 \ldots$ represent the shares issued to individual workers $L_1, L_2 \ldots, M_1, M_2 \ldots, N_1, N_2 \ldots$ Then the objective of the existing partners at any one time will be to maximise the return per share or

$$a = \frac{P_x X}{S + l_1 + l_2 + \ldots + m_1 + m_2 + \ldots + n_1 + n_2 + \ldots}$$

This will be achieved by following the rules (which are summarised in column 7 of the Table on page 405):

(i) increase or decrease S and so K as $P_x \frac{\partial X}{\partial K} \gtrless r\, P_k$

(ii) increase or decrease L as $P_x \frac{\partial X}{\partial L} \gtrless E_{ol}$

(iii) increase or decrease M as $P_x \frac{\partial X}{\partial M} \gtrless E_{om}$

(iv) increase or decrease N as $P_x \frac{\partial X}{\partial N} \gtrless E_{on}$

Reductions in L, M, N must be associated, as far as is necessary, with bargains by which existing partners buy their way out or are bribed by the remaining partners to withdraw.

The analysis which leads to these results is exactly the same as that which has been given above for an Inegalitarian Joint-Stock firm and for an Inegalitarian Co-operative.

Nor is this the only possibility of combination of structures. There is nothing in the nature of things to prevent some capitalists and some workers getting together and forming a partnership (on Inegalitarian Joint-Stock–Co-operative principles), but nevertheless borrowing some additional capital at fixed interest and hiring some additional labour at a fixed wage (thus introducing Entrepreneurial elements into the concern). Or, as with the usual profit-sharing arrangement, we may find labour being rewarded in an ordinary company partly with a fixed wage rate and partly with shares in the concern, which introduces a Co-operative element into an Inegalitarian Joint-Stock firm. All sorts of participatory profit sharing combinations are theoretically possible.

There is no place in the present article to discuss the historical and empirical questions as to which of these structures have flourished in which conditions. But it is interesting to ask why the Co-operative structure is not more common than it is in fact in the free-enterprise world. Two factors spring to mind.

First, there is the basic, though not strictly economic question whether a workers' Co-operative organisation is compatible with the maintenance of the discipline needed to ensure the efficient operation of a concern which employs a large body of workers.

Secondly, while property owners can spread their risks by putting small bits of their property into a large number of concerns, a worker cannot easily put small bits of his effort into a large number of different jobs. This presumably is a main reason why we find risk-bearing capital hiring labour rather than risk-bearing labour hiring capital. Moreover, since labour cannot spread its risks, we are likely to find Co-operative structures only in lines of activity in which the risk is not too great, and this means in lines of activity in which two conditions are fulfilled: first, the risk of fluctuations in the demand for the product must not be too great; and, secondly, the activity must be a labour-intensive activity in which the surplus accruing to labour does not constitute a small difference between two large quantities, the revenue from the sale of the product and the hire of capital plus the purchase of raw materials.[1] This may help to explain why such labour partnerships as do exist are usually to be found in labour-intensive services, such as lawyers, accountants, doctors, etc.

VIII

Many questions remain unconsidered. Neither Professor Vanek nor the author of the present article have attempted to answer a very important question concerning risk, namely whether, if a workers' Co-operative did exist in any given situation, it would (in its decisions concerning output, price, investment, employment, etc.) react differently from an Entrepreneurial firm in the face of a given set of risks. Nor has any systematic attempt been made to compare the behaviour of a Co-operative system with that of Managerial Capitalism,[2] though Professor Vanek does claim (*op. cit.*, page 119) that the Co-operative system would be less prone to the temptations of " gigantism " than any other economic regime.

In this article the author has made no attempt to argue for or against the institution of labour partnerships. Professor Vanek in his book which inspired this article professes himself to be a keen advocate of such participatory organisations; but in spite of this he maintains a most admirable scientific frankness in exposing the weaknesses as well as the strengths of such organisations. It has not been possible in this article to review all of Professor Vanek's arguments; his book should be read by all economists interested in the subject. The purpose of this article has been merely to analyse some of the implications of labour partnerships or profit-sharing structures. It may well be the case that the merits of participation should be so highly prized as to make the encouragement of such institutions a major objective of governmental policy. For governmental encouragement of one kind or another will almost certainly be necessary because of the natural tendency for risk-bearing capital to hire labour rather than the risk-bearing labour to hire captial.

If such governmental policies are to be devised, there are at least three main problems to be borne in mind.

First, as we have tried to show, the effective workings of labour partnerships will depend very much upon easy conditions for the formation of new

[1] In terms of Fig. 1 if the *MN* and the *PQ* curves were both raised substantially so as to leave the difference *CB* unchanged, a 1% fall in the *PQ* curve would have a much more marked effect in ducing *CB*.

[2] Of the kind described by such authors as Berle and Means, Burnham, Galbraith, and Marris.

partnerships to enter any profitable industry. But easy company promotion of this kind by unemployed or ill-paid workers will certainly be impossible without appropriate governmental interventions of a most extensive character—leading perhaps inevitably to a socialist ownership of the main capital resources of the community as in Yugoslavia.

Second, the labour partnership presents in its own special form a conflict between efficiency and equality. Some compromise rules on the distribution of the surplus among new and old workers must be found which does not introduce excessive inequalities on the one hand or excessive inefficiencies on the other.

Third, thought must be given to the extent to which labour partnerships involve workers risking all their eggs in one basket. Some compromise between the degree of participation and the degree of the spreading of risks would have to be sought.[1]

J. E. Meade

Christ's College,
Cambridge.

[1] In this connection it would be helpful to encourage a wide distribution of the ownership of property (what the present reviewer has called a Propdem in another connection) so that the representative worker is also a representative property owner. A citizen could then at least spread his property in small parcels over a lot of other concerns, even though he had to concentrate his earnings from work on one particular concern.

[18]

Some Economics of Property Rights

1. SCARCITY, COMPETITION, AND PROPERTY

In *every* society, conflicts of interest among the members of that society must be resolved. The process by which that resolution (not elimination!) occurs is known as competition. Since, by definition, there is no way to eliminate competition, the relevant question is what kind of competition shall be used in the resolution of the conflicts of interest. In more dramatic words designed to arouse emotional interest, What forms of discrimination among the members of that society shall be employed in deciding to what extent each person is able to achieve various levels of his goals? Discrimination, competition, and scarcity are three inseparable concepts.

2. CONSTRAINTS

That list of concepts can be expanded—scarcity, competition, discrimination, constraints, property. In other words,

Preparation of this paper was facilitated by a grant from the Lilly Endowment of Indianapolis, Indiana, to the University of California, Los Angeles, for a study of various forms of property rights.

constraints exist that prevent our individually achieving a level of want-fulfillment beyond which none of us wants more. In still other words, these constraints, even though imposed by nature, include also the constraints imposed by other people who because they achieve certain levels of want fulfillment leave other people with lower levels. (I do not mean that *all* activities that enable one person to have a greater level of goal fulfillment will also necessarily mean less for someone else; we know that some forms of exchange permit joint increases. But we also know that cooperative action is possible, and also that competitive action is also present.) If we concentrate attention on constraints and classes of permissible action we find ourselves studying the *property* aspect of behavior.

Economists are, I think, too prone to examine exchange as a cooperative act whereby the buyer and seller each act in an effort to reach a more desired position. Yet I find it more interesting (now that I understand the cooperative aspect of exchange) to examine the competitive, or property, aspect of exchange. The act of exchange is a means whereby the buyer is able to compete against other claimants for the goods being obtained from the seller. The kinds of offers, forms of competition and behavior that the members of society can employ in an endeavor to get more of the goods that would otherwise go to other people, is brought more into the focus of attention. More directly, the forms and kinds of property rights sanctioned in a society define or identify the kinds of competition, discrimination, or behavior characteristic of that society.

Yet if we look at the "fields" of economics, say as presented by the American Economic Association's classification of areas of interest or specialization, we find no mention of the word "property." Either we can infer that the profession is so obviously aware of the pervasiveness of the effects of various forms of property rights that property rights can not sensibly be regarded as merely a subfield; or else we can infer that economists have forgotten about the possibility of subjective rigorous systematic coherent analysis of the various forms of property rights. My conviction is that the latter inference is the more valid one. As evidence I cite that the only systematic analysis of choice among "goods" postulates utility maximization subject to a budget or *wealth* constraint, wherein the constraint is almost invariably a *private* property type of wealth constraint.

3. PROPERTY RIGHTS

If, in what follows, I talk as if the property rights were enforced by formal state police power, let me here emphasize that such an interpretation, regardless of what I may later say, is gross error. It seems to be a fact that individuals will not stand by idly while some other person's property is stolen. It seems to be a fact that *private* property rights are rights not merely because the state formally makes them so but because individuals want such rights to be enforced, at least for a vast, overwhelming majority of people. And yet if I recognize the number of socialist states, I must admit to some confusion (I appeal for edification).

The rights of individuals to the use of resources (i.e., property rights) in any society are to be construed as supported by the force of etiquette, social custom, ostracism, and formal legally enacted laws supported by the states' power of violence or punishment. Many of the constraints on the use of what we call private property involve the force of etiquette and social ostracism. The level of noise, the kind of clothes we wear, our intrusion on other people's privacy are restricted not merely by laws backed by the police force, but by social acceptance, reciprocity, and voluntary social ostracism for violators of accepted codes of conduct. The use of arabic numbers rather than roman, the use of certain types of clothing, or styles of speech and address, of printing from left to right and top to bottom, rather than the reverse, or keeping our garden up with Jones', all are subject to the force of social opprobrium. No laws require such behavior. Yet each of us (or nearly every one of us) will punish in one way or another those who violate these rules. Surely it is not the important rules that are left to the formal state power of enactment and compulsion. Obviously there is heated dispute as to which forms of behavior should be ''enforced'' by social voluntary ostracism and which by formal state police action.

By a system of property rights I mean a method of assigning to particular individuals the ''authority'' to select, for specific goods, any use from a nonprohibited class of uses. As suggested in the preceding remarks the concepts of ''authority'' and of ''nonprohibited'' rely on some concept of enforcement or inducement to respect the assignment and scope of prohibited choice. A property right for me means some protection against other people's choosing against my will one of the uses of resources, said to be ''mine.''

Often the idea or scope of *private* property rights is expressed as an assignment of exclusive authority to some individual to choose any use of the goods deemed to be his private property. In other words the ''owners,'' who are assigned the right to make the choice, have an unrestricted right to the choice of use of specified goods. Notice, that we did not add—''so long as the rights of other people are similarly respected.'' That clause is redundant in strict logic. Private property owners can use their goods in any way they choose. If some of these chosen uses involve the use or destruction of other people's private property, it follows that the private property system is being violated, for this use has denied to other people the control of use over the goods classed as private property. To say I have private property rights is to say that no one else has the right to make the choice of use of that good (contained in the class of private property). This means that if I select a use for the goods said to be my private property, the selection must not affect the physical attributes of your goods. If I own some iron, I can make window frames or fence posts out of it, but if I shove a piece of iron through "your" glass window, I shall be denying you the right of choice of the physical attributes of your private property. However, if I convert the iron to a special kind of good that other people are willing to buy instead of buying what you are selling, you may find that the reduced exchange value of your goods imposes a greater loss of exchange power (wealth) than if I had simply broken your window.

Although private property rights protect private property from physical changes chosen by other people, no immunity is implied for the exchange value of one's property. Nor does it imply that my use of my goods, which may not in any way affect your goods, cannot be a use that you find objectionable on moral or emotional grounds. If I use my resources to make lewd pictures for my own use or for exchange with other people, you may find your "utility" much affected. You may be more upset, annoyed, distressed, or hurt by my action than if I had broken your window or stolen some of your wealth.

Private property, as I understand it, does *not* imply that a person may use his property in any way he sees fit so long as no one else is "hurt." Instead, it seems to mean the right to use goods (or to transfer that right) in any way the owner wishes so long as the physical attributes or uses of all other people's private property is unaffected. And that leaves plenty of room for disturbance and alienation of affections of other people. If I open a restaurant near yours and win away business by my superior service, you are as hurt as if I had burned part of your building. If I open a restaurant and pour smells and smoke over your neighboring land then I have changed the physical attributes of your property; I have violated your private property rights—incidentally, a form of violation very common in most societies.

But if the right for me to open a business were denied, this could, if it also were part of a system in which your rights to enter into various businesses were similarly restricted, be considered by you to be an undesirable restriction and one that did you more harm than would be encountered by you in a less restrictive environment.

In sum, it is only the choice over physical attributes that is constrained to owners, not the value-in-exchange effects nor the psychological, emotional effects that you may suffer in the knowledge that I am behaving in what you consider improper ways (short of changing the physical attributes of your property).

4. PARTITIONING OF PROPERTY RIGHTS

Whether or not the preceding suggested definition is useful, we examine another issue. What are the effects of various partitionings of use rights? By this I refer to the fact that at the same time several people may each possess some portion of the rights to use the land. A may possess the right to grow wheat on it. B may possess the right to walk across it. C may possess the right to dump ashes and smoke on it. D may possess the right to fly an airplane over it. E may have the right to subject it to vibrations consequent to the use of some neighboring equipment. And each of these rights may be transferable. In sum, private property rights to various partitioned uses of the land are "owned" by different persons.[1]

A lease or rental agreement partitions the rights so that the renter gets the right to make decisions about particular uses of the item by the "owner." Normally the rights of the renter to decide where the furniture will be placed or when it will be sat on, etc., are not thought of as ownership rights, because they are so frequently allocated to the renter, and because the ultimate value consequence rests on the "owner." However, our main point here is that the rights can be partitioned, divided, and reallocated on a temporary—or even on a permanent—basis, so that the "ownership" rights are partitioned among two or more persons. This kind of division is not necessarily a cross-sectional division with each owner now having equal parts of all the ownership rights. Instead it is a selective partitioning with all of some of the subrights staying with the "owner" and all of some other rights being transferred temporarily at least to the "renter." Even though this is called a rental or leasing agreement, it does contain transfers of some of the rights that are included in ownership. The fact that these partitionings of owner are temporary makes it easy to decide who is the "owner" in the conventional sense.

The partitioning of various types of rights to use, has been

[1] A different form of interpersonal sharing of rights is that in which all rights are possessed in common and jointly by the group, but the decision as to any use must be reached by the group. Rights to each different kind of use are not separated and possessed by different people. Instead the rights are commonly owned; and the problem is in devising or specifying some choice process which will "declare" the decision of the "group" of joint owners.

explored by Ronald Coase.[2] He notes that what are commonly called nuisances and torts apply to just such situations in which rights are partitioned and the exercise of one owner's rights involves distress or nuisance for the owners of other rights. For example, if a railroad spreads sparks and ignites fires in wheatfields near the tracks, the wheat grower can pay the railroad not to spread sparks (if the law gives the railroad the right to spread such sparks). On the other hand, if the right to decide about such land use is reserved to the farmer, the railroad could pay him for the right to drop sparks on the land (and save costs of spark screens, etc.). If there were no costs of *negotiating* such exchanges of rights and policing them, the initial partitioning of rights would not affect the way resources are used. (Of course, wealth would be redistributed in accord with the initial assignment of the partitioned rights.)

But when we recognize that transaction costs do exist, it seems clear that the partitioned rights will be reaggregated into more convenient clusters of rights. If so, there should be an evolutionary force toward survival of larger clusters of certain types of rights in the sanctioned concept of property rights. But I am at a loss to formulate this more precisely, meaningfully, and fruitfully. Except for rare studies like those of Glanville Williams on the development of the laws of trespass and the two-volume work of Maitland and Pollack on the development of law (and property rights) in the 12th through 14th centuries, I suspect our main alternative is to initiate studies of our own.[3] For example, a study of the property rights in Ireland during the past three hundred years and of

[2] "The Problem of Social Costs," *Journal of Law and Economics* (1960): 1–5.

[3] Frederick Pollock and Frederic Maitland, *The History of English Law Before the Time of Edward I*, 2nd ed. (Cambridge, 1952); Glanville Williams, *Liability for Animals* (Cambridge: Cambridge University Press, 1939).

water law in the United States may (and I believe, will) enable us to discover more rigorous formulation of the laws of development of property law.

5. SHARING PROPERTY RIGHTS

At this point there is a temptation to start classifying various partitioning of property rights, e.g., private, public, bailments, easements, leases, licenses, franchises, inheritances, etc. This temptation is easy to avoid, because the task is so difficult. Another temptation is to list the various ways in which property rights of owners—ownership rights, as they are called hereafter—whatever they may be, can be shared among people as joint owners or as a partnership. Or corporations can be created as a means of sharing property rights of owners among voluntary sharers. Or public property may amount to everyone having a share—although, as we shall see, I think this is not the crucial difference between public and private ownership.

The ability of individuals to enter into mutually agreeable sharing of the rights they possess is evident from the tremendous variety of such arrangements, e.g., corporations, partnerships, nonprofit corporations, licenses, bailments, nonvoting common stock, trusts, agencies, employee-employer relationships, and marriages.

Should we be surprised that the government refuses to enforce some voluntary proposed sharing of legitimate property rights among owners? Presumably the "undesirable" effects justify the refusal to sanction some of the ownership sharing. For example, at one time, the state refused to enforce corporate ownership—even though all the members of the corporation entered voluntarily. Will it enforce every voluntary sharing and partitioning of ownership rights among individuals?

The variety of joint sharing of property and ownership rights is a testimony to man's ingenuity. But if one asked what the difference was between any two of them, say public and private ownership, he would find the answer not so easy. In one sense it is adequate to say that the public is the owner as contrasted to a private group. But that is not very helpful if one is interested in discovering what difference it makes for behavior and use of resources. Compare a privately owned golf course with a publicly owned course (or auditorium, bus service, water service, garbage collection, airport, school, or even spaghetti factory). There are differences in the way they are operated; at least anyone who has ever compared them will think so. Why do these differences occur? Are the objectives different? Is it because the kind of people who operate one are different from those who operate the other? Is it because of the form of ownership?

I believe (on the basis of something more than casual observation) that behavior under each institution is different, not because the objectives sought by organizations under each form are different, but, instead, because even with the same explicit organization goals, the costs-rewards system impinging on the employees and the "owners" of the organization are different. And I suspect that these differences are implied by economic theory, if the trouble is taken to apply the theory. Further, preliminary speculation suggests, for example, that the difference between a privately owned corporation with 1,000 owners and a state-owned entity in a democracy with 1,000 citizens is quite significant, because the 1,000 individuals are furthering their own individual interests in each entity under two different systems of property rights, i.e., the rewards-costs schedules differ.

6. PRIVATE AND PUBLIC OWNERSHIP

How do private and public ownership rights differ? To sharpen the issue, consider a small-town theater owned by 1,000 corporate shareholders (each with one share) and an auditorium owned by the 1,000 residents as public property. This eliminates the difference of sharing and differences in the number of joint "owners." Every activity conducted at one could, in principle, just as well be held at the other building. Assume also, the city auditorium is operated to make money, not to subsidize some group, and so is the private theater.

The public auditorium and the private theater both serve the public. It is not the case that the former is designed to provide a public service and the latter not. The privately owned theater will survive only if it can provide services that the public wants at the price asked. It is a source of public service, even though its purpose from the owners' point of view is to make money. But what about the publicly owned auditorium? Is its end that of public service or to make money for the public owners? Suppose its end is public service. This does not *require* that its means of action be any different than if its ends were profits to the owners—public or private. Furthermore, assume in both cases the managers and employees were induced to take their jobs only because the salary enhances their own wealth or well-being. They take the jobs—not because they want to provide a public service or wealth for the owners; but instead because they want a better living for themselves. We can assume that those resident citizens who "own" the auditorium and voted for it did so because each felt it would make his own situation preferable—not because he wanted to benefit someone else as a charity device.

But there are differences, and we conjecture the proposition that the differences between public and private ownership arise from *the inability of a public owner to sell his share of public ownership* (and the ability to acquire a share without a purchase of the right). But let us be clear about this. We are not yet asserting that there are no other differences, nor that this difference has not been noticed before. Instead we are emphasizing the *unique* importance of this difference in the ownership rights.

We are not begging the issue by assuming away one general difference—the profit incentive or criterion. Both public and private property can seek profits. The desire to avoid or suppress the effects of the profit-making incentive is, however, often the reason society resorts to public ownership. However, the objectives sought by public ownership cannot merely be announced to the managers or operators with expectation that exhortation will be either sufficient or necessary to achieve the objective. Since our general postulate is that people, as individuals, seek to increase their utility and that wealth is a source of utility, we cannot expect people to change their goals or desires. Instead, we rely upon changes in the rewards-costs structure to redirect their activities as they seek to increase their utility or level of satisfaction of their desires.[4] And we shall try to show that many differences, that do exist between behavior in public and privately owned institutions, reflect this ownership difference—viz., the presence or the absence of the right to sell a share of ownership to someone else.

The difference can be put somewhat less euphemistically.

[4] Friends of Adam Smith will recognize this as the major postulate of his *Wealth of Nations*, a postulate which seems to have served economists well when not forgotten.

Public ownership *must* be borne by all members of the public, and no member can divest himself of that ownership. Ownership of public property is not voluntary; it is compulsory as long as one is a member of the public. To call something "compulsory" usually is a good start towards condemning it.

A person must move from one town to another to change his ownership in public property. In one sense it is not compulsory because it is not compulsory that one lives in a particular community. But so long as one does live in any community with public property he is a public owner and cannot divest himself of public ownership; but he can sell and shift private property ownership rights without also having to leave the community.

It is tempting to emphasize the possibility, under public ownership, of someone joining the community and thereby acquiring a share of public ownership, without payment to any of the existing owners. This dilution of a person's share of ownership is presumably absent in private ownership. In fact, a community could close off immigration; but public ownership would continue even if this dilution effect were an important problem. Furthermore, many corporations issue new shares without preemptive rights to former owners. Presumably this is done only when the receiver of the new shares pays the corporation something of at least equivalent value. And it is a safe assumption that the management deems the *quid pro quo* to have been worthwhile so far as present purposes are concerned. Still, it is sufficient that even if dilution of public ownership were eliminated by restriction of entry, the inability to sell one's share of public ownership remains a potent factor in the costs-reward system impinging on all members of the public and on the employees and administrators of the publicly owned institution.

7. SOME IMPLICATIONS OF TRANSFERABILITY

To see what difference is made by the right to transfer ownership shares, suppose public ownership could be sold. It would be possible for me to sell to someone else my share in the publicly owned water, or bus or garbage, or parks, or school system. To separate out the fact that public ventures are usually run without the intent of making a profit, let us suppose that the water or bus system had been instructed to be as profitable as it could. Now that its ownership has become salable, with capitalized profits or losses accruing to the owners, will incentives be any different?

The answer is suggested by two implications of the specialization of "ownership" which is similar to the familiar specialization of other kinds of skills or activities. The two derivative implications are: (1) concentration of rewards and costs *more* directly on each person responsible for them, and (2) comparative advantage effects of specialized applications of (a) knowledge in control and (b) of risk bearing.

Degree of Dependency. The greater concentration of rewards and costs means simply that each person's wealth is more dependent upon his own activities. This is brought about as follows: the more he concentrates his wealth holding in particular resources, the more will his wealth respond to his own activities in those areas. Consider the following example: Suppose there are 100 people in a community, with 10 separate enterprises. Suppose that each person, by devoting one tenth of his time to some one enterprise as an owner, could produce a saving or gain of $1,000. Since the individual is a 1/100 part owner he will acquire $10. Suppose, further, that he does this for each of the 10 different enterprises, in each of which he owns 1/100 part. His total wealth gain will be $100, with the rest of the product, $9,900, going to the 99 other people. If the 99 other people act in the same way, he will get from their activities an increase of wealth of $990,000/100=$9,900, which gives him a total of $10,000. This is exactly equal to his product most of which was spread over the other owners.

However, if everyone each owns 1/10 part of *one* enterprise only (which means that ownership has been reshuffled from pro rata equal shares in all enterprises to a concentration in one enterprise by each person, although with the same total number of enterprises), the individual will now be assumed to devote his whole time during one year to the one enterprise, so he again produces $10,000. (We assume that his productivity is proportional to the number of hours of work, and that it is the same for everyone. Other assumptions will change the arithmetic, but will not destroy the main principle being elaborated.) Of this he gets $1,000. The remainder, $9,000, goes to the owners of the other 9/10 share. Like them, he too receives portions of the other owners' products, and if all are assumed to be exactly alike, then he gets from the 9 other joint owners of his enterprise $9.000 for a total of $10,000—precisely the same as in the preceding example. The difference is that now $1,000 of this is dependent upon his own activities whereas formerly only $100 was. Or more pertinently, the amount dependent upon the activities of other people is reduced from $9,900 to $9,000.

If we go to the extreme where the 10 enterprises are divided into 100, with each person as the sole owner of one enterprise, then all $10,000 of his year's wealth increase will depend upon his own activities. The first of these three examples corresponds to public ownership, the second to corporate joint private ownership, and the third to sole proprietorship.

If public ownership rights were made salable, they would in effect become private ownership rights and there would be a movement toward concentration of ownership of the type in the second example, at least. Why? In the second case, the wealth a person can get is more dependent upon his own activities than in the first case. Many people may prefer to let the situation stay as in example 1, hoping to collect a major portion of their wealth gain from other people's activities. If this were the case, the total wealth gain would decrease since everyone would have less incentive to work. But it suffices that there be at least one person who prefers to make himself less dependent upon other people's activities than in example 1 and who prefers at least some more wealth to some more leisure. He will then be prepared to buy up some ownership rights and pay a higher price for them than they are worth to some other people. That he values them more highly is precisely another way of saying that he values independence more than they do, or that he prefers more wealth to less wealth—even if it requires some work by him.

Comparative Advantage in Ownership: Control. The preceding example did not involve interpersonal differences of abilities, knowledge, or attitude toward risk. But if people differ in any of these respects, as they in fact do, it can be shown that specialization in various tasks—including that of owning a business—will increase wealth. This demonstration is simply the logical theorem of gains from comparative advantage, which we shall not explain here.

Usually the illustrations of comparative advantage are based on "labor" productivities with no reference to "ownership" productivities. But people differ in their talents as owners. Owners bear the risk of value changes, make the decisions of how much to produce, how much to invest, and how it shall be produced and who shall be employed as laborers and managers. Ownership ability includes attitude toward risk bearing, knowledge of different people's productive abilities, foresight and, of course, "judgment." These talents differ among people according to the particular industry, type of product, or productive resource one is considering. The differences in skills of people as owners make pertinent the principle of comparative advantage through specialization in ownership. If ownership rights are transferable, then specialization of ownership will yield gains. People will concentrate their ownership in those areas in which they believe they have a comparative advantage, if they want to increase their wealth. Just as specialization in typing, music, or various types of labor is more productive, so is specialization in ownership. Some people specialize in electronics industry knowledge, some in airlines, some in dairies, some in retailing, etc. Private property owners can specialize in knowledge about electronics, devoting much of their effort and study to learning which electronic devices show promise, which are now most efficient in various uses, which should be produced in larger numbers, where investment should take place, what kinds of research and development to finance, etc. But public ownership practically eliminates possibilities of specialization among owners—though not of employees in the publicly owned venture.

A person who is very knowledgeable about woodworking and cabinet or furniture building would have an advantage as an owner of a furniture company. He would, by being a stockholder, not necessarily make the company any better, but instead he would choose the better company—as judged by his knowledge—as one in which to own shares. The relative rise in the price of such companies enables the existing owners to issue new shares, borrow money more readily, and retain control. In this way the differences in knowledge enable people to specialize in the application of that knowledge to the management and operation of the company—albeit sometimes by indirect lines.

Comparative Advantage in Ownership: Risk Bearing. A second aspect of ownership specialization is risk bearing. People's attitudes toward risk differ. If various ventures or resources represent different prospects of values, then exchange of ownership will enable a reallocation of risks among people, leading to greater utility in the same sense that exchange of goods does. This risk-bearing difference reflects not only attitudes toward risk but beliefs about the prospects of future values of the assets whose ownership can be transferred. Differences in "knowledge" can be used not only in an effort to be more productive but also as a means for distinguishing different risk situations. For example, I may be the top administrator of the Carnation Milk Company, but I may choose to hold stocks in some electronic company because I prefer the risk pattern provided by that stock to that provided by ownership in Carnation. In this way a person can separate the productivity of knowledge and effort in what he owns from the risk bearing. He can, if he wants, combine them by holding stock in a company in which he is active. This possibility of separating the *control* (effective administration or operation of the company—an activity which rewards comparative superiority in ability and knowledge) from *risk bearing* is, of course, regarded as an advantage by those who act as employed managers or administrators, and by those who choose to act as corporate stock owners without also bothering to exercise their vote or worry about control. Yet, it is often criticized as undesirable.

Not all of the owners have to think of themselves as owners who are going to exercise their voting rights so effectively as to exert an influence on management. Most of the owners may go along simply because they believe the prospects for profits and losses are sufficiently promising relative to other assets they could own. If losses eventuate, their only alternative is to sell out. To whom? To other buyers who, because of the reduced profit prospects, will offer only a lower price. These "nonactive" owners perform a very important function in that they provide the willingness to bear some of the value consequences, at least. So long as scarce resources *exist*, value changes will occur. The question left is then which particular members are to bear the reduced value. Someone has to bear them. Those changes cannot be eliminated.

Often it is said that joint ownership in the modern corporation has separated ownership and control. What this means is that risk bearing and management are more separate. This is correct in that each owner does not have the kind of control he would as the sole owner. But it is a long logical leap to decrying this. It can be a good thing. Specialization in risk bearing and in management or decision-making about particular uses of resources is now possible. Complete separation does not exist for every joint owner, for to the extent that some share owners are inactive or indifferent to alternative choices or management problems, other stockholders (joint owners) will be more influential. In effect, the "passive" owners are betting on the decisions of "active" owners; "betting" in the sense that they are prepared to pay other people for any losses produced by these "activists" and in turn collect the profits, if any. In the absence of any right to buy and sell shared ownership rights voluntarily everyone would have to bet on the activists as a group (the case of public property). The right to sell concentrates this betting on these who are prepared to pay the most (or demand the least) for the right to do so. And it concentrates the control or management with those who believe they are relatively most able at that task—and these beliefs can be tested with the less able being eliminated more surely in private ownership than in public because (1) the evidence of poor management and the opportunity to capture wealth gains by eliminating it is revealed to outsiders by the lower selling price of the ownership rights, (2) the specialization of ownership functions is facilitated, and (3) the possibility of concentrating one's wealth in certain areas permits greater correlation of personal interest and effort in line with wealth holdings.

We conjecture from the preceding discussion the theorem: *Under public ownership the costs of any decision or choice are less fully thrust upon the selector than under private property*. In other words, the cost-benefit incentives system is changed toward lower costs. The converse of this implication is that the gains to any owner resulting from any cost-saving action are less fully effective. These do not mean that the true costs are reduced. The looser correlation between the costs borne by any chooser and the costs of the particular choices he makes is what is implied. Similarly, the capturable gains to the owners of their actions are reduced.

They are *less* fully borne than they would be if the same action were taken in a private property institution, with a similar number of owners.[5] From this theorem one would expect that public agencies would, in order to offset or counterbalance this reduced cost bearing, impose special extra costs or constraints on public employees or agents. Public agents who

[5] In other words, this difference between public and private ownership does not flow from differences in numbers of owners.

are authorized to spend public funds should be more severely constrained with extra restrictions precisely because the costs of their actions are less effectively thrust upon them. And of course these extra constraints do exist. Because of these extra constraints—or because of the "costs" of them—the public arrangement becomes a higher cost (in the sense of "less efficient") than that for private property agencies.

For example, civil service, nepotism restrictions, tenure, single-salary structures for public schoolteachers, sealed bids, and "lineitem" budget controls, to name a few, are some of the costly devices used.

But it is not easy—indeed impossible—in many instances to impose "corrective" costs as offsets. How would one impose full costs upon a city manager who decided to have a garbage collection system (that turned out to be a big money loser) that the city would tolerate? By not reelecting him. But this cost is less than that borne by the private owner who decides (erroneously) to start a garbage collection system. He loses his job *and* the sunk costs. Similarly, how do we make a voter bear the costs of bad judgment in his votes? Are the prospects of costs that may be imposed on a voter equivalent to the cost-prospects that will be laid on a private owner (with share rights) voting in a private corporation? Not according to the theorem derived from our analysis.

I should, I suppose, avow at random intervals that all this is not a condemnation of public ownership any more than certain "deficiencies" of marriage, the human eye, the upright position of the human being, or smoking are to be regarded as condemnations of marriage, eyes, walking on two feet, or smoking. The "lesser" evils in some institutions—and they exist in all—are borne for the greater good in some of them. We are not arguing that private property even in its purest form is perfect in the cost-bearing sense. No standard of perfection is available. All of our statements have been comparative in degrees of cost bearing.

The converse of this "apologia" is that one should not speak of the imperfections of the marketplace, either. Nor should one assume in those instances where the marketplace is inferior in certain respects to, say, public ownership or government control, that we ought to switch from the private property market to the government. The presence of one kind of relative deficiency does not justify a switch to another agency—which has other kinds of deficiencies.

8. WE SUMMARIZE

As we suggested earlier, public and private ownership are used for different purposes, and in some cases *because* of these different behavioral implications. If public ownership in some government activity were converted to private property, the method of achieving the government objectives would be changed. If city and national parks, or golf courses owned by cities were converted to private property, they would no longer be operated as subsidies for certain groups. If the fire and police department rights were converted to private property rights, vast changes would occur in their operation. And the same goes for the postal system, the garbage collection system, the bus lines, streets, the federal mortgage insurance companies, and the army, the navy, and the air force. When "we" do not want (whatever that means) these changes to occur, these activities are conducted via public ownership instead of privately. And if the effects of greater dependence of benefits and costs on one's own actions are not wanted, resort is made to government activity. Which is not to say that government activity is therefore for that reason good or bad. The extent to which ''society'' reduces risks that must be individually borne and instead has them borne by society at large—thus reducing the correlation between choice of action and consequences for people as individuals—the greater is the extent of public property. How much this depends upon a *choice* to socialize certain risks, and how much reflects the voting and decision-making *process* are questions I cannot answer.

[19]

Production, Information Costs, and Economic Organization

By ARMEN A. ALCHIAN AND HAROLD DEMSETZ*

The mark of a capitalistic society is that resources are owned and allocated by such nongovernmental organizations as firms, households, and markets. Resource owners increase productivity through cooperative specialization and this leads to the demand for economic organizations which facilitate cooperation. When a lumber mill employs a cabinetmaker, cooperation between specialists is achieved within a firm, and when a cabinetmaker purchases wood from a lumberman, the cooperation takes place across markets (or between firms). Two important problems face a theory of economic organization—to explain the conditions that determine whether the gains from specialization and cooperative production can better be obtained within an organization like the firm, or across markets, and to explain the structure of the organization.

It is common to see the firm characterized by the power to settle issues by fiat, by authority, or by disciplinary action superior to that available in the conventional market. This is delusion. The firm does not own all its inputs. It has no power of fiat, no authority, no disciplinary action any different in the slightest degree from ordinary market contracting between any two people. I can "punish" you only by withholding future business or by seeking redress in the courts for any failure to honor our exchange agreement. That is exactly all that any employer can do. He can fire or sue, just as I can fire my grocer by stopping purchases from him or sue him for delivering faulty products. What then is the content of the presumed power to manage and assign workers to various tasks? Exactly the same as one little consumer's power to manage and assign his grocer to various tasks. The single consumer can assign his grocer to the task of obtaining whatever the customer can induce the grocer to provide at a price acceptable to both parties. That is precisely all that an employer can do to an employee. To speak of managing, directing, or assigning workers to various tasks is a deceptive way of noting that the employer continually is involved in renegotiation of contracts on terms that must be acceptable to both parties. Telling an employee to type this letter rather than to file that document is like my telling a grocer to sell me this brand of tuna rather than that brand of bread. I have no contract to continue to purchase from the grocer and neither the employer nor the employee is bound by any contractual obligations to continue their relationship. Long-term contracts between employer and employee are not the essence of the organization we call a firm. My grocer can count on my returning day after day and purchasing his services and goods even with the prices not always marked on the goods —because I know what they are—and he adapts his activity to conform to my directions to him as to what I want each day . . . he is not my employee.

Wherein then is the relationship between a grocer and his employee different from that between a grocer and his cus-

* Professors of economics at the University of California, Los Angeles. Acknowledgment is made for financial aid from the E. Lilly Endowment, Inc. grant to UCLA for research in the behavioral effects of property rights.

tomers? It is in a *team* use of inputs and a centralized position of some party in the contractual arrangements of *all* other inputs. It is the *centralized contractual agent in a team productive process*—not some superior authoritarian directive or disciplinary power. Exactly what is a team process and why does it induce the contractual form, called the firm? These problems motivate the inquiry of this paper.

I. The Metering Problem

The economic organization through which input owners cooperate will make better use of their comparative advantages to the extent that it facilitates the payment of rewards in accord with productivity. If rewards were random, and without regard to productive effort, no incentive to productive effort would be provided by the organization; and if rewards were negatively correlated with productivity the organization would be subject to sabotage. Two key demands are placed on an economic organization—metering input productivity and metering rewards.[1]

Metering problems sometimes can be resolved well through the exchange of products across competitive markets, because in many situations markets yield a high correlation between rewards and productivity. If a farmer increases his output of wheat by 10 percent at the prevailing market price, his receipts also increase by 10 percent. This method of organizing economic activity meters the *output directly*, reveals the marginal product and apportions the *rewards* to resource owners in accord with that direct measurement of their outputs. The success of this decentralized, market exchange in promoting productive specialization requires that changes in market rewards fall on those responsible for changes in *output*.[2]

The classic relationship in economics that runs from marginal productivity to the distribution of income implicitly *assumes* the existence of an organization, be it the market or the firm, that allocates rewards to resources in accord with their productivity. The problem of economic organization, the economical means of metering productivity and rewards, is not confronted directly in the classical analysis of production and distribution. Instead, that analysis tends to assume sufficiently economic—or zero cost—means, as if productivity automatically created its reward. We conjecture the direction of causation is the reverse—the specific sys-

[1] Meter means to measure and also to apportion. One can meter (measure) output and one can also meter (control) the output. We use the word to denote both; the context should indicate which.

[2] A producer's wealth would be reduced by the present capitalized value of the future income lost by loss of reputation. Reputation, i.e., credibility, is an asset, which is another way of saying that reliable information about expected performance is both a costly and a valuable good. For acts of God that interfere with contract performance, both parties have incentives to reach a settlement akin to that which would have been reached if such events had been covered by specific contingency clauses. The reason, again, is that a reputation for "honest" dealings—i.e., for actions similar to those that would probably have been reached had the contract provided this contingency—is wealth.

Almost every contract is open-ended in that many contingencies are uncovered. For example, if a fire delays production of a promised product by *A* to *B*, and if *B* contends that *A* has not fulfilled the contract, how is the dispute settled and what recompense, if any, does *A* grant to *B*? A person uninitiated in such questions may be surprised by the extent to which contracts permit either party to escape performance or to nullify the contract. In fact, it is hard to imagine any contract, which, when taken solely in terms of its stipulations, could not be evaded by one of the parties. Yet that is the ruling, viable type of contract. Why? Undoubtedly the best discussion that we have seen on this question is by Stewart Macaulay.

There are means not only of detecting or preventing cheating, but also for deciding how to allocate the losses or gains of unpredictable events or quality of items exchanged. Sales contracts contain warranties, guarantees, collateral, return privileges and penalty clauses for specific nonperformance. These are means of assignment of *risks* of losses of cheating. A lower price without warranty—an "as is" purchase—places more of the risk on the buyer while the seller buys insurance against losses of his "cheating." On the other hand, a warranty or return privilege or service contract places more risk on the seller with insurance being bought by the buyer.

tem of rewarding which is relied upon stimulates a particular productivity response. If the economic organization meters poorly, with rewards and productivity only loosely correlated, then productivity will be smaller; but if the economic organization meters well productivity will be greater. What makes metering difficult and hence induces means of economizing on metering costs?

II. Team Production

Two men jointly lift heavy cargo into trucks. Solely by observing the total weight loaded per day, it is impossible to determine each person's marginal productivity. With team production it is difficult, solely by observing total output, to either define or determine *each* individual's contribution to this output of the cooperating inputs. The output is yielded by a team, by definition, and it is not a *sum* of separable outputs of each of its members. Team production of Z involves at least two inputs, X_i and X_j, with $\partial^2 Z/\partial X_i \partial X_j \neq 0$.[3] The production function is *not* separable into two functions each involving only inputs X_i or only inputs X_j. Consequently there is no *sum* of Z of two separable functions to treat as the Z of the team production function. (An example of a *separable* case is $Z = aX_i^2 + bX_j^2$ which is separable into $Z_i = aX_i^2$ and $Z_j = bX_j^2$, and $Z = Z_i + Z_j$. This is not team production.) There exist production techniques in which the Z obtained is greater than if X_i and X_j had produced separable Z. Team production will be used if it yields an output enough larger than the sum of separable production of Z to cover the costs of organizing and disciplining team members—the topics of this paper.[4]

[3] The function is separable into additive functions if the cross partial derivative is zero, i.e., if $\partial^2 Z/\partial X_i \partial X_j = 0$.

[4] With sufficient generality of notation and conception this team production function could be formulated as a case of the generalized production function interpretation given by our colleague, E. A. Thompson.

Usual explanations of the gains from cooperative behavior rely on exchange and production in accord with the comparative advantage specialization principle with separable additive production. However, as suggested above there is a source of gain from cooperative activity involving working as a *team*, wherein individual cooperating inputs do not yield identifiable, separate products which can be *summed* to measure the total output. For this cooperative productive activity, here called "team" production, measuring *marginal* productivity and making payments in accord therewith is more expensive by an order of magnitude than for separable production functions.

Team production, to repeat, is production in which 1) several types of resources are used and 2) the product is not a sum of separable outputs of each cooperating resource. An additional factor creates a team organization problem—3) not all resources used in team production belong to one person.

We do not inquire into why all the jointly used resources are not owned by one person, but instead into the types of organization, contracts, and informational and payment procedures used among owners of teamed inputs. With respect to the one-owner case, perhaps it is sufficient merely to note that (a) slavery is prohibited, (b) one might assume risk aversion as a reason for one person's not borrowing enough to purchase all the assets or sources of services rather than renting them, and (c) the purchase-resale spread may be so large that costs of short-term ownership exceed rental costs. Our problem is viewed basically as one of organization among different people, not of the physical goods or services, however much there must be selection and choice of combination of the latter.

How can the members of a team be rewarded and induced to work efficiently?

In team production, marginal products of cooperative team members are not so directly and separably (i.e., cheaply) observable. What a team offers to the market can be taken as the marginal product of the team but not of the team members. The costs of metering or ascertaining the marginal products of the team's members is what calls forth new organizations and procedures. Clues to each input's productivity can be secured by observing *behavior* of individual inputs. When lifting cargo into the truck, how rapidly does a man move to the next piece to be loaded, how many cigarette breaks does he take, does the item being lifted tilt downward toward his side?

If detecting such behavior were costless, neither party would have an incentive to shirk, because neither could impose the cost of his shirking on the other (if their cooperation was agreed to voluntarily). But since costs must be incurred to monitor each other, each input owner will have more incentive to shirk when he works as part of a team, than if his performance could be monitored easily or if he did not work as a team. If there is a net increase in productivity available by team production, net of the metering cost associated with disciplining the team, then team production will be relied upon rather than a multitude of bilateral exchange of separable individual outputs.

Both leisure and higher income enter a person's utility function.[5] Hence, each person should adjust his work and realized reward so as to equate the marginal rate of substitution between leisure and production of real output to his marginal rate of substitution in consumption. That is, he would adjust his rate of work to bring his demand prices of leisure and output to equality with their true costs. However, with detection, policing, monitoring, measuring or metering costs, each person will be induced to take more leisure, because the effect of relaxing on ***his realized*** (reward) rate of substitution between output and leisure will be less than the effect on the ***true*** rate of substitution. His realized cost of leisure will fall more than the true cost of leisure, so he "buys" more leisure (i.e., more nonpecuniary reward).

If his relaxation cannot be detected perfectly at zero cost, part of its effects will be borne by others in the team, thus making *his* realized cost of relaxation less than the true total cost to the team. The difficulty of detecting such actions permits the private costs of his actions to be less than their full costs. Since each person responds to his private realizable rate of substitution (in production) rather than the true total (i.e., social) rate, and so long as there are costs for other people to detect his shift toward relaxation, it will not pay (them) to force him to readjust completely by making him realize the true cost. Only enough efforts will be made to equate the marginal gains of detection activity with the marginal costs of detection; and that implies a lower rate of productive effort and more shirking than in a costless monitoring, or measuring, world.

In a university, the faculty use office telephones, paper, and mail for personal uses beyond strict university productivity. The university administrators could stop such practices by identifying *the* responsible person in each case, but they can do so only at higher costs than administrators are willing to incur. The extra costs of identifying each party (rather than merely identifying the presence of such activity) would exceed the savings from diminished faculty "turpitudinal peccadilloes." So the faculty is allowed some degree of "privileges, perquisites, or fringe benefits." And the total of the pecuniary wages paid

[5] More precisely: "if anything other than pecuniary income enters his utility function." Leisure stands for all nonpecuniary income for simplicity of exposition.

is lower because of this irreducible (at acceptable costs) degree of amenity-seizing activity. Pay is lower in pecuniary terms and higher in leisure, conveniences, and ease of work. But still every person would prefer to see detection made more effective (if it were somehow possible to monitor costlessly) so that he, as part of the now more effectively producing team, could thereby realize a higher pecuniary pay and less leisure. If everyone could, at zero cost, have his reward-realized rate brought to the true production possibility real rate, all could achieve a more preferred position. But detection of the responsible parties is costly; that cost acts like a tax on work rewards.[6] Viable shirking is the result.

What forms of organizing team production will lower the cost of detecting "performance" (i.e., marginal productivity) and bring personally realized rates of substitution closer to true rates of substitution? Market competition, in principle, could monitor some team production. (It already *organizes* teams.) Input owners who are not team members can offer, in return for a smaller share of the team's rewards, to replace excessively (i.e., overpaid) shirking members. Market competition among potential team members would determine team membership and individual rewards. There would be no team leader, manager, organizer, owner, or employer. For such decentralized organizational control to work, outsiders, possibly after observing each team's total output, can speculate about their capabilities as team members and, by a market competitive process, revised teams with greater productive ability will be formed and sustained. Incumbent members will be constrained by threats of replacement by outsiders offering services for lower reward shares or offering greater rewards to the other members of the team. Any team member who shirked in the expectation that the reduced output effect would not be attributed to him will be displaced if his activity is detected. Teams of productive inputs, like business units, would evolve in apparent spontaneity in the market—without any central organizing agent, team manager, or boss.

But completely effective control cannot be expected from individualized market competition for two reasons. First, for this competition to be completely effective, new challengers for team membership must know where, and to what extent, shirking is a serious problem, i.e., know they can increase net output as compared with the inputs they replace. To the extent that this is true it is probably possible for existing fellow team members to recognize the shirking. But, by definition, the detection of shirking by observing team output is costly for team production. Secondly, assume the presence of detection costs, and assume that in order to secure a place on the team a new input owner must accept a smaller share of rewards (or a promise to produce more). Then his incentive to shirk would still be at least as great as the incentives of the inputs replaced, because he still bears less than the entire reduction in team output for which he is responsible.

III. The Classical Firm

One method of reducing shirking is for someone to specialize as a monitor to check the input performance of team members.[7]

[6] Do not assume that the sole result of the cost of detecting shirking is one form of payment (more leisure and less take home money). With several members of the team, each has an incentive to cheat against each other by engaging in more than the average amount of such leisure if the employer can not tell at zero cost which employee is taking more than average. As a result the total productivity of the team is lowered. Shirking detection costs thus change the form of payment and also result in lower total rewards. Because the cross partial derivatives are positive, shirking reduces other people's marginal products.

[7] What is meant by performance? Input energy, initiative, work attitude, perspiration, rate of exhaustion?

(Continued)

But who will monitor the monitor? One constraint on the monitor is the aforesaid market competition offered by other monitors, but for reasons already given, that is not perfectly effective. Another constraint can be imposed on the monitor: give him title to the net earnings of the team, net of payments to other inputs. If owners of cooperating inputs agree with the monitor that he is to receive any residual product above prescribed amounts (hopefully, the marginal value products of the other inputs), the monitor will have an added incentive not to shirk as a monitor. Specialization in monitoring plus reliance on a residual claimant status will reduce shirking; but additional links are needed to forge the firm of classical economic theory. How will the residual claimant monitor the other inputs?

We use the term monitor to connote several activities in addition to its disciplinary connotation. It connotes measuring output performance, apportioning rewards, observing the input behavior of inputs as means of detecting or estimating their marginal productivity and giving assignments or instructions in what to do and how to do it. (It also includes, as we shall show later, authority to terminate or revise contracts.) Perhaps the contrast between a football coach and team captain is helpful. The coach selects strategies and tactics and sends in instructions about what plays to utilize. The captain is essentially an observer and reporter of the performance at close hand of the members. The latter is an inspector-steward and the former a supervisor manager. For the present all these activities are included in the rubric "monitoring." All these tasks are, in principle, negotiable across markets, but we are presuming that such market measurement of marginal productivities and job reassignments are not so cheaply performed for team production. And in particular our analysis suggests that it is not so much the costs of spontaneously negotiating contracts in the markets among groups for team production as it is the detection of the performance of individual members of the team that calls for the organization noted here.

The specialist *who receives the residual rewards* will be the monitor of the members of the team (i.e., will manage the use of cooperative inputs). The monitor earns his residual through the reduction in shirking that he brings about, not only by the prices that he agrees to pay the owners of the inputs, but also by observing and directing the actions or uses of these inputs. *Managing or examining the ways to which inputs are used in team production is a method of metering the marginal productivity of individual inputs to the team's output.*

To discipline team members and reduce shirking, the residual claimant must have power to revise the contract terms and incentives of *individual* members without having to terminate or alter every other input's contract. Hence, team members who seek to increase their productivity will assign to the monitor not only the residual claimant right but also the right to alter individual membership and performance on the team. Each team member, of course, can terminate his own membership (i.e., quit the team), but only the monitor may unilaterally terminate the membership of any of the

Or output? It is the latter that is sought—the *effect* or output. But performance is nicely ambiguous because it suggests both input and output. It is *nicely* ambiguous because as we shall see, sometimes by inspecting a team member's input activity we can better judge his output effect, perhaps not with complete accuracy but better than by watching the output of the *team*. It is not always the case that watching input activity is the only or best means of detecting, measuring or monitoring output effects of each team member, but in some cases it is a useful way. For the moment the word performance glosses over these aspects and facilitates concentration on other issues.

other members without necessarily terminating the team itself or his association with the team; and he alone can expand or reduce membership, alter the mix of membership, or sell the right to be the residual claimant-monitor of the team. It is this entire bundle of rights: 1) to be a residual claimant; 2) to observe input behavior; 3) to be the central party common to all contracts with inputs; 4) to alter the membership of the team; and 5) to sell these rights, that defines the *ownership* (or the employer) of the *classical* (capitalist, free-enterprise) firm. The coalescing of these rights has arisen, our analysis asserts, because it resolves the shirking-information problem of team production better than does the noncentralized contractual arrangement.

The relationship of each team member to the *owner* of the firm (i.e., the party common to all input contracts *and* the residual claimant) is simply a "quid pro quo" contract. Each makes a purchase and sale. The employee "orders" the owner of the team to pay him money in the same sense that the employer directs the team member to perform certain acts. The employee can terminate the contract as readily as can the employer, and long-term contracts, therefore, are not an essential attribute of the firm. Nor are "authoritarian," "dictational," or "fiat" attributes relevant to the conception of the firm or its efficiency.

In summary, two necessary conditions exist for the emergence of the firm on the prior assumption that more than pecuniary wealth enter utility functions: 1) It is possible to increase productivity through team-oriented production, a production technique for which it is costly to directly measure the marginal outputs of the cooperating inputs. This makes it more difficult to restrict shirking through simple market exchange between cooperating inputs. 2) It is economical to estimate marginal productivity by observing or specifying input behavior. The simultaneous occurrence of both these preconditions leads to the contractual organization of inputs, known as the *classical capitalist firms* with (a) joint input production, (b) several input owners, (c) one party who is common to all the contracts of the joint inputs, (d) who has rights to renegotiate any input's contract independently of contracts with other input owners, (e) who holds the residual claim, and (f) who has the right to sell his central contractual residual status.[8]

Other Theories of the Firm

At this juncture, as an aside, we briefly place this theory of the firm in the contexts of those offered by Ronald Coase and Frank Knight.[9] Our view of the firm is not necessarily inconsistent with Coase's; we attempt to go further and identify refutable implications. Coase's penetrating insight is to make more of the fact that markets do not operate costlessly, and he relies on the cost of using markets to *form* contracts as his basic explanation for the existence of firms. We do not disagree with the proposition that, *ceteris paribus*, the higher is the cost of transacting across markets the greater will be the comparative advantage of organizing resources within the firm; it is a difficult proposition to disagree with or to refute. We could with equal ease subscribe to a theory of the firm based on the cost of managing, for surely it is true that, *ceteris paribus*, the lower is the cost of managing the greater will be the comparative advantage of organizing resources within the firm. To move the theory forward, it is necessary to know what is meant by a firm and to

[8] Removal of (b) converts a capitalist proprietary firm to a socialist firm.

[9] Recognition must also be made to the seminal inquiries by Morris Silver and Richard Auster, and by H. B. Malmgren.

explain the circumstances under which the cost of "managing" resources is low relative to the cost of allocating resources through market transaction. The conception of and rationale for the classical firm that we propose takes a step down the path pointed out by Coase toward that goal. Consideration of team production, team organization, difficulty in metering outputs, and the problem of shirking are important to our explanation but, so far as we can ascertain, not in Coase's. Coase's analysis insofar as it had heretofore been developed would suggest open-ended contracts but does not appear to imply anything more—neither the residual claimant status nor the distinction between employee and subcontractor status (nor any of the implications indicated below). And it is not true that employees are generally employed on the basis of long-term contractual arrangements any more than on a series of short-term or indefinite length contracts.

The importance of our proposed additional elements is revealed, for example, by the explanation of why the person to whom the control monitor is responsible receives the residual, and also by our later discussion of the implications about the corporation, partnerships, and profit sharing. These alternative forms for organization of the firm are difficult to resolve on the basis of market transaction costs only. Our exposition also suggests a definition of the classical firm—something crucial that was heretofore absent.

In addition, sometimes a technological development will lower the cost of market transactions while, at the same time, it expands the role of the firm. When the "putting out" system was used for weaving, inputs were organized largely through market negotiations. With the development of efficient central sources of power, it became economical to perform weaving in proximity to the power source and to engage in team production. The bringing in of weavers surely must have resulted in a reduction in the cost of negotiating (forming) contracts. Yet, what we observe is the beginning of the factory system in which inputs are organized within a firm. Why? The weavers did not simply move to a common source of power that they could tap like an electric line, purchasing power while they used their own equipment. Now team production in the joint use of equipment became more important. The measurement of marginal productivity, which now involved interactions between workers, especially through their joint use of machines, became more difficult though contract negotiating cost was reduced, while managing the *behavior* of inputs became easier because of the increased centralization of activity. The firm as an organization expanded even though the cost of transactions was reduced by the advent of centralized power. The same could be said for modern assembly lines. Hence the emergence of central power sources expanded the scope of productive activity in which the firm enjoyed a comparative advantage as an organizational form.

Some economists, following Knight, have identified the bearing of risks of wealth changes with the director or central employer without explaining why that is a viable arrangement. Presumably, the more risk-averse inputs become employees rather than owners of the classical firm. Risk averseness and uncertainty *with regard to the firm's fortunes* have little, if anything, to do with our explanation although it helps to explain why all resources in a team are not owned by one person. That is, the role of risk taken in the sense of absorbing the windfalls that buffet the firm because of unforeseen competition, technological change, or fluctuations in demand are not central to our theory, although it is true that imperfect knowledge and, therefore, risk, in *this* sense of risk, underlie the problem of monitoring team behavior. We deduce the system of paying the manager with a residual claim (the equity) from the desire to have efficient means to reduce shirking so as to make team production economical and not from the smaller aversion to the risks of enterprise in a dynamic economy. We conjecture that "distribution-of-risk" is not a valid rationale for the *existence* and organization of the *classical* firm.

Although we have emphasized team production as creating a costly metering task and have treated team production as an essential (necessary?) condition for the firm, would not other obstacles to cheap metering also call forth the same kind of contractual arrangement here denoted as a firm? For example, suppose a farmer produces wheat in an easily ascertained quantity but with subtle and difficult to detect quality variations determined by how the farmer grew the wheat. A vertical integration could allow a purchaser to control the farmer's behavior in order to more economically estimate productivity. But this is not a case of joint or team production, unless "information" can be considered part of the product. (While a good case could be made for that broader conception of production, we shall ignore it here.) Instead of forming a firm, a buyer can contract to have his inspector on the site of production, just as home builders contract with architects to supervise building contracts; that arrangement is not a firm. Still, a firm might be organized in the production of many products wherein no team production or jointness of use of separately owned resources is involved.

This possibility rather clearly indicates a broader, or complementary, approach to that which we have chosen. 1) As we do in this paper, it can be argued that the firm is the particular policing device utilized when joint team production is present. If other sources of high policing costs arise, as in the wheat case just indicated, some other form of contractual arrangement will be used. Thus to each source of informational cost there may be a different type of policing and contractual arrangement. 2) On the other hand, one can say that where policing is difficult across markets, various forms of contractual arrangements are devised, but there is no reason for that known as the firm to be uniquely related or even highly correlated with team production, as defined here. It might be used equally probably and viably for other sources of high policing cost. We have not intensively analyzed other sources, and we can only note that our current and readily revisable conjecture is that 1) is valid, and has motivated us in our current endeavor. In any event, the test of the theory advanced here is to see whether the conditions we have identified are necessary for firms to have long-run viability rather than merely births with high infant mortality. Conglomerate firms or collections of separate production agencies into one owning organization can be interpreted as an investment trust or investment diversification device—probably along the lines that motivated Knight's interpretation. A holding company can be called a firm, because of the common association of the word firm with any ownership unit that owns income sources. The term firm as commonly used is so turgid of meaning that we can not hope to explain every entity to which the name is attached in common or even technical literature. Instead, we seek to identify and explain a particular contractual arrangement induced by the cost of information factors analyzed in this paper.

IV. Types of Firms

A. Profit-Sharing Firms

Explicit in our explanation of the capitalist firm is the assumption that the cost of *managing* the team's inputs by a central monitor, who disciplines himself because he is a residual claimant, is low relative to the cost of metering the marginal outputs of team members.

If we look within a firm to see who monitors—hires, fires, changes, promotes, and renegotiates—we should find him being a residual claimant or, at least, one whose pay or reward is more than any others correlated with fluctuations in the residual value of the firm. They more likely will have options or rights or bonuses than will inputs with other tasks.

An implicit "auxiliary" assumption of our explanation of the firm is that the cost of team production is increased if the residual claim is not held entirely by the central monitor. That is, we assume that if profit sharing had to be relied upon for *all* team members, losses from the resulting increase in central monitor shirking would exceed the output gains from the increased incentives of other team members not to shirk. If the optimal team size is only two owners of inputs, then an equal division of profits and losses between them will leave each with stronger incentives to reduce shirking than if the optimal team size is large, for in the latter case only a smaller percentage of the losses occasioned by the shirker will be borne by him. Incentives to shirk are positively related to the optimal size of the team under an equal profit-sharing scheme.[10]

The preceding does not imply that profit sharing is never viable. Profit sharing to encourage self-policing is more appropriate for small teams. And, indeed, where input owners are free to make whatever contractual arrangements suit them, as generally is true in capitalist economies, profit sharing seems largely limited to partnerships with a relatively small number of *active*[11] partners. Another advantage of such arrangements for smaller teams is that it permits more effective reciprocal monitoring among inputs. Monitoring need not be entirely specialized.

Profit sharing is more viable if small team size is associated with situations where the cost of specialized management of inputs is large relative to the increased productivity potential in team effort. We conjecture that the cost of managing team inputs increases if the productivity of a team member is difficult to correlate with his behavior. In "artistic" or "professional" work, watching a man's activities is not a good clue to what he is actually thinking or doing with his mind. While it is relatively easy to manage or direct the loading of trucks by a team of dock workers where input activity is so highly related in an obvious way to output, it is more difficult to manage and direct a lawyer in the preparation and presentation of a case. Dock workers can be directed in detail without the monitor himself loading the truck, and assembly line workers can be monitored by varying the speed of the assembly line, but detailed direction in the preparation of a law case would require in much greater degree that the monitor prepare the case himself. As a result, artistic or professional inputs, such as lawyers, advertising specialists, and doctors, will be given relatively freer reign with regard to individual behavior. If the management of inputs is relatively costly, or ineffective, as it would seem to be in these cases, but, nonetheless if team effort is more productive than separable production with exchange across markets, then there will develop a tendency to use profit-sharing schemes to provide incentives to avoid shirking.[12]

[10] While the degree to which residual claims are centralized will affect the size of the team, this will be only one of many factors that determine team size, so as an approximation, we can treat team size as exogenously determined. Under certain assumptions about the shape of the "typical" utility function, the incentive to avoid shirking with unequal profit-sharing can be measured by the Herfindahl index.

[11] The use of the word active will be clarified in our discussion of the corporation, which follows below.

[12] Some sharing contracts, like crop sharing, or rental

B. Socialist Firms

We have analyzed the classical proprietorship and the profit-sharing firms in the context of free association and choice of economic organization. Such organizations need not be the most viable when political constraints limit the forms of organization that can be chosen. It is one thing to have profit sharing when professional or artistic talents are used by small teams. But if political or tax or subsidy considerations induce profit-sharing techniques when these are not otherwise economically justified, then additional management techniques will be developed to help reduce the degree of shirking.

For example, most, if not all, firms in Jugoslavia are owned by the employees in the restricted sense that all share in the residual. This is true for large firms and for firms which employ nonartistic, or nonprofessional, workers as well. With a decay of political constraints, most of these firms could be expected to rely on paid wages rather than shares in the residual. This rests on our auxiliary assumption that general sharing in the residual results in losses from enhanced shirking by the monitor that exceed the gains from reduced shirking by residual-sharing employees. If this were not so, profit sharing with employees should have occurred more frequently in Western societies where such organizations are neither banned nor preferred politically. Where residual sharing by employees is politically imposed, as in Jugoslavia, we are led to expect that some management technique will arise to reduce the shirking by the central monitor, a technique that will not be found frequently in Western societies since the monitor retains all (or much) of the residual in the West and profit sharing is largely confined to small, professional-artistic team production situations. We do find in the larger scale residual-sharing firms in Jugoslavia that there are employee committees that can recommend (to the state) the termination of a manager's contract (veto his continuance) with the enterprise. We conjecture that the workers' committee is given the right to recommend the termination of the manager's contract precisely because the general sharing of the residual increases "excessively" the manager's incentive to shirk.[13]

payments based on gross sales in retail stores, come close to profit sharing. However, it is gross output sharing rather than profit sharing. We are unable to specify the implications of the difference. We refer the reader to S. N. Cheung.

C. The Corporation

All firms must initially acquire command over some resources. The corporation does so primarily by selling promises of future returns to those who (as creditors or owners) provide financial capital. In some situations resources can be acquired in advance from consumers by promises of future delivery (for example, advance sale of a proposed book). Or where the firm is a few artistic or professional persons, each can "chip in" with time and talent until the sale of services brings in revenues. For the most part, capital can be acquired more cheaply if many (risk-averse) investors contribute small portions to a large investment. The economies of raising large sums of equity capital in this way suggest that modifications in the relationship among corporate inputs are required to cope with the shirking problem

[13] Incidentally, investment activity will be changed. The inability to capitalize the investment value as "take-home" proviate property *wealth* of the members of the firm means that the benefits of the investment must be taken as annual income by those who are employed at the time of the income. Investment will be confined more to those with shorter life and with higher rates or pay-offs if the alternative of investing is paying out the firm's income to its employees to take home and use as private property. For a development of this proposition, see the papers by Eirik Furobotn and Svetozar Pejovich, and by Pejovich.

that arises with profit sharing among large numbers of corporate stockholders. One modification is limited liability, especially for firms that are large relative to a stockholder's wealth. It serves to protect stockholders from large losses no matter how they are caused.

If every stock owner participated in each decision in a corporation, not only would large bureaucratic costs be incurred, but many would shirk the task of becoming well informed on the issue to be decided, since the losses associated with unexpectedly bad decisions will be borne in large part by the many other corporate shareholders. More effective control of corporate activity is achieved for most purposes by transferring decision authority to a smaller group, whose main function is to negotiate with and manage (renegotiate with) the other inputs of the team. The corporate stockholders retain the authority to revise the membership of the management group and over major decisions that affect the structure of the corporation or its dissolution.

As a result a new modification of partnerships is induced—the right to sale of corporate shares without approval of any other stockholders. Any shareholder can remove his wealth from control by those with whom he has differences of opinion. Rather than try to control the decisions of the management, which is harder to do with many stockholders than with only a few, unrestricted salability provides a more acceptable escape to each stockholder from continued policies with which he disagrees.

Indeed, the policing of managerial shirking relies on across-market competition from new groups of would-be managers as well as competition from members within the firm who seek to displace existing management. In addition to competition from outside and inside managers, control is facilitated by the temporary congealing of share votes into voting blocs owned by one or a few contenders. Proxy battles or stock-purchases concentrate the votes required to displace the existing management or modify managerial policies. But it is more than a change in policy that is sought by the newly formed financial interests, whether of new stockholders or not. It is the capitalization of expected future benefits into stock prices that concentrates on the innovators the wealth gains of their actions if they own large numbers of shares. Without capitalization of future benefits, there would be less incentive to incur the costs required to exert informed decisive influence on the corporation's policies and managing personnel. Temporarily, the structure of ownership is reformed, moving away from diffused ownership into decisive power blocs, and this is a transient resurgence of the classical firm with power again concentrated in those who have title to the residual.

In assessing the significance of stockholders' power it is not the usual diffusion of voting power that is significant but instead the frequency with which voting congeals into decisive changes. Even a one-man owned company may have a long term with just one manager—continuously being approved by the owner. Similarly a dispersed voting power corporation may be also characterized by a long-lived management. The question is the probability of replacement of the management if it behaves in ways not acceptable to a majority of the stockholders. The unrestricted salability of stock and the transfer of proxies enhances the probability of decisive action in the event current stockholders or any outsider believes that management is not doing a good job with the corporation. We are not comparing the corporate responsiveness to that of a single proprietorship; instead, we are indicating features of the corporate structure that are induced by the problem of delegated authority to manager-monitors.[14]

D. Mutual and Nonprofit Firms

The benefits obtained by the new management are greater if the stock can be purchased and sold, because this enables *capitalization* of anticipated future improvements into present *wealth* of new managers who bought stock and created a larger capital by their management changes. But in nonprofit corporations, colleges, churches, country clubs, mutual savings banks, mutual insurance companies, and "coops," the future consequences of improved management are not

[14] Instead of thinking of shareholders as joint *owners*, we can think of them as investors, like bondholders, except that the stockholders are more optimistic than bondholders about the enterprise prospects. Instead of buying bonds in the corporation, thus enjoying smaller risks, shareholders prefer to invest funds with a greater realizable return if the firm prospers as expected, but with smaller (possibly negative) returns if the firm performs in a manner closer to that expected by the more pessimistic investors. The pessimistic investors, in turn, regard only the bonds as likely to pay off.

If the entrepreneur-organizer is to raise capital on the best terms to him, it is to his advantage, as well as that of prospective investors, to recognize these differences in expectations. The residual claim on earnings enjoyed by shareholders does not serve the function of enhancing their efficiency as monitors in the general situation. The stockholders are "merely" the less risk-averse or the more optimistic member of the group that finances the firm. Being more optimistic than the average and seeing a higher mean value future return, they are willing to pay more for a certificate that allows them to realize gain on their expectations. One method of doing so is to buy claims to the distribution of returns that "they see" while bondholders, who are more pessimistic, purchase a claim to the distribution that they see as more likely to emerge. Stockholders are then comparable to warrant holders. They care not about the voting rights (usually not attached to warrants); they are in the same position in so far as voting rights are concerned as are bondholders. The only difference is in the probability distribution of rewards and the terms on which they can place their bets.

If we treat bondholders, preferred and convertible preferred stockholders, and common stockholders and warrant holders as simply different classes of investors—differing not only in their risk averseness but in their beliefs about the probability distribution of the firm's future earnings, why should stockholders be regarded as "owners" in any sense distinct from the other financial investors? The entrepreneur-organizer, who let us assume is the chief operating officer and sole repository of control of the corporation, does not find his authority residing in common stockholders (except in the case of a take over). Does this type of control make any difference in the way the firm is conducted? Would it make any difference in the kinds of behavior that would be tolerated by competing managers and investors (and we here deliberately refrain from thinking of them as owner-stockholders in the traditional sense)?

Investment old timers recall a significant incidence of nonvoting common stock, now prohibited in corporations whose stock is traded on listed exchanges. (Why prohibited?) The entrepreneur in those days could hold voting shares while investors held nonvoting shares, which in every other respect were identical. Nonvoting share holders were simply investors devoid of ownership connotations. The control and behavior of inside owners in such corporations has never, so far as we have ascertained, been carefully studied. For example, at the simplest level of interest, does the evidence indicate that nonvoting shareholders fared any worse because of not having voting rights? Did owners permit the nonvoting holders the normal return available to voting shareholders? Though evidence is prohibitively expensive to obtain, it is remarkable that voting and nonvoting shares sold for essentially identical prices, even during some proxy battles. However, our casual evidence deserves no more than interest-initiating weight.

One more point. The facade is deceptive. Instead of nonvoting shares, today we have warrants, convertible preferred stocks all of which are solely or partly "equity" claims without voting rights, though they could be converted into voting shares.

In sum, is it the case that the stockholder-investor relationship is one emanating from the *division* of *ownership* among several people, or is it that the collection of investment funds from people of varying anticipations is the underlying factor? If the latter, why should any of them be thought of as the owners in whom voting rights, whatever they may signify or however exercisable, should reside in order to enhance efficiency? Why voting rights in any of the outside, participating investors?

Our initial perception of this possibly significant difference in interpretation was precipitated by Henry Manne. A reading of his paper makes it clear that it is hard to understand why an investor who wishes to back and "share" in the consequences of some new business should necessarily have to acquire voting power (i.e., power to change the manager-operator) in order to invest in the venture. In fact, we invest in some ventures in the hope that no other stockholders will be so "foolish" as to try to toss out the incumbent management. We want him to have the power to stay in office, and for the prospect of sharing in his fortunes we buy nonvoting common stock. Our willingness to invest is enhanced by the knowledge that we can act legally via fraud, embezzlement and other laws to help assure that we outside investors will not be "milked" beyond our initial discounted anticipations.

capitalized into present wealth of stockholders. (As if to make more difficult that competition by new would-be monitors, mutiple shares of ownership in those enterprises cannot be bought by one person.) One should, therefore, find greater shirking in nonprofit, mutually owned enterprises. (This suggests that nonprofit enterprises are especially appropriate in realms of endeavor where more shirking is desired and where redirected uses of the enterprise in response to market-revealed values is less desired.)

E. Partnerships

Team production in artistic or professional intellectual skills will more likely be by partnerships than other types of team production. This amounts to market-organized team activity and to a non-employer status. Self-monitoring partnerships, therefore, will be used rather than employer-employee contracts, and these organizations will be small to prevent an excessive dilution of efforts through shirking. Also, partnerships are more likely to occur among relatives or long-standing acquaintances, not necessarily because they share a common utility function, but also because each knows better the other's work characteristics and tendencies to shirk.

F. Employee Unions

Employee unions, whatever else they do, perform as monitors for employees. Employers monitor employees and similarly employees monitor an employer's performance. Are correct wages paid on time and in good currency? Usually, this is extremely easy to check. But some forms of employer performance are less easy to meter and are more subject to employer shirking. Fringe benefits often are in nonpecuniary, contingent form; medical, hospital, and accident insurance, and retirement pensions are contingent payments or performances partly in *kind* by employers to employees. Each employee cannot judge the character of such payments as easily as money wages. Insurance is a contingent payment—what the employee will get upon the contingent event may come as a disappointment. If he could easily determine what other employees had gotten upon such contingent events he could judge more accurately the performance by the employer. He could "trust" the employer not to shirk in such fringe contingent payments, but he would prefer an effective and economic monitor of those payments. We see a specialist monitor—the union employees' agent—hired by them and monitoring those aspects of employer payment most difficult for the employees to monitor. Employees should be willing to employ a specialist monitor to administer such hard-to-detect employer performance, even though their monitor has incentives to use pension and retirement funds not entirely for the benefit of employees.

V. Team Spirit and Loyalty

Every team member would prefer a team in which no one, not even himself, shirked. Then the true marginal costs and values could be equated to achieve more preferred positions. If one could enhance a common interest in nonshirking in the guise of a team loyalty or team spirit, the team would be more efficient. In those sports where team activity is most clearly exemplified, the sense of loyalty and team spirit is most strongly urged. Obviously the team is better, with team spirit and loyalty, because of the reduced shirking not because of some other feature inherent in loyalty or spirit as such.[15]

[15] *Sports Leagues:* Professional sports contests among teams is typically conducted by a *league* of teams. We assume that sports consumers are interested not only in absolute sporting skill but also in skills *relative* to other teams. Being slightly better than opposing teams enables one to claim a major portion of the receipts; the

Corporations and business firms try to instill a spirit of loyalty. This should not be viewed simply as a device to increase profits by *over*-working or misleading the employees, nor as an adolescent urge for belonging. It promotes a closer approximation to the employees' potentially available true rates of substitution between production and leisure and enables each team member to achieve a more preferred situation. The difficulty, of course, is to create economically that team spirit and loyalty. It can be preached with an aura of moral code of conduct—a morality with literally the same basis as the ten commandments—to restrict our conduct toward what we would choose if we bore our full costs.

inferior team does not release resources and reduce costs, since they were expected in the play of contest. Hence, absolute skill is developed beyond the equality of marginal investment in sporting skill with its true social marginal value product. It follows there will be a tendency to overinvest in training athletes and developing teams. "Reverse shirking" arises, as budding players are induced to overpractice hyperactively relative to the social marginal value of their enhanced skills. To prevent overinvestment, the teams seek an agreement with each other to restrict practice, size of teams, and even pay of the team members (which reduces incentives of young people to overinvest in developing skills). Ideally, if all the contestant teams were owned by one owner, overinvestment in sports would be avoided, much as ownership of common fisheries or underground oil or water reserve would prevent overinvestment. This hyperactivity (to suggest the opposite of shirking) is controlled by the league of teams, wherein the league adopts a common set of constraints on each team's behavior. In effect, the teams are no longer really owned by the team owners but are supervised by them, much as the franchisers of some product. They are not full-fledged owners of their business, including the brand name, and can not "do what they wish" as franchises. Comparable to the franchiser, is the league commissioner or conference president, who seeks to restrain hyperactivity, as individual team supervisors compete with each other and cause external diseconomies. Such restraints are usually regarded as anticompetitive, antisocial, collusive-cartel devices to restrain free open competition, and reduce players' salaries. However, the interpretation presented here is premised on an attempt to avoid hyperinvestment in team sports production. Of course, the team operators have an incentive, once the league is formed and restraints are placed on hyperinvestment activity, to go further and obtain the private benefits of monopoly restriction. To what extent overinvestment is replaced by monopoly restriction is not yet determinable; nor have we seen an empirical test of these two competing, but mutually consistent interpretations. (This interpretation of league-sports activity was proposed by Earl Thompson and formulated by Michael Canes.) Again, athletic teams clearly exemplify the specialization of monitoring with captains and coaches; a captain detects shirkers while the coach trains and selects strategies and tactics. Both functions may be centralized in one person.

VI. Kinds of Inputs Owned by the Firm

To this point the discussion has examined why firms, as we have defined them, exist? That is, why is there an owner-employer who is the common party to contracts with other owners of inputs in team activity? The answer to that question should also indicate the kind of the jointly used resources likely to be owned by the central-owner-monitor and the kind likely to be hired from people who are not team-owners. Can we identify characteristics or features of various inputs that lead to their being hired or to their being owned by the firm?

How can residual-claimant, central-employer-owner demonstrate ability to pay the other hired inputs the promised amount in the event of a loss? He can pay in advance or he can commit wealth sufficient to cover negative residuals. The latter will take the form of machines, land, buildings, or raw materials committed to the firm. Commitments of labor-wealth (i.e., human wealth) given the property rights in people, is less feasible. These considerations suggest that residual claimants—owners of the firm—will be investors of resalable capital equipment in the firm. The goods or inputs more likely to be invested, than rented, by the owners of the enterprise, will have higher resale values relative to the initial cost and will have longer expected use in a firm relative to the economic life of the good.

But beyond these factors are those developed above to explain the existence of the institution known as the firm—the costs of detecting output performance. When a durable resource is used it will have a marginal product and a depreciation. Its use requires payment to cover at least use-induced depreciation; unless that user cost is specifically detectable, payment for it will be demanded in accord with *expected* depreciation. And we can ascertain circumstances for each. An indestructible hammer with a readily detectable marginal product has zero user cost. But suppose the hammer were destructible and that careless (which is easier than careful) use is more abusive and causes greater depreciation of the hammer. Suppose in addition the abuse is easier to detect by observing the way it is used than by observing only the hammer after its use, or by measuring the output scored from a hammer by a laborer. If the hammer were rented and used in the absence of the owner, the depreciation would be greater than if the use were observed by the owner and the user charged in accord with the imposed depreciation. (Careless use is more likely than careful use—if one does not pay for the greater depreciation.) An absentee owner would therefore ask for a higher rental price because of the higher *expected* user cost than if the item were used by the owner. The expectation is higher because of the greater difficulty of observing specific user cost, by inspection of the hammer after use. Renting is therefore in this case more costly than owner use. This is the valid content of the misleading expressions about ownership being more economical than renting—ignoring all other factors that may work in the opposite direction, like tax provision, short-term occupancy and capital risk avoidance.

Better examples are tools of the trade. Watch repairers, engineers, and carpenters tend to own their own tools especially if they are portable. Trucks are more likely to be employee owned rather than other equally expensive team inputs because it is relatively cheap for the driver to police the care taken in using a truck. Policing the use of trucks by a nondriver owner is more likely to occur for trucks that are not specialized to one driver, like public transit busses.

The factor with which we are concerned here is one related to the costs of monitoring not only the gross product performance of an input but also the abuse or depreciation inflicted on the input in the course of its use. If depreciation or user cost is more cheaply detected when the owner can see its use than by only seeing the input before and after, there is a force toward owner use rather than renting. Resources whose user cost is harder to detect when used by someone else, tend on this count to be owner-used. Absentee ownership, in the lay language, will be less likely. Assume momentarily that labor service cannot be performed in the absence of its owner. The labor owner can more cheaply monitor any abuse of himself than if somehow labor-services could be provided without the labor owner observing its mode of use or knowing what was happening. Also his incentive to abuse himself is increased if he does not own himself.[16]

[16] Professional athletes in baseball, football, and basketball, where athletes having sold their source of service to the team owners upon entering into sports activity, are owned by team owners. Here the team owners must monitor the athletes' physical condition and behavior to protect the team owners' wealth. The athlete has *less* (not, *no*) incentive to protect or enhance his athletic prowess since capital value changes have less impact on his own wealth and more on the team owners. Thus, some athletes sign up for big initial bonuses (representing present capital value of future services). Future salaries are lower by the annuity value of the prepaid "bonus" and hence the athlete has *less* to lose by subsequent abuse of his athletic prowess. Any decline in his subsequent service value would in part be borne by the team owner who owns the players' future service. This does not say these losses of future salaries have no effect on preservation of athletic talent (we are not making a "sunk cost" error). Instead, we assert that the

The similarity between the preceding analysis and the question of absentee landlordism and of sharecropping arrangements is no accident. The same factors which explain the contractual arrangements known as a firm help to explain the incidence of tenancy, labor hiring or sharecropping.[17]

VII. Firms as a Specialized Market Institution for Collecting, Collating, and Selling Input Information

The firm serves as a highly specialized surrogate market. Any person contemplating a joint-input activity must search and detect the qualities of available joint inputs. He could contact an employment agency, but that agency in a small town would have little advantage over a large firm with many inputs. The employer, by virtue of monitoring many inputs, acquires special superior information about their productive talents. This aids his *directive* (i.e., market hiring) efficiency. He "sells" his information to employee-inputs as he aids them in ascertaining good input combinations for team activity. Those who work as employees or who rent services to him are using him to discern superior combinations of inputs. Not only does the director-employer "decide" what each input will produce, he also estimates which heterogeneous inputs will work together jointly more efficiently, and he does this in the context of a privately owned market for forming teams. The department store is a firm and is a superior private market. People who shop and work in one town can as well shop and work in a privately owned firm.

This marketing function is obscured in the theoretical literature by the assumption of homogeneous factors. Or it is tacitly left for individuals to do themselves via personal market search, much as if a person had to search without benefit of specialist retailers. Whether or not the firm arose because of this efficient information service, it gives the director-employer more knowledge about the productive talents of the team's inputs, and a basis for superior decisions about efficient or profitable combinations of those heterogeneous resources.

In other words, opportunities for profitable team production by inputs already within the firm may be ascertained more economically and accurately than for resources outside the firm. Superior combinations of inputs can be more economically identified and formed from resources already used in the organization than by obtaining new resources (and knowledge of them) from the outside. Promotion and revision of employee assignments (contracts) will be preferred by a firm to the hiring of new inputs. To the extent that this occurs there is reason to expect the firm to be able to operate as a conglomerate rather than persist in producing a single product. Efficient production with heterogeneous resources is a result not of having *better* resources but in *knowing more accurately* the relative productive performances of those resources. Poorer resources can be paid less in accord with their inferiority; greater accuracy of

preservation is reduced, not eliminated, because the amount of loss of wealth suffered is smaller. The athlete will spend less to maintain or enhance his prowess thereafter. The effect of this revised incentive system is evidenced in comparisons of the kinds of attention and care imposed on the athletes at the "expense of the team owner" in the case where atheletes' future servies are owned by the team owner with that where future labor service values are owned by the athlete himself. Why athletes' future athletic services are owned by the team owners rather than being hired is a question we should be able to answer. One presumption is cartelization and monopsony gains to team owners. Another is exactly the theory being expounded in this paper—costs of monitoring production of athletes; we know not on which to rely.

[17] The analysis used by Cheung in explaining the prevalence of sharecropping and land tenancy arrangements is built squarely on the same factors—the costs of detecting output performance of jointly used inputs in team production and the costs of detecting user costs imposed on the various inputs if owner used or if rented.

knowledge of the potential and actual productive actions of inputs rather than having high productivity resources makes a firm (or an assignment of inputs) profitable.[18]

VIII. Summary

While ordinary contracts facilitate efficient specialization according to comparative advantage, a special class of contracts among a group of joint inputs to a team production process is commonly used for team production. Instead of multilateral contracts among all the joint inputs' owners, a central common party to a set of bilateral contracts facilitates efficient organization of the joint inguts in team production. The terms of the contracts form the basis of the entity called the firm—especially appropriate for organizing team production processes.

Team productive activity is that in which a union, or joint use, of inputs yields a larger output than the sum of the products of the separately used inputs. This team production requires—like all other production processes—an assessment of marginal productivities if efficient production is to be achieved. Nonseparability of the products of several differently owned joint inputs raises the cost of assessing the marginal productivities of those resources or services of each input owner. Monitoring or metering the productivities to match marginal productivities to costs of inputs and thereby to reduce shirking can be achieved more economically (than by across market bilateral negotiations among inputs) in a firm.

The essence of the classical firm is identified here as a contractual structure with: 1) joint input production; 2) several input owners; 3) one party who is common to all the contracts of the joint inputs; 4) who has rights to renegotiate any input's contract independently of contracts with other input owners; 5) who holds the residual claim; and 6) who has the right to sell his central contractual residual status. The central agent is called the firm's owner and the employer. No authoritarian control is involved; the arrangement is simply a contractual structure subject to continuous renegotiation with the central agent. The contractual structure arises as a means of enhancing efficient organization of team production. In particular, the ability to detect shirking among owners of jointly used inputs in team production is enhanced (detection costs are reduced) by this arrangement and the discipline (by revision of contracts) of input owners is made more economic.

Testable implications are suggested by the analysis of different types of organizations—nonprofit, proprietary for profit, unions, cooperatives, partnerships, and by the kinds of inputs that tend to be owned by the firm in contrast to those employed by the firm.

We conclude with a highly conjectural

[18] According to our interpretation, the firm is a specialized surrogate for a market for team use of inputs; it provides superior (i.e., cheaper) collection and collation of knowledge about heterogeneous resources. The greater the set of inputs about which knowledge of performance is being collated within a firm the greater are the present costs of the collation activity. Then, the larger the firm (market) the greater the attenuation of monitor control. To counter this force, the firm will be divisionalized in ways that economize on those costs—just as will the market be specialized. So far as we can ascertain, other theories of the reasons for firms have no such implications.

In Japan, employees by custom work nearly their entire lives with one firm, and the firm agrees to that expectation. Firms will tend to be large and conglomerate to enable a broader scope of input revision. Each firm is, in effect, a small economy engaging in "intranational and international" trade. Analogously, Americans expect to spend their whole lives in the United States, and the bigger the country, in terms of variety of resources, the easier it is to adjust to changing tastes and circumstances. Japan, with its lifetime employees, should be characterized more by large, conglomerate firms. Presumably, at some size of the firm, specialized knowledge about inputs becomes as expensive to transmit across divisions of the firms as it does across markets to other firms.

but possibly significant interpretation. As a consequence of the flow of information to the central party (employer), the firm takes on the characteristic of an efficient market in that information about the productive characteristics of a large set of specific inputs is now more cheaply available. Better recombinations or new uses of resources can be more efficiently ascertained than by the conventional search through the general market. In this sense inputs compete with each other within and via a firm rather than solely across markets as conventionally conceived. Emphasis on interfirm competition obscures intrafirm competition among inputs. Conceiving competition as the *revelation and exchange* of knowledge or information about qualities, potential uses of different inputs in different potential applications indicates that the firm is a device for enchancing competition among sets of input resources as well as a device for more efficiently rewarding the inputs. In contrast to markets and cities which can be viewed as publicly or nonowned market places, the firm can be considered a privately owned market; if so, we could consider the firm and the ordinary market as competing types of markets, competition between private proprietary markets and public or communal markets. Could it be that the market suffers from the defects of communal property rights in organizing and influencing uses of valuable resources?

REFERENCES

M. Canes, "A Model of a Sports League," unpublished doctoral dissertation, UCLA 1970.

S. N. Cheung, *The Theory of Share Tenancy*, Chicago 1969.

R. H. Coase, "The Nature of the Firm," *Economica*, Nov. 1937, *4*, 386–405; reprinted in G. J. Stigler and K. Boulding, eds., *Readings in Price Theory*, Homewood 1952, 331–51.

E. Furobotn and S. Pejovich, "Property Rights and the Behavior of the Firm in a Socialist State," *Zeitschrift für Nationalökonomie*, 1970, *30*, 431–454.

F. H. Knight, *Risk, Uncertainty and Profit*, New York 1965.

S. Macaulay, "Non-Contractual Relations in Business: A Preliminary Study," *Amer. Sociological Rev.*, 1968, *28*, 55–69.

H. B. Malmgren, "Information, Expectations and the Theory of the Firm," *Quart J. Econ.*, Aug. 1961, *75*, 399–421.

H. Manne, "Our Two Corporation Systems: Law and Economics," *Virginia Law Rev.*, Mar. 1967, *53*, No. 2, 259–84.

S. Pejovich, "The Firm, Monetary Policy and Property Rights in a Planned Economy," *Western Econ. J.*, Sept. 1969, *7*, 193–200.

M. Silver and R. Auster, "Entrepreneurship, Profit, and the Limits on Firm Size," *J. Bus. Univ. Chicago*, Apr. 1969, *42*, 277–81.

E. A. Thompson, "Nonpecuniary Rewards and the Aggregate Production Function," *Rev. Econ. Statist.*, Nov. 1970, *52*, 395–404.

Part V
Other Applications of the Neoclassical Method

[20]

THE JOURNAL OF
POLITICAL ECONOMY

Volume LXX JUNE 1962 Number 3

THE INCIDENCE OF THE CORPORATION INCOME TAX

ARNOLD C. HARBERGER
University of Chicago

I. INTRODUCTION

THIS paper aims to provide a theoretical framework for the analysis of the effects of the corporation income tax and, also, to draw some inferences about the probable incidence of this tax in the United States. It is clear that a tax as important as the corporation income tax, and one with ramifications into so many sectors of the economy, should be analyzed in general-equilibrium terms rather than partial-equilibrium terms. The main characteristic of the theoretical framework that I present is its general-equilibrium nature. It was inspired by a long tradition of writings in the field of international trade, in which the names of Heckscher, Ohlin, Stolper, Samuelson, Metzler, and Meade are among the most prominent. These writers inquired into the effects of international trade, or of particular trade policies, on relative factor prices and the distribution of income. Here we shall examine the effects of the corporation income tax on these same variables.

Our model divides the economy into two industries or sectors, one corporate and the other non-corporate, each employing two factors of production, labor and capital. The corporation income tax is viewed as a tax which strikes the earnings of capital in the corporate sector, but not in the non-corporate sector. Both industries are assumed to be competitive, with production in each governed by a production function which is homogeneous of the first degree (embodying constant returns to scale). We do not inquire into the short-run effects of the imposition of the corporation tax, on the supposition that it is the long-run effects which are of greatest theoretical and practical interest. In the very short run, the tax will necessarily be borne out of the earnings of fixed capital equipment in the affected industry, so long as our assumption of competition applies. But this will entail a disequilibrium in the capital market, with the net rate of return to owners of capital in the taxed industry being less than the net rate of return received by owners of capital in the untaxed sector. A redistribution of the resources of the economy will result, moving toward a long-run equilibrium in which the net rates of return to capital are equal in both sectors. In this long-run equilibrium the wages of labor will also be equal in the two sectors, and the available quantities of labor and capital will be fully employed.

I also assume that the available quantities of labor and capital in the economy are not affected by the existence of the tax. This assumption is rather innocuous in the case of labor, but in the case of capital it is surely open to question. It is highly likely that as a result of the imposition of the corporation tax, the net rate of return received by owners of capital will be lower than it would be in the absence of this tax. This reduction in the return to capital can influence savings in two ways: first, because now the owners of capital have less total income, and second, because the rate of return facing them is lower. On the first, we must bear in mind that any alternative way of raising the same revenue would entail the same reduction in income in the private sector; the impact on saving of the corporation tax would thus differ from that, say, of a proportional income tax yielding the same revenue, only as a result of such differences as may exist among economic groups in their savings propensities. On the second, we must inquire into the elasticity of the supply of savings with respect to the rate of interest. If this elasticity is zero, the alteration in the net rate of interest facing savers will not influence the size of the capital stock at any given time, or the path along which the capital stock grows through time. In the United States, the fraction of national income saved has been reasonably constant, in periods of full employment, for nearly a century. Over this time span, income levels have increased greatly, and interest rates have fluctuated over a rather wide range. We have no clear evidence, from these data or from other sources, that variations in the rate of interest within the ranges observed in the United States exert a substantial influence on the level of savings out of any given level of income. We shall therefore proceed on the assumption that the level of the capital stock at any time is the same in the presence of the tax as it would be in its absence; but in the conclusion of this paper we shall briefly consider how the results based on this assumption might be altered if in fact the corporation income tax has influenced the total stock of capital.

The relevance of this approach for the analysis of real-world taxes might also be questioned on the ground that the economy cannot reasonably be divided into a set of industries which are overwhelmingly "corporate," and another set which is overwhelmingly non-corporate. This objection has little validity, at least in the case of the United States. In the period 1953–55, for example, the total return to capital in the private sector of the United States economy averaged some $60 billion per year, $34 billion being corporate profits and $26 billion being other return to capital. Of the $26 billion which was not corporate profits, more than 80 per cent accrued to two industries—agriculture and real estate, in which corporate profits were negligible. In all but seven industries in a forty-eight-industry classification, corporation taxes averaged more than 25 per cent of the total return to capital, and one can, for all practical purposes, say that no industries except agriculture, real estate, and miscellaneous repair services paid less than 20 per cent of their total return to capital in corporation taxes, while the three named industries all paid less than 4 per cent of their income from capital as corporation taxes. Within the "corporate" sector, different industries paid different fractions of their total return to capital in corporation tax, owing partly to differences in their relative use of debt and equity capital, partly to the presence in some of these industries of a fringe of unincorporated enterprises, and partly to special situations such as loss-carryovers from prior years, failure of full use of current losses to obtain tax offsets, and so on. But these differences, in my view, are not large enough to affect seriously the validity of the main distinction made here between the corporate and the non-corporate sectors.[1]

The relevance of the approach taken in this paper might also be questioned on the ground that the capital market does not in fact work to equalize the net rates of return on capital in different industries. If this objection is based on the idea that the capital market might be poorly organized, or that participants in it might not be very adept at seeking the best available net return on their invested funds, I believe it must be rejected for the United States case, for in the United States the capital market is obviously highly organized, and the bulk of the funds involved are commanded by able and knowledgeable people. The objection may, however, be based on the idea that rates of return in different industries, and perhaps on different types of obligations, will differ even in equilibrium because of the risk premiums which investors demand for different kinds of investments. At this point we must make clear that the "equalization" which our theory postulates is equalization net of such risk premiums. So long as the pattern of risk differentials is not itself significantly altered by the presence of the corporation income tax, our theoretical results will be applicable without modification. And even if the pattern of risk premiums applying to different types of activities and obligations has changed substantially as a result of the tax, it is highly likely that the consequent modification of our results would be of the second order of importance.

II. OUTLINES OF THE INCIDENCE PROBLEM: THE COBB-DOUGLAS CASE

So long as the capital market works to equilibrate rates of return net of taxes and risk premiums, and so long as the imposition of a corporation income tax does not itself have a significant effect on the (pattern of) risk premiums associated with different types of activities, it is inevitable that in the long run the corporation tax will be included in the price of the product. That is, of two industries, one corporate and one non-corporate, each using the same combination of labor and capital to produce a unit of product, the equilibrium price of the corporate product will be higher than the equilibrium price of the non-corporate product by precisely the amount of corporation tax paid per unit of product. This result is taken by some people as evidence that the burden of the corporation tax is borne by consumers, that is, that the tax is shifted forward. Such an inference is far wide of the mark.

Perhaps the easier way of demonstrating the error of the above inference is to present a simple counterexample. Consider an economy producing only two

[1] For the data from which the above figures were derived, see my paper, "The Corporation Income Tax: An Empirical Appraisal," in United States House of Representatives, Ways and Means Committee, *Tax Revision Compendium* (Washington: Government Printing Office, November, 1959), I, 231–50, esp. Table 20. That paper also contains a brief statement of the problem of the incidence of the corporation income tax (pp. 241–43), which in some ways foreshadows the work presented here. It is, however, principally concerned with the resource allocation costs of the corporation income tax rather than its incidence.

products—product X, produced by firms in the corporate form, and product Y, produced by unincorporated enterprises. Let the demand characteristics of the economy be such that consumers always spend half of their disposable income on X and half on Y. Let the production functions in both industries be of the Cobb-Douglas type, with coefficients of $\frac{1}{2}$ for both labor and capital: that is, $X = L_x^{1/2}K_x^{1/2}$, $Y = L_y^{1/2}K_y^{1/2}$, where L_x and L_y represent the amounts of labor used in the X and Y industries, and K_x and K_y the corresponding amounts of capital. The total amounts of labor and capital available to the economy are assumed to be fixed, at levels L and K, respectively.

Under competitive conditions, production in each industry will be carried to the point where the value of the marginal product of each factor is just equal to the price paid by entrepreneurs for the services of the factor. Thus, in the absence of taxes, we have $L_x p_L = \frac{1}{2}Xp_x$; $K_x p_k = \frac{1}{2}Xp_x$; $L_y p_L = \frac{1}{2}Yp_y$; $K_y p_k = \frac{1}{2}Yp_y$. If the total income of the economy is \$1,200, equally divided between X and Y, then labor in industry X will be earning \$300, labor in industry Y \$300, capital in industry X \$300, and capital in industry Y \$300. It is clear that both the labor force and the capital stock will have to be equally divided between industries X and Y. Choosing our units of labor and capital so that in this equilibrium position $p_L = p_k = \$1.00$, we have the result that without any taxes there will be 300 units of labor in industry X and 300 in industry Y, and that the capital stock will be similarly distributed.

Suppose now that a tax of 50 per cent is levied on the earnings of capital in industry X, and that the government, in spending the proceeds of the tax, also divides its expenditures equally between the two industries. Labor in industry X will once again earn \$300, as will labor in industry Y. Since the price paid by entrepreneurs for labor is also the price received by the workers, and since equilibrium in the labor market is assumed, the equilibrium distribution of the labor force will be the same in this case as in the previous one, that is, 300 workers in each industry.

The situation is different, however, when we come to capital. The price paid by entrepreneurs for capital, multiplied by the amount of capital used, will again be \$300 in each industry. But the price paid by entrepreneurs in industry X will include the tax, while that paid in industry Y will not. With a tax of 50 per cent on the total amount paid, capital in industry X will be receiving, net of tax, only \$150, while capital in industry Y will be getting \$300. For equilibrium in the capital market to obtain, there must be twice as much capital in industry Y as in industry X. Thus, as a result of the tax, the distribution of capital changes: instead of having 300 units of capital in each industry, we now have 200 units in industry X and 400 units in industry Y.

Out of the total of \$600 which entrepreneurs are paying for capital in both industries, one-half will go to capital in industry Y, on which no tax will be paid, one-quarter will go to capital in industry X, net of tax, and one-quarter will go to the government as a tax payment. The price of capital will fall from \$1.00 to \$0.75.

A crude calculation suffices to suggest the resulting tax incidence. Out of a national income of \$1,200, labor obtained \$600 before the imposition of the tax and after it, but capital obtained (net of tax) only \$450 after the tax was imposed as against \$600 before the tax, the difference of \$150 going to the government. Capital is clearly bearing the brunt of the tax, in spite of the fact that in the tax situation, the tax is included in what consumers are paying for commodity X.

Of course, this does not tell the whole story of the incidence of the tax. Since the price of commodity X rises, and the price of commodity Y falls, consumers with particularly strong preferences for one or the other of the two goods will be hurt or benefited in their role as consumers, in addition to whatever benefit they obtain or burden they bear in their role as owners of productive factors. It is important to realize, however, that the price of Y does fall, and that this brings to consumers as a group a benefit which counterbalances the burden they bear as a result of the rise in the price of X.[2]

I would sum up the analysis of the incidence of the assumed tax on capital in industry X as follows: capitalists as a group lose in income earned an aggregate amount equal to the amount received by the government. This reduction in the income from capital is spread over all capital, whether employed in industry X or in industry Y, as soon as the capital market is once again brought into equilibrium after imposition of the tax. Insofar as individual consumers have the same expenditure pattern as the average of all consumers, they neither gain nor lose in their role as consumers. Insofar as individual consumers differ from the average, they gain if they spend a larger fraction of their budget on Y than the average, and lose if they spend a larger fraction of their budget on X than the average. The gains of those consumers who prefer Y, however, are counterbalanced by the losses of those who prefer X. If we are prepared to accept this canceling of gains and losses as the basis for a statement that consumers as a group do not suffer as a consequence of the tax, then we can conclude that capital bears the tax. Otherwise, we must be content to note that the gross transfers from individuals as capitalists and consumers of X exceed the yield of the tax by an amount equal to the gross transfer to consumers of Y.

The above example is representative of the entire class of cases in which expenditures are divided among goods in given proportions, and production of each good is determined by a Cobb-Douglas function. The exponents of the Cobb-Douglas functions can differ from industry to industry, and even the tax rates on the earnings of capital can be different in different taxed industries; yet the conclusion that capital bears the tax, in the sense indicated above, remains. It is easy to demonstrate the truth of the above assertion. Let A_i be the fraction of the national income spent

[2] The counterbalancing is not precise owing to the fact that the corporation income tax carries an "excess burden." In the post-tax equilibrium, the value of the marginal product of capital in industry X exceeds that in industry Y by the amount of the tax, whereas efficient allocation of capital would require these two values to be equal. Moreover, the pattern of consumption in the economy is also rendered "inefficient" by the tax, because the marginal rate of substitution of X for Y in consumption (which is given by the ratios of their prices gross of tax) is different from the marginal rate of substitution of X for Y in production (which is given by the ratio of their prices net of tax). The result of this twofold inefficiency is that the same resources, even though fully employed, produce less national income in the presence of the tax than in its absence. If, as is customary in discussions of incidence, we neglect "excess burden," we can treat the effects of changes in the prices of X and Y as having exactly offsetting influences on consumer welfare and can determine the incidence of the tax by observing what happens to the prices of labor and capital. This approach does not preclude the full burden of the tax being borne by consumers, for in cases in which the prices (net of tax) of labor and capital move in the same proportions as a result of the tax, it is just as correct to say that the tax is borne by consumers as it is to say that the tax burden is shared by labor and capital in proportion to their initial contributions to the national income; examples of such cases are given below.

on the product of industry i, B_i be the coefficient of the labor input in the ith industry (equal to the fraction of the receipts of the ith industry which is paid in wages to labor), and C_i $(= 1 - B_i)$ be the coefficient of the capital input in the ith industry (equal to the fraction of the receipts of the ith industry which is paid [gross of tax] to capital). Then $\Sigma A_i B_i$ will be the fraction of national income going to labor, both in the tax situation and in the case in which taxes are absent. Immediately one can conclude that labor's share in the national income will remain the same in the two cases. Moreover, the distribution of labor among industries will also remain unchanged since each industry i will employ the fraction $A_i B_i / (\Sigma A_i B_i)$ of the labor force in both cases. Likewise, capital will receive a fixed fraction of the national income (gross of tax) equal to $\Sigma A_i C_i$. When a tax is levied on capital, capital will receive $\Sigma A_i C_i (1 - t_i)$ net of tax, and the government will receive $\Sigma A_i C_i t_i$, where t_i is the percentage rate of tax applying to income from capital in the ith industry. Thus capital as a whole will lose a fraction of the national income exactly equal to that garnered by the government in tax receipts. As in the case presented in the above example, the distribution of capital among industries will change as a result of the imposition of the tax, the fraction of the total capital stock in the ith industry being $A_i C_i / (\Sigma A_i C_i)$ in the absence of the tax and $A_i C_i (1 - t_i) / [\Sigma A_i C_i (1 - t_i)]$ in its presence. Except when the tax rate on income from capital is equal in each industry, there will be effects on relative prices, and transfers of income among consumers, of the same general nature as those outlined above for the simpler case. But, as before, the gains of those consumers who do gain as a result of the changes in relative prices will, to a first approximation, be offset by the losses of those consumers who lose; thus, if we accept this offsetting as a canceling of effects as far as people in their role as consumers are concerned, we can say that capital bears the full burden of the tax.

III. THE CASE OF FIXED PROPORTIONS IN THE TAXED INDUSTRY

Returning now to an example in which there are only two industries, let us assume that the taxed industry is not characterized by a Cobb-Douglas production function, but instead by a production function in which the factors combine in strictly fixed proportions. Let us retain all of the other assumptions of the preceding example—that expenditure is divided equally between the two products, that production in industry Y is governed by the function $Y = L_y^{1/2} K_y^{1/2}$, that there are 600 units of each factor, and that the prices of the two factors are initially each \$1.00. These assumptions determine that the initial, pre-tax equilibrium will be the same as before, with 300 units of each factor occupied in each industry. The fixed-proportions production function for industry X which is consistent with these assumptions is $X = \text{Min}\ (L_x, K_x)$.

What happens when a tax of 50 per cent is imposed on the income from capital in industry X? It is clear that whatever reduction in output may occur in industry X, the two factors of production will be released to industry Y in equal amounts. Since industry Y is already using one unit of capital per unit of labor, it can absorb increments in these two factors in the same ratio without altering the marginal productivity of either factor in physical terms. The price of Y will have to fall, however, in order to create an increased demand for it. Whatever may be this fall in the price of Y, it will induce a proportionate fall in the price of each of the factors (since their marginal physical productivities are unchanged). We thus have the result that, in the final equilibrium after the tax, \$600 will be spent on the product of industry Y, with half going to capital and half to labor, and \$600 will be spent on the product of industry X, with \$200 going to labor, \$200 to capital (net of tax), and \$200 to the government. The price of labor will have fallen from \$1.00 to \$(5/6), and the price of capital will also have fallen from \$1.00 to \$(5/6). The tax will have fallen on capital and labor in proportion to their initial contributions to the national income.

It should be evident that the result just obtained, of labor and capital suffering the same percentage burden, depends critically on the fact that in the above example industry Y was in a position to absorb capital and labor in precisely the proportions in which they were ejected from industry X without a change in the relative prices of the two factors. If industry X had ejected two units of labor for each unit of capital, while industry Y had initially been using equal quantities of the two factors, the price of labor would have had to fall relative to the price of capital in order to induce the necessary increase in the proportion of labor to capital in industry Y. In such a case, labor would bear more tax, relative to its share in the national income, than capital. The following example will demonstrate that this is so.

Suppose that in the initial equilibrium 300 units of labor and 300 units of capital are engaged in the production of Y, and that the production function here is, as before, $Y = L_y^{1/2}K_y^{1/2}$. Suppose also, however, that 400 units of labor and 200 units of capital were initially dedicated to the production of X, with the production function for X requiring that labor and capital be used in these fixed proportions, that is, $X = \text{Min}\,[(L_x/2), K_x]$. Assume as before that the initial prices of labor and capital were \$1.00, and that national income remains unchanged at \$1,200 after the imposition of the tax. Likewise retain the assumption that expenditure is divided equally between goods X and Y.

The post-tax equilibrium in this case will be one in which the price of labor is \$0.83916, the price of capital \$0.91255. Industry X will use 171.25 units of capital and 342.5 units of labor; capital in industry X will receive a net income of \$156.274, and the government, with a 50 per cent tax on the gross earnings of capital in industry X, will get an equal amount; labor in industry X will receive \$287.412. These three shares in the product of industry X add up (but for a small rounding error) to \$600, the amount assumed to be spent on X. Industry Y will employ 328.75 (= 500 − 171.25) units of capital and 357.5 (= 700 − 342.5) units of labor, and the total receipts of each factor in industry Y will be, as before, \$300.[3]

[3] Let W be the net earnings of capital in industry X. Our other assumptions require that capital in industry Y must receive \$300. Therefore, in the post-tax equilibrium $[W/(\$300 + W)]$ (500) units of capital must be employed in industry X. Since \$600 is the total amount spent on X, and since the government's take is equal to the net amount (W) received by capital in industry X, labor in X must receive, in the post-tax equilibrium, an amount equal to $\$600 - 2W$. Since labor in industry Y must receive, under our assumptions, \$300, total labor earnings will be $\$900 - 2W$, and the number of units of labor in industry X must be $[(\$600 - 2W)/(\$900 - 2W)](700)$. (Recall that in this example there are 500 units of capital and 700 units of labor in the economy.) The production function for X requires that the industry employ twice as many units of labor as of capital. Hence we have that $(2)[W/(\$300 + W)](500) = [(\$600 - 2W)/(\$900 - 2W)](700)$ in the post-tax equilibrium. Solution of this

Since the price of capital has gone down from \$1.00 to \$0.91255, and the price of labor has gone down from \$1.00 to \$0.83916, it is clear that labor is roughly twice as heavily burdened by this tax (a tax on the earnings of *capital* in industry *X!*) than is capital, each factor's burden being taken relative to its initial share in the national income. The more labor-intensive is industry X, relative to the proportions in which the factors are initially used in industry Y, the heavier will be the relative burden of the tax upon labor. For example, if initially industry X had used 500 units of labor and 100 units of capital, while industry Y again used 300 of each with the same production function as before, the end result of a tax of 50 per cent of the earnings of capital in industry X would have been a fall in the price of capital from \$1.00 to \$0.9775, and in the price of labor from \$1 to \$0.8974. The burden on labor, relative to its initial share in the national income, would be more than five times that on capital.[4]

Whereas, in the Cobb-Douglas case discussed in Section II, capital bore the whole tax regardless of the proportions in which capital and labor combined in the two industries, we find in the present case that the relative proportions are of critical importance. The fact is that once fixed proportions are assumed to prevail in the taxed industry, it matters little whether the tax is nominally placed on the earnings of capital in X, on the earnings of labor in X, or on the sales of industry X. A tax on any of these three bases will lead to the ejection of labor and capital from industry X precisely in the proportions in which they are there use. If industry Y is initially using the factors in just these proportions, there will be no change in their relative prices, and they will bear the tax in proportion to their initial contributions to the national income. If industry Y is initially more capital-intensive than X, the price of labor must fall relative to that of capital in order to induce the absorption in Y of the factors released by X, and labor will bear a greater proportion of the tax than its initial share in the national income. If, on the other hand, industry Y is initially more labor-intensive than X, the opposite result will occur, and capital will bear a larger fraction of the tax burden than its initial share in national income.

IV. THE CASE OF FIXED PROPORTIONS IN THE UNTAXED INDUSTRY

When production in the taxed industry is governed by a Cobb-Douglas function, and fixed proportions prevail in the untaxed industry, the results of the tax are very different from those in the case just discussed. Now the normal result is for capital to bear more than the full burden of the tax, while labor enjoys an absolute increase in its real income. The degree of increase in labor's real income depends on the relative factor proportions in the two industries, but the fact

quadratic for W permits us to calculate the proportion of the capital stock $[W/(\$300 + W)]$ used in industry X. Applying this proportion to the total capital stock (500 units), we obtain the number of units of capital used in X. Likewise, we obtain the proportion $[(\$600 - 2W)/(\$900 - 2W)]$ of the labor force used in X, and from it the number of workers employed in X. Once we have these, we calculate the number of units of labor and capital employed in Y, and using these results, together with the fact that labor and capital in Y each earn a total of \$300, we calculate the prices of the two factors. (Although the quadratic in W that must be solved has two solutions, one of these is economically inadmissible.)

[4] The key equation for arriving at this solution is $(5)[W/(\$300 + W)](400) = [(\$600 - 2W)/(\$900 - 2W)](800)$. The solution is $W = 91$, $K_x = 93.1$, $L_x = 465.7$, $K_y = 306.9$, $L_y = 334.3$. Capital in industry X gets, net of tax, \$91, the government gets \$91, and labor in industry X earns \$418.

that labor will get such an increase is not dependent on these proportions.

The reason for this apparently anomalous result is that, in order for the untaxed industry to absorb any capital at all from the taxed industry, it must also absorb some labor, for it uses the two factors in fixed proportions. However, since in our example the fraction of national income spent on the taxed industry is given, and since the Cobb-Douglas function determines that the share of this fraction going to labor is fixed, it follows that any reduction in the amount of labor used in the taxed industry will carry with it a rise in the wage of labor.

A few examples of the type presented in the preceding sector will serve both to clarify this general result and to show how the degree of labor's gain depends on the relative factor proportions in the two industries. Assume first that the initial proportions in which the factors are combined are the same in the two industries. Let the production function for X be $X = K_x^{1/2}L_x^{1/2}$, and that for Y be $Y = \text{Min}\ (K_y,\ L_y)$, and let there be initially 300 units of each factor in each industry, earning a price of $1.00. Once again let total expenditures be divided equally between the two products. It follows that, after a tax of 50 per cent is imposed on the earnings of capital in industry X, capital in X will be earning $150 net of tax while labor in X will be getting $300. Since there are just as many units of labor as of capital in the economy, and since industry Y uses one unit of labor per unit of capital, industry X must, in the final equilibrium, employ as many units of labor as of capital. Since the total earnings of labor in X must be twice the total after-tax earnings of capital in that industry, it follows that the unit price of labor must be twice the unit price of capital. Of the total national income of $1,200, the government will get $150, capital will get $350, and labor will get $700. The price of capital will have fallen from $1.00 to $0.5833, and that of labor will have risen from $1.00 to $1.1667. Capital will have lost a total of $250 in income, of which $150 will have gone to the government in taxes and $100 will have been gained by labor.

Now consider a case in which the taxed industry is more labor-intensive than the untaxed industry. Let industry Y use twice as many units of capital as of labor, and let Y's initial levels of factor use be 400 capital and 200 labor, otherwise keeping the same assumptions as before. In this case, as a result of a 50 per cent tax on the earnings of capital in industry X, the price of capital will fall from $1.00 to $0.677855, and that of labor will rise from $1.00 to $1.15100. Capital will have lost a total of $225.5 in income, of which $75.5 will have been gained by labor.[5]

In a more extreme case, let industry Y use five times as many units of capital as of labor, and let Y's initial levels of factor use be 500 capital and 100 labor, again retaining our other assumptions. Now the price of capital falls from $1.00 to

[5] Let Z stand for the (as yet unknown) total earnings of capital in industry Y in the new equilibrium. Our other assumptions determine that capital in X will be earning $150 net of tax. Therefore the fraction of the capital stock employed in Y will be $Z/(\$150 + Z)$, and the number of units of capital in Y will be this fraction times 700, the total amount of capital in the economy. Labor in Y, in the final equilibrium, will be getting $(\$600 - Z)$, and labor in X $300. Therefore the fraction of the labor force occupied in Y will be $(\$600 - Z)/(\$900 - Z)$, and the number of units of labor in Y will be this fraction times 500. Since the number of units of capital in Y must be twice the number of units of labor, we have as a necessary condition of equilibrium $[Z/(\$150 + Z)](700) = (2)[(\$600 - Z)/(\$900 - Z)](500)$. Z turns out to be $324.5, $K_y = 478.714$, $L_y = 239.357$. K_x is, therefore, 221.286, and p_k is $150 divided by this number. Likewise p_l ix $300 divided by 260.643, the number of units of labor in X.

\$0.774393, and that of labor rises from \$1.00 to \$1.076272. Capital loses a total of \$180.5 in income from the pre-tax to the post-tax situation, of which \$30.5 is gained by labor.[6]

It is clear that the more capital-intensive is the untaxed industry, the less is the percentage reduction in income that capital must sustain as a result of the tax. If the untaxed industry is more labor-intensive than the taxed industry, capital is made even worse off by the tax than in the case of initially equal factor proportions. Where the untaxed industry is twice as labor-intensive as the taxed industry, for example, the price of capital falls from \$1.00 to \$0.528 as a result of the tax, capital losing some \$236 in total income, of which \$86 is gained by labor.[7]

V. A GENERAL MODEL OF THE INCIDENCE OF THE CORPORATION TAX

Although the examples presented in the three preceding sections give some insight into the nature of the incidence problem and into the factors which are likely to govern the incidence of the corporation income tax, they suffer from the defect of being based on particular restrictive assumptions about the nature of demand and production functions. In this section I shall present a model of substantially greater generality.

Let there be two products in the economy, X and Y, with their units of quantity so chosen that their prices are initially equal to unity. Demand for each product will depend on its relative price and on the level of income of demanders. The incomes of consumers will naturally fall as a result of the imposition of the tax, and through the consequent restriction of their demand for goods, command over resources will be released to the government. The ultimate demand position will depend on how consumers react to the change in their income and to whatever price change takes place, and on how the government chooses to spend the proceeds of the tax. Assume for the sake of simplicity that the way in which the government would spend the tax proceeds, if the initial prices continued to prevail, would just counterbalance the reductions in private expenditures on the two goods. This assumption, plus the additional assumption that redistributions of income among consumers do not change the pattern of demand, enable us to treat changes in demand as a function of changes in relative prices alone. Since full employment is also assumed, the demand functions for X and Y are not independent; once the level of demand for X is known, for given prices and full employment income, the level of demand for Y can be derived from the available information. We may therefore summarize conditions of demand in our model by an equation in which the quantity of X demanded depends on (p_x/p_y). Differentiating this function we obtain

$$\frac{dX}{X} = E\frac{d(p_x/p_y)}{(p_x/p_y)} = E(dp_x - dp_y) \quad (1)$$

(Demand for X),

where E is the price elasticity of demand for X, and where the assumption that initial prices were unity is used to obtain the final expression.

[6] The key equation in this case is $[Z/(\$150 + Z)](800) = (5)[(\$600 - Z)/(\$900 - Z)](400)$.

[7] This assumes that initially there were 400 units of labor and 200 units of capital occupied in industry Y. The key equation is $(2)[Z/(\$150 + Z)](500) = [(\$600 - Z)/(\$900 - Z)](700)$. Though the amount of the induced transfer from capital to labor is in this case less in total than it was in the case of equal factor proportions (\$86 vs \$100), the transfer amounts to a greater fraction of capital's initial income, which in this case is \$500 as against \$600 in the equal-proportions case treated earlier.

Assume next that the production function for X is homogeneous of the first degree. This enables us to write

$$\frac{dX}{X}=f_L\frac{dL_x}{L_x}+f_K\frac{dK_x}{K_x} \quad (2)$$
(Supply of X),

where f_L and f_K are the initial shares of labor and capital, respectively, in the total costs of producing X.

In an industry characterized by competition and by a homogeneous production function, the percentage change in the ratio in which two factors of production are used will equal the elasticity of substitution (S) between those factors times the percentage change in the ratio of their prices. Thus we have, for industry Y,

$$\frac{d(K_y/L_y)}{(K_y/L_y)}=S_y\frac{d(p_k/p_L)}{(p_k/p_L)}. \quad (3)$$

If we choose units of labor and capital so that their initial prices are equal to unity, this can be simplified to

$$\frac{dK_y}{K_y}-\frac{dL_y}{L_y}=S_y(dp_k-dp_L) \quad (3')$$
(Factor response in Y).

(Note at this point that the elasticity of substitution, like the elasticity of demand, is here defined so as to make its presumptive sign negative.)

We may follow an analogous procedure to obtain an equation for factor response in industry X, but we must realize here that the return to capital is being subjected to a tax in X, but not in Y. If (dp_k) is the change in the price of capital relevant for production decisions in industry Y, it is clearly the change in the price of capital net of tax. The change in the price of capital including the tax will be (dp_k+T), where T is the amount of tax per unit of capital. The factor response equation for X will therefore be

$$\frac{dK_x}{K_x}-\frac{dL_x}{L_x}=S_x(dp_k+T-dp_L) \quad (4)$$
(Factor response in X),

where S_x is the elasticity of substitution between labor and capital in industry X.[8]

The four equations, (1), (2), (3′), and (4), contain the following nine unknowns: dX, dp_x, dp_y, dL_x, dL_y, dK_x, dK_y, dp_L, and dp_k. These can be reduced to four by the use of the following five additional equations:

$$dK_y=-dK_x \quad (5)$$

$$dL_y=-dL_x \quad (6)$$

$$dp_x=f_Ldp_L+f_k(dp_k+T) \quad (7)$$

$$dp_y=g_Ldp_L+g_Kdp_k \quad (8)$$

$$dp_L=0. \quad (9)$$

Equations (5) and (6) come from the assumption of fixed factor supplies: the amount of any factor released by one of the two industries must be absorbed by the other. Equations (7) and (8) come from the assumptions of homogeneous production functions in both industries, and of competition. These assumptions assure that factor payments exhaust the total receipts in each industry. Thus, for industry Y, we have $p_ydY+Ydp_y=p_LdL_y+L_ydp_L+p_kdK_y+K_ydp_k$, to a first-order approximation. Since the marginal product of labor in Y is (p_L/p_y),

[8] It is convenient in this exercise to treat the tax on capital as a fixed tax per unit of capital employed in X. The analysis, however, is equally applicable to a tax expressed in percentage terms. If t is the percentage rate of tax on the gross income from capital, then in the post-tax equilibrium the absolute tax T can be obtained from the equation $t=T/(1+dp_k+T)$. Thus a case in which the tax is expressed in percentage terms can be analyzed by substituting for T in equation (4) the expression $[t(1+dp_k)(1-t)]$.

and that of capital (p_k/p_y), we have, also to a first-order approximation, $p_y dY = p_L dL_y + p_k dK_y$. Subtracting, we obtain $Y dp_y = L_y dp_L + K_y dp_k$, which, dividing through by Y and recalling that the initial prices of both factors and products are assumed to be unity, we find to be equivalent to (8), where g_L and g_k represent the initial shares of labor and capital, respectively, in the product of industry Y. An exactly analogous procedure applied to industry X yields equation (7); here, however, it must be borne in mind that the change in the price of capital as seen by entrepreneurs in industry X is not dp_k but $(dp_k + T)$.

Equation (9) is of a different variety than the others. The equations of the model contain absolute price changes as variables, while in the underlying economic theory it is only relative prices that matter. We have need of some sort of *numeraire*, a price in terms of which the other prices are expressed, and equation (9) chooses the price of labor as that *numeraire*. This choice places no restriction on the generality of our results. The government invariably will gain $K_x T$ in tax revenue. If the price of capital, net of tax, falls by $TK_x/(K_x + K_y)$ as a result of the tax, we can conclude that capital bears the entire tax. The change in national income, measured in units of the price of labor, is $K_x T + (K_x + K_y)dp_k$, so the result assumed above would leave labor's share of the national income unchanged, while capital's share would fall by just the amount gained by the government. If the solution of our equations told us that dp_k was zero, on the other hand, we would have to conclude that labor and capital were bearing the tax in proportion to their initial contributions to the national income. The relative prices of labor and capital (net of tax) would remain the same as before, hence both factors would have suffered the same percentage decline in real income as a result of the tax. The case where labor bears the entire burden of the tax emerges when the percentage change in the net price of capital (measured in wage units) is equal to the percentage change in the national income (also measured in wage units). Since dp_k is already in percentage terms because the initial price of capital is unity, this condition can be written $dp_k = [K_x T + (K_x + K_y)dp_k]/(L_x + L_y + K_x + K_y)$, which in turn reduces to $dp_k = K_x T/(L_x + L_y)$. Thus the choice of the price of labor as the *numeraire* by no means predestines labor to bear none of the burden of the tax, as might at first be supposed; in fact this assumption in no way restricts the solution of the incidence problem.

Substituting equations (5)–(9) into equations (1), (2), (3′), and (4), we obtain:

$$\frac{dX}{X} = E\,[f_k(dp_k + T) - g_k dp_k] \qquad (1')$$

$$\frac{dX}{X} = f_L \frac{dL_x}{L_x} + f_k \frac{dK_x}{K_x} \qquad (2)$$

$$\frac{K_x(-dK_x)}{K_y K_x} - \frac{L_x(-dL_x)}{L_y L_x} = S_y dp_k \qquad (3'')$$

$$\frac{dK_x}{K_x} - \frac{dL_x}{L_x} = S_x(dp_k + T). \qquad (4')$$

Equating $(dX)/X$ in equations (1′) and (2), and rearranging terms, we have the following system of three equations:

$$E f_k T = E(g_k - f_k)\,dp_k + f_L \frac{dL_x}{L_x} + f_k \frac{dK_x}{K_x} \qquad (10)$$

$$0 = S_y dp_k - \frac{L_x}{L_y}\frac{dL_x}{L_x} + \frac{K_x}{K_y}\frac{dK_x}{K_x} \qquad (3'')$$

$$S_x T = -S_x dp_k - \frac{dL_x}{L_x} + \frac{dK_x}{K_x}. \quad (4')$$

The solution for dp_k, which gives us the answer to the incidence question, is

$$dp_k = \frac{\begin{vmatrix} Ef_k & f_L & f_k \\ 0 & \frac{-L_x}{L_y} & \frac{K_x}{K_y} \\ S_x & -1 & 1 \end{vmatrix}}{\begin{vmatrix} E(g_k - f_k) & f_L & f_k \\ S_y & \frac{-L_x}{L_y} & \frac{K_x}{K_y} \\ -S_x & -1 & 1 \end{vmatrix}} \cdot T. \quad (11)$$

Alternatively, (11) can be written:

$$\frac{Ef_k\left(\frac{K_x}{K_y} - \frac{L_x}{L_y}\right) + S_x\left(\frac{f_L K_x}{K_y} + \frac{f_k L_x}{L_y}\right)}{E(g_k - f_k)\left(\frac{K_x}{K_y} - \frac{L_x}{L_y}\right) - S_y - S_x\left(\frac{f_L K_x}{K_y} + \frac{f_k L_x}{L_x}\right)} \cdot T = dp_k. \quad (12)$$

In solving the determinant in the denominator of (11) to obtain the expression in the denominator of (12), use is made of the fact that $(f_L + f_k) = 1$.

Before turning to an examination of some of the economic implications of this solution, let us establish the fact that the denominator of (12), or of (11) is necessarily positive. S_x is necessarily negative; the expression in brackets which it multiplies in the denominator of (12) is necessarily positive; and S_x is preceded by a minus sign; therefore, the whole third term in the denominator of (12) is positive. $(-S_y)$ is also positive. In the first term, E is negative, so that if it can be shown that $(g_k - f_k)[(K_x/K_y) - (L_x/L_y)]$ is negative or zero, it will be established that the whole denominator is positive (or, in the limiting case, zero). If g_k is greater than f_k, industry Y is more capital-intensive than industry X and therefore $[(K_x/K_y) - (L_x/L_y)]$ must be negative; therefore, the indicated product must be negative. Likewise, if $(g_k - f_k)$ is negative, industry X will be the more capital-intensive of the two industries, and $[(K_x/K_y) - (L_x/L_y)]$ will be positive. The whole first term in the denominator of (12) is therefore positive, and the denominator also.

VI. DETAILED EXAMINATION OF THE GENERAL SOLUTION

In this section, I shall set out certain general conclusions which can be drawn on the basis of the solution given in (12).

1. *Only if the taxed industry is relatively labor-intensive can labor bear more of the tax, in proportion to its initial share in the national income, than capital.* Recall that when dp_k is zero, labor and capital bear the tax precisely in proportion to their initial shares in the national income. For labor to bear more than this, dp_k must be positive. Since the denominator of (12) is positive, the sign of dp_k will be determined by the sign of the numerator of (12). The second term in the numerator is necessarily negative, so dp_k can be positive only if the first term is positive and greater in absolute magnitude than the second term. Since E is negative, the first term can be positive only if $[(K_x/K_y) - (L_x/L_y)]$ is negative, and this can occur only if industry X is relatively more labor-intensive than industry Y. Q.E.D.

2. *If the elasticity of substitution between labor and capital in the taxed industry is as great or greater in absolute value than the elasticity of demand for the product of the taxed industry, capital must bear more of the tax than labor, relative to their initial income shares.* In this case the

term $Ef_k(-L_x/L_y)$, which is the only term which can give the numerator of (12) a positive sign, is dominated by the term $S_x f_k(L_x/L_y)$.

3. *If the elasticity of substitution between labor and capital in the taxed industry is as great in absolute value as the elasticity of substitution between the two final products, capital must bear more of the tax than labor, relative to their initial income shares.* This holds a fortiori from the above, since the elasticity of substitution between X and Y must be greater in absolute value than the elasticity of demand for X. The formula relating the elasticity of substitution between X and Y, which I shall denote by V, and the elasticity of demand for X, E, is $E = V[Y/(X+Y)]$.[9]

4. *The higher is the elasticity of substitution between labor and capital in the untaxed industry, the greater will be the tendency for labor and capital to bear the tax in proportion to their initial income shares.* This elasticity, S_y, appears only in the denominator of (12). It changes not the sign but the magnitude of the expression for dp_k. The larger is S_y in absolute value, the smaller will be the absolute value of dp_k. In the limit, where S_y is infinite, dp_k must be zero: in this case the relative prices of labor and capital are determined in the untaxed industry; the tax cannot affect them.

5. *The higher the elasticity of substitution between labor and capital in the taxed industry, the closer, other things equal, will be the post-tax rate of return on capital to the initial rate of return less the unit tax applied to capital in industry* X. This elasticity, S_x, appears in the numerator and the denominator of (12) with equal coefficients but with opposite signs. When S_x is infinite, and the other elasticities finite, the expression for dp_k is equal to $-T$. The price of capital in the taxed industry, gross of tax, must in this case bear the same relationship to the price of labor as existed in the pre-tax situation. The net price of capital must therefore fall by the amount of the tax per unit of capital in X. Since this fall in price applies to capital employed in Y as well as in X, the reduction in the income of capital must exceed the amount of revenue garnered by the government; labor's real income must therefore rise. When S_x is not infinite, its contribution is to move the value of dp_k toward $-T$, from whatever level would be indicated by the other terms in (12) taken alone.

6. *When factor proportions are initially the same in both industries, capital will bear the full burden of the tax if the elasticities of substitution between labor and capital are the same in both industries, will bear less than the full burden of the tax if the elasticity of substitution between labor and capital is greater in the untaxed than in the taxed industry, and will bear more than the full burden of the tax if the elasticity of substitution is greater in the taxed industry.* When $(K_x/K_y) = (L_x/L_y)$, the first terms in both the numerator and denominator of (12) vanish, and the expression simplifies to $dp_k = -TS_xK_x/(S_yK_y + S_xK_x)$. When, additionally, $S_x = S_y$, this reduces to $-TK_x/(K_y + K_x)$, which was indicated earlier to be the condition for capital's bearing exactly the full burden of the tax. When S_x is greater than S_y, capital's burden will be

[9] One of the many places in which the derivation of this relationship is presented is my paper, "Some Evidence on the International Price Mechanism," *Journal of Political Economy*, LXVI (December, 1957), 514. The relationship applies when the relevant elasticity of demand is one which excludes first-order income effects. This is the concept relevant for the present analysis, because we are treating government demand for goods on a par with consumer demand. The presentation of this relationship at this point may seem a bit out of context; I bring it in because it will be used later.

greater than in the case where the two elasticities are equal, and conversely.

7. *When the elasticity of demand for the taxed commodity is zero, the results are somewhat similar to those just reached. In this case, however, capital does not necessarily bear precisely the full burden of the tax even when the elasticities of substitution are equal in the two industries. It bears somewhat more if the taxed industry is labor-intensive and somewhat less if the taxed industry is capital-intensive.* When E is zero, the first terms in both the numerator and denominator of (12) again vanish, but now the expression for dp_k reduces to $-Tf_LK_xS_x/(g_LK_yS_y + f_LK_xS_x)$.[10] It is clear that, even when $S_x = S_y$, this is equal to $-TK_x/(K_y + K_x)$ only when $f_L = g_L$, that is, when the two industries are initially equally labor-intensive. The fall in the price of capital will be greater or less than this according as f_L is greater than or less than g_L.

8. *When the elasticity of substitution between labor and capital is zero in both industries, the incidence of the tax will depend solely on the relative proportions in which the factors are used in the two industries, labor bearing the tax more than in proportion to its initial contribution to national income when the taxed industry is relatively labor-intensive, and vice versa.* In this case (12) simplifies to $dp_k = f_kT/(g_k - f_k)$, which will be positive when g_k is greater than f_k (taxed industry relatively labor-intensive) and negative when f_k is greater than g_k (taxed industry relatively capital-intensive). A somewhat anomalous aspect of this solution is that the absolute value of dp_k varies inversely with the difference in factor proportions in the two industries. When f_k is $\frac{1}{4}$ and g_k is $\frac{1}{2}$, $dp_k = T$; but when f_k is $\frac{1}{4}$ and g_k is $\frac{3}{4}$, dp_k is only $\frac{1}{2}T$. To see the reason for this, it is useful first to recognize that when there are only two industries, each of which uses the two factors in different proportions, there is only one set of outputs of X and Y which will provide full employment. So long as the full-employment condition is not violated, demand conditions require that the relative prices of the two products must remain unchanged. In our notation, $dp_x - dp_y$ must be zero. Since $dp_x = f_k(dp_k + T)$, and $dp_y = g_kdp_k$, it is clear that this condition on the relative prices of final products is sufficient to give the solution $dp_k = f_kT/(g_k - f_k)$. If, for example, capital initially accounts for one-tenth of the value of output in X and one-half in Y, a rise in the price of capital by $0.25T$ will permit relative product prices to remain unchanged. Recalling that the price of labor is the *numeraire*, and therefore is assumed to remain unchanged, one can see that the rise in the price of X would be $(0.1)(0.25T + T) = 0.125T$, while the rise in the price of Y would be $(0.5)(0.25T)$, also equal to $0.125T$. Suppose, however, that capital initially accounts for four-tenths of the value of product in X, and one-half in Y. Then the price of capital will have to rise by $4T$ in order to yield the equilibrium ratio of product prices. The rise in the price of X would then be $(0.4)(4T + T) = 2T$, and the rise in the price of Y would be $(0.5)(4T)$, which is also equal to $2T$. In the limit, where the factor proportions are the same in both industries, and where the production functions are such that these proportions cannot be altered, the model does not give sufficient information to determine the prices of

[10] Since $f_L = L_x/(L_x + K_x)$ and $f_k = K_x/(L_x + K_x)$, it is clear that $f_LK_x = f_kL_x$. The coefficient of S_x in the numerator of (12) can therefore be written $f_LK_x[(1/K_y) + (1/L_y)] = f_LK_x[(L_y + K_y)/(L_yK_y)] = f_LK_x/g_LK_y$. Setting $E = 0$ in (12), and multiplying numerator and denominator by g_LK_y, one obtains the expression given above for dp_k.

capital and labor, either in the pre-tax or in the post-tax equilibrium.

9. *Where the elasticity of substitution in demand between goods X and Y is equal to −1, and the elasticities of substitution between labor and capital in the two industries are also equal to −1, capital will bear precisely the full burden of the tax.* This is the Cobb-Douglas case treated in Section II above. The easiest way to demonstrate this proposition is to substitute the solution for dp_k, dL_x/L_x, and dK_x/K_x directly into equations (10), (3″), and (4′). Since the determinant of this system of equations is non-zero, we know that there can be only one solution; thus, if we find one that works, we know we have the right one. The correct solution is $dp_k = -TK_x/(K_x + K_y)$; $(dL_x/L_x) = 0$; and $(dK_x/K_x) = -TK_y/(K_x + K_y)$. Substituting this solution, and $S_x = -1$, into (4′), we obtain $-T = [-TK_x/(K_x + K_y)] + [-TK_y/(K_x + K_y)]$. Equation (4′) is therefore satisfied. Substituting into (3″), with S_y set equal to −1, we obtain $[K_xT/(K_x + K_y)] + [-K_xT/(K_x + K_y)] = 0$. Equation (3″) is therefore satisfied. Recalling that when the elasticity of substitution between X and Y is −1, the elasticity of demand for X will be $-Y/(X + Y)$, we substitute this value for E in (10), together with the solution values for the three unknowns, obtaining

$$\frac{-f_kYT}{X+Y} = \frac{YK_xg_kT}{(X+Y)(K_x+K_y)} - \frac{YK_xf_kT}{(X+Y)(K_x+K_y)} - \frac{f_kK_yT}{K_x+K_y}.$$

First, add $YK_xf_kT/(X + Y)(K_x + K_y)$ to both sides of the equation, to obtain

$$\frac{-f_kYK_yT}{(X+Y)(K_x+K_y)} = \frac{YK_xg_kT}{(X+Y)(K_x+K_y)} - \frac{f_xK_yT}{K_x+K_y};$$

here we use the fact that

$$\frac{K_x}{K_x+K_y} + \frac{K_y}{K_x+K_y} = 1.$$

Now add $f_kK_yT/(K_x + K_y)$ to both sides of the equation, to get

$$\frac{f_kXK_yT}{(X+Y)(K_x+K_y)} = \frac{YK_xg_kT}{(X+Y)(K_x+K_y)};$$

here we use the fact that $[X/(X + Y)] + [Y/(X + Y)] = 1$. Now, noting that $f_k = K_x/X$ and $g_k = K_y/Y$ under our assumption that all prices are initially equal to unity, we make the corresponding substitutions to obtain

$$\frac{K_xK_yT}{(X+Y)(K_x+K_y)} = \frac{K_xK_yT}{(X+Y)(K_x+K_y)}.$$

Equation (10) is therefore satisfied, and the solution has been verified to be the correct one.

10. *In any case in which the three elasticities of substitution are equal (and non-zero), capital will bear precisely the full burden of the tax.* We have shown that when $S_x = S_y = V = -1$, the solution for dp_k is $-KT_x/(K_x + K_y)$, which is what is required for capital to lose precisely what the government gains. Recalling that $E = VY/(X + Y)$, we see from (12) that multiplying S_x, S_y, and V by any positive constant would change the numerator and denominator of (12) in the same proportion, leaving the solution for dp_k unchanged.

VII. APPLICATION TO THE UNITED STATES CASE

If we divide the United States economy into two broad sectors, one corporate and the other non-corporate, the most plausible broad division is between agriculture, real estate, and miscellaneous repair services on the non-corporate side, and the remainder of United States industries on the other. As was indicated in the introduction, the industries here classified as corporate all paid some 20 per cent or more of their total income from capital in corporation tax; and one may add at this point that two thirds of them paid corporation taxes amounting to more than 40 per cent of their return to capital.[11]

On this classification, the corporate sector, in 1953–55, earned roughly \$40 billion in return to capital, and paid roughly \$20 billion in corporation income taxes. Its wage bill averaged around \$200 billion per year. The non-corporate sector, on the other hand, contributed some \$40 billion per year to the national income, of which some \$20 billion was return to capital and \$20 billion return to labor; this sector paid practically no corporation income taxes (less than \$500 million).[12] These data are sufficient to enable us to estimate some of the key elements in formula (12).

If the corporation income tax were of small magnitude, the pre-tax values of (L_x/L_y), (K_x/K_y), f_L, f_k, and g_k would all be very close to their post-tax values, and the post-tax values could be inserted into equation (12) without fear of significant error. However, the tax is in fact substantial in the United States. I have accordingly decided to use two alternative sets of values for these elements in the formula: Set I is derived from the observed values in the period 1953–55, and Set II represents the values that would

[11] In making the computations that follow, I have eliminated from consideration the government and rest-of-the-world sectors, together with the financial intermediaries (banking, brokers, finance, insurance), and certain of the services (private households, commercial and trade schools, medical, health, legal, engineering, educational, and other professional services, and non-profit membership organizations). The industrial classification used was that given in the official statistics on national income by industry. Because net interest and income of unincorporated enterprises are not given in so detailed an industrial breakdown as national income, corporate profits, corporate profits taxes, and so forth, it was necessary to estimate the industrial breakdown for them independently. The methods used, and the tests applied to check the consistency of the resulting figures with official data available for broader aggregates, are given in the appendix to my earlier paper, "The Corporation Income Tax: An Empirical Appraisal," *op. cit.*

[12] Readers of my earlier paper may recall that I reported there on a set of calculations in which the national output was divided into two sectors, and that the two sectors turned out to have roughly equal factor proportions. That division differs from the present one because it was based on the assumption that in each of the many industries considered, fixed factor proportions prevailed. In such a case, a tax on the earnings of capital in each industry is equivalent to an excise tax on the value added to that industry at a rate equal to the ratio of corporation tax receipts to value added. In my example I compared the results of such a pattern of excises with the results of a flat-rate excise tax on the value added of all industries, the rate being so chosen as to yield the same revenue as the present corporation tax. I then divided industries into two groups according to whether their ratios of corporation tax payments to value added were greater or less than this calculated flat rate. Under the assumption of no substitutability between capital and labor, those industries whose actual rate was higher than the flat rate would presumably contract, as a result of substituting the flat-rate excise for the present tax. Those that would contract would eject labor and capital, and the others would expand their use of both factors. The calculation I made was of the total amounts that would be demanded by the expanding industries, assuming unit elasticities of substitution among final products and also that relative factor prices did not change as a result of the alteration in tax provisions. It turned out that the expanding industries would demand new labor and capital in almost precisely the same amounts as contracting industries would eject them and that therefore the relative prices of the factors would remain substantially unchanged. I note this merely to explain the difference in concept between my earlier calculation of factor proportions and the present one. In the earlier case, the ratio of corporate tax payments to value added was the basic variable considered; here the basic variable is the ratio of corporate tax payments to total income from capital.

have emerged in 1953–55 in the absence of the tax if each sector were characterized by a Cobb-Douglas production function and if the elasticity of substitution between the products of the two sectors were unity. In both cases $(L_x/L_y) = 10$. This is the ratio of the wage bill in the taxed sector to the wage bill in the untaxed sector that was observed in 1953–55, and it will be recalled from the analysis of the Cobb-Douglas case in Section II that the pre-tax and post-tax distributions of the labor force are the same. Likewise, $g_k = 0.5$ in both cases, this being the share of capital in the untaxed industry in 1953–55; under Cobb-Douglas assumptions this fraction also is invariant between the pre-tax and post-tax situation. The observed value of (K_x/K_y) is 1, the after-tax receipts of capital being the same in the two sectors in 1953–55. The hypothetical initial value, however, is 2 under Cobb-Douglas assumptions, for these assumptions imply that in the absence of the tax the capital stock would be distributed between the industries in the same proportions as the gross-of-tax earnings of capital in the two industries after the tax had been imposed. Since under Cobb-Douglas assumptions the shares of the gross earnings of the factors in the total product of the industry are constant, we have for this case $f_k = (1/6)$ and $f_L = (5/6)$. For our alternative assumptions (Set I) we shall take the observed net-of-tax ratios in 1953–55: $f_k = (1/11)$ and $f_L = (10/11)$. The assumed initial values for these magnitudes are summarized below:

	(K_x/K_y)	(L_x/L_y)	f_k	f_L	g_k
Set I......	1	10	1/11	10/11	0.5
Set II.....	2	10	1/6	5/6	0.5

Substituting these figures into equation (12), we obtain expressions for dp_k in which the incidence of the corporation tax is expressed directly in terms of the elasticities of substitution and of demand:

$$dp_k = \frac{T[-9E + 20S_x]}{-40.5E - 11S_y - 20S_x} \qquad (13)$$

(based on Set I);

$$dp_k = \frac{T[-8E + 20S_x]}{-16E - 6S_y - 20S_x} \qquad (14)$$

(based on Set II).

We have evidence which I believe permits us to estimate the order of magnitude of E reasonably well, albeit by an indirect route. The untaxed sector, Y consists overwhelmingly of two industries—agriculture and real estate—and the activity of the latter is principally the provision of residential housing services. We know that the elasticity of demand for agricultural products lies well below unity, and recent evidence suggests strongly that the price elasticity of demand for residential housing in the United States is somewhere in the neighborhood of unity, perhaps a bit above it.[13] It is thus highly unlikely that the price elasticity of demand for the products of our non-corporate sector (which would be a weighted average of the price elasticities of the component commodities, adjusted downward to eliminate the contribution of substitutability among the products in the group) would exceed unity in absolute value; in all likelihood it is somewhat below this figure. This evidence permits us to use unity as a reasonable upper bound for the elasticity of substitution between X and Y. A value of unity for this elasticity of substitution implies a value of $-\frac{6}{7}$ for the elasticity of demand for the products of the non-

[13] See Richard F. Muth, "The Demand for Nonfarm Housing," in A. C. Harberger (ed.), *The Demand for Durable Goods* (Chicago: University of Chicago Press, 1960), pp. 29–96.

corporate sector, and a value of $-\frac{1}{7}$ for the elasticity of demand for the products of the corporate sector.[14] Only if one feels that the elasticity of demand for the non-corporate sector's product is higher than $\frac{6}{7}$ in absolute value can he place a higher value than $\frac{1}{7}$ on the elasticity of demand for the corporate sector's product.

Evidence on the elasticity of substitution (S_x) between labor and capital in the corporate sector is both more meager and less reliable than the evidence on elasticities of demand. However, two recent studies, one by Solow and the other by Minasian, suggest rather strongly that the elasticity of substitution between labor and capital in manufacturing industries in the United States tends to be near unity. Of nineteen elasticities of substitution measured by Solow for two-digit manufacturing industries, ten were greater than and nine less than unity. Of fourteen elasticities of substitution measured by Minasian for two-digit industries, six were greater than and eight less than unity. Of forty-six elasticities measured by Minasian for three-digit and four-digit industries, twenty-two were greater and twenty-four less than unity. Only in a small fraction of the cases were the differences between the estimated elasticities and unity statistically significant; and the majority of the estimated elasticities for which this difference was significant were greater than unity.[15]

We can be still less sure about the elasticity of substitution, S_y, between labor and capital in the untaxed sector. We may recognize the relative success that agriculture economists have had in fitting Cobb-Douglas production functions to data for different components of agriculture and perhaps tentatively accept an elasticity of substitution of unity as applying there. However, close to half the contribution of the non-corporate sector to national income comes from real estate and not from agriculture. It is difficult to see how the elasticity of substitution between labor and capital in the provision of housing services could be very great. Very little labor is in fact used in this industry (compensation of employees is only one-tenth of the value added in the industry), and it is hard to imagine that even fairly substantial changes in relative prices would bring about a much greater relative use of labor. Taking the non-corporate sector as a whole, I think it is fair to assume that the elasticity of substitution between labor and capital in this sector is below, and probably quite substantially below, that in the corporate sector.

We may now attempt to assess the burden of the corporation income tax in the United States. Let us take as a first approximation the Cobb-Douglas case, in which all three elasticities of substitution are unity. We have seen that this case

[14] Recall that V, the elasticity of substitution between X and Y, is related to the own-price elasticities of demand for those commodities by the formulas: $E_x = V[Y/(X+Y)]$, and $E_y = V[X/(X+Y)]$. In our 1953–55 data $[X/(X+Y)] = \$240/\$280$, and $[Y/(X+Y)] = \$40/\$280$.

[15] See R. M. Solow, "Capital, Labor, and Income in Manufacturing" (paper presented at the Conference on Income and Wealth, April, 1961, sponsored by the National Bureau of Economic Research [to be published]), and Jora R. Minasian, "Elasticities of Substitution and Constant-Output Demand Curves for Labor," *Journal of Political Economy*, LXIX, June, 1961), 261–70. Both of these studies were based on cross-section data, Solow's data being classified by regions and Minasian's by states. Though the over-all statistical significance of the conclusion that the substitution elasticity between labor and capital in most manufacturing industries is not far from unity is good, there is the possibility of bias toward unity in the results due to errors of measurement or to differences in the quality of labor among states or regions. It is on this ground that I regard these results as less firm than those on elasticities of demand.

implies that capital will bear precisely the full burden of the tax. This means, using Set I of initial conditions, that $dp_k = -\frac{1}{2}T$, and using Set II that $dp_k = -\frac{2}{3}T$. Inserting the values $E = -\frac{1}{7}$; $S_x = S_y = -1$ in equations (13) and (14), we find that, under Set I, $dp_k = -0.509T$, while under Set II $dp_k = -\frac{2}{3}T$.[16]

The most plausible alteration to make in the above assumptions is to reduce the value of S_y This will clearly operate to increase the burden on capital. To see how sensitive is the incidence of the tax to a reduction in S_y, let us assume $E = -\frac{1}{7}$; $S_x = -1$; $S_y = -\frac{1}{2}$. Here we find that under Set I $dp_k = -0.598T$, while under Set II $dp_k = -0.746T$. Comparing these results with the levels of dp_k, which would mean capital's just bearing the tax, we find that in this case capital's burden is 120 per cent of the tax under Set I and 112 per cent under Set II.

The results are even less sensitive to changes in the assumed demand elasticity than to changes in S_y. If we assume the elasticity of substitution between X and Y to be only $-\frac{1}{2}$ (which is implausibly low, since it implies an elasticity of demand for the non-corporate sector's product of only -0.42, even though we have strong evidence that this magnitude is much higher), while the elasticities of substitution in production are both -1, capital turns out to bear 114 per cent of the burden of the tax under Set I and 107 per cent under Set II of initial values. Raising the elasticity of substitution between X and Y to -1.5 (implying an elasticity of demand for the non-corporate sector's product of around -1.25), we obtain the result that capital bears 91 per cent of the tax under Set I and 93 per cent under Set II.

Raising S_x to -1.2 (which is perhaps a rather high value in the light of the Solow-Minasian evidence), and leaving the other elasticities of substitution at unity, gives the result that capital bears 111 per cent of the tax under Set I and 106 per cent under Set II of initial conditions. If we set S_x at $-.8$, we find that capital bears 90 per cent of the burden of the tax under Set I, and 92 per cent under Set II.

To reduce S_x below unity while not reducing S_y appears unrealistic, since our evidence suggests that S_x is near -1, while evidence and presumption suggest that S_y is lower. Let us accordingly test the consequences of a substantial reduction of S_x and S_y simultaneously, say, to $-\frac{2}{3}$, while leaving the elasticity of substitution between X and Y at -1. This gives the same relationship among the elasticities as existed when we assumed the elasticity of substitution between X and Y to be -1.5, and the elasticities of substitution in production to be -1; again we find that capital bears 91 per cent of the tax under Set I and 93 per cent under Set II of initial conditions.

It is hard to avoid the conclusion that plausible alternative sets of assumptions about the relevant elasticities all yield results in which capital bears very close to 100 per cent of the tax burden.[17] The

[16] Set I does not yield exact results because the assumed initial conditions are inconsistent with the assumed values of the three elasticities. However, the error is so small as to be negligible for practical purposes.

[17] Actually, the method used to estimate the percentages of the tax borne by capital in the above examples is biased away from this conclusion. The method was to divide the estimated value of dp_k by the value that dp_k would have if capital bore the whole tax. This method would tell us that capital bore none of the tax if the estimated dp_k were zero; yet we know that when $dp_k = 0$ the tax is shared by labor and capital in proportion to their initial contributions to total income. The method is precise only when $dp_k = -K_xT/(K_x + K_y)$. If p_k falls more than this, with the price of labor con-

most plausible assumptions imply that capital bears more than the full burden of the tax.

Let us now consider how this result would be modified if, as a result of the existence of the tax, the rate of saving was less than it would have been in the absence of this particular tax. I shall assume that, in the absence of the corporation income tax, the government would have raised the same amount of revenue by other means, and hence that there is no "income effect" of the tax on the volume of saving. However, our analysis implies that the net rate of return on capital is lowered as a result of the tax, and this would have an effect on capital accumulation if the elasticity of savings with respect to the rate of interest were not zero. Let the capital stock that we now observe be called K_1, and the capital stock that we would have had at the present time in the absence of the corporation tax be K_2. Let R be the percentage excess of K_2 over K_1. An increase in the capital stock from K_1 to K_2 would have caused an increase in output of h_kR per cent, where h_k is the fraction of the national income earned by capital. If, as is probably true, Cobb-Douglas assumptions apply, the shares of capital and labor in the national income will remain constant. Therefore, of the increase in output stemming from the increase in capital stock, a fraction h_L would accrue to labor, where h_L is the share of labor in the national income. Thus in the absence of the tax there would have occurred a transfer of h_Lh_kR per cent of the national income to labor. This transfer does not take place because of the existence of the tax; hence in a sense it may be said that the potential amount of this unrealized transfer is a burden imposed on labor by the tax.

How large is the amount of the potential transfer relative to the burden of the tax itself? Using our 1953–55 data, we find that h_k is about 0.22 and h_L is about 0.78, while the tax represents 1/14 of the total income produced in the two sectors considered. In order for (0.22)(0.78) R to equal 1/14 of the national income, R would have to be about 0.42. That is to say, the capital stock that would have existed in the absence of the corporation tax would have had to be some 42 per cent greater than the capital stock we now have.

It is quite implausible that the influence of the corporation tax on the capital stock could have been this great. If the tax did not influence the capital stock at all, it would have reduced the net rate of return on capital by a third; to the extent that it did influence the capital stock, the reduction in the net rate of return would have been less than this. K_2 is made different from K_1 by the influence of the reduction in the rate of return upon the rate of saving. If there is such an influence, its effect increases through time. In the first few years after the tax is imposed, only small differences between K_2 and K_1 can emerge. As time goes on, and the capital stock comes to consist more and more of capital accumulated after the imposition of the tax, the difference becomes larger. The percentage excess of K_2 over K_1 can, however, never be greater than the percentage excess of the savings rate that would have existed in the absence of the tax over the savings rate in the presence of

stant, the general price level will fall somewhat; capital will not suffer in real terms by as much as our approximation indicates. If p_k falls by less than this, the general price level will rise, and capital will suffer a greater burden (will come closer to bearing the full weight of the tax) than our approximation indicates. Correcting the above percentages for this bias would accordingly strengthen the conclusion stated above. The corrections would, however, be minor in the cases presented in the text.

the tax. Thus, if one thinks that in the absence of the corporation tax the net savings rate in the United States might be 20 per cent higher than it is now, he may set the maximum value for R at 0.2. This would mean that a maximum of half the burden of the corporation tax would be "shifted" to labor. If one thinks that the savings rate in the absence of the tax would be no more than 10 per cent higher than at present, a maximum of one-quarter of the burden of the tax would be "shifted" to labor. The observed constancy of the savings rate in the United States in the face of rather wide variations in the rate of return on capital suggests that the effect of the tax on the rate of saving is probably small. Moreover, no more than half of the present capital stock of the United States is the result of accumulations made after corporation tax rates became substantial in the mid-thirties. Thus even if savings in this period would have been 20 per cent greater in the absence of the tax, the current capital stock would be only 10 per cent less than it would have been in the absence of the tax. And if the effect of the tax was to reduce savings by 10 per cent, the current value of R would be only 5 per cent.

I conclude from this exercise that even allowing for a rather substantial effect of the corporation income tax on the rate of saving leads to only a minor modification of my over-all conclusion that capital probably bears close to the full burden of the tax. The savings effect here considered might well outweigh the presumption that capital bears more than the full burden of the tax, but it surely is not sufficiently large to give support to the frequently heard allegations that large fractions of the corporation income tax burden fall on laborers or consumers or both.

APPENDED NOTES

At the presentation of this paper at the 1961 meetings of the International Association for Research in Income and Wealth, and in other discussions of its content, some questions have been raised that clearly merit treatment, yet that do not quite fit as integral parts of, or as footnotes to, particular statements in the main text. These notes discuss two of these points.

1. OTHER SPECIAL TAX PROVISIONS RELATING TO CAPITAL

In this paper I have tried to get at what might be called the partial or particular effects of the corporation income tax. In the simple models presented, the corporation income tax was the only tax in the system, but the analysis can easily be adapted to cases where other taxes exist. In such cases the effects of adding the corporation income tax to a set of pre-existing taxes will be essentially the same as those derived in this paper for the case where there were no pre-existing taxes. Differences of detail in formulas such as equation (12) may appear as one considers different patterns of pre-existing taxes, but the basic roles played by relative factor proportions, by substitutability between corporate and non-corporate products in demand, and by the relative degrees of substitutability between labor and capital in producing the two classes of products will remain the same.

One may, however, accept the approach presented in the text as appropriate for analyzing the effects of the corporation income tax and may have no quarrel with the empirical exercise of Section VII as indicating the particular effect of the corporation income tax in the United States, and yet may doubt that capital is as heavily discriminated against in the corporate sector, or that capital as a whole bears as heavy a weight of "special" taxation, as is indicated in Section VII. Such doubts have been expressed to me on several occasions, the argument being that other "special" provisions of our tax laws operate to offset, to some extent, the particular effects of the corporation income tax.

The capital gains provisions of the personal income tax are a case in point. Capital gains in the United States are taxed only upon realization, and then (except for short term gains) at a preferential rate that cannot exceed 25 per cent. Accrued gains that have not been realized before the death of the owner escape capital gains tax altogether and are subject only to the estate tax. These provisions operate to make the tax load on owners of capital lighter than it would be in their absence. They also operate to attract capital to the corporate sector, for it is here that capital gains can be expected to accrue in the normal course of events (as a result of corporate saving), whereas in the non-corporate sector capital gains come mainly from less normal causes such as general price inflation or relative price changes.

To get an idea of how taking capital gains provisions into account would alter the results of Section VII, let us assume that corporate saving of a given amount tends to generate an equal amount of capital gains, and that no capital gains normally accrue in the non-corporate sector. Let us, moreover, assume that the special provisions regarding capital gains lead to a reduction in personal income-tax liabilities (as against a situation in which capital gains would be taxed as ordinary income) equal to half the amount of the gains themselves. This last assumption implies a "typical" marginal income-tax rate for corporate shareholders somewhere between 50 per cent (what it would be if no capital gains tax were in fact paid on the gains generated in the corporate sector) and 75 per cent (what it would be if the maximum long-term capital gains tax of 25 per cent were actually paid on all the gains generated in the corporate sector). These assumptions are meant to be extreme rather than realistic, so that we may see how large the possible offsetting effects of the capital gains provisions may be.

In the period 1953–55, from which the data used in Section VII were taken, corporate savings averaged slightly less than $10 billion per year. The assumptions above imply a personal tax offset, due to the capital gains provisions, of about $5 billion per year. Thus, in analyzing corporation-tax-cum-capital-gains-provisions we would set up an example in which corporate capital paid $15 billion in special taxes and non-corporate capital nothing, as compared with the $20 billion and nothing, respectively, used in the example of Section VII. The argument would run along precisely the same lines, and we would come to the conclusion that the $15 billion in special taxes was borne predominantly by capital.

Two other special tax provisions relating to income from capital deserve notice here. One consists of the property taxes levied by state and local governments. These averaged about $10 billion per year during 1953–55, with about three-quarters of this amount falling upon residences and farms, and about one-quarter falling on commercial and industrial property.[18] The other provision is the exclusion from personal income subject to tax of the imputed net rent on owner-occupied dwellings. The official national income statistics of the United States estimate the value of this net rent to have been slightly over $5 billion per year in the period 1953–55.[19] We may estimate that at least $1 billion of potential tax yield is foregone by the government as a result of the failure to tax imputed rent.

Taking all four special provisions together, we may estimate that non-corporate capital is liable in the first instance to no more than $6.5 billion ($7.5 billion of property taxes minus at least $1 billion of

[18] United States Bureau of the Census, *Statistical Abstract of the United States*, 1960 (Washington: Government Printing Office, 1960), p. 417.

[19] United States Department of Commerce, *U.S. Income and Output* (Washington: Government Printing Office, 1958), p. 229.

tax forgiveness on net rent) of special taxes. Corporate capital, on the other hand, is liable to at least $17.5 billion ($20 billion of corporation income tax plus $2.5 billion of property taxes minus at most $5 billion in personal tax offsets due to the capital gains provisions). Since there are roughly equal amounts of capital in each of the two sectors, it is clear that corporate capital is taxed substantially more heavily than non-corporate capital. To get at the incidence of the roughly $24 billion accruing to the government on account of all four special provisions taken together, we can break up the problem into two parts. The $6.5 billion paid by non-corporate capital together with the first $6.5 billion paid by corporate capital function in roughly the same way as would a flat-rate, across-the-board tax on all capital. So long as the total supply of capital is not sensitive to changes in the net rate of return in the relevant range, capital will bear the full burden of this $13 billion. The remaining $11 billion paid by corporate capital is not matched by any corresponding tax on non-corporate capital. This can be treated as a special levy on corporate capital, over and above the flat-rate levy on all capital represented by the $6.5 billion figure above. The analysis of the incidence of this special levy would follow exactly the same lines as my analysis in the main body of this paper of the incidence of the corporation income tax. This leads to the conclusion that the bulk of the $11 billion is probably also borne by capital.

To sum up this survey of the impact of other tax provisions relating to capital we can say that no more than a quarter of the burden of the corporation income tax is offset as a result of the capital gains provisions. The fact that property taxes strike non-corporate capital more heavily than corporate capital mitigates, to a limited extent, the tendency induced by the corporation tax for capital to be driven out of the corporate sector. This fact also, however, practically assures us that half or more (represented by the $13 billion figure above) of the total burden resulting from all four provisions taken together is solidly borne by capital. There remains a substantial amount of corporation tax (represented by the $11 billion figure above) that is neither offset by the capital gains provisions nor matched by the higher property taxes on non-corporate capital. It is to study the incidence of this residual amount of corporation tax that the methods outlined in this paper would apply, and I want to emphasize that the amount is substantial even when possible offsets are taken into account. In all likelihood, the proper figure would be greater than $11 billion, for I have consciously overstated the offsetting effect of the capital gains provisions and understand the amount by which the imputed rent provisions reduce the tax burden on non-corporate capital. Adjusting either of these in the appropriate direction would raise the amount of "special" taxation striking corporate capital above $11 billion. I would therefore claim that the analysis presented in the text is relevant not only for estimating the incidence of the corporation income tax itself, but also for understanding the effects of the combination of special provisions with regard to income from capital that prevails in the United States.

2. MONOPOLY ELEMENTS IN THE CORPORATE SECTOR

Several readers of the original draft of this paper have been disturbed by the assumption of competition in the corporate sector. Rather than attempt to argue for the applicability of this assumption, I propose here to outline how the analysis of the paper can be adjusted to accommodate the presence of monopoly elements in the corporate sector. I shall leave untouched as much of the basic model as possible: production functions, demand functions, the equalization of returns to labor and to capital in the two sectors all remain as before. Monopoly elements are introduced by means of a "monopoly markup," M, which represents the percentage by which the price charged by the monopoly firm exceeds unit cost including the equilibrium return on capital.

It is important to realize at this point that I am not treating the entire corporate sector as one huge monopoly firm. If it were such, it could surely extract a huge monopoly markup from consumers in the economy, to say nothing of the gains it could achieve through the monopsony power that such a great aggregate could wield in the markets for labor and capital. M is kept down to modest size by the existence of many independent firms within the corporate sector; by the availability, elsewhere in the corporate sector, of reasonably close substitutes for the products of any one firm; and by the perennial threat of new entry into any field in which the monopoly markup is large. The strength of these forces, which determine what M will be, is not likely to be altered by the imposition or removal of a corporation income tax. Thus M is assumed to be the same in the pre-tax and the post-tax situations.

The effects of introducing monopoly elements can be seen quite clearly in a simple example similar to that of Section II above. Suppose that consumers always spend 50 per cent of their income on X, the corporate product, and 50 per cent on Y, the noncorporate product, and that production of both X and Y is governed by Cobb-Douglas production functions in which the exponents applying to labor and capital are each one-half. Suppose, moreover, that the monopoly markup in X is 25 per cent. These assumptions dictate that 50 per cent of the national income is spent on Y, of which half goes to labor and half to capital; and that 50 per cent of the national income is spent on X, of which $\frac{2}{5}$ goes to labor, $\frac{2}{5}$ to capital, and $\frac{1}{5}$ is monopoly profit.

Imposing a corporation income tax of 50 per cent on the profits of industry X (including the monopoly profits, of course), will not alter the fractions of the national income spent on X and Y, nor the shares earned by labor in X and Y, and by capital in Y. It will also not alter the gross earnings of capital in X, or the gross amount of monopoly profit. But net earnings on capital in industry X will be reduced by the tax from 20 per cent to 10 per cent of the national income, and net monopoly profits will be reduced by the tax from 10 per cent to 5 per cent of the national income. The distribution of capital between the two industries will change so as to equalize net returns. Whereas before the tax $\frac{4}{9}$ of the capital stock was located in industry X, after the tax only $\frac{2}{7}$ of the capital stock would be occupied there.

The only difference between this example and that of Section II is that here the tax bites into monopoly profits as well as into the return on capital as such. It is no longer quite proper to say that the tax is exclusively borne by capital, but it is proper to say that the tax is exclusively borne by profits (in the broad sense of the term which includes interest, rent, return on equities, and monopoly profits).

It is also quite straightforward to incorporate the monopoly markup into the more general model of section V. Of the basic equations (1) through (9), only (7) is altered. It becomes:

$$dp_x = [f_L dp_L + f_k(dp_k + T)](1+M). \qquad (7')$$

In the reduction of the system to equations (10), (3″) and (4′), only (10) is altered. It becomes:

$$Ef_k(1+M)T = E[g_k - f_k(1+M)]\,dp_k + f_L\frac{dL_x}{L_x} + f_k\frac{dK_x}{K_x}. \qquad (10')$$

Finally, the solution for dp_k, given in equation (12), now becomes:

$$dp_k = \frac{Ef_k(1+M)\left(\frac{K_x}{K_y} - \frac{L_x}{L_y}\right) + S_x\left(f_L\frac{K_x}{K_y} + f_k\frac{L_x}{L_y}\right)}{E[g_k - f_k(1+M)]\left(\frac{K_x}{K_y} - \frac{L_x}{L_y}\right) - S_y - S_x\left(f_L\frac{K_x}{K_y} + f_k\frac{L_x}{L_y}\right)}\cdot T. \qquad (12')$$

Comparison of (12′) with (12) reveals that the determinants of the incidence of the corporation income tax play essentially the same roles in the "monopoly" case as they did in the competitive case treated in the text. And for plausible values of the key parameters and ratios, the magnitude of dp_k/T is not likely to be very sensitive to a change in the value of M from zero to something like 0.05 or 0.1 or 0.2.

A word should be said, however, about the interpretation of T in the monopoly case. Recall that the basic model treats T as a specific tax per unit of capital. If such a tax were in fact levied, it would not strike monopoly profits as such. If, however, a tax of a given percentage, t, is levied on all profits in the corporate sector, it will strike monopoly profits as well as the normal return to capital. Its total yield will be $t(MXp_x + K_x p_k')$, where the magnitudes in parentheses are measured in the post-tax situation, and p_k' represents the gross-of-tax price of capital in industry X. To fit such a tax into our model, it is convenient to view it as two different taxes: one, a direct tax taking a percentage t of all monopoly profits, and the other, a specific tax at the rate $T = tp_k'$ per unit of capital in industry X. The incidence of the first tax is purely upon monopoly profits. Equation (12′) gives us the answer to the incidence of the second tax.

We may summarize the results of this note as follows: the main effect of introducing monopoly elements in the corporate sector is that now a corporation income tax of the usual type will fall on monopoly profits as well as on the ordinary return to capital. The part that falls on monopoly profits will be borne by them. The part, however, that falls on the ordinary return to capital in the corporate sector will introduce a disequilibrium in the capital market. To restore a full equilibrium in factor and product markets, the distribution of factors of production between the corporate and noncorporate sectors, the relative quantities of the two classes of products, and the relative prices of factors and products will all typically change. The ultimate resting place of the part of the burden of the tax that is not directly borne by monopoly profits will be determined by a mechanism that differs only in minute detail from that which determines the incidence of the corporation income tax in the competitive case.

[21]

Journal of Public Economics 1 (1972) 323–338. © North-Holland Publishing Company

INCOME TAX EVASION: A THEORETICAL ANALYSIS

Michael G. ALLINGHAM and Agnar SANDMO *

University of Pennsylvania, Philadelphia, U.S.A. and
The Norwegian School of Economics and Business Administration, Bergen, Norway

First version received May 1972, revised version received August 1972

1. Introduction

Theoretical analysis of the connection between taxation and risk-taking has mainly been concerned with the effect of taxes on portfolio decisions of consumers, Mossin (1968b) and Stiglitz (1969). However, there are some problems which are not naturally classified under this heading and which, although of considerable practical interest, have been left out of the theoretical discussions. One such problem is tax evasion. This takes many forms, and one can hardly hope to give a completely general analysis of all these. Our objective in this paper is therefore the more limited one of analyzing the individual taxpayer's decision on whether and to what extent to avoid taxes by deliberate underreporting. On the one hand our approach is related to the studies of economics of criminal activity, as e.g. in the papers by Becker (1968) and by Tulkens and Jacquemin (1971). On the other hand it is related to the analysis of optimal portfolio and insurance policies in the economics of uncertainty, as in the work by Arrow (1970), Mossin (1968a) and several others.

We shall start by considering a simple static model where this decision is the only one with which the individual is concerned, so that we ignore the interrelationships that probably exist with other types of economic choices. After a detailed study of this simple case (sections

* Tax evasion as a topic for theoretical investigation was suggested by J.A. Mirrlees (1971) in a paper prepared for the International Economic Association's Workshop in Economic Theory, which was held in Bergen in the summer of 1971. This provided us with the initial stimulus to write the present article. We have received valuable comments and suggestions from A.B. Atkinson, Karl Borch, Jacques Drèze, Leif Johansen and a referee.

2–4) we proceed with an analysis of the dynamic case where the individual has to make a sequence of tax declaration decisions (section 5). We conclude (section 6) with an informal discussion of some further problems in this field, including the optimal design of tax systems.

2. The nature of the optimum

The tax declaration decision is a decision under uncertainty. The reason for this is that failure to report one's full income to the tax authorities does not automatically provoke a reaction in the form of a penalty. The taxpayer has the choice between two main strategies: (1) He may declare his actual income. (2) He may declare less than his actual income. If he chooses the latter strategy his payoff will depend on whether or not he is investigated by the tax authorities. If he is not, he is clearly better off than under strategy (1). If he is, he is worse off. The choice of a strategy is therefore a non-trivial one.

We shall assume that the tax-payer's behaviour conforms to the Von Neumann–Morgenstern axioms for behaviour under uncertainty. His cardinal utility function has income as its only argument; this must be understood as the indirect utility function with constant prices. Marginal utility will be assumed to be everywhere positive and strictly decreasing, so that the individual is risk averse.

Actual income, W, is exogenously given and is known by the taxpayer but not by the government's tax collector.[1] Tax is levied at a constant rate, θ, on declared income, X, which is the taxpayer's decision variable. However, with some probability p the taxpayer will be subjected to investigation by the tax authorities, who will then get to know the exact amount of his actual income. It this happens the taxpayer will have to pay tax on the undeclared amount, W-X, at a penalty rate π which is higher than θ.

This formal representation of the taxpayer's choice situation is in some ways a significant simplification of his real world situation; in particular, the present formulation ignores some of the uncertainty elements. First, it abstracts from the fact that the tax laws to some

[1] The analysis would be essentially unchanged if we were to assume (more realistically) that a part of the actual income were known by the government. Clearly, it would never pay to try to avoid taxes on that part, so the analysis would then be valid for that part of actual income which is unknown by the government.

extent leave it to the discretion of the courts to determine whether the penalty will be of the type discussed here or take the form of a jail sentence; it may also be a combination of both. Second, even if jail is not an alternative, the penalty rate θ may itself be uncertain from the point of view of the taxpayer. Even though we ignore these points, we hope to have retained enough of the structure of the problem to make the theoretical analysis worthwhile.

The taxpayer will now choose X so as to maximize

$$E[U] = (1-p)\,U(W-\theta X) + pU(W-\theta X-\pi(W-X))\,. \tag{1}$$

For notational convenience we define

$$\begin{aligned} Y &= W-\theta X\,,\\ Z &= W-\theta X-\pi(W-X)\,. \end{aligned} \tag{2}$$

The first-order condition for an interior maximum of (1) can then be written as

$$-\theta(1-p)\,U'(Y)-(\theta-\pi)\,pU'(Z)=0\,. \tag{3}$$

The second-order condition

$$D=\theta^2(1-p)\,U''(Y)+(\theta-\pi)^2pU''(Z)\,, \tag{4}$$

is satisfied by the assumption of concavity of the utility function.

In this analysis the conditions for an interior maximum to exist are of particular importance. Clearly, it cannot be assumed a priori that $0 < X < W$, because whether or not this will be true, should depend on the values of the parameters. To see what conditions on parameter values are required for an interior solution we evaluate expected utility at $X = 0$ and $X = W$. Since expected marginal utility is decreasing with X, we must have that

$$\left.\frac{\partial E[U]}{\partial X}\right|_{X=0} = -\theta(1-p)\,U'(W)-(\theta-\pi)\,pU'(W(1-\pi)) > 0 \tag{5}$$

and

$$\left.\frac{\partial E[U]}{\partial X}\right|_{X=W} = -\theta(1-p)\,U'(W(1-\theta)) - (\theta-\pi)pU'(W(1-\theta)) < 0\,. \tag{6}$$

These conditions can be rewritten as

$$p\pi > \theta\left[p + (1-p)\,\frac{U'(W)}{U'(W(1-\theta))}\right], \tag{5'}$$

$$p\pi < \theta\,. \tag{6'}$$

(6′) implies that the taxpayer will declare less than his actual income if the expected tax payment on undeclared income is less than the regular rate. Since the bracketed factor in (5′) is obviously positive and less than one, the two conditions do give us a set of positive parameter values which will guarantee an interior solution. It is with such solutions that we shall be concerned in later selections.

This is a very simple theory, and it may perhaps be criticized for giving too little attention to nonpecuniary factors in the taxpayer's decision on whether or not to evade taxes. It need hardly be stressed that in addition to the income loss there may be other factors affecting utility if one's attempt at tax evasion is detected. These factors may perhaps be summarily characterized as affecting adversely one's reputation as a citizen of the community; we may represent this by an additional variable, s, in the utility function. We now write expected utility as

$$E[U] = (1-p)\,U(Y,s_0) + pU(Z,s_1)\,. \tag{7}$$

Thus, the variable s takes on different values according to what state of the world obtains (whether or not the evasion is detected). As a convention we assume $U(Y, s_0) > U(Y, s_1)$. The first-order condition is then

$$-\theta(1-p)\,U_1(Y,s_0) - (\theta-\pi)pU_1(Z,s_1) = 0\,, \tag{8}$$

where U_1 now denotes the derivative of U with respect to the income variable. Of special interest is now the condition on parameter values which must hold for $X < W$. Proceeding as in the cases studied above we obtain this condition as

$$p\pi < \theta \left[p + (1-p) \frac{U_1(W(1-\theta), s_0)}{U_1(W(1-\theta), s_1)} \right] . \tag{9}$$

Observe first that (9) reduces to (6′) if $U_1(W(1-\theta), s_0) = U_1(W(1-\theta), s_1)$, so that a change in the state variable leaves the *marginal* utility of income unaffected. The most natural assumption is perhaps $U_1(W(1-\theta), s_0) < U_1(W(1-\theta), s_1)$; a better reputation decreases the marginal utility of income so that "reputation" and income are substitutes in the cardinal sense. This would make the expression in brackets in (9) less than one and the right-hand side of the inequality less than θ, so that the condition for "profitable" tax evasion would become stricter. Depending on the value of $U_1(W(1-\theta), s_0)/U_1(W(1-\theta), s_1)$, one might observe different "break-even" values of the parameters for different taxpayers.[2]

3. Comparative static results

We shall now examine the way in which reported income depends on the parameters of the model, W, θ, π and p. We shall do this using the simpler of the two models above, in which the only argument in the taxpayer's utility function is his net income. This does represent some simplification of the argument compared to the alternative model, in so far as the various derivatives with respect to income will depend upon the value of s. The reader will notice that some but not all of our results are affected by this simplification. Moreover, if the reader is prepared to accept the view that the influence on e.g. the relative risk aversion function of a change in s is insignificant compared to the effect of a change in income, then the results reported here can be seen as approximative results for the more complicated model.

We shall make use of the well-known Arrow–Pratt risk aversion measures to evaluate our results. These are the absolute and the relative risk aversion functions, defined as

$$R_A(Y) = -\frac{U''(Y)}{U'(Y)}, \qquad R_R(Y) = -\frac{U''(Y)Y}{U'(Y)}, \tag{10}$$

[2] One should be aware that in a cross-section of taxpayers θ and π might also vary considerably if they are interpreted as *marginal* tax rates. One might also expect the subjective assessment of the probability of detection to differ a lot between taxpayers.

respectively. (The functions could of course equally well have been written with Z or any income variable as the argument.)

There seems to be a general presumption that absolute risk aversion is decreasing with income; the case of relative risk aversion is more complicated, and we shall not commit ourselves to any specific hypothesis as to its shape.[3] Differentiating (3) with respect to W and solving for $\partial X/\partial W$, we obtain

$$\frac{\partial X}{\partial W}=\frac{1}{D}\Big[\theta(1-p)\,U''(Y)+(\theta-\pi)(1-\pi)\,pU''(Z)\Big]\,. \tag{11}$$

Substituting from (3) we can rewrite this as

$$\frac{\partial X}{\partial W}=-\frac{1}{D}\,\theta(1-p)\,U'(Y)\left[-\frac{U''(Y)}{U'(Y)}+(1-\pi)\,\frac{U''(Z)}{U'(Z)}\right]$$

or, using (10),

$$\frac{\partial X}{\partial W}=-\frac{1}{D}\,\theta(1-p)\,U'(Y)[R_A(Y)-(1-\pi)R_A(Z)]\,. \tag{12}$$

On the assumption of decreasing absolute risk aversion $R_A(Y)<R_A(Z)$. However, the sign of the bracketed expression depends on the value of π. Only in the case of $\pi\geqslant 1$ can we conclude that the derivative is unambigously positive.

It is perhaps of somewhat greater interest to study the sign of the derivative $\partial(X/W)/\partial W$; i.e. how does the fraction of actual income declared vary as actual income changes? Since we have that

$$\frac{\partial(X/W)}{\partial W}=\frac{1}{W^2}\left(\frac{\partial X}{\partial W}W-X\right),$$

we can substitute from (11) and (4) to obtain

[3] For a lucid discussion of these measures see Arrow (1970). They have been used in the analysis of taxation and risk-taking by Mossin (1968b) and Stiglitz (1969).

$$\frac{\partial(X/W)}{\partial W} = \frac{1}{W^2}\frac{1}{D}\Big[\theta(1-p)\,U''(Y)W + (\theta-\pi)(1-\pi)pU''(Z)W$$

$$-\,\theta^2(1-p)\,U''(Y)X - (\theta-\pi)^2pU''(Z)X\Big]\,.$$

Collecting terms and substituting from (2) we can write

$$\frac{\partial(X/W)}{\partial W} = \frac{1}{W^2}\frac{1}{D}\,[\theta(1-p)\,U''(Y)Y + (\theta-\pi)pU''(Z)Z]\ .$$

We can now substitute in this expression from the first-order condition (3). This yields

$$\frac{\partial(X/W)}{\partial W} = -\frac{1}{W^2}\frac{1}{D}\,\theta(1-p)\,U'(Y)[R_R(Y) - R_R(Z)]\ . \qquad (13)$$

We can then conclude that when actual income varies, the fraction declared increases, stays constant or decreases according as relative risk aversion is an increasing, constant or decreasing function of income.

It is not easy to select one of these hypotheses about the relative risk aversion function as the most realistic one. We shall therefore be content with adding this result to those of a similar nature that already exist in the economics of uncertainty. However, it is of some interest in itself to observe that even a model a simple as the present one does not generate any simple result concerning the relationship between income and tax evasion.

We now differentiate (3) with respect to θ. This yields

$$\frac{\partial X}{\partial\theta} = -\frac{1}{D}X[\theta(1-p)\,U''(Y) + (\theta-\pi)pU''(Z)]$$

$$+\frac{1}{D}\,[(1-p)\,U'(Y) + pU'(Z)]\ .$$

Substituting from (3) we can rewrite this as

$$\frac{\partial X}{\partial\theta} = \frac{1}{D}\,X\theta(1-p)\,U'(Y)[R_A(Y) - R_A(Z)]$$

$$+\frac{1}{D}\,[(1-p)\,U'(Y) + pU'(Z)]\ . \qquad (14)$$

The second of the two terms on the right is unambiguously negative. The first term is positive, zero or negative according as absolute risk aversion is decreasing, constant or increasing. Of these decreasing absolute risk aversion seems to be the most attractive assumption, but we must then conclude that no clearcut hypothesis emerges as to the connection between the regular tax rate and reported income.

The economic meaning of this result is best seen if we regard the two terms in (14) as the income effect and the substitution effect, respectively. The latter is negative because an increase in the tax rate makes it more profitable to evade taxes on the margin. The former is positive because an increased tax rate makes the tax payer less wealthy, reducing both Y and Z for any level of X, and this, under decreasing absolute risk aversion, tends to reduce evasion.

The next question we investigate is how reported income depends on the penalty rate. From (3) we get

$$\frac{\partial X}{\partial \pi} = -\frac{1}{D}(W-X)(\theta-\pi)pU''(Z) - \frac{1}{D}pU'(Z)\,. \qquad (15)$$

These terms are both positive, so that an increase in the penalty rate will always increase the fraction of actual income declared.

Finally, we differentiate (3) with respect to p to obtain

$$\frac{\partial X}{\partial p} = \frac{1}{D}\left[-\theta U'(Y) + (\theta-\pi)\,U'(Z)\right]\,. \qquad (16)$$

This derivative is positive; an increase in the probability of detection will always lead to a larger income being declared.

Summing up the comparative static analysis of our model, we may note that although it does not yield any clear-cut results in the analysis of changes in actual income and in the tax rate, unambiguous results can be derived for the two parameters of the model which are of particular interest for policy purposes in this field, viz. the penalty rate and the probability of detection. The former is a parameter over which the tax authority exercises direct control; the latter it may be assumed to control indirectly through the amount and efficiency of resources spent on detecting tax evasion. The model implies that these two policy tools are substitutes for each other. While the expected tax yield would fall with a decrease of p, the loss of tax revenue could be compensated by an increase of π.

4. Variable probability of detection

We have assumed the probability of detection to be exogenously given to the individual taxpayer; consequently it is independent of the amount of income he reports. This may not be entirely satisfactory, but a natural hypothesis on the nature of the dependence does not immediately suggest itself. If we write $p = p(X)$, should $p'(X)$ be positive or negative? On the one hand the tax authorities might believe that the rich are most likely to evade taxes, thus making $p'(X) > 0$. On the other hand they might base their policy on the statistical hypothesis that in the absence of any knowledge about actual income, a person with a low reported income is more likely to be an evader; the tax authorities would then formulate a rule according to which $p'(X) < 0$.

It seems difficult to choose between these two hypotheses unless we introduce the further assumption that although the tax authorities do not know the taxpayer's actual income they do know his profession, and they have some ideas about normal incomes in the various professions. They would then formulate a $p(X)$ function for each profession, and each such function would have $p'(X) < 0$; a person reporting an income below the average of his profession is more likely to be investigated than one reporting an income above the average. This might well be consistent with the first of the two hypotheses mentioned above, since the $p(X)$ functions might shift upward with increasing average professional income. Within our framework of individual choice $p'(X) < 0$ seems the more natural hypothesis and will be adopted in the following.

It is interesting to see how this added complication affects our comparative static results. Expected utility must now be written as

$$E[U] = [1 - p(X)]\, U(Y) + p(X)\, U(Z)\,, \tag{17}$$

and the first-order condition becomes

$$\begin{aligned} &-p'(X)\, U(Y) - \theta[1 - p(X)]\, U'(Y) \\ &+p'(X)\, U(Z) - (\theta - \pi)\, p(X)\, U'(Z) = 0\,. \end{aligned} \tag{18}$$

One small problem arises now because the dependence of p on X might create non-concavities in $E[U]$. Although we shall only be concerned with local properties of $E[U]$ we may as well eliminate this problem by assuming very naturally that $p''(X) \geqslant 0$. Then all terms in the second-order derivative, which we shall now write as D^*, will be negative.

We now limit ourselves to an investigation of the effect of changes in the two policy parameters which are presumably most relevant for the control of tax evasion, viz. the penalty rate and the probability of detection. Differentiating (18) with respect to π yields

$$\frac{\partial X}{\partial \pi} = -\frac{1}{D^*}(W-X)(\theta-\pi)p(X)U''(Z) - \frac{1}{D^*}p(X)U'(Z) + \frac{1}{D^*}(W-X)p'(X)U'(Z)\,. \tag{19}$$

The first two terms on the right correspond to the two terms in (15) and are both positive. The dependence of p on X adds a third term which is also unambiguously positive. The conclusion from the simpler model therefore carries over; a rise in the penalty rate will lead to an increase in declared income.

Our previous derivative $\partial X/\partial p$ has no direct counterpart in the present model, since p is now endogenously determined. However, it is possible to study a shift in the $p(X)$ function, e.g. by writing it as $p(X) + \epsilon$, differentiating with respect to ϵ and evaluating the derivative at $\epsilon = 0$. The result is then

$$\frac{\partial X}{\partial \epsilon} = \frac{1}{D^*}[-\theta U'(Y) + (\theta-\pi)U'(Z)]\,, \tag{20}$$

which is an expression of exactly the same form as the previous one in (16) and therefore positive. A positive shift in the $p(X)$ function will increase declared income and reduce tax evasion.

5. The dynamic case

We now leave the problem where the individual has only to make one declaration, or where his problems in different time periods are independent, and consider the more general case where the individual must make a sequence of (interrelated) decisions. Essentially, the problem arises because it is plausible that if the individual is discovered cheating today he will be investigated, and thus if he was cheating discovered, for yesterday.

The purpose of this section is to investigate the dynamic rather than the comparative static aspects of his declarations: for example whether for fixed parameters (tax rates, etc.) his declarations will increase or decrase over time, rather than whether in a fixed period the declaration will increase or decrase if a parameter is changed. The latter question is still of interest, but as it may be investigated using the methods of the previous sections is not discussed here.

We work in discrete time, and to simplify the analysis we assume that the individual has an infinite life expectancy; as we shall see the individual breaks his planning period down into a number of finite length subperiods, so this involves no serious loss of generality – except for the individual who would be near the end of his life. To abstract from other problems we will also assume that the individual has no time preference, and does not anticipate or postpone income by borrowing or saving.

To formalize our rationale for examining the dynamic problem we continue to assume that there is a fixed probability p of the individual's being discovered in period t evading tax in that period, if he does evade. However, if he is discovered in period t he is now investigated, and therefore discovered, for all preceding periods back to the time when he last paid the full amount – either voluntarily or because he was discovered. The individual has a fixed income in all periods, which, as we no longer change, we shall normalize to unity; he may, however, vary the amount he declares X_t in each period t (measured from some time when a full declaration was last made), provided that he neither declares a negative income nor more than he receives, that is $0 \leqslant X_t \leqslant 1$. Now if the individual is not discovered in period t his post tax income is simply

$$Y_t = 1 - \theta X_t \,, \tag{21}$$

while if he is discovered he must pay a penalty on all he has evaded since the time when he last paid the full amount, so his post-tax income is

$$Z_t = 1 - \theta X_t - \Pi \sum_{\tau=1}^{t} (1 - X_\tau) \,. \tag{22}$$

Such a penalty rule is clearly arbitrary, but is not without interest. Investigation is obviously costly for the authorities (or otherwise $p = 1$), and a plausible rule-of-thumb for rationing these investigations would be to make a preliminary random investigation in each period, and then continue investigating backwards as long as this yielded some revenue, stopping when it did not. Our rule would be consistent with such behaviour. We latter comment on the alternative of investigating the entire past of a discovered evader, but ignore the possibility of his being discovered today affecting his future p.

The problem involves interrelationships between declarations at different times in two ways: firstly today's decision must be influenced by past declarations, since these determine the penalty if caught; and secondly, a decision to cheat today involves mortgaging the future, since the stochastic penalty is in effect delayed. Before considering the consistent individual who appreciates both of these interdepencies it is constructive to consider the simpler case of the myopic individual who appreciates only the first.

The myopic individual then ignores the effect of his actions today on his future, and as he must take the past as given he is essentially in a static framework. This case is, however, worth a brief examination here as the form of the problem is slightly different to that of the static problem (specifically the penalty is no longer proportional to the underdeclaration), and also as it simply illustrates the concepts we shall be interested in.

The questions we shall consider are the following: (1) whether the individual will initially make a partial underdeclaration, that is whether $0 < X < 1$; (2) whether in some period, say T, he will declare his full income, that is whether there exists a T such that $X_T = 1$; and (3) whether his declarations will increase (or decrease) over time, that is whether $X_t > X_s$ for $t > s$. These three properties essentially define the qualitative nature of his declaration path over time.

Since the myopic individual ignores the future and must take the past as given he maximizes, in each period t, the expected value of his utility level in that period, that is

$$E[U_t] = (1-p)\,U(Y_t) + pU(Z_t)\,, \tag{23}$$

where Y_t (post-tax income if not discovered) and Z_t (post-tax income if discovered) are as defined above.

We first note that for $t = 1$ we have $Y_1 = 1 - \theta X_1$ and $Z_1 = 1 - \theta X_1 - \Pi(1 - X_1)$, so the problem is identical to the static case. It follows that there will be situations where an initial partial underdeclaration is made, which answers our first question; these are the interesting cases which we shall consider.

To answer our second question we first show that X_t does not tend asymptotically to 1 (for we later require $\inf \{1 - X_t\} > 0$). If $X_t < 1$ for all t it is clear that

$$(1-p)\,U(Y_t) + pU(Z_t) > U(1-\theta)\,. \tag{24}$$

Then taking $t \to \infty$ we would have, if $X_t \to 1$,

$$pU\Big(1 - \theta - \Pi \sum_{1}^{\infty} (1-X_\tau)\Big) > pU(1-\theta)\,,$$

which would imply $\Sigma_1^\infty\ (1 - X_\tau) < 0$, which is impossible as $X_t < 1$. Having cleared up this minor point we now show that the left side of (24) tends to minus infinity; since the right side is constant this means that (24) cannot hold for all t, so that at some t, $X_t = 1$. The first term $(1 - p)\ U\ (Y_t) \leqslant (1 - p)\ U\ (1)$ is clearly bounded. In the second we have

$$Z_t = 1 - \theta X_t - \Pi \sum_{1}^{t} (1-X_\tau) \leqslant 1 - \theta X_t - \Pi t K \to -\infty\,,$$

where $K = \inf \{1 - X_\tau\} > 0$; it follows that the second term itself, $U(Z_t)$, and thus the left side, tend to minus infinity.

The answer to our third question is in the affirmative, that is declarations increase over time. To show this we first digress to consider our simple static model with a fixed penalty C, so we have $Z = 1 - \theta X - \Pi(1 - X) - C$, rather than $Z = 1 - \theta X - \Pi(1 - X)$. Proceeding as in section 3 we may obtain the effect of a change in this fixed penalty as

$$\frac{\partial X}{\partial C} = -\frac{1}{D}(\theta - \Pi)\,pU''(Z) > 0\,.$$

By integrating it follows that if $C' > C$ then $X' > X$ (providing X and X' are both interior solutions). The relevance of this to our problem is immediate, for the passage of time is equivalent to the increase of a fixed penalty; this is because we may always write Z_t as $1 - \theta X_t - \Pi(1-X_t) - C_t$ where $C_t = \Pi \sum_1^{t-1} (1-X_\tau)$. Since $C_{t+1} = C_t + \Pi(1-X_t) > C_t$ it follows that $X_{t+1} > X_t$.

We now turn to the consistent individual, and recall that the essential difference between this and the myopic is that the consistent appreciates that by cheating today he is placing himself in a worse position tomorrow. Because of this we may obtain at least intuitive ideas on his declaration path from that of the myopic individual.

Since the individual considers the whole of the future he maximizes lifetime utility, which we specify to take the simple form $\sum_1^\infty E[U_t]$. When this infinite sum does not converge, which will typically be the case, we specify that he maximizes $1/T \sum_1^T E[U_t]$, where T is some time which divides the future into independent periods; specifically, $E[U_s]$ is independent of X_t if $s \leqslant T < t$. Clearly T will be the period when the individual first plans to declare his full income, or alternatively is discovered. For this to be well-defined we must of course ensure that $T < \infty$, but this is simply our second question, which we consider below.

First, however, we note that an initial partial underdeclaration is possible, so $0 < X_1 < 1$, or equivalently, $T > 1$. This may be shown in exactly the same way as in the static or myopic cases.

To answer our second question, we use the analysis for the myopic individual. If in some period t the taxpayer declares his full income the sum of his future expected utilities is

$$[U(1-\theta)] + [(1-p)\,U(1-\theta X_{t+1}) + pU(1-\theta X_{t+1} - \Pi(1-X_{t+1}))] + \dots , \tag{25}$$

while if $X_t < 1$ the corresponding sum, if he is not discovered in period t, is

$$[(1-p)\,U(Y_t) + pU(Z_t)] + [(1-p)\,U(1-\theta X'_{t+1}) + pU(1-\theta X'_{t+1} - \Pi(1-X'_{t+1}) - \Pi \sum_1^t (1-X_\tau))] + \dots \tag{26}$$

though if he is discovered it is

$$[(1-p)\,U(Y_t)+pU(Z_t)]$$
$$+\,[(1-p)\,U(1-\theta X''_{t+1})+pU(1-\theta X''_{t+1}-\Pi(1-X''_{t+1}))]\;+\;\dots\,. \tag{27}$$

In these expressions X_{t+1}, X'_{t+1}, and X''_{t+1} are the respective optimal declarations in period $t+1$; of course he only knows if he is discovered in period t at the end of that period, so the probabilistic nature of the first terms in (26) and (27) make sense. In parallel with the myopic individual it is clear that T is finite if the individual terms of (25) are not less than the corresponding terms of both (26) and (27), with strict inequality from some term. Now it is clear that the second term in (26) is less than the second term in (25), for it is the highest expected utility level achievable with the positive fixed penalty $\Pi\Sigma_1^t(1-X_\tau)$ as opposed to that achievable with zero fixed penalty; the second term in (27) is of course equal to that in (25). This argument may be repeated for all subsequent terms, so the (weak inequality) condition is fulfilled for all terms beyond the first. For the first term, however, the myopic argument immediately tells us that the (strong inequality) condition is fulfilled for some t. It follows that T is finite.

An interesting corollary to this, apart from the choice process being well-defined, is that the consistent individual will always declare more than the myopic: it is then indeed "short-sighted to evade taxes". Finally, if the individual knows that once he is discovered his whole past will be investigated, his behaviour is straightforward: he will act exactly as he would in the case we have considered until period T, and thereafter declare everything.

6. Concluding remarks

We have examined some static and dynamic aspects of the decision to evade income taxes. The model we have used is clearly rather special, and we can claim no more for it than that it seems to yield some insight into the structure of the problem. We also hope that the approach will suggest other topics for research in the field, both theoretical and empirical.

Of theoretical topics the ones which immediately suggest themselves are perhaps various generalizations of the present model. One possibility is to extend the model to take account of labour supply decisions;

one might hope to discover some interesting connections between incentives to avoid taxes and to supply work effort. However, although we have studied this case, we have not been able to come up with any interesting and reasonably simple results. Another possible extension would be to incorporate saving and portfolio decisions. It might also be worthwhile to analyze more complicated income tax schemes than the simple proportional case which we have examined.

It would also be of interest to see a discussion of tax evasion within the framework of optimal taxation theory. This theory assumes of course that there is no evasion whatever. One conclusion which is classic is that to promote an efficient allocation of resources taxes should be levied primarily on commodities that are inelastic in demand or supply. In particular, it seems to be widely agreed that an income tax is the best means by which to effect a redistribution of incomes if labour is perfectly inelastic in supply. This conclusion stands in obvious need of modification if it is realized that an income tax probably offers much larger opportunities for tax evasion than commodity taxes do. The policy tools available to the government for the purpose of counteracting the tendency to evasion are the tax rates themselves, the penalty rates and the expenditure on investigation, which determines the probability of being detected. To assess the efficiency of these tools one would need empirical estimates of the effects discussed in this paper.

References

Arrow, K.J., 1970, Essays in the theory of risk-bearing (North-Holland, ch. 3).

Becker, G.S., 1968, Crime and punishment: an economic approach, Journal of Political Economy 76, 169–217.

Mirrlees, J.A., 1971, Notes on some special cases of the taxation of risk-taking, mimeographed.

Mossin, J., 1968a, Aspects of rational insurance purchasing, Journal of Political Economy 76, 553–568.

Mossin, J., 1968b, Taxation and risk-taking: an expected utility approach, Economica 35, 74–82.

Stiglitz, J.E., 1969, The effects of income, wealth and capital gains taxation on risk-taking, Quarterly Journal of Economics 83, 263–283.

Tulkens, H. and A. Jacquemin, 1971, The cost of delinquency: a problem of optimal allocation of private and public expenditure (CORE Discussion Paper 7133).

[22]

A Rational Theory of the Size of Government

Allan H. Meltzer and Scott F. Richard

Carnegie-Mellon University

In a general equilibrium model of a labor economy, the size of government, measured by the share of income redistributed, is determined by majority rule. Voters rationally anticipate the disincentive effects of taxation on the labor-leisure choices of their fellow citizens and take the effect into account when voting. The share of earned income redistributed depends on the voting rule and on the distribution of productivity in the economy. Under majority rule, the equilibrium tax share balances the budget and pays for the voters' choices. The principal reasons for increased size of government implied by the model are extensions of the franchise that change the position of the decisive voter in the income distribution and changes in relative productivity. An increase in mean income relative to the income of the decisive voter increases the size of government.

I. Introduction

The share of income allocated by government differs from country to country, but the share has increased in all countries of western Europe and North America during the past 25 years (Nutter 1978). In the United States, in Britain, and perhaps elsewhere, the rise in tax payments relative to income has persisted for more than a century (Peacock and Wiseman 1961; Meltzer and Richard 1978). There is, as

We are indebted to Karl Brunner, Dennis Epple, Peter Ordeshook, and Tom Romer for many helpful discussions and to the participants in the Carnegie-Mellon Public Economics Workshop, an anonymous referee, the editor, and the Interlaken Seminar for constructive comments on an earlier version.

[*Journal of Political Economy*, 1981, vol. 89, no. 5]

yet, no generally accepted explanation of the increase and no single accepted measure of the size of government.

In this paper, the budget is balanced.[1] We use the share of income redistributed by government, in cash and in services, as our measure of the relative size of government and develop a theory in which the government's share is set by the rational choices of utility-maximizing individuals who are fully informed about the state of the economy and the consequences of taxation and income redistribution.[2]

The issues we address have a long intellectual history. Wicksell (1958) joined the theory of taxation to the theory of individual choice. His conclusion, that individual maximization requires government spending and taxes to be set by unanimous consent, reflects the absence of a mechanism for grouping individual choices to reach a collective decision. Following Downs (1957), economists turned their attention to the determination of an equilibrium choice of public goods, redistribution, and other outcomes under voting rules that do not require unanimity.

Several recent surveys of the voluminous literature on the size or growth of government are now available (see Brunner 1978; Peacock 1979; Aranson and Ordeshook 1980; and Larkey, Stolp, and Winer 1980).[3] Many of the hypotheses advanced in this literature emphasize the incentives for bureaucrats, politicians, and interest groups to increase their incomes and power by increasing spending and the control of resources or rely on specific institutional details of the budget, taxing, and legislative processes. Although such studies contribute to an understanding of the processes by which particular programs are chosen, they often neglect general equilibrium aspects. Of particular importance is the frequent failure to close many of the models by balancing the budget in real terms and considering the effect on voters of the taxes that pay for spending and redistribution (see, e.g., Olson 1965; Niskanen 1971; and Hayek 1979). A recent empirical study by Cameron (1978) suggests that decisions about the size of the budget are not the result of "fiscal illusion," so the neglect of budget balance cannot be dismissed readily.

We differ from much of the recent literature in three main ways.

[1] All variables are real. There is no inflation. Budget balance means that redistribution uses real resources. Public goods are neglected.

[2] Ideally the size of government would be measured by the net burden imposed (or removed) by government programs.

[3] Larkey et al. (1980) include a survey of previous surveys. Recent surveys by Mueller (1976) and Sahota (1978) summarize recent contributions by Downs (1957), Musgrave (1959), Olson (1965), Niskanen (1971), Buchanan and Tullock (1972), Riker and Ordeshook (1973), and others to such related topics as the determination of equilibrium collective decisions and the effects of government policies on the distribution of income.

First, voters do not suffer from "fiscal illusion" and are not myopic. They know that the government must extract resources to pay for redistribution. Second, we concentrate on the demand for redistribution and neglect any "public goods" provided by government (see also Peltzman 1979). Third, we return to the earlier tradition of de Tocqueville ([1835] 1965) who associated the size of government, measured by taxes and spending, with two factors: the spread of the franchise and the distribution of wealth (property).[4]

Our hypothesis implies that the size of government depends on the relation of mean income to the income of the decisive voter. With universal suffrage and majority rule, the median voter is the decisive voter as shown by Roberts (1977) in an extension of the well-known work of Hotelling (1929) and Downs (1957). Studies of the distribution of income show that the distribution is skewed to the right, so the mean income lies above the median income. Any voting rule that concentrates votes below the mean provides an incentive for redistribution of income financed by (net) taxes on incomes that are (relatively) high. Extensions of the franchise to include more voters below mean income increase votes for redistribution and, thus, increase this measure of the size of government.

The problem with this version of the de Tocqueville hypothesis is that it explains too much. Nothing limits the amount of redistribution or prevents the decisive voter from equalizing incomes or, at a minimum, eliminating any difference between his disposable income and the disposable income of those who earn higher incomes. Incentives have been ignored. Higher taxes and redistribution reduce the incentive to work and thereby lower earned income. Once we take account of incentives, there is a limit to the size of government. To bring together the effect of incentives, the desire for redistribution, and the absence of fiscal illusion or myopia, we develop a general equilibrium model.

Section II sets out a static model. Individuals who differ in productivity, and therefore in earned income, choose their preferred combination of consumption and leisure. Not all individuals work, but those who do pay a portion of their income in taxes. The choice between labor and leisure, and the amount of earned income and taxes, depend on the tax rate and on the size of transfer payments.

The tax rate and the amount of income redistributed depend on the voting rule and the distribution of income. Section III shows how income redistribution, taxes, and the size of the government budget

[4] We are indebted to Larkey et al. (1980) for pointing out the similarity between de Tocqueville and the conclusion we reached in an earlier version and in Meltzer and Richard (1978). De Tocqueville's distribution of property finds an echo in the concerns about "mob rule" by the writers of the Constitution.

change with the voting rule and the distribution of productivity. A conclusion summarizes the findings and main implications.

II. The Economic Environment

The economy we consider has relatively standard features. There are a large number of individuals. Each treats prices, wages, and tax rates as givens, determined in the markets for goods and labor and by the political process, respectively. Differences in the choice of labor, leisure, and consumption and differences in wages arise solely because of differences in endowments which reflect differences in productivity. In this section, we extend this standard model to capture the salient features of the process by which individuals choose to work or subsist on welfare payments and show the conditions under which these choices are uniquely determined by the tax rate.

The utility function is assumed to be a strictly concave function, $u(c, l)$, for consumption, c, and leisure, l. Consumption and leisure are normal goods, and the marginal utility of consumption or leisure is infinite when the level of consumption or leisure is zero, respectively. There is no capital and no uncertainty.

The individual's endowment consists of ability to produce, or productivity, and a unit of time that he allocates to labor, n, or leisure, $l = 1 - n$. Individual incomes reflect the differences in individual productivity and the use of a common, constant-returns-to-scale technology to produce consumption goods. An individual with productivity x earns pretax income, y:

$$y(x) = xn(x). \tag{1}$$

Income is measured in units of consumption.

Tax revenues finance lump-sum redistribution of r units of consumption per capita. Individual productivity cannot be observed directly, so taxes are levied against earned income. The tax rate, t, is a constant fraction of earned income but a declining fraction of disposable income. The fraction of income paid in taxes net of transfers, however, rises with income.[5] There is no saving; consumption equals

[5] Reliance on a linear tax follows a well-established tradition. Romer (1975) analyzed problems of unimodality using a linear tax and predetermined government spending. Roberts (1977), using a linear tax and a predetermined budget, showed that the median voter dominates the solution if incomes are ordered by productivity. Linear tax functions are used also when the social welfare function is used to determine the optimal tax (see Sheshinski 1972). The degree to which actual taxes differ from linear taxes has generated a large literature. Pechman and Okner (1974) find that the tax rate is approximately constant. King (1980) writes that most redistribution in the United States and the United Kingdom comes from the transfer system, not from the tax system. Browning and Johnson (1979) show that conclusions about proportionality of the tax rate depend heavily on assumptions used to allocate the burden of indirect business taxes.

disposable income as shown in (2):

$$c(x) = (1 - t)nx + r, \qquad c \geqslant 0. \tag{2}$$

If there are individuals without any ability to produce, $x = 0$, their consumption is $r \geqslant 0$.

Each individual is a price taker in the labor market, takes t and r as givens, and chooses n to maximize utility. The maximization problem is:

$$\max_{n \in [0,1]} u(c, l) = \max_{n \in [0,1]} u[r + nx(1 - t), 1 - n]. \tag{3}$$

The first-order condition,

$$0 = \frac{\partial u}{\partial n} = u_c[r + nx(1 - t), 1 - n]x(1 - t) - u_l[r + nx(1 - t), 1 - n], \tag{4}$$

determines the optimal labor choice, $n[r, x(1 - t)]$, for those who choose to work. The choice depends only on the size of the welfare payment, r, and the after-tax wage, $x(1 - t)$.[6]

Some people subsist on welfare payments. From (4) we know that the productivity level at which $n = 0$ is the optimal choice is

$$x_0 = \frac{u_l(r, 1)}{u_c(r, 1)(1 - t)}. \tag{5}$$

Individuals with productivity below x_0 subsist on welfare payments and choose not to work; $n = 0$ for $x \leqslant x_0$.

Increases in redistribution increase consumption. For those who subsist on welfare, $c = r$, so $\partial c/\partial r = 1$. Those who work must consider not only the direct effect on consumption but also the effect of redistribution on their labor-leisure choice. The assumption that consumption is a normal good means that $\partial c/\partial r > 0$. Differentiating (4) and using the second-order condition, $D < 0$, in footnote 6 restricts u_{cl}:

$$\frac{\partial c}{\partial r} = \frac{u_{cl}x(1 - t) - u_{ll}}{-D} > 0. \tag{6}$$

Consumption increases with r for both workers and nonworkers provided consumption is a normal good.

The positive response of c to r takes one step toward establishing conditions under which we find a unique value of r that determines

[6] By assumption, u is strictly concave, so the second-order condition is negative and (4) defines a maximum. The second-order condition is $\partial^2 u/\partial n^2 = D = u_{cc}x^2(1 - t)^2 - 2u_{cl}x(1 - t) + u_{ll} < 0$.

the amount of earned income and amount of redistribution for each tax rate. The next step is to show that normality of consumption is sufficient to establish that earned income (income before taxes) increases with productivity.

Pretax income is

$$y(r, t, x) = xn[r, x(1 - t)]. \tag{7}$$

People who do not work, $x \leqslant x_0$, have $y = 0$ and $\partial y/\partial x = 0$. For all others,

$$\frac{\partial y}{\partial x} = n + x\frac{\partial n}{\partial x}. \tag{8}$$

The first-order condition (eq. [4]) yields

$$\frac{\partial n}{\partial x} = \frac{u_c(1 - t) + u_{cc}nx(1 - t)^2 - u_{cl}n(1 - t)}{-D}. \tag{9}$$

The sign of $\partial n/\partial x$ is indeterminate; as productivity increases, the supply of labor can be backward bending. Pretax income, $y = nx$, does not decline, however, even if n falls. Substituting (9) into (8) and rearranging terms shows that the bracketed term in (10) is the numerator of $\partial c/\partial r$ in (6). Hence, $\partial y/\partial x$ is positive for all $x > x_0$ provided that consumption is a normal good:

$$\frac{\partial y}{\partial x} = \frac{u_c(1 - t)x + n[u_{cl}x(1 - t) - u_{ll}]}{-D} > 0. \tag{10}$$

The final step in establishing that there is a unique equilibrium solution for any tax rate uses our assumption that leisure is a normal good. The government budget is balanced and all government spending is for redistribution of income. If per capita income is $\bar{y}$, then

$$t\bar{y} = r. \tag{11}$$

Let $F(\cdot)$ denote the distribution function for individual productivity, so that $F(x)$ is the fraction of the population with productivity less than x. Per capita income is obtained by integrating:

$$\bar{y} = \int_{x_0}^{\infty} xn[r, (1 - t)x]dF(x). \tag{12}$$

Equation (12) shows that per capita income, and therefore total earned income, is determined once we know x_0, t, and r. From (5), we know that x_0 depends only on t and r, and from (11) we know that, for any tax rate, there is at least one value of r that balances the budget.[7]

[7] The left side of (11) is nonnegative and is a continuous function of r that is bounded by $t\bar{x}$, where $\bar{x}$ is the average of x.

If leisure is a normal good, the value of r that satisfies (11) for each t is unique.[8]

Once r or t is chosen, the other is determined. The individual's choices of consumption and the distribution of his time between labor and leisure are determined also. The choice of r or t uniquely determines each individual's welfare and sets the size of government.

III. The Size of Government

The political process determines the share of national income taxed and redistributed. The many ways to make this choice range from dictatorship to unanimous consent, and each produces a different outcome. We call each political process that determines the tax rate a voting rule.

In this section, we consider any voting rule that allows a decisive individual to choose the tax rate. Two examples are dictatorship and universal suffrage with majority rule. A dictator is concerned about the effect of his decisions on the population's decisions to work and consume, but he alone makes the decision about the tax rate. Under majority rule, the voter with median income is decisive as we show below. We then show that changes in the voting rules and changes in productivity change the tax rate and the size of government.

The decisive voter chooses the tax rate that maximizes his utility. In making his choice, he is aware that his choice affects everyone's decision to work and consume. Increases in the tax rate have two effects. Each dollar of earned income raises more revenue but earned income declines; everyone chooses more leisure, and more people choose to subsist on redistribution. "High" and "low" tax rates have opposite effects on the choice of labor or leisure and, therefore, on earned income.

Formally, the individual is constrained to find a tax rate that balances the government budget, equation (11), and maximizes utility subject to his own budget constraint, equation (3). The first-order condition for the decisive voter is solved to find his preferred tax rate:

$$\bar{y} + t\frac{d\bar{y}}{dt} - y_d = 0, \tag{13}$$

where y_d is the income of the decisive voter.

[8] The normality of leisure means that $\partial l/\partial r > 0$ and, therefore, $\partial n/\partial r = -\partial l/\partial r < 0$. Since

$$\frac{\partial \bar{y}}{\partial r} = \int_{x_0}^{\infty} x \frac{\partial n}{\partial r}\, dF(x) < 0,$$

the left side of (11) is a strictly decreasing, continuous function of r. The right side of (11) strictly increases with r. This implies that there is a unique value of r that satisfies (11).

Roberts (1977) showed that if the ordering of individual incomes is independent of the choice of r and t, individual choice of the tax rate is inversely ordered by income. This implies that with universal suffrage the voter with median income is decisive, and the higher one's income, the lower the preferred tax rate. By making the additional assumption that consumption is a normal good, we have shown that incomes are ordered by productivity for all r and t. Combining Roberts's lemma 1 (1977, p. 334) with our results, we can order the choice of tax rate by the productivity of the decisive voter.[9] The higher an individual's productivity, the lower is his preferred tax rate.

Figure 1 illustrates the proposition and shows the effect on the tax rate of changing the voting rule. The negatively sloped line is the relation between individual productivity, x, and the individual's preferred tax rate. This line need not be linear.

The maximum tax rate, $t_{\max}$, is chosen if the decisive voter does not work. An example is $x = x_{d1}$. In this case, $x \leq x_0$; the decisive voter consumes only r, so he chooses the tax rate ($t_{\max}$) that maximizes r. Any higher tax rate reduces aggregate earned income, tax collections, and the amount available for redistribution. From equation (5), we see that the maximum tax rate must be less than $t = 1$.

As productivity rises from x_0 to $\bar{x}$, the tax rate declines from $t_{\max}$ to 0. At $x_d = \bar{x}$, the decisive voter is endowed with average productivity and cannot gain from lump-sum redistribution, so he votes for no redistribution by choosing $t = 0$.[10] From equation (5) and $u_c(0, \cdot) = \infty$, we see that everyone works when $r = 0$. If the decisive voter's productivity exceeds $\bar{x}$, t and r remain at zero and aggregate earned income remains at society's maximum.

Changes in the voting rule that spread the franchise up or down the productivity distribution change the decisive voter and raise or lower the tax rate. Our hypothesis implies that changing the position of the decisive voter in the distribution of productivity changes the size of government provided $x_0 < x_d < \bar{x}$. Major changes in x_d have occurred in two ways. Wealth and income requirements for voting were reduced or eliminated, gradually broadening the franchise and lowering the income of the decisive voter. Social security retirement systems grew in most countries after the franchise was extended. By increas-

[9] The formal statement of the result is: Consider any two pairs (r_1, t_1) and (r_2, t_2). If $t_2 > t_1$, then for all x: x is indifferent between (r_1, t_1) and (r_2, t_2) implies that x' weakly prefers (r_2, t_2) to (r_1, t_1) for all $x' < x$ and x'' weakly prefers (r_1, t_1) to (r_2, t_2) for all $x'' > x$; x strictly prefers (r_1, t_1) to (r_2, t_2) implies that x'' strictly prefers (r_1, t_1) to (r_2, t_2) for all $x'' > x$; x strictly prefers (r_2, t_2) to (r_1, t_1) implies that x' strictly prefers (r_2, t_2) to (r_1, t_1) for all $x' < x$. Note that this result does not require unimodality of voter preferences for tax rates.

[10] We have omitted public goods. In an earlier version we showed that under carefully specified conditions, public goods can be included without changing the result for redistribution.

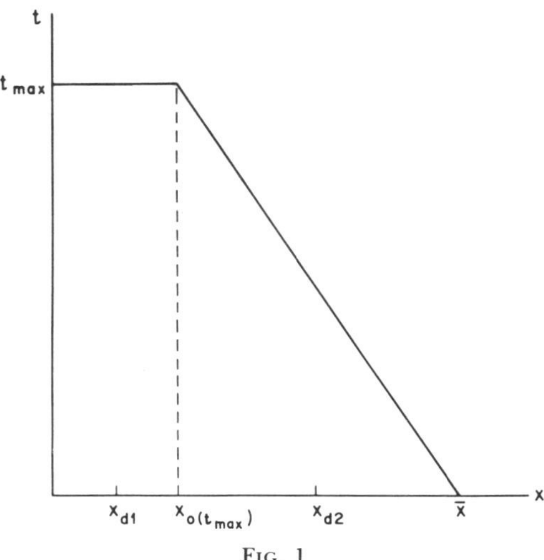

FIG. 1

ing the number of retired persons, social security systems increase the number of voters who favor increased redistribution financed by taxes on wages. Some of the retired who favor redistribution also favor low taxes on capital, property, and the income from capital.

The size of government changes also if there are changes in relative income, as shown by equation (13), or relative productivity. Conclusions about the precise effect of changes of this kind are difficult to draw. We cannot observe productivity directly and can only infer changes in the distribution of productivity, $F(\cdot)$, by observing changes in relative income. Recent literature makes clear that these effects are disputed (see Sahota 1978; King 1980; and others). Further, we cannot deduce the effect of changes in productivity on t directly from equation (13). The reason is that $\bar{y}$ depends on t, so finding the effect of changes in relative productivity requires the solution to a nonlinear equation in t. Instead, we rewrite (13) in a form which involves the (partial) elasticities of per capita income ($\bar{y}$) with respect to redistribution (r) and the wage rate ($x[1 - t]$).

Let $\tau = 1 - t$ be the fraction of earned income retained. From (12), $\bar{y}$ depends on r and τ only. The total derivative

$$\frac{d\bar{y}}{dt} = \frac{\bar{y}_r\bar{y} - \bar{y}_\tau}{1 - t\bar{y}_r}, \tag{14}$$

where $\bar{y}_r$ and $\bar{y}_\tau$ are the two partial derivatives. Substituting (14) into (13), we solve for t:

$$t = \frac{m - 1 + \eta(\bar{y}, r)}{m - 1 + \eta(\bar{y}, r) + m\eta(\bar{y}, \tau)}, \tag{15}$$

where m is the ratio of mean income to the income of the decisive voter, $\bar{y}/y_d$, and the η's are partial elasticities. Using the common economic assumption that the elasticities are constant, the tax rate rises as mean income rises relative to the income of the decisive voter, and taxes fall as m falls:

$$\frac{dt}{dm} = \frac{\eta(\bar{y}, \tau)[1 - \eta(\bar{y}, r)]}{[m - 1 + \eta(\bar{y}, r) + m\eta(\bar{y}, \tau)]^2} > 0. \tag{16}$$

Relaxing the assumption of constant elasticities weakens the conclusion, but we expect the sign of (16) to remain positive provided the change in the elasticities is small.

One of the oldest and most frequently tested explanations of the growth of government is known as Wagner's law. This law has been interpreted in two ways. The traditional interpretation is that government is a luxury good so that there is a positive relation between the relative size of government and the level of real income. Recently Alt (1980) has questioned this interpretation of Wagner's idea. Alt (1980, p. 4) notes that Wagner argued that there is "a proportion between public expenditure and national income which may not be permanently overstepped." This suggests an equilibrium relative size of government rather than an ever-growing government sector.

The traditional statement of Wagner's law—that government grows more rapidly than income—has been tested many times, but with mixed results. Peacock and Wiseman (1961), Cameron (1978), and Larkey et al. (1980) discuss these tests. Our hypothesis suggests that the results are ambiguous because Wagner's law is incomplete. The effect of absolute income on the size of government is conditional on relative income. Average or absolute income affects the elasticities in equation (15), and the relative income effect is given by m.

To make our hypothesis testable, we must identify the decisive voter. The applicable voting rule in the United States is universal franchise and majority rule. Under this rule, the voter with median income is decisive in single-issue elections, as we argued above. Hence the median voter is decisive in elections to choose the tax rate, so m is the ratio of mean to median income.[11]

[11] The many tests of the median-voter hypothesis using regression analyses are inconclusive. One reason is that many of the tests do not discriminate between the median and any other fractile of the income distribution (see Romer and Rosenthal 1979). Cooter and Helpman (1974) use income before and after taxes net of transfers to estimate the shape of the social welfare function implicit in U.S. data. They conclude that "the assumption that ability is distributed as wages per hour . . . —perhaps the best assumption on distribution of ability—vindicates the median voter rule."

IV. Conclusion

Government spending and taxes have grown relative to output in most countries with elected governments for the past 30 years or longer. Increased relative size of government appears to be independent of budget and tax systems, federal or national governments, the size of the bureaucracy, and other frequently mentioned institutional arrangements, although the relative rates of change in different countries may depend on these arrangements.

Our explanation of the size of government emphasizes voter demand for redistribution. Using a parsimonious, general equilibrium model in which the only government activities are redistribution and taxation, the real budget is balanced, and voters are fully informed, we show that the size of government is determined by the welfare-maximizing choice of a decisive individual. The decisive individual may be a dictator, absolute monarch, or marginal member of a junta.

With majority rule the voter with median income among the enfranchised citizens is decisive. Voters with income below the income of the decisive voter choose candidates who favor higher taxes and more redistribution; voters with income above the decisive voter desire lower taxes and less redistribution. The decisive voter chooses the tax share. When the mean income rises relative to the income of the decisive voter, taxes rise, and vice versa. The spread of the franchise in the nineteenth and twentieth centuries increased the number of voters with relatively low income. The position of the decisive voter shifted down the distribution of income, so tax rates rose. In recent years, the proportion of voters receiving social security has increased, raising the number of voters favoring taxes on wage and salary income to finance redistribution. A rational social security recipient with large property income supports taxes on labor income to finance redistribution but opposes taxes on income from property. In our analysis, there is neither capital nor taxes on property, so the increase in social security recipients has an effect similar to an extension of the franchise.

Our assumption that voters are fully informed about the size of government differs from much recent literature. There, taxpayers are portrayed as the prey sought by many predators who conspire to raise taxes relative to income by diffusing costs and concentrating benefits, or in other ways (Buchanan and Tullock 1962; Olson 1965; Niskanen 1971; Hayek 1979). We acknowledge that voters are ill informed about the costs of particular projects when, as is often the case, it is rational to avoid learning details. Knowledge of detail is not required to learn that the size of government has increased and that taxes have increased relative to output or income. Long ago it became rational for voters to anticipate this outcome of the political process.

Wagner's law, relating taxation to income, has generated a large literature and has been tested in various ways. Our analysis shows that Wagner's law should be amended to include the effect of relative income in addition to absolute income.

Kuznets (1955) observed that economic growth raises the incomes of skilled individuals relative to the incomes of the unskilled. In this way, economic growth can lead to rising inequality and, if our hypothesis is correct, to votes for redistribution. The rising relative size of government slows when the relative changes come to an end and reverses if the relative changes reverse in a mature stationary economy.

The distinctive feature of our analysis is not the voting rule but the relation between individual and collective choice. Each person chooses consumption and leisure by maximizing in the usual way. Anyone who works receives a wage equal to his marginal product. Taxes on labor income provide revenues for redistribution, however, so everyone benefits from decisions to work and incurs a cost when leisure increases.

The analysis explains why the size of government and the tax rate can remain constant yet be criticized by an overwhelming majority of citizens. The reason is that at the voting equilibrium nearly everyone prefers a different outcome. If unconstrained by the voting rule, everyone but the decisive voter would choose a different outcome. But only the decisive voter can assure a majority.

An extension of our argument may suggest why real government debt per capita, as measured in the budget, has increased more than 20-fold in this century. The decisive voter has as much incentive to tax the future rich as the current rich. An optimal distribution of the cost of redistribution would not tax only the current generation because, with economic growth, the future generation will be richer than the current generation. By shifting the burden of taxation toward the future, income is redistributed intertemporally.

To pursue these questions more fully and to analyze any effect of defense and public goods, it seems necessary to embed the analysis in a model with saving, capital accumulation, and public goods and to explore the effect of permitting relative shares to change as income changes. From an analysis of a growing economy, we can expect to develop a rational theory of the growth of government to complement our analysis of the government's size.

References

Alt, James. "Democracy and Public Expenditure." Multilithed. St. Louis: Washington Univ., 1980.

Aranson, Peter, and Ordeshook, Peter C. "Alternative Theories of the Growth of Government and Their Implications for Constitutional Tax and Spending Limits." Multilithed. Pittsburgh: Carnegie-Mellon Univ., 1980.

Browning, Edgar K., and Johnson, William R. *The Distribution of the Tax Burden.* Washington: American Enterprise Inst., 1979.

Brunner, Karl. "Reflections on the Political Economy of Government: The Persistent Growth of Government." *Schweizerische Zeitschrift Volkwirtschaft und Statis.* 114 (September 1978): 649–80.

Buchanan, James M., and Tullock, Gordon. *The Calculus of Consent: Logical Foundations of Constitutional Democracy.* Ann Arbor: Univ. Michigan Press, 1962.

Cameron, David. "The Expansion of the Public Economy: A Comparative Analysis." *American Polit. Sci. Rev.* 72 (December 1978): 1243–61.

Cooter, Robert, and Helpman, Elhanan. "Optimal Income Taxation for Transfer Payments under Different Social Welfare Criteria." *Q.J.E.* 88 (November 1974): 656–70.

Downs, Anthony. *An Economic Theory of Democracy.* New York: Harper & Row, 1957.

Hayek, Friedrich A. *Law, Legislation and Liberty.* Vol. 3, *The Political Order of a Free People.* Chicago: Univ. Chicago Press, 1979.

Hotelling, Harold. "Stability in Competition." *Econ. J.* 39 (March 1929): 41–57.

King, Mervyn A. "How Effective Have Fiscal Policies Been in Changing the Distribution of Income and Wealth?" *A.E.R. Papers and Proc.* 70 (May 1980): 72–76.

Kuznets, Simon. "Economic Growth and Income Inequality." *A.E.R.* 45 (March 1955): 1–28.

Larkey, P. D.; Stolp, C.; and Winer, M. "Theorizing about the Growth and Decline of Government: A Research Assessment." Multilithed. Pittsburgh: Carnegie-Mellon Univ., 1980.

Meltzer, Allan H., and Richard, Scott F. "Why Government Grows (and Grows) in a Democracy." *Public Interest* 52 (Summer 1978): 111–18.

Mueller, Dennis C. "Public Choice: A Survey." *J. Econ. Literature* 14 (June 1976): 395–433.

Musgrave, Richard A. *The Theory of Public Finance: Study in Public Economy.* New York: McGraw-Hill, 1959.

Niskanen, William A. *Bureaucracy and Representative Government.* Chicago: Aldine-Atherton, 1971.

Nutter, G. Warren. *Growth of Government in the West.* Washington: American Enterprise Inst., 1978.

Olson, Mancur, Jr. *The Logic of Collective Action: Public Goods and the Theory of Groups.* Cambridge, Mass.: Harvard Univ. Press, 1965.

Peacock, Alan T. *Economic Analysis of Government and Related Theories.* New York: St. Martin's, 1979.

Peacock, Alan T., and Wiseman, Jack. *The Growth of Public Expenditure in the United Kingdom.* Princeton, N.J.: Princeton Univ. Press, 1961.

Pechman, Joseph A., and Okner, Benjamin A. *Who Bears the Tax Burden?* Washington: Brookings Inst., 1974.

Peltzman, Sam. "The Growth of Government." Multilithed. Chicago: Univ. Chicago, 1979.

Riker, William H., and Ordeshook, Peter C. *An Introduction to Positive Political Theory.* Englewood Cliffs, N.J.: Prentice-Hall, 1973.

Roberts, Kevin W. S. "Voting over Income Tax Schedules." *J. Public Econ.* 8 (December 1977): 329–40.

Romer, Thomas. "Individual Welfare, Majority Voting, and the Properties of a Linear Income Tax." *J. Public Econ.* 4 (February 1975): 163–85.

Romer, Thomas, and Rosenthal, Howard. "The Elusive Median Voter." *J. Public Econ.* 12 (October 1979): 143–70.

Sahota, Gian Singh. "Theories of Personal Income Distribution: A Survey." *J. Econ. Literature* 16 (March 1978): 1–55.

Sheshinski, Eytan. "The Optimal Linear Income Tax." *Rev. Econ. Studies* 39 (July 1972): 297–302.

de Tocqueville, Alexis. *Democracy in America.* 1835. Reprint ed. Oxford: Oxford Univ. Press, 1965.

Wicksell, Knut. "A New Principle of Just Taxation." Reprinted in *Classics in the Theory of Public Finance,* edited by Richard A. Musgrave and Alan T. Peacock. New York: St. Martin's, 1958.

Name Index